1-28-00

# Multiagent Systems

# Multiagent Systems

## A Modern Approach to Distributed Artificial Intelligence

edited by Gerhard Weiss

The MIT Press
Cambridge, Massachusetts
London, England

This book was set in Computer Modern by Gerhard Weiss.

Printed and bound in the United States of America.

Library of Congress Cataloging-in-Publication Data

Multiagent systems: a modern approach to distributed artificial intelligence / edited by Gerhard Weiss
      p. cm.
    Includes bibliographical references and index.
    ISBN 0-262-23203-0 (hardcover: alk. paper)
    1. Intelligent agents (Computer software) 2. Distributed artificial intelligence.
I. Weiss, Gerhard, 1962– .
QA76.76.I58M85 1999
006.3—dc21                                     98-49797
                                                               CIP

# Contents in Brief

# Part II: Related Themes

# Contents in Detail

## 5   Distributed Rational Decision Making    201

*Tuomas W. Sandholm*

## 6    Learning in Multiagent Systems    259

*Sandip Sen and Gerhard Weiss*

## 9   Industrial and Practical Applications of DAI   377

*H. Van Dyke Parunak*

# Part II: Related Themes

## 10   Groupware and Computer Supported Cooperative Work   425

*Clarence Ellis and Jacques Wainer*

## 11  Distributed Models for Decision Support   459

*Jose Cuena and Sascha Ossowski*

## 12  Concurrent Programming for DAI   505

*Gul A. Agha and Nadeem Jamali*

## 13  Distributed Control Algorithms for AI    539

*Gerard Tel*

---

# Contributing Authors

**Gul A. Agha**
Open Systems Laboratory
Department of Computer Science
University of Illinois at
    Urbana-Champaign
1304 West Springfield Avenue
Urbana, IL 61801, USA

**Kathleen M. Carley**
Department of Social and
    Decision Sciences
Carnegie Mellon University
Pittsburgh, PA 15213, USA

**Jose Cuena**
Department of Artificial Intelligence
Technical University of Madrid
Campus de Montegancedo s/n
28660 Boadilla del Monte, Spain

**Edmund H. Durfee**
Artificial Intelligence Laboratory
Department of Electrical Engineering
    and Computer Science
University of Michigan
Ann Arbor, MI 48109, USA

**Clarence (Skip) Ellis**
Department of Computer Science
University of Colorado
Boulder CO 80309-0430, USA

**Les Gasser**
Information Technology and
    Organizations Program
National Science Foundation
4201 Wilson Blvd.
Arlington, Va. 22230, USA

**Michael P. Georgeff**
Australian AI Institute
171 La Trobe Street
Melbourne, Victoria 3000, Australia

**Michael N. Huhns**
Center for Information Technology
Department of Electrical &
    Computer Engineering
University of South Carolina
Columbia, SC 29208, USA

**Toru Ishida**
Department of Information Science
Kyoto University
Yoshida-honmachi, Sakyo-ku
Kyoto, 606-01, Japan

**Nadeem Jamali**
Open Systems Laboratory
University of Illinois at
    Urbana-Champaign
1304 West Springfield Avenue
Urbana, IL 61801, USA

**Sascha Ossowski**
Department of Artificial Intelligence
Technical University of Madrid
Campus de Montegancedo s/n
28660 Boadilla del Monte, Spain

**H. Van Dyke Parunak**
Industrial Technology Institute
PO Box 1485
Ann Arbor, MI 48106 USA

**Anand S. Rao**
Mitchell Madison Group
Level 49, 120 Collins Street
Melbourne, Vic 3000, Australia

**Tuomas Sandholm**
Department of Computer Science
Campus Box 1045
Washington University
One Brookings Drive
St. Louis, MO 63130-4899, USA

**Sandip Sen**
Department of Mathematical &
    Computer Science
University of Tulsa
600 South College Avenue
Tulsa, OK 74104-3189, USA

**Munindar P. Singh**
Department of Computer Science
446 EGRC/Box 7534
1010 Main Campus Drive
North Carolina State University
Raleigh, NC 27695-7534, USA

**Larry N. Stephens**
Center for Information Technology
Department of Electrical &
    Computer Engineering
University of South Carolina
Columbia, SC 29208, USA

**Gerard Tel**
Utrecht University
Department of Computer Science
Padualaan 14, 3584 CH Utrecht
The Netherlands

**Jacques Wainer**
Instituto de Computação
Universidade Estadual de Campinas
Caixa Postal 6176
Campinas, SP 13083-970, Brazil

**Gerhard Weiss**
Institut für Informatik
Technische Universität München
D-80290 München, Germany

**Mike Wooldridge**
Dept of Electronic Engineering
Queen Mary & Westfield College
University of London
London E1 4NS, United Kingdom

**Makoto Yokoo**
NTT Communication Science
    Laboratories
2-2 Hikaridai, Seika-cho, Soraku-gun
Kyoto 619-02, Japan

# Preface

**Purpose** – The study of multiagent systems began in the field of distributed artificial intelligence (DAI) about 20 years ago. Today these systems are not simply a research topic, but are also beginning to become an important subject of academic teaching and industrial and commercial application. While there are several high-quality collections of articles on multiagent systems and DAI in print, most of these are proceedings of conferences and workshops. What is urgently needed is a book that offers a comprehensive and up-to-date introduction and is suitable as a textbook for the field. The purpose of this volume is to fulfill this need.

**Features** – The book offers a number of features that make it especially useful to readers:

- *Scope.* It is designed as an introductory text and a textbook that covers the whole range of multiagent systems. The book reflects the state of the art in this field, and treats basic themes (Part I) as well as several closely related themes (Part II) in detail.

- *Theory.* It gives a clear and careful presentation of the key concepts, methods, and algorithms that form the core of the field. Many illustrations and examples are provided.

- *Practice.* The emphasis is not only on theory, but also on practice. In particular, the book includes a number of thought-provoking exercises of varying degrees of difficulty at the end of each chapter that allow the reader to gain practical experience.

- *Glossary.* It contains an extensive glossary that provides the reader with compact explanations of relevant terminology used in the field.

- *Expertise.* Its chapters have been written by leading and outstanding authorities. This guarantees that the book is built on a very broad and diverse basis of knowledge and experience.

It is worth saying a little more about the last-mentioned feature. It is clear that a book prepared by just a few authors, as textbooks usually are, is likely to be more coherent than a book in which many authors are involved. But as the reader will see, the contributors to *Multiagent Systems* have invested considerable effort in ensuring the coherence of this book (and, in so doing, they practiced some of the basic issues—cooperation and negotiation—described in their chapters).

**Readership** – The book is primarily intended to meet the interests of the following audiences:

- *Professors and students* who require an up-to-date, in-depth source of material for their courses on multiagent systems and DAI. Below it is described how the book can be used as the basis of a number of different courses.
- *Researchers in the field* who wish to branch out beyond the area in which they are specialized to better understand the field as a whole, to investigate relationships between their own work and work by others, and to obtain valuable stimuli for their future research activities.
- *Software practitioners and professionals from industry* who want to find out whether and how the technologies available in the field can be usefully applied in their working domains.

Owing to the potential impact of multiagent systems on a variety of disciplines, this book can also serve as a repository and primary reference volume for computer scientists, sociologists, economists, management and organization scientists, engineers, psychologists, and philosophers.

**How to Use This Book** – The book can be used for teaching as well as self-study. The chapters and consequently the overall book are designed to be self-contained and understandable without additional material. Of course, there are many relationships between the chapters, but in principle they can be treated independently and read in any sequence. I recommended, however, to start with Chapters 1 and 2.

This book can be used as a text for a *graduate or advanced undergraduate course*. A one-quarter course should concentrate on the first three chapters of Part I of the book; with whatever time remains, further chapters of Part I, or parts of them, could be covered. A course based on Part I could comfortably occupy a full semester. A course fully covering Part I, Part II, and some separate material could take an entire year. The book is also useful as a *supplementary text for a general AI course*; for instance, within such a course the considerations on "classical" AI topics like problem solving and search could be enriched by Chapter 3 and Chapter 4, respectively. Moreover, most chapters could be also used as the *starting material for speciality courses and seminars*; for instance, Chapter 5, Chapter 6, and Chapter 7 could be used for courses devoted to distributed decision making, distributed machine learning, and computational organization theory, respectively. Although it is obvious, I finally want to mention that Chapter 8 should be part of courses with an emphasis on theory, while Chapter 9 should be part of courses with a focus on applications.

The exercises allow the reader to further deepen her or his knowledge, and course instructors might use them for putting more emphasis on practical aspects. Some exercises are fairly simple and are intended to make sure that the material provided in the chapters is mastered. Others are much more difficult and may serve as a subject of class discussions or advanced team work.

Throughout the book numerous references to the source literature are provided. They enable interested students to further pursue specific aspects, and they support professors in choosing additional course material.

The chapters can be understood without specific prior knowledge. However, a background in computer science and mathematics/logic definitely would be helpful in using all parts of the book most efficiently.

**One Final Word** – When working through this book, the reader is asked to keep in mind that multiagent systems and DAI constitute a young and dynamic field of interdisciplinary nature whose defining boundaries are not yet fully clear. It is my particular hope that this book contributes to the search for sharper boundaries by spurring further research, teaching, and application in this fascinating field.

**Acknowledgments** – This book would not have happened without the help of many people. I am most greateful to the authors for participating in this challenging project. They contributed significantly to this book not only by preparing and coordinating their texts—the chapters, the chapter descriptions included in the Prologue, and the index and glossary entries—but also by providing many useful comments and suggestions on how the book's overall quality could be further improved. It was the authors' enthusiasm and encouragement that often made my editorial work easier. Particular thanks are due to Mike Wooldridge and Munindar Singh for reading a draft of the Prologue.

At The MIT Press, I am grateful to Robert Prior for providing expert assistance and support during this project whenever necessary.

I give my warmest thanks to my wife, Tina, for her tolerance and patience at the many evenings and weekends I worked on this book.

Over the course of this project I have been financially supported by DFG (German National Science Foundation) under grant We1718/6-1.

Of course, despite the authors' influencing comments and suggestions, responsibility for the conception of this book and the final selection of the chapter themes ultimately lies with me.

*Gerhard Weiß*

# Prologue

## Multiagent Systems and Distributed Artificial Intelligence

Since its inception in the mid to late 1970s distributed artificial intelligence (DAI) evolved and diversified rapidly. Today it is an established and promising research and application field which brings together and draws on results, concepts, and ideas from many disciplines, including artificial intelligence (AI), computer science, sociology, economics, organization and management science, and philosophy. Its broad scope and multi-disciplinary nature make it difficult to precisely characterize DAI in a few words. The following definition is intended to serve as a starting point for exploring this arena and as a constant point of reference for reading through this book:

> *DAI is the study, construction, and application of multiagent systems, that is, systems in which several interacting, intelligent agents pursue some set of goals or perform some set of tasks.*

An agent is a computational entity such as a software program or a robot that can be viewed as perceiving and acting upon its environment and that is autonomous in that its behavior at least partially depends on its own experience. As an intelligent entity, an agent operates flexibly and rationally in a variety of environmental circumstances given its perceptual and effectual equipment. Behavioral flexibility and rationality are achieved by an agent on the basis of key processes such as problem solving, planning, decision making, and learning. As an interacting entity, an agent can be affected in its activities by other agents and perhaps by humans. A key pattern of interaction in multiagent systems is goal- and task-oriented coordination, both in cooperative and in competitive situations. In the case of cooperation several agents try to combine their efforts to accomplish as a group what the individuals cannot, and in the case of competition several agents try to get what only some of them can have. The long-term goal of DAI is to develop mechanisms and methods that enable agents to interact as well as humans (or even better), and to understand interaction among intelligent entities whether they are computational, human, or both. This goal raises a number of challenging issues that all are centered around the elementary question of *when and how to interact with whom*.

Two main reasons to deal with DAI can be identified, and these two reasons are the primary driving forces behind the growth of this field in recent years. The first is that multiagent systems have the capacity to play a key role in current and future computer science and its application. Modern computing platforms and information environments are distributed, large, open, and heterogeneous. Computers are no longer stand-alone systems, but have became tightly connected both with each other and their users. The increasing complexity of computer and information systems goes together with an increasing complexity of their applications. These often exceed the level of conventional, centralized computing because they require, for instance, the processing of huge amounts of data, or of data that arises at geographically distinct locations. To cope with such applications, computers have to act more as "individuals" or agents, rather than just "parts." The technologies that DAI promises to provide are among those that are urgently needed for managing high-level interaction in and intricate applications for modern computing and information processing systems.

The second reason is that multiagent systems have the capacity to play an important role in developing and analyzing models and theories of interactivity in human societies. Humans interact in various ways and at many levels: for instance, they observe and model one another, they request and provide information, they negotiate and discuss, they develop shared views of their environment, they detect and resolve conflicts, and they form and dissolve organizational structures such as teams, committees, and economies. Many interactive processes among humans are still poorly understood, although they are an integrated part of our everyday life. DAI technologies enable us to explore their sociological and psychological foundations.

**Intelligent Agents that Interact**

To make the above considerations more concrete, a closer look has to be taken on multiagent systems and thus on "interacting, intelligent agents":

- "Agents" are autonomous, computational entities that can be viewed as perceiving their environment through sensors and acting upon their environment through effectors. To say that agents are computational entities simply means that they physically exist in the form of programs that run on computing devices. To say that they are autonomous means that to some extent they have control over their behavior and can act without the intervention of humans and other systems. Agents pursue goals or carry out tasks in order to meet their design objectives, and in general these goals and tasks can be supplementary as well as conflicting.

- "Intelligent" indicates that the agents pursue their goals and execute their tasks such that they optimize some given performance measures. To say that agents are intelligent does not mean that they are omniscient or omnipotent, nor does it mean that they never fail. Rather, it means that they operate flexibly and rationally in a variety of environmental circumstances, given the information they have and their perceptual and effectual capabilities. A major focus of DAI therefore is on processes such as problem solving, planning, search, decision making, and learning that make it possible for agents to show flexibility and rationality in their behavior, and on the realization of such processes in multiagent scenarios.

- "Interacting" indicates that the agents may be affected by other agents or perhaps by humans in pursuing their goals and executing their tasks. Interaction can take place indirectly through the environment in which they are embedded (e.g., by observing one another or by carrying out an action that modifies the environmental state) or directly through a shared language (e.g., by providing information in which other agents are interested or which confuses other agents). DAI primarily focuses on coordination as a form of interaction that is particularly important with respect to goal attainment and task completion. The purpose of coordination is to achieve or avoid states of affairs that are considered as desirable or undesirable by one or several agents. To coordinate their goals and tasks, agents have to explicitly take dependencies among their activities into consideration. Two basic, contrasting patterns of coordination are cooperation and competition. In the case of cooperation, several agents work together and draw on the broad collection of their knowledge and capabilities to achieve a common goal. Against that, in the case of competition, several agents work against each other because their goals are conflicting. Cooperating agents try to accomplish as a team what the individuals cannot, and so fail or succeed together. Competitive agents try to maximize their own benefit at the expense of others, and so the success of one implies the failure of others.

It has to be stressed that there is no universally accepted definition of agency or of intelligence, and the above explanations are just intended to show how these terms are generally understood and what is generally considered as essential for an entity to be an intelligent agent. The concept of an intelligent agent that interacts allows various degrees of degradation, and is perhaps best viewed as a "guideline" for designing and analyzing systems rather than an "instruction" that allows no variation, or a precise "criterion" that always allows one to determine whether an object does or does not fulfill it. A useful catalog of agent theories and systems is provided in [45]. Another popular text on agents is [38, Chapter 2]. A recent overview of key themes in agent research is given in [22].

In [25] the following major characteristics of multiagent systems are identified:

- each agent has just incomplete information and is restricted in its capabilities;
- system control is distributed;
- data is decentralized; and
- computation is asynchronous.

Multiagent systems can differ in the agents themselves, the interactions among the agents, and the environments in which the agents act. The following table gives an overview of some attributes of multiagent systems, together with their potential range (an extensive overview is offered in [22]):

| | attribute | range |
|---|---|---|
| **agents** | number | from two upward |
| | uniformity | homogeneous ... heterogeneous |
| | goals | contradicting ... complementary |
| | architecture | reactive ... deliberative |
| | abilities (sensors, effectors, cognition) | simple ... advanced |
| **interaction** | frequency | low ... high |
| | persistence | short-term ... long-term |
| | level | signal-passing ... knowledge-intensive |
| | pattern (flow of data and control) | decentralized ... hierarchical |
| | variability | fixed ... changeable |
| | purpose | competitive ... cooperative |
| **environment** | predictability | forseeable ... unforseeable |
| | accessibility and knowability | unlimited ... limited |
| | dynamics | fixed ... variable |
| | diversity | poor ... rich |
| | availability of resources | restricted ... ample |

Traditionally two primary types of DAI systems have been distinguished [2]: multiagent systems in which several agents coordinate their knowledge and activities and reason about the processes of coordination; and distributed problem solving systems in which the work of solving a particular problem is divided among a number of nodes that divide and share knowledge about the problem and the developing solution. Whereas initially the emphasis of work on multiagent systems was on behavior coordination, the emphasis of work on distributed problem solving systems was on task decomposition and solution synthesis. The modern concept of multiagent systems as described above covers both types of systems. For that reason, and in accordance with contemporary usage, in this book no explicit distinction is made between multiagent systems and distributed problem solving systems, and the terms multiagent system and DAI system are used synonymously.

The role that the concept of a multiagent system plays in DAI is comparable to the role that the concept of an individual agent plays in traditional AI (see, e.g., [33, 36, 38]). Broadly construed, both DAI and traditional AI deal with computational aspects of intelligence, but they do so from different points of view and under different assumptions. Where traditional AI concentrates on agents as "intelligent stand-alone systems" and on intelligence as a property of systems that act in isolation, DAI concentrates on agents as "intelligent connected systems" and on intelligence as a property of systems that interact. Where traditional AI focuses on "cognitive processes" within individuals, DAI focuses on "social processes" in groups of individuals. Where traditional AI considers systems having a single locus of internal reasoning and control and requiring just minimal help from others to act successfully, DAI considers systems in which reasoning and control is distributed and successful activity is a joint effort. And where traditional AI uses psychology and behaviorism for ideas, inspiration, and metaphor, DAI uses sociology and economics. In this way, DAI is not so much a specialization of traditional AI, but a generalization of it.

**Challenging Issues**

To build a multiagent system in which the agents "do what they should do" turns out to be particularly difficult in the light of the basic system characteristics mentioned above. The only way to cope with these characteristics is to enable the agents to interact appropriately, and thus the elementary question faced by DAI is *When and how should which agents interact—cooperate and compete—to successfully meet their design objectives?* Based on the common distinction between the *"micro"* or agent level and the *"macro"* or group level (e.g., see [31]), in principle one can follow two different routes to answer this question:

- bottom up: to search for specific agent-level capabilities that result in appropriate interaction at the overall group level; or

- top down: to search for specific group-level rules—called conventions, norms, and so on—that appropriately constrain the interaction repertoire at the level of the individual agents.

(The question how agent-level—individual—activity and group-level—societal—rules and structures are related to each other is known as the micro-macro problem in sociology.) No matter which route is chosen, this question raises several challenging, intertwined issues (items 1 to 5 were first mentioned in [2], and item 6 and items 7 and 8 were additionally formulated in [31] and [25], respectively):

1. How to enable agents to decompose their goals and tasks, to allocate sub-goals and sub-tasks to other agents, and to synthesize partial results and solutions.

2. How to enable agents to communicate. What communication languages and protocols to use.

3. How to enable agents to represent and reason about the actions, plans, and knowledge of other agents in order to appropriately interact with them.

4. How to enable agents to represent and reason about the state of their interaction processes. How to enable them to find out whether they have achieved progress in their coordination efforts, and how to enable them to improve the state of their coordination and to act coherently.

5. How to enable agents to recognize and reconcile disparate viewpoints and conflicts. How to syntheze views and results.

6. How to engineer and constrain practical multiagent systems. How to design technology platforms and development methodologies for DAI.

7. How to effectively balance local computation and communication.

8. How to avoid or mitigate harmful (e.g., chaotic or oscillatory) overall system behavior.

9. How to enable agents to negotiate and contract. What negotiation and contract protocols should they use.

10. How to enable agents to form and dissolve organizational structures—teams, alliances, and so on—that are suited for attaining their goals and completing their tasks.

11. How to formally describe multiagent systems and the interactions among agents. How to make sure that they are correctly specified.

12. How to realize "intelligent processes" such as problem solving, planning, decision making, and learning in multiagent contexts. How to enable agents to collectively carry out such processes in a coherent way.

To provide solutions to these issues is the core request of DAI.

## Applications

Many existing and potential industrial and commercial applications for DAI and multiagent systems are described in the literature (e.g., see [23, 24] and also [26]). Basically following [25] (here the readers find a number of pointers to specific work), examples of such applications are:

- Electronic commerce and electronic markets, where "buyer" and "seller" agents purchase and sell goods on behalf of their users.

- Real-time monitoring and management of telecommunication networks, where agents are responsible, e.g., for call forwarding and signal switching and transmission.

- Modelling and optimization of in-house, in-town, national- or world-wide transportation systems, where agents represent, e.g., the transportation vehicles or the goods or customers to be transported.

- Information handling in information environments like the Internet, where multiple agents are responsible, e.g., for information filtering and gathering.

- Improving the flow of urban or air traffic, where agents are responsible for appropriately interpreting data arising at different sensor stations.

- Automated meeting scheduling, where agents act on behalf of their users to fix meeting details like location, time, and agenda.

- Optimization of industrial manufacturing and production processes like shop-floor scheduling or supply chain management, where agents represent, e.g., different workcells or whole enterprises.

- Analysis of business processes within or between enterprises, where agents represent the people or the distinct departments involved in these processes in different stages and at different levels.

- Electronic entertainment and interactive, virtual reality-based computer games, where, e.g., animated agents equipped with different characters play against each other or against humans.

- Design and re-engineering of information- and control-flow patterns in large-scale natural, technical, and hybrid organizations, where agents represent the entities responsible for these patterns.

- Investigation of social aspects of intelligence and simulation of complex social phenomena such as the evolution of roles, norms, and organzational structures, where agents take on the role of the members of the natural societies under consideration.

What these applications have in common is that they show one or several of the following features [2]:

- *Inherent Distribution* – They are inherently distributed in the sense that the data and information to be processed

  □ arise at geographically different locations ("spatial distribution");

  □ arise at different times ("temporal distribution");

  □ are structured into clusters whose access and use requires familiarity with different ontologies and languages ("semantic distribution"); and/or

  □ are structured into clusters whose access and use requires different perceptual, effectual, and cognitive capabilities ("functional distribution").

- *Inherent Complexity* – They are inherently complex in the sense that they are too large to be solved by a single, centralized system because of limitations available at a given level of hardware or software technology. To enlarge a centralized system such that it meets the requirements of inherently complex applications usually is very difficult, time-consuming, and costly. Moreover, such an enlargement often results in solutions that are brittle and that become useless as soon as the application requirements change only slightly.

Solving inherently distributed and complex applications in a centralized way is obviously not only counter-intuitive, but often not even possible at all. The alternative is to distribute the solution process across multiple entities capable of intelligent coordination—and DAI aims at developing technologies and methodologies for realizing this alternative in a very natural way [15].

## Rationales for Multiagent Systems

The two major reasons that cause people to study multiagent systems are:

- *Technological and Application Needs* – Multiagent systems offer a promising and innovative way to understand, manage, and use distributed, large-scale, dynamic, open, and heterogeneous computing and information systems. The Internet is the most prominent example of such systems; other examples are multi-database systems and in-house information systems. Computers and computer applications play an increasingly important and influencing part in our everyday life, as they become more powerful and more tightly connected both with each other through long-range and local-area networks and with humans through user-interfaces. These systems are too complex to be completely characterized and precisely described. As their control becomes more and more decentralized, their components act more and more like "individuals" that deserve attributes like autonomous, rational, intelligent, and so forth rather than just as "parts." DAI does not only aim at providing know-how for building sophisticated interactive systems from scratch, but also for interconnecting existing legacy systems such that they coherently act as a whole. Moreover, like no other discipline, DAI aims at providing solutions to inherently distributed and inherently complex applications. As we saw above, these applications are hard to solve with centralized computing technology. Many real world applications, if not most, fall into this class, and they are present in many domains such as scheduling, manufacturing, control, diagnosis, and logistics.

- *Natural View of Intelligent Systems* – Multiagent systems offer a natural way to view and characterize intelligent systems. Intelligence and interaction are deeply and inevitably coupled, and multiagent systems reflect this insight. Natural intelligent systems, like humans, do not function in isolation. Instead, they are at the very least a part of the environment in which they and other intelligent systems operate. Humans interact in various ways and at various levels, and most of what humans have achieved is a result of interaction. DAI can provide insights and understanding about poorly understood interactions among natural, intelligent beings, as they organize themselves into various groups, committees, societies, and economies in order to achieve improvement.

In addition, multiagent systems, as distributed systems, have the capacity to offer several desirable properties [2]:

- *Speed-up and Efficiency* – Agents can operate asynchronously and in parallel, and this can result in an increased overall speed (provided that the overhead of necessary coordination does not outweigh this gain).

- *Robustness and Reliability* – The failure of one or several agents does not necessarily make the overall system useless, because other agents already available in the system may take over their part.

- *Scalability and Flexibility* – The system can be adopted to an increased problem size by adding new agents, and this does not necessarily affect the operationality of the other agents.

- *Costs* – It may be much more cost-effective than a centralized system, since it could be composed of simple subsystems of low unit cost.

- *Development and Reusability* – Individual agents can be developed separately by specialists (either from scratch or on the basis of already available hardware and/or software facilities), the overall system can be tested and maintained more easily, and it may be possible to reconfigure and reuse agents in different application scenarios.

The available computer and network technology forms a sound platform for realizing these systems. In particular, recent developments in object-oriented programming, parallel and distributed computing, and mobile computing, as well as ongoing progress in programming and computing standardization efforts such as KSE (e.g., http://www.cs.umbc.edu/kse/), FIPA (e.g., http://drogo.cselt.stet.it/fipa/), and CORBA (e.g., http://www.rhein-neckar.de/~cetus/oo_corba.html and http://industry.ebi.ac.uk/~corba/) are expected to further improve the possibilities of implementing and applying DAI techniques and methods.

---

## A Guide to This Book

### The Chapters

The book is divided into two parts. Part I contains nine chapters, each treating a core theme in the field of multiagent systems and DAI:

- Chapter 1 concentrates on agents—the "micro" level referred to above.

- Chapter 2 expands the considerations of Chapter 1 by focusing on systems of agents and the computational infrastructure required for interaction—the "macro" level referred to above.

- Chapters 3 to 6 address elementary "intelligent activities" and their realization in multiagent systems, namely,

  - problem solving and planning,
  - search,
  - decision making, and
  - learning.

- Chapter 7 shows how processes of organizing, as they occur among agents and humans, can be computationally modelled.

- Chapter 8 describes formal methods for studying and constructing agents and multiagent systems.

- Chapter 9 concentrates on applications of agent and multiagent system technology.

Part II includes chapters on closely related, selected themes from computer science and software engineering:

- Chapter 10 focuses on groupware and computer supported cooperative work.

- Chapter 11 concentrates on distributed decision support systems.

- Chapter 12 discusses various issues of concurrent programming.

- Chapter 13 describes distributed control algorithms.

The relevance of these themes for the field can be easily seen. Agents in a multiagent system often have to coordinate their activities, and so there is a need for technologies that support them in acting coherently as a group; additionally, groupware and computer supported cooperative work constitute an important application domain for multiagent systems. Agents in a multiagent system often have to jointly make decisions, and so there is a need for technologies that support them in their distributed decision processes; moreover, distributed decision making is another obvious application domain for multiagent systems. There is a need for powerful concurrent programming techniques that allow to efficiently implement multiagent systems as parallel and distributed systems. And finally, there is an obvious need for mechanisms and methods that enable agents to control their distributed computations.

In the following, the individual chapters and their themes are motivated in more detail.

**Chapter 1, "Intelligent Agents" by Michael Wooldridge** – This chapter aims to introduce the reader to the basic issues surrounding the design and implementation of intelligent agents. It begins by motivating the idea of an agent, presents a definition of agents and intelligent agents, and then discusses the relationship between agents and other software paradigms (in particular, objects and expert systems). The chapter then goes on to discuss four major approaches to building agents. First, *logic based architectures* are reviewed. In logic based architectures, decision-making is viewed as logical deduction: the process of deciding which action to perform is reduced to a theorem proving problem. Such architectures have the advantage of semantic clarity, and in addition allow us to bring to bear all the apparatus of logic and theorem proving that has been developed in AI and computer science over the years. However, such architectures suffer from a number of drawbacks, not the least of which being that purely logical architectures do not seem well suited to domains that are subject to real time constraints. Second, *reactive architectures* are discussed. The characteristic of such architectures is that they eschew symbolic representations and reasoning in favour of a closer relationship between agent perception and action. Such architectures are more economical in computational terms, making them well-suited to episodic environments that require real-time performance. However, the process of engineering such architectures is not well understood. Third, *belief-desire-intention* architectures are discussed. In such architectures, decision making is viewed as *practical reasoning* from beliefs about how the world is and will be to the options available to an agent, and finally to intentions and actions. The process is somewhat similar to the kind of "folk reasoning" that humans use every day in deciding what to do. Belief-desire-intention architectures also have an attractive formalization, discussed elsewhere in this book. Fourth, layered agent architectures are reviewed. In such architectures, decision making is partitioned into a number of different decision making layers, each dealing with the agent's environment at a different level of abstraction. Layered agent architectures provide a natural way of decomposing agent functionality, and are currently a popular approach to agent design. In particular, the *horizontally layered* TOURINGMACHINES architecture and the *vertically layered* INTERRAP architecture are discussed. Finally, some prototypical agent programming languages are reviewed: Shoham's AGENT0 language, and Fisher's Concurrent METATEM language.

**Chapter 2, "Multiagent Systems and Societies of Agents" by Michael N. Huhns and Larry M. Stephens** – Agents operate and exist in some environment, which typically is both computational and physical. The environment might be open or closed, and it might or might not contain other agents. Although there are situations where an agent can operate usefully by itself, the increasing interconnection and networking of computers is making such situations rare. In Chapter 2, environments in which agents can operate effectively and interact with each other productively are analyzed, described, and designed.

The environments provide a computational infrastructure for such interactions to take place. The infrastructure includes communication protocols, which enable agents to exchange and understand messages, and interaction protocols, which enable agents to have conversations—structured exchanges of messages. For example, a communication protocol might specify that the messages for a particular course of action to be exchanged between two agents are of the types Propose, Accept, Reject, and Counterpropose. Based on these message types, two agents might use the following interaction protocol for negotiation: Agent1 proposes a course of action to Agent2; Agent2 evaluates the proposal and sends a counterproposal to Agent1; Agent1 accepts the counterproposal.

Interaction protocols enable agents to coordinate their activities, which can then be performed more efficiently. The degree of coordination is the extent to which they avoid extraneous activity by reducing resource contention, avoiding livelock and deadlock, and maintaining applicable safety conditions. Cooperation is coordination among nonantagonistic agents, while negotiation is coordination among competitive or simply self-interested agents. Chapter 2 describes protocols for coordination, cooperation, and negotiation.

Chapter 2 also shows how environments in which large numbers of agents exist must have different interaction protocols, based on social commitments, laws, and conventions.

**Chapter 3, "Distributed Problem Solving and Planning" by Edmund H. Durfee** – The interaction protocols introduced in Chapter 2 provide a means for agents to communicate about working together to solve problems, including coordination problems. Chapter 3 focuses on strategies for using protocols and reasoning capabilities to realize the benefits of cooperation. *Distributed problem solving* focuses on techniques for exploiting the distributed computational power and expertise in a MAS to accomplish large complex tasks. Of particular interest are strategies for moving tasks or results among agents to realize the benefits of cooperative problem solving. One main thread of work is the development of *task-passing techniques* to decide where to allocate subtasks to exploit the available capabilities of agents when large tasks initially arrive at a few agents. A second main thread of work is the study of *result-sharing strategies* to decide how agents that might be working on pieces of larger task can discover the relationships among their activities and coordinate them.

Coordinating problem-solving activities can involve anticipating the activities being undertaken by various agents and modifying those *plans* to make them more coordinated. Solving this planning problem is thus both a means to an end (distributed problem solving) and a distributed problem to be solved in its own right. The specific requirements and representations of planning problems, however, allow us to identify techniques that are particularly suited for *distributed planning*. We distinguish between the planning process and the execution of plans, and recognize that either, or both, of these can be distributed. We can then consider techniques for each. An interesting issue arises as to whether the coordination process should precede or succeed the planning processes of the agents; different decisions lead to different flavors of distributed planning, and a perspective is presented that allows these approaches to be seen as extremes of a more general process. It is also considered how throwing execution into the mix of planning and coordination can complicate matters, and algorithms for interleaving planning, coordination, and execution for dynamic applications are presented.

**Chapter 4, "Search Algorithms for Agents" by Makoto Yokoo and Toru Ishida** – This chapter deals with search algorithms for agents. Search is an umbrella term for various problem solving techniques in AI, where the sequence of actions required for solving a problem cannot be known *a priori* but must be determined by a trial-and-error exploration of alternatives. Search problems are divided into three classes: *(i)* path-finding problems, where the objective is to find a path from an initial state to a goal state, *(ii)* constraint satisfaction problems, where the objective is to find a combination of variable values that satisfies the given constraints, and *(iii)* two-player games such as chess and checkers. While two-player games deal with situations in which two *competitive* agents exist, most algorithms for the other two classes (constraint satisfaction and path-finding) were originally developed for single-agent problem solving. Various *asynchronous search* algorithms for these two classes are described. These algorithms are useful for cooperative problem solving by multiple agents each with *limited rationality*, since in these algorithms, a problem can be solved by accumulating local computations for each agent, and the execution order of these local computations can be arbitrary or highly flexible. More specifically, with respect constraint satisfaction problems the following asynchronous search algorithms are presented: the filtering algorithm, the hyper-resolution-based consistency algorithm, the asynchronous backtracking algorithm, and the asynchronous weak-commitment search algorithm. With respect to path-finding problems, first asynchronous dynamic programming as the basis for other algorithms is introduced. Then the Learning Real-time A* algorithm, the Real-time A* algorithm, the Moving Target Search algorithm, Real-time Bidirectional Search algorithms, and real-time multiagent search algorithms as special cases of asynchronous dynamic programming are described. With respect to two-player games, the basic minimax procedure and the alpha-beta pruning method to speed up the minimax procedure are presented.

**Chapter 5, "Distributed Rational Decision Making" by Tuomas W. Sandholm** − Multiagent systems consisting of self-interested agents are becoming increasingly important. One reason for this is the technology push of a growing standardized communication infrastructure over which separately designed agents belonging to different organizations can interact in an open environment in real-time and safely carry out transactions. The second reason is strong application pull for computer support for negotiation at the operative decision making level. For example, we are witnessing the advent of small transaction electronic commerce on the Internet for purchasing goods, information, and communication bandwidth. There is also an industrial trend toward virtual enterprises: dynamic alliances of small, agile enterprises which together can take advantage of economies of scale when available—e.g., respond to more diverse orders than individual agents can—but do not suffer from diseconomies of scale. Automated negotiation can save labor time of human negotiators, but in addition, other savings are possible because computational agents can be more effective at finding beneficial short-term contracts than humans are in strategically and combinatorially complex settings.

This chapter discusses methods for making socially desirable decisions among rational agents that only care of their own good, and may act insincerely to promote it. The techniques covered include

- voting,
- auctions,
- bargaining,
- market mechanisms,
- contracting, and
- coalition formation.

The chapter cites results from microeconomics—especially game theory—but it is not a general overview of those topics. Instead it deals relatively deeply with some of the topics which are particularly relevant to the design of computational multiagent systems. Special emphasis is placed on the implications of limited computation on the classic results. This is one area where game theory and computer science fruitfully blend within the field of DAI.

**Chapter 6, "Learning in Multiagent Systems" by Sandip Sen and Gerhard Weiss** – Multiagent systems typically are of considerable complexity with respect to both their structure and their function. For most application tasks, and even in environments that appear to be more or less simple at a first glance, it is extremely difficult or even impossible to correctly specify the behavioral repertoires and concrete activities of multiagent sytems at design time. This would require, for instance, that it is known in advance which environmental requirements will emerge in the future, which agents will be available at the time of emergence, and how the available agents have to interact in response to these requirements. Obviously, often the only feasible way to cope with this kind of problems is to endow the agents themselves with the ability to learn appropriate activity and interaction patterns. This chapter focuses on important aspects of learning in multiagent systems.

The chapter starts with a more general characterization of learning in multiagent systems. This includes an identification of *principle categories* of this kind of learning, an overview of *differencing features* that help to structure the broad variety of forms of learning that may occur in multiagent systems, and (from the point of view of multiagent systems) a description of the basic learning problem known as the *credit-assignment problem*. Then several typical learning approaches are described and illustrated. These approaches are ordered according to their main focus:

- learning and activity coordination;
- learning about and from other agents; and
- learning and communication.

The chapter also offers a brief guide to relevant related work from machine learning, psychology, and economics, and shows potential directions of future research.

**Chapter 7, "Computational Organization Theory" by Kathleen M. Carley and Les Gasser** – Chapter 7 provides an overview of the emergent field of Computational Organization Theory (COT). Researchers in COT use mathematical and computational models to theorize about and analyze organizations and the processes of organizing. Research in this area blends some of the traditional concerns of AI and distributed computing with work by organizational and social theorists, to develop a more comprehensive understanding. In most of this work, organizations are characterized as multiagent systems in which agents are embedded in particular social roles, have particular cognitive capabilities, and are engaged in specific organizationally-relevant tasks. Using computationally intensive techniques and empirical data, researchers are examining how organizations composed of people, artificial agents (such as webbots, robots, or other information technologies), or both, should be coordinated and how work should be distributed within and across such systems. Much of the work in this area focuses on issues of representation, organizational design, knowledge sharing, learning, and adaptivity. Some issues currently being addressed include:

- What is the nature of coordination and how can it be made most effective?

- How do organizations of people and organizations of automated agents differ? Should they be coordinated in similar ways?

- How socially intelligent do artifical agents need to be to communicate effectively with people during a team decision task?

and so on. In general, the aim of research in this area is to build new concepts, theories, and knowledge about organizing and organization in the abstract, to develop tools and procedures for the validation and analysis of computational organizational models, and to reflect these computational abstractions back to actual organizational practice through both tools and knowledge. This chapter reviews the dominant approaches and models in this area, potential toolkits, new findings, directions, and trends.

**Chapter 8, "Formal Methods in DAI" by Munindar P. Singh, Anand S. Rao, and Michael P. Georgeff** – As DAI moves into larger and more critical applications, it is becoming increasingly important to develop techniques to ensure that DAI systems behave appropriately. Safety and assurance can be addressed by development methodologies, as in traditional software engineering. But for methodologies to be effective in improving safety and correctness, they must be founded upon rigorous characterizations of the architecture and behavior of the given class of systems. In the case of DAI, this means that we develop formal bases for the abstractions and constructions that arise in the study of agents and multiagent systems.

Chapter 8 studies precisely such formalizations. It begins with background material on some logics that are commonly used in traditional computer science, especially in the verification of concurrent programs. It presents DAI-specific enhancements to these logics, covering the concepts of knowledge, beliefs, desires, goals, intentions, and know-how. Such cognitive concepts have long been informally studied in the context of agents, because they offer high-level specifications of the agents' design and behavior that are independent of most implementation details. In order to give a flavor of how the formal techniques might be applied, this chapter also describes how the above concepts may be realized in a practical interpreter.

Next, this chapter discusses a range of additional phenomena, such as coordination, teamwork, interagent communications, and social primitives. In conjunction with concepts such as joint and group intentions, which lift single-agent primitives to multiagent systems, these topics provide the essential conceptual basis for multiagent systems.

The chapter concludes with a discussion of tools and systems that either directly implement the associated DAI-specific formal theories, are inspired by those theories, or bring in traditional formal approaches.

**Chapter 9, "Industrial and Practical Applications of DAI" by H. Van Dyke Parunak** – Successful application of agents (as of any technology) must reconcile two perspectives. The researcher (exemplified in Chapters 1 to 8) focuses on a particular capability (e.g., communication, planning, learning), and seeks practical problems to demonstrate the usefulness of this capability (and justify further funding). The industrial practitioner has a practical problem to solve, and cares much more about the speed and cost-effectiveness of the solution than about its elegance or sophistication. Chapter 9 attempts to bridge these perspectives. To the agent researcher, it offers an overview of the kinds of problems that industrialists face, and some examples of agent technologies that have made their way into practical application. To the industrialist, it explains why agents are not just the latest technical fad, but a natural match to the characteristics of a broad class of real problems. Chapter 9 emphasizes agent applications in manufacturing and physical control because good examples are available, the problems of interfacing agents to the environment are more challenging than in all-electronic domains, and the evidence of success or failure is clearer when a system must directly confront the laws of physics. The chapter begins by describing the main *industrial motivations* for choosing an agent architecture for a particular problem. It then explains the concept of a *system life cycle*, which is widely used in industry to manage the progress of a project toward its intended results. The life cycle serves as an organizing framework for two sets of case studies. The first shows where in the life cycle agent-based systems are used, while the second discusses the design and construction of an agent-based system in terms of the life cycle. The chapter includes a review of some *development tools* that will hasten deployment of agent technology in industry.

**Chapter 10, "Groupware and Computer Supported Cooperative Work" by Clarence Ellis and Jacques Wainer** – The explosive growth of internet, intranet, and related technologies is leading to an explosive growth of the interest in groupware. Within our society, we see technologies that appear to greatly advance the conditions for human life (e.g., water purification technology), and others that seem to be questionable in their societal effects (e.g., television technology). Convergence of computer and communications technologies makes the world a "global village." Groupware is an emerging technology that promises to conceptually bring people together. Whether people are in the same conference room or scattered around the world, groupware can potentially help them to coordinate, collaborate, and cooperate.

Chapter 10 provides an introduction to groupware and computer supported cooperative work. Groupware is defined as computing and communications technology-based systems that assist groups of participants, and help to support a shared environment. Computer supported cooperative work is defined as the study of how groups work, and how technology to enhance group interaction and collaboration can be implemented.

The chapter, which primarily emphasizes technical issues of groupware, offers a taxonomy of groupware that is based on four aspects. The first aspect, *keeper*, groups functionalities that are related to storage and access of shared data; the second aspect, *coordinator*, is related to the ordering and synchronization of individual activities that make up the group process; the third aspect, *communicator*, groups functionalities related to unconstrained and explicit communication among the participants; and the fourth aspect, *team-agents*, refers to intelligent or semi-intelligent software components that perform specialized functions and contribute as participants to the dynamics of the group. Most current groupware systems have functionalities that are covered by the first three aspects. However, the most promising aspect is the fourth one—and because this aspect is most closely related to DAI, particular attention is paid to it throughout the chapter.

**Chapter 11, "Distributed Models for Decision Support" by Jose Cuena and Sascha Ossowski** – Decision support systems (DSS) assist the responsible persons in generating action plans in order to influence the behavior of natural or artificial systems in a desired direction. Knowledge-based DSSs have shown to perform well in a variety of different domains, as they allow for a meaningful dialogue with the control personnel. Still, the growing complexity of todays decision support problems makes the design process of such systems increasingly difficult and cost intensive.

This chapter introduces the notion of distributed knowledge-based DSSs. Setting out from concepts described in Part 1 of this book, an agent-based decision support architecture is proposed. On the basis of this architecture, the possibilities of a distributed, agent-based approach to DSS design are discussed by means of three case studies taken from literature:

- Environmental Emergency Management – The objective of Environmental Emergency Management is to minimize the negative impact of natural disasters or industrial accidents. The architecture of a multiagent DSS is presented, in which each agent corresponds to a preestablished organizational entity. An example of the operation of this system is given within the frame of a flood management scenario.

- Energy Management – Energy Management aims to maintain high quality supply of electrical energy despite damages to transport and distribution networks caused by wind, icing, lightning etc. A multiagent decision support architecture for this task is described, that integrates both preexisting and purposefully designed agents. In an example, it is shown how these agents cooperate to perform fault diagnosis and service restauration in a distributed fashion.

- Road Traffic Management – Road Traffic Management is concerned with the smooth flow of traffic in a road network along the different rush hour demands and despite events such as accidents or road works. A multiagent architecture is presented, where each traffic agent is responsible for specific parts of the road network. An example illustrates how the interaction between these agents leads to the coordinated proposals of traffic control actions.

**Chapter 12, "Concurrent Programming for DAI" by Gul A. Agha and Nadeem Jamali** – As processors and networks have become faster and cheaper, parallelism and distribution to achieve performance gains has become more attractive. This chapter describes the Actor model of concurrent computation and extends it to define mobile *agents*. Mobile agents may travel over a network of processors in search for resources that they need to achieve their goals.

An economic model is useful as a basis on which hosts could be provided incentives to allow agents to migrate and also to limit the resources that the agents consume. The chapter defines agents that are allocated limited units of a global currency which they can expend on purchasing physical resources needed for carrying out their activities on different hosts.

Reasoning about concurrent systems has traditionally been a challenging task. The chapter discusses ways of modifying semantics of Actor systems to support mobility and control of resource consumption. The semantics of Agent systems provides guidelines for designing systems of agents, for supporting non-intrusive monitoring of the system, allows the systematic use computational reflection, and enables agents to develop proofs of safe execution which may be offered to prospective hosts.

The dynamicity and uncertainty in the behavior of ensembles of agents poses challenging problems. The chapter describes how the context in which agents execute, and in which their interactions are mediated, may be dynamically customized. Programming constructs for naming in open systems and scalable communication are also described. The chapter also includes a number of programming examples and a discussion of open issues.

**Chapter 13, "Distributed Control Algorithms for AI" by Gerard Tel** – This chapter discusses a number of elementary problems in distributed computing and a couple of well-known algorithmic "building blocks," which are used as procedures in distributed applications. The chapter is not intended to be complete, as an enumeration of the many known distributed algorithms would be pointless and endless. The chapter is even not intended to touch all relevant sub-areas and problems studied in distributed computing, because they are not all relevant to DAI. Rather than an algorithm catalogue, the chapter aims to be an eye-opener for the possibilities of the distributed computing model, an introduction to designing and reasoning about the algorithms, and a pointer to some literature.

The chapter introduces the distributed model and illustrates the various possibilities and difficulties with algorithms to compute spanning trees in a network. It is shown how the communication and time complexities of the algorithms are evaluated. Then a more complicated, but relevant control problem is studied, namely termination detection. This study reveals how intricate it is to make information about a distributed global state available to a node locally. Termination detection occurs in distributed applications of all areas and is not specific for DAI.

Application of some distributed control techniques is exemplified in the later sections in distributed computations for AI problems. A distributed implementation of Arc Consistency and Constraint Satisfaction is discussed, and it is shown how termination detection and distributed evaluation of functions play a role. The chapter finally presents a distributed graph algorithm, illustrating another termination detection principle, and providing an example of broadcast/convergecast and controller movement.

## The Exercises

To enable the reader to gain practice in multiagent systems and DAI, a number of exercises of varying levels of difficulty are provided at the end of each chapter. The following rating system is applied to roughly indicate the amount of effort required for solving the exercises:

1. *[Level 1]* Exercises of Level 1 are solvable within a day (e.g., simple test of comprehension or a small program).

2. *[Level 2]* Solving exercises of Level 2 can take days or weeks (e.g., writting a fairly complex program). Usually the chapters provide all the information necessary for solving Level-1 and Level-2 exercises.

3. *[Level 3]* Exercises of Level 3 are even harder and their solution can take several weeks or months. Many of these exercises are related to "hot" topics of current research.

4. *[Level 4]* Exercises of Level 4 concern open research questions and could be topics of PhD theses. Solving Level-3 and Level-4 exercises typically requires to read further literature and/or to conduct extensive experiments.

It is recommend to do the Level-1 and Level-2 exercises, and to attack at least some of the exercises of Levels 3 and 4. Carefully working through Level-1 and Level-2 exercises will reward a reader with a real understanding of the material of the chapters, and solving Level-3 and Level-4 exercises will turn a reader into a real expert!

## The Glossary

The glossary at the end of the book is the result of a joint effort of the chapter authors. It provides compact explanations of a number of terms used in the field of multiagent systems and DAI. This glossary is neither intended to be complete nor to offer "definitions" in the strict sense of this word. Instead, the focus is on key terms and on their common usage. The primary purpose of the glossary is to make it easier for the readers to get acquainted with basic terminology.

## A Few Pointers to Further Readings

The number of publications on multiagent systems and DAI has grown rapidly in the past decade. The reader not familiar with the field and the available literature may find the following, by no means complete, list of pointers useful as an initial point of orientation:

- *Introductory texts, surveys, and overviews*:
  There are several general texts on multiagent systems and DAI (e.g., [2, 8, 20, 22, 25, 31, 40]), distributed problem solving (e.g., [10, 11, 17]), and agents (e.g., [5, 22, 45]).

- *Collections*:
  A detailed treatment of many key aspects of DAI is provided in [34]. A recent compendium that covers both agent and multiagent themes is [23]. A "classic" collection of DAI articles is [3]. Journal special issues on DAI and multiagent systems are, e.g., [9, 16, 46]. There is a number of proceedings of conferences and workshops on multiagent systems and DAI. For instance, the "International Conference on Multi-Agent Systems (ICMAS)" series resulted in three proceedings [12, 18, 30] that broadly cover the whole range of multiagent systems. The AAAI-sponsored "Workshop on DAI" series led to two other "classic" collections of DAI papers [19, 21]. The papers presented at the "European Workshop on Modelling Agents in a Multi-Agent World (MAAMAW)" series are published in [1, 7, 6, 13, 14, 35, 42, 43]. There are several conference and workshop series on agents. Among them are, for instance, the "International Conference on Autonomous Agents (Agents)" series [37, 41], the "International Workshop on Agent Theories, Architectures, and Languages (ATAL)" series [32, 39, 44, 47], and the "Cooperative Information Agents (CIA)" series [27, 28].

- *Bibliographies*:
  A useful list of pointers to published material on DAI and related areas is provided in [29]. A subject-indexed bibliography that comprehensively covers early DAI publications is [4].

- The first journal in the field is *Autonomous Agents and Multi-Agent Systems* (Kluwer Academic Publishers).

Pointers to papers that deal with specific aspects of multiagent systems are extensively included in the individual chapters.

# References

1. M. Boman and W. Van der Velde, editors. *Decentralized Artificial Intelligence. Proceedings of the Eighth European Workshop on Modelling Autonomous Agents in a Multi-Agent World (MAAMAW'97)*. Lecture Notes in Artificial Intelligence, Vol. 1237. Springer-Verlag, Berlin, 1997.

2. A.H. Bond and L. Gasser. An analysis of problems and research in DAI. In A.H. Bond and L. Gasser, editors, *Readings in Distributed Artificial Intelligence*, pages 3–35. Morgan Kaufmann, San Mateo, CA, 1988.

3. A.H. Bond and L. Gasser, editors. *Readings in Distributed Artificial Intelligence*. Morgan Kaufmann, San Mateo, CA, 1988.

4. A.H. Bond and L. Gasser. A subject-indexed bibliography of distributed artificial intelligence. In A.H. Bond and L. Gasser, editors, *Readings in Distributed Artificial Intelligence*, pages 37–56. Morgan Kaufmann, San Mateo, CA, 1988.

5. J.M. Bradshaw. An introduction to software agents. In J.M. Bradshaw, editor, *Software Agents*, pages 3–46. AAAI Press/The MIT Press, 1997.

6. C. Castelfranchi and J.-P. Müller, editors. *Decentralized Artificial Intelligence. Proceedings of the Fifth European Workshop on Modelling Autonomous Agents in a Multi-Agent World (MAAMAW'93)*. Lecture Notes in Artificial Intelligence, Vol. 957. Springer-Verlag, Berlin, 1995.

7. C. Castelfranchi and E. Werner, editors. *Decentralized Artificial Intelligence. Proceedings of the Fourth European Workshop on Modelling Autonomous Agents in a Multi-Agent World (MAAMAW'92)*. Lecture Notes in Artificial Intelligence, Vol. 830. Springer-Verlag, Berlin, 1994.

8. B. Chaib-draa, B. Moulin, R. Mandiau, and P. Millot. Trends in distributed artificial intelligence. *Artificial Intelligence Review*, 6(1):35–66, 1992.

9. B. Chandrasekaran, editor. Special Issue on Distributed Artificial Intelligence of the *IEEE Transactions on Systems, Man, and Cybernetics*. Vol. SMC-11, 1981.

10. K.S. Decker. Distributed problem solving techniques: A survey. *IEEE Transactions on Systems, Man, and Cybernetics*, SMC-17:729–740, 1987.

11. K.S. Decker, E.H. Durfee, and V.R. Lesser. Evaluating research in cooperative distributed problem solving. In M.N. Huhns and L. Gasser, editors, *Distributed Artificial Intelligence, Volume 2*, pages 487–519. Pitman/Morgan Kaufmann, Cambridge, MA, 1989.

12. Y. Demazeau, editor. *Proceedings of the Third International Conference on Multi-Agent Systems (ICMAS-98)*. IEEE Computer Society, 1998.

13. Y. Demazeau and J.-P. Müller, editors. *Decentralized Artificial Intelligence. Proceedings of the First European Workshop on Modelling Autonomous Agents in a Multi-Agent World (MAAMAW'89)*. North-Holland, 1990.

14. Y. Demazeau and J.-P. Müller, editors. *Decentralized Artificial Intelligence. Proceedings of the Second European Workshop on Modelling Autonomous Agents in a Multi-Agent World (MAAMAW'90)*. Elsevier Science, 1991.

15. E.H. Durfee. The distributed artificial intelligence melting pot. *IEEE Transactions on Systems, Man, and Cybernetics*, SMC-21(6):1301–1306, 1991.

16. E.H. Durfee, editor. Special Issue on Distributed Artificial Intelligence of the *IEEE Transactions on Systems, Man, and Cybernetics*. Vol. SMC-21, 1991.

17. E.H. Durfee, V.R. Lesser, and D.D. Corkill. Distributed problem solving. In S.C. Shapiro, editor, *Encyclopedia of Artificial Intelligence*, pages 379–388. John Wiley, 1992.

18. E.H. Durfee and M. Tokoro, editors. *Proceedings of the Second International Conference on Multi-Agent Systems (ICMAS-96)*. AAAI Press, 1996.

19. L. Gasser and M.N. Huhns, editors. *Distributed Artificial Intelligence, Volume 2*. Pitman/Morgan Kaufmann, 1989.

20. L. Gasser and M.N. Huhns. Themes in distributed artificial intelligence research. In L. Gasser and M.N. Huhns, editors, *Distributed Artificial Intelligence, Volume 2*, pages vii–xv. Pitman/Morgan Kaufmann, 1989.

21. M.N. Huhns, editor. *Distributed Artificial Intelligence*. Pitman/Morgan Kaufmann, 1987.

22. M.N. Huhns and M.P. Singh. Agents and multiagent systems: Themes, approaches, and challenges. In M.N. Huhns and M.P. Singh, editors, *Readings in Agents*, pages 1–23. Morgan Kaufmann, San Francisco, CA, 1998.

23. M.N. Huhns and M.P. Singh, editors. *Readings in Agents*. Morgan Kaufmann, San Francisco, CA, 1998.

24. N.R. Jennings, editor. *Cooperation in Industrial Multi-Agent Systems*. World Scientific, Singapore, 1994.

25. N.R. Jennings, K. Sycara, and M. Wooldridge. A roadmap of agent research and development. *Autonomous Agents and Multi-Agent Systems*, 1:7–38, 1998.

26. N.R. Jennings and M.J. Wooldridge, editors. *Agent Technology. Foundations, Applications, and Markets*. Springer-Verlag, Berlin, 1998.

27. P. Kandzia and M. Klusch, editors. *Cooperative Information Agents*. Lecture Notes in Artificial in Artificial Intelligence, Vol. 1202. Springer-Verlag, Berlin, 1997.

28. M. Klusch and G. Weiß, editors. *Cooperative Information Agents II*. Lecture Notes in Artificial in Artificial Intelligence, Vol. 1435. Springer-Verlag, Berlin, 1998.

29. D. Kwek and S. Kalenka. Distributed artificial intelligence references and resources. In G.M.P. O'Hare and N.R. Jennings, editors, *Foundations of Distributed Artificial Intelligence*, pages 557–572. John Wiley & Sons Inc., New York, 1996.

30. V.R. Lesser and L. Gasser, editors. *Proceedings of the First International Conference on Multi-Agent Systems (ICMAS-95)*. AAAI Press/The MIT Press, 1995.

31. B. Moulin and B. Chaib-Draa. An overview of distributed artificial intelligence. In G.M.P. O'Hare and N.R. Jennings, editors, *Foundations of Distributed Artificial Intelligence*, pages 3–55. John Wiley & Sons Inc., New York, 1996.

32. J.P. Müller, M. Wooldridge, and N.R. Jennings, editors. *Intelligent Agents III*. Lecture Notes in Artificial in Artificial Intelligence, Vol. 1193. Springer-Verlag, Berlin, 1997.

33. N.J. Nilsson. *Artificial Intelligence. A New Synthesis*. Morgan Kaufmann Publ., San Francisco, CA, 1998.

34. G.M.P. O'Hare and N.R. Jennings, editors. *Foundations of Distributed Artificial Intelligence*. John Wiley & Sons Inc., New York, 1996.

35. J.W. Perram and J.-P. Müller, editors. *Decentralized Artificial Intelligence. Proceedings of the Sixth European Workshop on Modelling Autonomous Agents in a*

*Multi-Agent World (MAAMAW'94)*. Lecture Notes in Artificial Intelligence, Vol. 1069. Springer-Verlag, Berlin, 1996.

36. D. Poole, A. Machworth, and R. Goebel. *Computational Intelligence*. Oxford University Press, New York, 1998.

37. *Proceedings of the First International Conference on Autonomous Agents (Agents'97)*. http://www.isi.edu/isd/Agents97/materials-order-form.html, 1997.

38. S.J. Russell and P. Norwig. *Artificial Intelligence. A Modern Approach*. Prentice Hall, Englewood Cliffs, New Jersey, 1995.

39. M.P. Singh, A. Rao, and M.J. Wooldridge, editors. *Intelligent Agents IV*. Lecture Notes in Artificial in Artificial Intelligence, Vol. 1365. Springer-Verlag, Berlin, 1998.

40. K. Sycara. Multiagent systems. *AI Magazine*, Summer:79–92, 1998.

41. K.P. Sycara and M. Wooldridge, editors. *Proceedings of the Second International Conference on Autonomous Agents (Agents'98)*. Association for Computing Machinery, Inc. (ACM), 1998.

42. W. Van der Velde and J.W. Perram, editors. *Decentralized Artificial Intelligence. Proceedings of the Seventh European Workshop on Modelling Autonomous Agents in a Multi-Agent World (MAAMAW'96)*. Lecture Notes in Artificial Intelligence, Vol. 1038. Springer-Verlag, Berlin, 1996.

43. E. Werner and Y. Demazeau, editors. *Decentralized Artificial Intelligence. Proceedings of the Third European Workshop on Modelling Autonomous Agents in a Multi-Agent World (MAAMAW'91)*. Elsevier Science, 1992.

44. M. Wooldridge and N.R. Jennings, editors. *Intelligent Agents*. Lecture Notes in Artificial in Artificial Intelligence, Vol. 890. Springer-Verlag, Berlin, 1995.

45. M. Wooldridge and N.R. Jennings. Intelligent agents: Theory and practice. *The Knowledge Engineering Review*, 10(2):115–152, 1995.

46. M. Wooldridge and N.R. Jennings, editors. Special Issue on Intelligent Agents and Multi-Agent Systems *Applied Artificial Intelligence Journal*. Vol. 9(4), 1995 and Vol. 10(1), 1996.

47. M. Wooldridge, J.P. Müller, and M. Tambe, editors. *Intelligent Agents II*. Lecture Notes in Artificial in Artificial Intelligence, Vol. 1037. Springer-Verlag, Berlin, 1996.

# Part I:

# Basic Themes

# 1    Intelligent Agents

Michael Wooldridge

## 1.1  Introduction

Computers are not very good at knowing what to do: every action a computer performs must be explicitly anticipated, planned for, and coded by a programmer. If a computer program ever encounters a situation that its designer did not anticipate, then the result is not usually pretty—a system crash at best, multiple loss of life at worst. This mundane fact is at the heart of our relationship with computers. It is so self-evident to the computer literate that it is rarely mentioned. And yet it comes as a complete surprise to those encountering computers for the first time.

For the most part, we are happy to accept computers as obedient, literal, unimaginative servants. For many applications (such as payroll processing), it is entirely acceptable. However, for an increasingly large number of applications, we require systems that can *decide for themselves* what they need to do in order to satisfy their design objectives. Such computer systems are known as *agents*. Agents that must operate robustly in rapidly changing, unpredictable, or open environments, where there is a significant possibility that actions can *fail* are known as *intelligent agents*, or sometimes *autonomous agents*. Here are examples of recent application areas for intelligent agents:

- When a space probe makes its long flight from Earth to the outer planets, a ground crew is usually required to continually track its progress, and decide how to deal with unexpected eventualities. This is costly and, if decisions are required *quickly*, it is simply not practicable. For these reasons, organisations like NASA are seriously investigating the possibility of making probes more autonomous—giving them richer decision making capabilities and responsibilities.

- Searching the Internet for the answer to a specific query can be a long and tedious process. So, why not allow a computer program—an agent—do searches for us? The agent would typically be given a query that would require synthesising pieces of information from various different Internet information sources. Failure would occur when a particular resource was unavailable, (perhaps due to network failure), or where results could not be obtained.

This chapter is about intelligent agents. Specifically, it aims to give you a thorough introduction to the main issues associated with the design and implementation of intelligent agents. After reading it, you will understand:

- why agents are believed to be an important new way of conceptualising and implementing certain types of software application;

- what intelligent agents are (and are not), and how agents relate to other software paradigms—in particular, expert systems and object-oriented programming;

- the main approaches that have been advocated for designing and implementing intelligent agents, the issues surrounding these approaches, their relative merits, and the challenges that face the agent implementor;

- the characteristics of the main programming languages available for building agents today.

The chapter is structured as follows. First, section 1.2 describes what is meant by the term *agent*. Section 1.3, presents some *abstract architectures* for agents. That is, some general models and properties of agents are discussed without regard to how they might be implemented. Section 1.4, discusses *concrete* architectures for agents. The various major design routes that one can follow in implementing an agent system are outlined in this section. In particular, *logic-based* architectures, *reactive* architectures, *belief-desire-intention* architectures, and finally, *layered* architectures for intelligent agents are described in detail. Finally, section 1.5 introduces some prototypical programming languages for agent systems.

### Comments on Notation

This chapter makes use of simple mathematical notation in order to make ideas precise. The formalism used is that of discrete maths: a basic grounding in sets and first-order logic should be quite sufficient to make sense of the various definitions presented. In addition: if $S$ is an arbitrary set, then $\wp(S)$ is the powerset of $S$, and $S^*$ is the set of sequences of elements of $S$; the symbol $\neg$ is used for logical negation (so $\neg p$ is read "not $p$"); $\wedge$ is used for conjunction (so $p \wedge q$ is read "$p$ and $q$"); $\vee$ is used for disjunction (so $p \vee q$ is read "$p$ or $q$"); and finally, $\Rightarrow$ is used for material implication (so $p \Rightarrow q$ is read "$p$ implies $q$").

## 1.2   What Are Agents?

An obvious way to open this chapter would be by presenting a definition of the term *agent*. After all, this is a book about multiagent systems—surely we must all agree on what an agent is? Surprisingly, there is no such agreement: there is no universally accepted definition of the term agent, and indeed there is a good deal of ongoing debate and controversy on this very subject. Essentially, while there is a general consensus that *autonomy* is central to the notion of agency, there is little agreement beyond this. Part of the difficulty is that various attributes associated with agency

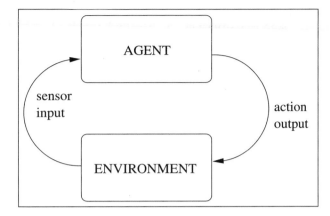

**Figure 1.1**  An agent in its environment. The agent takes sensory input from the environment, and produces as output actions that affect it. The interaction is usually an ongoing, non-terminating one.

are of differing importance for different domains. Thus, for some applications, the ability of agents to *learn* from their experiences is of paramount importance; for other applications, learning is not only unimportant, it is undesirable.

Nevertheless, some sort of definition is important—otherwise, there is a danger that the term will lose all meaning (cf. "user friendly"). The definition presented here is adapted from [71]: An *agent* is a computer system that is *situated* in some *environment*, and that is capable of *autonomous action* in this environment in order to meet its design objectives.

There are several points to note about this definition. First, the definition refers to "agents" and not "intelligent agents." The distinction is deliberate: it is discussed in more detail below. Second, the definition does not say anything about what *type* of environment an agent occupies. Again, this is deliberate: agents can occupy many different types of environment, as we shall see below. Third, we have not defined *autonomy*. Like agency itself, autonomy is a somewhat tricky concept to tie down precisely. In this chapter, it is used to mean that agents are able to act without the intervention of humans or other systems: they have control both over their own internal state, and over their behavior. In section 1.2.3, we will contrast agents with the objects of object-oriented programming, and we will elaborate this point there. In particular, we will see how agents embody a much stronger sense of autonomy than objects do.

Figure 1.1 gives an abstract, top-level view of an agent. In this diagram, we can see the action output generated by the agent in order to affect its environment. In most domains of reasonable complexity, an agent will not have *complete* control over its environment. It will have at best *partial* control, in that it can *influence* it. From the point of view of the agent, this means that the same action performed twice in apparently identical circumstances might appear to have entirely different effects, and in particular, it may *fail* to have the desired effect. Thus agents in all but the most trivial of environments must be prepared for the possibility of *failure*. We can sum this situation up formally by saying that environments are *non-deterministic*.

Normally, an agent will have a repertoire of actions available to it. This set of possible actions represents the agents *effectoric capability*: its ability to modify its environments. Note that not all actions can be performed in all situations. For example, an action "lift table" is only applicable in situations where the weight of the table is sufficiently small that the agent *can* lift it. Similarly, the action "purchase a Ferrari" will fail if insufficient funds area available to do so. Actions therefore have *pre-conditions* associated with them, which define the possible situations in which they can be applied.

The key problem facing an agent is that of deciding *which* of its actions it should perform in order to best satisfy its design objectives. *Agent architectures*, of which we shall see several examples later in this chapter, are really software architectures for decision making systems that are embedded in an environment. The complexity of the decision-making process can be affected by a number of different environmental properties. Russell and Norvig suggest the following classification of environment properties [59, p46]:

- *Accessible* vs *inaccessible*.
  An accessible environment is one in which the agent can obtain complete, accurate, up-to-date information about the environment's state. Most moderately complex environments (including, for example, the everyday physical world and the Internet) are inaccessible. The more accessible an environment is, the simpler it is to build agents to operate in it.

- *Deterministic* vs *non-deterministic*.
  As we have already mentioned, a deterministic environment is one in which any action has a single guaranteed effect—there is no uncertainty about the state that will result from performing an action. The physical world can to all intents and purposes be regarded as non-deterministic. Non-deterministic environments present greater problems for the agent designer.

- *Episodic* vs *non-episodic*.
  In an episodic environment, the performance of an agent is dependent on a number of discrete episodes, with no link between the performance of an agent in different scenarios. An example of an episodic environment would be a mail sorting system [60]. Episodic environments are simpler from the agent developer's perspective because the agent can decide what action to perform based only on the current episode—it need not reason about the interactions between this and future episodes.

- *Static* vs *dynamic*.
  A static environment is one that can be assumed to remain unchanged except by the performance of actions by the agent. A dynamic environment is one that has other processes operating on it, and which hence changes in ways beyond the agent's control. The physical world is a highly dynamic environment.

- *Discrete* vs *continuous*.

  An environment is discrete if there are a fixed, finite number of actions and percepts in it. Russell and Norvig give a chess game as an example of a discrete environment, and taxi driving as an example of a continuous one.

As Russell and Norvig observe [59, p46], if an environment is sufficiently complex, then the fact that it is *actually* deterministic is not much help: to all intents and purposes, it may as well be non-deterministic. The most complex general class of environments are those that are inaccessible, non-deterministic, non-episodic, dynamic, and continuous.

### 1.2.1   Examples of Agents

At this point, it is worth pausing to consider some examples of agents (though not, as yet, intelligent agents):

- Any *control* system can be viewed as an agent. A simple (and overused) example of such a system is a thermostat. Thermostats have a sensor for detecting room temperature. This sensor is directly embedded within the environment (i.e., the room), and it produces as output one of two signals: one that indicates that the temperature is too low, another which indicates that the temperature is OK. The actions available to the thermostat are "heating on" or "heating off". The action "heating on" will generally have the effect of raising the room temperature, but this cannot be a *guaranteed* effect—if the door to the room is open, for example, switching on the heater may have no effect. The (extremely simple) decision making component of the thermostat implements (usually in electro-mechanical hardware) the following rules:

$$\text{too cold} \longrightarrow \text{heating on}$$
$$\text{temperature OK} \longrightarrow \text{heating off}$$

  More complex environment control systems, of course, have considerably richer decision structures. Examples include autonomous space probes, fly-by-wire aircraft, nuclear reactor control systems, and so on.

- Most software daemons, (such as background processes in the UNIX operating system), which monitor a software environment and perform actions to modify it, can be viewed as agents. An example is the X Windows program `xbiff`. This utility continually monitors a user's incoming email, and indicates via a GUI icon whether or not they have unread messages. Whereas our thermostat agent in the previous example inhabited a *physical* environment—the physical world—the `xbiff` program inhabits a *software* environment. It obtains information about this environment by carrying out software functions (by executing system programs such as `ls`, for example), and the actions it performs are software actions (changing an icon on the screen, or executing a program). The decision making component is just as simple as our thermostat example.

To summarize, agents are simply computer systems that are capable of autonomous action in some environment in order to meet their design objectives. An agent will typically sense its environment (by physical sensors in the case of agents situated in part of the real world, or by software sensors in the case of software agents), and will have available a repertoire of actions that can be executed to modify the environment, which may appear to respond non-deterministically to the execution of these actions.

### 1.2.2    Intelligent Agents

We are not used to thinking of thermostats or UNIX daemons as agents, and certainly not as *intelligent* agents. So, when do we consider an agent to be intelligent? The question, like the question *what is intelligence?* itself, is not an easy one to answer. But for the purposes of this chapter, an intelligent agent is one that is capable of *flexible* autonomous action in order to meet its design objectives, where flexibility means three things [71]:

- *reactivity*: intelligent agents are able to perceive their environment, and respond in a timely fashion to changes that occur in it in order to satisfy their design objectives;

- *pro-activeness*: intelligent agents are able to exhibit goal-directed behavior by *taking the initiative* in order to satisfy their design objectives;

- *social ability*: intelligent agents are capable of interacting with other agents (and possibly humans) in order to satisfy their design objectives.

These properties are more demanding than they might at first appear. To see why, let us consider them in turn. First, consider *pro-activeness*: goal directed behavior. It is not hard to build a system that exhibits goal directed behavior—we do it every time we write a procedure in PASCAL, a function in C, or a method in JAVA. When we write such a procedure, we describe it in terms of the *assumptions* on which it relies (formally, its *pre-condition*) and the *effect* it has if the assumptions are valid (its *post-condition*). The effects of the procedure are its *goal*: what the author of the software intends the procedure to achieve. If the pre-condition holds when the procedure is invoked, then we expect that the procedure will execute *correctly*: that it will terminate, and that upon termination, the post-condition will be true, i.e., the goal will be achieved. This is goal directed behavior: the procedure is simply a plan or recipe for achieving the goal. This programming model is fine for many environments. For example, its works well when we consider *functional systems*—those that simply take some input $x$, and produce as output some some function $f(x)$ of this input. Compilers are a classic example of functional systems.

But for non-functional systems, this simple model of goal directed programming is not acceptable, as it makes some important limiting assumptions. In particular, it assumes that the environment *does not change* while the procedure is executing. If the environment does change, and in particular, if the assumptions (pre-condition) underlying the procedure become false while the procedure is executing, then the behavior of the procedure may not be defined—often, it will simply crash. Also, it is assumed that the goal, that is, the reason for executing the procedure, remains valid at least until the procedure terminates. If the goal does *not* remain valid, then there is simply no reason to continue executing the procedure.

In many environments, neither of these assumptions are valid. In particular, in domains that are *too complex* for an agent to observe completely, that are *multi-agent* (i.e., they are populated with more than one agent that can change the environment), or where there is *uncertainty* in the environment, these assumptions are not reasonable. In such environments, blindly executing a procedure without regard to whether the assumptions underpinning the procedure are valid is a poor strategy. In such dynamic environments, an agent must be *reactive*, in just the way that we described above. That is, it must be responsive to events that occur in its environment, where these events affect either the agent's goals or the assumptions which underpin the procedures that the agent is executing in order to achieve its goals.

As we have seen, building purely goal directed systems is not hard. As we shall see later in this chapter, building *purely reactive* systems—ones that *continually* respond to their environment—is also not difficult. However, what turns out to be hard is building a system that achieves an effective *balance* between goal-directed and reactive behavior. We want agents that will attempt to achieve their goals systematically, perhaps by making use of complex procedure-like patterns of action. But we don't want our agents to continue blindly executing these procedures in an attempt to achieve a goal either when it is clear that the procedure will not work, or when the goal is for some reason no longer valid. In such circumstances, we want our agent to be able to react to the new situation, in time for the reaction to be of some use. However, we do not want our agent to be *continually* reacting, and hence never focussing on a goal long enough to actually achieve it.

On reflection, it should come as little surprise that achieving a good balance between goal directed and reactive behavior is hard. After all, it is comparatively rare to find humans that do this very well. How many of us have had a manager who stayed blindly focussed on some project long after the relevance of the project was passed, or it was clear that the project plan was doomed to failure? Similarly, how many have encountered managers who seem unable to stay focussed at all, who flit from one project to another without ever managing to pursue a goal long enough to achieve *anything*? This problem—of effectively integrating goal-directed and reactive behavior—is one of the key problems facing the agent designer. As we shall see, a great many proposals have been made for how to build agents that can do this—but the problem is essentially still open.

Finally, let us say something about *social ability*, the final component of flexible autonomous action as defined here. In one sense, social ability is trivial: every day, millions of computers across the world routinely exchange information with both humans and other computers. But the ability to exchange bit streams is not really social ability. Consider that in the human world, comparatively few of our meaningful goals can be achieved without the *cooperation* of other people, who cannot be assumed to *share* our goals—in other words, they are themselves autonomous, with their own agenda to pursue. To achieve our goals in such situations, we must *negotiate* and *cooperate* with others. We may be required to understand and reason about the goals of others, and to perform actions (such as paying them money) that we would not otherwise choose to perform, in order to get them to cooperate with us, and achieve our goals. This type of social ability is much more complex, and much less well understood, than simply the ability to exchange binary information. Social ability in general (and topics such as negotiation and cooperation in particular) are dealt with elsewhere in this book, and will not therefore be considered here. In this chapter, we will be concerned with the decision making of *individual* intelligent agents in environments which may be dynamic, unpredictable, and uncertain, but do not contain other agents.

### 1.2.3   Agents and Objects

Object-oriented programmers often fail to see anything novel or new in the idea of agents. When one stops to consider the relative properties of agents and objects, this is perhaps not surprising. Objects are defined as computational entities that *encapsulate* some state, are able to perform actions, or *methods* on this state, and communicate by message passing.

While there are obvious similarities, there are also significant differences between agents and objects. The first is in the degree to which agents and objects are autonomous. Recall that the defining characteristic of object-oriented programming is the principle of encapsulation—the idea that objects can have control over their own internal state. In programming languages like JAVA, we can declare instance variables (and methods) to be `private`, meaning they are only accessible from within the object. (We can of course also declare them `public`, meaning that they can be accessed from anywhere, and indeed we must do this for methods so that they can be used by other objects. But the use of `public` instance variables is usually considered poor programming style.) In this way, an object can be thought of as exhibiting autonomy over its state: it has control over it. But an object does not exhibit control over it's *behavior*. That is, if a method m is made available for other objects to invoke, then they can do so whenever they wish—once an object has made a method `public`, then it subsequently has no control over whether or not that method is executed. Of course, an object *must* make methods available to other objects, or else we would be unable to build a system out of them. This is not normally an issue, because if we build a system, then we design the objects that go in it, and they can thus be assumed to share a "common goal". But in many types of multiagent system, (in particular, those that contain agents built by different organisations or individuals), no such common goal can be assumed. It cannot be for granted that an agent $i$ will execute an action (method) $a$ just because another agent $j$ wants it to—$a$ may not be in the best interests of $i$. We thus do not think of agents as invoking methods upon one-another, but rather as *requesting* actions to be performed. If $j$ requests $i$ to perform $a$, then $i$ may perform the action or it may not. The locus of control with respect to the decision about whether to execute an action is thus different in agent and object systems. In the object-oriented case, the decision lies with the object that invokes the method. In the agent case, the decision lies with the agent that receives the request. This distinction between objects and agents has been nicely summarized in the following slogan: *Objects do it for free; agents do it for money.*

Note that there is nothing to stop us implementing agents using object-oriented techniques. For example, we can build some kind of decision making about whether to execute a method into the method itself, and in this way achieve a stronger kind of autonomy for our objects. The point is that autonomy of this kind is not a component of the basic object-oriented model.

The second important distinction between object and agent systems is with respect to the notion of flexible (reactive, pro-active, social) autonomous behavior. The standard object model has nothing whatsoever to say about how to build systems that integrate these types of behavior. Again, one could object that we can build object-oriented programs that *do* integrate these types of behavior. But this argument misses the point, which is that the standard object-oriented programming model has nothing to do with these types of behavior.

The third important distinction between the standard object model and our view of agent systems is that agents are each considered to have their own thread of control—in the standard object model, there is a single thread of control in the system. Of course, a lot of work has recently been devoted to *concurrency* in object-oriented programming. For example, the JAVA language provides built-in constructs for multi-threaded programming. There are also many programming languages available (most of them admittedly prototypes) that were specifically designed to allow concurrent object-based programming. But such languages do not capture the idea we have of agents as *autonomous* entities. Perhaps the closest that the object-oriented community comes is in the idea of *active objects*:

*An active object is one that encompasses its own thread of control [...]. Active objects are generally autonomous, meaning that they can exhibit some behavior without being operated upon by another object. Passive objects, on the other hand, can only undergo a state change when explicitly acted upon. [5, p91]*

Thus active objects are essentially agents that do not necessarily have the ability to exhibit flexible autonomous behavior.

To summarize, the traditional view of an object and our view of an agent have at least three distinctions:

- agents embody stronger notion of autonomy than objects, and in particular, they decide for themselves whether or not to perform an action on request from another agent;
- agents are capable of flexible (reactive, pro-active, social) behavior, and the standard object model has nothing to say about such types of behavior;

■ a multiagent system is inherently multi-threaded, in that each agent is assumed to have at least one thread of control.

### 1.2.4   Agents and Expert Systems

Expert systems were the most important AI technology of the 1980s [31]. An expert system is one that is capable of solving problems or giving advice in some knowledge-rich domain [32]. A classic example of an expert system is MYCIN, which was intended to assist physicians in the treatment of blood infections in humans. MYCIN worked by a process of interacting with a user in order to present the system with a number of (symbolically represented) facts, which the system then used to derive some conclusion. MYCIN acted very much as a *consultant*: it did not operate directly on humans, or indeed any other environment. Thus perhaps the most important distinction between agents and expert systems is that expert systems like MYCIN are inherently *disembodied*. By this, we mean that they do not interact directly with any environment: they get their information not via sensors, but through a user acting as middle man. In the same way, they do not *act* on any environment, but rather give feedback or advice to a third party. In addition, we do not generally require expert systems to be capable of co-operating with other agents. Despite these differences, some expert systems, (particularly those that perform real-time control tasks), look very much like agents. A good example is the ARCHON system [33].

#### *Sources and Further Reading*

A view of artificial intelligence as the process of agent design is presented in [59], and in particular, Chapter 2 of [59] presents much useful material. The definition of agents presented here is based on [71], which also contains an extensive review of agent architectures and programming languages. In addition, [71] contains a detailed survey of *agent theories*—formalisms for reasoning about intelligent, rational agents, which is outside the scope of this chapter. This question of "what is an agent" is one that continues to generate some debate; a collection of answers may be found in [48]. The relationship between agents and objects has not been widely discussed in the literature, but see [24]. Other readable introductions to the idea of intelligent agents include [34] and [13].

## 1.3   Abstract Architectures for Intelligent Agents

We can easily formalize the abstract view of agents presented so far. First, we will assume that the state of the agent's environment can be characterized as a set $S = \{s_1, s_2, \ldots\}$ of *environment states*. At any given instant, the environment is assumed to be in one of these states. The effectoric capability of an agent is assumed to be represented by a set $A = \{a_1, a_2, \ldots\}$ of *actions*. Then abstractly, an agent can be viewed as a function

$$action : S^* \rightarrow A$$

which maps sequences of environment states to actions. We will refer to an agent modelled by a function of this form as a *standard agent*. The intuition is that an agent decides what action to perform on the basis of its history—its experiences to date. These experiences are represented as a sequence of environment states—those that the agent has thus far encountered.

The (non-deterministic) behavior of an an environment can be modelled as a function

$$env : S \times A \rightarrow \wp(S)$$

which takes the current state of the environment $s \in S$ and an action $a \in A$ (performed by the agent), and maps them to a set of environment states $env(s, a)$—those that could result from performing action $a$ in state $s$. If all the sets in the range of $env$ are all singletons, (i.e., if the result of performing any action in any state is a set containing a single member), then the environment is *deterministic*, and its behavior can be accurately predicted.

We can represent the interaction of agent and environment as a *history*. A history $h$ is a sequence:

$$h : s_0 \xrightarrow{a_0} s_1 \xrightarrow{a_1} s_2 \xrightarrow{a_2} s_3 \xrightarrow{a_3} \cdots \xrightarrow{a_{u-1}} s_u \xrightarrow{a_u} \cdots$$

where $s_0$ is the initial state of the environment (i.e., its state when the agent starts executing), $a_u$ is the $u$'th action that the agent chose to perform, and $s_u$ is the $u$'th environment state (which is one of the possible results of executing action $a_{u-1}$ in state $s_{u-1}$). If $action : S^* \rightarrow A$ is an agent, $env : S \times A \rightarrow \wp(S)$ is an environment, and $s_0$ is the initial state of the environment, then the sequence

$$h : s_0 \xrightarrow{a_0} s_1 \xrightarrow{a_1} s_2 \xrightarrow{a_2} s_3 \xrightarrow{a_3} \cdots \xrightarrow{a_{u-1}} s_u \xrightarrow{a_u} \cdots$$

will represent a possible history of the agent in the environment iff the following two conditions hold:

$$\forall u \in I\!N, a_u = action((s_0, s_1, \ldots, s_u))$$

and

$$\forall u \in I\!N \text{ such that } u > 0, s_u \in env(s_{u-1}, a_{u-1}).$$

The *characteristic behavior* of an agent $action : S^* \rightarrow A$ in an environment $env : S \times A \rightarrow \wp(S)$ is the set of all the histories that satisfy these properties. If some property $\phi$ holds of all these histories, this property can be regarded as an invariant property of the agent in the environment. For example, if our agent is a nuclear reactor controller, (i.e., the environment is a nuclear reactor), and in all possible histories of the controller/reactor, the reactor does not blow up, then this can be regarded as a (desirable) invariant property. We will denote by *hist*(*agent*, *environment*) the set of all histories of *agent* in *environment*. Two agents $ag_1$ and $ag_2$ are said to be *behaviorally equivalent* with respect to environment *env* iff *hist*($ag_1$, *env*) = *hist*($ag_2$, *env*), and simply behaviorally equivalent iff they are behaviorally equivalent with respect to all environments.

In general, we are interested in agents whose interaction with their environment *does not end*, i.e., they are *non-terminating*. In such cases, the histories that we consider will be infinite.

### 1.3.1   Purely Reactive Agents

Certain types of agents decide what to do without reference to their history. They base their decision making entirely on the present, with no reference at all to the past. We will call such agents *purely reactive*, since they simply respond directly to their environment. Formally, the behavior of a purely reactive agent can be represented by a function

$$action : S \rightarrow A.$$

It should be easy to see that for every purely reactive agent, there is an equivalent standard agent; the reverse, however, is not generally the case.

Our thermostat agent is an example of a purely reactive agent. Assume, without loss of generality, that the thermostat's environment can be in one of two states—either too cold, or temperature OK. Then the thermostat's action function is simply

$$action(s) = \begin{cases} \text{heater off} & \text{if } s = \text{temperature OK} \\ \text{heater on} & \text{otherwise.} \end{cases}$$

### 1.3.2   Perception

Viewing agents at this abstract level makes for a pleasantly simply analysis. However, it does not help us to construct them, since it gives us no clues about how to design the decision function *action*. For this reason, we will now begin to *refine* our abstract model of agents, by breaking it down into sub-systems in exactly the way that one does in standard software engineering. As we refine our view of agents, we find ourselves making *design choices* that mostly relate to the subsystems that go to make up an agent—what data and control structures will be present. An *agent architecture* is essentially a map of the internals of an agent—its data structures, the operations that may be performed on these data structures, and the control flow between these data structures. Later in this chapter, we will discuss a number of different types of agent architecture, with very different views on the data structures and algorithms that will be present within an agent. In the remainder of this section, however, we will survey some fairly high-level design decisions. The first of these is the separation of an agent's decision function into *perception* and *action* subsystems: see Figure 1.2.

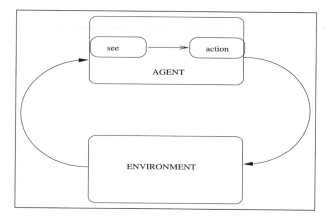

**Figure 1.2**    Perception and action subsystems.

The idea is that the function *see* captures the agent's ability to observe its environment, whereas the *action* function represents the agent's decision making process. The *see* function might be implemented in hardware in the case of an agent situated in the physical world: for example, it might be a video camera or an infra-red sensor on a mobile robot. For a software agent, the sensors might be system commands that obtain information about the software environment, such as `ls`, `finger`, or suchlike. The *output* of the *see* function is a *percept*—a perceptual input. Let $P$ be a (non-empty) set of percepts. Then *see* is a function

$$see : S \to P$$

which maps environment states to percepts, and *action* is now a function

$$action : P^* \to A$$

which maps sequences of percepts to actions.

These simple definitions allow us to explore some interesting properties of agents and perception. Suppose that we have two environment states, $s_1 \in S$ and $s_2 \in S$, such that $s_1 \neq s_2$, but $see(s_1) = see(s_2)$. Then two *different* environment states are mapped to the *same* percept, and hence the agent would receive the same perceptual information from different environment states. As far as the agent is concerned, therefore, $s_1$ and $s_2$ are *indistinguishable*. To make this example concrete, let us return to the thermostat example. Let $x$ represent the statement

"the room temperature is OK"

and let $y$ represent the statement

"John Major is Prime Minister."

If these are the only two facts about our environment that we are concerned with, then the set $S$ of environment states contains exactly four elements:

$$S = \{\underbrace{\{\neg x, \neg y\}}_{s_1}, \underbrace{\{\neg x, y\}}_{s_2}, \underbrace{\{x, \neg y\}}_{s_3}, \underbrace{\{x, y\}}_{s_4}\}$$

Thus in state $s_1$, the room temperature is not OK, and John Major is not Prime Minister; in state $s_2$, the room temperature is not OK, and John Major *is* Prime Minister. Now, our thermostat is sensitive *only* to temperatures in the room. This room temperature is not causally related to whether or not John Major is Prime Minister. Thus the states where John Major is and is not Prime Minister are literally *indistinguishable* to the thermostat. Formally, the *see* function for the thermostat would have two percepts in its range, $p_1$ and $p_2$, indicating that the temperature is too cold or OK respectively. The *see* function for the thermostat would behave as follows:

$$see(s) = \begin{cases} p_1 & \text{if } s = s_1 \text{ or } s = s_2 \\ p_2 & \text{if } s = s_3 \text{ or } s = s_4. \end{cases}$$

Given two environment states $s \in S$ and $s' \in S$, let us write $s \equiv s'$ if $see(s) = see(s')$. It is not hard to see that $\equiv$ is an *equivalence relation* over environment states, which partitions $S$ into mutually indistinguishable sets of states. Intuitively, the coarser these equivalence classes are, the less effective is the agent's perception. If $|\equiv| = |S|$, (i.e., the number of distinct percepts is equal to the number of different environment states), then the agent can distinguish *every* state—the agent has perfect perception in the environment; it is *omniscient*. At the other extreme, if $|\equiv| = 1$, then the agent's perceptual ability is non-existent—it cannot distinguish between *any* different states. In this case, as far as the agent is concerned, all environment states are identical.

### 1.3.3   Agents with State

We have so far been modelling an agent's decision function *action* as from *sequences* of environment states or percepts to actions. This allows us to represent agents whose decision making is influenced by history. However, this is a somewhat unintuitive representation, and we shall now replace it by an equivalent, but somewhat more natural scheme. The idea is that we now consider agents that *maintain state*—see Figure 1.3.

These agents have some internal data structure, which is typically used to record information about the environment state and history. Let $I$ be the set of all internal states of the agent. An agent's decision making process is then based, at least in part, on this information. The perception function *see* for a state-based agent is unchanged, mapping environment states to percepts as before:

$$see : S \rightarrow P$$

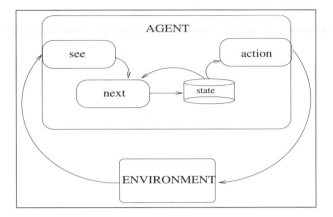

**Figure 1.3**   Agents that maintain state.

The action-selection function *action* is now defined a mapping

$$action : I \to A$$

from internal states to actions. An additional function *next* is introduced, which maps an internal state and percept to an internal state:

$$next : I \times P \to I$$

The behavior of a state-based agent can be summarized as follows. The agent starts in some initial internal state $i_0$. It then observes its environment state $s$, and generates a percept $see(s)$. The internal state of the agent is then updated via the *next* function, becoming set to $next(i_0, see(s))$. The action selected by the agent is then $action(next(i_0, see(s)))$. This action is then performed, and the agent enters another cycle, perceiving the world via *see*, updating its state via *next*, and choosing an action to perform via *action*.

It is worth observing that state-based agents as defined here are in fact no more powerful than the standard agents we introduced earlier. In fact, they are *identical* in their expressive power—every state-based agent can be transformed into a standard agent that is behaviorally equivalent.

### *Sources and Further Reading*

The abstract model of agents presented here is based on that given in [25, Chapter 13], and also makes use of some ideas from [61, 60]. The properties of perception as discussed in this section lead to *knowledge theory*, a formal analysis of the information implicit within the state of computer processes, which has had a profound effect in theoretical computer science. The definitive reference is [14], and an introductory survey is [29].

## 1.4   Concrete Architectures for Intelligent Agents

Thus far, we have considered agents only in the abstract. So while we have examined the properties of agents that do and do not maintain state, we have not stopped to consider what this state might look like. Similarly, we have modelled an agent's decision making as an abstract function *action*, which somehow manages to indicate which action to perform—but we have not discussed how this function might be implemented. In this section, we will rectify this omission. We will consider four classes of agents:

- *logic based agents*—in which decision making is realized through logical deduction;
- *reactive agents*—in which decision making is implemented in some form of direct mapping from situation to action;
- *belief-desire-intention agents*—in which decision making depends upon the manipulation of data structures representing the beliefs, desires, and intentions of the agent; and finally,
- *layered architectures*—in which decision making is realized via various software layers, each of which is more-or-less explicitly reasoning about the environment at different levels of abstraction.

In each of these cases, we are moving away from the abstract view of agents, and beginning to make quite specific commitments about the internal structure and operation of agents. Each section explains the nature of these commitments, the assumptions upon which the architectures depend, and the relative advantages and disadvantages of each.

### 1.4.1   Logic-Based Architectures

The "traditional" approach to building artificially intelligent systems, (known as *symbolic AI*) suggests that intelligent behavior can be generated in a system by giving that system a *symbolic* representation of its environment and its desired behavior, and syntactically manipulating this representation. In this section, we focus on the apotheosis of this tradition, in which these symbolic representations are *logical formulae*, and the syntactic manipulation corresponds to *logical deduction*, or *theorem proving*.

The idea of agents as theorem provers is seductive. Suppose we have some theory of agency—some theory that explains how an intelligent agent should behave. This theory might explain, for example, how an agent generates goals so as to satisfy its design objective, how it interleaves goal-directed and reactive behavior in order to achieve these goals, and so on. Then this theory $\phi$ can be considered as a *specification* for how an agent should behave. The traditional approach to implementing a system that will satisfy this specification would involve *refining* the specification through a series of progressively more concrete stages, until finally an implementation was reached. In the view of agents as theorem provers, however, no such refinement takes place. Instead, $\phi$ is viewed as an *executable specification*: it is *directly executed* in order to produce the agent's behavior.

To see how such an idea might work, we shall develop a simple model of logic-based agents, which we shall call *deliberate* agents. In such agents, the internal state is assumed to be a database of formulae of classical first-order predicate logic. For example, the agent's database might contain formulae such as:

$Open(valve221)$

$Temperature(reactor4726, 321)$

$Pressure(tank776, 28)$

It is not difficult to see how formulae such as these can be used to represent the properties of some environment. The database is the *information* that the agent has about its environment. An agent's database plays a somewhat analogous role to that of *belief* in humans. Thus a person might have a belief that valve 221 is open— the agent might have the predicate $Open(valve221)$ in its database. Of course, just like humans, agents can be wrong. Thus I might believe that valve 221 is open when it is in fact closed; the fact that an agent has $Open(valve221)$ in its database does not mean that valve 221 (or indeed any valve) is open. The agent's sensors may be faulty, its reasoning may be faulty, the information may be out of date, or the interpretation of the formula $Open(valve221)$ intended by the agent's designer may be something entirely different.

Let $L$ be the set of sentences of classical first-order logic, and let $D = \wp(L)$ be the set of $L$ *databases*, i.e., the set of sets of $L$-formulae. The internal state of an agent is then an element of $D$. We write $\Delta, \Delta_1, \ldots$ for members of $D$. The internal state of an agent is then simply a member of the set $D$. An agent's decision making process is modelled through a set of *deduction rules*, $\rho$. These are simply rules of inference for the logic. We write $\Delta \vdash_\rho \phi$ if the formula $\phi$ can be proved from the database $\Delta$ using only the deduction rules $\rho$. An agents perception function *see* remains unchanged:

$see : S \rightarrow P.$

Similarly, our *next* function has the form

$next : D \times P \rightarrow D$

It thus maps a database and a percept to a new database. However, an agent's action selection function, which has the signature

$action : D \rightarrow A$

is defined in terms of its deduction rules. The pseudo-code definition of this function is as follows.

```
1.      function action(Δ : D) : A
2.      begin
3.          for each a ∈ A do
4.              if Δ ⊢_ρ Do(a) then
5.                  return a
6.              end-if
7.          end-for
8.          for each a ∈ A do
9.              if Δ ⊬_ρ ¬Do(a) then
10.                 return a
11.             end-if
12.         end-for
13.         return null
14.     end function action
```

The idea is that the agent programmer will encode the deduction rules $\rho$ and database $\Delta$ in such a way that if a formula $Do(a)$ can be derived, where $a$ is a term that denotes an action, then $a$ is the best action to perform. Thus, in the first part of the function (lines (3)–(7)), the agent takes each of its possible actions $a$ in turn, and attempts to prove the form the formula $Do(a)$ from its database (passed as a parameter to the function) using its deduction rules $\rho$. If the agent succeeds in proving $Do(a)$, then $a$ is returned as the action to be performed.

What happens if the agent fails to prove $Do(a)$, for all actions $a \in A$? In this case, it attempts to find an action that is *consistent* with the rules and database, i.e., one that is not explicitly forbidden. In lines (8)–(12), therefore, the agent attempts to find an action $a \in A$ such that $\neg Do(a)$ cannot be derived from its database using its deduction rules. If it can find such an action, then this is returned as the action to be performed. If, however, the agent fails to find an action that is at least consistent, then it returns a special action *null* (or *noop*), indicating that no action has been selected.

In this way, the agent's behavior is determined by the agent's deduction rules (its "program") and its current database (representing the information the agent has about its environment).

To illustrate these ideas, let us consider a small example (based on the vacuum cleaning world example of [59, p51]). The idea is that we have a small robotic agent that will clean up a house. The robot is equipped with a sensor that will tell it whether it is over any dirt, and a vacuum cleaner that can be used to suck up dirt. In addition, the robot always has a definite orientation (one of *north*, *south*, *east*, or *west*). In addition to being able to suck up dirt, the agent can move forward one "step" or turn right 90°. The agent moves around a room, which is divided grid-like into a number of equally sized squares (conveniently corresponding to the unit of movement of the agent). We will assume that our agent does nothing but clean—it never leaves the room, and further, we will assume in the interests of simplicity that the room is a $3 \times 3$ grid, and the agent always starts in grid square $(0, 0)$ facing

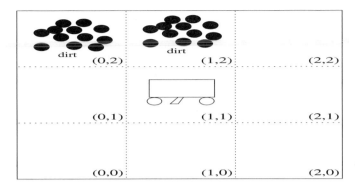

**Figure 1.4**   Vacuum world

north.

To summarize, our agent can receive a percept *dirt* (signifying that there is dirt beneath it), or *null* (indicating no special information). It can perform any one of three possible actions: *forward*, *suck*, or *turn*. The goal is to traverse the room continually searching for and removing dirt. See Figure 1.4 for an illustration of the vacuum world.

First, note that we make use of three simple *domain predicates* in this exercise:

$$In(x, y) \qquad \text{agent is at } (x, y)$$
$$Dirt(x, y) \quad \text{there is dirt at } (x, y)$$
$$Facing(d) \quad \text{the agent is facing direction } d$$

Now we specify our *next* function. This function must look at the perceptual information obtained from the environment (either *dirt* or *null*), and generate a new database which includes this information. But in addition, it must *remove* old or irrelevant information, and also, it must try to figure out the new location and orientation of the agent. We will therefore specify the *next* function in several parts. First, let us write $old(\Delta)$ to denote the set of "old" information in a database, which we want the update function *next* to remove:

$$old(\Delta) = \{P(t_1, \ldots, t_n) \mid P \in \{In, Dirt, Facing\} \text{ and } P(t_1, \ldots, t_n) \in \Delta\}$$

Next, we require a function *new*, which gives the set of new predicates to add to the database. This function has the signature

$$new : D \times P \to D$$

The definition of this function is not difficult, but it is rather lengthy, and so we will leave it as an exercise. (It must generate the predicates $In(\ldots)$, describing the new position of the agent, $Facing(\ldots)$ describing the orientation of the agent, and $Dirt(\ldots)$ if dirt has been detected at the new position.) Given the *new* and *old* functions, the *next* function is defined as follows:

$$next(\Delta, p) = (\Delta \setminus old(\Delta)) \cup new(\Delta, p)$$

Now we can move on to the rules that govern our agent's behavior. The deduction rules have the form

$$\phi(\ldots) \longrightarrow \psi(\ldots)$$

where $\phi$ and $\psi$ are predicates over some arbitrary list of constants and variables. The idea being that if $\phi$ matches against the agent's database, then $\psi$ can be concluded, with any variables in $\psi$ instantiated.

The first rule deals with the basic cleaning action of the agent: this rule will take priority over all other possible behaviors of the agent (such as navigation).

$$In(x,y) \wedge Dirt(x,y) \longrightarrow Do(suck) \tag{1.1}$$

Hence if the agent is at location $(x,y)$ and it perceives dirt, then the prescribed action will be to suck up dirt. Otherwise, the basic action of the agent will be to traverse the world. Taking advantage of the simplicity of our environment, we will hardwire the basic navigation algorithm, so that the robot will always move from $(0,0)$ to $(0,1)$ to $(0,2)$ and then to $(1,2)$, $(1,1)$ and so on. Once the agent reaches $(2,2)$, it must head back to $(0,0)$. The rules dealing with the traversal up to $(0,2)$ are very simple.

$$In(0,0) \wedge Facing(north) \wedge \neg Dirt(0,0) \longrightarrow Do(forward) \tag{1.2}$$

$$In(0,1) \wedge Facing(north) \wedge \neg Dirt(0,1) \longrightarrow Do(forward) \tag{1.3}$$

$$In(0,2) \wedge Facing(north) \wedge \neg Dirt(0,2) \longrightarrow Do(turn) \tag{1.4}$$

$$In(0,2) \wedge Facing(east) \longrightarrow Do(forward) \tag{1.5}$$

Notice that in each rule, we must explicitly check whether the antecedent of rule (1.1) fires. This is to ensure that we only ever prescribe one action via the $Do(\ldots)$ predicate. Similar rules can easily be generated that will get the agent to $(2,2)$, and once at $(2,2)$ back to $(0,0)$. It is not difficult to see that these rules, together with the *next* function, will generate the required behavior of our agent.

At this point, it is worth stepping back and examining the pragmatics of the logic-based approach to building agents. Probably the most important point to make is that a literal, naive attempt to build agents in this way would be more or less entirely impractical. To see why, suppose we have designed out agent's rule set $\rho$ such that for any database $\Delta$, if we can prove $Do(a)$ then $a$ is an *optimal* action—that is, $a$ is the best action that could be performed when the environment is as described in $\Delta$. Then imagine we start running our agent. At time $t_1$, the agent has generated some database $\Delta_1$, and begins to apply its rules $\rho$ in order to find which action to perform. Some time later, at time $t_2$, it manages to establish $\Delta_1 \vdash_\rho Do(a)$ for some $a \in A$, and so $a$ is the optimal action that the agent could perform at time $t_1$. But if the environment has *changed* between $t_1$ and $t_2$, then there is no guarantee that $a$ will *still* be optimal. It could be far from optimal, particularly if much time has elapsed between $t_1$ and $t_2$. If $t_2 - t_1$ is infinitesimal—that is, if decision making is effectively instantaneous—then we could safely disregard this problem. But in fact, we know that reasoning of the kind our logic-based agents use will be anything *but* instantaneous. (If our agent uses classical first-order predicate logic to represent the environment, and its rules are sound and complete, then there is no guarantee that the decision making procedure will even *terminate*.) An agent is said to enjoy the property of *calculative rationality* if and only if its decision making apparatus will suggest an action that was optimal *when the decision making process began*. Calculative rationality is clearly not acceptable in environments that change faster than the agent can make decisions—we shall return to this point later.

One might argue that this problem is an artifact of the pure logic-based approach adopted here. There is an element of truth in this. By moving away from strictly logical representation languages and complete sets of deduction rules, one can build agents that enjoy respectable performance. But one also loses what is arguably the greatest advantage that the logical approach brings: a simple, elegant logical semantics.

There are several other problems associated with the logical approach to agency. First, the *see* function of an agent, (its perception component), maps its environment to a percept. In the case of a logic-based agent, this percept is likely to be symbolic—typically, a set of formulae in the agent's representation language. But for many environments, it is not obvious how the mapping from environment to symbolic percept might be realized. For example, the problem of transforming an image to a set of declarative statements representing that image has been the object of study in AI for decades, and is still essentially open. Another problem is that actually *representing* properties of dynamic, real-world environments is extremely hard. As an example, representing and reasoning about *temporal information*—how a situation changes over time—turns out to be extraordinarily difficult. Finally, as the simple vacuum world example illustrates, representing even rather simple *procedural* knowledge (i.e., knowledge about "what to do") in traditional logic can be rather unintuitive and cumbersome.

To summarize, in logic-based approaches to building agents, decision making is viewed as deduction. An agent's "program"—that is, its decision making strategy—is encoded as a logical theory, and the process of selecting an action reduces to a problem of proof. Logic-based approaches are elegant, and have a clean (logical) semantics—wherein lies much of their long-lived appeal. But logic-based approaches have many disadvantages. In particular, the inherent computational complexity of theorem proving makes it questionable whether agents as theorem provers can operate effectively in time-constrained environments. Decision making in such agents is predicated on the assumption of calculative rationality—the assumption that the world will not change in any significant way while the agent is deciding what to do, and that an action which is rational when decision making begins will be rational when it concludes. The problems associated with representing and reasoning about complex, dynamic, possibly physical environments are also essentially unsolved.

### *Sources and Further Reading*

My presentation of logic based agents is based largely on the discussion of *deliberate agents* presented in [25, Chapter 13], which represents the logic-centric view of AI and agents very well. The discussion is also partly based on [38]. A number of more-or-less "pure" logical approaches to agent programming have been developed. Well-known examples include the CONGOLOG system of Lespérance and colleagues [39] (which is based on the *situation calculus* [45]) and the METATEM and Concurrent METATEM programming languages developed by Fisher and colleagues [3, 21] (in which agents are programmed by giving them *temporal logic* specifications of the behavior they should exhibit). Concurrent METATEM is discussed as a case study in section 1.5. Note that these architectures (and the discussion above) assume that if one adopts a logical approach to agent-building, then this means agents are essentially theorem provers, employing explicit symbolic reasoning (theorem proving) in order to make decisions. But just because we find logic a useful tool for conceptualising or specifying agents, this does not mean that we must view decision-making as logical manipulation. An alternative is to *compile* the logical specification of an agent into a form more amenable to efficient decision making. The difference is rather like the distinction between interpreted and compiled programming languages. The best-known example of this work is the *situated automata* paradigm of Leslie Kaelbling and Stanley Rosenschein [58]. A review of the role of logic in intelligent agents may be found in [70]. Finally, for a detailed discussion of calculative rationality and the way that it has affected thinking in AI, see [60].

### 1.4.2   Reactive Architectures

The seemingly intractable problems with symbolic/logical approaches to building agents led some researchers to question, and ultimately reject, the assumptions upon which such approaches are based. These researchers have argued that minor changes to the symbolic approach, such as weakening the logical representation language, will not be sufficient to build agents that can operate in time-constrained environments: nothing less than a whole new approach is required. In the mid-to-late 1980s, these researchers began to investigate alternatives to the symbolic AI paradigm. It is difficult to neatly characterize these different approaches, since their advocates are united mainly by a rejection of symbolic AI, rather than by a common manifesto. However, certain themes do recur:

- the rejection of symbolic representations, and of decision making based on syntactic manipulation of such representations;

- the idea that intelligent, rational behavior is seen as innately linked to the *environment* an agent occupies—intelligent behavior is not disembodied, but is a product of the *interaction* the agent maintains with its environment;

- the idea that intelligent behavior *emerges* from the interaction of various simpler behaviors.

Alternative approaches to agency are sometime referred to as *behavioral* (since a common theme is that of developing and combining individual behaviors), *situated* (since a common theme is that of agents actually situated in some environment, rather than being disembodied from it), and finally—the term used in this chapter—*reactive* (because such systems are often perceived as simply reacting to an environment, without reasoning about it). This section presents a survey of the *subsumption architecture*, which is arguably the best-known reactive agent architecture. It was developed by Rodney Brooks—one of the most vocal and influential critics of the symbolic approach to agency to have emerged in recent years.

There are two defining characteristics of the subsumption architecture. The first is that an agent's decision-making is realized through a set of *task accomplishing behaviors*; each behavior may be though of as an individual *action* function, as we defined above, which continually takes perceptual input and maps it to an action to perform. Each of these behavior modules is intended to achieve some particular task. In Brooks' implementation, the behavior modules are finite state machines. An important point to note is that these task accomplishing modules are assumed to include *no* complex symbolic representations, and are assumed to do *no* symbolic reasoning at all. In many implementations, these behaviors are implemented as rules of the form

situation $\longrightarrow$ action

which simple map perceptual input directly to actions.

The second defining characteristic of the subsumption architecture is that many behaviors can "fire" simultaneously. There must obviously be a mechanism to choose between the different actions selected by these multiple actions. Brooks proposed arranging the modules into a *subsumption hierarchy*, with the behaviors arranged into *layers*. Lower layers in the hierarchy are able to *inhibit* higher layers: the lower a layer is, the higher is its priority. The idea is that higher layers represent more abstract behaviors. For example, one might desire a behavior in a mobile robot for the behavior "avoid obstacles". It makes sense to give obstacle avoidance a high priority—hence this behavior will typically be encoded in a *low-level* layer, which has *high* priority. To illustrate the subsumption architecture in more detail, we will now present a simple formal model of it, and illustrate how it works by means of a short example. We then discuss its relative advantages and shortcomings, and point at other similar reactive architectures.

The *see* function, which represents the agent's perceptual ability, is assumed to remain unchanged. However, in implemented subsumption architecture systems, there is assumed to be quite tight coupling between perception and action—raw sensor input is not processed or transformed much, and there is certainly no attempt to transform images to symbolic representations.

The decision function *action* is realized through a set of behaviors, together with an *inhibition* relation holding between these behaviors. A behavior is a pair $(c, a)$, where $c \subseteq P$ is a set of percepts called the *condition*, and $a \in A$ is an action. A behavior $(c, a)$ will *fire* when the environment is in state $s \in S$ iff $see(s) \in c$. Let $Beh = \{(c, a) \mid c \subseteq P$ and $a \in A\}$ be the set of all such rules.

Associated with an agent's set of behavior rules $R \subseteq Beh$ is a binary *inhibition relation* on the set of behaviors: $\prec \subseteq R \times R$. This relation is assumed to be a total ordering on $R$ (i.e., it is transitive, irreflexive, and antisymmetric). We write $b_1 \prec b_2$ if $(b_1, b_2) \in \prec$, and read this as "$b_1$ inhibits $b_2$", that is, $b_1$ is lower in the hierarchy than $b_2$, and will hence get priority over $b_2$. The action function is then defined as follows:

```
1.      function action(p : P) : A
2.      var fired : ℘(R)
3.      var selected : A
4.      begin
5.          fired := {(c, a) | (c, a) ∈ R and p ∈ c}
6.          for each (c, a) ∈ fired do
7.              if ¬(∃(c′, a′) ∈ fired such that (c′, a′) ≺ (c, a)) then
8.                  return a
9.              end-if
10.         end-for
11.         return null
12.     end function action
```

Thus action selection begins by first computing the set *fired* of all behaviors that fire (5). Then, each behavior $(c, a)$ that fires is checked, to determine whether there is some other higher priority behavior that fires. If not, then the action part of the behavior, $a$, is returned as the selected action (8). If no behavior fires, then the distinguished action *null* will be returned, indicating that no action has been chosen.

Given that one of our main concerns with logic-based decision making was its theoretical complexity, it is worth pausing to examine how well our simple behavior-based system performs. The overall time complexity of the subsumption action function is no worse than $O(n^2)$, where $n$ is the larger of the number of behaviors or number of percepts. Thus, even with the naive algorithm above, decision making is tractable. In practice, we can do *considerably* better than this: the decision making logic can be encoded into hardware, giving *constant* decision time. For modern hardware, this means that an agent can be guaranteed to select an action within nano-seconds. Perhaps more than anything else, this computational simplicity is the strength of the subsumption architecture.

To illustrate how the subsumption architecture in more detail, we will show how subsumption architecture agents were built for the following scenario (this example is adapted from [66]):

*The objective is to explore a distant planet, more concretely, to collect samples of a particular type of precious rock. The location of the rock samples is not known in advance, but they are typically clustered in certain spots. A number of autonomous vehicles are available that can drive around the planet collecting samples and later reenter the a mothership spacecraft to go back to earth. There is no detailed map of the planet available, although it is known that the terrain is full of obstacles—hills, valleys, etc.—which prevent the vehicles from exchanging any communication.*

The problem we are faced with is that of building an agent control architecture for each vehicle, so that they will cooperate to collect rock samples from the planet surface as efficiently as possible. Luc Steels argues that logic-based agents, of the type we described above, are "entirely unrealistic" for this problem [66]. Instead, he proposes a solution using the subsumption architecture.

The solution makes use of two mechanisms introduced by Steels: The first is a *gradient field*. In order that agents can know in which direction the mothership lies, the mothership generates a radio signal. Now this signal will obviously weaken as distance to the source increases—to find the direction of the mothership, an agent need therefore only travel "up the gradient" of signal strength. The signal need not carry any information—it need only exist.

The second mechanism enables agents to communicate with one another. The characteristics of the terrain prevent direct communication (such as message passing), so Steels adopted an *indirect* communication method. The idea is that agents will carry "radioactive crumbs", which can be dropped, picked up, and detected by passing robots. Thus if an agent drops some of these crumbs in a particular location, then later, another agent happening upon this location will be able to detect them. This simple mechanism enables a quite sophisticated form of cooperation.

The behavior of an individual agent is then built up from a number of behaviors, as we indicated above. First, we will see how agents can be programmed to *individually* collect samples. We will then see how agents can be programmed to generate a *cooperative* solution.

For individual (non-cooperative) agents, the lowest-level behavior, (and hence the behavior with the highest "priority") is obstacle avoidance. This behavior can can be represented in the rule:

*if* detect an obstacle *then* change direction.                                   (1.6)

The second behavior ensures that any samples carried by agents are dropped back at the mother-ship.

*if* carrying samples *and* at the base *then* drop samples                         (1.7)

*if* carrying samples and *not* at the base *then* travel up gradient.              (1.8)

Behavior (1.8) ensures that agents carrying samples will return to the mother-ship (by heading towards the origin of the gradient field). The next behavior ensures that agents will collect samples they find.

*if* detect a sample *then* pick sample up.                     (1.9)

The final behavior ensures that an agent with "nothing better to do" will explore randomly.

*if* true *then* move randomly.                                (1.10)

The pre-condition of this rule is thus assumed to always fire. These behaviors are arranged into the following hierarchy:

$$(1.6) \prec (1.7) \prec (1.8) \prec (1.9) \prec (1.10)$$

The subsumption hierarchy for this example ensures that, for example, an agent will *always* turn if any obstacles are detected; if the agent is at the mother-ship and is carrying samples, then it will *always* drop them if it is not in any immediate danger of crashing, and so on. The "top level" behavior—a random walk—will only every be carried out if the agent has nothing more urgent to do. It is not difficult to see how this simple set of behaviors will solve the problem: agents will search for samples (ultimately by searching randomly), and when they find them, will return them to the mother-ship.

If the samples are distributed across the terrain entirely at random, then equipping a large number of robots with these very simple behaviors will work extremely well. But we know from the problem specification, above, that this is not the case: the samples tend to be located in clusters. In this case, it makes sense to have agents *cooperate* with one-another in order to find the samples. Thus when one agent finds a large sample, it would be helpful for it to communicate this to the other agents, so they can help it collect the rocks. Unfortunately, we also know from the problem specification that *direct* communication is impossible. Steels developed a simple solution to this problem, partly inspired by the foraging behavior of ants. The idea revolves around an agent creating a "trail" of radioactive crumbs whenever it finds a rock sample. The trail will be created when the agent returns the rock samples to the mother ship. If at some later point, another agent comes across this trail, then it need only follow it down the gradient field to locate the source of the rock samples. Some small refinements improve the efficiency of this ingenious scheme still further. First, as an agent follows a trail to the rock sample source, it picks up some of the crumbs it finds, hence making the trail fainter. Secondly, the trail is *only* laid by agents returning to the mothership. Hence if an agent follows the trail out to the source of the nominal rock sample only to find that it contains no samples, it will reduce the trail on the way out, and will not return with samples to reinforce it. After a few agents have followed the trail to find no sample at the end of it, the trail will in fact have been removed.

The modified behaviors for this example are as follows. Obstacle avoidance, (1.6), remains unchanged. However, the two rules determining what to do if carrying a sample are modified as follows.

*if* carrying samples *and* at the base *then* drop samples                    (1.11)

*if* carrying samples and *not* at the base
*then* drop 2 crumbs *and* travel up gradient.                    (1.12)

The behavior (1.12) requires an agent to drop crumbs when returning to base with
a sample, thus either reinforcing or creating a trail. The "pick up sample" behavior,
(1.9), remains unchanged. However, an additional behavior is required for dealing
with crumbs.

*if* sense crumbs *then* pick up 1 crumb *and* travel down gradient                    (1.13)

Finally, the random movement behavior, (1.10), remains unchanged. These behavior
are then arranged into the following subsumption hierarchy.

$$(1.6) \prec (1.11) \prec (1.12) \prec (1.9) \prec (1.13) \prec (1.10)$$

Steels shows how this simple adjustment achieves near-optimal performance in
many situations. Moreover, the solution is *cheap* (the computing power required
by each agent is minimal) and *robust* (the loss of a single agent will not affect the
overall system significantly).

   In summary, there are obvious advantages to reactive approaches such as that
Brooks' subsumption architecture: simplicity, economy, computational tractability,
robustness against failure, and elegance all make such architectures appealing. But
there are some fundamental, unsolved problems, not just with the subsumption
architecture, but with other purely reactive architectures:

- If agents do not employ models of their environment, then they must have
  sufficient information available in their *local* environment for them to determine
  an acceptable action.

- Since purely reactive agents make decisions based on *local* information, (i.e.,
  information about the agents *current* state), it is difficult to see how such decision
  making could take into account *non-local* information—it must inherently take
  a "short term" view.

- It is difficult to see how purely reactive agents can be designed that *learn* from
  experience, and improve their performance over time.

- A major selling point of purely reactive systems is that overall behavior *emerges*
  from the interaction of the component behaviors when the agent is placed in
  its environment. But the very term "emerges" suggests that the relationship
  between individual behaviors, environment, and overall behavior is not understandable. This necessarily makes it very hard to *engineer* agents to fulfill specific
  tasks. Ultimately, there is no principled *methodology* for building such agents:
  one must use a laborious process of experimentation, trial, and error to engineer
  an agent.

- While effective agents can be generated with small numbers of behaviors (typically less that ten layers), it is *much* harder to build agents that contain many layers. The dynamics of the interactions between the different behaviors become too complex to understand.

Various solutions to these problems have been proposed. One of the most popular of these is the idea of *evolving* agents to perform certain tasks. This area of work has largely broken away from the mainstream AI tradition in which work on, for example, logic-based agents is carried out, and is documented primarily in the *artificial life* (alife) literature.

### Sources and Further Reading

Brooks' original paper on the subsumption architecture—the one that started all the fuss—was published as [8]. The description and discussion here is partly based on [15]. This original paper seems to be somewhat less radical than many of his later ones, which include [9, 11, 10]. The version of the subsumption architecture used in this chapter is actually a simplification of that presented by Brooks. The subsumption architecture is probably the best-known reactive architecture around—but there are many others. The collection of papers edited by Pattie Maes [41] contains papers that describe many of these, as does the collection by Agre and Rosenschein [2]. Other approaches include:

- the *agent network architecture* developed by Pattie Maes [40, 42, 43];
- Nilsson's *teleo reactive programs* [49];
- Rosenchein and Kaelbling's *situated automata* approach, which is particularly interesting in that it shows how agents can be *specified* in an abstract, logical framework, and *compiled* into equivalent, but computationally very simple machines [57, 36, 35, 58];
- Agre and Chapman's PENGI system [1];
- Schoppers' *universal plans*—which are essentially decision trees that can be used to efficiently determine an appropriate action in any situation [62];
- Firby's *reactive action packages* [19].

Kaelbling [34] gives a good discussion of the issues associated with developing resource-bounded rational agents, and proposes an agent architecture somewhat similar to that developed by Brooks.

### 1.4.3   Belief-Desire-Intention Architectures

In this section, we shall discuss *belief-desire-intention* (BDI) architectures. These architectures have their roots in the philosophical tradition of understanding *practical reasoning*—the process of deciding, moment by moment, which action to perform in the furtherance of our goals.

Practical reasoning involves two important processes: deciding *what* goals we want to achieve, and *how* we are going to achieve these goals. The former process is known as *deliberation*, the latter as *means-ends* reasoning. To gain an understanding of the BDI model, it is worth considering a simple example of practical reasoning. When you leave university with a first degree, you are faced with a decision to make—about what to do with your life. The decision process typically begins by trying to understand what the *options* available to you are. For example, if you gain a good first degree, then one option is that of becoming an academic. (If you fail to obtain a good degree, this option is not available to you.) Another option is entering industry. After generating this set of alternatives, you must *choose between them*, and *commit* to some. These chosen options become *intentions*, which then determine the agent's actions. Intentions then feed back into the agent's future practical reasoning. For example, if I decide I want to be an academic, then I should commit to this objective, and devote time and effort to bringing it about.

Intentions play a crucial role in the practical reasoning process. Perhaps the most obvious property of intentions is that they tend to lead to action. If I truly have an intention to become an academic, then you would expect me to *act* on that intention—to try to achieve it. For example, you might expect me to apply to various PhD programs. You would expect to make a *reasonable attempt* to achieve the intention. Thus you would expect me to carry our some course of action that I believed would best satisfy the intention. Moreover, if a course of action fails to achieve the intention, then you would expect me to *try again*—you would not expect me to simply give up. For example, if my first application for a PhD programme is rejected, then you might expect me to apply to alternative universities.

In addition, once I have adopted an intention, then the very fact of having this intention will constrain my future practical reasoning. For example, while I hold some particular intention, I will not entertain options that are inconsistent with that intention. Intending to become an academic, for example, would preclude the option of partying every night: the two are mutually exclusive.

Next, intentions *persist*. If I adopt an intention to become an academic, then I should *persist* with this intention and attempt to achieve it. For if I immediately drop my intentions without devoting resources to achieving them, then I will never achieve anything. However, I should not persist with my intention for too long—if it becomes clear to me that I will *never* become an academic, then it is only rational to drop my intention to do so. Similarly, if the reason for having an intention goes away, then it is rational of me to drop the intention. For example, if I adopted the intention to become an academic because I believed it would be an easy life, but then discover that I would be expected to actually *teach*, then the justification for the intention is no longer present, and I should drop the intention.

Finally, intentions are closely related to beliefs about the future. For example, if I intend to become an academic, then I should believe that I will indeed become an academic. For if I truly believe that I will never be an academic, it would be non-sensical of me to have an intention to become one. Thus if I intend to become an academic, I should at least believe that there is a good chance I will indeed become one.

From this discussion, we can see that intentions play a number of important roles in practical reasoning:

- *Intentions drive means-ends reasoning.*
  If I have formed an intention to become an academic, then I will attempt to achieve the intention, which involves, amongst other things, deciding *how* to achieve it, for example, by applying for a PhD programme. Moreover, if one particular course of action fails to achieve an intention, then I will typically attempt others. Thus if I fail to gain a PhD place at one university, I might try another university.

- *Intentions constrain future deliberation.*
  If I intend to become an academic, then I will not entertain options that are inconsistent with this intention. For example, a rational agent would not consider being rich as an option while simultaneously intending to be an academic. (While the two are not actually mutually exclusive, the probability of simultaneously achieving both is infinitesimal.)

- *Intentions persist.*
  I will not usually give up on my intentions without good reason—they will persist, typically until either I believe I have successfully achieved them, I believe I cannot achieve them, or else because the purpose for the intention is no longer present.

- *Intentions influence beliefs upon which future practical reasoning is based.*
  If I adopt the intention to become an academic, then I can plan for the future on the assumption that I *will* be an academic. For if I intend to be an academic while simultaneously believing that I will never be one, then I am being irrational.

A key problem in the design of practical reasoning agents is that of of achieving a good *balance* between these different concerns. Specifically, it seems clear that an agent should at times drop some intentions (because it comes to believe that either they will never be achieved, they are achieved, or else because the reason for having the intention is no longer present). It follows that, from time to time, it is worth an agent stopping to *reconsider* its intentions. But reconsideration has a cost—in terms of both time and computational resources. But this presents us with a dilemma:

- an agent that does not stop to reconsider sufficiently often will continue attempting to achieve its intentions even after it is clear that they cannot be achieved, or that there is no longer any reason for achieving them;

- an agent that *constantly* reconsiders its attentions may spend insufficient time actually working to achieve them, and hence runs the risk of never actually achieving them.

This dilemma is essentially the problem of balancing pro-active (goal directed) and reactive (event driven) behavior, that we introduced in section 1.2.2.

There is clearly a tradeoff to be struck between the degree of commitment and reconsideration at work here. The nature of this tradeoff was examined by David Kinny and Michael Georgeff, in a number of experiments carried out with a BDI agent framework called dMARS [37]. They investigate how *bold* agents (those that never stop to reconsider) and *cautious* agents (those that are constantly stopping to reconsider) perform in a variety of different environments. The most important parameter in these experiments was the *rate of world change*, $\gamma$. The key results of Kinny and Georgeff were as follows.

- If $\gamma$ is low, (i.e., the environment does not change quickly), then bold agents do well compared to cautious ones, because cautious ones waste time reconsidering their commitments while bold agents are busy working towards—and achieving—their goals.

- If $\gamma$ is high, (i.e., the environment changes frequently), then cautious agents tend to outperform bold agents, because they are able to recognize when intentions are doomed, and also to take advantage of serendipitous situations and new opportunities.

The lesson is that different types of environment require different types of decision strategies. In static, unchanging environment, purely pro-active, goal directed behavior is adequate. But in more dynamic environments, the ability to react to changes by modififying intentions becomes more important.

The process of practical reasoning in a BDI agent is summarized in Figure 1.5. As this Figure illustrates, there are seven main components to a BDI agent:

- a set of current *beliefs*, representing information the agent has about its current environment;

- a *belief revision function*, $(brf)$, which takes a perceptual input and the agent's current beliefs, and on the basis of these, determines a new set of beliefs;

- an *option generation function*, $(options)$, which determines the options available to the agent (its desires), on the basis of its current beliefs about its environment and its current *intentions*;

- a set of *current options*, representing possible courses of actions available to the agent;

- a *filter* function $(filter)$, which represents the agent's *deliberation* process, and which determines the agent's intentions on the basis of its current beliefs, desires, and intentions;

- a set of current *intentions*, representing the agent's current focus—those states of affairs that it has committed to trying to bring about;

- an *action selection function* $(execute)$, which determines an action to perform on the basis of current intentions.

It is straightforward to formally define these components. First, let *Bel* be the set of all possible beliefs, *Des* be the set of all possible desires, and *Int* be the set of

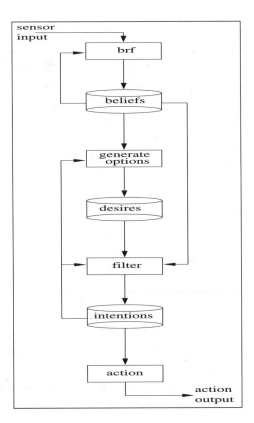

**Figure 1.5**   Schematic diagram of a generic belief-desire-intention architecture.

all possible intentions. For the purposes of this chapter, the content of these sets is not important. (Often, beliefs, desires, and intentions are represented as logical formulae, perhaps of first-order logic.) Whatever the content of these sets, its is worth noting that they should have some notion of *consistency* defined upon them, so that one can answer the question of, for example, whether having an intention to achieve $x$ is consistent with the belief that $y$. Representing beliefs, desires, and intentions as logical formulae permits us to cast such questions as questions as questions of determining whether logical formulae are consistent—a well known and well-understood problem. The state of a BDI agent at any given moment is, unsurprisingly, a triple $(B, D, I)$, where $B \subseteq Bel$, $D \subseteq Des$, and $I \subseteq Int$.

An agent's belief revision function is a mapping

$$brf : \wp(Bel) \times P \to \wp(Bel)$$

which on the basis of the current percept and current beliefs determines a new set of beliefs. Belief revision is out of the scope of this chapter (and indeed this book), and so we shall say no more about it here.

The option generation function, *options*, maps a set of beliefs and a set of intentions to a set of desires.

$options : \wp(Bel) \times \wp(Int) \to \wp(Des)$

This function plays several roles. First, it must be responsible for the agent's means-ends reasoning—the process of deciding how to achieve intentions. Thus, once an agent has formed an intention to $x$, it must subsequently consider options to *achieve* $x$. These options will be more concrete—less abstract—than $x$. As some of these options then become intentions themselves, they will also feedback into option generation, resulting in yet more concrete options being generated. We can thus think of a BDI agent's option generation process as one of recursively elaborating a hierarchical plan structure, considering and committing to progressively more specific intentions, until finally it reaches the intentions that correspond to immediately executable actions.

While the main purpose of the *options* function is thus means-ends reasoning, it must in addition satisfy several other constraints. First, it must be *consistent*: any options generated must be consistent with both the agent's current beliefs and current intentions. Secondly, it must be *opportunistic*, in that it should recognize when environmental circumstances change advantageously, to offer the agent new ways of achieving intentions, or the possibility of achieving intentions that were otherwise unachievable.

A BDI agent's deliberation process (deciding *what* to do) is represented in the *filter* function,

$filter : \wp(Bel) \times \wp(Des) \times \wp(Int) \to \wp(Int)$

which updates the agent's intentions on the basis of its previously-held intentions and current beliefs and desires. This function must fulfill two roles. First, it must *drop* any intentions that are no longer achievable, or for which the expected cost of achieving them exceeds the expected gain associated with successfully achieving them. Second, it should *retain* intentions that are not achieved, and that are still expected to have a positive overall benefit. Finally, it should *adopt* new intentions, either to achieve existing intentions, or to exploit new opportunities.

Notice that we do not expect this function to introduce intentions from nowhere. Thus *filter* should satisfy the following constraint:

$\forall B \in \wp(Bel), \forall D \in \wp(Des), \forall I \in \wp(Int), filter(B, D, I) \subseteq I \cup D.$

In other words, current intentions are either previously held intentions or newly adopted options.

The *execute* function is assumed to simply return any executable intentions—one that corresponds to a directly executable action:

$execute : \wp(Int) \to A$

The agent decision function, *action* of a BDI agent is then a function

$action : P \to A$

and is defined by the following pseudo-code.

```
1.      function action(p : P) : A
2.      begin
3.            B := brf(B, p)
4.            D := options(D, I)
5.            I := filter(B, D, I)
6.            return execute(I)
7.      end function action
```

Note that representing an agent's intentions as a *set* (i.e., as an unstructured collection) is generally too simplistic in practice. A simple alternative is to associate a *priority* with each intention, indicating its relative importance. Another natural idea is to represent intentions as a *stack*. An intention is pushed on to the stack when it is adopted, and popped when it is either achieved or else not achievable. More abstract intentions will tend to be at the bottom of the stack, with more concrete intentions towards the top.

To summarize, BDI architectures are practical reasoning architectures, in which the process of deciding what to do resembles the kind of practical reasoning that we appear to use in our everyday lives. The basic components of a BDI architecture are data structures representing the beliefs, desires, and intentions of the agent, and functions that represent its deliberation (deciding *what* intentions to have— i.e., deciding what to do) and means-ends reasoning (deciding how to do it). Intentions play a central role in the BDI model: they provide stability for decision making, and act to focus the agent's practical reasoning. A major issue in BDI architectures is the problem of striking a *balance* between being committed to and overcommitted to one's intentions: the deliberation process must be finely tuned to its environment, ensuring that in more dynamic, highly unpredictable domains, it reconsiders its intentions relatively frequently—in more static environments, less frequent reconsideration is necessary.

The BDI model is attractive for several reasons. First, it is intuitive—we all recognize the processes of deciding what to do and then how to do it, and we all have an informal understanding of the notions of belief, desire, and intention. Second, it gives us a clear functional decomposition, which indicates what sorts of subsystems might be required to build an agent. But the main difficulty, as ever, is knowing how to efficiently implement these functions.

### Sources and Further Reading

Belief-desire-intention architectures originated in the work of the Rational Agency project at Stanford Research Institute in the mid 1980s. The origins of the model lie in the theory of human practical reasoning developed by the philosopher Michael Bratman [6], which focusses particularly on the role of intentions in practical reasoning. The conceptual framework of the BDI model is described in [7], which also describes a specific BDI agent architecture called IRMA. The description of the BDI model given here (and in particular Figure 1.5) is adapted from [7]. One of the interesting aspects of the BDI model is that it has been used in one of the most successful agent architectures to date. The Procedural Resoning System (PRS), originally developed by Michael Georgeff and Amy Lansky [26], has been used to build some of the most exacting agent applications to date, including fault diagnosis for the reaction control system of the space shuttle, and an air traffic management system at Sydney airport in Australia—overviews of these systems are described in [27]. In the PRS, an agent is equipped with a library of *plans* which are used to perform means-ends reasoning. Deliberation is achieved by the use of *meta-level plans*, which are able to modify an agent's intention structure at runtime, in order to change the focus of the agent's practical reasoning. Beliefs in the PRS are represented as PROLOG-like facts—essentially, as atoms of first-order logic.

The BDI model is also interesting because a great deal of effort has been devoted to formalising it. In particular, Anand Rao and Michael Georgeff have developed a range of BDI logics, which they use to axiomatize properties of BDI-based practical reasoning agents [52, 56, 53, 54, 55, 51]. These models have been extended by others to deal with, for example, communication between agents [28].

### 1.4.4 Layered Architectures

Given the requirement that an agent be capable of reactive and pro-active behavior, an obvious decomposition involves creating separate subsystems to deal with these different types of behaviors. This idea leads naturally to a class of architectures in which the various subsystems are arranged into a hierarchy of interacting *layers*. In this section, we will consider some general aspects of layered architectures, and then go on to consider two examples of such architectures: INTERRAP and TOURINGMACHINES.

Typically, there will be at least two layers, to deal with reactive and pro-active behaviors respectively. In principle, there is no reason why there should not be many more layers. However many layers there are, a useful typology for such architectures is by the information and control flows within them. Broadly speaking, we can identify two types of control flow within layered architectures (see Figure 1.6):

- *Horizontal layering.*
  In horizontally layered architectures (Figure 1.6(a)), the software layers are each directly connected to the sensory input and action output. In effect, each layer itself acts like an agent, producing suggestions as to what action to perform.

- *Vertical layering.*
  In vertically layered architectures (Figure 1.6(b) and 1.6(c)), sensory input and action output are each dealt with by at most one layer each.

The great advantage of horizontally layered architectures is their conceptual simplicity: if we need an agent to exhibit $n$ different types of behavior, then we imple-

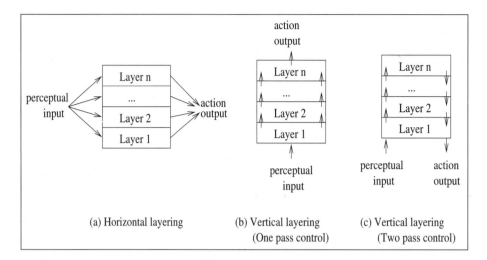

**Figure 1.6**  Information and control flows in three types of layered agent architecture (Source: [47, p263]).

ment $n$ different layers. However, because the layers are each in effect competing with one-another to generate action suggestions, there is a danger that the *overall* behavior of the agent will not be coherent. In order to ensure that horizontally layered architectures *are* consistent, they generally include a *mediator* function, which makes decisions about which layer has "control" of the agent at any given time. The need for such central control is problematic: it means that the designer must potentially consider all possible interactions between layers. If there are $n$ layers in the architecture, and each layer is capable of suggesting $m$ possible actions, then this means there are $m^n$ such interactions to be considered. This is clearly difficult from a design point of view in any but the most simple system. The introduction of a central control system also introduces a *bottleneck* into the agent's decision making.

These problems are partly alleviated in a vertically layered architecture. We can subdivide vertically layered architectures into *one pass* architectures (Figure 1.6(b)) and *two pass* architectures (Figure 1.6(c)). In one-pass architectures, control flows sequentially through each layer, until the final layer generates action output. In two-pass architectures, information flows up the architecture (the first pass) and control then flows back down. There are some interesting similarities between the idea of two-pass vertically layered architectures and the way that organisations work, with information flowing up to the highest levels of the organisation, and commands then flowing down. In both one pass and two pass vertically layered architectures, the complexity of interactions between layers is reduced: since there are $n - 1$ interfaces between $n$ layers, then if each layer is capable of suggesting $m$ actions, there are at most $m^2(n - 1)$ interactions to be considered between layers. This is clearly much simpler than the horizontally layered case. However, this simplicity comes at the cost of some flexibility: in order for a vertically layered architecture to

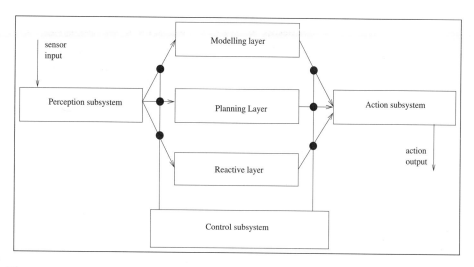

**Figure 1.7** TOURINGMACHINES: a horizontally layered agent architecture

make a decision, control must pass between *each* different layer. This is not fault tolerant: failures in any one layer are likely to have serious consequences for agent performance.

In the remainder of this section, we will consider two examples of layered architectures: Innes Ferguson's TOURINGMACHINES, and Jörg Müller's INTERRAP. The former is an example of a horizontally layered architecture; the latter is a (two pass) vertically layered architecture.

### *TouringMachines*

The TOURINGMACHINES architecture is illustrated in Figure 1.7. As this Figure shows, TOURINGMACHINES consists of three *activity producing layers*. That is, each layer continually produces "suggestions" for what actions the agent should perform. The *reactive layer* provides a more-or-less immediate response to changes that occur in the environment. It is implemented as a set of situation-action rules, like the behaviors in Brooks' subsumption architecture (section 1.4.2). These rules map sensor input directly to effector output. The original demonstration scenario for TOURINGMACHINES was that of autonomous vehicles driving between locations through streets populated by other similar agents. In this scenario, reactive rules typically deal with functions like obstacle avoidance. For example, here is an example of a reactive rule for avoiding the kerb (from [16, p59]):

```
rule-1: kerb-avoidance
    if
        is-in-front(Kerb, Observer) and
        speed(Observer) > 0 and
        separation(Kerb, Observer) < KerbThreshHold
```

```
then
    change-orientation(KerbAvoidanceAngle)
```

Here `change-orientation(...)` is the action suggested if the rule fires. The rules can only make references to the agent's current state—they cannot do any explicit reasoning about the world, and on the right hand side of rules are *actions*, not predicates. Thus if this rule fired, it would not result in any central environment model being updated, but would just result in an action being suggested by the reactive layer.

The TOURINGMACHINES *planning layer* achieves the agent's pro-active behavior. Specifically, the planning layer is responsible for the "day-to-day" running of the agent—under normal circumstances, the planning layer will be responsible for deciding what the agent does. However, the planning layer does not do "first-principles" planning. That is, it does not attempt to generate plans from scratch. Rather, the planning layer employs a *library* of plan "skeletons" called *schemas*. These skeletons are in essence hierarchically structured plans, which the TOURINGMACHINES planning layer elaborates at run time in order to decide what to do. So, in order to achieve a goal, the planning layer attempts to find a schema in its library which matches that goal. This schema will contain sub-goals, which the planning layer elaborates by attempting to find other schemas in its plan library that match these sub-goals.

The *modeling* layer represents the various entities in the world (including the agent itself, as well as other agents). The modeling layer thus predicts conflicts between agents, and generates new goals to be achieved in order to resolve these conflicts. These new goals are then posted down to the planning layer, which makes use of its plan library in order to determine how to satisfy them.

The three control layers are embedded within a *control subsystem*, which is effectively responsible for deciding which of the layers should have control over the agent. This control subsystem is implemented as a set of *control rules*. Control rules can either *suppress* sensor information between the control rules and the control layers, or else *censor* action outputs from the control layers. Here is an example censor rule [18, p207]:

```
censor-rule-1:
    if
        entity(obstacle-6) in perception-buffer
    then
        remove-sensory-record(layer-R, entity(obstacle-6))
```

This rule prevents the reactive layer from ever knowing about whether `obstacle-6` has been perceived. The intuition is that although the reactive layer will in general be the most appropriate layer for dealing with obstacle avoidance, there are certain obstacles for which other layers are more appropriate. This rule ensures that the reactive layer never comes to know about these obstacles.

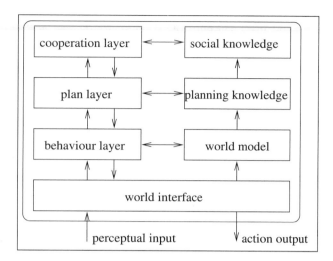

**Figure 1.8**   INTERRAP—a vertically layered two-pass agent architecture.

### *InteRRaP*

INTERRAP is an example of a vertically layered two-pass agent architecture—see Figure 1.8.

As Figure 1.8 shows, INTERRAP contains three control layers, as in TOURINGMA-CHINES. Moreover, the purpose of each INTERRAP layer appears to be rather similar to the purpose of each corresponding TOURINGMACHINES layer. Thus the lowest (*behavior based*) layer deals with reactive behavior; the middle (*local planning*) layer deals with everyday planning to achieve the agent's goals, and the uppermost (*cooperative planning*) layer deals with social interactions. Each layer has associated with it a *knowledge base*, i.e., a representation of the world appropriate for that layer. These different knowledge bases represent the agent and its environment at different levels of abstraction. Thus the highest level knowledge base represents the plans and actions of other agents in the environment; the middle-level knowledge base represents the plans and actions of the agent itself; and the lowest level knowledge base represents "raw" information about the environment. The explicit introduction of these knowledge bases distinguishes TOURINGMACHINES from INTERRAP.

The way the different layers in INTERRAP conspire to produce behavior is also quite different from TOURINGMACHINES. The main difference is in the way the layers interract with the environment. In TOURINGMACHINES, each layer was directly coupled to perceptual input and action output. This necessitated the introduction of a supervisory control framework, to deal with conflicts or problems between layers. In INTERRAP, layers interact with *each other* to achieve the same end. The two main types of interaction between layers are *bottom-up activation* and *top-down execution*. Bottom-up activation occurs when a lower layer passes control to a higher layer because it is not *competent* to deal with the current situation. Top-down execution occurs when a higher layer makes use of the facilities provided by a lower layer to achieve one of its goals. The basic flow of control in INTERRAP begins when perceptual input arrives at the lowest layer in the achitecture. If the reactive layer can deal with this input, then it will do so; otherwise, bottom-up activation will occur, and control will be passed to the local planning layer. If the local planning layer can handle the situation, then it will do so, typically by making use of top-down execution. Otherwise, it will use bottom-up activation to pass control to the highest layer. In this way, control in INTERRAP will flow from the lowest layer to higher layers of the architecture, and then back down again.

The internals of each layer are not important for the purposes of this chapter. However, it is worth noting that each layer implements two general functions. The first of these is a *situation recognition and goal activation* function. This function acts rather like the *options* function in a BDI architecture (see section 1.4.3). It maps a knowledge base (one of the three layers) and current goals to a new set of goals. The second function is responsible for *planning and scheduling*—it is responsible for selecting which plans to execute, based on the current plans, goals, and knowledge base of that layer.

Layered architectures are currently the most popular general class of agent architecture available. Layering represents a natural decomposition of functionality: it is easy to see how reactive, pro-active, social behavior can be generated by the reactive, pro-active, and social layers in an architecture. The main problem with layered architectures is that while they are arguably a *pragmatic* solution, they lack the conceptual and semantic clarity of unlayered approaches. In particular, while logic-based approaches have a clear logical semantics, it is difficult to see how such a semantics could be devised for a layered architecture. Another issue is that of interactions between layers. If each layer is an independent activity producing process (as in TOURINGMACHINES), then it is necessary to consider all possible ways that the layers can interact with one another. This problem is partly alleviated in two-pass vertically layered architecture such as INTERRAP.

### Sources and Further Reading

The introductory discussion of layered architectures given here draws heavily upon [47, pp262–264]. The best reference to TOURINGMACHINES is [16]; more accessible references include [17, 18]. The definitive reference to INTERRAP is [46], although [20] is also a useful reference. Other examples of layered architectures include the subsumption architecture [8] (see also section 1.4.2), and the 3T architecture [4].

## 1.5   Agent Programming Languages

As agent technology becomes more established, we might expect to see a variety of software tools become available for the design and construction of agent-based

systems; the need for software support tools in this area was identified as long ago
as the mid-1980s [23]. In this section, we will discuss two of the better-known agent
programming languages, focussing in particular on Yoav Shoham's AGENT0 system.

### 1.5.1  Agent-Oriented Programming

Yoav Shoham has proposed a "new programming paradigm, based on a societal
view of computation" which he calls *agent-oriented programming*. The key idea
which informs AOP is that of directly programming agents in terms of *mentalistic*
notions (such as belief, desire, and intention) that agent theorists have developed
to represent the properties of agents. The motivation behind the proposal is
that humans use such concepts as an *abstraction* mechanism for representing the
properties of complex systems. In the same way that we use these mentalistic
notions to describe and explain the behavior of humans, so it might be useful
to use them to program machines.

The first implementation of the agent-oriented programming paradigm was the
AGENT0 programming language. In this language, an agent is specified in terms of a
set of capabilities (things the agent can do), a set of initial *beliefs* (playing the role
of beliefs in BDI architectures), a set of initial *commitments* (playing a role similar
to that of intentions in BDI architectures), and a set of *commitment rules*. The key
component, which determines how the agent acts, is the commitment rule set. Each
commitment rule contains a *message condition*, a *mental condition*, and an action.
In order to determine whether such a rule fires, the message condition is matched
against the messages the agent has received; the mental condition is matched against
the beliefs of the agent. If the rule fires, then the agent becomes committed to the
action. Actions may be *private*, corresponding to an internally executed subroutine,
or *communicative*, i.e., sending messages. Messages are constrained to be one of
three types: "requests" or "unrequests" to perform or refrain from actions, and
"inform" messages, which pass on information—Shoham indicates that he took his
inspiration for these message types from speech act theory [63, 12]. Request and
unrequest messages typically result in the agent's commitments being modified;
inform messages result in a change to the agent's beliefs.

Here is an example of an AGENT0 commitment rule:

```
COMMIT(
   ( agent, REQUEST, DO(time, action)
   ), ;;; msg condition
   ( B,
     [now, Friend agent] AND
     CAN(self, action) AND
     NOT [time, CMT(self, anyaction)]
   ), ;;; mental condition
   self,
   DO(time, action)  )
```

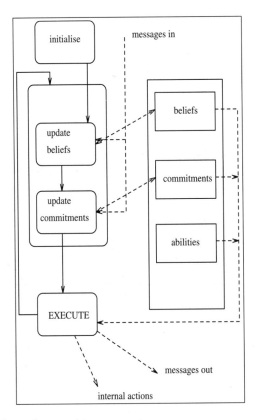

**Figure 1.9**   The flow of control in AGENT-0.

This rule may be paraphrased as follows:

*if I receive a message from agent which requests me to do action at time, and I believe that:*

- *agent is currently a friend;*
- *I can do the action;*
- *at time, I am not committed to doing any other action,*

*then commit to doing action at time.*

The operation of an agent can be described by the following loop (see Figure 1.9):

1.   Read all current messages, updating beliefs—and hence commitments—where necessary;

2.   Execute all commitments for the current cycle where the capability condition of the associated action is satisfied;

3.   Goto (1).

It should be clear how more complex agent behaviors can be designed and built in AGENT0. However, it is important to note that this language is essentially a *prototype*, not intended for building anything like large-scale production systems. But it does at least give a feel for how such systems might be built.

### 1.5.2  Concurrent METATEM

The Concurrent METATEM language developed by Fisher is based on the direct execution of logical formulae [21]. A Concurrent METATEM system contains a number of concurrently executing agents, each of which is able to communicate with its peers via asynchronous broadcast message passing. Each agent is programmed by giving it a *temporal logic* specification of the behavior that it is intended the agent should exhibit. An agent's specification is executed directly to generate its behavior. Execution of the agent program corresponds to iteratively building a logical model for the temporal agent specification. It is possible to prove that the procedure used to execute an agent specification is correct, in that if it is possible to satisfy the specification, then the agent will do so [3].

The logical semantics of Concurrent METATEM are closely related to the semantics of temporal logic itself. This means that, amongst other things, the specification and verification of Concurrent METATEM systems is a realistic proposition [22].

An agent program in Concurrent METATEM has the form $\bigwedge_i P_i \Rightarrow F_i$, where $P_i$ is a temporal logic formula referring only to the present or past, and $F_i$ is a temporal logic formula referring to the present or future. The $P_i \Rightarrow F_i$ formulae are known as *rules*. The basic idea for executing such a program may be summed up in the following slogan:

on the basis of the past do the future.

Thus each rule is continually matched against an internal, recorded *history*, and if a match is found, then the rule *fires*. If a rule fires, then any variables in the future time part are instantiated, and the future time part then becomes a *commitment* that the agent will subsequently attempt to satisfy. Satisfying a commitment typically means making some predicate true within the agent. Here is a simple example of a Concurrent METATEM agent definition:

$rc(ask)[give]$ :

$\quad \bigcirc\!\!\!\bullet\, ask(x) \Rightarrow \Diamond give(x)$

$\quad (\neg ask(x) \; \mathcal{Z} \; (give(x) \wedge \neg ask(x))) \Rightarrow \neg give(x)$

$\quad give(x) \wedge give(y) \Rightarrow (x = y)$

The agent in this example is a controller for a resource that is infinitely renewable, but which may only be possessed by one agent at any given time. The controller must therefore enforce mutual exclusion over this resource. The first line of the program defines the *interface* to the agent: its name is $rc$ (for resource controller), and it will accept *ask* messages and send *give* messages. The following three lines constitute the agent program itself. The predicate $ask(x)$ means that agent $x$ has asked for the resource. The predicate $give(x)$ means that the resource controller has given the resource to agent $x$. The resource controller is assumed to be the only agent able to "give" the resource. However, many agents may ask for the resource simultaneously. The three rules that define this agent's behavior may be summarized as follows:

Rule 1: if someone has just asked for the resource, then eventually give them the resource;

Rule 2: don't give unless someone has asked since you last gave; and

Rule 3: if you give to two people, then they must be the same person (i.e., don't give to more than one person at a time).

Concurrent METATEM is a good illustration of how a quite pure approach to logic-based agent programming can work, even with a quite expressive logic.

### Sources and Further Reading

The main references to AGENT0 are [64, 65]. Michael Fisher's Concurrent METATEM language is described in [21]; the execution algorithm that underpins it is described in [3]. Since Shoham's proposal, a number of languages have been proposed which claim to be agent-oriented. Examples include Becky Thomas's Planning Communicating Agents (PLACA) language [67, 68], MAIL [30], and Anand Rao's AGENTS-PEAK(L) language [50]. APRIL is a language that is intended to be used for building multiagent systems, although it is not "agent-oriented" in the sense that Shoham describes [44]. The TELESCRIPT programming language, developed by General Magic, Inc., was the first *mobile* agent programming language [69]. That is, it explicitly supports the idea of agents as processes that have the ability to autonomously move themselves across a computer network and recommence executing at a remote site. Since TELESCRIPT was announced, a number of mobile agent extensions to the JAVA programming language have been developed.

## 1.6    Conclusions

I hope that after reading this chapter, you understand what agents are and why they are considered to be an important area of research and development. The requirement for systems that can operate autonomously is very common. The requirement for systems capable of *flexible* autonomous action, in the sense that I have described in this chapter, is similarly common. This leads me to conclude that intelligent agents have the potential to play a significant role in the future of software engineering. Intelligent agent research is about the theory, design, construction, and application of such systems. This chapter has focussed on the design of intelligent agents. It has presented a high-level, abstract view of intelligent agents, and described the sort of properties that one would expect such an agent to enjoy. It went on to show how this view of an agent could be refined into various different types of agent architecture—purely logical agents, purely reactive/behavioral agents, BDI agents, and layered agent architectures.

## 1.7 Exercises

1.  *[Level 1]* Give other examples of agents (not necessarily intelligent) that you know of. For each, define as precisely as possible:

    (a)   the environment that the agent occupies (physical, software, ...), the states that this environment can be in, and whether the environment is: accessible or inaccessible; deterministic or non-deterministic; episodic or non-episodic; static or dynamic; discrete or continuous.

    (b)   the action repertoire available to the agent, and any pre-conditions associated with these actions;

    (c)   the goal, or design objectives of the agent—what it is intended to achieve.

2.  *[Level 1]* Prove that

    (a)   for every purely reactive agent, these is a behaviorally equivalent standard agent.

    (b)   there exist standard agents that have no behaviorally equivalent purely reactive agent.

3.  *[Level 1]* Prove that state-based agents are equivalent in expressive power to standard agents, i.e., that for every state-based agent there is a behaviorally equivalent standard agent and vice versa.

4.  *[Level 2]* The following few questions refer to the vacuum world example described in section 1.4.1.
    Give the full definition (using pseudo-code if desired) of the *new* function, which defines the predicates to add to the agent's database.

5.  *[Level 2]* Complete the vacuum world example, by filling in the missing rules. How intuitive do you think the solution is? How elegant is it? How compact is it?

6.  *[Level 2]* Try using your favourite (imperative) programming language to code a solution to the basic vacuum world example. How do you think it compares to the logical solution? What does this tell you about trying to encode essentially *procedural* knowledge (i.e., knowledge about what action to perform) as purely logical rules?

7.  *[Level 2]* If you are familiar with PROLOG, try encoding the vacuum world example in this language and running it with randomly placed dirt. Make use of the `assert` and `retract` meta-level predicates provided by PROLOG to simplify your system (allowing the program itself to achieve much of the operation of the *next* function).

8. *[Level 2]* Develop a solution to the vacuum world example using the behavior-based approach described in section 1.4.2. How does it compare to the logic-based example?

9. *[Level 2]* Try scaling the vacuum world up to a $10 \times 10$ grid size. Approximately how many rules would you need to encode this enlarged example, using the approach presented above? Try to generalize the rules, encoding a more general decision making mechanism.

10. *[Level 3]* Suppose that the vacuum world could also contain *obstacles*, which the agent needs to avoid. (Imagine it is equipped with a sensor to detect such obstacles.) Try to adapt the example to deal with obstacle detection and avoidance. Again, compare a logic-based solution to one implemented in a traditional (imperative) programming language.

11. *[Level 3]* Suppose the agent's sphere of perception in the vacuum world is enlarged, so that it can see the *whole* of its world, and see *exactly* where the dirt lay. In this case, it would be possible to generate an *optimal* decision-making algorithm—one which cleared up the dirt in the smallest time possible. Try and think of such general algorithms, and try to code them both in first-order logic and a more traditional programming language. Investigate the effectiveness of these algorithms when there is the possibility of *noise* in the perceptual input the agent receives, (i.e., there is a non-zero probability that the perceptual information is wrong), and try to develop decision-making algorithms that are robust in the presence of such noise. How do such algorithms perform as the level of perception is reduced?

12. *[Level 2]* Try developing a solution to the Mars explorer example from section 1.4.2 using the logic-based approach. How does it compare to the reactive solution?

13. *[Level 3]* In the programming language of your choice, implement the Mars explorer example using the subsumption architecture. (To do this, you may find it useful to implement a simple subsumption architecture "shell" for programming different behaviors.) Investigate the performance of the two approaches described, and see if you can do better.

14. *[Level 3]* Using the simulator implemented for the preceding question, see what happens as you increase the number of agents. Eventually, you should see that overcrowding leads to a sub-optimal solution—agents spend too much time getting out of each other's way to get any work done. Try to get around this problem by allowing agents to pass samples to each other, thus implementing *chains*. (See the description in [15, p305].)

15. *[Level 4]* Read about traditional *control theory*, and compare the problems and techniques of control theory to what are trying to accomplish in building intelligent agents. How are the techniques and problems of traditional control theory similar to those of intelligent agent work, and how do they differ?

16. *[Level 4]* One advantage of the logic-based approach to building agents is that

the logic-based architecture is *generic*: first-order logic turns out to extremely powerful and useful for expressing a range of different properties. Thus it turns out to be possible to use the logic-based architecture to *encode* a range of other architectures. For this exercise, you should attempt to use first-order logic to encode the different architectures (reactive, BDI, layered) described in this chapter. (You will probably need to read the original references to be able to do this.) Once completed, you will have a logical *theory* of the architecture, that will serve both as a formal specification of the architecture, and also as a precise mathematical model of it, amenable to proof. Once you have your logically-specified architecture, try to *animate* it, by mapping your logical theory of it into, say the PROLOG programming language. What compromises do you have to make? Does it seem worthwhile trying to directly program the system in logic, or would it be simpler to implement your system in a more pragmatic programming language (such as JAVA)?

## 1.8   References

1.  P. Agre and D. Chapman. PENGI: An implementation of a theory of activity. In *Proceedings of the Sixth National Conference on Artificial Intelligence (AAAI-87)*, pages 268–272, Seattle, WA, 1987.

2.  P. E. Agre and S. J. Rosenschein, editors. *Computational Theories of Interaction and Agency.* The MIT Press: Cambridge, MA, 1996.

3.  H. Barringer, M. Fisher, D. Gabbay, G. Gough, and R. Owens. METATEM: A framework for programming in temporal logic. In *REX Workshop on Stepwise Refinement of Distributed Systems: Models, Formalisms, Correctness (LNCS Volume 430)*, pages 94–129. Springer-Verlag: Berlin, Germany, June 1989.

4.  R. P. Bonasso, D. Kortenkamp, D. P. Miller, and M. Slack. Experiences with an architecture for intelligent, reactive agents. In M. Wooldridge, J. P. Müller, and M. Tambe, editors, *Intelligent Agents II (LNAI Volume 1037)*, pages 187–202. Springer-Verlag: Berlin, Germany, 1996.

5.  G. Booch. *Object-Oriented Analysis and Design (second edition).* Addison-Wesley: Reading, MA, 1994.

6.  M. E. Bratman. *Intentions, Plans, and Practical Reason.* Harvard University Press: Cambridge, MA, 1987.

7.  M. E. Bratman, D. J. Israel, and M. E. Pollack. Plans and resource-bounded practical reasoning. *Computational Intelligence*, 4:349–355, 1988.

8.  R. A. Brooks. A robust layered control system for a mobile robot. *IEEE Journal of Robotics and Automation*, 2(1):14–23, 1986.

9.  R. A. Brooks. Elephants don't play chess. In P. Maes, editor, *Designing Autonomous Agents*, pages 3–15. The MIT Press: Cambridge, MA, 1990.

10. R. A. Brooks. Intelligence without reason. In *Proceedings of the Twelfth International Joint Conference on Artificial Intelligence (IJCAI-91)*, pages 569–595, Sydney, Australia, 1991.

11. R. A. Brooks. Intelligence without representation. *Artificial Intelligence*, 47:139–159, 1991.

12. P. R. Cohen and C. R. Perrault. Elements of a plan based theory of speech acts. *Cognitive Science*, 3:177–212, 1979.

13. Oren Etzioni. Intelligence without robots. *AI Magazine*, 14(4), December 1993.

14. R. Fagin, J. Y. Halpern, Y. Moses, and M. Y. Vardi. *Reasoning About Knowledge*. The MIT Press: Cambridge, MA, 1995.

15. J. Ferber. Reactive distributed artificial intelligence. In G. M. P. O'Hare and N. R. Jennings, editors, *Foundations of Distributed Artificial Intelligence*, pages 287–317. John Wiley, 1996.

16. I. A. Ferguson. *TouringMachines: An Architecture for Dynamic, Rational, Mobile Agents*. PhD thesis, Clare Hall, University of Cambridge, UK, November 1992. (Also available as Technical Report No. 273, University of Cambridge Computer Laboratory).

17. I. A. Ferguson. Towards an architecture for adaptive, rational, mobile agents. In E. Werner and Y. Demazeau, editors, *Decentralized AI 3 — Proceedings of the Third European Workshop on Modelling Autonomous Agents in a Multi-Agent World (MAAMAW-91)*, pages 249–262. Elsevier Science Publishers B.V.: Amsterdam, The Netherlands, 1992.

18. I. A. Ferguson. Integrated control and coordinated behaviour: A case for agent models. In M. Wooldridge and N. R. Jennings, editors, *Intelligent Agents: Theories, Architectures, and Languages (LNAI Volume 890)*, pages 203–218. Springer-Verlag: Berlin, Germany, January 1995.

19. J. A. Firby. An investigation into reactive planning in complex domains. In *Proceedings of the Tenth International Joint Conference on Artificial Intelligence (IJCAI-87)*, pages 202–206, Milan, Italy, 1987.

20. K. Fischer, J. P. Müller, and M. Pischel. A pragmatic BDI architecture. In M. Wooldridge, J. P. Müller, and M. Tambe, editors, *Intelligent Agents II (LNAI Volume 1037)*, pages 203–218. Springer-Verlag: Berlin, Germany, 1996.

21. M. Fisher. A survey of Concurrent METATEM — the language and its applications. In D. M. Gabbay and H. J. Ohlbach, editors, *Temporal Logic — Proceedings of the First International Conference (LNAI Volume 827)*, pages 480–505. Springer-Verlag: Berlin, Germany, July 1994.

22. M. Fisher and M. Wooldridge. Specifying and verifying distributed intelligent systems. In M. Filgueiras and L. Damas, editors, *Progress in Artificial Intelligence — Sixth Portuguese Conference on Artificial Intelligence (LNAI Volume 727)*, pages 13–28. Springer-Verlag: Berlin, Germany, October 1993.

23. L. Gasser, C. Braganza, and N. Hermann. MACE: A flexible testbed for distributed AI research. In M. Huhns, editor, *Distributed Artificial Intelligence*, pages 119–152. Pitman Publishing: London and Morgan Kaufmann: San Mateo, CA, 1987.

24. L. Gasser and J. P. Briot. Object-based concurrent programming and DAI. In *Distributed Artificial Intelligence: Theory and Praxis*, pages 81–108. Kluwer Academic Publishers: Boston, MA, 1992.

25. M. R. Genesereth and N. Nilsson. *Logical Foundations of Artificial Intelligence*. Morgan Kaufmann Publishers: San Mateo, CA, 1987.

26. M. P. Georgeff and A. L. Lansky. Reactive reasoning and planning. In *Proceedings of the Sixth National Conference on Artificial Intelligence (AAAI-87)*, pages 677–682, Seattle, WA, 1987.

27.  M. P. Georgeff and A. S. Rao. A profile of the Australian AI Institute. *IEEE Expert*, 11(6):89–92, December 1996.

28.  A. Haddadi. *Communication and Cooperation in Agent Systems (LNAI Volume 1056)*. Springer-Verlag: Berlin, Germany, 1996.

29.  J. Y. Halpern. Using reasoning about knowledge to analyze distributed systems. *Annual Review of Computer Science*, 2:37–68, 1987.

30.  H. Haugeneder, D. Steiner, and F. G. M$^c$Cabe. IMAGINE: A framework for building multi-agent systems. In S. M. Deen, editor, *Proceedings of the 1994 International Working Conference on Cooperating Knowledge Based Systems (CKBS-94)*, pages 31–64, DAKE Centre, University of Keele, UK, 1994.

31.  F. Hayes-Roth, D. A. Waterman, and D. B. Lenat, editors. *Building Expert Systems*. Addison-Wesley: Reading, MA, 1983.

32.  P. Jackson. *Introduction to Expert Systems*. Addison-Wesley: Reading, MA, 1986.

33.  N. R. Jennings, J. Corera, I. Laresgoiti, E. H. Mamdani, F. Perriolat, P. Skarek, and L. Z. Varga. Using ARCHON to develop real-world DAI applications for electricity transportation management and particle accelerator control. *IEEE Expert*, dec 1996.

34.  L. P. Kaelbling. An architecture for intelligent reactive systems. In M. P. Georgeff and A. L. Lansky, editors, *Reasoning About Actions & Plans — Proceedings of the 1986 Workshop*, pages 395–410. Morgan Kaufmann Publishers: San Mateo, CA, 1986.

35.  L. P. Kaelbling. A situated automata approach to the design of embedded agents. *SIGART Bulletin*, 2(4):85–88, 1991.

36.  L. P. Kaelbling and S. J. Rosenschein. Action and planning in embedded agents. In P. Maes, editor, *Designing Autonomous Agents*, pages 35–48. The MIT Press: Cambridge, MA, 1990.

37.  D. Kinny and M. Georgeff. Commitment and effectiveness of situated agents. In *Proceedings of the Twelfth International Joint Conference on Artificial Intelligence (IJCAI-91)*, pages 82–88, Sydney, Australia, 1991.

38.  K. Konolige. *A Deduction Model of Belief*. Pitman Publishing: London and Morgan Kaufmann: San Mateo, CA, 1986.

39.  Y. Lésperance, H. J. Levesque, F. Lin, D. Marcu, R. Reiter, and R. B. Scherl. Foundations of a logical approach to agent programming. In M. Wooldridge, J. P. Müller, and M. Tambe, editors, *Intelligent Agents II (LNAI Volume 1037)*, pages 331–346. Springer-Verlag: Berlin, Germany, 1996.

40.  P. Maes. The dynamics of action selection. In *Proceedings of the Eleventh International Joint Conference on Artificial Intelligence (IJCAI-89)*, pages 991–997, Detroit, MI, 1989.

41.  P. Maes, editor. *Designing Autonomous Agents*. The MIT Press: Cambridge, MA, 1990.

42.  P. Maes. Situated agents can have goals. In P. Maes, editor, *Designing Autonomous Agents*, pages 49–70. The MIT Press: Cambridge, MA, 1990.

43.  P. Maes. The agent network architecture (ANA). *SIGART Bulletin*, 2(4):115–120, 1991.

44.  F. G. M$^c$Cabe and K. L. Clark. `April` — agent process interaction language. In M. Wooldridge and N. R. Jennings, editors, *Intelligent Agents: Theories, Architectures, and Languages (LNAI Volume 890)*, pages 324–340. Springer-Verlag:

Berlin, Germany, January 1995.

45. J. McCarthy and P. J. Hayes. Some philosophical problems from the standpoint of artificial intelligence. In B. Meltzer and D. Michie, editors, *Machine Intelligence 4*. Edinburgh University Press, 1969.

46. J. Müller. A cooperation model for autonomous agents. In J. P. Müller, M. Wooldridge, and N. R. Jennings, editors, *Intelligent Agents III (LNAI Volume 1193)*, pages 245–260. Springer-Verlag: Berlin, Germany, 1997.

47. J. P. Müller, M. Pischel, and M. Thiel. Modelling reactive behaviour in vertically layered agent architectures. In M. Wooldridge and N. R. Jennings, editors, *Intelligent Agents: Theories, Architectures, and Languages (LNAI Volume 890)*, pages 261–276. Springer-Verlag: Berlin, Germany, January 1995.

48. J. P. Müller, M. Wooldridge, and N. R. Jennings, editors. *Intelligent Agents III (LNAI Volume 1193)*. Springer-Verlag: Berlin, Germany, 1995.

49. N. J. Nilsson. Towards agent programs with circuit semantics. Technical Report STAN–CS–92–1412, Computer Science Department, Stanford University, Stanford, CA 94305, January 1992.

50. A. S. Rao. AgentSpeak(L): BDI agents speak out in a logical computable language. In W. Van de Velde and J. W. Perram, editors, *Agents Breaking Away: Proceedings of the Seventh European Workshop on Modelling Autonomous Agents in a Multi-Agent World, (LNAI Volume 1038)*, pages 42–55. Springer-Verlag: Berlin, Germany, 1996.

51. A. S. Rao. Decision procedures for propositional linear-time Belief-Desire-Intention logics. In M. Wooldridge, J. P. Müller, and M. Tambe, editors, *Intelligent Agents II (LNAI Volume 1037)*, pages 33–48. Springer-Verlag: Berlin, Germany, 1996.

52. A. S. Rao and M. P. Georgeff. Asymmetry thesis and side-effect problems in linear time and branching time intention logics. In *Proceedings of the Twelfth International Joint Conference on Artificial Intelligence (IJCAI-91)*, pages 498–504, Sydney, Australia, 1991.

53. A. S. Rao and M. P. Georgeff. Modeling rational agents within a BDI-architecture. In R. Fikes and E. Sandewall, editors, *Proceedings of Knowledge Representation and Reasoning (KR&R-91)*, pages 473–484. Morgan Kaufmann Publishers: San Mateo, CA, April 1991.

54. A. S. Rao and M. P. Georgeff. An abstract architecture for rational agents. In C. Rich, W. Swartout, and B. Nebel, editors, *Proceedings of Knowledge Representation and Reasoning (KR&R-92)*, pages 439–449, 1992.

55. A. S. Rao and M. P. Georgeff. A model-theoretic approach to the verification of situated reasoning systems. In *Proceedings of the Thirteenth International Joint Conference on Artificial Intelligence (IJCAI-93)*, pages 318–324, Chambéry, France, 1993.

56. A. S. Rao, M. P. Georgeff, and E. A. Sonenberg. Social plans: A preliminary report. In E. Werner and Y. Demazeau, editors, *Decentralized AI 3 — Proceedings of the Third European Workshop on Modelling Autonomous Agents in a Multi-Agent World (MAAMAW-91)*, pages 57–76. Elsevier Science Publishers B.V.: Amsterdam, The Netherlands, 1992.

57. S. Rosenschein and L. P. Kaelbling. The synthesis of digital machines with provable epistemic properties. In J. Y. Halpern, editor, *Proceedings of the 1986 Conference on Theoretical Aspects of Reasoning About Knowledge*, pages 83–98. Morgan Kaufmann Publishers: San Mateo, CA, 1986.

58. S. J. Rosenschein and L. P. Kaelbling. A situated view of representation and control. In P. E. Agre and S. J. Rosenschein, editors, *Computational Theories of Interaction and Agency*, pages 515–540. The MIT Press: Cambridge, MA, 1996.

59. S. Russell and P. Norvig. *Artificial Intelligence: A Modern Approach*. Prentice-Hall, 1995.

60. S. Russell and D. Subramanian. Provably bounded-optimal agents. *Journal of AI Research*, 2:575–609, 1995.

61. S. J. Russell and E. Wefald. *Do the Right Thing — Studies in Limited Rationality*. The MIT Press: Cambridge, MA, 1991.

62. M. J. Schoppers. Universal plans for reactive robots in unpredictable environments. In *Proceedings of the Tenth International Joint Conference on Artificial Intelligence (IJCAI-87)*, pages 1039–1046, Milan, Italy, 1987.

63. J. R. Searle. *Speech Acts: An Essay in the Philosophy of Language*. Cambridge University Press: Cambridge, England, 1969.

64. Y. Shoham. Agent-oriented programming. Technical Report STAN–CS–1335–90, Computer Science Department, Stanford University, Stanford, CA 94305, 1990.

65. Y. Shoham. Agent-oriented programming. *Artificial Intelligence*, 60(1):51–92, 1993.

66. L. Steels. Cooperation between distributed agents through self organization. In Y. Demazeau and J.-P. Müller, editors, *Decentralized AI — Proceedings of the First European Workshop on Modelling Autonomous Agents in a Multi-Agent World (MAAMAW-89)*, pages 175–196. Elsevier Science Publishers B.V.: Amsterdam, The Netherlands, 1990.

67. S. R. Thomas. *PLACA, an Agent Oriented Programming Language*. PhD thesis, Computer Science Department, Stanford University, Stanford, CA 94305, August 1993. (Available as technical report STAN–CS–93–1487).

68. S. R. Thomas. The PLACA agent programming language. In M. Wooldridge and N. R. Jennings, editors, *Intelligent Agents: Theories, Architectures, and Languages (LNAI Volume 890)*, pages 355–369. Springer-Verlag: Berlin, Germany, January 1995.

69. J. E. White. Telescript technology: The foundation for the electronic marketplace. White paper, General Magic, Inc., 2465 Latham Street, Mountain View, CA 94040, 1994.

70. M. Wooldridge. Agent-based software engineering. *IEE Transactions on Software Engineering*, 144(1):26–37, February 1997.

71. M. Wooldridge and N. R. Jennings. Intelligent agents: Theory and practice. *The Knowledge Engineering Review*, 10(2):115–152, 1995.

# 2 Multiagent Systems and Societies of Agents

Michael N. Huhns and Larry M. Stephens

## 2.1 Introduction

Agents operate and exist in some environment, which typically is both computational and physical. The environment might be open or closed, and it might or might not contain other agents. Although there are situations where an agent can operate usefully by itself, the increasing interconnection and networking of computers is making such situations rare, and in the usual state of affairs the agent interacts with other agents. Whereas the previous chapter defined the structure and characteristics of an individual agent, the focus of this chapter is on systems with multiple agents. At times, the number of agents may be too numerous to deal with them individually, and it is then more convenient to deal with them collectively, as a society of agents.

In this chapter, we will learn how to analyze, describe, and design environments in which agents can operate effectively and interact with each other productively. The environments will provide a computational infrastructure for such interactions to take place. The infrastructure will include protocols for agents to communicate and protocols for agents to interact.

Communication protocols enable agents to exchange and understand messages. Interaction protocols enable agents to have conversations, which for our purposes are structured exchanges of messages. As a concrete example of these, a communication protocol might specify that the following types of messages can be exchanged between two agents:

- Propose a course of action
- Accept a course of action
- Reject a course of action
- Retract a course of action
- Disagree with a proposed course of action
- Counterpropose a course of action

Based on these message types, the following conversation—an instance of an interaction protocol for negotiation—can occur between Agent1 and Agent2:

- Agent1 proposes a course of action to Agent2
  Agent2 evaluates the proposal and
- sends acceptance to Agent1
  or
- sends counterproposal to Agent1
  or
- sends disagreement to Agent1
  or
- sends rejection to Agent1

This chapter describes several protocols for communication and interaction among both large and small groups of agents.

### 2.1.1  Motivations

But why should we be interested in distributed systems of agents? Indeed, centralized solutions are generally more efficient: anything that can be computed in a distributed system can be moved to a single computer and optimized to be at least as efficient. However, distributed computations are sometimes easier to understand and easier to develop, especially when the problem being solved is itself distributed. Distribution can lead to computational algorithms that might not have been discovered with a centralized approach. There are also times when a centralized approach is impossible, because the systems and data belong to independent organizations that want to keep their information private and secure for competitive reasons.

The information involved is necessarily distributed, and it resides in information systems that are large and complex in several senses: (1) they can be geographically distributed, (2) they can have many components, (3) they can have a huge content, both in the number of concepts and in the amount of data about each concept, and (4) they can have a broad scope, i.e., coverage of a major portion of a significant domain. Also, the components of the systems are typically distributed and heterogeneous. The topology of these systems is dynamic and their content is changing so rapidly that it is difficult for a user or an application program to obtain correct information, or for the enterprise to maintain consistent information.

There are four major techniques for dealing with the size and complexity of these enterprise information systems: modularity, distribution, abstraction, and intelligence, i.e., being smarter about how you seek and modify information. The use of intelligent, distributed modules combines all four of these techniques, yielding a distributed artificial intelligence (DAI) approach [25, 18].

In accord with this approach, computational agents need to be distributed and embedded throughout the enterprise. The agents could function as intelligent application programs, active information resources, "wrappers" that surround and buffer conventional components, and on-line network services. The agents would be knowledgeable about information resources that are local to them, and cooperate to provide global access to, and better management of, the information. For the practical reason that the systems are too large and dynamic (i.e., open) for global solutions to be formulated and implemented, the agents need to execute autonomously and be developed independently.

The rationale for interconnecting computational agents and expert systems is to enable them to cooperate in solving problems, to share expertise, to work in parallel on common problems, to be developed and implemented modularly, to be fault tolerant through redundancy, to represent multiple viewpoints and the knowledge of multiple experts, and to be reusable.

The possibility of an agent interacting with other agents in the future, in unanticipated ways, causes its developer to think about and construct it differently. For example, the developer might consider "What exactly does my agent know?" and "How can another agent access and use the knowledge my agent has?" This might lead to an agent's knowledge being represented declaratively, rather than being buried in procedural code.

Multiagent systems are the best way to characterize or design distributed computing systems. Information processing is ubiquitous. There are computer processors seemingly everywhere, embedded in all aspects of our environment. Your kitchen likely has many, in such places as the microwave oven, toaster, and coffee maker, and this number does not consider the electrical power system, which probably uses hundreds in getting electricity to the kitchen. The large number of processors and the myriad ways in which they interact makes distributed computing systems the dominant computational paradigm today.

When the processors in the kitchen are intelligent enough to be considered agents, then it becomes convenient to think of them in anthropomorphic terms. For example, "the toaster *knows* when the toast is done," and "the coffee pot *knows* when the coffee is ready." When these systems are interconnected so they can interact, then they should also *know* that the coffee and toast should be ready at approximately the same time. In these terms, your kitchen becomes more than just a collection of processors—a distributed computing system—it becomes a *multiagent system.*

Much of traditional AI has been concerned with how an agent can be constructed to function intelligently, with a single locus of internal reasoning and control implemented in a Von Neumann architecture. But intelligent systems do not function in isolation—they are at the very least a part of the environment in which they operate, and the environment typically contains other such intelligent systems. Thus, it makes sense to view such systems in societal terms.

### 2.1.2 Characteristics of Multiagent Environments

1.  Multiagent environments provide an infrastructure specifying communication and interaction protocols.

2.   Multiagent environments are typically open and have no centralized designer.

3.   Multiagent environments contain agents that are autonomous and distributed, and may be self-interested or cooperative.

A multiagent execution environment includes a number of concerns, which are enumerated as possible characteristics in Table 2.1.

| Property | Range of values |
|---|---|
| *Design Autonomy* | Platform/Interaction Protocol /Language/Internal Architecture |
| *Communication Infrastructure* | Shared memory (blackboard) or Message-based Connected or Connection-less (email) Point-to-Point, Multicast, or Broadcast Push or Pull Synchronous or Asynchronous |
| *Directory Service* | White pages, Yellow pages |
| *Message Protocol* | KQML HTTP and HTML OLE, CORBA, DSOM |
| *Mediation Services* | Ontology-based? Transactions? |
| *Security Services* | Timestamps/Authentication |
| *Remittance Services* | Billing/Currency |
| *Operations Support* | Archiving/Redundancy /Restoration/Accounting |

**Table 2.1**   Characteristics of multiagent environments.

| Property | Definition |
|---|---|
| *Knowable* | To what extent is the environment known to the agent |
| *Predictable* | To what extent can it be predicted by the agent |
| *Controllable* | To what extent can the agent modify the environment |
| *Historical* | Do future states depend on the entire history, or only the current state |
| *Teleological* | Are parts of it purposeful, i.e., are there other agents |
| *Real-time* | Can the environment change while the agent is deliberating |

**Table 2.2**   Environment-agent characteristics.

Table 2.2 lists some key properties of an environment with respect to a specific agent that inhabits it. These generalize the presentation in [38].

## 2.2  Agent Communications

We first provide a basic definition for an agent, which we need in order to describe the languages and protocols needed by multiagent systems. Fundamentally, an agent is an active object with the ability to perceive, reason, and act. We assume that an agent has explicitly represented knowledge and a mechanism for operating on or drawing inferences from its knowledge. We also assume that an agent has the ability to communicate. This ability is part perception (the receiving of messages) and part action (the sending of messages). In a purely computer-based agent, these may be the agent's only perceptual and acting abilities.

### 2.2.1  Coordination

Agents communicate in order to achieve better the goals of themselves or of the society/system in which they exist. Note that the goals might or might not be known to the agents explicitly, depending on whether or not the agents are goal-based. Communication can enable the agents to coordinate their actions and behavior, resulting in systems that are more coherent.

Coordination is a property of a system of agents performing some activity in a shared environment. The degree of coordination is the extent to which they avoid extraneous activity by reducing resource contention, avoiding livelock and deadlock, and maintaining applicable safety conditions. Cooperation is coordination among nonantagonistic agents, while negotiation is coordination among competitive or simply self-interested agents. Typically, to cooperate successfully, each agent must maintain a model of the other agents, and also develop a model of future interactions. This presupposes sociability.

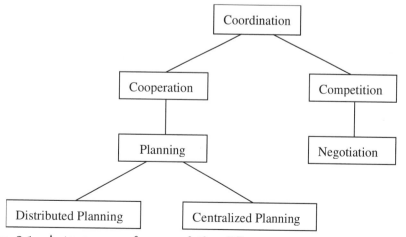

**Figure 2.1**  A taxonomy of some of the different ways in which agents can coordinate their behavior and activities.

Coherence is how well a system behaves as a unit. A problem for a multiagent system is how it can maintain global coherence without explicit global control. In this case, the agents must be able on their own to determine goals they share with other agents, determine common tasks, avoid unnecessary conflicts, and pool knowledge and evidence. It is helpful if there is some form of organization among the agents. Also, social commitments can be a means to achieving coherence, which is addressed in Section 2.4.

Section 2.3.7 discusses another means, based on economic principles of markets. In this regard, Simon [40] argues eloquently that although markets are excellent for clearing all goods, i.e., finding a price at which everything is sold, they are less effective in computing optimal allocations of resources. Organizational structures are essential for that purpose. It is believed that coherence and optimality are intimately related.

### 2.2.2  Dimensions of Meaning

There are three aspects to the formal study of communication: syntax (how the symbols of comunication are structured), semantics (what the symbols denote), and pragmatics (how the symbols are interpreted). Meaning is a combination of semantics and pragmatics. Agents communicate in order to understand and be understood, so it is important to consider the different dimensions of meaning that are associated with communication [42].

**Descriptive vs. Prescriptive.** Some messages describe phenomena, while others prescribe behavior. Descriptions are important for human comprehension, but are difficult for agents to mimic. Appropriately, then, most agent communication languages are designed for the exchange of information about activities and behavior.

**Personal vs. Conventional Meaning.** An agent might have its own meaning for a message, but this might differ from the meaning conventionally accepted by the other agents with which the agent communicates. To the greatest extent possible, multiagent systems should opt for conventional meanings, especially since these systems are typically open environments in which new agents might be introduced at any time.

**Subjective vs. Objective Meaning** Similar to conventional meaning, where meaning is determined external to an agent, a message often has an explicit effect on the environment, which can be perceived objectively. The effect might be different than that understood internally, i.e., subjectively, by the sender or receiver of the message.

**Speaker's vs. Hearer's vs. Society's Perspective** Independent of the conventional or objective meaning of a message, the message can be expressed according to the viewpoint of the speaker or hearer or other observers.

**Semantics vs. Pragmatics** The pragmatics of a communication are concerned with how the communicators use the communication. This includes considerations of the mental states of the communicators and the environment in which they exist, considerations that are external to the syntax and semantics of the communication.

**Contextuality** Messages cannot be understood in isolation, but must be interpreted in terms of the mental states of the agents, the present state of the environment, and the environment's history: how it arrived at its present state. Interpretations are directly affected by previous messages and actions of the agents.

**Coverage** Smaller languages are more manageable, but they must be large enough so that an agent can convey the meanings it intends.

**Identity** When a communication occurs among agents, its meaning is dependent on the identities and roles of the agents involved, and on how the involved agents are specified. A message might be sent to a particular agent, or to just any agent satisfying a specified criterion.

**Cardinality** A message sent privately to one agent would be understood differently than the same message broadcast publicly.

### 2.2.3  Message Types

It is important for agents of different capabilities to be able to communicate. Communication must therefore be defined at several levels, with communication at the lowest level used for communication with the least capable agent. In order to be of interest to each other, the agents must be able to participate in a dialogue. Their role in this dialogue may be either active, passive, or both, allowing them to function as a master, slave, or peer, respectively. In keeping with the above definition for and assumptions about an agent, we assume that an agent can send and receive messages through a communication network. The messages can be of several types, as defined next.

There are two basic message types: assertions and queries. Every agent, whether active or passive, must have the ability to accept information. In its simplest form, this information is communicated to the agent from an external source by means of an assertion. In order to assume a passive role in a dialog, an agent must additionally be able to answer questions, i.e., it must be able to 1) accept a query from an external source and 2) send a reply to the source by making an assertion. Note that from the standpoint of the communication network, there is no distinction between an unsolicited assertion and an assertion made in reply to a query.

In order to assume an active role in a dialog, an agent must be able to issue queries and make assertions. With these capabilities, the agent then can potentially control another agent by causing it to respond to the query or to accept the information asserted. This means of control can be extended to the control of subagents, such as neural networks and databases.

An agent functioning as a peer with another agent can assume both active and passive roles in a dialog. It must be able to make and accept both assertions and queries. A summary of the capabilities needed by different classes of agents is shown in Table 2.3.

| | Basic Agent | Passive Agent | Active Agent | Peer Agent |
|---|:---:|:---:|:---:|:---:|
| Receives assertions | • | • | • | • |
| Receives queries | | • | | • |
| Sends assertions | | • | • | • |
| Sends queries | | | • | • |

**Table 2.3**  Agent capabilities.

| Communicative Action | Illocutionary Force | Expected Result |
|---|---|---|
| Assertion | Inform | Acceptance |
| Query | Question | Reply |
| Reply | Inform | Acceptance |
| Request | Request | |
| Explanation | Inform | Agreement |
| Command | Request | |
| Permission | Inform | Acceptance |
| Refusal | Inform | Acceptance |
| Offer/Bid | Inform | Acceptance |
| Acceptance | | |
| Agreement | | |
| Proposal | Inform | Offer/Bid |
| Confirmation | | |
| Retraction | | |
| Denial | | |

**Table 2.4**  Interagent message types.

Other types of messages, derived from work on speech-act theory [43], are listed in Table 2.4.

### 2.2.4   Communication Levels

Communication protocols are typically specified at several levels. The lowest level of the protocol specifies the method of interconnection; the middle level specifies the format, or syntax, of the information being transfered; the top level specifies the meaning, or semantics, of the information. The semantics refers not only to the substance of the message, but also to the type of the message.

There are both binary and n-ary communication protocols. A binary protocol involves a single sender and a single receiver, whereas an n-ary protocol involves a single sender and multiple receivers (sometimes called broadcast or multicast). A protocol is specified by a data structure with the following five fields:

1.   sender

2.  receiver(s)

3.  language in the protocol

4.  encoding and decoding functions

5.  actions to be taken by the receiver(s).

### 2.2.5  Speech Acts

Spoken human communication is used as the model for communication among computational agents. A popular basis for analyzing human communication is *speech act theory* [1, 39]. Speech act theory views human natural language as *actions*, such as requests, suggestions, commitments, and replies. For example, when you request something, you are not simply making a statement, but creating the request itself. When a jury declares a defendant guilty, there is an action taken: the defendant's social status is changed.

A speech act has three aspects:

1.  Locution, the physical utterance by the speaker

2.  Illocution, the intended meaning of the utterance by the speaker

3.  Perlocution, the action that results from the locution.

For example, John might say to Mary, "Please close the window." This act consists of the physical sounds generated by John (or the character sequences typed by John), John's intent for the message as a request or a command, and if all goes well, the window being shut.

In communication among humans, the intent of the message is not always easily identified. For example, "I am cold," can be viewed as an assertion, a request for a sweater, or a demand for an increase in room temperature. However, for communication among agents, we want to insure that there is no doubt about the type of message.

Speech act theory uses the term *performative* to identify the illocutionary force of this special class of utterance. Example performative verbs include *promise, report, convince, insist, tell, request,* and *demand.* Illocutionary force can be broadly classified as assertives (statements of fact), directives (commands in a master-slave structure), commissives (commitments), declaratives (statements of fact), and expressives (expressions of emotion).

Performatives are usually represented in the stylized syntatic form "I hereby tell..." or "I hereby request..." Because performatives have the special property that "saying it makes it so," not all verbs are performatives. For example, stating that "I hereby solve this problem" does not create the solution. Although the term speech is used in this discussion, speech acts have to do with communication in forms other than the spoken word.

In summary, speech act theory helps define the type of message by using the concept of the illocutionary force, which constrains the semantics of the communication act itself. The sender's intended communication act is clearly defined, and the receiver has no doubt as to the type of message sent. This constraint simplifies the design of our software agents.

The message contained *within* the protocol may be ambiguous, may have no simple response, or may require decomposition and the assistance of other agents; however, the communication protocol itself should clearly identify the type of message being sent.

### 2.2.6    Knowledge Query and Manipulation Language (KQML)

A fundamental decision for the interaction of agents is to separate the semantics of the communication protocol (which must be domain independent) from the semantics of the enclosed message (which may depend on the domain). The communication protocol must be universally shared by all agents. It should be concise and have only a limited number of primitive communication acts.

The knowledge query and manipulation language (KQML) is a protocol for exchanging information and knowledge, as illustrated in Figure 2.2. The elegance of KQML is that all information for understanding the content of the message is included in the communication itself. The basic protocol is defined by the following structure:

(KQML-performative

|  | |
|---|---|
| :sender | \<word\> |
| :receiver | \<word\> |
| :language | \<word\> |
| :ontology | \<word\> |
| :content | \<expression\> |
| ...) | |

The syntax is Lisp-like; however, the arguments—identified by keywords preceded

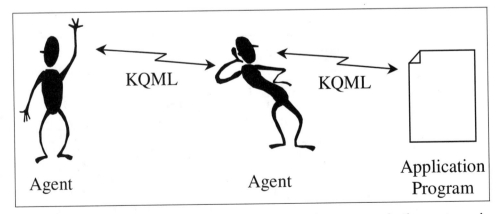

**Figure 2.2**   KQML is a protocol for communications among both agents and application programs.

by a colon—may be given in any order. The KQML-performatives are modeled on speech act performatives. Thus, the semantics of KQML performatives is domain independent, while the semanatics of the message is defined by the fields `:content` (the message itself), `:language` (the langauge in which the message is expressed), and `:ontology` (the vocabulary of the "words" in the message). In effect, KQML "wraps" a message in a *structure* that can be understood by any agent. (To understand the message itself, the recipient must understand the language and have access to the ontology.)

The terms `:content`, `:language`, and `:ontology` delineate the semantics of the message. Other arguments, including `:sender`, `:receiver`, `:reply-with`, and `:in-reply-to`, are parameters of the message passing. KQML assumes asynchronous communications; the fields `:reply-with` from a sender and `:in-reply-to` from a responding agent link an outgoing message with an expected response.

KQML is part of a broad research effort to develop a methodology for distributing information among different systems [35]. One part of the effort involves defining the Knowledge Interchange Format (KIF), a formal syntax for representing knowledge. Described in the next section, KIF is largely based on first-order predicate calculus. Another part of the effort is defining ontologies that define the common concepts, attributes, and relationships for different subsets of world knowledge. The definitions of the ontology terms give meaning to expressions represented in KIF. For example, in a Blocks-World ontology, if the concept of a wooden block of a given size is represented by the unary predicate Block, then the fact that block A is on top of block B could be communicated as follows:

```
(tell
        :sender       Agent1
        :receiver     Agent2
        :language:    KIF
        :ontology:    Blocks-World
        :content      (AND (Block A) (Block B) (On A B))
```

The language in a KQML message is not restricted to KIF; other languages such as PROLOG, LISP, SQL, or any other defined agent communication language can be used.

KQML-speaking agents appear to each other as clients and servers. Their communications can be either synchronous or asynchronous, as illustrated in Figure 2.3. For a synchronous communication, a sending agent waits for a reply. For an asynchronous communication, the sending agent continues with its reasoning or acting, which would then be interrupted when replies arrive at a later time.

Interestingly, KQML messages can be "nested" in that the content of a KQML message may be another KQML message, which is self contained. For example, if Agent1 cannot communicate directly with Agent2 (but can communicate with Agent3), Agent1 might ask Agent3 to forward a message to Agent2:

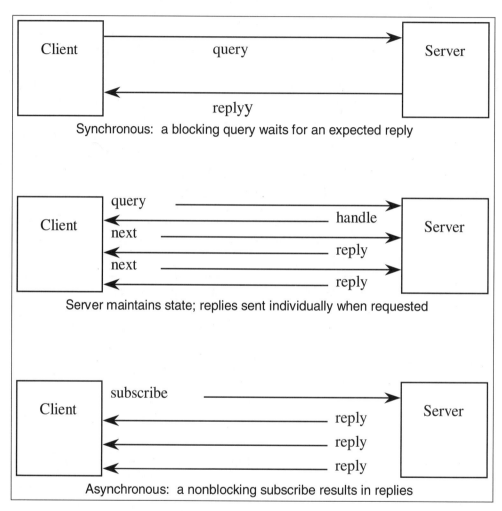

**Figure 2.3**   Synchronous and asynchronous communications among agents that understand KQML.

```
(forward
            :from        Agent1
            :to          Agent2
            :sender      Agent1
            :receiver    Agent3
            :language    KQML
            :ontology    kqml-ontology
            :content     (tell
                                :sender     Agent1
                                :receiver   Agent2
                                :language   KIF
                                :ontology:  Blocks-World
                                :content    (On (Block A) (Block B))))
```

In a forwarded KQML message, the value of the :from field becomes the value in the :sender field of the `:content` message, and the value of the `:to` field in the forward becomes the value of the `:receiver` field.

The KQML performatives may be organized into seven basic categories:

- Basic query performatives (evaluate, ask-one, ask-all, ...)
- Multiresponse query performatives (stream-in, stream-all, ...)
- Response performatives (reply, sorry, ...)
- Generic informational performatives (tell, achieve, cancel, untell, unachieve, ...)
- Generator performatives (standby, ready, next, rest, ...)
- Capability-definition performatives (advertise, subscribe, monitor, ...)
- Networking performatives (register, unregister, forward, broadcast, ...)

The advertise performative is used by a :sender agent to inform a `:receiver` about the `:sender`'s capabilities:

```
(advertise
            :sender      Agent2
            :receiver    Agent1
            :language    KQML
            :ontology    kqml-ontology
            :content     (ask-all
                                :sender      Agent1
                                :receiver    Agent2
                                :in-reply-to id1
                                :language    Prolog
                                :ontology:   Blocks-World
                                :content     "on(X,Y)"))
```

Now Agent1 may query Agent2:

```
(ask-all
        :sender        Agent1
        :receiver      Agent2
        :in-reply-to   id1
        :reply-with    id2
        :language:     Prolog
        :ontology:     Blocks-World
        :content       "on(X,Y)"
```

Agent2 could respond with matching assertions from its knowledge base:

```
(tell
        :sender        Agent2
        :receiver      Agent1
        :in-reply-to   id2
        :language:     Prolog
        :ontology:     Blocks-World
        :content       "[on(a,b),on(c,d)]"
```

**Issues:**

The sender and receiver must understand the agent communication language being used; the ontology must be created and be accesssible to the agents who are communicating.

KQML must operate within a communication infrastructure that allows agents to locate each other. The infrastructure is not part of the KQML specification, and implemented systems use custom-made utility programs called *routers* or *facilators* to perform this function. In the advertise example above, if Agent2 sent the message to a facilator agent, then other agents could query the facilitator to find out about Agent2's capabilities.

KQML is still a work in progress and its semantics have not been completely defined. Labrou and Finin [31] have recently proposed a new KQML specification that refines the original draft [15]. However, there is yet no offical KQML specification that agent builders can rely on.

### 2.2.7   Knowledge Interchange Format (KIF)

Agents need descriptions of real-world things. The descriptions could be expressed in natural languages, such as English and Japanese, which are capable of describing a wide variety of things and situations. However, the meaning of a natural language statement is often subject to different interpretations.

Symbolic logic is a general mathematical tool for describing things. Rather simple logics (e.g., the first order predicate calculus) have been found to be capable of describing almost anything of interest or utility to people and other intelligent agents. These things include simple concrete facts, definitions, abstractions, inference rules, constraints, and even metaknowledge (knowledge about knowledge).

KIF, a particular logic language, has been proposed as a standard to use to describe things within expert systems, databases, intelligent agents, etc. It is readable by both computer systems and people. Moreover, it was specifically designed to serve as an "interlingua," or mediator in the translation of other languages. For example, there is a translation program that can map a STEP/PDES expression about products into an equivalent KIF expression and vice versa. If there were a translation program for mapping between the healthcare language HL7 and KIF, then there would be a way to translate between STEP/PDES and HL7 (to exchange information about healthcare products) using KIF as an intermediate representation.

KIF is a prefix version of first order predicate calculus with extensions to support nonmonotonic reasoning and definitions. The language description includes both a specification for its syntax and one for its semantics. KIF provides for the expression of simple data. For example, the sentences shown below encode 3 tuples in a personnel database (arguments stand for employee ID number, department assignment, and salary, respectively):

```
(salary 015-46-3946 widgets 72000)
(salary 026-40-9152 grommets 36000)
(salary 415-32-4707 fidgets 42000)
```

More complicated information can be expressed through the use of complex terms. For example, the following sentence states that one chip is larger than another:

```
(> (* (width chip1) (length chip1))
   (* (width chip2) (length chip2)))
```

KIF includes a variety of logical operators to assist in the encoding of logical information, such as negation, disjunction, rules, and quantified formulas. The expression shown below is an example of a complex sentence in KIF. It asserts that the number obtained by raising any real-number ?x to an even power ?n is positive:

```
(=> (and (real-number ?x)
         (even-number ?n))
    (> (expt ?x ?n) 0))
```

KIF provides for the encoding of knowledge about knowledge, using the back-quote (') and comma (,) operators and related vocabulary. For example, the following sentence asserts that agent Joe is interested in receiving triples in the salary relation. The use of commas signals that the variables should not be taken literally.

Without the commas, this sentence

```
(interested joe '(salary ,?x ,?y ,?z))
```

would say that agent joe is interested in the sentence (`salary ?x ?y ?z`) instead of its instances.

KIF can also be used to describe procedures, i.e., to write programs or scripts for agents to follow. Given the prefix syntax of KIF, such programs resemble Lisp or Scheme. The following is an example of a three-step procedure written in KIF. The first step ensures that there is a fresh line on the standard output stream; the second step prints "Hello!" to the standard output stream; the final step adds a carriage return to the output.

```
(progn (fresh-line t)
       (print "Hello!")
       (fresh-line t))
```

The semantics of the KIF core (KIF without rules and definitions) is similar to that of first-order logic. There is an extension to handle nonstandard operators (like backquote and comma), and there is a restriction that models must satisfy various axiom schemata (to give meaning to the basic vocabulary in the format). Despite these extensions and restrictions, the core language retains the fundamental characteristics of first-order logic, including compactness and the semi-decidability of logical entailment.

### 2.2.8   Ontologies

An ontology is a specification of the objects, concepts, and relationships in an area of interest. In the Blocks-World example above, the term Block represents a concept and the term On represents a relationship. Concepts can be represented in first-order logic as unary predicates; higher-arity predicates represent relationships. To express the idea that a block is a physical object, we might use the first-order expression

$$\forall x \; (\text{Block } x) \Rightarrow (\text{PhysicalObject } x)$$

There are other, more general representations. Instead of (`Block A`), the expression (`instanceOf A Block`) could be used. Both `A` and `Block` are now objects in the universe of discourse, and new relationships `instanceOf` and `subclassOf` are introduced:

```
(class Block)
(class PhysicalObject)
(subclassOf Block PhysicalObject)
```
$$\forall x,y,z \; (\text{instanceOf } x \; y) \land (\text{subclassOf } y \; z) \Rightarrow (\text{instanceOf } x \; z)$$

The last sentence is a rule that expresses the notion of a type hierarchy.

An ontology is more than a taxonomy of classes (or types); the ontology must describe the relationships. The classes and relationships must be represented in the ontology; the instances of classes need not be represented. For example, there is no need to represent `A` in the ontology for either (`Block A`) or (`instanceOf A Block`). An ontology is analogous to a database schema, not the contents of a database itself.

Implicit in this discussion is that an agent must represent its knowledge in the vocabulary of a specified ontology. Since agents are constructed by people, the effect is that the agent's creator must use a specified ontology to represent the agent's knowledge. All agents that share the same ontology for knowledge representation have an understanding of the "words" in the agent communication language.

Many agents have knowledge bases in which relationships are defined in more detail than just a character string. For example, the domain and range of a binary relationship can be specified;

```
(domain On PhysicalObject)
(range On PhysicalObject)
```

These restrictions limit the values allowed in *using* a relationship. (`On A B`) is permitted since both `A` and `B` are instances of `PhysicalObject` via transitive closure of `subclassOf`; (`On A Dream1`) would be prohibited assuming that `Dream1` is not of type `PhysicalObject`.

Ontology editors, such as those developed at Stanford [14] and the University of South Carolina [32], are typically frame-based knowledge-representation systems that allow users to define ontologies and their components: classes, instances, relationships, and functions. Figure 2.4 shows an example of such an ontology. Ontology editors offer a variety of features, such as the ability to translate ontologies into several representation languages or the ability for distributed groups to develop ontologies jointly over the Internet.

### 2.2.9  Other Communication Protocols

The above protocols for interagent communication in no way preclude *other* means by which computational agents can interact, communicate, and be interconnected. For example, one agent may be able to view a second agent with a camera, and use the resulting images to coordinate its own actions with those of the second agent.

Once communication protocols are defined and agreed upon by a set of agents, higher level protocols can be readily implemented. The next section describes some of these.

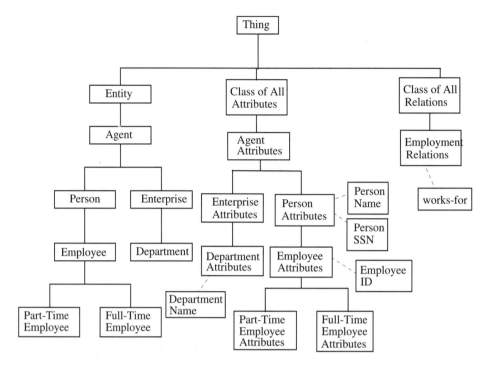

**Figure 2.4**  Example ontology for a simple business, showing classes and their subclasses, relationships, and instances (indicated by a dashed line).

## 2.3   Agent Interaction Protocols

The previous section describes mechanisms for agents to communicate *single* messages. Interaction protocols govern the exchange of a *series* of messages among agents—a conversation. Several interaction protocols have been devised for systems of agents. In cases where the agents have conflicting goals or are simply self-interested, the objective of the protocols is to maximize the payoffs (utilities) of the agents [37]. In cases where the agents have similar goals or common problems, as in distributed problem solving (DPS), the objective of the protocols is to maintain globally coherent performance of the agents without violating autonomy, i.e., without explicit global control [11]. For the latter cases, important aspects include how to

- determine shared goals
- determine common tasks
- avoid unnecessary conflicts
- pool knowledge and evidence.

### 2.3.1   Coordination Protocols

In an environment with limited resources, agents must coordinate their activities
with each other to further their own interests or satisfy group goals. The actions
of multiple agents need to be coordinated because there are dependencies between
agents' actions, there is a need to meet global constraints, and no one agent has
sufficient competence, resources or information to achieve system goals. Examples
of coordination include supplying timely information to other agents, ensuring the
actions of agents are synchronized, and avoiding redundant problem solving.

To produce coordinated systems, most DAI research has concentrated on techniques for distributing both control and data. Distributed control means that agents
have a degree of autonomy in generating new actions and in deciding which goals to
pursue next. The disadvantage of distributing control and data is that knowledge
of the system's overall state is dispersed throughout the system and each agent has
only a partial and imprecise perspective. There is an increased degree of uncertainty
about each agent's actions, so it is more difficult to attain coherent global behavior.

The actions of agents in solving goals can be expressed as search through a
classical AND/OR goal graph. The goal graph includes a representation of the
dependencies between the goals and the resources needed to solve the primitive goals
(leaf nodes of the graph). Indirect dependencies can exist between goals through
shared resources.

Formulating a multiagent system in this manner allows the activities requiring
coordination to be clearly identified. Such activities include: (1) defining the goal
graph, including identification and classification of dependencies; (2) assigning
particular regions of the graph to appropriate agents; (3) controlling decisions about
which areas of the graph to explore; (4) traversing the graph; and (5) ensuring that
successful traversal is reported. Some of the activities may be collaborative, while
some may be carried out by an agent acting in isolation. Determining the approach
for each of the phases is a matter of system design.

While the distributed goal search formalism has been used frequently to characterize both global and local problems, the key agent structures are commitment and
convention [29]. *Commitments* are viewed as pledges to undertake a specified course
of action, while *conventions* provide a means of managing commitments in changing circumstances. Commitments provide a degree of predictability so that agents
can take the future activities of others into consideration when dealing with inter-
agent dependencies, global constraints, or resource utilization conflicts. As situations
change, agents must evaluate whether existing commitments are still valid. Conventions constrain the conditions under which commitments should be reassessed
and specify the associated actions that should then be undertaken: either retain,
rectify or abandon the commitments.

If its circumstances do not change, an agent will endeavor to honor its commitments. This obligation constrains the agent's subsequent decisions about making
new commitments, since it knows that sufficient resources must be reserved to honor
its existing ones. For this reason, an agent's commitments should be both internally

consistent and consistent with its beliefs.

Conventions help an agent manage its commitments, but they do not specify how the agent should behave towards others if it alters or modifies its commitments. However for goals that are dependent, it is essential that the relevant agents be informed of any substantial change that affects them. A convention of this type is a social one. If communication resources are limited, the following social convention might be appropriate:

LIMITED-BANDWIDTH SOCIAL CONVENTION

INVOKE WHEN
        Local commitment dropped
        Local commitment satisfied

ACTIONS
RULE1:  IF Local commitment satisfied
       THEN inform all related commitments

Rule2:  IF local commitments dropped because unattainable or
          motivation not present
       THEN inform all strongly related commitments

Rule3:  IF local commitments dropped because unattainable or
          motivation not present
       AND communication resources not overburdened
       THEN inform all weakly related commitments

When agents decide to pursue a joint action, they jointly commit themselves to a common goal, which they expect will bring about the desired state of affairs. The minimum information that a team of cooperating agents should share is (1) the status of their commitment to the shared objective, and (2) the status of their commitment to the given team framework. If an agent's beliefs about either of these issues change, then the semantics of joint commitments requires that all team members be informed. As many joint actions depend upon the participation of an entire team, a change of commitment by one participant can jeopardize the team's efforts. Hence, if an agent comes to believe that a team member is no longer jointly committed, it also needs to reassess its own position with respect to the joint action. These three basic assumptions are encoded in a convention that represents the minimum requirement for joint commitments, as shown below.

BASIC JOINT-ACTION CONVENTION

INVOKE WHEN
        Status of commitment to joint action changes
        Status of commitment to attaining joint action in present

```
                      team context changes
               Status of joint commitment of a team member changes

     ACTIONS
     Rule1:  IF Status of commitment to joint action changes
                 OR
             IF Status of commitment to present team
                   context changes
             THEN inform all other team member of these changes


     Rule2:  IF Status of joint commitment of a team member changes
             THEN Determine whether joint commitment still viable
```

Commitments and conventions are the cornerstones of coordination: commitments provide the necessary structure for predictable interactions, and social conventions provide the necessary degree of mutual support.

### 2.3.2  Cooperation Protocols

A basic strategy shared by many of the protocols for cooperation is to decompose and then distribute tasks. Such a divide-and-conquer approach can reduce the complexity of a task: smaller subtasks require less capable agents and fewer resources. However, the system must decide among alternative decompositions, if available, and the decomposition process must consider the resources and capabilities of the agents. Also, there might be interactions among the subtasks and conflicts among the agents.

Task decomposition can be done by the system designer, whereby decomposition is programmed during implementation, or by the agents using hierarchical planning, or it might be inherent in the representation of the problem, as in an AND-OR graph. Task decomposition might be done spatially, based on the layout of information sources or decision points, or functionally, according to the expertise of available agents.

Once tasks are decomposed, they can be distributed according to the following criteria [13]:

- Avoid overloading critical resources
- Assign tasks to agents with matching capabilities
- Make an agent with a wide view assign tasks to other agents
- Assign overlapping responsibilities to agents to achieve coherence
- Assign highly interdependent tasks to agents in spatial or semantic proximity. This minimizes communication and synchronization costs
- Reassign tasks if necessary for completing urgent tasks.

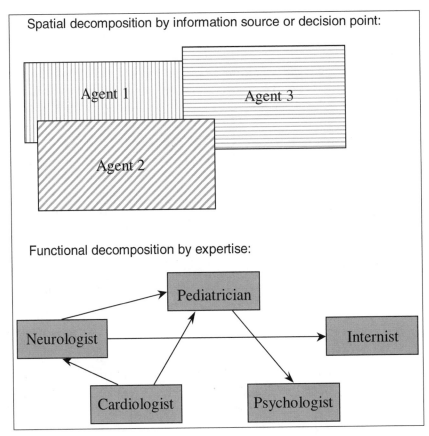

**Figure 2.5**   Two commonly used methods for distributing tasks among cooperative agents.

The following mechanisms are commonly used to distribute tasks:

- Market mechanisms: tasks are matched to agents by generalized agreement or mutual selection (analogous to pricing commodities)
- Contract net: announce, bid, and award cycles
- Multiagent planning: planning agents have the responsibility for task assignment
- Organizational structure: agents have fixed responsibilities for particular tasks.

Figure 2.5 illustrates two of the methods of task distribution. Details of additional methods are described in the sections that follow.

### 2.3.3   Contract Net

Of the above mechanisms, the best known and most widely applied is the contract net protocol [44, 9]. The contract net protocol is an interaction protocol for cooperative problem solving among agents. It is modeled on the contracting mechanism used by businesses to govern the exchange of goods and services. The contract net provides a solution for the so-called *connection problem*: finding an appropriate agent to work on a given task. Figure 2.6 illustrates the basic steps in this protocol.

An agent wanting a task solved is called the *manager*; agents that might be able to solve the task are called potential *contractors*. From a manager's perspective, the process is

- Announce a task that needs to be performed
- Receive and evaluate bids from potential contractors
- Award a contract to a suitable contractor
- Receive and synthesize results.

From a contractor's perspective, the process is

- Receive task announcements
- Evaluate my capability to respond
- Respond (decline, bid)
- Perform the task if my bid is accepted
- Report my results.

The roles of agents are not specified in advance. Any agent can act as a manager by making task announcements; any agent can act as a contractor by responding to task announcements. This flexibility allows for further task decomposition: a contractor for a specific task may act as a manager by soliciting the help of other agents in solving parts of that task. The resulting manager-contractor links form a control hierarchy for task sharing and result synthesis.

The contract net offers the advantages of graceful performance degradation. If a contractor is unable to provide a satisfactory solution, the manager can seek other potential contractors for the task.

The structure of a task announcement includes slots for *addressee, eligibility specification, task abstraction, bid specification,* and *expiration time*. The tasks may be addressed to one or more potential contractors who must meet the criteria of the eligibility specification. The task abstraction, a brief description of the task, is used by contractors to rank tasks from several task announcements. The bid specification tells potential contractors what information must be provided with the bid; returned bid specifications give the manager a basis for comparing bids from different potential contractors. The expiration time is a deadline for receiving bids.

Each potential contractor evaluates unexpired task announcements to determine if it is eligible to offer a bid. The contractor then chooses the most attractive task (based on some criteria) and offers a bid to the corresponding manager.

A manager receives and evaluates bids for each task announcement. Any bid deemed satisfactory may be accepted before the expiration time of the task announcement. The manager notifies the contractor of bid acceptance with an *an-*

A manager announces the existence of tasks via a (possibly selective) multicast

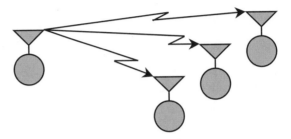

Agents evaluate the announcement. Some of these agents submit bids

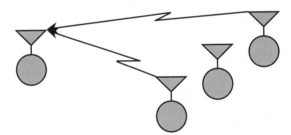

The manager awards a contract to the most appropriate agent

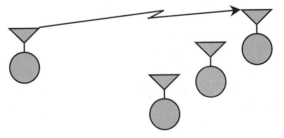

The manager and contractor communicate privately as necessary

**Figure 2.6**   The basic steps in the contract net, an important generic protocol for interactions among cooperative agents.

*nounced award* message. (A limitation of the contract net protocol is that a task might be awarded to a contractor with limited capability if a better qualified contractor is busy at award time. Another limitation is that a manager is under no obligation to inform potential contractors that an award has already been made.)

A manager may not receive bids for several reasons: (1) all potential contractors are busy with other tasks, (2) a potential contractor is idle but ranks the proposed task below other tasks under consideration, (3) no contractors, even if idle, are capable of working on the task. To handle these cases, a manager may request immediate response bids to which contractors respond with messages such as *eligible but busy*, *ineligible*, or *uninterested* (task ranked too low for contractor to bid). The manager can then make adjustments in its task plan. For example, the manager can wait until a busy potential contractor is free.

The contract net provides for *directed contracts* to be issued without negotiation. The selected contractor responds with an *acceptance* or *refusal*. This capability can simplify the protocol and improve effiency for certain tasks.

### 2.3.4   Blackboard Systems

Blackboard-based problem solving is often presented using the following metaphor:

"Imagine a group of human or agent specialists seated next to a large blackboard. The specialists are working cooperatively to solve a problem, using the blackboard as the workplace for developing the solution. Problem solving begins when the problem and initial data are written onto the blackboard. The specialists watch the blackboard, looking for an opportunity to apply their expertise to the developing solution. When a specialist finds sufficient information to make a contribution, he records the contribution on the blackboard. This additional information may enable other specialists to apply their expertise. This process of adding contributions to the blackboard continues until the problem has been solved."

This metaphor captures a number of the important characteristics of blackboard systems, each of which is described below.

**Independence of expertise.** The specialists (called knowledges sources or KSs) are not trained to work solely with that specific group of specialists. Each is an expert on some aspects of the problem and can contribute to the solution independently of the particular mix of other specialists in the room.

**Diversity in problem-solving techniques.** In blackboard systems, the internal representation and inferencing machinery used by each KS are hidden from direct view.

**Flexible representation of blackboard information.** The blackboard model does not place any prior restrictions on what information can be placed on the blackboard.

**Common interaction language.** KSs in blackboard systems must be able to correctly interpret the information recorded on the blackboard by other KSs. In practice, there is a tradeoff between the representational expressiveness of a specialized representation shared by only a few KSs and a fully general representation understood by all KSs.

**Event-based activation.** KSs in blackboard systems are triggered in response to blackboard and external events. Blackboard events include the addition of new information to the blackboard, a change in existing information, or the removal of existing information. Rather than having each KS scan the blackboard, each KS informs the blackboard system about the kind of events in which it is interested. The blackboard system records this information and directly considers the KS for activation whenever that kind of event occurs.

**Need for control.** A control component that is separate from the individual KSs is responsible for managing the course of problem solving. The control component can be viewed as a specialist in directing problem solving, by considering the overall benefit of the contributions that would be made by triggered KSs. When the currently executing KS activation completes, the control component selects the most appropriate pending KS activation for execution.

When a KS is triggered, the KS uses its expertise to evaluate the quality and importance of its contribution. Each triggered KS informs the control component of the quality and costs associated with its contribution, without actually performing the work to compute the contribution. The control component uses these estimates to decide how to proceed.

**Incremental solution generation.** KSs contribute to the solution as appropriate, sometimes refining, sometimes contradicting, and sometimes initiating a new line of reasoning.

Figure 2.7 shows the architecture of a basic blackboard system.

### 2.3.5   Negotiation

A frequent form of interaction that occurs among agents with different goals is termed negotiation. *Negotiation* is a process by which a joint decision is reached by two or more agents, each trying to reach an individual goal or objective. The agents first communicate their positions, which might conflict, and then try to move towards agreement by making concessions or searching for alternatives.

The major features of negotiation are (1) the language used by the participating agents, (2) the protocol followed by the agents as they negotiate, and (3) the decision process that each agent uses to determine its positions, concessions, and criteria for agreement.

Many groups have developed systems and techniques for negotiation. These can be either environment-centered or agent-centered. Developers of environment-centered techniques focus on the following problem: "How can the rules of the environment be designed so that the agents in it, regardless of their origin, capabilities, or intentions, will interact productively and fairly?" The resultant negotiation mechanism should ideally have the following attributes:

**Efficiency:** the agents should not waste resources in coming to an agreement.

**Stability:** no agent should have an incentive to deviate from agreed-upon strategies.

**Simplicity:** the negotiation mechanism should impose low computational and bandwidth demands on the agents.

**Distribution:** the mechanism should not require a central decision maker.

**Symmetry:** the mechanism should not be biased against any agent for arbitrary or inappropriate reasons.

An articulate and entertaining treatment of these concepts is found in [36]. In particular, three types of environments have been identified: worth-oriented domains, state-oriented domains, and task-oriented domains.

A task-oriented domain is one where agents have a set of tasks to achieve, all resources needed to achieve the tasks are available, and the agents can achieve the tasks without help or interference from each other. However, the agents can benefit by sharing some of the tasks. An example is the "Internet downloading domain," where each agent is given a list of documents that it must access over the Internet. There is a cost associated with downloading, which each agent would like to minimize. If a document is common to several agents, then they can save

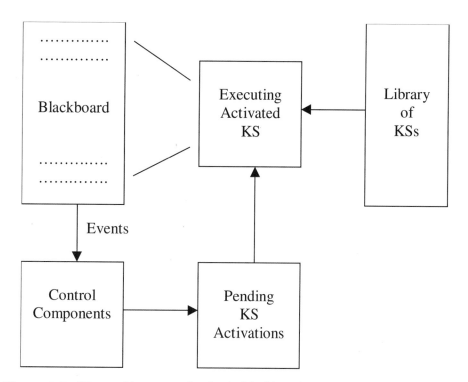

**Figure 2.7**  The architecture of a basic blackboard system, showing the blackboard, knowledge sources or agents, and control components.

downloading cost by accessing the document once and then sharing it.

The environment might provide the following simple negotiation mechanism and constraints: (1) each agent declares the documents it wants, (2) documents found to be common to two or more agents are assigned to agents based on the toss of a coin, (3) agents pay for the documents they download, and (4) agents are granted access to the documents they download, as well as any in their common sets. This mechanism is simple, symmetric, distributed, and efficient (no document is downloaded twice). To determine stability, the agents' strategies must be considered.

An optimal strategy is for an agent to declare the true set of documents that it needs, regardless of what strategy the other agents adopt or the documents they need. Because there is no incentive for an agent to diverge from this strategy, it is stable.

Developers of agent-centered negotiation mechanisms focus on the following problem: "Given an environment in which my agent must operate, what is the best strategy for it to follow?" Most such negotiation strategies have been developed for specific problems, so few general principles of negotiation have emerged. However, there are two general approaches, each based on an assumption about the particular type of agents involved.

For the first approach, speech-act classifiers together with a possible world semantics are used to formalize negotiation protocols and their components. This clarifies the conditions of satisfaction for different kinds of messages. To provide a flavor of this approach, we show in the following example how the commitments that an agent might make as part of a negotiation are formalized [21]:

$$
\forall x (x \neq y) \wedge
$$
$$
\neg (Precommit_a \; y \; x \; \phi) \wedge (Goal \; y \; Eventually(Achieves \; y \; \phi)) \wedge (Willing \; y \; \phi)
$$
$$
\Longleftrightarrow (Intend \; y \; Eventually(Achieves \; y \; \phi))
$$

This rule states that an agent forms and maintains its commitment to achieve $\phi$ individually iff (1) it has not precommitted itself to another agent to adopt and achieve $\phi$, (2) it has a goal to achieve $\phi$ individually, and (3) it is willing to achieve $\phi$ individually. The chapter on "Formal Methods in DAI" provides more information on such descriptions.

The second approach is based on an assumption that the agents are economically rational. Further, the set of agents must be small, they must have a common language and common problem abstraction, and they must reach a common solution. Under these assumptions, Rosenschein and Zlotkin [37] developed a unified negotiation protocol. Agents that follow this protocol create a *deal*, that is, a joint plan between the agents that would satisfy all of their goals. The *utility* of a deal for an agent is the amount he is willing to pay minus the cost of the deal. Each agent wants to maximize its own utility. The agents discuss a *negotiation set*, which is the set of all deals that have a positive utility for every agent.

In formal terms, a task-oriented domain under this approach becomes a tuple

$$< T, \ A, \ c >$$

where $T$ is the set of tasks, $A$ is the set of agents, and $c(X)$ is a monotonic function for the cost of executing the tasks $X$. A deal is a redistribution of tasks. The utility of deal $d$ for agent $k$ is

$$U_k(d) = c(T_k) - c(d_k)$$

The conflict deal $D$ occurs when the agents cannot reach a deal. A deal $d$ is individually rational if $d > D$. Deal $d$ is pareto optimal if there is no deal $d' > d$. The set of all deals that are individually rational and pareto optimal is the negotiation set, $NS$. There are three possible situations:

1.  conflict: the negotiation set is empty

2.  compromise: agents prefer to be alone, but since they are not, they will agree to a negotiated deal

3.  cooperative: all deals in the negotiation set are preferred by both agents over achieving their goals alone.

When there is a conflict, then the agents will not benefit by negotiating—they are better off acting alone. Alternatively, they can "flip a coin" to decide which agent gets to satisfy its goals. Negotiation is the best alternative in the other two cases.

Since the agents have some execution autonomy, they can in principle deceive or mislead each other. Therefore, an interesting research problem is to develop protocols or societies in which the effects of deception and misinformation can be constrained. Another aspect of the research problem is to develop protocols under which it is rational for agents to be honest with each other.

The connections of the economic approaches with human-oriented negotiation and argumentation have not yet been fully worked out.

### 2.3.6 Multiagent Belief Maintenance

A multiagent truth-maintenance system can serve as a detailed example of a high-level interaction among agents. A truth-maintenance system (TMS) [10] is designed to ensure the integrity of an agent's knowledge, which should be stable, well-founded, and logically consistent. Depending on how beliefs, justifications, and data are represented, a *stable* state of a knowledge base is one in which 1) each datum that has a valid justification is believed, and 2) each datum that lacks a valid justification is disbelieved. A *well-founded* knowledge base permits no set of its beliefs to be mutually dependent. A *logically consistent* knowledge base is one that is stable at the time that consistency is determined and in which no logical contradiction exists. A consistent knowledge base is one in which no datum is both believed and disbelieved (or neither), or in which no datum and its negation are both believed. Other desirable properties for a knowledge base are that it be complete, concise, accurate, and efficient.

A single-agent TMS attempts to maintain well-founded stable states of a knowledge base by adjusting which data are believed and which are disbelieved. However, it is important for a group of agents to be able to assess and maintain the integrity of communicated information, as well as of their own knowledge. A multiagent TMS can provide this integrity [27].

We consider a modified *justification-based* TMS, in which every datum has a set of justifications and an associated status of INTERNAL (believed, because of a valid local justification), EXTERNAL (believed, because another agent asserted it), or OUT (disbelieved). Consider a network of many agents, each with a partially-independent system of beliefs. The agents interact by communicating data, either unsolicited or in response to a query. For well-foundedness, a communicated datum must be INTERNAL to at least one of the agents that believes it and either INTERNAL or EXTERNAL to the rest.

The support status of a communicated datum is jointly maintained by several agents. Hence, a single agent is generally not free to change the status on its own accord. It must coordinate with the other agents so that they are all consistent on the status of the datum.

The multiagent TMS is invoked by the addition or removal of a justification, and obeys the following principles:

- Belief changes should be resolved with as few agents as possible.
- Belief changes should be resolved by changing as few beliefs as possible.

When invoked, it does the following three things:

1.  Unlabels some data, including the newly justified datum and, presumably, its consequences. This unlabeled data set might be confined to a single agent or it might span several agents. If a communicated datum is unlabeled in some agent, it must be unlabeled in all the agents that share it.

2.  Chooses labelings for all the unlabeled shared data, as defined above.

3.  Initiates labeling by each of the affected agents with respect to the requirements imposed by the shared data. If any of the affected agents fails to label successfully, it then backtracks. It either chooses different labelings for the shared data (step 2), or unlabels a different set of data (step 1).

Consider the justification network in Figure 2.8. There are two agents, Agent 1 and Agent 2, and they share the communicated datum T. Assume that the initial labeling shown in the diagram is perturbed by the addition of a new justification for Q. Agent 1 initially unlabels just the changed datum and private data downstream, P and Q, but there is no consistent relabeling. Hence, Agent 1 unlabels all shared data downstream of P and Q, and all private data downstream from there: P, Q, both Ts, and U. Again labeling fails. Since there is no further shared data downstream, Agent 1 and Agent 2 unlabel upstream and privately downstream

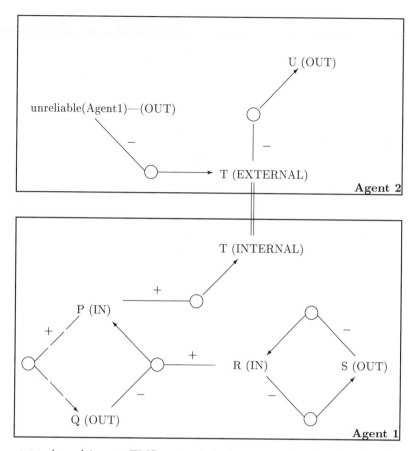

**Figure 2.8**  A multiagent TMS network before a new justification for datum Q (shown dashed) is added; this invokes the multiagent TMS algorithm and results in a relabeling of the network.

from there: P, Q, Ts, U, R, and S. Now labeling succeeds, with S and U IN and everything else OUT, as shown in Figure 2.9. Had labeling failed, **unlabel** would not be able to unlabel more data, and would report that the network is inconsistent.

### 2.3.7  Market Mechanisms

Most of the protocols and mechanisms described earlier in this chapter require agents to communicate with each other directly, so are appropriate for small numbers of agents only. Other mechanisms for coordination are needed when there are a large or unknown number of agents. One mechanism is based on voting, where agents choose from a set of alternatives, and then adopt the alternative receiving the most votes. This mechanism is simple, equitable, and distributed, but it requires significant amounts of communication and organization, and is most useful when there are just a few well defined issues to be decided.

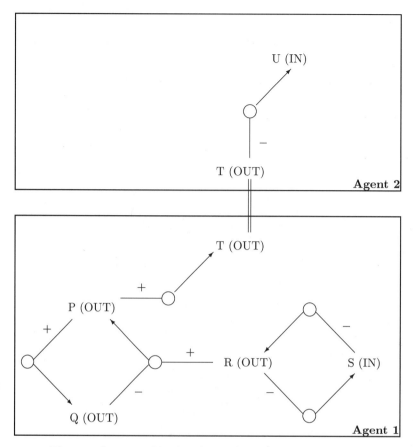

**Figure 2.9** The resultant stable labeling of the justification network that is produced by the multiagent TMS algorithm.

Computational economies, based on market mechanisms, are another approach [47]. These are effective for coordinating the activities of many agents with minimal direct communication among the agents. The research challenge is to build computational economies to solve specific problems of distributed resource allocation.

Everything of interest to an agent is described by current prices—the preferences or abilities of others are irrelevant except insofar as they (automatically) affect the prices. There are two types of agents, *consumers*, who exchange goods, and *producers*, who transform some goods into other goods. Agents bid for goods at various prices, but all exchanges occur at current market prices. All agents bid so as to maximize either their profits or their utility.

To cast a problem in terms of a computational market, one needs to specify

- the goods being traded
- the consumer agents that are trading the goods

- the producer agents, with their technologies for transforming some goods into others

- the bidding and trading behaviors of the agents.

Since the markets for goods are interconnected, the price of one good will affect the supply and demand of others. The market will reach a competitive equilibrium such that (1) consumers bid to maximize their utility, subject to their budget constraints, (2) producers bid to maximize their profits, subject to their technological capability, and (3) net demand is zero for all goods.

The important property is that an equilibrium corresponds—in some sense optimally—to an allocation of resources and dictates the activities and consumptions of the agents. In general, equilibria need not exist or be unique, but under certain conditions, such as when the effect of an individual on the market is assumed negligible, they can be guaranteed to exist uniquely.

In an open market, agents are free to choose their own strategy, and they do not have to behave rationally. Economic rationality assumes that the agent's preferences are given along with knowledge of the effects of the agent's actions. From these, the rational action for an agent is the one that maximizes its preferences.

Economic rationality has the charm of being a simple, "least common denominator" approach—if you can reduce everything to money, you can talk about maximizing it. But to apply it well requires a careful selection of the target problem.

One of the oldest applications of economic rationality is in decision-theoretic planning, which models the costs and effects of actions quantitatively and probabilistically. For many applications, where the probabilities can be estimated reliably, this leads to highly effective plans of actions [24, 22].

The need to maximize preferences essentially requires that there be a scalar representation for all the true preferences of an agent. In other words, all of the preferences must be reduced to a single scalar that can be compared effectively with other scalars. This is often difficult unless one can carefully circumscribe the application domain. Otherwise, one ends up essentially recreating all of the other concepts under a veneer of rationality. For example, if we would like an agent to be governed by its past commitments, not just the most attractive choice at the present time, then we can develop a utility function that gives additional weight to past commitments. This approach may work in principle, but, in practice, it only serves to hide the structure of commitments in the utility function that one chooses. The next section describes social commitments more fully.

## 2.4  Societies of Agents

Much of traditional AI has been concerned with how an agent can be constructed to function intelligently, with a single locus of internal reasoning and control implemented in a Von Neumann architecture. But intelligent systems do not function in isolation—they are at the very least a part of the environment in which they operate, and the environment typically contains other such intelligent systems. Thus, it makes sense to view such systems in societal terms.

There are promising opportunities engendered by the combination of increasingly large information environments, such as the national information infrastructure and the intelligent vehicle highway system, and recent advances in multiagent systems. Planned information environments are too large, complex, dynamic, and open to be managed centrally or via predefined techniques—the only feasible alternative is for computational intelligence to be embedded at many and sundry places in such environments to provide distributed control. Each locus of embedded intelligence is best thought of as an autonomous agent that finds, conveys, or manages information. Because of the nature of the environments, the agents must be long-lived (they should be able to execute unattended for long periods of time), adaptive (they should be able to explore and learn about their environment, including each other), and social (they should interact and coordinate to achieve their own goals, and the goals of their society; they should rely on other agents to know things so they do not have to know everything).

Techniques for managing societies of autonomous computational agents are useful not only for large open information environments, but also for large open physical environments. For example, such techniques can yield new efficiencies in defense logistics: by considering each item of materiel to be an intelligent entity whose goal is to reach a destination, a distribution system could manage more complicated schedules and surmount unforeseen difficulties.

A group of agents can form a small society in which they play different roles. The group defines the roles, and the roles define the commitments associated with them. When an agent joins a group, he joins in one or more roles, and acquires the commitments of that role. Agents join a group autonomously, but are then constrained by the commitments for the roles they adopt. The groups define the *social context* in which the agents interact.

Social agency involves abstractions from sociology and organizational theory to model societies of agents. Since agents are often best studied as members of multiagent systems, this view of agency is important and gaining recognition. Sociability is essential to cooperation, which itself is essential for moving beyond the somewhat rigid client-server paradigm of today to a true peer-to-peer distributed and flexible paradigm that modern applications call for, and where agent technology finds its greatest payoffs.

Although mental primitives, such as beliefs, desires, and intentions, are appropriate for a number of applications and situations, they are not suitable in themselves for understanding all aspects of social interactions. Further, economic models of agency, although quite general in principle, are typically limited in practice. This is because the value functions that are tractable essentially reduce an agent to a selfish agent. [7] argue that a self-interested agent need not be selfish, because it may have other interests than its immediate personal gain. This is certainly true in many cases when describing humans, and is likely to be a richer assumption for modeling artificial agents in settings that are appropriately complex.

*Social commitments* are the commitments of an agent to another agent. These must be carefully distinguished from internal commitments. Social commitments have been studied by a number of researchers, including [17, 28]. There are a number of definitions in the literature, which add components such as witnesses [5] or contexts [41]. Social commitments are a flexible means through which the behavior of autonomous agents is constrained. An important concept is that of social dependence, defined as

$$(SocialDependence\ x\ y\ a\ p) \equiv (Goal\ x\ p)\ \land$$
$$\neg(CanDo\ x\ a)\ \land$$
$$(CanDo\ y\ a)\ \land$$
$$((DoneBy\ y\ a) \implies Eventually\ p)$$

that is, agent $x$ depends on agent $y$ with regard to act $a$ for realizing state $p$, when $p$ is a goal of $x$ and $x$ is unable to realize $p$ while $y$ is able to do so.

Social dependence can be voluntary when the agents adopt the roles that bind them to certain commitments. However, it is an objective relationship, in that it holds independently of the agents' awareness of it. Of course, there may be consequences that occur when the agents become aware of it, such as $x$ might try to influence $y$ to pursue $p$.

Social dependencies may be compound. For example, mutual dependence occurs when $x$ and $y$ depend on each other for realizing a common goal $p$, which can be achieved by a plan including at least two different actions, such that $x$ depends on $y$ doing $a_y$ and $y$ depends on $x$ doing $a_x$, as

$$\exists p((SocialDependence\ x\ y\ a_y\ p) \land (SocialDependence\ y\ x\ a_x\ p))$$

Cooperation is a form of such mutual dependence.

Reciprocal dependence occurs when $x$ and $y$ depend on each other for realizing different goals, $p_x$ for $x$ and $p_y$ for $y$, as

$$\exists p_x \exists p_y((SocialDependence\ x\ y\ a_y\ p_x) \land (SocialDependence\ y\ x\ a_x\ p_y))$$

Social exchange is a form of such reciprocal dependence.

With this as a basis, a group of agents form a cooperative team when

- All agents share a common goal.

- Each agent is required to do its share to achieve the common goal by the group itself or a subgroup.

- Each agent adopts a request to do its share.

Beyond social dependencies, social laws may govern the behaviors of large numbers of agents in a society. See [34] for a treatment of this concept.

## 2.5   Conclusions

This chapter described elements of a computational environment that are needed for the interaction of multiple software agents. The elements enable agents to communicate, cooperate, and negotiate while they act in the interests of themselves or their society.

Further research is needed to develop the basis and techniques for societies of autonomous computational agents that execute in open environments for indefinite periods. This research will rely on the ability of agents to acquire and use representations of each other. This is what is needed for negotiation, cooperation, coordination, and multiagent learning. What should be the contents of these representations? Subsequent chapters of this textbook provide the answers.

## 2.6   Exercises

1.   *[Level 1]* What are some of the advantages and disadvantages of synchronous versus asynchronous communications among agents?

2.   *[Level 1]* Imagine that two agents are negotiating a contract. In the course of the negotiation, they engage in the following speech acts: *propose, counterpropose, accept, reject, retract, explain, ask-for-clarification, agree, disagree.* Draw a state diagram for the negotiation protocol followed by each agent.

3.   *[Level 3]* Consider an environment having one broker agent with which many information agents can advertise. When an information agent advertises, it provides the broker with a list of predicate calculus expressions summarizing its knowledge. To find information agents who are knowledgeable about certain topics, a query agent supplies predicate calculus expressions to the broker and asks for pointers to the relevant information agents. The broker then returns a list of all relevant information agents.

   (a)   List the KQML message that would be sent when query agent Q1 asks broker agent B1 for pointers to information agents knowledgeable about the predicate calculus expression `weight(Automobile ?x)`. Hint: the following is an example KQML message for an information agent advertising with a broker:

```
(advertise
        :content weight(Automobile ?z)
        :language Predicate-Calculus
        :ontology Transportation-Domain
        :sender info-agent-3
        :receiver broker-1)
```

   (b)   The `Transportation-Domain` ontology is common to all agents. Draw a state transition diagram for each agent. Be sure that every speech act sent and received serves as a "condition" for a state transition. State any simplifying assumptions used.

4.  *[Level 1]* What is the difference between the concepts coherence and coordination?

5.  *[Level 1]* Give an advantage and disadvantage of the use of the contract net protocol.

6.  *[Level 2]* Formalize the following protocol for the contract net in KQML. Clearly state which parts must be in the :content part of the communications. "One agent, the Manager, has a task that it wants to be solved. The Manager announces the task by broadcasting the task description in a task-announcement message to the other agents, the potential contractors. When contractors receives a task announcement, they evaluate it and some of them respond with a bid message, containing an estimate of their ability and a cost. The manager evaluates the bids, chooses the best one, and sends an award message to the winning contractor."

7.  *[Level 2]* List the sequence of KQML performatives that must the generated by agents A, B, and C in solving the following problem: "Agent A wants to find out the cost of football tickets. Agent A does not know the cost, but Agent A knows that Agent B exists. Agent B does not know the cost either, but Agent B knows that Agent C exists. Agent C knows the cost." Assume that the agents are cooperative and truthful.

8.  *[Level 2]* Describe how three agents might negotiate to find a common telephone line for a conference call. Assume that Agent A has telephones lines 1, 2, 3; Agent B, 1, 3; and Agent C, 2, 3.
    The negotiation proceeds pair-wise: two agents at a time. The agents negotiate in order: A, B, C, A, B, C, A,... Also, alternate lines are chosen in the order specified above for each agent.
    Initially,
    Agent A proposes line 1 to Agent B, and Agent B accepts it.
    Agent B proposes line 1 to Agent C, but Agent C rejects it.
    Complete the process until all agents have picked a common line.

9.  *[Level 3]* "Multiagent Truth Maintenance:" A single agent who knows P and P $\Rightarrow$ Q would have its knowledge labeled as follows:

**fact1:**     P

     status:            (IN)

     shared with:   (NIL)

     justification:  (PREMISE)

**rule1:**     $P \Rightarrow Q$

     status:            (IN)

     shared with:   (NIL)

     justification:  (PREMISE)

**fact2:**     Q

     status:            (IN)

     shared with:   (NIL)

     justification:  (fact1, rule1)

If the agent shares fact1 with another agent, fact1's status changes to IN-TERNAL, and the agent receiving the knowledge labels its new fact as having status EXTERNAL.

Now consider the following situation in which the knowledge is initially local to each agent:

| Agent A | Agent B | Agent C |
|---------|---------|---------|
| fact1: P | rule1: $P \Rightarrow Q$ | fact1: R |
| rule1: $S \Rightarrow V$ | rule2: $R \Rightarrow Q$ | |
| | rule3: $R \Rightarrow S$ | |
| | rule4: $Q \Rightarrow W$ | |

(a) Suppose that Agent A shares fact1 with Agent B, who uses forward chaining to make all possible conclusions from his knowledge. Show the effect of Agent A sharing fact1 on the `status`, `shared with`, and `justification` fields for all data in each agent.

(b) Now suppose Agent C shares fact1 with Agent B. Show the effect of sharing this knowledge on the `status`, `shared with`, and `justification` fields for all data in each agent.

(c) Now suppose that Agent A retracts fact1 by making fact1 have status OUT. Show the changes that would occur to the `status`, `shared with`, and `justification` fields for all data in each agent.

10. *[Level 1]* In the discussion of the unified negotiation protocol, it is stated that the agents might decide to "flip a coin" when the negotiation set is empty. Under what conditions might this be beneficial to the agents.

11. *[Level 4]* Imagine a two-dimensional domain consisting of packages and destinations (Figure 2.10). In this domain, robots must move the packages to the correct destinations. Robots can carry only one package at a time, and they

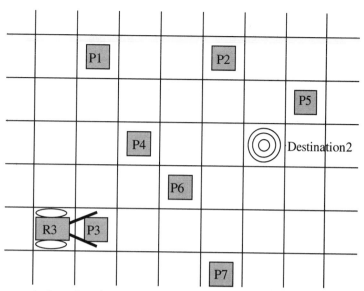

**Figure 2.10**   A domain where robots must move packages to their destinations.

are not allowed to travel through a package—they must maneuver around it. There is a cost associated with moving a package, but not with picking it up or setting it down. If a robot encounters a package when it is already carrying another, it can either move the package out of the way, or it can go around it. Moving it has a higher cost, but it might be beneficial to itself or other robots in the future to have the package out of the way. Assume that a robot is rewarded according to the amount that it moves a package closer to its destination. Develop a computer simulation of this domain, and try to establish answers to the following questions:

(a) Will the robots develop any social conventions regarding which direction they move packages that are obstacles?

(b) Under what conditions will "roadways" (paths without obstacles) form for the robots to travel on?

(c) Destination points will likely become congested with robots attempting to drop off their packages. Gridlock might even occur. Will the robots become specialized in their operation, where some robots bring packages near the destinations and other robots move them from the drop-off points to the final destinations?

(d) If the robots communicate information about their intentions regarding the packages they are moving, will other robots be able to take advantage of the information?

Suggestions: choose a grid of size NxN containing P packages, R robots, and D destinations, where initial values for the parameters are N=100, P=50, R=8, and D=3. Assume that a robot and a package each take up one square of the grid. Assume that a robot can move to any of its 8 adjoining squares, or stay where it is, in each time interval.

12. *[Level 1]* The initial state in a Block's World is On(B,C), On(D,A), Table(A), and Table(C). The desired goal state is On(A,B), On(B,C), Table(C), and Table(D). Agent1 can manipulate only blocks A and B; Agent2 can manipulate only blocks C and D. In solving this problem, the action MoveToTable(agent, block) can be used to place block D on the table. Express the movement of block D to the table in terms of the social dependence formula in this chapter.

## 2.7   References

1.  John L. Austin. *How to do Things with Words.* Clarendon, Oxford, UK, 1962.

2.  Will Briggs and Diane Cook. Flexible Social Laws. In *Proc. 14th IJCAI*, 1995.

3.  Birgit Burmeister, Afsaneh Haddadi, and Kurt Sundermeyer. Generic Configurable Cooperation Protocols for Multi-Agent Systems. In *Proceedings of the 3rd European Workshop on Modelling Autonomous Agents in a Multi-Agent World (MAAMAW)*, 1993.

4.  Stefan Bussman and Jurgen Muller. A Communication Architecture for Cooperating Agents. *Computers and Artificial Intelligence*, Vol. 12, No. 1, pages 37–53, 1993.

5.  Cristiano Castelfranchi. Commitments: From individual intentions to groups and organizations. In *Proceedings of the International Conference on Multiagent Systems*, pages 41–48, 1995.

6.  Man Kit Chang. *SANP: A Communication Level Protocol for Supporting Machine-to-Machine Negotiation in Organization.* MS Thesis, U. of British Columbia, Vancouver, B.C., Canada, 1991.

7.  Rosaria Conte and Cristiano Castelfranchi. *Cognitive and Social Action.* UCL Press, London, 1995.

8.  Daniel D. Corkill, Kevin Q. Gallagher, and Kelly E. Murray. GBB: A Generic Blackboard Development System. In *Proc. AAAI-86*, Philadelphia, PA, pages 1008–1014, 1986.

9.  Randall Davis and Reid G. Smith. Negotiation as a Metaphor for Distributed Problem Solving. *Artificial Intelligence*, Vol. 20, No. 1, pages 63–109, January 1983.

10.  Jon Doyle. A Truth Maintenance System. *Artificial Intelligence*, Vol. 12, No. 3, pages 231–272, 1979.

11.  Edmund H. Durfee. *Coordination of Distributed Problem Solvers.* Kluwer, 1988.

12.  Edmund H. Durfee and Thomas A. Montgomery. A Hierarchical Protocol for Coordinating Multiagent Behaviors. In *Proc. AAAI-90*, 1990.

13.  Edmund H. Durfee, Victor R. Lesser, and Daniel D. Corkill. Coherent Cooperation among Communicating Problem Solvers. *IEEE Transactions on Computers*, C-36(11):1275–1291, 1987.

14.  Adam Farquhar, Richard Fikes, and James Rice. The Ontolingua Server: A tool for Collaborative Ontology Construction. Technical Report KSL-96-26, Knowledge Systems Laboratory, Stanford University, September 1996.

15. Tim Finin, Don McKay, and Rich Fritzson. An Overview of KQML: A Knowledge Query and Manipulation Language. Technical Report, U. of Maryland CS Department, 1992.

16. S. Fiske and S. E. Taylor. *Social Cognition*. Addison Wesley, New York, 1984.

17. Les Gasser. Social Conceptions of Knowledge and Action: DAI Foundations and Open Systems Semantics. *Artificial Intelligence*, 47:107–138, 1991.

18. Les Gasser and Michael N. Huhns, editors. *Distributed Artificial Intelligence, Volume II*. Pitman Publishing, London, 1989.

19. N. Gilbert and J. E. Doran, editors. Simulating Societies: The Computer Simulation of Social Phenomena. In *Proceedings of the Symposium on Simulating Societies*. University College Press, London, 1994.

20. N.Gilbert and R.Conte, editors. *Artificial Societies: Computer Simulation of Social Life*. University College Press, London, 1995.

21. Afsaneh Haddadi. Towards a Pragmatic Theory of Interactions. In *Proc. International Conference on MultiAgent Systems (ICMAS)*, San Francisco, 1995.

22. Peter Haddawy. Believing Change and Changing Belief. *IEEE Transactions on Systems, Man, and Cybernetics Special Issue on Higher-Order Uncertainty*, 26(5), 1996.

23. Carl Hewitt. Open Information Systems Semantics for Distributed Artificial Intelligence. *Artificial Intelligence*, Vol. 47, pages 79-106, 1991.

24. Eric Horvitz and Geoffrey Rutledge. Time-dependent Utility and Action under Uncertainty. In *Proceedings of the 7th Conference on Uncertainty in Artificial Intelligence*, pages 151–158, 1991.

25. M. N. Huhns, U. Mukhopadhyay, L. M. Stephens, and R. D. Bonnell. DAI for Document Retrieval: The MINDS Project. In M. N. Huhns, editor, *Distributed Artificial Intelligence*. Pittman, London, 1987.

26. Michael N. Huhns and Munindar P. Singh. A Mediated Approach to Open, Large-Scale Information Management. In *Proc. IEEE Int. Phoenix Conf. on Computers and Communications*, 1995.

27. Michael N. Huhns and David M. Bridgeland. Multiagent Truth Maintenance. *IEEE Transactions on Systems, Man, and Cybernetics*, Vol. 21, No. 6, pages 1437–1445, December 1991.

28. N. R. Jennings. Commitments and Conventions: The Foundation of Coordination in Multi-Agent Systems. *The Knowledge Engineering Review*, 2(3):223–250, 1993.

29. Nick R. Jennings. Coordination Techniques for distributed Artificial Intelligence. In G. M. P. O'Hare and N. R. Jennings, editors, *Foundations of Distributed Artificial Intelligence*, pages 187–210. John Wiley & Sons, Inc., New York, 1996.

30. R. Kakehi and M. Tokoro. A Negotiation Protocol for Conflict Resolution in Multi-Agent Environments. In *Proc. ICICIS*, pages 185–196, 1993.

31. Yannis Labrou and Tim Finin. A Semantics approach for KQML—A General Purpose Communication Language for Software Agents. In *Proc. Int. Conf on Information and Knowledge Management*, 1994.

32. Kuha Mahalingam and Michael N. Huhns. An Ontology Tool for Distributed Information Environments. *IEEE Computer*, 30(6):80–83, June 1997.

33. Robin Milner. Elements of Interaction. *CACM*, Vol. 36, No. 1, pages 78–89, 1993.

34. Yoram Moses and Moshe Tenenholtz. On Computational Aspects of Artificial Social Systems. In *Proc. 11th DAI Workshop*, Glen Arbor, MI, 1992.

35. R. Neches, R. Fikes, T. Finin, R. Gruber, R. Patil, T. Senator, and W. Swartout. Enabling Technology for Knowledge Sharing. AI Magazine, 12(3):36–56, Fall 1991.

36. Jeffrey S. Rosenschein and Gilad Zlotkin. *Rules of Encounter.* The MIT Press, Cambridge, MA, 1994.

37. Jeffrey S. Rosenschein and Gilad Zlotkin. Designing Conventions for Automated Negotiation. *AI Magazine*, pages 29–46, 1994.

38. Stuart J. Russell and Peter Norvig. *Artificial Intelligence: A Modern Approach.* Prentice Hall, Upper Saddle River, NJ, 1995.

39. John R. Searle. *Speech Acts: An Essay in the Philosophy of Language.* Cambridge U. Press, 1970.

40. Herbert Simon. *The Sciences of the Artificial.* MIT Press, Cambridge, MA, third edition, 1996.

41. Munindar P. Singh. Commitments among autonomous agents in information-rich environments. In *Proceedings of the 8th European Workshop on Modelling Autonomous Agents in a Multi-Agent World (MAAMAW)*, 1997.

42. Munindar P. Singh. "Considerations on Agent Communication," presented at FIPA Workshop, 1997.

43. Munindar P. Singh. A Semantics for Speech Acts. *Annals of Mathematics and AI*, Vol.8, No.I-II, pages 47–71, 1993.

44. Reid G. Smith. The Contract Net Protocol: High Level Communication and Control in a Distributed Problem Solver. *IEEE Transactions on Computers*, Vol. C-29, No. 12, pages 1104–1113, December 1980.

45. Reid G. Smith and Randall Davis. Frameworks for Cooperation in Distributed Problem Solving. *IEEE Transactions on Systems, Man, and Cybernetics*, Vol. SMC-11, No. 1, pages 61–70, January 1981.

46. Katia Sycara. Resolving Goal Conflicts via Negotiation. In *Proc. AAAI-88*, pages 245–250, 1988.

47. Michael P. Wellman. A Computational Market Model for Distributed Configuration Design. *AI EDAM*, 9:125–133, 1995.

48. Eric Werner. Cooperating Agents: A Unified Theory of Communication and Social Structure. In L. Gasser and M. Huhns, editors, *Distributed Artificial Intelligence*, Volume II, pages 3–36. Pittman, London, 1989.

49. Gio Wiederhold. Mediators in the Architecture of Future Information Systems, *IEEE Computer*, Vol. 25, No. 3, pages 38–49, March 1992.

50. Carson Woo and Frederick H. Lochovsky. Knowledge Communication in Intelligent Information Systems. *International Journal of Intelligent and Cooperative Information Systems*, Vol. 1, No. 1, pages 203–228, 1992.

# 3     Distributed Problem Solving and Planning

Edmund H. Durfee

---

## 3.1   Introduction

Distributed problem solving is the name applied to a subfield of distributed artificial intelligence (AI) in which the emphasis is on getting agents to work together well to solve problems that require collective effort. Due to an inherent distribution of resources such as knowledge, capability, information, and expertise among the agents, an agent in a distributed problem-solving system is unable to accomplish its own tasks alone, or at least can accomplish its tasks better (more quickly, completely, precisely, or certainly) when working with others.

Solving distributed problems well demands both group coherence (that is, agents need to want to work together) and **competence** (that is, agents need to know how to work together well). As the reader by now recognizes, group coherence is hard to realize among individually-motivated agents (see Chapters 2 and 5, for example). In distributed problem solving, we typically assume a fair degree of coherence is already present: the agents have been designed to work together; or the payoffs to self-interested agents are only accrued through collective efforts; or social engineering has introduced disincentives for agent individualism; etc. Distributed problem solving thus concentrates on competence; as anyone who has played on a team, worked on a group project, or performed in an orchestra can tell you, simply having the desire to work together by no means ensures a competent collective outcome!

Distributed problem solving presumes the existence of problems that need to be solved and expectations about what constitute solutions. For example, a problem to solve might be for a team of (computational) agents to design an artifact (say, a car). The solution they formulate must satisfy overall requirements (it should have four wheels, the engine should fit within the engine compartment and be powerful enough to move the car, etc.), and must exist in a particular form (a specification document for the assembly plant). The teamed agents formulate solutions by each tackling (one or more) subproblems and synthesizing these subproblem solutions into overall solutions.

Sometimes the problem the agents are solving is to construct a plan. And often, even if the agents are solving other kinds of problems, they also have to solve

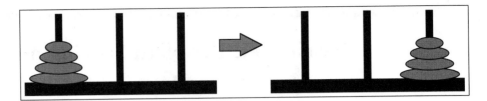

**Figure 3.1**   Tower of Hanoi (ToH).

planning problems as well. That is, how the agents should plan to work together—decompose problems into subproblems, allocate these subproblems, exchange subproblem solutions, and synthesize overall solutions—is itself a problem the agents need to solve. Distributed planning is thus tightly intertwined with distributed problem solving, being both a problem in itself and a means to solving a problem.

In this chapter, we will build on the topics of the previous chapters to describe the concepts and algorithms that comprise the foundations of distributed problem solving and planning. The reader is already familiar with protocols of interaction; here we describe how those protocols are used in the context of distributed problem solving and planning. The reader is also assumed to be familiar with traditional AI search techniques; since problem solving and planning are usually accomplished through search, we make liberal use of the relevant concepts. The subsequent chapter delves more formally into distributed search specifically.

The remainder of the chapter is structured as follows. We begin by introducing some representative example problems, as well as overviewing a variety of other applications of the techniques to be described. Working from these motivating examples, we work our way up through a series of algorithms and concepts as we introduce increasingly complicated requirements into the kinds of problems to solve, including planning problems.

## 3.2   Example Problems

There are several motivations for distributed problem solving and distributed planning. One obvious motivation is that using distributed resources concurrently can allow a speedup of problem solving thanks to parallelism. The possible improvements due to parallelism depend, of course, on the degree of parallelism inherent in a problem.

One problem that permits a large amount of parallelism during planning is a classic toy problem from the AI literature: the **Tower of Hanoi** (ToH) problem (see Figure 3.1). As the reader will recall from an introductory AI course, ToH consists of 3 pegs and $n$ disks of graduated sizes. The starting situation has all of the disks on one peg, largest at bottom to smallest at top. The goal is to move the disks from the start peg to another specified peg, moving only one disk at a time, without ever placing a larger disk on top of a smaller disk. The problem, then, is to find a sequence of moves that will achieve the goal state.

A second motivation for distributed problem solving and planning is that expertise or other problem-solving capabilities can be inherently distributed. For example, in concurrent engineering, a problem could involve designing and manufacturing an artifact (such as a car) by allowing specialized agents to individually formulate components and processes, and combining these into a collective solution. Or, supervisory systems for air-traffic control, factory automation, or crisis management can involve an interplay between separate pieces for event monitoring, situation assessment, diagnosis, prioritization, and response generation. In these kinds of systems, the problem is to employ diverse capabilities to solve problems that are not only large (the ToH can itself be arbitrarily large) but also multi-faceted.

As a simple example of distributed capability, we will use the example of **distributed sensor network establishment** for monitoring a large area for vehicle movements. In this kind of problem, the overall task of monitoring cannot be done in a central location since the large area cannot be sensed from any single location. The establishment problem is thus to decompose the larger monitoring task into subtasks that can be allocated appropriately to geographically distributed agents.

A third motivation is related to the second, and that is that beliefs or other data can be distributed. For example, following the successful solution of the distributed sensor network *establishment* problem just described, the problem of actually doing the **distributed vehicle monitoring** could in principle be centralized: each of the distributed sensor agents could transmit raw data to a central site to be interpreted into a global view. This centralized strategy, however, could involve tremendous amounts of unnecessary communication compared to allowing the separate sensor agents to formulate local interpretations that could then be transmitted selectively.

Finally, a fourth motivation is that the results of problem solving or planning might need to be distributed to be acted on by multiple agents. For example, in a task involving the delivery of objects between locations, **distributed delivery** agents can act in parallel (see Figure 3.2). The formation of the plans that they execute could be done at a centralized site (a dispatcher) or could involve distributed problem- solving among them. Moreover, during the execution of their plans, features of the environment that were not known at planning time, or that unexpectedly change, can trigger changes in what the agents should do. Again, all such decisions could be routed through a central coordinator, but for a variety of reasons (exploiting parallelism, sporadic coordinator availability, slow communication channels, etc.) it could be preferable for the agents to modify their plans unilaterally or with limited communication among them.

In the above, we have identified several of the motivations for distributed problem solving and planning, and have enumerated examples of the kinds of applications for which these techniques make sense. In the rest of this chapter, we will refer back to several of these kinds of application problems, specifically:

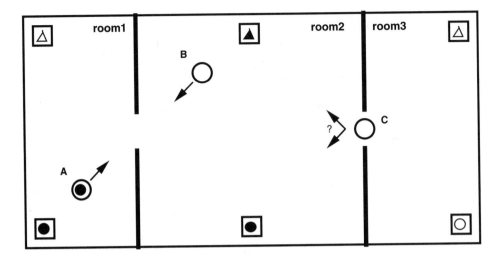

**Figure 3.2**   Distributed delivery example.

- Tower of Hanoi (ToH)
- Distributed Sensor Network Establishment (DSNE)
- Distributed Vehicle Monitoring (DVM)
- Distributed Delivery (DD)

## 3.3   Task Sharing

The first class of distributed problem-solving strategies that we will consider have been called "task sharing" or "task passing" strategies in the literature. The idea is simple. When an agent has many tasks to do, it should enlist the help of agents with few or no tasks. The main steps in task sharing are:

1. **Task decomposition**: Generate the set of tasks to potentially be passed to others. This could generally involve decomposing large tasks into subtasks that could be tackled by different agents.

2. **Task allocation**: Assign subtasks to appropriate agents.

3. **Task accomplishment**: The appropriate agents each accomplish their subtasks, which could include further decomposition and subsubtask assignment, recursively to the point that an agent can accomplish the task it is handed alone.

4. **Result synthesis**: When an agent accomplishes its subtask, it passes the result to the appropriate agent (usually the original agent, since it knows the

decomposition decisions and thus is most likely to know how to compose the results into an overall solution).

Note that, depending on the circumstances, different steps might be more or less difficult. For example, sometimes an overburdened agent begins with a bundle of separate tasks, so decomposition is unnecessary; sometimes the agent can pass tasks off to any of a number of identical agents, so allocation is trivial; and sometimes accomplishing the tasks does not yield any results that need to be synthesized in any complex way.

### 3.3.1  Task Sharing in the ToH Problem

To get a feel for the possibilities of task sharing, we start with the very simple ToH problem. Consider the task-sharing steps when it comes to this problem:

1. Task decomposition: Means-ends analysis (see Figure 3.3), where moving the largest disk that is not at its destination peg is considered the most important difference, leads to a recursive decomposition: solve the problem of getting to the state where the largest disk can be moved, and get from the state after it is moved to the goal state. These subproblems can be further decomposed into problems of moving the second largest disk to the middle peg to get it out of the way, so the state where that can be done needs to be reached, etc.

2. Task allocation: If we assume an indefinite number of identical idle agents capable of solving (pieces of) the ToH problem, then allocation reduces to just assigning a task randomly to one of these agents.

3. Task accomplishment: In general, an agent can use means-ends analysis to find the most significant difference between the start and goal states that it is responsible for, and will decompose the problem based on these. If the decomposed problems are such that the start and goal states are the same (that is, where the most significant difference is also the only difference), then the recursive decomposition terminates.

4. Result synthesis: When an agent has solved its problem, it passes the solution back on up. When an agent has received solutions to all of the subproblems it passed down, it can compose these into a more comprehensive sequence of moves, and then pass this up as its solution.

ToH represents an ideal case of the possibilities of distributed problem solving due to the hierarchical nature of the problem. In general, for a problem like ToH, the search space is exponential in size. If we assume a branching factor of $b$ (meaning that from a state, there are $b$ alternative states that can be reached by moving some disk to some peg), and assuming that in the best case it will take $n$ disk movements to go from the start state to the end state, then the search complexity is $b^n$.

Thanks to the hierarchical structure of the problem, the means-ends heuristic can reduce this complexity dramatically. Let us assume that ultimately the hierarchy

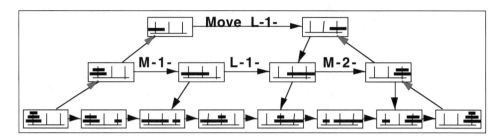

**Figure 3.3**  Means-ends decomposition for ToH.

divides the problem of size $n$ into problems each of size $k$, yielding $n/k$ subproblems, each of which requires $f(k)$ time to solve. These solutions are fed to the next level up in the hierarchy such that $k$ are given to each of the agents at this level. Each of these $n/k^2$ agents has to synthesize $k$ results, again requiring $f(k)$ time. This aggregation process continues up the hierarchy, such that at the next-to-topmost level, $n/k^{l-1}$ agents are combining $k$ results from below in the hierarchy with $l$ levels. The topmost agent then combines these $n/k^{l-1}$ results together, requiring $f(n/k^{l-1})$ time. The total expenditure is thus:

$$f(n/k^{l-1}) + (n/k^{l-1} \cdot f(k)) + (n/k^{l-2} \cdot f(k)) + \ldots + (n/k \cdot f(k)) \quad .$$

Since $k$ is a constant, and we can choose $l = \log_k n$, the equation can be reduced to $O([(k^l - 1)/(k - 1)]f(k))$ which can be simplified simply to $O(n)$ [23, 23]. More importantly, if each level of the hierarchy has agents that solve their subproblems in parallel, then the time needed below the top of the hierarchy (assuming negligible distribution and communication time) is simply $f(k)$ for each level, so $(l - 1)f(k)$. This is added to the top agent's calculation $f(n/k^{l-1})$. Again, since $k$ (and hence $f(k)$) is constant, and $l = \log_k n$, this reduces simply to $O(\log_k n)$. This means that through decomposition and parallel problem solving, the exponential ToH problem can be reduced to logarithmic time complexity [33].

What the ToH problem illustrates is the potential for improved parallelism due to distributed problem solving in the ideally decomposable case. Unfortunately, few problems satisfy the assumptions in this analysis of ToH, including:

1.  There is no backtracking back upward in the abstraction hierarchy, meaning that each distributed subproblem is solvable independently and the solution of one does not affect the solution of others. We will consider the effects of relaxing this assumption in Subection 3.3.4.

2.  The solution found hierarchically approximates (is linear in length to) the solution that would be found using brute-force centralized search. This depends on having hierarchical abstraction spaces that do not exclude good solutions as a consequence of reducing complexity.

3. The number of abstraction levels grows with the problem size. While doing this is easy for ToH, often the number of levels is fixed by the domain rather than the specific problem instance.

4. The ratio between levels is the base of the logarithm, $k$. Again, this depends on how the abstraction space is constructed.

5. The problems can be decomposed into equal-sized subproblems. This is very difficult in domains where problems are decomposed into qualitatively different pieces, requiring different expertise. We consider the effects of relaxing this assumption in Subsection 3.3.2.

6. There are at least as many agents as there are "leaf" subproblems. Clearly, this will be difficult to scale!

7. The processes of decomposing problems, distributing subproblems, and collecting results takes negligible time. We consider some of the effects of relaxing this assumption at various places in this chapter.

### 3.3.2 Task Sharing in Heterogeneous Systems

One of the powerful motivations for distributed problem solving is that it is difficult to build artifacts (or train humans) to be competent in every possible task. Moreover, even if it feasible to build (or train) an omni-capable agent, it is often overkill because, at any given time, most of those capabilities will go to waste. The strategy in human systems, and adopted in many distributed problem-solving systems, is to bring together on demand combinations of specialists in different areas to combine their expertise to solve problems that are beyond their individual capabilities.

In the ToH example, the subproblems required identical capabilities, and so the decisions about where to send tasks was extremely simple. When agents can have different capabilities, and different subproblems require different capabilities, then the assignment of subproblems to agents is not so simple.

Conceptually, it is possible for an agent to have a table that identifies the capabilities of agents, so that it can simply select an appropriate agent and send the subproblem off, but usually the decisions need to be based on more dynamic information. For example, if several candidate agents are capable of solving a subproblem, but some are already committed to other subproblems, how is this discovered? One way is to use the Contract Net protocol (Chapter 2) with directed contracts or focused addressing: the agent (in Contract-Net terms, the *manager*) announces a subproblem to a specific agent (in the case of directed contracts) or a focused subset of other agents (in focused addressing) based on the table of capabilities, and requests that returned bids describe acceptance/availability. The manager can then award the subproblem to the directed contractor if it accepts, or to one of the available contractors in the focused addressing set. However, if none of the agents are available, the manager has several options, described in the following paragraphs.

### Broadcast Contracting

In the kind of open environment for which Contract Net was envisioned, it is unlikely that a manager will be acquainted with all of the possible contractors in its world. Thus, while directed contracts and focused addressing might be reasonable first tries (to minimize communication in the network), a manager might want to update its knowledge of eligible contractors by broadcasting its announcement to reach agents that it is currently unaware of as well. This is the most commonly considered mode of operation for Contract Net. Directed contracts and focused addressing can be thought of as caching results of such broadcasts, but since the cached results can become outdated, many implementations of Contract Net do not include this function. It is interesting to note, however, that this kind of "capabilities database" has found renewed favor in knowledge sharing efforts such as KQML (Chapter 2), where some agents explicitly adopt the task of keeping track of what other agents purport to be good at.

### Retry

One very simple strategy is to retry the announcement periodically, assuming that eventually a contractor will free up. The retry interval then becomes an important parameter: if retries happen too slowly, then many inefficiencies can arise as agents do not utilize each other well; but if retries happen to quickly, the network can get bogged down with messages. One strategy for overcoming such a situation is to turn the protocol on its head. Rather than announcing tasks and collecting bids, which implies that usually there are several bidders for each task, instead the protocol can be used by potential contractors to announce availability, and managers can respond to the announcements by bidding their pending tasks! It is possible to have a system alternate between the task and availability announcement strategies depending on where the bottlenecks are in the system at various times [41].

### Announcement Revision

Part of the announcement message that a manager sends is the eligibility specification for potential contractors. When no (satisfactory) contractors respond to an announcement, it could be that the manager was being too exclusive in whom it would entertain bids from. Thus, the manager could engage in iterative revision of its announcement, relaxing eligibility requirements until it begins to receive bids.

An interesting aspect of this relaxation process is that the eligibility specifications could well reflect preferences over different classes of contractors – or, more specifically, over the quality of services that different contractors provide. In concert with other methods of handling a lack of bids (described above), a manager will be deciding the relative importance of having a preferred contractor eventually pursue the subproblem compared to finding a suboptimal contractor sooner. In many cases, these preferences and tradeoffs between them can be captured using economic representations. By describing parts of its marginal utility curve, for example, a manager can provide tradeoff information to an auction, which can then apply principled algorithms to optimize the allocation of capabilities (see Chapter 5).

### *Alternative Decompositions*

The manager can try decomposing the overall problem differently such that contractors are available for the alternative subproblems. In general, the relationship between problem decomposition and subproblem allocation is extremely complex and has not received sufficient attention. Sometimes a manager should first determine the space of alternative contractors to focus problem decomposition, while other times the space of decompositions can be very restrictive. Moreover, decisions about the number of problems to decompose into and the granularity of those subproblems will depend on other features of the application environment, including communication delays. We say no more about these issues here, other than to stress the research opportunities in this area.

### 3.3.3  Task Sharing for DSNE

Smith and Davis (and others since) have explored the use of the Contract Net protocol for a variety of problems, including the Distributed Sensor Net Establishment (DSNE) problem [4]. To give the reader a flavor of this approach, we briefly summarize the stages of this application.

At the outset, it is assumed that a particular agent is given the task of monitoring a wide geographic area. This agent has expertise in how to perform the overall task, but is incapable of sensing all of the area from its own locality. Therefore, the first step is that an agent recognizes that it can perform its task better (or at all) if it enlists the help of other agents. Given this recognition, it then needs to create subtasks to offload to other agents. In the DSNE problem, it can use its representation of the structure of the task to identify that it needs sensing done (and sensed data returned) from remote areas. Given this decomposition, it then uses the protocol to match these sensing subtasks with available agents. It announces (either directed, focused, or broadcast) a subtask; we leave out the details of the message fields since they were given in Chapter 2.

The important aspects of the announcement for our purposes here are the eligibility specification, the task abstraction, and the bid specification. To be eligible for this task requires that the bidding agent have a sensor position within the required sensing area identified and that it have the desired sensing capabilities. Agents that meet these requirements can then analyze the task abstraction (what, at an abstract level, is the task being asked of the bidders) and can determine the degree to which it is willing and able to perform the task, from its perspective. Based on this analysis, an eligible agent can bid on the task, where the content of a bid is dictated by the bid specification.

The agent with the task receives back zero or more bids. If it gets back no bids, then it faces the options previously described: it can give up, try again, broaden the eligibility requirements to increase the pool of potential bidders, or decompose the task differently to target a different pool of bidders. If it gets back bids, it could be that none are acceptable to it, and it is as if it got none back. If one or more is acceptable, then it can award the sensing subtask to one (or possible several) of the bidding agents. Note that, because the agent with the task has a choice over what it announces and what bids it accepts, and an eligible agent has a choice over whether it wants to bid and what content to put into its bid, no agent is forced to be part of a contract. The agents engage in a rudimentary form of negotiation, and form teams through *mutual selection*.

### 3.3.4  Task Sharing for Interdependent Tasks

For problems like ToH, tasks can be accomplished independently; the sequence of actions to get from the start state to an intermediate state can be found completely separately from the sequence to get from that intermediate state to the goal state. Thus, the subtasks can be accomplished in any order (or concurrently), and synthesis need only wait to complete until they are all done.

In some cases, contracted tasks are not independent. In a concurrent engineering application, for example, process planning subtasks usually need to wait until product design tasks have progressed beyond a certain point. For relatively clearcut subtask relationships, a manager for the subtasks can coordinate their execution by initiating a subtask based on the progress of another, or by relaying interim results for one subtask to contractors of related subtasks.

More generally, however, aspects of subtask relationships might only become apparent during the course of problem solving, rather than being dictated ahead of time by the problem decomposition. For example, when using a distributed sensor network to perform vehicle monitoring, the runtime relationships between what is being monitored in different areas is as variable as the possible movements of vehicles through the areas. While a task-sharing strategy, exemplified in the Contract Net protocol, can *establish* a distributed sensor network, it does not provide a sufficient basis for using the network. Or, put more correctly, when task sharing is used to allocate *classes* of tasks among agents, then if different instances of those tasks have different interrelationships, discovering and exploiting those relationships requires the generation and sharing of tentative results.

## 3.4 Result Sharing

A problem-solving task is accomplished within the context of the problem solver, so the results of the task if performed by one problem solver could well differ from the results of the same task being performed by another problem solver. For example, students in a class are often given the same task (homework problem), but their independently derived solutions will not (better not!) be identical.

By sharing results, problem solvers can improve group performance in combinations of the following ways:

1. **Confidence**: Independently derived results for the same task can be used to corroborate each other, yielding a collective result that has a higher confidence of being correct. For example, when studying for an exam, students might separately work out an exercise and then compare answers to increase confidence in their solutions.

2. **Completeness**: Each agent formulates results for whichever subtasks it can (or has been contracted to) accomplish, and these results altogether cover a more complete portion of the overall task. For example, in distributed vehicle monitoring, a more complete map of vehicle movements is possible when agents share their local maps.

3. **Precision**: To refine its own solution, an agent needs to know more about the solutions that others have formulated. For example, in a concurrent engineering application, each agent might separately come up with specifications for part of an artifact, but by sharing these the specifications can be further honed to fit together more precisely.

4. **Timeliness**: Even if an agent could in principle solve a large task alone, solving subtasks in parallel can yield an overall solution faster.

Accruing the benefits of result sharing obviously means that agents need to share results. But making this work is harder than you might think! First of all, agents need to know what to do with shared results: how should an agent assimilate results shared from others in with its own results? Second, given that assimilation might be non-trivial, that communicating large volumes of results can be costly, and that managing many assimilated results incurs overhead, agents should attempt to be as selective as possible about what they exchange. In the remainder of this section, we look at these issues.

### 3.4.1 Functionally Accurate Cooperation

In task-passing applications like ToH, the separate problem-solving agents are completely accurate in their computations (they have all information and a complete specification for their subtasks) and operate independently. In contrast, agents doing Distributed Vehicle Monitoring (DVM) lack information about what is happening elsewhere that could impact their calculations. As a result, these agents need to cooperate to solve their subtasks, and might formulate tentative results along the way that turn out to be unnecessary. This style of collective problem solving has been termed functionally-accurate (it gets the answer eventually, but with possibly many false starts) and cooperative (it requires iterative exchange) [28].

Functionally-accurate cooperation has been used extensively in distributed problem solving for tasks such as interpretation and design, where agents only discover the details of how their subproblem results interrelate through tentative formulation and iterative exchange. For this method to work well, participating agents need to treat the partial results they have formulated and received as tentative, and therefore might have to entertain and contrast several competing partial hypotheses at once. A variety of agent architectures can support this need; in particular, blackboard architectures (Chapter 2) have often been employed as semi-structured repositories for storing multiple competing hypotheses.

Exchanging tentative partial solutions can impact completeness, precision, and confidence. When agents can synthesize partial solutions into larger (possibly still partial) solutions, more of the overall problem is covered by the solution. When an agent uses a result from another to refine its own solutions, precision is increased. And when an agent combines confidence measures of two (corroborating or competing) partial solutions, the confidence it has in the solutions changes. In general, most distributed problem-solving systems assume similar representations of partial solutions (and their certainty measures) which makes combining them straightforward, although some researchers have considered challenges in crossing between representations, such as combining different uncertainty measurements [47].

In functionally accurate cooperation, the iterative exchange of partial results is expected to lead, eventually, to some agent having enough information to keep moving the overall problem solving forward. Given enough information exchange, therefore, the overall problem will be solved. Of course, without being tempered by some control decisions, this style of cooperative problem solving could incur dramatic amounts of communication overhead and wasted computation. For example, if agents share too many results, a phenomenon called **distraction** can arise: it turns out that they can begin to all gravitate toward doing the same problem-solving actions (synthesizing the same partial results into more complete solutions). That is, they all begin exploring the same part of the search space (Chapter 4). For this reason, limiting communication is usually a good idea, as is giving agents some degree of skepticism in how they assimilate and react to information from others. We address these issues next.

### 3.4.2   Shared Repositories and Negotiated Search

One strategy for reducing potential flurry of multicast messages is to instead concentrate tentative partial results in a single, shared repository. The blackboard architecture, for example, allows cooperating knowledge sources to exchange results and build off of them by communicating through a common, structured blackboard (Chapter 2).

This strategy has been adopted in a variety of distributed problem-solving approaches, including those for design applications [25, 45]. In essence, using a shared repository can support search through alternative designs, where agents with different design criteria can revise and critique the alternatives. In many ways, this is a distributed constraint satisfaction problem (Chapter 4), but it differs from traditional formulations in a few respects.

Two important differences are: agents are not assumed to know whose constraints might be affected by their design choices, and agents can relax constraints in a pinch. The first difference motivates the use of a shared repository, since agents would not know whom to notify of their decisions (as is assumed in typical DCSP formulations as in Chapter 4). The second difference motivates the need for heuristics to control the distributed search, since at any given time agents might need to choose between improving some solutions, rejecting some solutions, or relaxing expectations (thus making some solutions that were previously considered as rejected now acceptable).

For example, agents engaged in negotiated search [25] have at their disposal a variety of operators for progressing the distributed problem-solving effort: *initiate-solution* (propose a new starting point for a solution); *extend-solution* (revise an already existing partial solution); *critique-solution* (provide feedback on the viability of an already existing partial solution); and *relax-solution-requirement* (change local requirements for solution acceptability). At any given time, an agent needs to decide which of these operators to apply, and where. While a systematic exploration of the space can be considered (Chapter 4), the problem domains for negotiated search are typically complex enough that heuristic guidance is preferred. Heuristic measures for when to invoke operators (such as invoking the *relax-solution-requirement* operator when lack of progress is detected) and on what (such as relaxing requirements corresponding to the most constrained component) are generally application-specific.

### 3.4.3   Distributed Constrained Heuristic Search

Constraint satisfaction problems in distributed environments also arise due to contention for resources. Rather than assuming a shared repository for tentative partial solutions, a search strategy that has been gainfully employed for distributed resource allocation problems has been to associate an "agent" with each resource, and have that agent process the contending demands for the resource. One form that this strategy takes is so-called market-oriented programming [44] where associated with resources are auctions that support the search for equilibria in which resources are allocated efficiently. Market mechanisms are covered in detail in Chapter 5.

A second form that this strategy takes is to allow resources to compute their aggregate demands, which then the competing agents can take into account as they attack their constraint-satisfaction problem. For example, distributed constrained heuristic search (DCHS) uses aggregate demand to inform a heuristic search for solving a distributed constraint satisfaction problem [43]. The idea is that more informed search decisions decrease wasted backtracking effort, and that constraint satisfaction heuristics such as variable and value ordering can be gainfully employed in a distributed environment.

DCHS works as follows (Figure 3.4):

1. An agent begins with a problem state comprised of a problem topology (the tasks to do and their relationships including constraints).

2. An agent propagates constraints within its state; it backtracks if an inconsistency is detected. Otherwise, it determines what resources it requires for what time intervals and computes a demand profile for those resources.

3. If the system is just beginning, or if the demand profiles differ from previous profiles, an agent sends the profile(s) to the resource(s).

4. A resource computes aggregate demand and informs the agents making the demands.

5. An agent uses the aggregate demands to order its variables (resource-and-time-interval pairs) and order the activities that it might assign to the highest-demand pair. It identifies a preferred resource/time-interval/activity assignment.

6. An agent requests that the resource reserve the interval for it.

7. The resource in turn grants the reservation if possible and updates the resource schedule. Otherwise the request is denied.

8. An agent processes the response from the resource. If the reservation is granted, the agent goes to step 2 (to propagate the effects of concretely scheduling the activity). If the reservation is not granted, the agent attempts another reservation, going to step 6.

This view of the search strategy, while simplified, highlights the use of resources being contended for to focus communication, and of an exchange of information that tends to decrease the amount of backtracking. That is, by giving agents an opportunity to settle the "difficult" contention issues first, much useless work is avoided in settling the easier issues and then discovering that these fail to allow the hard issues to be settled.

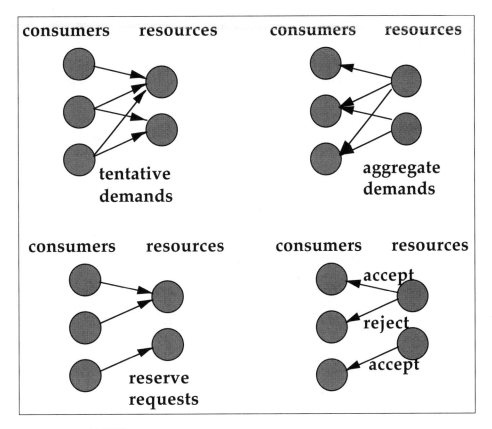

**Figure 3.4**   DCHS steps.

### 3.4.4   Organizational Structuring

When a shared repository cannot be supported or when problem-solving is not tantamount to resource scheduling, an alternative strategy for reducing communication is to exploit the task decomposition structure, to the extent that it is known. In a distributed design problem, for example, it makes sense to have designers working on components that must "connect" speak with each other more frequently than they speak with designers working on more remote parts of the design (of course, physical proximity might be only one heuristic!). Or, in a DVM task, agents monitoring neighboring parts of the space should communicate when their maps show activity at or near their mutual boundary. The notion is that agents have general roles to play in the collective effort, and by using knowledge of these roles the agents can make better interaction decisions.

This notion can be explicitly manifested in an organizational structure, which defines roles, responsibilities, and preferences for the agents within a cooperative society, and thus in turn defines control and communication patterns between them. From a global view, the organizational structure associates with each agent the types of tasks that it can do, and usually some prioritization over the types such that an agent that currently could do any of a number of tasks can identify the most important tasks as part of its organizational role. Allowing prioritization allows the structure to permit overlapping responsibilities (to increase the chances of success despite the loss of some of the agents) while still differentiating agents based on their primary roles.

Since each agent has responsibilities, it is important that an agent be informed of partial results that could influence how it carries out its responsibilities. More importantly, agents need not be told of results that could not affect their actions, and this can be determined based on the organizational structure. Thus, an organizational structure provides the basis for deciding who might potentially be interested in a partial result. It also can dictate the degree to which an agent should believe and act on (versus remain skeptical about) a received result.

While an organizational structure needs to be coherent from an overall perspective, it is important to note that, as in human organizations, an agent only needs to be aware of its local portion of the structure: what it is supposed to be doing (and how to decide what to do when it has choices), who to send what kinds of information to, who to accept what kinds of information from and how strongly to react to that information, etc. For practical purposes, therefore, organizational structures are usually implemented in terms of stored pattern-response rules: when a partial result that matches the pattern is generated/received, then the response actions are taken (to transmit the partial result to a particular agent, or to act on it locally, or to decrement its importance, etc.). Note that a single partial result could trigger multiple actions.

Finally, we have briefly mentioned that an organizational structure can be founded upon the problem decomposition structure, such as for the DSNE problem where agents would be made aware of which other agents are responsible for neighboring areas so that partial results that matched the overlapping regions of interest would be shared. The design of organizational structures for multi- agent systems, however, is generally a complex search problem in its own right. The search can be conducted in a bottom-up distributed manner, where boundaries between the roles of agents can be determined as the problem instance is initialized [5] or as problem solving progresses [19, 35], where adjustments to the structure can be based on reacting to performance inefficiencies of the current structure. In some cases, the organizational structure can be equated to a priority order for a distributed constraint satisfaction problem, and the agents are trying to discover an effective ordering to converge on a solution efficiently (see Chapter 4).

Alternatively, organizational structuring can be viewed as a top-down design problem, where the space of alternative designs can be selectively explored and candidate designs can be evaluated prior to their implementation [3, 34, 40]. The use of computational techniques to study, and prescribe, organizational structures is covered in Chapter 7.

### 3.4.5 Communication Strategies

Organization structures, or similar knowledge, can provide static guidelines about who is generally interested in what results. But this ignores timing issues. When deciding whether to send a result, an agent really wants to know whether the potential recipient is likely to be interested in the result now (or soon). Sending a result that is potentially useful but that turns out to not be at best clutters up the memory of the recipient, and at worst can distract the recipient away from the useful work that it otherwise would have done. On the other hand, refraining from sending a result for fear of these negative consequences can lead to delays in the pursuit of worthwhile results and even to the failure of the system to converge on reasonable solutions at all because some links in the solution chain were broken.

When cluttering memory is not terrible and when distracting garden paths are short, then the communication strategy can simply be to send all partial results. On the other hand, when it is likely that an exchange of a partial result will lead a subset of agents into redundant exploration of a part of the solution space, it is better to refrain, and only send a partial result when the agent that generated it has completed everything that it can do with it locally. For example, in a distributed theorem-proving problem, an agent might work forward through a number of resolutions toward the sentence to prove, and might transmit the final resolvent that it has formed when it could progress no further.

Between the extremes of sending everything and sending only locally complete results are a variety of gradations [7], including sending a small partial result early on (to potentially spur the recipient into pursuing useful related results earlier). For example, in the DVM problem, agents in neighboring regions need to agree when they map vehicles from one region to the other. Rather than waiting until it forms its own local map before telling its neighbor, an agent can send a preliminary piece of its map near the boundary early on, to stimulate its neighbor into forming a complementary map (or determining that no such map is possible and that the first agent is working down a worthless interpretation path).

So far, we have concentrated on how agents decide when and with whom to voluntarily share results. But the decision could clearly be reversed: agents could only send results when requested. Just like the choice between announcing tasks versus announcing availability in the Contract Net depends on which is more scarce, the same holds true in result sharing. When the space of possible interesting results is large compared to the actual results that are generated, then communicating results makes sense. But when the space of results formed is large and only few are really needed by others, then sending requests (or more generally, goals) to others makes more sense. This strategy has been explored in the DVM problem [3], as well as in distributed theorem proving [15, 31]. For example, in DARES [31], when a theorem proving agent would fail to make progress, it would request to import clauses from other such agents, where the set of desired literals would be heuristically chosen (Figure 3.5).

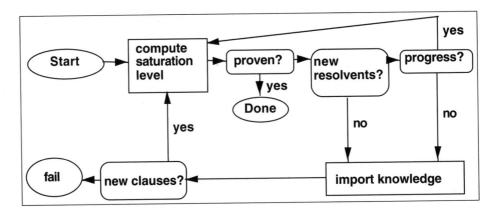

**Figure 3.5**   DARES agent control flow.

It is also important to consider the delays in iterative exchange compared to a blind inundation of information. A request followed by a reply incurs two communication delays, compared to the voluntary sharing of an unrequested result. But sharing too many unrequested results can introduce substantial overhead. Clearly, there is a tradeoff between reducing information exchanged by iterative messaging versus reducing delay in having the needed information reach its destination by sending many messages at the same time. Sen, for example, has looked at this in the context of distributed meeting scheduling [38]. Our experience as human meeting schedulers tells us that finding a meeting time could involve a series of proposals of specific times until one is acceptable, or it could involve having the participants send all of their available times at the outset. Most typically, however, practical considerations leave us somewhere between these extremes, sending several options at each iteration.

Finally, the communication strategies outlined have assumed that messages are assured of getting through. If messages get lost, then results (or requests for results) will not get through. But since agents do not necessarily expect messages from each other, a potential recipient will be unable to determine whether or not messages have been lost. One solution to this is to require that messages be acknowledged, and that an agent sending a message will periodically repeat the message (sometimes called "murmuring") until it gets an acknowledgment [29]. Or, a less obtrusive but more uncertain method is for the sending agent to predict how the message will affect the recipient, and to assume the message made it through when the predicted change of behavior is observed (see discussion of plan recognition in Subsection 7.4).

### 3.4.6   Task Structures

Up to this point, we have made intuitive appeals to why agents might need to communicate results. The TAEMS work of Decker and Lesser has investigated this question much more concretely [6]. In their model, an agent's local problem solving can have non-local effects on the activity of other agents. Perhaps it is supplying a result that another agent must have to *enable* its problem-solving tasks. Or the result might *facilitate* the activities of the recipient, allowing it to generate better results and/or generate results faster. The opposites of these (*inhibit* and *hinder*, respectively) are among the other possible relationships.

By representing the problem decomposition structure explicitly, and capturing within it these kinds of task relationships, we can employ a variety of coordination mechanisms. For example, an agent that provides an enabling result to another can use the task structure representation to detect this relationship, and can then bias its processing to provide this result earlier. In fact, it can use models of task quality versus time curves to make commitments to the recipient as to when it will generate a result with sufficiently high quality. In situations where there are complex networks of non-local task interrelationships, decisions of this kind of course get more difficult. Ultimately, relatively static organizational structures, relationships, and communication strategies can only go so far. Going farther means that the problem-solving agents need to analyze their current situation and construct plans for how they should interact to solve their problems.

## 3.5  Distributed Planning

In many respects, distributed planning can be thought of simply as a specialization of distributed problem solving, where the problem being solved is to design a plan. But because of the particular features of planning problems, it is generally useful to consider techniques that are particularly suited to planning.

Distributed planning is something of an ambiguous term, because it is unclear exactly what is "distributed." It could be that the operative issue is that, as a consequence of planning, a plan is formulated that can be distributed among a variety of execution systems. Alternatively, the operative issue could be that the planning process should be distributed, whether or not the resulting plan(s) can be. Or perhaps both issues are of interest. In this section, we consider both distributed plans and distributed plan formation as options; we of course skip over the case where neither holds (since that is traditional centralized planning) and consider where one or both of these distributions exists.

### 3.5.1  Centralized Planning for Distributed Plans

Plans that are to be executed in a distributed fashion can nonetheless be formulated in a centralized manner. For example, a partial order planner can generate plans where there need not be a strict ordering between some actions, and in fact where those actions can be executed in parallel. A centralized coordinator agent with such a plan can break it into separate threads, possibly with some synchronization actions. These separate plan pieces can be passed (using task-passing technology) to agents that can execute them. If followed suitably, and under assumptions of correctness of knowledge and predictability of the world, the agents operating in parallel achieve a state of the world consistent with the goals of the plan.

Let us consider this process more algorithmically. It involves:

1. Given a goal description, a set of operators, and an initial state description, generate a partial order plan. When possible, bias the search to find a plan in which the steps have few ordering constraints among them.

2. Decompose the plan into subplans such that ordering relationships between steps tend to be concentrated within subplans and minimized across subplans. [26].

3. Insert synchronization (typically, communication) actions into subplans.

4. Allocate subplans to agents using task-passing mechanisms. If failure, return to previous steps (decompose differently, or generate a different partial order plan, ...). If success, insert remaining bindings into subplans (such as binding names of agents to send synchronization messages to).

5. Initiate plan execution, and optionally monitor progress (synthesize feedback from agents to ensure complete execution, for example).

Notice that this algorithm is just a specialization of the decompose-allocate-execute-synthesize algorithm used in task passing. The specific issues of decomposition and allocation that are involved in planning give it a special flavor. Essentially, the objective is to find, of all the possible plans that accomplish the goal, the plan that can be decomposed and distributed most effectively. But since the availability of agents for the subplans is not easy to determine without first having devised the subplans, it is not certain that the most decomposable and distributable plan can be allocated in any current context.

Moreover, the communication infrastructure can have a big impact on the degree to which plans should be decomposed and distributed. As an extreme, if the distributed plans require synchronization and if the communication channels are slow or undependable, then it might be better to form a more efficient centralized plan. The monetary and/or time costs of distributing and synchronizing plans should thus be taken into account. In practical terms, what this usually means is that there is some minimal subplan size smaller than which it does not make sense to decompose a plan. In loosely-coupled networks, this leads to systems with fewer agents each accomplishing larger tasks, while in tightly-connected (or even shared-memory) systems the degree of decomposition and parallelism can be increased.

### 3.5.2   Distributed Planning for Centralized Plans

Formulating a complex plan might require collaboration among a variety of **cooperative planning** specialists, just like generating the solution to any complex problem would. Thus, for complex planning in fields such as manufacturing and logistics, the process of planning could well be distributed among numerous agents, each of which contributes pieces to the plan, until an overarching plan is created.

Parallels to task-sharing and result-sharing problem solving are appropriate in this context. The overall problem-formulation task can be thought of as being decomposed and distributed among various planning specialists, each of which might then proceed to generate its portion of the plan. For some types of problems, the interactions among the planning specialists might be through the exchange of a partially-specified plan. For example, this model has been used in the manufacturing domain, where a general-purpose planner has been coupled with specialist planners for geometric reasoning and fixturing [21]. In this application, the geometric specialist considers the shape of a part to be machined, and generates an abstract plan as an ordering over the geometric features to put into the part. The general-purpose planner then uses these ordering constraints to plan machining operations, and the augmented plan is passed on to the fixture specialist, which ensures that the operations can be carried out in order (that the part can be held for each operation, given that as each operation is done the shape of the part can become increasingly irregular). If any of these planners cannot perform its planning subtask with the partially- constructed plan, they can backtrack and try other choices (See Chapter 4 on DCSPs). Similar techniques have been used for planning in domains such as mission planning for unmanned vehicles [7] and for logistics planning [46].

The more asynchronous activity on the part of planning problem-solvers that is characteristic of most distributed problem-solving systems can also be achieved through the use of result sharing. Rather than pass around a single plan that is elaborated and passed on (or discovered to be a deadend and passed back), a result-sharing approach would have each of the planning agents generate a partial plan in parallel and then share and merge these to converge on a complete plan in a negotiated search mode. For example, in the domain of communication networks, localized agents can tentatively allocate network connections to particular circuits and share these tentative allocations with neighbors [2]. When inconsistent allocations are noticed, some agents try other allocations, and the process continues until a consistent set of allocations have been found. In this example, result-sharing amounts to a distributed constraint satisfaction search, with the usual concerns of completeness and termination (See Chapter 4 on DCSPs).

### 3.5.3  Distributed Planning for Distributed Plans

The most challenging version of distributed planning is when both the planning process and its results are intended to be distributed. In this case, it might be unnecessary to ever have a multi-agent plan represented in its entirety anywhere in the system, and yet the distributed pieces of the plan should be compatible, which at a minimum means that the agents should not conflict with each other when executing the plans, and preferably should help each other achieve their plans when it would be rational to do so (e.g. when a helping agent is no worse off for its efforts).

The literature on this kind of distributed planning is relatively rich and varied. In this chapter, we will hit a few of the many possible techniques that can be useful.

### Plan Merging

We begin by considering the problem of having multiple agents formulate plans for themselves as individuals, and then having to ensure that their separate plans can be executed without conflict. Assume that the assignment of goals to agents has been done, either through task-sharing techniques, or because of the inherent distributivity of the application domain (such as in a distributed delivery (DD) task, where different agents are contacted by users to provide a delivery service). Now the challenge is to identify and resolve potential conflicts.

We begin by considering a centralized plan coordination approach. Let us say that an agent collects together these individual plans. It then has to analyze the plans to discover what sequences of actions might lead to conflicts, and to modify the plans to remove the conflicts. In general, the former problem amounts to a *reachability analysis* – given a set of possible initial states, and a set of action sequences that can be executed asynchronously, enumerate all possible states of the world that can be reached. Of these, then, find the subset of worlds to avoid, and insert constraints on the sequences to eliminate them.

In general, enumerating the reachable state space can be intractable, so strategies for keeping this search reasonable are needed. From the planning literature, many assumptions about the limited effects of actions and minimal interdependence between agents' goals can be used to reduce the search. We will look at one way of doing this, adapted from Georgeff [16] next.

As is traditional, assume that the agents know the possible initial states of the world, and each agent builds a totally-ordered plan using any planning technology. The plan is comprised of actions $a_1$ through $a_n$, such that $a_1$ is applicable to any of the initial states, and $a_i$ is applicable in all states that could arise after action $a_{i-1}$. The state arising after $a_n$ satisfies the agent's goal.

We represent an action as a **STRIPS operator**, with preconditions that must hold for the action to take place, effects that the action has (where features of the world not mentioned in the effects are assumed unaffected), and "during" conditions to indicate changes to the world that occur only during the action. The STRIPS assumption simplifies the analysis for interactions by allowing us to avoid having to search through all possible interleavings of actions; it is enough to identify specific actions that interact with other specific actions, since the effects of any sequence is just the combined effects of the sequence's actions.

The merging method thus proceeds as follows. Given the plans of several agents (where each is assume to be a correct individual plan), the method begins by analyzing for interactions between pairs of actions to be taken by different agents. Arbitrarily, let us say we are considering the actions $a_i$ and $b_j$ are the next to be executed by agents $A$ and $B$, respectively, having arrived at this point through the asynchronous execution of plans by $A$ and $B$. Actions $a_i$ and $b_j$ can be executed in parallel if the preconditions, during conditions, and effects of each are satisfiable at the same time as any of those conditions of the other action. If this is the case, then the actions can commute, and are essentially independent. If this is not the case, then it might still be possible for both actions to be taken but in a stricter order. If the situation before either action is taken, modified by the effects of $a_i$, can satisfy the preconditions of $b_j$, then $a_i$ can precede $b_j$. It is also possible for $b_j$ to precede $a_i$. If neither can precede the other, then the actions conflict.

From the interaction analysis, the set of unsafe situations can be identified. Clearly, it is unsafe to begin both $a_i$ and $b_j$ if they do not commute. It is also unsafe to begin $a_i$ before $b_j$ unless $a_i$ has precedence over $b_j$. Finally, we can propagate these unsafe interactions to neighboring situations:

- the situation of beginning $a_i$ and $b_j$ is unsafe if either of its successor situations is unsafe;

- the situation of beginning $a_i$ and ending $b_j$ is unsafe if the situation of ending $a_i$ and ending $b_j$ is unsafe;

- the situation of ending $a_i$ and ending $b_j$ is unsafe if both of its successor states are unsafe.

To keep this safety analysis tractable, actions that commute with all others can be dropped from consideration. Given a loosely-coupled multiagent system, where agents mostly bring their own resources and capabilities to bear and thus have few opportunities to conflict, dropping commuting actions would reduce the agents' plans to relatively short sequences. From these simplified sequences, then, the process can find the space of unsafe interactions by considering the (exponential) number of interleavings. And, finally, given the discovered unsafe interactions, synchronization actions can be added to the plans to force some agents to suspend activities during regions of their plans that could conflict with others' ongoing actions, until those others release the waiting agents.

Plan synchronization need not be accomplished strictly through communication only. Using messages as signals allows agents to synchronize based on the completion of events rather than reaching specific time points. But many applications have temporal features for goals. Manufacturing systems might have deadlines for fabricating an artifact, or delivery systems might have deadlines for dropping off objects. For these kinds of applications, where temporal predictions for individual tasks are fundamentally important, the formulation of distributed plans can be based on scheduling activities during fixed time intervals. Thus, in these kinds of systems, the individual planners can formulate a desired schedule of activities assuming independence, and then plan coordination requires that the agents search for revisions to their schedules to find non-conflicting times for their activities (which can be accomplished by DCHS (see 3.4.3)). More importantly, different tasks that the agents pursue might be related in a precedence ordering (e.g. a particular article needs to be dropped off before another one can be picked up). Satisfying these constraints, along with deadlines and resource limitation constraints, turns the search for a workable collective schedule into a distributed constraint satisfaction problem (see Chapter 4).

A host of approaches to dealing with more complex forms of this problem exist, but are beyond the scope of this chapter. We give the flavor of a few of these to illustrate some of the possibilities. When there are uncertainties about the time needs of tasks, or of the possibility of arrival of new tasks, the distributed scheduling problem requires mechanisms to maximize expected performance and to make forecasts about future activities [30]. When there might not be feasible schedules to satisfy all agents, issues arise about how agents should decide which plans to combine to maximize their global performance [12]. More complex representations of reactive plans and techniques for coordinating them based on model-checking and Petri-net-based mechanisms have also been explored [20, 27, 37].

### Iterative Plan Formation

Plan merging is a powerful technique for increasing parallelism in the planning process as well as during execution. The synchronization and scheduling algorithms outlined above can be carried out in centralized and decentralized ways, where the flow is generally that of (1) assign goals to agents; (2) agents formulate local plans; (3) local plans are exchanged and combined; (4) messaging and/or timing commitments are imposed to resolve negative plan interactions. The parallels between this method of planning and the task-sharing style of distributed problem-solving should be obvious. But just as we discovered in distributed problem solving, not all problems are like the Tower of Hanoi; sometimes, local decisions are dependent on the decisions of others. This raises the question of the degree to which local plans should be formulated with an eye on the coordination issues, rather than as if the agent could work alone.

One way of tempering proposed local plans based on global constraints is to require agents to search through larger spaces of plans rather than each proposing a single specific plan. Thus, each agent might construct the set of *all* feasible plans for accomplishing its own goals. The distributed planning process then consists of a search through how subsets of agents' plans can fit together.

Ephrati and Rosenschein [11] have developed a **plan combination search** approach for doing this kind of search, where the emphasis is on beginning with encompassing sets of possible plans and refining these to converge on a nearly optimal subset. They avoid commitment to sequences of actions by specifying sets of propositions that hold as a result of action sequences instead. The agents engage in the search by proposing, given a particular set of propositions about the world, the changes to that set that they each can make with a single action from their plans. These are all considered so as to generate candidate next sets of propositions about the world, and these candidates can be ranked using an A* heuristic (where each agent can use its plans to estimate the cost from the candidate to completing its own goals). The best candidate is chosen and the process repeats, until no agent wants to propose any changes (each has accomplished its goal).

Note that, depending on the more global movement of the plan, an agent will be narrowing down the plan it expects to use to accomplish its own private goals. Thus, agents are simultaneously searching for which local plan to use as well as for synchronization constraints on their actions (since in many cases the optimal step forward in the set of achieved propositions might omit the possible contributions of an agent, meaning that the agent should not perform an action at the time).

An alternative to this approach instead exploits the hierarchical structure of a plan space to perform **distributed hierarchical planning**. By now, hierarchical planning is well-established in the AI literature. It has substantial advantages (as exemplified in the ToH problem) in that some interactions can be worked out in more abstract plan spaces, thereby pruning away large portions of the more detailed spaces. In the distributed planning literature, the advantages of hierarchical planning were first investigated by Corkill.

Corkill's work considered a distributed version of Sacerdoti's NOAH system. He added a "decompose plan" critic that would look for conjunctive goals to distribute. Thus, in a blocks-world problem (the infamous Sussman's Anomaly, for instance), the initial plan refinement of (AND (ON A B) (ON B C)) leads to a plan network with two concurrent paths, one for each of the conjuncts. The decompose-plan critic gives a copy of the plan network to a second agent, where each of the two agents now represents the goal it is to achieve as well as a parallel node in the network that represents a model of the other agent's plan. Then the agents proceed refine their abstract plans to successively detailed levels. As an agent does so, it can communicate with the other one about the changes that it expects to make to the world state, so that each can separately detect conflicts. For example, when an agent learns that the other is going to make block B not clear (it does not know the details of how) it can determine that this will interfere with stacking B on C, and can ask the first agent to WAIT on the action that causes that change until it has received permission to go on. This process can continue until a synchronized set of detailed plans are formed.

A variation on the hierarchical distributed planning approach is to allow each agent to represent its local planned behaviors at multiple levels of abstraction, any of which can suffice to resolve all conflicts. In this **hierarchical behavior-space search** approach to distributed planning, the outer loop of the protocol identifies a particular level of abstraction to work with, and whether conflicts should be resolved at this level or passed to more detailed levels. The inner loop of the protocol conducts what can be thought of as a distributed constraint satisfaction search to resolve the conflicts. Because the plans at various abstraction levels dictate the behaviors of agents to a particular degree, this approach has been characterized

1. Initialize the current-abstraction-level to the most abstract level.

2. Agents exchange descriptions of the plans and goals of interest at the current level.

3. Remove plans with no potential conflicts. If the set is empty, then done; otherwise determine whether to resolve conflicts at the current level or at a deeper level.

4. If conflicts are to be resolved at a deeper level, set the current level to the next deeper level and set the plans/goals of interest to the refinements of the plans with potential conflicts. Go to step 2.

5. If conflicts are to be resolved at this level:

   (a) Agents form a total order. Top agent is the current superior.

   (b) Current superior sends down its plan to the others.

   (c) Other agents change their plans to work properly with those of the current superior. Before confirming with the current superior, an agent also doublechecks that its plan changes do not conflict with previous superiors.

   (d) Once no further changes are needed among the plans of the inferior agents, the current superior becomes a previous superior and the next agent in the total order becomes the superior. Return to step (b). If there is no next agent, then the protocol terminates and the agents have coordinated their plans.

**Algorithm 3.1**    Hierarchical behavior-space search algorithm.

as search through hierarchical behavior space [9]. The algorithm is presented in Algorithm 3.1. Provided that there are finite abstraction levels and that agents are restricted in the changes to their plans that they can make such that they cannot get into cyclic plan generation patterns, the above protocol is assured to terminate. A challenge lies in the outer loop, in terms of deciding whether to resolve at an abstract level or to go deeper. The advantage of resolving a conflict at an abstract level is that it reduces the amount of search, and thus yields coordinated plans with less time and messaging. The disadvantage is that the coordination constraints at an abstract level might impose unnecessary limits on more detailed actions. At more detailed levels, the precise interaction problems can be recognized and resolved, while at abstract levels more inefficient coordination solutions might work. The tradeoffs between long-term, simple, but possibly inefficient coordination decisions versus more responsive but complex runtime coordination decisions is invariably domain-dependent. The goal is to have mechanisms that support the broad spectrum of possibilities.

As a concrete example of this approach, consider the DD problem of two delivery robots making repeated deliveries between two rooms as in Figure 3.6 (left side). Since R1 always delivers between the upper locations, and R2 between the lower ones, the robots could each inform the other about where they might be into the

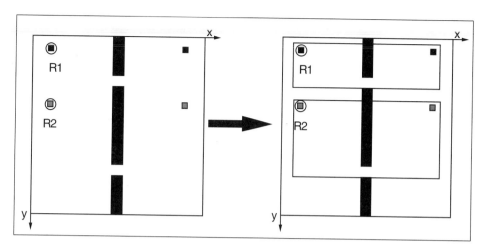

**Figure 3.6** An organizational solution.

indefinite future (between the locations, passing through the closest door). Their long-term delivery behaviors potentially conflict over that door, so the robots can choose either to search in greater detail around the door, or to eliminate the conflict at the abstract behavior level. The latter leads to a strategy for coordinating that statically assigns the doors. This leads to the permanent allocation of spatial regions shown in Figure 3.6 (right side), where R2 is always running around the long way. This "organizational" solution avoids any need for further coordination, but it can be inefficient, especially when R1 is not using its door, since R2 is still taking the long route. If they choose to examine their behaviors in more detail, they can find other solutions. If they consider a particular delivery, for example, R1 and R2 might consider their time/space needs, and identify that pushing their activities apart in space or time would suffice (Figure 3.7, top). With temporal resolution, R2 waits until R1 is done before beginning to move through the central door. Or the robots could use information from this more abstract level to further focus communication on exchanging more detailed information about the trouble spots. They could resolve the potential conflict at an intermediate level of abstraction; temporal resolution has R2 begin once R1 has cleared the door (Figure 3.7, middle). Or they could communicate more details (Figure 3.7, bottom), where now R2 moves at the same time as R1, and stops just before the door to let R1 pass through first. Clearly, this last instance of coordination is crispest, but it is also the most expensive to arrive at and the least tolerant of failure, since the robots have less distance between them in general, so less room to avoid collisions if they deviate from planned paths.

Of course, there are even more strategies for coordination even in a simple domain such as the distributed delivery task. One interesting strategy is for the robots to move up a level to see their tasks as part of a single, team task. By doing so, they can recognize alternative decompositions. For example, rather than decompose by

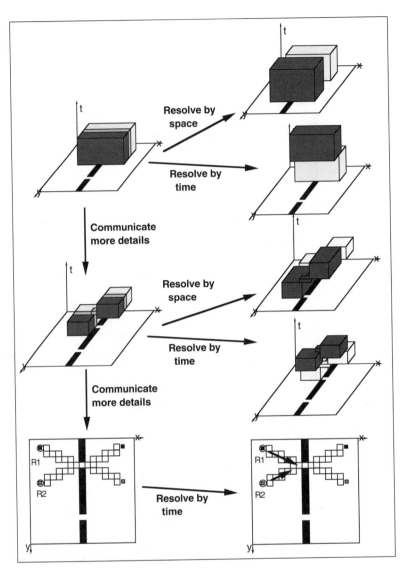

**Figure 3.7**   Alternative levels of abstraction.

items to deliver, they could decompose by spatial areas, leading to a solution where one robot picks up items at the source locations and drops them off at the doorway, and the other picks up at the doorway and delivers to the final destinations. By seeing themselves as part of one team, the agents can coordinate to their mutual benefit (they can cooperate) by searching through an enlarged behavior space.

### Negotiation in Distributed Planning

In the above, we considered how agents can determine that conflicts exist between their plans and how to impose constraints on (usually when they take) their actions to avoid conflict. Sometimes, determining which agent should wait for another is fairly random and arbitrary. Exceptions, however, exist. A large amount of work in negotiation (see Chapter 2) is concerned with these issues, so we only touch on them briefly here.

Sometimes the selection of the agent that should revise its local plans is based on models of the possibilities open to the agents. For example, Steeb and Cammarata, in the air-traffic control domain, were concerned with which of the various aircraft should alter direction to decrease potentially dangerous congestion. Their agents exchanged descriptions indicating their flexibility, and the agent that had the most other options was asked to change its plan, in an early distributed AI application of the least-constrained agent heuristic (see Subsection 3.4.3 and Chapter 4 on DCSPs).

Of course, these and other negotiation mechanisms for resolving goals presume that agents are honest about the importance of their goals and their options for how to achieve them. Issues of how to encourage self-interested agents to be honest are covered elsewhere in this book (see Chapter 5). However, clearly agents have self-interest in looking for opportunities to work to their mutual benefit by accomplishing goals that each other need. However, although the space of possible conflicts between agents is large, the space of possible cooperative activities can be even larger, and introduces a variety of utility assessments. That is, while it can be argued that agents that have conflicts always should resolve them (since the system might collapse if conflicts are manifested), the case for potential cooperative actions is not so strong. Usually, cooperation is "better," but the degree to which agents benefit might not outweigh the efforts they expend in finding cooperative opportunities. Thus, work on distributed planning that focuses on planning for mutually beneficial actions even though they were not strictly necessary has been limited to several forays into studies within well-defined boundaries. For example, partial global planning (see Subsection 3.7.3) emphasized a search for generating partial solutions near partial solution boundaries with other agents, so as to provide them with useful focusing information early on (see Subsection 3.4.5 on communication strategies). The work of von Martial [32] concentrated on strategies that agents can use to exploit "favor relations" among their goals, such as accomplishing a goal for another agent while pursuing its own goal.

## 3.6 Distributed Plan Representations

Distributed problem solving, encompassing distributed planning, generally relies heavily on agents being able to communicate about tasks, solutions, goals, plans, and so on. Of course, much work has gone into low-level networking protocols for interprocess communication in computer science generally, which forms the foundation upon which the particular communication mechanisms for multiagent systems build. At a much higher level, general-purpose protocols for agent interaction have been developed over the years, ranging from the Contract Net protocol which we have already seen to a broader variety of languages based on speech acts, such as KQML and agent-oriented programming (see Chapter 2). With speech-act-based languages, sending a message can be seen as invoking a behavior at the recipient. For example, sending a message of the type "query" might be expected to evoke in the recipient a good-faith effort to generate an answer followed by sending a message of the type "response" back to the sender.

This is all well and good, but what should the query itself look like? And the response? Different kinds of information might be asked about, and talked about, very differently. For this reason, a high-level speech-act-based language usually leaves the definition of the "content" of a message up to the designer. For any application domain, therefore, one or more relevant content languages need to be defined such that agents can understand not only the intent behind a message, but also the content of the message. In general, the definition of content languages is difficult and open-ended. By restricting our considerations to distributed planning, however, there is some hope in developing characteristics of a sharable planning language.

A planning content language needs to satisfy all of the constituencies that would use the plan. If we think of a plan as being comprised of a variety of fields (different kinds of related information), then different combinations of agents will need to access and modify different combinations of fields. In exchanging a plan, the agents need to be able to find the information they need so as to take the actions that they are expected to take in interpreting, modifying, or executing the plan. They also need to know how to change the plan in ways that will be interpreted correctly by other agents and lead to desirable effects.

To date, there are few standards for specifying plans for computer-based agents. Some conventions certainly exist (such as the "STRIPS operator" format [14]), but these are usually useful only within a narrow context. In most distributed planning systems, it is assumed that the agents use identical representations and are built to interpret them in the same ways.

One effort for formulating a more general description of a plan has been undertaken by SRI, in the development of their Cypress system [46]. In a nutshell, Cypress combined existing systems for plan generation and for plan execution. These existing systems were initially written to be stand-alone; Cypress needed to define a language that the two systems could use to exchange plans, despite the fact that what each system did with plans was very different. In their formalism, an **ACT** is composed of the following fields:

- Name – a unique label

- Cue – goals which the ACT is capable of achieving

- Precondition – features of the world state that need to hold for the ACT to be applicable
- Setting – world-state features that are bound to ACT variables
- Resources – resources required by the ACT during execution
- Properties – other properties associated with the ACT
- Comment – documentation information
- Plot – specification of the procedure (partially-ordered sequences of goals/actions) to be executed

Of course, each of these fields in turn needs a content language that can be understood by the relevant agents.

Other efforts have sought planning languages grounded in temporal logics and operational formalisms such as Petri Nets and Graphcet [20, 27, 37]. By appealing to a representation with a well-understood operational interpretation, the planning agents are freed from having to use identical internal representations so long as their interpretations are consistent with the operational semantics.

## 3.7 Distributed Planning and Execution

Of course, distributed planning does not occur in a vacuum. The product of distributed planning needs to be executed. The relationships between planning and execution are an important topic in AI in general, and the added complexity of coordinating plans only compounds the challenges. In this section, we consider strategies for combining coordination, planning, and execution.

### 3.7.1 Post-Planning Coordination

The distributed planning approach based on plan merging essentially sequentialized the processes in terms of allowing agents to plan, then coordinating the plans, and then executing them. This is reasonable approach given that the agents individually build plans that are likely to be able to be coordinated, and that the coordinated result is likely to executed successfully. If, during execution, one (or more) plans for agents fail to progress as expected, the coordinated plan set is in danger of failing as a whole.

As in classical planning systems, there are several routes of recourse to this problem. One is **contingency planning**. Each agent formulates not only its expected plan, but also alternative (branches of) plans to respond to possible contingencies that can arise at execution time. These larger plans, with their conditional branches, can then be merged and coordinated. The coordination process of course is more complicated because of the need to consider the various combinations of plan execution threads that could be pursued. By annotating the plan choices with the conditions, a more sophisticated coordination process can ignore combinations of conditional plans whose conditions cannot be satisfied in the same run.

A second means of dealing with dynamics is through monitoring and replanning: Each agent monitors its plan execution, and if there is a deviation it stops all agents' progress, and the plan-coordinate-execute cycle is repeated. Obviously, if this happens frequently, a substantial expenditure of effort for planning and coordination can result. Sometimes, strategies such as repairing the previous plans, or accessing a library of reusable plans [42] can reduce the effort to make it managable.

Significant overhead can of course be saved if a plan deviation can be addressed locally rather than having to require coordination. For example, rather than coordinating sequences of actions, the agents might coordinate their plans at an abstract level. Then, during execution, an agent can replan details without requiring coordination with others so long as its plan revision fits within the coordinated abstract plan. This approach has been taken in the team plan execution work of Kinney and colleagues, for example [22]. The perceptive reader will also recognize in this approach the flavor of organizational structuring and distributed planning in a hierarchical behavior space: so long as it remains within the scope of its roles and responsibilities, an agent can individually decide what is the best way of accomplishing its goals. By moving to coordinate at the most abstract plan level, the process essentially reverses from post-planning to pre-planning coordination.

### 3.7.2   Pre-Planning Coordination

Before an agent begins planning at all, can coordination be done to ensure that, whatever it plans to do, the agent will be coordinated with others? The answer is of course yes, assuming that the coordination restrictions are acceptable. This was the answer in organizational structuring in distributed problem solving, where an agent could choose to work on any part of the problem so long as it fit within its range of responsibilities.

A variation on this theme is captured in the work on **social laws** [39]. A social law is a prohibition against particular choices of actions in particular contexts. For example, entering an intersection on a red light is prohibited, as might be *not* entering the intersection on a green light. These laws can be derived by working from undesirable states of the world backwards to find combinations of actions that lead to those states, and then imposing restrictions on actions so that the combinations cannot arise. A challenge is to find restrictions that prevent undesirable states without handcuffing agents from achieving states that are acceptable and desirable. When overly constrictive, relaxations of social laws can be made [1].

Alternatively, in domains where conflict avoidance is not a key consideration, it is still possible that agents might mutually benefit if they each prefer to take actions that benefit society as a whole, even if not directly relevant to the agent's goal. For example, in a Distributed Delivery application, it could be that a delivery agent is passing by a location where an object is awaiting pickup by a different agent. The agent passing by could potentially pick up the object and deliver it itself, or deliver it to a location along its route that will be a more convenient pickup point for the other agent. For example, the delivery agents might pass through a "hub" location. The bias toward doing such favors for other agents could be encoded into cooperative state-changing rules [17] that require agents to take such cooperative actions even to their individual detriment, as long as they are not detrimental beyond some threshold.

### 3.7.3 Interleaved Planning, Coordination, and Execution

More generally, between approaches that assume agents have detailed plans to coordinate and approaches that assume general-purpose coordination policies can apply to all planning situations, lies work that is more flexible about at what point between the most abstract and most detailed plan representations different kinds of coordination should be done. Perhaps the search for the proper level is conducted through a hierarchical protocol, or perhaps it is predefined. In either case, planning and coordination are interleaved with each other, and often with execution as well.

Let us consider a particular example of an approach that assumes that planning and coordination decisions must be continually revisited and revised. The approach we focus on is called **Partial Global Planning** [8].

*Task Decomposition* – Partial Global Planning starts with the premise that tasks are inherently decomposed – or at least that they could be. Therefore, unlike planning techniques that assume that the overall task to be planned for is known by one agent, which then decomposes the task into subtasks, which themselves might be decomposed, and so on, partial global planning assumes that an agent with a task to plan for might be unaware at the outset as to what tasks (if any) other agents might be planning for, and how (and whether) those tasks might be related to its own as in the DVM task. A fundamental assumption in Partial Global Planning is that no individual agent might be aware of the global task or state, and the purpose of coordination is to allow agents to develop sufficient awareness to accomplish their tasks nonetheless.

*Local Plan Formulation* – Before an agent can coordinate with others using Partial Global Planning, it must first develop an understanding of what goals it is trying to achieve and what actions it is likely to take to achieve them. Hence, purely reactive agents, which cannot explicitly represent goals that they are trying to achieve and actions to achieve them, cannot gainfully employ Partial Global Planning (or, for that matter, distributed planning at all). Moreover, since most agents will be concurrently concerned with multiple goals (or at least will be able to identify several achievable outcomes that satisfy a desired goal), local plans will most often be uncertain, involving branches of alternative actions depending on the results of previous actions and changes in the environmental context in carrying out the plan.

*Local Plan Abstraction* – While it is important for an agent to identify alternative courses of action for achieving the same goal in an unpredictable world, the details of the alternatives might be unnecessary as far as the agent's ability to coordinate with others. That is, an agent might have to commit to activities at one level of detail (to supply a result by a particular time) without committing to activities at more detailed levels (specifying how the result will be constructed over time). Abstraction plays a key role in coordination, since coordination that is both correct and computationally efficient requires that agents have models of themselves and others that are only detailed enough to gainfully enhance collective performance. In Partial Global Planning, for example, agents are designed to identify their major plan steps that could be of interest to other agents.

*Communication* – Since coordination through Partial Global Planning requires agents to identify how they could and should work together, they must somehow communicate about their abstract local plans so as to build models of joint activity. In Partial Global Planning, the knowledge to guide this communication is contained in the **Meta-Level Organization** (MLO). The MLO specifies information and control flows among the agents: Who needs to know the plans of a particular agent, and who has authority to impose new plans on an agent based on having a more global view. The declarative MLO provides a flexible means for controlling the process of coordination.

*Partial Global Goal Identification* – Due to the inherent decomposition of tasks among agents, the exchange of local plans (and their associated goals) gives agents an opportunity to identify when the goals of one or more agents could be considered subgoals of a single global goal. Because, at any given time, only portions of the global goal might be known to the agents, it is called a partial global goal. Construction of partial global goals is, in fact, an interpretation problem, with a set of operators that attempts to generate an overall interpretation (global goal) that explains the component data (local goals). The kinds of knowledge needed are abstractions of the knowledge needed to synthesize results of the distributed tasks. And, just as interpretations can be ambiguous, so too is it possible that a local goal can be seen as contributing to competing partial global goals.

*Partial Global Plan Construction and Modification* – Local plans that can be seen as contributing to a single partial global goal can be integrated into a partial global plan, which captures the planned concurrent activities (at the abstract plan step level) of the individuals. By analyzing these activities, an agent that has constructed the partial global plan can identify opportunities for improved coordination. In particular, the coordination relationships emphasized in PGP are those of facilitating task achievement of others by performing related tasks earlier, and of avoiding redundant task achievement. PGP uses a simple hill-climbing algorithm, coupled with an evaluation function on ordered actions, to search for an improved (although not necessarily optimal) set of concurrent actions for the

---

1. For the current ordering, rate the individual actions and sum the ratings.

2. For each action, examine the later actions for the same agent and find the most highly-rated one. If it is higher rated, then swap the actions.

3. If the new ordering is more highly rated than the current one, then replace the current ordering with the new one and go to step 2.

4. Return the current ordering.

---

**Algorithm 3.2**   The algorithm for PGP plan step reordering.

---

1. Initialize the set of partial task results to integrate.

2. While the set contains more than one element:

   (a) For each pair of elements: find the earliest time and agent at which they can be combined.

   (b) For the pair that can be combined earliest: add a new element to the set of partial results for the combination and remove the two elements that were combined.

3. Return the single element in the set.

---

**Algorithm 3.3**   The algorithm for planning communication actions.

partial global plan (see Algorithm 3.2). The evaluation function sums evaluations of each action, where the evaluation of an action is based on features such as whether the task is unlikely to have been accomplished already by another agent, how long it is expected to take, and on how useful its results will be to others in performing their tasks.

*Communication Planning* – After reordering the major local plan steps of the participating agents so as to yield a more coordinated plan, an agent must next consider what interactions should take place between agents. In PGP, interactions, in the form of communicating the results of tasks, are also planned. By examining the partial global plan, an agent can determine when a task will be completed by one agent that could be of interest to another agent, and can explicitly plan the communication action to transmit the result. If results need to be synthesized, an agent using PGP will construct a tree of exchanges such that, at the root of the tree, partially synthesized results will be at the same agent which can then construct the complete result (see Algorithm 3.3).

*Acting on Partial Global Plans* – Once a partial global plan has been constructed and the concurrent local and communicative actions have been ordered, the collective activities of the agents have been planned. What remains is for these activities to be translated back to the local level so that they can be carried out. In PGP, an agent responds to a change in its partial global plans by modifying the abstract representation of its local plans accordingly. In turn, this modified representation is used by an agent when choosing its next local action, and thus the choice of local actions is guided by the abstract local plan, which in turn represents the local component of the planned collective activity.

*Ongoing Modification* – As agents pursue their plans, their actions or events in the environment might lead to changes in tasks or in choices of actions to accomplish tasks. Sometimes, these changes are so minor that they leave the abstract local plans used for coordination unchanged. At other times, they do cause changes. A challenge in coordination is deciding when the changes in local plans are significant enough to warrant communication and recoordination. The danger in being too sensitive to changes is that an agent that informs others of minor changes can cause a chain reaction of minor changes, where the slight improvement in coordination is more than offset by the effort spent in getting it. On the other hand, being too insensitive can lead to very poor performance, as agents' local activities do not mesh well because each is expecting the other to act according to the partial global plan, which is not being followed very closely anymore. In PGP, a system designer has the ability to specify parametrically the threshold that defines significant temporal deviation from planned activity.

*Task Reallocation* – In some circumstances, the exogenous task decomposition and allocation might leave agents with disproportionate task loads. Through PGP, agents that exchange abstract models of their activities will be able to detect whether they are overburdened, and candidate agents that are underburdened. By generating and proposing partial global plans that represent others taking over some of its tasks, an agent essentially suggests a contracting relationship among the agents. A recipient has an option of counter proposing by returning a modified partial global plan, and the agents could engage in protracted negotiations. If successful, however, the negotiations will lead to task reallocation among the agents, allowing PGP to be useful even in situations where tasks are quite centralized.

*Summary* – PGP fills a distributed planning niche, being particularly suited to applications where some uncoordinated activity can be tolerated and overcome, since the agents are individually revisiting and revising their plans midstream, such that the system as a whole might at times (or even through the whole task episode) never settle down into a stable collection of local plans. PGP focuses on dynamically revising plans in cost-effective ways given an uncertain world, rather than on optimizing plans for static and predictable environments. It works well for many tasks, but could be inappropriate for domains such as air-traffic control where guarantees about coordination must be made prior to any execution.

### 3.7.4 Runtime Plan Coordination Without Communication

While tailored for dynamic domains, PGP still assumes that agents can and will exchange planning information over time to coordinate their actions. In some applications, however, runtime recoordination needs to be done when agents cannot or should not communicate. We briefly touch on plan coordination mechanisms for such circumstances.

One way of coordinated without explicit communication is to allow agents to infer each others plans based on observations. The plan recognition literature focuses on how observed actions can lead to hypotheses about the plans being executed by others. While generally more uncertain than coordination using explicit communication, **observation-based plan coordination** can still achieve high-quality results and, under some circumstances can outperform communication-based distributed planning [18].

Another way of coordinating without explicit communication is to allow agents to make inferences about the choices others are likely to make based on assumptions about their rationality [36] or about how they view the world. For example, if Distributed Delivery agents are going to hand off objects to each other, they might infer that some locations (such as a hub) are more likely to be mutually recognized as good choices. Such solutions to choice problems have been referred to as **focal points** [13].

## 3.8   Conclusions

Distributed planning has a variety of reasonably well-studied tools and techniques in its repertoire. One of the important challenges to the field is in characterizing these tools and undertanding where and when to apply each. To some extent, the lack of specificity in the term "distributed planning" in terms of whether the process or the product or both of planning is distributed has hampered communication within the field, but more fundamental issues of articulating the foundational assumptions behind different approaches still need to be addressed. Until many of the assumed context and semantics for plans are unveiled, the goal of having heterogeneous plan generation and plan execution agents work together is likely to remain elusive.

The field of distributed problem solving is even more wide open, because the characterization of a "problem" is that much broader. As we have tried to emphasize, distributed plan formation and, in many cases, execution can be thought of as distributed problem solving tasks. Representations and general-purpose strategies for distributed problem solving are thus even more elusive. In this chapter we have characterized basic classes of strategies such as task- sharing and result-sharing. Ultimately, the purpose of any strategy is to share the right information about tasks, capabilities, availabilities, partial results, or whatever so that each agent is doing the best thing that it can for the group at any given time. Of course, exchanging and using the information that renders such choices can itself be costly, and opens the door to misinterpretation that makes matters worse rather than better. All of these considerations factor into the definition and implementation of a distributed problem strategy, but formulating such a strategy still has more "art" to it than we like to see in an engineering discipline.

**Acknowledgements:** The effort of compiling (and in some cases developing) the ideas in this chapter was supported, in part, by the NSF under PYI award 91-58473, and by DARPA under contract N66001-93-D-0058. I would like to thank my colleagues and my current and former graduate students, who have contributed the partial solutions assembled here.

## 3.9   Exercises

1.  *[Level 1]* The ToH time complexity analysis that reduces the complexity to logarithmic time assumed that the number of levels was a function of the problem size. More realistically, an organization would be developed for a variety of problems, rather than on a case-by-case basis. Assume the number of levels is fixed (and so the ratio between hierarchy levels will vary with the problem size). Now what is the expected time complexity for the ToH in a distributed problem-solving scenario. What does this answer tell you?

2.  *[Level 1]* Consider Contract Net without focused addressing (that is, announcements are broadcast).

    (a)  Name a real-life example where task announcment makes much more sense than availability announcement. Justify why.

    (b)  Now name a real-life example where availability announcement makes much more sense. Justify why.

    (c)  Let's say that you are going to build a mechanism that oversees a distributed problem-solving system, and can "switch" it to either a task or availability announcement mode.

        i.   Assuming communication costs are negligible, what criteria would you use to switch between modes? Be specific about what you would test.

        ii.  If communication costs are high, now what criteria would you use? Be specific about what you would test.

3.  *[Level 2/3]* We noted that task announcing can be tricky: If a manager is too fussy about eligibility, it might get no bids, but if it is too open it might have to process too many bids, including those from inferior contractors. Let us say that the manager has $n$ levels of eligibility specifications from which it needs to choose one. Describe how it would make this choice based on a decision-theoretic formulation. How would this formulation change if it needed to consider competition for contractors from other managers?

4.  *[Level 2]* A folk theorem in the organization literature is that, in human organizations, task decompositions invariably lead to clear assignments of subtasks to members of the organization. Give an example of where decomposition with-

out look-ahead to available contractors can be detrimental. Give an example where biasing decomposition based on available contractors can instead be detrimental. Finally, give an algorithm for alternating between decomposition and assignment to incrementally formulate a distributed problem-solving system. Is your algorithm assured of yielding an optimal result? Is it complete?

5. *[Level 1]* Consider the pursuit task, with four predators attempting to surround and capture a prey. Define an organizational structure for the predators. What are the roles and responsibilities of each? How does the structure indicate the kinds of communication patterns (if any) that will lead to success?

6. *[Level 2]* In the problem of distributed meeting scheduling, let us say that the chances that a specific meeting time proposal will be accepted is $p$.

   (a) If each iteration of the scheduling protocol has an agent propose a specific time to the others, what is the probability that the meeting will be scheduled in exactly $I$ iterations? What is the expected number of iterations to schedule the meeting?

   (b) If each iteration instead proposes $N$ specific times, now what is the probability that the meeting will be scheduled in exactly $I$ iterations? What is the expected number of iterations to schedule the meeting? What happens when $N$ approaches 1? How about when $N$ grows very large?

   (c) Based on the above, how would you choose a value for $N$ to use in a distributed meeting scheduling system? What other considerations might need to be taken into account besides a desire to keep the number of iterations low?

7. *[Level 2]* Consider the following simple instance of the distributed delivery task. Robot $A$ is at position $\alpha$ and robot $B$ is at position $\beta$. Article $X$ is at position $\xi$ and needs to go to position $\psi$, and article $Y$ is at position $\psi$ and needs to go to $\zeta$. Positions $\alpha$, $\beta$, $\xi$, $\psi$, and $\zeta$ are all different.

   (a) Define in STRIPS notation, suitable for Partial Order Planning, simple operators Pickup, Dropoff, PickDrop, and Return, where Pickup moves the robot from its current position to a Pickup position where it then has the article associated with that position; Dropoff moves a robot and an article it holds to a dropoff position where it no longer has the article; PickDrop combines the two (it drops off its article and picks up another associated with that position); and Return moves a robot back to its original position.

   (b) Using these operators, generate the partial order plan with the shortest sequence of plan steps to accomplish the deliveries. Decompose and distribute this plan to the robots for parallel execution, inserting any needed synchronization actions. How does the use of multiple robots affect the plan execution?

   (c) Using the operators, generate the partial order plan that, when distributed, will accomplish the deliveries as quickly as possible. Is this the same plan as in the previous part of this problem? Why or why not?

8. *[Level 2]* Given the problem of question 7, include in the operator descriptions conditions that disallow robots to be at the same position at the same time (for example, a robot cannot do a pickup in a location where another is doing a dropoff). Assuming each robot was given the task of delivering a different one of the articles, generate the individual plans and then use the plan merging algorithm to formulate the synchronized plans, including any synchronization actions into the plans. Show your work.

9. *[Level 2]* Consider the problem of question 7. Assume that delivery plans can be decomposed into 3 subplans (pickup, dropoff, and return), and that each of these subplans can further be decomposed into individual plan steps. Furthermore, assume that robots should not occupy the same location at the same time not just at dropoff/pickup points, but throughout their travels. Use the hierarchical protocol to resolve potential conflicts between the robots plans, given a few different layouts of the coordinates for the various positions (that is, where path-crossing is maximized and minimized). What kinds of coordinated plans arise depending on what level of the hierarchy the plans' conflicts are resolved through synchronization?

10. *[Level 2]* Assume that agents in the distributed delivery domain could be given delivery requests at any given time, and operate in a finite, fully shared delivery region. Describe social laws that can assure that no matter what deliveries are asked of them and when, the agents can be assured of avoiding collisions no matter where the pickup and dropoff positions are. You may assume that the world begins in a legal state. In what circumstances would using these laws be very inefficient?

11. *[Level 3]* Assume that distributed delivery robots are in an environment where delivery tasks pop up dynamically. When a delivery needs to be done, the article to be delivered announces that it needs to be delivered, and delivery agents within a particular distance from the article hear the announcement.

    (a) Assume that the distance from which articles can be heard is small. What characteristics would an organizational structure among the delivery agents have to have to minimize the deliveries that might be overlooked?

    (b) Assume that the distance is instead large. Would an organizational structure be beneficial anyway? Justify your answer.

    (c) As they become aware of deliveries to be done, delivery agents try to incorporate those into their current delivery plans. But the dynamic nature of the domain means that these plans are undergoing evolution. Under what assumptions would partial global planning be a good approach for coordinating the agents in this case?

    (d) Assume you are using partial global planning for coordination in this problem. What would you believe would be a good planning level for the agents to communicate and coordinate their plans? How would the agents determine whether they were working on related plans? How would they use this view to change their local plans? Would a hill-climbing strategy work well for this?

## 3.10 References

1. W. Briggs and D.J. Cook. Flexible social laws. In *Proceedings of the Fourteenth International Joint Conference on Artificial Intelligence (IJCAI-95)*, August 1995.

2. Susan E. Conry, Kazuhiro Kuwabara, Victor R. Lesser, and Robert A. Meyer. Multistage negotiation for distributed constraint satisfaction. *IEEE Transactions on Systems, Man, and Cybernetics*, SMC-21(6):1462-1477, Nov. 1991.

3. Daniel D. Corkill. *A Framework for Organizational Self-Design in Distributed Problem Solving Networks*. PhD thesis, University of Massachusetts, December 1982.

4. Randall Davis and Reid Smith. Negotiation as a metaphor for distributed problem solving. *Artificial Intelligence*, 20:63-109, 1983.

5. Keith Decker and Victor Lesser. A one-shot dynamic coordination algorithm for distributed sensor networks. In *Proceedings of the Eleventh National Conference on Artificial Intelligence (AAAI-93)*, pages 210-216, July 1993.

6. Keith Decker and Victor Lesser. Designing a family of coordination mechanisms. In *Proceedings of the First International Conf. on Multi-Agent Systems (ICMAS-95)*, pages 73-80, June 1995.

7. Edmund H. Durfee, Victor R. Lesser, and Daniel D. Corkill. Cooperation Through Communication in a Distributed Problem Solving Network. In M. Huhns, editor, *Distributed Artificial Intelligence*, Chapter 2, Pitman 1987.

8. Edmund H. Durfee. *Coordination of Distributed Problem Solvers*, Kluwer Academic Press, Boston 1988.

9. Edmund H. Durfee and Thomas A. Montgomery. Coordination as Distributed Search in a Hierarchical Behavior Space. *IEEE Transactions on Systems, Man, and Cybernetics*, Special Issue on Distributed Artificial Intelligence, SMC-21(6):1363-1378, November 1991.

10. Edmund H. Durfee, Patrick G. Kenny, and Karl C. Kluge. Integrated Premission Planning and Execution for Unmanned Ground Vehicles. In *Proceedings of the First International Conference on Autonomous Agents*, pages 348-354, February 1997.

11. Eithan Ephrati and Jeffrey S. Rosenschein. Divide and conquer in multi-agent planning. In *Proceedings of the Twelfth National Conference on Artificial Intelligence (AAAI-94)*, pages 375-380, July 1994.

12. Eithan Ephrati, Martha E. Pollack, and Jeffrey S. Rosenschein. A tractable heuristic that maximizes global utility through local plan combination. In *Proceedings of the First International Conference on Multi-Agent Systems (ICMAS-95)*, pages 94-101, June 1995.

13. Maier Fenster, Sarit Kraus, and Jeffrey S. Rosenschein. Coordination without communication: experimental validation of focal point techniques. In *Proceedings of the First International Conference on Multi-Agent Systems (ICMAS-95)*, pages 102-108, June 1995.

14. R.E. Fikes and N.J. Nilsson. STRIPS: A new approach to the application of theorem proving to problem solving. *Artificial Intelligence*, 2(3-4):189-208, 1971.

15. Michael Fisher and Michael Wooldridge. Distributed problem-solving as concurrent theorem-proving. In *Proceedings of MAAMAW'97*, Lecture Notes in Artificial Intelligence, Springer-Verlag.

16. Michael Georgeff. Communication and Interaction in multi-agent planning. In *Proceedings of the Third National Conference on Artificial Intelligence (AAAI-83)*, pages 125-129, July 1983.

17. Claudia Goldman and Jeffrey S. Rosenschein. Emergent coordination through the use of cooperative state-changing rules. In *Proceedings of the Twelfth National Conference on Artificial Intelligence (AAAI-94)*, pages 408-413, July 1994.

18. Marcus J. Huber and Edmund H. Durfee. An initial assessment of plan-recognition-based coordination for multi-agent teams. In *Proceedings of the Second International Conference on Multi-Agent Systems (ICMAS-96)*, pages 126-133, December 1996.

19. Toru Ishida, Les Gasser, and Makoto Yokoo. Organization self-design of distributed production systems, *IEEE Trans on Knowl. and Data Sys.*, DKE4(2):123-134.

20. Froduald Kabanza. Synchronizing multiagent plans using temporal logic specifications. In *Proceedings of the First International Conference on Multi-Agent Systems (ICMAS-95)*, pages 217-224, June 1995.

21. Subbarao Kambhampati, Mark Cutkosky, Marty Tenenbaum, and Soo Hong Lee. Combining specialized reasoners and general purpose planners: A case study. In *Proceedings of the Ninth National Conference on Artificial Intelligence*, pages 199-205, July 1991.

22. David Kinney, Magus Ljungberg, Anand Rao, Elizabeth Sonenberg, Gil Tidhar, and Eric Werner. Planned Team Activity, *Preproceedings of the Fourth European Workshop on Modeling Autonomous Agents in a MultiAgent World*, July 1992.

23. Craig A. Knoblock. *Generating Abstraction Hierarchies: An Automated Approach to Reducing Search in Planning*. Kluwer Academic Publishers, 1993.

24. Richard E. Korf. Planning as search: A qualitative approach. *Artificial Intelligence*, 33(1):65-88, 1987.

25. Susan E. Lander and Victor R. Lesser. Understanding the role of negotiation in distributed search among heterogeneous agents. In *Proceedings of the Thirteenth International Joint Conference on Artificial Intelligence (IJCAI-93)*, pages 438-444, August 1993.

26. Amy L. Lansky. Localized Search for Controlling Automated Reasoning. In *Proceedings of the DARPA Workshop on Innovative Approaches to Planning, Scheduling, and Control*, pages 115-125, November 1990.

27. Jaeho Lee. *An Explicit Semantics for Coordinated Multiagent Plan Execution*. PhD dissertation. University of Michigan, 1997.

28. Victor R. Lesser and Daniel D. Corkill. Functionally accurate, cooperative distributed systems. *IEEE Transactions on Systems, Man, and Cybernetics*, SMC-11(1):81-96, 1981.

29. Victor R. Lesser and Lee D. Erman. Distributed interpretation: A model and an experiment. *IEEE Transactions on Computers* (Special Issue on Distributed Processing), C-29(12):1144-1163.

30. Jyi-Shane Liu and Katia P. Sycara. Multiagent coordination in tightly coupled task

scheduling. In *Proceedings of the Second International Conference on Multi-Agent Systems (ICMAS-96)*, pages 181-188, December 1996.

31. Douglas MacIntosh, Susan Conry, and Robert Meyer. Distributed automated reasoning: Issues in coordination, cooperation, and performance. *IEEE Transactions on Systems, Man, and Cybernetics*, SMC-21(6):1307-1316.

32. Frank von Martial. *Coordinating Plans of Autonomous Agents*. Lecture Notes in Artificial Intelligence, Springer-Verlag, 1992.

33. Thomas A. Montgomery and Edmund H. Durfee. Search Reduction in Hierarchical Distributed Problem Solving. *Group Decision and Negotiation*, 2:301-317 (Special issue on Distributed Artificial Intelligence), 1993.

34. H. Edward Pattison, Daniel D. Corkill, and Victor R. Lesser. Instantiating descriptions of organizational structures. In M. Huhns, editor, *Distributed Artificial Intelligence*. London, Pittman.

35. M.V. Nagendra Prasad, Keith Decker, Alan Garvey, and Victor Lesser. Exploring organizational designs with TAEMS: A case study of distributed data processing. In *Proceedings of the Second International Conference on Multi-Agent Systems (ICMAS-96)*, pages 283-290, December 1996.

36. Jeffrey S. Rosenschein and John S. Breese. Communication-free interactions among rational agents: A probabilistic approach. In L. Gasser and M. Huhns, editors, *Distributed Artificial Intelligence volume II*, pages 99-118, Morgan Kaufmann Publishers.

37. Amal El Fallah Seghrouchni and Serge Haddad. A recursive model for distributed planning. In *Proceedings of the Second International Conference on Multi-Agent Systems (ICMAS-96)*, pages 307-314, December 1996.

38. Sandip Sen and Edmund H. Durfee. A contracting model for flexible distributed scheduling. *Annals of Operations Research*, 65, pp. 195-222, 1996.

39. Yoav Shaham and Moshe Tennenholtz. On the synthesis of useful social laws for artificial agent societies. In *Proceedings of the Tenth National Conference on Artificial Intelligence (AAAI-92)*, pages 276-281-380, July 1992.

40. Young-pa So and Edmund H. Durfee. Designing tree-structured organizations for computational agents. *Computational and Mathematical Organization Theory*, 2(3):219-246, Fall 1996.

41. John A. Stankovic, Krithi Ramamritham, and S.-C. Cheng. Evaluation of a flexible task scheduling algorithm for distributed hard real- time systems. *IEEE Transactions on Computers*, C-34(12):1130-1143, 1985.

42. Toshiharu Sugawara. Reusing past plans in distributed planning. In *Proceedings of the First International Conference on Multi-Agent Systems (ICMAS-95)*, pages 360-367, June 1995.

43. Katia Sycara, Steven Roth, Norman Sadeh, and Mark Fox. Distributed constrained heuristic search. *IEEE Transactions on Systems, Man, and Cybernetics*, SMC-21(6):1446-1461.

44. Michael P. Wellman. A market-oriented programming environment and its application to distributed multicommodity flow problems. *Journal of Artificial Intelligence Research*, 1:1-23, 1993.

45. Keith J. Werkman. Multiple agent cooperative design evaluation using negotiation. In *Proceedings of the Second International Conference on Artificial Intelligence in Design*, Pittsburgh PA, June 1992.

46. D.E. Wilkins and K.L. Myers. A common knowledge representation for plan generation and reactive execution. *Journal of Logic and Computation*, 5(6):731-761, 1995.

47. Chenqi Zhang. Cooperation under uncertainty in distributed expert systems. *Artificial Intelligence*, 56:21-69, 1992.

# 4 Search Algorithms for Agents

Makoto Yokoo and Toru Ishida

## 4.1 Introduction

In this chapter, we introduce several search algorithms that are useful for problem solving by multiple agents. Search is an umbrella term for various problem solving techniques in AI. In search problems, the sequence of actions required for solving a problem cannot be known *a priori* but must be determined by a trial-and-error exploration of alternatives. Since virtually all AI problems require some sort of search, search has a long and distinguished history in AI.

The problems that have been addressed by search algorithms can be divided into three classes: path-finding problems, constraint satisfaction problems, and two-player games.

A typical example of the first class, i.e., path-finding problems, is a puzzle called the *n-puzzle*. Figure 4.1 shows the 8-puzzle, which consists of eight numbered tiles arranged on a $3 \times 3$ board (in a generalized case, there are $n = k^2 - 1$ tiles on a $k \times k$ board). The allowed moves are to slide any tile that is horizontally or vertically adjacent to the empty square into the position of the empty square. The objective is to transform the given initial configuration to the goal configuration by making allowed moves. Such a problem is called a path-finding problem, since the objective is to find a path (a sequence of moves) from the initial configuration to the goal configuration.

A constraint satisfaction problem (CSP) involves finding a goal configuration rather than finding a path to the goal configuration. A typical example of a CSP is a puzzle called 8-queens. The objective is to place eight queens on a chess board ($8 \times 8$ squares) so that these queens will not threaten each other. This problem is called a constraint satisfaction problem since the objective is to find a configuration that satisfies the given conditions (constraints).

Another important class of search problems is two-player games, such as chess. Since two-player games deal with situations in which two *competitive* agents exist, it is obvious that these studies have a very close relation with DAI/multiagent systems where agents are competitive.

On the other hand, most algorithms for the other two classes (constraint satisfaction and path-finding) were originally developed for single-agent problem solving.

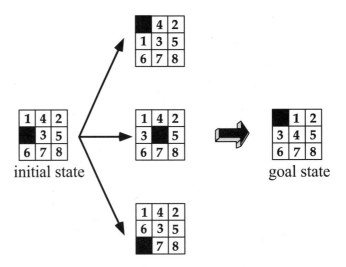

**Figure 4.1**   Example of a path-finding problem (8-puzzle).

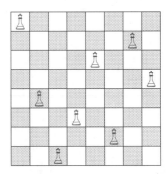

**Figure 4.2**   Example of a constraint satisfaction problem (8-queens).

Among them, what kinds of algorithms would be useful for cooperative problem solving by multiple agents?

In general, an agent is assumed to have *limited rationality*. More specifically, the computational ability or the recognition ability of an agent is usually limited. Therefore, getting the complete picture of a given problem may be impossible. Even if the agent can manage to get complete information on the problem, dealing with the global information of the problem can be too expensive and beyond the computational capability of the agent. Therefore, the agent must do a limited amount of computations using only partial information on the problem and then take appropriate actions based on the available resources.

In most standard search algorithms (e.g., the A* algorithm [20] and backtracking algorithms [26]), each step is performed sequentially, and for each step, the global knowledge of the problem is required. For example, the A* algorithm extends the wavefront of explored states from the initial state and chooses the most promising state within the whole wavefront.

On the other hand, a search problem can be represented by using a graph, and there exist search algorithms with which a problem is solved by accumulating local computations for each node in the graph. The execution order of these local computations can be arbitrary or highly flexible, and can be executed asynchronously and concurrently. We call these algorithms *asynchronous search* algorithms.

When a problem is solved by multiple agents each with limited rationality, asynchronous search algorithms are appropriate based on the following reasons.

- We can assume that the computational and recognition abilities required to perform the local computations of each node will be small enough for the agents. On the other hand, if each step of the algorithm requires the global knowledge of the problem, it may be beyond the capability of an agent.

- If multiple agents are cooperatively solving a problem using the asynchronous search algorithm, the execution order of these agents can be highly flexible or arbitrary. Otherwise, we need to synchronize the computations of the agents, and the overhead for such control can be very high.

The importance of solving a problem by combining such local and asynchronous computations was first pointed out by Lesser [24], and this idea has been widely acknowledged in DAI studies.

In the following, we give a formal definition of a constraint satisfaction problem and a path-finding problem and introduce asynchronous search algorithms for solving these problems. Then, we show the formalization of and algorithms for two-player games.

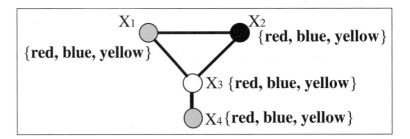

**Figure 4.3**   Example of a constraint satisfaction problem (graph-coloring).

## 4.2   Constraint Satisfaction

### 4.2.1   Definition of a Constraint Satisfaction Problem

A constraint satisfaction problem (CSP) is a problem to find a consistent value assignment of variables that take their values from finite, discrete domains. Formally, a CSP consists of $n$ variables $x_1, x_2, \ldots, x_n$, whose values are taken from finite, discrete domains $D_1, D_2, \ldots, D_n$, respectively, and a set of constraints on their values. A constraint is defined by a predicate. That is, the constraint $p_k(x_{k1}, \ldots, x_{kj})$ is a predicate that is defined on the Cartesian product $D_{k1} \times \ldots \times D_{kj}$. This predicate is true iff the value assignment of these variables satisfies this constraint. Solving a CSP is equivalent to finding an assignment of values to all variables such that all constraints are satisfied. Since constraint satisfaction is NP-complete in general, a trial-and-error exploration of alternatives is inevitable.

For example, in the 8-queens problem, it is obvious that only one queen can be placed in each row. Therefore, we can formalize this problem as a CSP, in which there are eight variables $x_1, x_2, \ldots, x_8$, each of which corresponds to the position of a queen in each row. The domain of a variable is $\{1, 2, \ldots, 8\}$. A solution is a combination of values of these variables. The constraints that the queens will not threaten each other can be represented as predicates, e.g., a constraint between $x_i$ and $x_j$ can be represented as $x_i \neq x_j \wedge |i - j| \neq |x_i - x_j|$.

Another typical example problem is a graph-coloring problem (Figure 4.3). The objective of a graph-coloring problem is to paint nodes in a graph so that any two nodes connected by a link do not have the same color. Each node has a finite number of possible colors. This problem can be formalized as a CSP by representing the color of each node as a variable, and the possible colors of the node as a domain of the variable.

If all constraints are binary (i.e., between two variables), a CSP can be represented as a graph, in which a node represents a variable, and a link between nodes represents a constraint between the corresponding variables. Figure 4.4 shows a constraint graph representing a CSP with three variables $x_1, x_2, x_3$ and constraints $x_1 \neq x_3$, $x_2 \neq x_3$. For simplicity, we will focus our attention on binary CSPs in

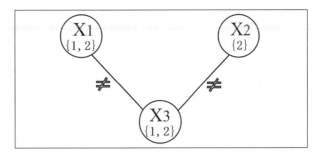

**Figure 4.4** Constraint graph.

the following chapter. However, the algorithms described in this chapter are also applicable to non-binary CSPs.

Then, how can the CSP formalization be related to DAI? Let us assume that the variables of a CSP are distributed among agents. Solving a CSP in which multiple agents are involved (such a problem is called a *distributed* CSP) can be considered as achieving coherence among the agents. Many application problems in DAI, e.g., interpretation problems, assignment problems, and multiagent truth maintenance tasks, can be formalized as distributed CSPs.

An interpretation problem can be viewed as a problem to find a compatible set of hypotheses that correspond to the possible interpretations of input data. An interpretation problem can be mapped into a CSP by viewing possible interpretations as possible variable values. If there exist multiple agents, and each of them is assigned a different part of the input data, such a problem can be formalized as a distributed CSP. The agents can eliminate the number of hypotheses by using the filtering algorithm or the hyper-resolution-based consistency algorithm, both of which are described in the following.

If the problem is to allocate tasks or resources to multiple agents, and there exist inter-agent constraints, such a problem can be formalized as a distributed CSP by viewing each task or resource as a variable and the possible assignments as values. Furthermore, we can formalize multiagent truth maintenance tasks described in Chapter 2 as a distributed CSP, where each item of the uncertain data is represented as a variable whose value can be IN or OUT.

In the following, we describe asynchronous search algorithms in which each process corresponds to a variable, and the processes act asynchronously to solve a CSP.

We assume the following communication model.

- Processes communicate by sending messages. A process can send messages to other processes iff the process knows the addresses/identifiers of other processes.

- The delay in delivering a message is finite, though random.

- For the transmission between any pair of processes, messages are received in the order in which they were sent.

Furthermore, we call the processes that have links to $x_i$ *neighbors* of $x_i$. We assume that a process knows the identifiers of its neighbors.

### 4.2.2   Filtering Algorithm

In the filtering algorithm [36], each process communicates its domain to its neighbors and then removes values that cannot satisfy constraints from its domain. More specifically, a process $x_i$ performs the following procedure **revise**$(x_i, x_j)$ for each neighboring process $x_j$.

procedure **revise**$(x_i, x_j)$
  **for all** $v_i \in D_i$ **do**
    **if** there is no value $v_j \in D_j$ such that $v_j$ is consistent with $v_i$
    **then** delete $v_i$ from $D_i$; **end if; end do;**

If some value of the domain is removed by performing the procedure **revise**, process $x_i$ sends the new domain to neighboring processes. If $x_i$ receives a new domain from a neighboring process $x_j$, the procedure **revise**$(x_i, x_j)$ is performed again. The execution order of these processes is arbitrary.

We show an example of an algorithm execution in Figure 4.5. The example problem is a smaller version of the 8-queens problem (3-queens problem). There are three variables $x_1, x_2, x_3$, whose domains are $\{1,2,3\}$. Obviously, this problem is over-constrained and has no solution. After exchanging the domains (Figure 4.5 (a)), $x_1$ performs **revise**$(x_1, x_2)$ and removes 2 from its domain (if $x_1 = 2$, none of $x_2$'s values satisfies the constraint with $x_1$). Similarly, $x_2$ performs **revise**$(x_2, x_3)$, $x_3$ performs **revise**$(x_3, x_2)$, and each process removes 2 from its domain. After exchanging the new domains (Figure 4.5 (b)), $x_1$ performs **revise**$(x_1, x_3)$, and removes 1 and 3 from its domain. The domain of $x_1$ then becomes an empty set, so the process discovers that this problem has no solution.

By applying the filtering algorithm, if a domain of some variable becomes an empty set, the problem is over-constrained and has no solution. Also, if each domain has a unique value, then the combination of the remaining values becomes a solution. On the other hand, if there exist multiple values for some variable, we cannot tell whether the problem has a solution or not, and further trial-and-error search is required to find a solution.

Figure 4.6 shows a graph-coloring problem. Since there are three variables and the only possible colors of each variable are red or blue, this problem is over-constrained. However, in the filtering algorithm, no process can remove a value from its domain. Furthermore, in the 8-queens problem (which has many solutions), no process can remove a value from its domain by using the filtering algorithm.

Since the filtering algorithm cannot solve a problem in general, it should be considered a preprocessing procedure that is invoked before the application of other search methods. Even though the filtering algorithm alone cannot solve a problem, reducing the domains of variables for the following search procedure is worthwhile.

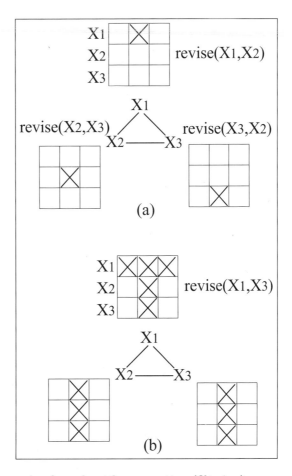

(a)

(b)

**Figure 4.5**   Example of an algorithm execution (filtering).

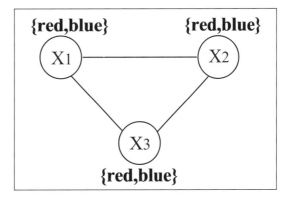

**Figure 4.6**   Example that the filtering algorithm cannot solve.

### 4.2.3  Hyper-Resolution-Based Consistency Algorithm

The filtering algorithm is one example of a general class of algorithms called *consistency algorithms*. Consistency algorithms can be classified by the notion of k-consistency [9]. A CSP is k-consistent iff the following condition is satisfied.

- Given any instantiation of any $k-1$ variables satisfying all the constraints among those variables, it is possible to find an instantiation of any $k$th variable such that these $k$ variable values satisfy all the constraints among them.

The filtering algorithm achieves 2-consistency (also called arc-consistency), i.e., any variable value has at least one consistent value of another variable. A k-consistency algorithm transforms a given problem into an equivalent (having the same solutions as the original problem) k-consistent problem. If the problem is k-consistent and j-consistent for all $j < k$, the problem is called *strongly* k-consistent. If there are $n$ variables in a CSP and the CSP is strongly n-consistent, then a solution can be obtained immediately without any trial-and-error exploration, since for any instantiation of $k - 1$ variables, we can always find at least one consistent value for $k$-th variables.

In the following, we describe a consistency algorithm using the the hyper-resolution rule [6]. In this algorithm, all constraints are represented as a nogood, which is a prohibited combination of variable values. For example, in Figure 4.6, a constraint between $x_1$ and $x_2$ can be represented as two nogoods $\{x_1 = red, x_2 = red\}$ and $\{x_1 = blue, x_2 = blue\}$.

A new nogood is generated from several existing nogoods by using the hyper-resolution rule. For example, in Figure 4.6, there are nogoods such as $\{x_1 = red, x_2 = red\}$ and $\{x_1 = blue, x_3 = blue\}$. Furthermore, since the domain of $x_1$ is $\{red, blue\}$, $(x_1 = red) \vee (x_1 = blue)$ holds. The hyper-resolution rule combines nogoods and the condition that a variable takes one value from its domain, and generates a new nogood, e.g., $\{x_2 = red, x_3 = blue\}$.

The meaning of this nogood is as follows. If $x_2$ is red, $x_1$ cannot be red. Also, if $x_3$ is blue, $x_1$ cannot be blue. Since $x_1$ is either red or blue, if $x_2$ is red and $x_3$ is blue, there is no possible value for $x_1$. Therefore, this combination cannot satisfy all constraints.

The hyper-resolution rule is described as follows ($A_i$ is a proposition such as $x_1 = 1$).

$$
\begin{array}{c}
A_1 \vee A_2 \vee \ldots \vee A_m \\
\neg(A_1 \wedge A_{11} \ldots), \\
\neg(A_2 \wedge A_{21} \ldots), \\
\vdots \\
\neg(A_m \wedge A_{m1} \ldots) \\
\hline
\neg(A_{11} \wedge \ldots \wedge A_{21} \wedge \ldots \wedge A_{m1} \ldots)
\end{array}
$$

In the hyper-resolution-based consistency algorithm, each process represents its constraints as nogoods. The process then generates new nogoods by combining the information about its domain and existing nogoods using the hyper-resolution rule. A newly obtained nogood is communicated to related processes. If a new nogood is communicated, the process tries to generate further new nogoods using the communicated nogood.

For example, in Figure 4.6, assume $x_1$ generates a new nogood $\{x_2 = red, x_3 = blue\}$ using nogood $\{x_1 = red, x_2 = red\}$ and nogood $\{x_1 = blue, x_3 = blue\}$. This nogood is communicated to $x_2$ and $x_3$. $x_2$ generates a new nogood $\{x_3 = blue\}$ using this communicated nogood and nogood $\{x_2 = blue, x_3 = blue\}$. Similarly, $x_1$ generates a new nogood $\{x_2 = blue, x_3 = red\}$ from $\{x_1 = blue, x_2 = blue\}$ and $\{x_1 = red, x_3 = red\}$. $x_2$ generates a new nogood $\{x_3 = red\}$ using this nogood and nogood $\{x_2 = red, x_3 = red\}$. Then, $x_3$ can generate $\{\}$ from nogood$\{x_3 = blue\}$ and $\{x_3 = red\}$, which is an empty set. Recall that a nogood is a combination of variable values that is prohibited. Therefore, a superset of a nogood cannot be a solution. Since any set is a superset of an empty set, if an empty set becomes a nogood, the problem is over-constrained and has no solution.

The hyper-resolution rule can generate a very large number of nogoods. If we restrict the application of the rules so that only nogoods whose lengths (the length of a nogood is the number of variables that constitute the nogood) are less than $k$ are produced, the problem becomes strongly k-consistent.

### 4.2.4 Asynchronous Backtracking

The asynchronous backtracking algorithm [39] is an asynchronous version of a backtracking algorithm, which is a standard method for solving CSPs. In the asynchronous backtracking algorithm, the priority order of variables/processes is determined, and each process communicates its tentative value assignment to neighboring processes. The priority order is determined by alphabetical order of the variable identifiers, i.e., preceding variables in the alphabetical order have higher priority. A process changes its assignment if its current value assignment is not consistent with the assignments of higher priority processes. If there exists no value that is consistent with the higher priority processes, the process generates a new nogood, and communicates the nogood to a higher priority process; thus the higher priority process changes its value.

The generation procedure of a new nogood is basically identical to the hyper-resolution rule described in Section 4.2.3. However, in the consistency algorithm, all constraints (nogoods) are considered for generating new nogoods. On the other hand, the asynchronous backtracking algorithm generates only the constraints that are not satisfied in the current situation. In other words, a new nogood is generated only if the nogood actually occurs in the asynchronous backtracking.

Each process maintains the current value assignment of other processes from its viewpoint (local_view). It must be noted that since each process acts asynchronously and concurrently and processes communicate by sending messages, the local_view

**when received** (**ok?**, $(x_j, d_j)$) **do** — (i)
    add $(x_j, d_j)$ to *local_view*;
    **check_local_view**;
**end do**;

**when received** (**nogood**, *nogood*) **do** — (ii)
    record *nogood* as a new constraint;
    **when** $(x_k, d_k)$ where $x_k$ is not a neighbor **do**
      request $x_k$ to add $x_i$ to its neighbors;
      add $x_k$ to neighbors;
      add $(x_k, d_k)$ to *local_view*; **end do**;
    **check_local_view**;
**end do**;

procedure **check_local_view**
    **when** *local_view* and *current_value* are not consistent **do**
      **if** no value in $D_i$ is consistent with *local_view*
        **then** resolve a new nogood using hyper-resolution rule
          and send the nogood to the lowest priority process in the nogood;
          **when** an empty nogood is found **do**
            broadcast to other processes that there is no solution,
            terminate this algorithm; **end do**;
        **else** select $d \in D_i$ where *local_view* and $d$ are consistent;
        *current_value* $\leftarrow d$;
        send (**ok?**, $(x_i, d)$) to neighbors; **end if**; **end do**;

**Algorithm 4.1**   Procedures for receiving messages (asynchronous backtracking).

may contain obsolete information. Even if $x_i$'s local_view says that $x_j$'s current assignment is 1, $x_j$ may already have changed its value. Therefore, if $x_i$ does not have a consistent value with the higher priority processes according to its local_view, we cannot use a simple control method such as $x_i$ orders a higher priority process to change its value, since the local_view may be obsolete. Therefore, each process needs to generate and communicate a new constraint (nogood), and the receiver of the new nogood must check whether the nogood is actually violated from its own local_view.

The main message types communicated among processes are *ok?* messages to communicate the current value, and *nogood* messages to communicate a new nogood. The procedures executed at process $x_i$ after receiving an *ok?* message and a *nogood* message are described in Algorithm 4.1 (i) and Algorithm 4.1 (ii), respectively.

We show an example of an algorithm execution in Figure 4.7. In Figure 4.7 (a), after receiving *ok?* messages from $x_1$ and $x_2$, the *local_view* of $x_3$ will be $\{(x_1, 1), (x_2, 2)\}$. Since there is no possible value for $x_3$ consistent with this *local_view*, a new nogood $\{(x_1, 1), (x_2, 2)\}$ is generated. $x_3$ chooses the lowest priority process in the nogood, i.e., $x_2$, and sends a *nogood* message. By receiving this *nogood* message, $x_2$ records this nogood. This nogood, $\{(x_1, 1), (x_2, 2)\}$, contains process $x_1$, which is not a neighbor $x_2$. Therefore, a new link must be added be-

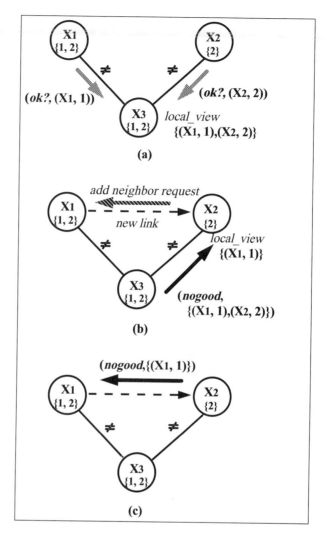

**Figure 4.7**   Example of an algorithm execution (asynchronous backtracking).

tween $x_1$ and $x_2$. $x_2$ requests $x_1$ to send $x_1$'s value to $x_2$, and adds $(x_1, 1)$ to its *local_view* (Figure 4.7 (b)). $x_2$ checks whether its value is consistent with the local_view. The *local_view* $\{(x_1, 1)\}$ and the assignment $(x_2, 2)$ violate the received nogood $\{(x_1, 1), (x_2, 2)\}$. However, there is no other possible value for $x_2$. Therefore, $x_2$ generates a new nogood $\{(x_1, 1)\}$, and sends a *nogood* message to $x_1$ (Figure 4.7 (c)).

The completeness of the algorithm (always finds a solution if one exists, and terminates if no solution exists) is guaranteed. The outline of the proof is as follows.

We can show that this algorithm never falls into an infinite processing loop by induction. In the base case, assume that the process with the highest priority, $x_1$, is in an infinite loop. Because it has the highest priority, $x_1$ only receives *nogood* messages. When it proposes a possible value, $x_1$ either receives a *nogood* message back, or else gets no message back. If it receives *nogood* messages for all possible values of its variable, then it will generate an empty nogood (any choice leads to a constraint violation) and the algorithm will terminate. If it does not receive a nogood message for a proposed value, then it will not change that value. Either way, it cannot be in an infinite loop.

Now, assume that processes $x_1$ to $x_{k-1}$ ($k > 2$) are in a stable state, and the process $x_k$ is in an infinite processing loop. In this case, the only messages process $x_k$ receives are *nogood* messages from processes whose priorities are lower than $k$, and these *nogood* messages contain only the processes $x_1$ to $x_k$. Since processes $x_1$ to $x_{k-1}$ are in a stable state, the *nogoods* process $x_k$ receives must be compatible with its *local_view*, and so $x_k$ will change instantiation of its variable with a different value. Because its variable's domain is finite, $x_k$ will either eventually generate a value that does not cause it to receive a nogood (which contradicts the assumption that $x_k$ is in an infinite loop), or else it exhausts the possible values and sends a nogood to one of $x_1 \ldots x_{k-1}$. However, this nogood would cause a process, which we assumed as being in a stable state, to not be in a stable state. Thus, by contradiction, $x_k$ cannot be in an infinite processing loop.

Since the algorithm does not fall in an infinite processing loop, the algorithm eventually reaches a solution if one exists, and if the problem is over-constrained, some process will eventually generate a nogood that is an empty set.

### 4.2.5   Asynchronous Weak-Commitment Search

One limitation of the asynchronous backtracking algorithm is that the process/variable ordering is statically determined. If the value selection of a higher priority process is bad, the lower priority processes need to perform an exhaustive search to revise the bad decision.

We can reduce the chance of a process making a bad decision by introducing value ordering heuristics, such as the *min-conflict* heuristic [27]. In this heuristic, when a variable value is to be selected, a value that minimizes the number of constraint violations with other variables is preferred. Although this heuristic has been found to be very effective [27], it cannot completely avoid bad decisions.

The asynchronous weak-commitment search algorithm[38] introduces a method for dynamically ordering processes so that a bad decision can be revised without an exhaustive search. More specifically, a *priority value* is determined for each variable, and the priority order among processes is determined using these priority values by the following rules.

- For each variable/process, a non-negative integer value representing the priority order of the variables/processes is defined. We call this value the *priority value*.

- The order is defined such that any variable/process with a larger priority value has higher priority.

- If the priority values of multiple processes are the same, the order is determined by the alphabetical order of the identifiers.

- For each variable/process, the initial priority value is 0.

- If there exists no consistent value for $x_i$, the priority value of $x_i$ is changed to $k + 1$, where $k$ is the largest priority value of related processes.

In the asynchronous weak-commitment search, as in the asynchronous backtracking, each process concurrently assigns a value to its variable, and sends the variable value to other processes. After that, processes wait for and respond to incoming messages. Although the following algorithm is described in a way that a process reacts to messages sequentially, a process can handle multiple messages concurrently, i.e., the process first revises the *local_view* and constraints according to the messages, and then performs **check_local_view** only once.

In Algorithm 4.2, the procedure executed at process $x_i$ by receiving an *ok?* message is described (the procedure for a *nogood* message is basically identical to that for the asynchronous backtracking algorithm). The differences between these procedures and the procedures for the asynchronous backtracking algorithm are as follows.

- The priority value, as well as the current value assignment, is communicated through the *ok?* message (Algorithm 4.2 (i)).

- The priority order is determined using the communicated priority values. If the current value is not *consistent* with the *local_view*, i.e., some constraint with variables of higher priority processes is not satisfied, the agent changes its value using the *min-conflict* heuristic, i.e., it selects a value that is not only consistent with the *local_view*, but also minimizes the number of constraint violations with variables of lower priority processes (Algorithm 4.2 (iii)).

- When $x_i$ cannot find a consistent value with its *local_view*, $x_i$ sends *nogood* messages to other processes, and increments its priority value. If $x_i$ cannot resolve a new nogood, $x_i$ will not change its priority value but will wait for the next message (Algorithm 4.2 (ii)). This procedure is needed to guarantee the completeness of the algorithm. In the asynchronous weak-commitment algorithm, processes try to avoid situations previously found to be nogoods. However, due to the delay of messages, a *local_view* of a process can occasionally be identical to a previously found nogood. In order to avoid reacting to such unstable situations, and performing unnecessary changes of priority values, each process records the nogoods that have been resolved. If no new nogood is found, the process will not change the priority value and waits for the next message.

We illustrate an execution of the algorithm using the distributed 4-queens problem, i.e., there exist four processes, each of which corresponds to a queen in one of the rows. The goal of the process is to find positions on a $4 \times 4$ chess board so that the queens do not threaten each other.

The initial values are shown in Figure 4.8 (a). Processes communicate these values with each other. The values within parentheses represent the priority values. The initial priority values are 0. Since the priority values are equal, the priority order is

```
when received (ok?, (x_j, d_j, priority)) do — (i)
    add (x_j, d_j, priority) to local_view;
    check_local_view;
end do;

procedure check_local_view
    when local_view and current_value are not consistent do
        if no value in D_i is consistent with local_view
        then resolve a new nogood using hyper-resolution rule;
            when an empty nogood is found do
                broadcast to other processes that there is no solution,
                terminate this algorithm; end do;
            when a new nogood is found do — (ii)
                send the nogood to the processes in the nogood;
                current_priority ← 1 + p_max,
                    where p_max is the maximal priority value of neighbors;
                select_best_value; end do;
        else select_best_value; end if; end do;

procedure select_best_value
    select d ∈ D_i where local_view and d are consistent, and d minimizes
        the number of constraint violations with lower priority processes; — (iii)
    current_value ← d;
    send (ok?, (x_i, d, current_priority)) to neighbors; end do;
```

**Algorithm 4.2** Procedures for receiving messages (asynchronous weak-commitment search).

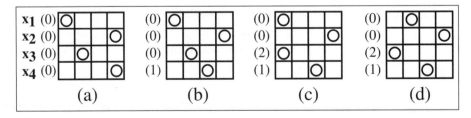

**Figure 4.8** Example of an algorithm execution (asynchronous weak-commitment search).

determined by the alphabetical order of the identifiers. Therefore, only the value of $x_4$ is not consistent with its *local_view*. Since there is no consistent value, $x_4$ sends *nogood* messages and increments its priority value. In this case, the value minimizing the number of constraint violations is 3, since it conflicts with $x_3$ only. Therefore, $x_4$ selects 3 and sends *ok?* messages to the other processes (Figure 4.8 (b)). Then, $x_3$ tries to change its value. Since there is no consistent value, $x_3$ sends *nogood* messages, and increments its priority value. In this case, the value that minimizes the number of constraint violations is 1 or 2. In this example, $x_3$ selects 1 and sends *ok?* messages to the other processes (Figure 4.8 (c)). After that, $x_1$ changes its value to 2, and a solution is obtained (Figure 4.8 (d)).

In the distributed 4-queens problem, there exists no solution when $x_1$'s value is 1. We can see that the bad decision of $x_1$ (assigning its value to 1) can be revised without an exhaustive search in the asynchronous weak-commitment search.

The completeness of the algorithm is guaranteed. The outline of the proof is as follows. The priority values are changed if and only if a new nogood is found. Since the number of possible nogoods is finite, the priority values cannot be changed infinitely. Therefore, after a certain time point, the priority values will be stable. If the priority values are stable, the asynchronous weak-commitment search algorithm is basically identical to the asynchronous backtracking algorithm. Since the asynchronous backtracking is guaranteed to be complete, the asynchronous weak-commitment search algorithm is also complete.

However, the completeness of the algorithm is guaranteed by the fact that the processes record all nogoods found so far. Handling a large number of nogoods is time/space consuming. We can restrict the number of recorded nogoods, i.e., each process records only a fixed number of the most recently found nogoods. In this case, however, the theoretical completeness cannot be guaranteed (the algorithm may fall into an infinite processing loop in which processes repeatedly find identical nogoods). Yet, when the number of recorded nogoods is reasonably large, such an infinite processing loop rarely occurs. Actually, when solving large-scale problems, the theoretical completeness has only theoretical importance.

## 4.3   Path-Finding Problem

### 4.3.1   Definition of a Path-Finding Problem

A path-finding problem consists of the following components: a set of nodes $N$, each representing a state, and a set of directed links $L$, each representing an operator available to a problem solving agent. We assume that there exists a unique node $s$ called the start node, representing the initial state. Also, there exists a set of nodes $G$, each of which represents a goal state. For each link, the weight of the link is defined, which represents the cost of applying the operator. We call the weight of the link between two nodes the *distance* between the nodes. We call the nodes that

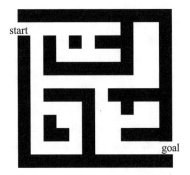

**Figure 4.9**   Example of a path-finding problem (maze).

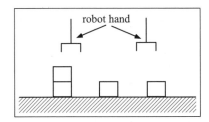

**Figure 4.10**   Planning for multiple robot hands.

have directed links from node $i$ *neighbors* of node $i$.

The 8-puzzle problem can be formalized as a path-finding problem by representing possible arrangements of tiles as nodes, and allowed moves as links. The arrangements that can be reached by sliding one tile are the neighbors of the original arrangement. In this problem, the weights of all links are 1, and for each link, there exists a link in the opposite direction.

Another example of a path-finding problem is a maze in a grid state space (Figure 4.9). There exists a grid state-space with obstacles. We allow moves along the horizontal and vertical dimensions, but not diagonal motions. The initial state is at the upper-left corner and the goal state is at the bottom-right corner.

Then, how can the path-finding problem formalization be related to DAI? Assume that multiple robots are exploring an unknown environment for finding a certain location. Such a problem can be formalized as a path-finding problem. Furthermore, the planning problem of multiple robot hands shown in Figure 4.10 can be represented as a path-finding problem.

In the following, we first introduce asynchronous dynamic programming as the basis of other algorithms. Then, we present the Learning Real-time A* algorithm, the Real-time A* algorithm, the Moving Target Search algorithm, Real-time Bidirectional Search algorithms, and real-time multiagent search algorithms, as special cases of asynchronous dynamic programming.

### 4.3.2 Asynchronous Dynamic Programming

In a path-finding problem, the *principle of optimality* holds. In short, the principle of optimality states that a path is optimal if and only if every segment of it is optimal. For example, if there exists an optimal (shortest) path from the start node to a goal node, and there exists an intermediate node $x$ on the path, the segment from the start node to node $x$ is actually the optimal path from the start node to node $x$. Similarly, the segment from node $x$ to the goal state is also the optimal path from node $x$ to the goal state.

Let us represent the shortest distance from node $i$ to goal nodes as $h^*(i)$. ¿From the principle of optimality, the shortest distance via a neighboring node $j$ is given by $f^*(j) = k(i,j) + h^*(j)$, where $k(i,j)$ is the cost of the link between $i, j$. If node $i$ is not a goal node, the path to a goal node must visit one of the neighboring nodes. Therefore, $h^*(i) = min_j f^*(j)$ holds.

If $h^*$ is given for each node, the optimal path can be obtained by repeating the following procedure.

- For each neighboring node $j$ of the current node $i$, compute $f^*(j) = k(i,j) + h^*(j)$. Then, move to the $j$ that gives $min_j f^*(j)$.

Asynchronous dynamic programming [4] computes $h^*$ by repeating the local computations of each node.

Let us assume the following situation.

- For each node $i$, there exists a process corresponding to $i$.
- Each process records $h(i)$, which is the estimated value of $h^*(i)$. The initial value of $h(i)$ is arbitrary (e.g., $\infty$, 0) except for goal nodes.
- For each goal node $g$, $h(g)$ is 0.
- Each process can refer to $h$ values of neighboring nodes (via shared memory or message passing)

In this situation, each process updates $h(i)$ by the following procedure. The execution order of the processes is arbitrary.

- For each neighboring node $j$, compute $f(j) = k(i,j) + h(j)$, where $h(j)$ is the current estimated distance from $j$ to a goal node, and $k(i,j)$ is the cost of the link from $i$ to $j$. Then, update $h(i)$ as follows: $h(i) \leftarrow min_j f(j)$.

We show an example of an algorithm execution in Figure 4.11. Assume that the initial value of $h$ is infinity except for the goal node (Figure 4.11 (i)). Then, $h$ values are changed at the nodes adjoining the goal node (Figure 4.11 (ii)). It must be noted that these values do not have to be the true values. For example, though the estimated cost from node $d$ is currently 3, there exists a path from node $d$ to the goal node via node $c$, and the cost of the path is 2.

However, $h$ values are further changed at the nodes that can be reached to the goal node (Figure 4.11 (iii)). Now, the $h$ value of $d$ is equal to the true value. We

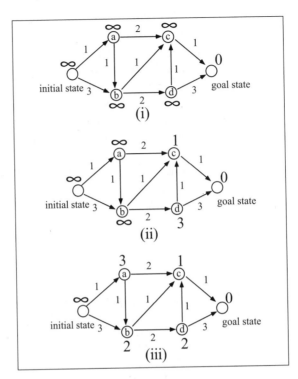

**Figure 4.11**    Example of an algorithm execution (asynchronous dynamic programming).

can see that the $h$ values converge to the true values from the nodes that are close to the goal node. By repeating the local computations, it is proved that for each node $i$, $h(i)$ will eventually converge to the true value $h^*(i)$ if the costs of all links are positive.

In reality, we cannot use asynchronous dynamic programming for a reasonably large path-finding problem. In a path-finding problem, the number of nodes can be huge, and we cannot afford to have processes for all nodes. However, asynchronous dynamic programming can be considered a foundation for the other algorithms introduced in this section. In these algorithms, instead of allocating processes for all nodes, some kind of control is introduced for enabling the execution by a reasonable number of processes (or *agents*).

### 4.3.3    Learning Real-Time A*

When only one agent is solving a path-finding problem, it is not always possible to perform local computations for all nodes. For example, autonomous robots may not have enough time for planning and should interleave planning and execution. Therefore, the agent must selectively execute the computations for certain nodes. Given this requirement, which node should the agent choose? One intuitively natural way is to choose the current node where the agent is located. It is easily to imagine that the sensing area of an autonomous robot is always limited. First, the agent updates the $h$ value of the current node, and then moves to the best neighboring node. This procedure is repeated until the agent reaches a goal state. This method is called the Learning Real-time A* (LRTA*) algorithm [19].

More precisely, in the LRTA* algorithm, each agent repeats the following procedure (we assume that the current position of the agent is node $i$). As with asynchronous dynamic programming, the agent records the estimated distance $h(i)$ for each node.

1. Lookahead:
   Calculate $f(j) = k(i,j) + h(j)$ for each neighbor $j$ of the current node $i$, where $h(j)$ is the current estimate of the shortest distance from $j$ to goal nodes, and $k(i,j)$ is the link cost from $i$ to $j$.

2. Update:
   Update the estimate of node $i$ as follows.

$$h(i) \leftarrow \min_j f(j)$$

3. Action selection:
   Move to the neighbor $j$ that has the minimum $f(j)$ value. Ties are broken randomly.

One characteristic of this algorithm is that the agent determines the next action in a constant time, and executes the action. Therefore, this algorithm is called an *on-line, real-time* search algorithm.

In the LRTA*, the initial value of $h$ must be optimistic, i.e., it must never overestimate the true value. Namely, the condition $h(i) \leq h^*(i)$ must be satisfied. If the initial values satisfy this condition, $h(i)$ will not be greater than the true value $h^*(i)$ by updating.

We call a function that gives the initial values of $h$ a *heuristic function*. For example, in the 8-puzzle, we can use the number of mismatched tiles, or the sum of the Manhattan distances (the sum of the horizontal and vertical distances) of the mismatched tiles, for the heuristic function (the latter is more accurate). In the maze problem, we can use the Manhattan distance to the goal as a heuristic function.

A heuristic function is called *admissible* if it never overestimates. The above examples satisfy this condition. If we cannot find any good heuristic function, we can satisfy this condition by simply setting all estimates to 0.

In asynchronous dynamic programming, the initial values are arbitrary and can be infinity. What makes this difference? In asynchronous dynamic programming, it is assumed that the updating procedures are performed in all nodes. Therefore, the $h$ value of a node eventually converges to the true value, regardless of its initial value. On the other hand, in LRTA*, the updating procedures are performed only for the nodes that the agent actually visits. Therefore, if the initial value of node $i$

is larger than the true value, it is possible that the agent never visits node $i$; thus, $h(i)$ will not be revised.

The following characteristic is known [19].

- In a finite number of nodes with positive link costs, in which there exists a path from every node to a goal node, and starting with non-negative admissible initial estimates, LRTA* is *complete*, i.e., it will eventually reach a goal node.

Furthermore, since LRTA* never overestimates, it *learns* the optimal solutions through repeated trials, i.e., if the initial estimates are admissible, then over repeated problem solving trials, the values learned by LRTA* will eventually converge to their actual distances along every optimal path to the goal node.

A sketch of the proof for completeness is given in the following. Let $h^*(i)$ be the cost of the shortest path between state $i$ and the goal state, and let $h(i)$ be the heuristic value of $i$. First of all, for each state $i$, $h(i) \leq h^*(i)$ always holds, since this condition is true in the initial situation where all $h$ values are admissible, meaning that they never overestimate the actual cost, and this condition will not be violated by updating. Define the *heuristic error* at a given point of the algorithm as the sum of $h^*(i) - h(i)$ over all states $i$. Define a positive quantity called *heuristic disparity*, as the sum of the heuristic error and the heuristic value $h(i)$ of the current state $i$ of the problem solver. It is easy to show that in any move of the problem solver, this quantity decreases. Since it cannot be negative, and if it ever reaches zero the problem is solved, the algorithm must eventually terminate successfully. This proof can be easily extended to cover the case where the goal is moving as well. See [11] for more details.

Now, the convergence of LRTA* is proven as follows. Define the *excess cost* at each trial as the difference between the cost of actual moves of the problem solver and the cost of moves along the shortest path. It can be shown that the sum of the excess costs over repeated trials never exceeds the initial heuristic error. Therefore, the problem solver eventually moves along the shortest path. It is said that $h(i)$ is correct if $h(i) = h^*(i)$. If the problem solver on the shortest path moves from state $i$ to the neighboring state $j$ and $h(j)$ is correct, $h(i)$ will be correct after updating. Since the $h$ values of goal states are always correct, and the problem solver eventually moves only along the shortest path, $h(i)$ will eventually converge to the true value $h^*(i)$. The details are given in [33].

### 4.3.4   Real-Time A*

Real-time A* (RTA*) updates the value of $h(i)$ in a different way from LRTA*. In the second step of RTA*, instead of setting $h(i)$ to the smallest value of $f(j)$ for all neighbors $j$, the second smallest value is assigned to $h(j)$. Thus, RTA* learns more efficiently than LRTA*, but can overestimate heuristic costs. The RTA* algorithm is shown below. Note that *secondmin* represents the function that returns the second smallest value.

1.   Lookahead:
     Calculate $f(j) = k(i,j) + h(j)$ for each neighbor $j$ of the current state $i$, where $h(j)$ is the current lower bound of the actual cost from $j$ to the goal state, and $k(i,j)$ is the edge cost from $i$ to $j$.

2.   Consistency maintenance:
     Update the lower bound of state $i$ as follows.

$$h(i) \leftarrow \text{secondmin}_j f(j)$$

3.   Action selection:
     Move to the neighbor $j$ that has the minimum $f(j)$ value. Ties are broken randomly.

Similar to LRTA*, the following characteristic is known [19].

- In a finite problem space with positive edge costs, in which there exists a path from every state to the goal, and starting with non-negative admissible initial heuristic values, RTA* is *complete* in the sense that it will eventually reach the goal.

Since the second smallest values are always maintained, RTA* can make *locally optimal decisions* in a tree problem space, i.e., each move made by RTA* is along a path whose estimated cost toward the goal is minimum based on the already-obtained information. However, this result cannot be extended to cover general graphs with cycles.

### 4.3.5   Moving Target Search

Heuristic search algorithms assume that the goal state is fixed and does not change during the course of the search. For example, in the problem of a robot navigating from its current location to a desired goal location, it is assumed that the goal location remains stationary. In this subsection, we relax this assumption, and allow the goal to change during the search. In the robot example, instead of moving to a particular fixed location, the robot's task may be to reach another robot which is in fact moving as well. The target robot may cooperatively try to reach the problem solving robot, actively avoid the problem solving robot, or independently move around. There is no assumption that the target robot will eventually stop, but the goal is achieved when the position of the problem solving robot and the position of the target robot coincide. In order to guarantee success in this task, the problem solver must be able to move faster than the target. Otherwise, the target could evade the problem solver indefinitely, even in a finite problem space, merely by avoiding being trapped in a dead-end path.

We now present the *Moving Target Search* (MTS) algorithm, which is a generalization of LRTA* to the case where the target can move. MTS must acquire heuristic information for each target location. Thus, MTS maintains a matrix of heuristic values, representing the function $h(x,y)$ for all pairs of states $x$ and $y$.

Conceptually, all heuristic values are read from this matrix, which is initialized to the values returned by the static evaluation function. Over the course of the search, these heuristic values are updated to improve their accuracy. In practice, however, we only store those values that differ from their static values. Thus, even though the complete matrix may be very large, it is typically quite sparse.

There are two different events that occur in the algorithm: a move of the problem solver, and a move of the target, each of which may be accompanied by the updating of a heuristic value. We assume that the problem solver and the target move alternately, and can each traverse at most one edge in a single move. The problem solver has no control over the movements of the target, and no knowledge to allow it to predict, even probabilistically, the motion of the target. The task is accomplished when the problem solver and the target occupy the same node. In the description below, $x_i$ and $x_j$ are the current and neighboring positions of the problem solver, and $y_i$ and $y_j$ are the current and neighboring positions of the target. To simplify the following discussions, we assume that all edges in the graph have unit cost.

*When the problem solver moves:*

1. Calculate $h(x_j, y_i)$ for each neighbor $x_j$ of $x_i$.

2. Update the value of $h(x_i, y_i)$ as follows:

$$h(x_i, y_i) \leftarrow max \left\{ \begin{array}{l} h(x_i, y_i) \\ min_{x'}\{h(x_j, y_i) + 1\} \end{array} \right\}$$

3. Move to the neighbor $x_j$ with the minimum $h(x_j, y_i)$, i.e., assign the value of $x_j$ to $x_i$. Ties are broken randomly.

*When the target moves:*

1. Calculate $h(x_i, y_j)$ for the target's new position $y_j$.

2. Update the value of $h(x_i, y_i)$ as follows:

$$h(x_i, y_i) \leftarrow max \left\{ \begin{array}{l} h(x_i, y_i) \\ h(x_i, y_j) - 1 \end{array} \right\}$$

3. Reflect the target's new position as the new goal of the problem solver, i.e., assign the value of $y_j$ to $y_i$.

A problem solver executing MTS is guaranteed to eventually reach the target. The following characteristic is known [11]. The proof is obtained by extending the one for LRTA*.

- In a finite problem space with positive edge costs, in which there exists a path from every state to the goal state, starting with non-negative admissible initial heuristic values, and allowing motion of either a problem solver or the target along any edge in either direction with unit cost, the problem solver executing MTS will eventually reach the target, if the target periodically skips moves.

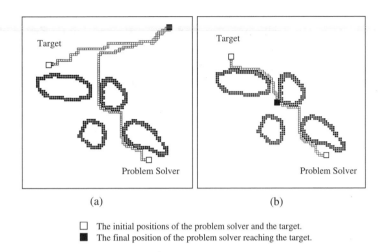

□   The initial positions of the problem solver and the target.
■   The final position of the problem solver reaching the target.

**Figure 4.12**   Sample Tracks of MTS.

An interesting target behavior is obtained by allowing a human user to indirectly control the motion of the target. Figure 4.12 shows the experimental setup along with sample tracks of the target (controlled by a human user) and problem solver (controlled by MTS) with manually placed obstacles. The initial positions of the problem solver and the target are represented by white rectangles, while their final positions are denoted by black rectangles. In Figure 4.12 (a), the user's task is to avoid the problem solver, which is executing MTS, for as long as possible, while in Figure 4.12 (b), the user's task is to meet the problem solver as quickly as possible. We can observe that if one is trying to avoid a faster pursuer as long as possible, the best strategy is not to run away, but to hide behind obstacles. The pursuer then reaches the opposite side of obstacles, and moves back and forth in confusion.

### 4.3.6   Real-Time Bidirectional Search

Moving target search enables problem solvers to adapt to changing goals. This allows us to investigate various organizations for problem solving agents. Suppose there are two robots trying to meet in a fairly complex maze: one is starting from the entrance and the other from the exit. Each of the robots always knows its current location in the maze, and can communicate with the other robot; thus, each robot always knows its goal location. Even though the robots do not have a map of the maze, they can gather information around them through various sensors.

For further sensing, however, the robots are required to physically move (as opposed to state expansion): planning and execution must be interleaved. In such a situation, how should the robots behave to efficiently meet with each other? Should they negotiate their actions, or make decisions independently? Is the two-robot organization really superior to a single robot one?

All previous research on bidirectional search focused on offline search [29] [5].

In RTBS, however, two problem solvers starting from the initial and goal states physically move toward each other. As a result, unlike the offline bidirectional search, the coordination cost is expected to be limited within some constant time. Since the planning time is also limited, the moves of the two problem solvers may be inefficient.

In RTBS, the following steps are repeatedly executed until the two problem solvers meet in the problem space.

1. *Control strategy*:
   Select a forward (*Step2*) or backward move (*Step3*).

2. *Forward move*:
   The problem solver starting from the initial state (i.e., the *forward problem solver*) moves toward the problem solver starting from the goal state.

3. *Backward move*:
   The problem solver starting from the goal state (i.e., the *backward problem solver*) moves toward the problem solver starting from the initial state.

RTBS algorithms can be classified into the following two categories depending on the autonomy of the problem solvers. One is called *centralized RTBS* where the best action is selected from among all possible moves of the two problem solvers, and the other is called *decoupled RTBS* where the two problem solvers independently make their own decisions. Let us take an *n*-puzzle example. The real-time unidirectional search algorithm utilizes a single game board, and interleaves both planning and execution; it evaluates all possible actions at a current puzzle state and physically performs the best action (slides one of the movable tiles). On the other hand, the RTBS algorithm utilizes two game boards. At the beginning, one board indicates the initial state and the other indicates the goal state. What is pursued in this case is to equalize the two puzzle states. Centralized RTBS behaves as if one person operates both game boards, while decoupled RTBS behaves as if each of two people operates his/her own game board independently.

In centralized RTBS, the control strategy selects the best action from among all of the possible forward and backward moves to minimize the estimated distance to the goal state. Two centralized RTBS algorithms can be implemented, which are based on LRTA* and RTA*, respectively. In decoupled RTBS, the control strategy merely selects the forward or backward problem solver alternately. As a result, each problem solver independently makes decisions based on its own heuristic information. MTS can be used for both forward and backward moves for implementing decoupled RTBS.

The evaluation results show that, in clear situations, (i.e., heuristic functions return accurate values), decoupled RTBS performs better than centralized RTBS, while in uncertain situations (i.e., heuristic functions return inaccurate values), the latter becomes more efficient. Surprisingly enough, compared to real-time unidirectional search, RTBS dramatically reduces the number of moves for 15- and 24-puzzles, and even solves larger games such as 35- 48- and 63- puzzles. On the other hand, it increases the number of moves for randomly generated mazes: the number of moves for centralized RTBS is around 1/2 in 15-puzzles and 1/6 in 24-puzzles that for real-time unidirectional search; In mazes, however, as the number of obstacles increases, the number of moves for RTBS is roughly double that for unidirectional search [12].

Why is RTBS efficient for $n$-puzzles but not for mazes? The key to understanding the real-time bidirectional search performance is to view that RTBS algorithms solve a totally different problem from unidirectional search, i.e., the difference between real-time unidirectional search and bidirectional search is not the number of problem solvers, but their problem spaces. Let $x$ and $y$ be the locations of two problem solvers. We call a pair of locations $(x, y)$ a *p-state*, and the problem space consisting of p-states a *combined problem space*. When the number of states in the original problem space is $n$, the number of p-states in the combined problem space becomes $n^2$. Let $i$ and $g$ be the initial and goal states; then $(i, g)$ becomes the initial p-state in the combined problem space. The goal p-state requires both problem solvers to share the same location. Thus, the goal p-state in the combined problem space is not unique, i.e., when there are $n$ locations, there are $n$ goal p-states. Each state transition in the combined problem space corresponds to a move by one of the problem solvers. Thus, the branching factor in the combined problem space is the sum of the branching factors of the two problem solvers.

Centralized RTBS can be naturally explained by using a combined problem space. In decoupled RTBS, two problem solvers independently make their own decisions and alternately move toward the other problem solver. We can view, however, that even in decoupled RTBS, the two problem solvers move in a combined problem space. Each problem solver selects the best action from possible moves, but does not examine the moves of the other problem solver. Thus, the selected action might not be the best among the possible moves of the two problem solvers.

The performance of real-time search is sensitive to the topography of the problem space, especially to *heuristic depressions*, i.e., a set of connected states with heuristic values less than or equal to those of the set of immediate and completely surrounding states. This is because, in real-time search, erroneous decisions seriously affect the consequent problem solving behavior. Heuristic depressions in the original problem space have been observed to become *large* and *shallow* in the combined problem space. If the original heuristic depressions are deep, they become large and that makes the problem harder to solve. If the original depressions are shallow, they become very shallow and this makes the problem easier to solve. Based on the above observation, we now have a better understanding of real-time bidirectional search: in $n$-puzzles, where heuristic depressions are shallow, the performance increases significantly, while in mazes, where deep heuristic depressions exist, the performance seriously decreases.

Let us revisit the example at the beginning of this section. The two robots first make decisions independently to move toward each other. However, this method hardly solves the problem. To overcome this inefficiency, the robots then introduce centralized decision making to choose the appropriate robot to move next. They are going to believe that two is better than one, because a two-robot organization has more freedom for selecting actions; better actions can be selected through sufficient coordination. However, the result appears miserable. The robots are not aware of the changes that have occurred in their problem space.

### 4.3.7   Real-Time Multiagent Search

Even if the number of agents is two, RTBS is not the only way for organizing problem solvers. Another possible way is to have both problem solvers start from the initial state and move toward the goal state. In the latter case, it is natural to adopt the original problem space. This means that the selection of the problem solving organization is the selection of the problem space, which determines the baseline of the organizational efficiency; once a difficult problem space is selected, the local coordination among the problem solvers hardly overcomes the deficit.

If there exist multiple agents, how can these agents cooperatively solve a problem? Again, the key issue is to select an appropriate organization for the agents. Since the number of possible organizations is quite large, we start with the most simple organization: the multiple agents share the same problem space with a single fixed goal. Each agent executes the LRTA* algorithm independently, but they share the updated $h$ values (this algorithm is called multiagent LRTA*). In this case, when one of the agents reaches the goal, the objective of the agents as a whole is satisfied. How efficient is this particular organization? Two different effects are observed as follows:

1.  Effects of sharing experiences among agents:
    As the execution order of the local computations of processes is arbitrary in asynchronous dynamic programming, the LRTA* algorithm inherits this property. Although the agents start from the same initial node, since ties are broken randomly, the current nodes of the agents are gradually dispersed even though the agents share $h$ values. This algorithm is complete and the $h$ values will eventually converge to the true values, in the same way as the LRTA*.

2.  Effects of autonomous decision making:
    If there exists a critical choice in the problem, solving the problem with multiple agents becomes a great advantage. Assume the maze problem shown in Figure 4.13. If an agent decides to go down at the first branching point, the problem can be solved straightforwardly. On the other hand, if the agent goes right, it will take a very long time before the agent returns to this point.
    If the problem is solved by one agent, since ties are broken randomly, the probability that the agent makes a correct decision is $1/2$, so the problem can be solved efficiently with the probability 0.5, but it may take a very long time with the probability of 0.5. If the problem is solved by two agents, if one of the agents goes down, the problem can be solved efficiently. The probability that a solution can be obtained straightforwardly becomes $3/4$ (i.e., $1-1/4$, where the probability that both agents go right is $1/4$). If there exist $k$ agents, the

**Figure 4.13**   Example of a critical choice.

probability that a solution can be obtained straightforwardly becomes $1 - 1/2^k$.

By solving a problem with multiple agents concurrently, we can increase both the efficiency and robustness. For further study on problem solving organizations, there exist several typical example problems such as *Tileworld* [30] and the *Pursuit Game* [2]. There are several techniques to create various organizations: explicitly break down the goal into multiple subgoals which may change during the course of problem solving; dynamically assign multiple subgoals to multiple agents; or assign problem solving skills by allocating relevant operators to multiple agents. Real-time search techniques will provide a solid basis for further study on problem solving organizations in dynamic uncertain multiagent environments.

## 4.4   Two-Player Games

### 4.4.1   Formalization of Two-Player Games

For games like chess or checkers, we can describe the sequence of possible moves using a tree. We call such a tree a *game tree*. Figure 4.14 shows a part of a game tree for tic-tac-toe (noughts and crosses). There are two players; we call the player who plays first the *MAX player*, and his opponent the *MIN player*. We assume MAX marks crosses ($\times$) and MIN marks circles ($\bigcirc$). This game tree is described from the viewpoint of MAX. We call a node that shows MAX's turn a MAX node, and a node for MIN's turn a MIN node. There is a unique node called a *root node*, representing the initial state of the game. If a node $n'$ can be obtained by a single move from a node $n$, we say $n'$ is a child node of $x$, and $n$ is a parent of $n'$. Furthermore, if a node $n''$ is obtained by a sequence of moves from a node $n$, we call $n$ an ancestor of $n''$.

If we can generate a complete game tree, we can find a winning strategy, i.e., a strategy that guarantees a win for MAX regardless of how MIN plays, if such a strategy exists. However, generating a complete game tree for a reasonably complicated game is impossible. Therefore, instead of generating a complete game

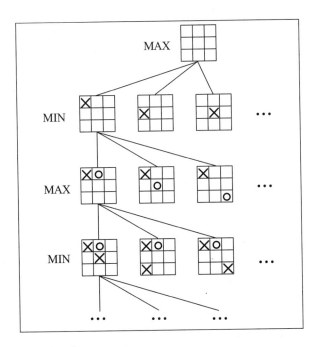

**Figure 4.14**   Example of a game tree.

tree, we need to find out a good move by creating only a reasonable portion of a game tree.

### 4.4.2   Minimax Procedure

In the minimax procedure, we first generate a part of the game tree, evaluate the merit of the nodes on the search frontier using a static evaluation function, then use these values to estimate the merit of ancestor nodes. An evaluation function returns a value for each node, where a node favorable to MAX has a large evaluation value, while a node favorable to MIN has a small evaluation value. Therefore, we can assume that MAX will choose the move that leads to the node with the maximum evaluation value, while MIN will choose the move that leads to the node with the minimum evaluation value. By using these assumptions, we can define the evaluation value of each node recursively as follows.

- The evaluation value of a MAX node is equal to the maximum value of any of its child nodes.
- The evaluation value of a MIN node is equal to the minimum value of any of its child nodes.

By backing up the evaluation values from frontier nodes to the root node, we can obtain the evaluation value of the root node. MAX should choose a move that gives the maximum evaluation value.

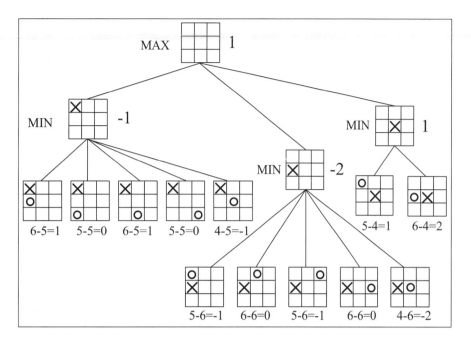

**Figure 4.15**   Example of evaluation values obtained by the minimax procedure.

Figure 4.15 shows the evaluation values obtained using the minimax algorithm, where nodes are generated by a search to depth 2 (symmetries are used to reduce the number of nodes). We use the following evaluation function for frontier nodes: (the number of complete rows, columns, or diagonals that are still open for MAX) – (the number of complete rows, columns, or diagonals that are still open for MIN). In this case, MAX chooses to place a × in the center.

### 4.4.3   Alpha-Beta Pruning

The alpha-beta pruning method is commonly used to speed up the minimax procedure without any loss of information. This algorithm can prune a part of a tree that cannot influence the evaluation value of the root node. More specifically, for each node, the following value is recorded and updated.

$\alpha$ value: represents the lower bound of the evaluation value of a MAX node.

$\beta$ value: represents the upper bound of the evaluation value of a MIN node.

While visiting nodes in a game tree from the root node by a depth-first order to a certain depth, these values are updated by the following rules.

- The $\alpha$ value of a MAX node is the maximum value of any of its child nodes visited so far.

- The $\beta$ value of a MIN node is the minimum value of any of its child nodes visited so far.

We can prune a part of the tree if one of the following conditions is satisfied.

**$\alpha$-cut:** If the $\beta$ value of a MIN node is smaller than or equal to the maximum $\alpha$ value of its ancestor MAX nodes, we can use the current $\beta$ value as the evaluation value of the MIN node, and can prune a part of the search tree under the MIN node. In other words, the MAX player never chooses a move that leads to the MIN node, since there exists a better move for the MAX player.

**$\beta$-cut:** If the $\alpha$ value of a MAX node is larger than or equal to the minimum $\beta$ value of its ancestor MIN nodes, we can use the current $\alpha$ value as the evaluation value of the MAX node, and can prune a part of the search tree under the MAX node. In other words, the MIN player never chooses a move that leads to the MAX node, since there exists a better move for the MIN player.

Figure 4.16 shows examples of these pruning actions. In this figure, a square shows a MAX node, and a circle shows a MIN node. A number placed near each node represents an $\alpha$ or $\beta$ value. Also, $\times$ shows a pruning action. A pruning action under a MAX node represents an $\alpha$-cut, and that under a MIN node represents a $\beta$-cut.

The effect of the alpha-beta pruning depends on the order in which the child nodes are visited. If the algorithm first examines the nodes that will likely be chosen (i.e., MAX nodes with large $\alpha$ values, and MIN nodes with small $\beta$ values), the effect of the pruning becomes great. One popular approach for obtaining a good ordering is to do an iterative deepening search, and use the backed-up values from one iteration to determine the ordering of child nodes in the next iteration.

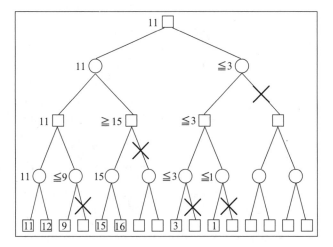

**Figure 4.16**   Example of alpha-beta pruning.

## 4.5   Conclusions

In this chapter, we presented several search algorithms that will be useful for problem solving by multiple agents. For constraint satisfaction problems, we presented the filtering algorithm, the hyper-resolution-based consistency algorithm, the asynchronous backtracking algorithm, and the weak-commitment search algorithm. For path-finding problems, we introduced asynchronous dynamic programming as the basis for other algorithms; we then described the LRTA* algorithm, the RTA* algorithm, the MTS algorithm, RTBS algorithms, and real-time multiagent search algorithms as special cases of asynchronous dynamic programming. For two-player games, we presented the basic minimax procedure, and alpha-beta pruning to speed up the minimax procedure.

There are many articles on constraint satisfaction, path-finding, two-player games, and search in general. Pearl's book [28] is a good textbook for path-finding and two-player games. Tsang's textbook [35] on constraint satisfaction covers topics from basic concepts to recent research results. Concise overviews of path-finding can be found in [18, 20], and one for constraint satisfaction is in [26].

The first application problem of CSPs was a line labeling problem in vision research. The filtering algorithm [36] was developed to solve this problem. The notion of k-consistency was introduced by Freuder [9]. The hyper-resolution-based consistency algorithm [6] was developed during the research of an assumption-based truth maintenance system (ATMS). Forbus and de Kleer's textbook [8] covers ATMS and truth maintenance systems in general. Distributed CSPs and the asynchronous backtracking algorithm were introduced in [39], and the asynchronous weak-commitment search algorithm was described in [38]. An iterative improvement search algorithm for distributed CSPs was presented in [40].

Dynamic programming and the principle of optimality were proposed by Bellman [3], and have been widely used in the area of combinatorial optimization and control. Asynchronous dynamic programming [4] was initially developed for distributed/parallel processing in dynamic programming. The Learning Real-time A* algorithm and its variant Real-time A* algorithm were presented in [19]. Barto *et al.* [1] later clarified the relationship between asynchronous dynamic programming and various learning algorithms such as the Learning Real-time A* algorithm and Q-learning [37]. The multiagent real-time A* algorithm was proposed in [16], where a path-finding problem is solved by multiple agents, each of which uses the Real-time A* algorithm. Methods for improving the multiagent Real-time A* algorithm by organizing these agents was presented in [15, 41].

Although real-time search provides an attractive framework for resource-bounded problem solving, the behavior of the problem solver is not rational enough for autonomous agents: the problem solver tends to perform superfluous actions before attaining the goal; the problem solver cannot utilize and improve previous experiments; the problem solver cannot adapt to the dynamically changing goals; and the problem solver cannot cooperatively solve problems with other problem solvers.

Various extensions of real-time search, including Moving Target Search and Real-time Bidirectional Search, have been studied in recent years [31, 13, 14].

The idea of the minimax procedure using a static evaluation function was proposed in [32]. The alpha-beta pruning method was discovered independently by many of the early AI researchers [17]. Another approach for improving the efficiency of the minimax procedure is to control the search procedure in a best-first fashion [21]. Best-first minimax procedure always expands the leaf node which determines the $\alpha$ value of the root node.

There are other DAI works that are concerned with search, which were not covered in this chapter due to space limitations. Lesser [23] formalized various aspects of cooperative problem solving as a search problem. Attempts to formalize the negotiations among agents in real-life application problems were presented in [7, 22, 34].

## 4.6    Exercises

1.  *[Level 1]* Implement the A* and LRTA* algorithms to solve the 8-puzzle problem. Compare the number of states expanded by each algorithm. Use the sum of the Manhattan distance of each misplaced tile as the heuristic function.

2.  *[Level 1]* Implement the filtering algorithm to solve graph-coloring problems. Consider a graph structure in which the filtering algorithm can always tell whether the problem has a solution or not without further trial-and-error search.

3.  *[Level 1]* Implement a game-tree search algorithm for tic-tac-toe, which introduces the alpha-beta pruning method. Use the static evaluation function described in this chapter. Increase the search depth and see how the strategy of the MAX player changes.

4.  *[Level 2]* Implement the asynchronous backtracking algorithm to solve the n-queens problem. If you are not familiar with programming using multiprocess and inter-process communications, you may use shared memories, and assume that agents act sequentially in a round-robin order.

5.  *[Level 2]* Implement the asynchronous weak-commitment algorithm to solve the n-queens problem. Increase *n* and see how large you can make it to solve the problem in a reasonable amount of time.

6.  *[Level 2]* In Moving Target Search, it has been observed that if one is trying to avoid a faster pursuer as long as possible, the best strategy is not to run away, but to hide behind obstacles. Explain how this phenomenon comes about.

7.  *[Level 3]* When solving mazes by two problem solvers, there are at least two possible organizations: One way is to have the two problem solvers start from the initial and the goal states and meet in the middle of the problem space; Another way is to have both problem solvers start from the initial state and

move toward the goal state. Make a small maze and compare the efficiency of the two organizations. Try to create original organizations that differ from the given two organizations.

8. *[Level 3]* In the multiagent LRTA* algorithm, each agent chooses its action independently without considering the actions nor the current states of other agents. Improve the efficiency of the multiagent LRTA* algorithm by introducing coordination among the agents, i.e., agents coordinate their actions by considering the actions and current states of other agents.

9. *[Level 4]* When a real-life problem is formalized as a CSP, it is often the case that the problem is over-constrained. In such a case, we hope that the algorithm will find an incomplete solution that satisfies most of the important constraints, while violating some less important constraints [10]. One way for representing the subjective importance of constraints is to introduce a hierarchy of constraints, i.e., constraints are divided into several groups, such as $C_1, C_2, \ldots, C_k$. If all constraints cannot be satisfied, we will give up on satisfying the constraints in $C_k$. If there exists no solution that satisfies all constraints in $C_1, C_2, \ldots, C_{k-1}$, we will further give up on satisfying the constraints in $C_{k-1}$, and so on. Develop an asynchronous search algorithm that can find the best incomplete solution of a distributed CSP when a hierarchy of constraints is defined.

10. *[Level 4]* The formalization of a two-player game can be generalized to an *n-player game* [25], i.e., there exist $n$ players, each of which takes turns alternately. Rewrite the minimax procedure so that it works for n-player games. Consider what kinds of pruning techniques can be applied.

## 4.7   References

1. A. Barto, S. J. Bradtke, and S. Singh. Learning to act using real-time dynamic programming. *Artificial Intelligence*, 72:81–138, 1995.

2. M. Benda, V. Jagannathan and R. Dodhiawalla, On optimal cooperation of knowledge sources. *Technical Report BCS-G2010-28*, Boeing AI Center, 1985.

3. R. Bellman. *Dynamic programming*. Princeton University Press, Princeton, NJ, 1957.

4. D. P. Bertsekas. Distributed dynamic programming. *IEEE Trans. Automatic Control*, AC-27(3):610–616, 1982.

5. D. de Champeaux and L. Sint. An improved bidirectional heuristic search algorithm. *Journal of ACM*, 24(2), 177–191, 1977.

6. J. de Kleer. A comparison of ATMS and CSP techniques. In *Proceedings of the Eleventh International Joint Conference on Artificial Intelligence*, pages 290–296, 1989.

7. E. Durfee and T. Montgomery. Coordination as distributed search in a hierarchical behavior space. *IEEE Transactions on Systems, Man and Cybernetics*,

21(6):1363–1378, 1991.

8. K. D. Forbus and J. de Kleer. *Building Problem Solvers*. MIT Press, 1993.

9. E. C. Freuder. Synthesizing constraint expressions. *Communications ACM*, 21(11):958–966, 1978.

10. E. C. Freuder and R. J. Wallance. Partial constraint satisfaction. *Artificial Intelligence*, 58(1–3):21–70, 1992.

11. T. Ishida and R. E. Korf, A moving target search: A real-time search for changing goals. *IEEE Transaction on Pattern Analysis and Machine Intelligence*, 17(6): 609–619, 1995.

12. T. Ishida. Real-time bidirectional search: Coordinated problem solving in uncertain situations. *IEEE Transaction on Pattern Analysis and Machine Intelligence*, 18(6): 617–628, 1996.

13. T. Ishida and M. Shimbo. Improving the learning efficiencies of realtime search. *Proceedings of the Thirteenth National Conference on Artificial Intelligence*, pages 305–310, 1996.

14. T. Ishida. *Real-time search for learning autonomous agents*. Kluwer Academic Publishers, 1997.

15. Y. Kitamura, K. Teranishi, and S. Tatsumi. Organizational strategies for multiagent real-time search. In *Proceedings of the Second International Conference on Multi-Agent Systems*. MIT Press, 1996.

16. K. Knight. Are many reactive agents better than a few deliberative ones? In *Proceedings of the Thirteenth International Joint Conference on Artificial Intelligence*, pages 432–437, 1993.

17. D. E. Knuth and R. W. Moore. An analysis of alpha-beta pruning. *Artificial Intelligence*, 6(4):293–326, 1975.

18. R. E. Korf. Search in AI: A survey of recent results. In H. Shrobe, editor, *Exploring Artificial Intelligence*. Morgan-Kaufmann, 1988.

19. R. E. Korf. Real-time heuristic search. *Artificial Intelligence*, 42(2–3):189–211, 1990.

20. R. E. Korf. Search. In S. C. Shapiro, editor, *Encyclopedia of Artificial Intelligence*, pages 1460–1467. Wiley-Interscience Publication, New York, 1992.

21. R. E. Korf and D. M. Chickering. Best-first minimax search. *Artificial Intelligence*, 84:299–337, 1996.

22. S. E. Lander and V. R. Lesser. Understanding the role of negotiation in distributed search among heterogeneous agents. In *Proceedings of the Thirteenth International Joint Conference on Artificial Intelligence*, pages 438–444, 1993.

23. V. R. Lesser. A retrospective view of FA/C distributed problem solving. *IEEE Transactions on Systems, Man and Cybernetics*, 21(6):1347–1362, 1991.

24. V. R. Lesser and D. D. Corkill. Functionally accurate, cooperative distributed systems. *IEEE Transactions on Systems, Man and Cybernetics*, 11(1):81–96, 1981.

25. C. A. Luchhardt and K. B. Irani. An algorithmic solution of n-person games. In *Proceedings of the Fifth National Conference on Artificial Intelligence*, pages 99–111, 1986.

26. A. K. Mackworth. Constraint satisfaction. In S. C. Shapiro, editor, *Encyclopedia of Artificial Intelligence*, pages 285–293. Wiley-Interscience Publication, New York, 1992.

27. S. Minton, M. D. Johnston, A. B. Philips, and P. Laird. Minimizing conflicts: a heuristic repair method for constraint satisfaction and scheduling problems. *Artificial Intelligence*, 58(1–3):161–205, 1992.

28. J. Pearl. *Heuristics: Intelligent Search Strategies for Computer Problem Solving.* Addison-Wesley, 1984.

29. I. Pohl. Bi-directional search. *Machine Intelligence*, 6, 127–140, 1971.

30. M. E. Pollack and M. Ringuette. *Introducing the Tileworld: Experimentally evaluating agent architectures. Proceedings of the Eighth National Conference on Artificial Intelligence*, pages 183-189, 1990.

31. S. Russell and E. Wefald. *Do the Right Thing.* The MIT Press, 1991.

32. C. E. Shannon. Programming a computer for playing chess. *Philosophical Magazine (series 7)*, 41:256–275, 1950.

33. M. Shimbo and T. Ishida. On the convergence of realtime search. *Journal of Japanese Society for Artificial Intelligence*, 1998.

34. K. R. Sycara. Multiagent compromise via negotiation. In L. Gasser and M. N. Huhns, editors, *Distributed Artificial Intelligence, Volume II*, pages 245–258. Morgan Kaufmann, 1989.

35. E. Tsang. *Foundations of Constraint Satisfaction.* Academic Press, 1993.

36. D. Waltz. Understanding line drawing of scenes with shadows. In P. Winston, editor, *The Psychology of Computer Vision*, pages 19–91. McGraw-Hill, 1975.

37. C. Watkins and P. Dayan. Technical note: Q-learning. *Machine Learning*, 8(3/4), 1992.

38. M. Yokoo. Asynchronous weak-commitment search for solving distributed constraint satisfaction problems. In *Proceedings of the First International Conference on Principles and Practice of Constraint Programming (Lecture Notes in Computer Science 976)*, pages 88–102. Springer-Verlag, 1995.

39. M. Yokoo, E. H. Durfee, T. Ishida, and K. Kuwabara. Distributed constraint satisfaction for formalizing distributed problem solving. In *Proceedings of the Twelfth IEEE International Conference on Distributed Computing Systems*, pages 614–621, 1992.

40. M. Yokoo and K. Hirayama. Distributed breakout algorithm for solving distributed constraint satisfaction problems. In *Proceedings of the Second International Conference on Multi-Agent Systems*, pages 401–408. MIT Press, 1996.

41. M. Yokoo and Y. Kitamura. Multiagent Real-time-A* with selection: Introducing competition in cooperative search. In *Proceedings of the Second International Conference on Multi-Agent Systems*, pages 409–416. MIT Press, 1996.

# 5 Distributed Rational Decision Making

Tuomas W. Sandholm

## 5.1 Introduction

Automated negotiation systems with self-interested agents are becoming increasingly important. One reason for this is the *technology push* of a growing standardized communication infrastructure—Internet, WWW, NII, EDI, KQML, FIPA, Concordia, Voyager, Odyssey, Telescript, Java, *etc.*—over which separately designed agents belonging to different organizations can interact in an open environment in real-time and safely carry out transactions. The second reason is strong *application pull* for computer support for negotiation at the operative decision making level. For example, we are witnessing the advent of small transaction electronic commerce on the Internet for purchasing goods, information, and communication bandwidth [31]. There is also an industrial trend toward virtual enterprises: dynamic alliances of small, agile enterprises which together can take advantage of economies of scale when available (e.g., respond to more diverse orders than individual agents can), but do not suffer from diseconomies of scale.

Multiagent technology facilitates such negotiation at the operative decision making level. This automation can save labor time of human negotiators, but in addition, other savings are possible because computational agents can be more effective at finding beneficial short-term contracts than humans are in strategically and combinatorially complex settings.

This chapter discusses multiagent negotiation in situations where agents may have different goals, and each agent is trying to maximize its own good without concern for the global good. Such self-interest naturally prevails in negotiations among independent businesses or individuals. In building computer support for negotiation in such settings, the issue of self-interest has to be dealt with. In *cooperative distributed problem solving* [12, 9], the system designer imposes an interaction *protocol*[1] and a *strategy* (a mapping from state history to action; a

---

1. Here a protocol does not mean a low level communication protocol, but a negotiation protocol which determines the possible actions that agents can take at different points of the interaction. The *sealed-bid first-price auction* is an example protocol where each bidder is free to submit one bid for the item, which is awarded to the highest bidder at the price of his bid.

way to use the protocol) for each agent. The main question is what social outcomes follow given the protocol and *assuming that the agents use the imposed strategies*. On the other hand, in *multiagent systems* [67, 63, 61, 56, 34], the agents are provided with an interaction protocol, but each agent will choose its own strategy. A self-interested agent will choose the best strategy for itself, which cannot be explicitly imposed from outside. Therefore, the protocols need to be designed using a *noncooperative, strategic* perspective: the main question is what social outcomes follow given a protocol which *guarantees that each agent's desired local strategy is best for that agent—and thus the agent will use it*. This approach is required in designing robust non-manipulable multiagent systems where the agents may be constructed by separate designers and/or may represent different real world parties.

The rest of this chapter discusses protocols for voting, auctions, bargaining, markets, contracting, and coalition formation. However, first some central evaluation criteria for protocols are presented.

## 5.2    Evaluation Criteria

Negotiation protocols—i.e. mechanisms—can be evaluated according to many types of criteria, as listed below. The choice of protocol will then depend on what properties the protocol designer wants the overall system to have.

### 5.2.1    Social Welfare

*Social welfare* is the sum of all agents' payoffs or utilities in a given solution. It measures the global good of the agents. It can be used as a criterion for comparing alternative mechanisms by comparing the solutions that the mechanisms lead to. When measured in terms of utilities, the criterion is somewhat arbitrary, because it requires interagent utility comparisons, and really each agent's utility function can only be specified up to positive affine transformations [39].

### 5.2.2    Pareto Efficiency

*Pareto efficiency* is another solution evaluation criterion that takes a global perspective. Again, alternative mechanisms can be evaluated according to Pareto efficiency by comparing the solutions that the mechanisms lead to. A solution $x$ is Pareto efficient—i.e. Pareto optimal—if there is no other solution $x'$ such that at least one agent is better off in $x'$ than in $x$ and no agent is worse off in $x'$ than in $x$. So, Pareto efficiency measures global good, and it does not require questionable interagent utility comparisons.

Social welfare maximizing solutions are a subset of Pareto efficient ones. Once the sum of the payoffs is maximized, an agent's payoff can increase only if another agent's payoff decreases.

### 5.2.3   Individual Rationality

Participation in a negotiation is individually rational to an agent if the agent's payoff in the negotiated solution is no less than the payoff that the agent would get by not participating in the negotiation. A mechanism is individually rational if participation is individually rational for all agents. Only individually rational mechanisms are viable: if the negotiated solution is not individually rational for some agent, that self-interested agent would not participate in that negotiation.

### 5.2.4   Stability

Among self-interested agents, mechanism should be designed to be stable (non-manipulable), i.e. they should motivate each agent to behave in the desired manner. This is because if a self-interested agent is better off behaving in some other manner than desired, it will do so.

Sometimes it is possible to design mechanisms with *dominant strategies*. This means that an agent is best off by using a specific strategy no matter what strategies the other agents use.

However, often an agent's best strategy depends on what strategies other agents choose. In such settings, dominant strategies do not exist, and other stability criteria are needed. The most basic one is the *Nash equilibrium* [48, 39, 17, 35]. The strategy profile $S_A^* = \langle S_1^*, S_2^*, ..., S_{|A|}^* \rangle$ among agents $A$ is in Nash equilibrium if for each agent $i$, $S_i^*$ is the agent's best strategy—i.e. best response—given that the other agents choose strategies $\langle S_1^*, S_2^*, ..., S_{i-1}^*, S_{i+1}^*, ..., S_{|A|}^* \rangle$. In other words, in Nash equilibrium, each agent chooses a strategy that is a best response to the other agents' strategies.

There are two main problems in applying Nash equilibrium. First, in some games no Nash equilibrium exists [39, 17, 35]. Second, some games have multiple Nash equilibria, and it is not obvious which one the agents should actually play [35].

There are also limitations regarding what the Nash equilibrium guarantees even when it exists and is unique.

First, in sequential games it only guarantees stability in the beginning of the game. At a later stage the strategies need not be in equilibrium anymore. A refined solution concept called the *subgame perfect Nash equilibrium* is defined to be a Nash equilibrium that remains a Nash equilibrium in every subgame (even subgames that are not along the actual path of play and will thus never be reached) [71, 39, 17, 35]. This solution concept also suffers from existence and uniqueness problems.

Second, the Nash equilibrium is often too weak because subgroups of agents can deviate in a coordinated manner. Some refinements of the Nash equilibrium solution concept guarantee stability against such collusive deviations as well. This will be discussed in Section 5.8.

Sometimes efficiency goals and stability goals conflict. A simple example of this is the Prisoner's Dilemma game where the unique welfare maximizing and Pareto efficient strategy profile is the one where both agents cooperate, Table 5.1. On the other hand, the only dominant strategy equilibrium and Nash equilibrium is the one where both agents defect.

|  |  | column player | |
|---|---|---|---|
|  |  | cooperate | defect |
| row | cooperate | 3, 3 | 0, 5 |
| player | defect | 5, 0 | 1, 1 |

**Table 5.1**  Prisoner's Dilemma game. The row player's payoff is listed first.

### 5.2.5  Computational Efficiency

Clearly, mechanisms should be designed so that when agents use them, as little computation is needed as possible. Classically, mechanisms have been designed so that they lead to domain solutions that satisfy some of the above evaluation criteria. Of these mechanisms, the ones with the lowest computational overhead have been preferred. However, a more advanced approach would be to explicitly trade off the cost of the process against the solution quality [62].

### 5.2.6  Distribution and Communication Efficiency

All else being equal, distributed protocols should be preferred in order to avoid a single point of failure and a performance bottleneck—among other reasons. Simultaneously one would like to minimize the amount of communication that is required to converge on a desirable global solution. In some cases these two goals conflict.

The rest of this chapter discusses different interaction protocols using the evaluation criteria presented so far. These mechanisms include voting, auctions, bargaining, markets, contracting, and coalition formation.

## 5.3  Voting

In a *voting* (social choice) setting, all agents give input to a mechanism, and the outcome that the mechanism chooses based on these inputs is a solution for all of the agents. In most settings, this outcome is enforced so that all agents have to abide to the solution prescribed by the mechanisms.

### 5.3.1 Truthful Voters

The classic goal has been to derive a social choice rule that ranks feasible social outcomes based on individuals' rankings of those outcomes. Let the set of agents be $A$, and let $O$ be the set of feasible outcomes for the society. Furthermore, let each agent $i \in A$ have an asymmetric and transitive strict preference relation $\succ_i$ on $O$. A social choice rule takes as input the agents' preference relations $(\succ_1, ..., \succ_{|A|})$ and produces as output the social preferences denoted by a relation $\succ^*$. Intuitively, the following properties of a social choice rule seem desirable:

- A social preference ordering $\succ^*$ should exist for all possible inputs (individual preferences).

- $\succ^*$ should be defined for every pair $o, o' \in O$.

- $\succ^*$ should be asymmetric and transitive over $O$.

- The outcome should be Pareto efficient: if $\forall i \in A, o \succ_i o'$, then $o \succ^* o'$.

- The scheme should be independent of irrelevant alternatives. Specifically, if $\succ$ and $\succ'$ are arrays of consumer rankings that satisfy $o \succ_i o'$ iff $o \succ'_i o'$ for all $i$, then the social ranking of $o$ and $o'$ is the same in these two situations.

- No agent should be a dictator in the sense that $o \succ_i o'$ implies $o \succ^* o'$ for all preferences of the other agents.

Unfortunately it is not possible to satisfy these desiderata:

**Theorem 5.1 *Arrow's impossibility theorem***
No social choice rule satisfies all of these six conditions [4, 35].

So, to design social choice rules, the desiderata have to be relaxed. Commonly the first property is relaxed in the sense that the domain (combinations of individual preferences) on which the rule works is restricted. This will be discussed later in conjunction with insincere voting.

The third desideratum can also be relaxed. This is done e.g. in the *plurality protocol* which is a majority voting protocol where all alternatives are compared simultaneously, and the one with the highest number of votes wins. Introducing an irrelevant alternative can split the majority; some in favor of the old most favored alternative, and some in favor of the newly introduced alternative. This may cause both the old favorite, and the newly introduced irrelevant alternative to drop below one of the originally less preferred alternatives, which then would become the social choice.

In a *binary protocol*, the alternatives are voted on pairwise, and the winner stays to challenge further alternatives while the loser is eliminated. As in plurality protocols, also in binary protocols the introduction of irrelevant alternatives often changes the outcome. Furthermore, in binary protocols, the *agenda*—i.e. order of the pairings—can totally change the socially chosen outcome. For example, Figure 5.1 shows four different agendas which all lead to a different outcome under the given preferences of the agents. Interestingly, in the last agenda, alternative

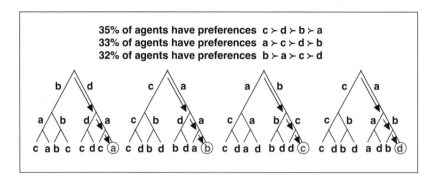

**Figure 5.1**   Four different agendas for a binary protocol with four alternatives: $a$, $b$, $c$, and $d$.

$d$ wins although every agent prefers $c$ over $d$. In other words, the social choice is Pareto dominated in this case.

If the number of alternative outcomes is large, pairwise voting may be slow, and an alternative called the *Borda protocol* is often used. The Borda count assigns an alternative $|O|$ points whenever it is highest in some agent's preference list, $|O| - 1$ whenever it is second and so on. These counts are then summed across voters. The alternative with the highest count becomes the social choice. The Borda protocol can also lead to paradoxical results, for example via irrelevant alternatives. Table 5.2 shows an example (from [49]) where removing the lowest ranked (irrelevant) alternative $d$ from the set of possible outcomes leads to the worst of the remaining alternatives turning best and the best turning worst.

| Agent | Preferences |
|---|---|
| 1 | $a \succ b \succ c \succ d$ |
| 2 | $b \succ c \succ d \succ a$ |
| 3 | $c \succ d \succ a \succ b$ |
| 4 | $a \succ b \succ c \succ d$ |
| 5 | $b \succ c \succ d \succ a$ |
| 6 | $c \succ d \succ a \succ b$ |
| 7 | $a \succ b \succ c \succ d$ |
| Borda count | $c$ wins with 20, $b$ has 19, $a$ has 18, $d$ loses with 13 |
| Borda count with $d$ removed | $a$ wins with 15, $b$ has 14, $c$ loses with 13 |

**Table 5.2**   Winner turns loser and loser turns winner paradox in the Borda protocol.

### 5.3.2  Strategic (Insincere) Voters

So far it was assumed that in executing the social choice method, all agents'
preferences are known. In reality this is seldom the case. Instead, agents usually
have to reveal, i.e. declare, their preferences. Assuming knowledge of the preferences
is equivalent to assuming that the agents reveal their preferences truthfully. But if
an agent can benefit from insincerely declaring his preferences, he will do so. This
further complicates the design of social choice mechanisms.

An area of game theory called *mechanism design* explores such interaction
mechanisms among rational agents. The goal is to generate protocols such that
when agents use them according to some stability solution concept—e.g. dominant
strategy equilibrium [45, 17, 35], Nash equilibrium or its refinements [40, 52, 17, 35],
or some other type of equilibrium [46, 17, 35]—then desirable social outcomes follow.
The strategies are not externally imposed on the agents, but instead each agent uses
the strategy that is best for itself.

Let each agent $i \in A$ have some *type* $\theta_i \in \Theta_i$ which totally characterizes his
preferences (which are affected by his possible private information). Now, a social
choice function $f : \theta \to O$ chooses a social outcome given the agents' types. With
insincere agents this is hard to implement because one needs to somehow motivate
the agents to reveal the types. A protocol (i.e. rules of the game) is said to implement
a particular social choice function if the protocol has an equilibrium—which may
involve insincere play by the agents—whose outcome is the same as the outcome of
the social choice function would be if the agents revealed their types truthfully. The
following positive result conceptually allows one to restrict the search for desirable
protocols to ones where revelation occurs truthfully in a single step.

### *Theorem 5.2  Revelation principle*
Suppose some protocol (which may include multiple steps) implements social
choice function $f(\cdot)$ in Nash (or dominant strategy) equilibrium (where the agents'
strategies are not necessarily truthful). Then $f(\cdot)$ is implementable in Nash (or
dominant strategy, respectively) equilibrium via a single-step protocol where the
agents reveal their entire types truthfully [39, 35, 45, 40, 52].

The proof is based on changing the protocol so that it will construct the best (i.e.
according to the original equilibrium) strategic revelation on behalf of each agent
(this revelation depends on the agent's truthful preferences), and then simulate the
old protocol as if the agents had constructed these insincere revelations themselves.
Under this new protocol, each agent is motivated to reveal his type truthfully in
a single step because the protocol will take care of optimally lying on the agent's
behalf.

The idea of incorporating the strategy generation into the protocol is problematic
among computationally limited agents. In the original protocol it may have been infeasible or prohibitively costly for an agent to compute its best strategy. Therefore,
in a complex protocol the agents might not play the equilibrium. This may be undesirable because agents may play uncoordinated strategies leading to undesirable

outcomes. On the other hand, if most equilibrium outcomes are undesirable, the protocol designer can construct a complex protocol—where agents cannot find the equilibrium—in the hope that a more desirable outcome will emerge. In the revised protocol of the proof, it is assumed that the protocol can solve for the equilibrium. However, if computation is costly, who pays for the computation that is required to solve for equilibrium? For some protocols, solving for equilibrium might be hard or even noncomputable.

The Nash equilibrium version of Theorem 5.2 has additional weaknesses. First, it assumes that the agents and the protocol designer have common knowledge about the joint probabilities of the agents' types. Second, the revised protocol may have other Nash equilibria in addition to the truthful one: Theorem 5.2 only says that a truthful one exists. This problem can be partially alleviated by what are called *augmented revelation mechanisms* [35].

While Theorem 5.2 is positive in nature, the following negative result establishes that in the general case, non-manipulable protocols are dictatorial:

### Theorem 5.3 Gibbard-Satterthwaite impossibility theorem

Let each agent's type $\theta_i$ consist of a preference order $\succ_i$ on $O$. Let there be no restrictions on $\succ_i$, i.e. each agent may rank the outcomes $O$ in any order.[2] Let $|O| \geq 3$. Now, if the social choice function $f(\cdot)$ is truthfully implementable in a dominant strategy equilibrium, then $f(\cdot)$ is dictatorial, i.e. there is some agent $i$ who gets (one of) his most preferred outcomes chosen no matter what types the others reveal [18, 70].

### Circumventing the Gibbard-Satterthwaite Impossibility Theorem: Restricted Preferences and the Groves-Clarke Tax Mechanism

The design of nonmanipulable protocols is not as impossible as it may seem in light of Theorem 5.3. The individual preferences may happen to belong to some restricted domain—thus invalidating the conditions of the impossibility theorem—and it is known that there are islands in the space of agents' preferences for which nonmanipulable nondictatorial protocols can be constructed.

Let us go through an example. Let the outcomes be of the form $o = (g, \pi_1, \ldots, \pi_{|A|})$, where $\pi_i$ is the amount of some divisible numeraire (e.g. money) that agent $i$ receives in the outcome, and $g$ encodes the other features of the outcome. The agents' preferences are called *quasilinear* if they can be represented by utility functions of the form $u_i(o) = v_i(g) + \pi_i$.

For example, in voting whether to build a joint pool, say $g = 1$ if the pool is built and $g = 0$ if not. Call each agent's gross benefit from the pool $v_i^{gross}(g)$, and say that the cost $P$ of the pool would be divided equally among the agents, i.e. $\pi_i = -P/|A|$. So, an agent's (net) benefit is $v_i(g) = v_i^{gross}(g) - P/|A|$.

---

2. Theorem 5.3 applies even if each agent's preferences are restricted to being complete, transitive, and strict.

> Every agent $i \in A$ reveals his valuation $\hat{v}_i(g)$ for every possible $g$
> The social choice is $g^* = \arg\max_g \sum_i \hat{v}_i(g)$
> Every agent is levied a tax: $tax_i = \sum_{j \neq i} \hat{v}_j(g^*) - \sum_{j \neq i} \hat{v}_j(\arg\max_g \sum_{k \neq i} \hat{v}_k(g))$

**Algorithm 5.1**  The Clarke tax algorithm.

Quasilinearity of the environment would require several things. First, no agent should care how others divide payoffs among themselves. This might be violated e.g. if an agent wants his enemies to pay more than his friends. Second, an agent's valuation $v_i^{gross}(g)$ of the pool should not depend on the amount of money that the agent will have. This might be violated for example if rich agents have more time to enjoy the pool because they do not have to work.

When voting whether to build the pool or not, the agents that vote for the pool impose an externality on the others because the others have to pay as well. On the other hand, if only the pro-pool voters would have to pay, there would be an incentive for them to vote for no pool, and free ride the pool that might be built anyway due to the others' votes. The solution is to make the agents precisely internalize this externality by imposing a tax on those agents whose vote changes the outcome. The size of an agent's tax is exactly how much his vote lowers the others' utility. Agents that do not end up changing the outcome do not pay any tax.

### Theorem 5.4

If each agent has quasilinear preferences, then, under Algorithm 5.1, each agent's dominant strategy is to reveal his true preferences, i.e. $\hat{v}_i(g) = v_i(g)$ for all $g$. [11, 21]

So, in the example, if the pool is built, the utility for each agent $i$ becomes $u_i(o) = v_i(1) - P/|A| - tax_i$, and if not, $u_i(o) = v_i(0)$.

The mechanism leads to the socially most preferred $g$ to be chosen. Also, because truthtelling is every agents dominant strategy, the agents need not waste effort in counterspeculating each others' preference declarations. Furthermore, participation in the mechanism can only increase an agent's utility, which makes participation individually rational.

Unfortunately the mechanism does not maintain budget balance: too much tax is collected. There are other truth-dominant algorithms for this problem where too little tax is collected (negative taxes are paybacks), but none that guarantee that the sum of the taxes is zero. The schemes where too little is collected require an external benefactor to operate. The schemes that collect too much are not Pareto efficient because the extra tax revenue has to be burnt. It cannot be given back to the agents or donated to any cause that any of the agents care about. Such redistribution would affect the agents' utilities, and truthtelling would no longer be dominant.

Another problem with Algorithm 5.1 is that it is not coalition proof. Some coalition of voters might coordinate their insincere preference revelations and achieve higher utilities. Table 5.3 presents a 3-agent example of this where the cost of building the pool is $P = 9,000$, and $v_i(0) = 0$ for every agent. We study the case where agents 1 and 2 collude.

| $i$ | $v_i^{gross}(1)$ | $v_i(1)$ | No collusion | | | | Agents 1 and 2 collude | | | |
|---|---|---|---|---|---|---|---|---|---|---|
| | | | $\hat{v}_i(1)$ | $g^*$ | $tax_i$ | $u_i$ | $\hat{v}_i(1)$ | $g^*$ | $tax_i$ | $u_i$ |
| 1 | 5,000 | 2,000 | 2,000 | | 1,500 | 500 | 2,500 | | 1000 | 1,000 |
| 2 | 4,000 | 1,000 | 1,000 | 1(build) | 500 | 500 | 1,500 | 1(build) | 0 | 1,000 |
| 3 | 500 | −2,500 | −2,500 | | 0 | −2,500 | −2,500 | | 0 | −2,500 |

**Table 5.3**  Example of collusion in the Clarke tax algorithm.

Traditionally, the Clarke tax mechanism has been used to solve a single isolated social choice problem. In multiagent planning—e.g. in AI—this would mean voting over all possible multiagent plans. This is is often intractable. To reduce this complexity, Ephrati has used a variant of the method where the agents repeatedly use the Clarke tax mechanism to do planning over one timestep of the plan at a time [14, 15, 13]. In such multistep approaches one has to be careful that truthtelling is still a dominant strategy. If the outcomes of the different votings are not independent in value to every agent, there is a risk e.g. that an agent will speculatively reveal higher than truthful valuations for some outcomes because he anticipates future outcomes that will be synergic with those particular ones of the currently available outcomes.

### Other Ways to Circumvent the Gibbard-Satterthwaite Impossibility Theorem

Even if the agents do not happen to have preferences that are restricted in some particular way that allows one to avoid the negative conclusion of Theorem. 5.3, there are ways to circumvent the seemingly unavoidable tradeoff between manipulability and dictatoriality.

For example, *ex ante* fairness can be achieved by choosing the dictator randomly in the protocol. This can be done via a protocol where every agent submits a vote into a hat, and the decisive vote is pulled out of the hat at random. Clearly, each agent's dominant strategy is to vote truthfully: if his vote gets chosen, he would have been best off voting for his most preferred alternative, and if his vote is not chosen, it does not matter what the agent voted for.

Another possible way of getting around Theorem. 5.3 is to use a protocol for which computing an untruthful revelation—that is better than the truthful one— is prohibitively costly computationally. One difficulty with this approach is that to guarantee that an agent can never manipulate, manipulation would have to be provably hard for every instance (combination of agents' preferences), not just in the worst case. Another difficulty is that even if it were possible to prove that deterministically finding a beneficial manipulation is hard, the agent can (e.g. randomly) generate insincere revelations, and simulate the protocol (given that the others' strategies cannot matter in a dominant strategy equilibrium) to check whether his guessed manipulations are beneficial.

## 5.4   Auctions

Within mechanism design, auctions provide a special setting which is important and often relatively easily analyzable. Auctions also have many practical computer science applications [60, 81, 37, 25], and several successful web sites exist for buying and selling items using auction protocols. Unlike voting where the outcome binds all agents, in auctions the outcome is usually a deal between two agents: the auctioneer and one bidder. Also, in voting the protocol designer is assumed to want to enhance the social good, while in auctions, the auctioneer wants to maximize his own profit.

Auction theory analyzes protocols and agents' strategies in auctions. An auction consists of an auctioneer and potential bidders. Auctions are usually discussed in situations where the auctioneer wants to sell an item and get the highest possible payment for it while the bidders want to acquire the item at the lowest possible price. The discussion of this section will pertain to the classical setting, although in a contracting setting, the auctioneer wants to subcontract out tasks at the lowest possible price while the bidders who handle the tasks want to receive the highest possible payment for doing so. The mechanisms for the latter setting are totally analogous to mechanisms for the former.

### 5.4.1   Auction Settings

There are three qualitatively different auction settings depending on how an agent's value (monetary equivalent of utility) of the item is formed.

In *private value* auctions, the value of the good depends only on the agent's own preferences. An example is auctioning off a cake that the winning bidder will eat. The key is that the winning bidder will not resell the item or get utility from showing it off to others, because in such cases the value would depend on other agents' valuations (a valuation is the monetary equivalent of expected utility). The agent is often assumed to know its value for the good exactly.

On the other hand, in *common value* auctions, an agent's value of an item depends entirely on other agents' values of it, which are identical to the agent's by symmetry of this criterion. For example, auctioning treasury bills fulfills this criterion. Nobody inherently prefers having the bills, and the value of the bill comes entirely from reselling possibilities.

In *correlated value* auctions, an agent's value depends partly on its own preferences and partly on others' values. For example, a negotiation within a contracting setting fulfills this criterion. An agent may handle a task itself in which case the agent's local concerns define the cost of handling the task. On the other hand, the agent can recontract out the task in which case the cost depends solely on other agents' valuations.

The next section discusses different auction protocols. Those protocols have different properties under the three different auction settings presented above.

### 5.4.2   Auction Protocols

In the *English (first-price open-cry) auction*, each bidder is free to raise his bid. When no bidder is willing to raise anymore, the auction ends, and the highest bidder wins the item at the price of his bid. An agent's strategy is a series of bids as a function of his private value, his prior estimates of other bidder's valuations, and the past bids of others. In private value English auctions, an agent's dominant strategy is to always bid a small amount more than the current highest bid, and stop when his private value price is reached. In correlated value auctions the rules are often varied to make the auctioneer increase the price at a constant rate or at a rate he thinks appropriate. Also, sometimes *open-exit* is used where a bidder has to openly declare exiting without a re-entering possibility. This provides the other bidders more information regarding the agent's valuation.

In the *first-price sealed-bid auction*, each bidder submits one bid without knowing the others' bids. The highest bidder wins the item and pays the amount of his bid. An agent's strategy is his bid as a function of his private value and prior beliefs of others' valuations. In general there is no dominant strategy for bidding in this auction. An agent's best strategy is to bid less than his true valuation, but how much less depends on what the others bid. The agent would want to bid the lowest amount that still wins the auction—given that this amount does not exceed his valuation. With common knowledge assumptions regarding the probability distributions of the agents' values, it is possible to determine Nash equilibrium strategies for the agents. For example, in a private value auction where the valuation $v_i$ for each agent $i$ is drawn independently from a uniform distribution between 0 and $\bar{v}$, there is a Nash equilibrium where every agent $i$ bids $\frac{|A|-1}{|A|} v_i$, see [54].

In the *Dutch (descending) auction*, the seller continuously lowers the price until one of the bidders takes the item at the current price. The Dutch auction is strategically equivalent to the first-price sealed-bid auction, because in both games, an agent's bid matters only if it is the highest, and no relevant information is revealed during the auction process. Dutch auctions are efficient in terms of real time because the auctioneer can decrease the price at a brisk pace. You can observe this e.g. by participating in a Dutch auction simulation at http://www.mcsr.olemiss.edu/ ccjimmy/auction.

In the *Vickrey (second-price sealed-bid) auction*, each bidder submits one bid without knowing the others' bids. The highest bidder wins, but at the price of the second highest bid [80, 42]. An agent's strategy is his bid as a function of his private value and prior beliefs of others' valuations.

**Theorem 5.5**

A bidder's dominant strategy in a private value Vickrey auction is to bid his true valuation [80].[3]

If he bids more than his valuation, and the increment made the difference between winning or not, he will end up with a loss if he wins. If he bids less, there is a smaller chance of winning, but the winning price is unaffected[4]. Theorem 5.5 means that an agent is best off bidding truthfully no matter what the other bidders are like: what are their capabilities, operating environments, bidding plans, *etc.* This has two desirable sides. First, the agents reveal their preferences truthfully which allows globally efficient decisions to be made. Second, the agents need not waste effort in counterspeculating other agents because they do not matter in making the bidding decision.

Vickrey auctions have been widely advocated and adopted for use in computational multiagent systems. For example, versions of the Vickrey auction have been used to allocate computation resources in operating systems [81], to allocate bandwidth in computer networks [37], and to computationally control building heating [25]. On the other hand, Vickrey auctions have not been widely adopted in auctions among humans [57, 58] even though the protocol was invented over 25 years ago [80]. Limitations of the Vickrey auction protocol—especially in computational multiagent systems—are discussed in [61].

*All-pay auctions* are another family of auction protocols. In such mechanisms, each participating bidder has to pay the amount of his bid (or some other amount) to the auctioneer. The schemes have been used in computational multiagent systems for tool reallocation [36]. These methods are often susceptible to infinite escalations of bids [53], and will not be discussed further here.

### 5.4.3  Efficiency of the Resulting Allocation

In isolated private value or common value auctions, each one of the four auction protocols (English, Dutch, first-price sealed-bid, and Vickrey) allocates the auctioned item Pareto efficiently to the bidder who values it the most.[5] Although all

---

3. If the bidders know their own values, this result does not depend on the bidders' risk neutrality. On the other hand, if a bidder has some uncertainty about his own valuation, this result only holds for a risk-neutral bidder: e.g. a risk averse bidder can be better off by bidding less than his expected valuation [61].

4. In private value auctions, the Vickrey auction is strategically equivalent to the English auction. They will produce the same allocation at the same prices. On the other hand, in correlated value auctions, the other agents' bids in the English auction provide information to the agent about his own valuation. Therefore English and Vickrey auctions are not strategically equivalent in general, and may lead to different results.

5. This holds at least as long as the auctioneer always sells the item. On the other hand, if the auctioneer has a reservation price, he may inefficiently end up with the item even though the highest bidder really values the item more than the auctioneer.

four are Pareto efficient in the allocation, the ones with dominant strategies (Vickrey auction and English auction) are more efficient in the sense that no effort is wasted in counterspeculating the other bidders.

### 5.4.4   Revenue Equivalence and Non-Equivalence

One could imagine that the first-price auctions give higher expected revenue to the auctioneer because in second-price auctions the auctioneer only gets the second price. On the other hand, in first-price auctions the bidders underbid while in the second-price auctions they bid truthfully. Now, which of these effects is stronger, i.e. which protocol should the auctioneer choose to maximize his expected revenue? It turns out that the two effects are exactly equally strong:

*Theorem 5.6 Revenue equivalence*
All of the four auction protocols produce the same expected revenue to the auctioneer in private value auctions where the values are independently distributed, and bidders are risk-neutral [80, 42, 54].

Among risk averse bidders, the Dutch and the first-price sealed-bid protocols give higher expected revenue to the auctioneer than the Vickrey or English auction protocols. This is because in the former two protocols, a risk averse agent can insure himself by bidding more than what is optimal for a risk-neutral agent. On the other hand, a risk averse auctioneer achieves higher expected utility via the Vickrey or English auction protocols than via the Dutch or the first-price sealed-bid protocol.

The fact that revenue equivalence holds in private value auctions does not mean that it usually holds in practice: most auctions are not pure private value auctions. In non-private value auctions with at least three bidders, the English auction (especially the open-exit variant) leads to higher revenue than the Vickrey auction. The reason is that other bidders willing to go high up in price causes a bidder to increase his own valuation of the auctioned item. In this type of auctions, both the English and the Vickrey protocols produce greater expected revenue to the auctioneer than the first-price sealed-bid auction—or its equivalent, the Dutch auction.

### 5.4.5   Bidder Collusion

One problem with all four of the auction protocols (English, Dutch, first-price sealed-bid, and Vickrey) is that they are not collusion proof. The bidders could coordinate their bid prices so that the bids stay artificially low. In this manner, the bidders get the item at a lower price than they normally would.

The English auction and the Vickrey auction actually self-enforce some of the most likely collusion agreements. Therefore, from the perspective of deterring collusion, the first-price sealed-bid and the Dutch auctions are preferable. The following example from [54] shows this. Let bidder Smith have value 20, and every other bidder have value 18 for the auctioned item. Say that the bidders collude by deciding that Smith will bid 6, and everyone else will bid 5. In an English auction this is self-enforcing, because if one of the other agents exceeds 5, Smith will observe this, and will be willing to go all the way up to 20, and the cheater will not gain anything from breaking the coalition agreement. In the Vickrey auction, the collusion agreement can just as well be that Smith bids 20, because Smith will get the item for 5 anyway. Bidding 20 removes the incentive from any bidder to break the coalition agreement by bidding between 5 and 18, because no such bid would win the auction. On the other hand, in a first-price sealed-bid auction, if Smith bids anything below 18, the other agents have an incentive to bid higher than Smith's bid because that would cause them to win the auction. The same holds for the Dutch auction.

However, for collusion to occur under the Vickrey auction, the first-price sealed-bid auction, or the Dutch auction, the bidders need to identify each other before the submission of bids—otherwise a non-member of the coalition could win the auction. On the other hand, in the English auction this is not necessary, because the bidders identify themselves by shouting bids. To prevent this, the auctioneer can organize a computerized English auction where the bidding process does not reveal the identities of the bidders.

### 5.4.6 Lying Auctioneer

Insincerity of the auctioneer may be a problem in the Vickrey auction. The auctioneer may overstate the second highest bid to the highest bidder unless that bidder can verify it. An overstated second offer would give the highest bidder a higher bill than he would receive if the auctioneer were truthful. Cheating by the auctioneer has been suggested to be one of the main reasons why the Vickrey auction protocol has not been widely adopted in auctions among humans [58]. To solve the problem, cryptographic electronic signatures could be used by the bidders so that the auctioneer could actually present the second best bid to the winning bidder—and would not be able to alter it. The other three auction protocols (English, Dutch, and first-price sealed-bid) do not suffer from lying by the auctioneer because the highest bidder gets the item at the price of his bid.

In non-private value auctions with the English (or all-pay) auction protocol, the auctioneer can use *shills* that bid in the auction in order to make the real bidders increase their valuations of the item. This is not possible in the sealed-bid protocols or the Dutch protocol, because the bidders do not observe the others' bids.

The auctioneer may also have other tools at his disposal. For example, he may place a bid himself to guarantee that the item will not be sold below a certain price (this can also be achieved by having a reservation price which may or may not be public to the bidders). However, for example in the Vickrey auction, the auctioneer is motivated to bid more than his true reservation price. This is because there is a chance that his bid will be second highest in which case it determines the item's price. Such overbidding leads to the possibility that the auctioneer ends up inefficiently keeping the item even though some bidders' valuations exceed his true reservation price.

### 5.4.7  Bidders Lying in Non-Private-Value Auctions

Most auctions are not pure private value auctions: an agent's valuation of a good depends at least in part on the other agents' valuations of that good. For example in contracting settings, a bidder's evaluation of a task is affected by the prices at which the agent can subcontract the task or parts of it out to other agents. This type of recontracting is commonly allowed in automated versions of the contract net protocol also [60, 77].

Common value (and correlated value) auctions suffer from the *winner's curse*. If an agent bids its valuation and wins the auction, it will know that its valuation was too high because the other agents bid less. Therefore winning the auction amounts to a monetary loss. Knowing this in advance, agents should bid less than their valuations [42, 54]. This is the best strategy in Vickrey auctions also. So, even though the Vickrey auction promotes truthful bidding in private-value auctions, it fails to induce truthful bidding in most auction settings.

### 5.4.8  Undesirable Private Information Revelation

Because the Vickrey auction has truthful bidding as the dominant strategy in private value auctions, agents often bid truthfully. This leads to the bidders revealing their true valuations. Sometimes this information is sensitive, and the bidders would prefer not to reveal it. For example, after winning a contract with a low bid, a company's subcontractors figure out that the company's production cost is low, and therefore the company is making larger profits than the subcontractors thought. It has been observed that when such auction results are revealed, the subcontractors will want to renegotiate their deals to get higher payoff [58]. This has been suggested—along with the problem of a lying auctioneer—as one of the main reasons why the Vickrey auction protocol is not widely used in auctions among humans [58]. First-price auction protocols do not expose a bidder's valuation as clearly because the bid is based on the agent's model of other bidders, and this (possibly inaccurate) model is not known by the subcontractors. Therefore, these auction types may be more desirable than the Vickrey auction when valuations are sensitive.

### 5.4.9  Roles of Computation in Auctions

Auction theory does not usually study the computational aspects of auctions. However, from a DAI perspective they are crucial. Two issues that arise from computation in auctions will be discussed: the computationally complex lookahead that arises when auctioning interrelated items one at a time, and the implications of costly local marginal cost (valuation) computation or information gathering in a single-shot auction.

### Inefficient Allocation and Lying in Interrelated Auctions

In addition to single-item auctions, Vickrey auctions have been widely studied in the allocation of multiple items of a homogeneous good [42], and the dominance of truth-teling can be maintained. However, the case of auctioning heterogeneous interrelated goods has received less attention. This is the setting of many real world problems, including several where computational agents are used [66, 68, 67, 60, 62, 56].

This section discusses cases where heterogeneous items are auctioned one at a time, and an agent's valuations of these items are interdependent (not additive). This occurs for example in task allocation in transportation problems. Figure 5.2 presents a simple example of such a problem with two delivery tasks: $t_1$ and $t_2$. Task $t_1$ is auctioned before $t_2$. The auctioneer wants to get the tasks handled while paying agents 1 and 2 as little as possible for handling them. The initial locations of the two agents are presented in the figure. To handle a task, an agent needs to move to the beginning of the delivery task (arrow), and take a parcel from there to the end of the arrow. An agent's movement incurs the same cost irrespective of whether it is carrying a parcel. The agents need not return to their initial locations. The costs for handling tasks (subscripted by the name of the agent) can be measured from the figure: $c_1(\{t_1\}) = 2$, $c_1(\{t_2\}) = 1$, $c_1(\{t_1, t_2\}) = 2$, $c_2(\{t_1\}) = 1.5$, $c_2(\{t_2\}) = 1.5$, and $c_2(\{t_1, t_2\}) = 2.5$. Say that these costs are common knowledge to the agents. Clearly the globally optimal allocation is the one where agent 1 handles both tasks.

This allocation is not reached if agents treat the auctions independently and bid truthfully [61]. In the first auction of the example, task $t_1$ is allocated. Agent 1 bids $c_1(\{t_1\}) = 2$, and agent 2 bids $c_2(\{t_1\}) = 1.5$. The task is allocated to agent 2. In the second auction, task $t_2$ is allocated. Agent 1 bids $c_1(\{t_2\}) = 1$, and agent 2 bids $c_2(\{t_2\}) = 1.5$, so $t_2$ is allocated to agent 1. The resulting allocation of the two tasks is suboptimal. If agent 2 takes the ownership of $t_1$ into account when bidding for $t_2$, then it will bid $c_2(\{t_1, t_2\}) - c_2(\{t_1\}) = 2.5 - 1.5 = 1$. In this case $t_2$ may be allocated to either agent. In both cases the resulting allocation of the two tasks is still suboptimal.

Alternatively, the agents could incorporate full lookahead into their auction strategies. This way the optimal allocation is reached, but agents do not bid their true per-item costs [61]. In the last auction of the example, an agent is best off bidding its own costs that takes into account the tasks that the agent

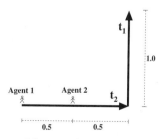

**Figure 5.2** Small example problem with two agents and two delivery tasks.

already has. Let us look at the auction of $t_2$. If agent 1 has $t_1$, it will bid $c_1(\{t_1, t_2\}) - c_1(\{t_1\}) = 2 - 2 = 0$, and $c_1(\{t_2\}) = 1$ otherwise. If agent 2 has $t_1$, it will bid $c_2(\{t_1, t_2\}) - c_2(\{t_1\}) = 2.5 - 1.5 = 1$, and $c_2(\{t_2\}) = 1.5$ otherwise. So, if agent 1 has $t_1$, it will win $t_2$ at the price 1.5, and get a payoff of $1.5 - 0 = 1.5$ in the second auction, while agent 2 gets zero. On the other hand, if agent 2 has $t_1$, the bids for $t_2$ are equal, and both agents get a zero payoff in the second auction irrespective of who $t_2$ gets allocated to. Therefore it is known that getting $t_1$ in the first auction is worth an extra 1.5 to agent 1 while nothing extra to agent 2. So, in the auction for $t_1$, agent 1's dominant strategy is to bid $c_1(\{t_1\}) - 1.5 = 2 - 1.5 = 0.5$. This is lower than agent 2's bid $c_2(\{t_1\}) - 0 = 1.5 - 0 = 1.5$, so agent one gets $t_1$. In the second auction agent 1 gets $t_2$ as discussed above. So the globally optimal allocation is reached. However, agent 1 bids 0.5 for $t_1$ instead of 2, which would be the truthful bid if the auctions were treated independently without lookahead.

Put together, lookahead is a key feature in auctions of multiple interrelated items. To date it has not been adequately addressed in computational multiagent systems that use Vickrey auctions, and it is a common misunderstanding that Vickrey auctions promote single-shot truth-telling even in interrelated auctions. In auctions by humans, such interrelationships are sometimes addressed by allowing a bidder to pool all of the interrelated items under one *entirety bid* [42]. Another method for enhancing the efficiency of interrelated auctions is to allow agents to backtrack from commitments by paying penalties. This allows a winning agent to beneficially decommit from an auctioned item in case that agent does not get synergic items from other related auctions [41, 67, 62]. This question will be revisited in Section 5.7.

While avoidance of counterspeculation was one of the original reasons suggested for adopting the Vickrey auction, lookahead requires speculation in the sense of trying to guess which items are going to be auctioned in the future, and which agents are going to win those auctions. Other speculative issues in sequential Vickrey auctions have been discussed for example in [28].

Even under complete information, the computational cost of full lookahead (searching the game tree which is deep if there are many items to be auctioned sequentially) may be prohibitively great. Further work is required to devise methods for controlling the search: the advantages of (partial) lookahead should be traded off against the cost.

### Counterspeculation When Computing One's Valuation

Sometimes even the Vickrey auction protocol fails to avoid counterspeculation—even in a single-shot auction. Let us look at a situation where an agent has uncertainty regarding its own valuation of the auction item, but can pay to remove this uncertainty. This situation often occurs among computational agents, where the value of a good (or task contract [66, 68, 67, 60, 62, 56]) can only be determined via carrying out a costly computation—e.g. a solution of a combinatorial problem [60, 66]. Alternatively the payment can be viewed as the cost of solving a prediction problem, or as the cost of performing an information gathering action, or as the cost paid to an expert oracle.

### Theorem 5.7 Incentive to counterspeculate

In a single-shot private value Vickrey auction with uncertainty about an agent's own valuation, a risk neutral agent's best (deliberation or information gathering) action can depend on the other agents. It follows that (if counterspeculation is cheap enough) it is worth counterspeculating [61].

**Proof by example.** Let there be two bidders: 1 and 2. Let 1's valuation $v_1$ for the auctioned item be uniformly distributed between 0 and 1, i.e. agent 1 does not know its own valuation exactly. Let 2's exact valuation $v_2$ be common knowledge. Say $0 \leq v_2 < \frac{1}{2}$, which implies $E[v_1] > v_2$.

Let agent 1 have the choice of finding out its exact valuation $v_1$ before the auction by paying a cost $c$. Now, should agent 1 take this informative but costly action?

No matter what agent 1 chooses here, agent 2 will bid $v_2$ because bidding ones valuation is a dominant strategy in a single-shot private value Vickrey auction.

If agent 1 chooses not to pay $c$, agent 1 should bid $E[v_1] = \frac{1}{2}$, because bidding ones expected valuation is a risk neutral agent's dominant strategy in a single-shot private value Vickrey auction. Now agent 1 gets the item at price $v_2$. If agent 1's valuation $v_1$ turns out to be less than $v_2$, agent 1 will suffer a loss. Agent 1's expected payoff is

$$E[\pi_{noinfo}] = \int_0^1 v_1 - v_2 dv_1 = \frac{1}{2} - v_2$$

If agent 1 chooses to pay $c$ for the exact information, it should bid $v_1$ because bidding ones valuation is a dominant strategy in a single-shot private value Vickrey auction. Agent 1 gets the item if *and only if* $v_1 \geq v_2$. Note that now the agent has no chance of suffering a loss, but on the other hand it has invested $c$ in the information. Agent 1's expected payoff is

$$E[\pi_{info}] = \int_0^{v_2} -cdv_1 + \int_{v_2}^1 v_1 - v_2 - cdv_1 = \frac{1}{2}v_2^2 - v_2 + \frac{1}{2} - c$$

Agent 1 should choose to buy the information iff

$$E[\pi_{info}] \geq E[\pi_{noinfo}]$$
$$\Leftrightarrow \frac{1}{2}v_2^2 - v_2 + \frac{1}{2} - c \geq \frac{1}{2} - v_2$$
$$\Leftrightarrow \frac{1}{2}v_2^2 \geq c$$
$$\Leftrightarrow v_2 \geq \sqrt{2c} \qquad \text{(because } v_2 \geq 0\text{)}$$

So, agent 1's best choice of action depends on agent 2's valuation $v_2$. Therefore, agent 1 can benefit from counterspeculating agent 2. ∎

## 5.5   Bargaining

In a *bargaining* setting, agents can make a mutually beneficial agreement, but have a conflict of interest about which agreement to make. In classical microeconomics, assumptions of monopoly (or monopsony) or perfect competition are often made. A monopolist gets all of the gains from interaction while an agent facing perfect competition can make no profit. Real world settings usually consist of a finite number of competing agents, so neither monopoly nor perfect competition assumptions strictly apply. Bargaining theory fits in this gap [50]. There are two major subfields of bargaining theory: axiomatic and strategic.

### 5.5.1   Axiomatic Bargaining Theory

Unlike noncooperative (strategic) game theory, *axiomatic bargaining theory* does not use the idea of a solution concept where the agents' strategies form some type of equilibrium. Instead, desirable properties for a solution, called axioms of the bargaining solution, are postulated, and then the solution concept that satisfies these axioms is sought [50, 30, 54, 51].

The *Nash bargaining solution* is a historically early solution concept that uses this approach. Nash analyzed a 2-agent setting where the agents have to decide on an outcome $o \in O$, and the fallback outcome $o_{fallback}$ occurs if no agreement is reached. There is a utility function $u_i : O \rightarrow \Re$ for each agent $i \in [1,2]$. It is assumed that that the set of feasible utility vectors $\{(u_1(o), u_2(o)) | o \in O\}$ is convex. This occurs, for example, if outcomes include all possible lotteries over actual alternatives.

When many deals are individually rational—i.e. have higher utility than the fallback—to both agents, multiple Nash equilibria often exist. For example, if the agents are bargaining over how to split a dollar, all splits that give each agent more than zero are in equilibrium. If agent one's strategy is to offer $\rho$ and no more, agent two's best response is to take the offer as opposed to the fallback which is zero. Now, one's best response to this is to offer $\rho$ and no more. Thus, a Nash equilibrium exists for any $\rho$ that defines a contract that is individually rational for both agents, and feasible ($0 < \rho < 1$). Due to the nonuniqueness of the equilibrium, a stronger (axiomatic) solution concept such as the Nash bargaining solution is needed to prescribe a unique solution.

The axioms of the Nash bargaining solution $u^* = (u_1(o^*), u_2(o^*))$ are:

- Invariance: The agents' numeric utility functions really only represent ordinal preferences among outcomes—the actual cardinalities of the utilities do not matter. Therefore, it should be possible to transform the utility functions in the following way: for any strictly increasing linear function $f$, $u^*(f(o), f(o_{fallback})) = f(u^*(o, o_{fallback}))$.

- Anonymity (symmetry): switching labels on the players does not affect the outcome.

- Independence of irrelevant alternatives: if some outcomes $o$ are removed, but $o^*$ is not, then $o^*$ still remains the solution.

- Pareto efficiency: it is not feasible to give both players higher utility than under $u^* = (u_1(o^*), u_2(o^*))$.

### *Theorem 5.8   Nash bargaining solution*
The unique solution that satisfies these four axioms is [47]:

$$o^* = \arg\max_{o}[u_1(o) - u_1(o_{fallback})][u_2(o) - u_2(o_{fallback})]$$

The Nash bargaining solution can be directly extended to more than two agents, as long as the fallback occurs if at least one agent disagrees. The 2-agent Nash bargaining solution is also the 2-agent special case of the Shapley value—a particular solution concept for payoff division in coalition formation, discussed later in Section 5.8.3—where coalitions of agents can cooperate even if all agents do not agree.

Other bargaining solutions also exist. They postulate different desiderata as axioms and arrive at a different utility combination as the outcome [30].

### 5.5.2   Strategic Bargaining Theory

Unlike axiomatic bargaining theory, *strategic bargaining theory* does not postulate desiderata as axioms on the solution concept. Instead, the bargaining situation is modeled as a game, and the solution concept is based on an analysis of which of the players' strategies are in equilibrium. It follows that for some games, the solution is not unique. On the other hand, strategic bargaining theory explains the behavior of rational utility maximizing agents better than axiomatic approaches. The latter are not based on what the agents can choose for strategies, but instead rely on the agents pertaining to axiomatic, imposed notions of fairness.

Strategic bargaining theory usually analyses sequential bargaining where agents alternate in making offers to each other in a prespecified order [50, 54, 51, 35]. Agent 1 gets to make the first offer. As an example, one can again think of deciding how to split a dollar. In a protocol with a finite number of offers and no time discount, the unique payoffs of the subgame perfect Nash equilibria are such that the last offerer will get the whole dollar (minus $\epsilon$), because the other agent is better off accepting $\epsilon$ than by rejecting and receiving nothing. For simplicity in the rest of this section, say that in similar situations, $\epsilon$ can be zero, and the other agent will still accept.

A time discount factor $\delta$ can be incorporated in the model. In round 1 the dollar is worth 1, in round two it is worth $\delta$, in round three it is worth $\delta^2$, and so on. With time discount, a subgame perfect Nash equilibrium of a finite game of length $T$ can be solved starting from the end. For example, if $\delta = 0.9$, then Table 5.4 represents the offerer's maximal claims that are acceptable to the other agent. In the last round, 2 would again accept zero. However, in the next to last round, 2 could keep 0.1, because it knows that this is how much 1 would loose by waiting to the next round. The same reasoning works for the previous rounds.

| Round | 1's share | 2's share | Total value | Offerer |
|-------|-----------|-----------|-------------|---------|
| ⋮ | ⋮ | ⋮ | ⋮ | ⋮ |
| $T-3$ | 0.819 | 0.181 | $0.9^{T-4}$ | 2 |
| $T-2$ | 0.91 | 0.09 | $0.9^{T-3}$ | 1 |
| $T-1$ | 0.9 | 0.1 | $0.9^{T-2}$ | 2 |
| $T$ | 1 | 0 | $0.9^{T-1}$ | 1 |

**Table 5.4**   Offerer's maximal acceptable claims in a finite game.

| Round | 1's share | 2's share | Offerer |
|-------|-----------|-----------|---------|
| ⋮ | ⋮ | ⋮ | ⋮ |
| $t-2$ | $1 - \delta_2(1 - \delta_1\bar{\pi}_1)$ | | 1 |
| $t-1$ | | $1 - \delta_1\bar{\pi}_1$ | 2 |
| $t$ | $\bar{\pi}_1$ | | 1 |
| ⋮ | ⋮ | ⋮ | ⋮ |

**Table 5.5**   Offerer's maximal acceptable claims in an infinite game with different discount factors.

When the protocol in a non-discounted setting allows an infinite number of bargaining rounds, the solution concept is powerless because any split of the dollar can be supported in subgame perfect Nash equilibrium—just as in the single-shot case. On the other hand, with discounting, even the infinite game can be solved:

**Theorem 5.9 Rubinstein bargaining solution**
In a discounted infinite round setting, the subgame perfect Nash equilibrium outcome is unique. Agent 1 gets $(1 - \delta_2)/(1 - \delta_1\delta_2)$, where $\delta_1$ is 1's discount factor, and $\delta_2$ is 2's. Agent 2 gets one minus this. Agreement is reached in the first round [59].

**Proof**   Let us denote by $\bar{\pi}_1$ the maximum undiscounted share that 1 can get in any subgame perfect Nash equilibrium on his turn to offer. Following the same logic as in the example above, Table 5.5 can be filled. Now we have two ways to represent the maximum undiscounted share that 1 can get in any subgame perfect Nash equilibrium on his turn to offer. Setting them equal gives

$$\bar{\pi}_1 = 1 - \delta_2(1 - \delta_1\bar{\pi}_1) \Leftrightarrow \bar{\pi}_1 = \frac{1 - \delta_2}{1 - \delta_1\delta_2},$$

which is an upper bound for the undiscounted share that 1 can get in any subgame perfect Nash equilibrium on his turn to offer. But now we can go through the same argument by replacing $\bar{\pi}_1$ by $\underline{\pi}_1$, the minimum undiscounted share that 1 can get in any subgame perfect Nash equilibrium on his turn to offer. The minimum will equal the maximum, which completes the proof.  ∎

This proof technique allows one to solve for subgame perfect Nash equilibrium payoffs even though it is impossible to carry out complete lookahead in the game tree because it is infinitely long.

Another model of sequential bargaining does not use discounts, but assumes a fixed bargaining cost per negotiation round.

- If the agents have symmetric bargaining costs, the solution concept is again powerless because any split of the dollar can be supported in subgame perfect Nash equilibrium.

- If 1's bargaining cost $c_1$ is even slightly smaller than 2's cost $c_2$, then 1 gets the entire dollar. If 2 offered $\pi$ in round $t$, then in period $t-1$, 1 could offer $1-\pi-c_2$, and keep $\pi + c_2$ to himself. In round $t-2$, 2 would offer $\pi + c_2 - c_1$, and keep $1 - \pi - c_2 + c_1$. Following this reasoning, in round $t-2k$, agent 2 would get to keep $1 - \pi - k(c_2 - c_1)$ which approaches $-\infty$ as $k$ increases. Realizing this, 2 would not bargain, but accept zero up front.

- If 1's bargaining cost is greater than 2's, then 1 receives a payoff that equals the second agent's bargaining cost, and agent 2 receives the rest. Agreement is again reached on the first round. This case is equivalent to the previous case except that the agent with the smaller bargaining cost is willing to give the other agent $c_2$ in order to avoid going through the first period of bargaining.

Kraus et al. have extended the work on sequential bargaining to the case with outside options [34]. They also analyze the case where one agent gains and one loses over time. Finally, they discuss negotiation over time when agents do not know each others' types.

### 5.5.3   Computation in Bargaining

All of the bargaining models discussed above assume perfect rationality from the agents. No computation is required in finding a mutually desirable contract. The space of deals is assumed to be fully comprehended by the agents, and the value of each potential contract known. On the other hand, future work should focus on developing methods where the cost of search (deliberation) for solutions is explicit, and it is decision-theoretically traded off against the bargaining gains that the search provides. This becomes particularly important as the bargaining techniques are scaled up to combinatorial problems with a multidimensional negotiation space as opposed to combinatorially simple ones like splitting the dollar.

There are actually two searches occurring in bargaining. In the intra-agent *deliberative search*, an agent locally generates alternatives, evaluates them, counterspeculates, does lookahead in the negotiation process *etc.* In the inter-agent *committal search*, the agents make (binding) agreements with each other regarding the solution. The agreements may occur over one part of the solution at a time. The agreed issues provide context for more focused intra-agent deliberative search—thus reducing the amount of costly computation required. The committal search may also involve iteratively renegotiating some parts of the solution that have already been agreed on, but have become less desirable in light of the newer agreements regarding other parts of the solution [60]. The two-search model proposed here is similar to the Real-Time A* search where an agent has to trade off thorough deliberation against more real-world actions [33]. Similarly, in modeling bargaining settings that require nontrivial computations, each agent's strategy should incorporate both negotiation actions and deliberation actions. The bargaining setting is more complex than the single agent setting of Real-Time A* in that there are multiple self-interested agents: the agents' strategies should be in equilibrium.

## 5.6   General Equilibrium Market Mechanisms

This section presents *general equilibrium theory*, a microeconomic market framework that has recently been successfully adapted for and used in computational multiagent systems in many application domains [82, 83, 44, 85, 10]. General equilibrium theory provides a distributed method for efficiently allocating goods and resources among agents—i.e. striking the best tradeoffs in a moderately complex multidimensional search space—based on market prices.

Such a market has $n > 0$ *commodity goods* $g$. The commodities can be physicals, e.g. coffee and meat, or they can be more abstract, e.g. parameters of an airplane design [83], flows in a traffic network [82], electricity in a power network [85], or mirror sites on the Internet [44]. The amount of each commodity is unrestricted, and each commodity is assumed arbitrarily divisible (continuous as opposed to discrete). Different elements within a commodity are not distinguishable, but different commodities are distinguishable from each other. The market also has prices $\mathbf{p} = [p_1, p_2, \ldots, p_n]$, where $p_g \in \Re$ is the price for good $g$.

The market can have two types of agents, *consumers* and *producers*. Each consumer $i$ has a *utility function* $u_i(\mathbf{x_i})$ which encodes its preferences over different *consumption bundles* $\mathbf{x_i} = [x_{i1}, x_{i2}, \ldots, x_{in}]^T$, where $x_{ig} \in \Re_+$ is consumer $i$'s allocation of good $g$. Each consumer $i$ also has an initial *endowment* $\mathbf{e_i} = [e_{i1}, e_{i2}, \ldots, e_{in}]^T$, where $e_{ig} \in \Re$ is his endowment of commodity $g$.

The producers—if there are any—can use some commodities to produce others. Let $\mathbf{y_j} = [y_{j1}, y_{j2}, \ldots, y_{jn}]^T$ be the *production vector*, where $y_{jg}$ is the amount of good $g$ that producer $j$ produces. Net usage of a commodity is denoted by a negative number. A producer's capability of turning inputs into outputs is characterized by its *production possibilities set* $Y_j$, which is the set of feasible production vectors. The *profit* of producer $j$ is $\mathbf{p} \cdot \mathbf{y_j}$, where $\mathbf{y_j} \in Y_j$. The producer's profits are divided among the consumers according to predetermined proportions which need not be equal (one can think of the consumers owning stocks of the producers). Let $\theta_{ij}$ be the fraction of producer $j$ that consumer $i$ owns. The producers' profits are divided among consumers according to these shares. However, the consumers are assumed to have no say-so in the producers' production decisions.

Prices may change, and the agents may change their consumption and production plans, but actual production and consumption only occur once the market has reached a *general equilibrium*. We say that $(\mathbf{p}^*, \mathbf{x}^*, \mathbf{y}^*)$ is a general (Walrasian) equilibrium if

**I** markets clear:

$$\sum_i \mathbf{x_i^*} = \sum_i \mathbf{e_i} + \sum_j \mathbf{y_j^*}, \text{ and}$$

**II** each consumer $i$ maximizes its preferences given the prices:

$$\mathbf{x_i^*} = \arg \max_{\mathbf{x_i} \in \Re_+^n \ | \ \mathbf{p}^* \cdot \mathbf{x_i} \leq \mathbf{p}^* \cdot \mathbf{e_i} + \sum_j \theta_{ij} \mathbf{p}^* \cdot \mathbf{y_j}} u_i(\mathbf{x_i}), \text{ and}$$

**III** each producer $j$ maximizes its profits given the prices:

$$\mathbf{y_j^*} = \arg \max_{\mathbf{y_j} \in Y_j} \mathbf{p}^* \cdot \mathbf{y_j}$$

### 5.6.1   Properties of General Equilibrium

General equilibrium solutions have some very desirable properties:

***Theorem 5.10  Pareto efficiency***
Each general equilibrium is Pareto efficient, i.e. no agent can be made better off without making some other agent worse off [39].

This means that there is no possible methodology for finding solutions to the agents' problem such that every agent is better off than in the general equilibrium. The solution is also stable against collusion:

***Theorem 5.11  Coalitional stability***
Each general equilibrium with no producers is stable in the sense of the *core* solution concept of coalition formation games: no subgroup of consumers can increase their utilities by pulling out of the equilibrium and forming their own market [39].

The situation is more complex when producers are present: for example, if a set of consumers colludes, and they own part of a producer via the shares, what can the coalition produce?

Unfortunately, in some domains no general equilibrium exists. For example, it may be best for some producer to produce an infinite amount of some good. However, sufficient conditions for existence are known:

***Theorem 5.12  Existence***
Let the production possibilities sets be closed (i.e. include their boundaries), convex (i.e. if bundles $y$ and $y'$ are producible, then so is $\alpha y + (1 - \alpha) y'$  $\forall \alpha \in [0, 1]$),

and bounded above (i.e. an infinite amount of no good can be produced). Let the consumers' preferences be continuous (i.e. the preferences have no "jumps"), strictly convex (i.e. if the consumer prefers $y$ to $y''$ and $y'$ to $y''$, then he prefers $\alpha y + (1-\alpha)y'$ to $y'' \ \forall \alpha \in [0,1]$), and strongly monotone (i.e. each consumer strictly prefers more to less of each commodity). Now, if a society-wide bundle is producible where the amount of each commodity is positive (positive endowments trivially imply this), a general equilibrium exists [39].

For example, economies of scale in production violate convexity of production possibilities. Continuity of the consumer's preferences is violated e.g. in bandwidth allocation if an agent's welfare jumps as the threshold for being able to participate in a video conference is reached. Similarly, the consumer's preferences are not convex if the consumer starts to prefer a good (relative to other goods) more as he gets more of that good. Drugs and Web surfing are examples of this.

Even if a general equilibrium exists, it might not be unique. However, there is an easily understood sufficient condition for uniqueness:

**Theorem 5.13 Uniqueness under gross substitutes**
A general equilibrium is unique if the society-wide demand for each good is nondecreasing in the prices of the other goods [39].

For example, as the price of meat increases, consumers have to convert to satisfying their hunger with less expensive foods. It follows that the demand of potatoes increases. On the other hand, the conditions of this theorem are not always met. For example, as the price of bread increases, the demand of butter decreases. Complementarities are also very common in production, where the producers often need all of the inputs to create the outputs.

The basic general equilibrium framework does not account for *externalities*. In *consumption externalities*, one agent's consumption affects another agent's utility. In *production externalities*, one agent's production possibilities set is directly affected by another agent's actions. Glance and Hogg have presented examples of computational ecologies (not based on general equilibrium theory) where externalities are so dominant that, counterintuitively, adding resources to the system makes it operate less efficiently [19]. Hogg has also shown that externality problems are likely to be common in computational ecosystems [23]. Evolutionary aspects of such systems have also been discussed [43], and the behaviors under incomplete and delayed information analyzed [26]. Some mechanisms to attack externality problems include taxes and viewing some of the externality issues as commodities themselves [79].

### 5.6.2 Distributed Search for a General Equilibrium

The operational motivation behind market mechanisms is that the agents can find an efficient joint solution—which takes into account tradeoffs between agents and the fact that the values of different goods to a single agent may be interdependent—

Algorithm for the price adjustor:
  $p_g = 1$ for all $g \in [1..n]$
  Set $\lambda_g$ to a positive number for all $g \in [1..n-1]$
  Repeat
      Broadcast $\mathbf{p}$ to consumers and producers
      Receive a production plan $\mathbf{y_j}$ from each producer $j$
      Broadcast the plans $\mathbf{y_j}$ to consumers
      Receive a consumption plan $\mathbf{x_i}$ from each consumer $i$
      For $g = 1$ to $n - 1$
          $p_g = p_g + \lambda_g(\sum_i (x_{ig} - e_{ig}) - \sum_j y_{jg})$
  Until $|\sum_i (x_{ig} - e_{ig}) - \sum_j y_{jg}| < \epsilon$ for all $g \in [1..n]$
  Inform consumers and producers that an equilibrium has been reached
Algorithm for consumer $i$:
  Repeat
      Receive $\mathbf{p}$ from the adjustor
      Receive a production plan $\mathbf{y_j}$ for each $j$ from the adjustor
      Announce to the adjustor a consumption plan $\mathbf{x_i} \in \Re^n_+$ that
          maximizes $u_i(\mathbf{x_i})$ given the budget constraint $\mathbf{p} \cdot \mathbf{x_i} \le \mathbf{p} \cdot \mathbf{e_i} + \sum_j \theta_{ij} \mathbf{p} \cdot \mathbf{y_j}$
  Until informed that an equilibrium has been reached
  Exchange and consume
Algorithm for producer $j$:
  Repeat
      Receive $\mathbf{p}$ from the adjustor
      Announce to the adjustor a production plan $\mathbf{y_j} \in Y_j$ that maximizes $\mathbf{p} \cdot \mathbf{y_j}$
  Until informed that an equilibrium has been reached
  Exchange and produce

**Algorithm 5.2**  The distributed price tâtonnement algorithm.

while never centralizing all the information or control. There are many algorithms that can be used to search for a general equilibrium, some centralized, and some decentralized. The most common decentralized algorithm for this purpose is the *price tâtonnement process*, (Algorithm 5.2) which is a steepest descent search method.

Clearly, if no general equilibrium exists, no algorithm can find it. Furthermore, sometimes the price tâtonnement algorithm fails to find an equilibrium even if equilibria exist. However, there are sufficient conditions that guarantee that an equilibrium is found if it exists. One such sufficient condition is the gross substitutes property which was used in Theorem. 5.13. More generally,

### Theorem 5.14  Convergence

The price tâtonnement algorithm convergences to a general equilibrium if $\mathbf{p}^* \cdot (\sum_i (\mathbf{x_i}(\mathbf{p}) - \mathbf{e_i}) - \sum_j \mathbf{y_j}(\mathbf{p})) > 0$ for all $\mathbf{p}$ not proportional to an equilibrium price vector $\mathbf{p}^*$ [39].

Strictly speaking, these convergence guarantees only apply to the continuous variant

$$\frac{dp_g}{dt} = \lambda_g \Big( \sum_i (x_{ig}(\mathbf{p}) - e_{ig}) - \sum_j y_{jg}(\mathbf{p}) \Big),$$

not to the more realistic discrete step version (Algorithm 5.2). However, these results suggest that even the discrete variant often converges—e.g. under gross substitutes—as long as the $\lambda$-multipliers in the algorithm are sufficiently small. If the $\lambda$-multipliers are too large, the search may keep "overshooting" the equilibrium. On the other hand, too small $\lambda$-multipliers will make the convergence slow. One potential solution to this problem is to dynamically adjust the step size, e.g. via the Newton method

$$\frac{dp_g}{dt} = -\lambda_g [J(\mathbf{p})]^{-1} \Big( \sum_i (x_{ig}(\mathbf{p}) - e_{ig}) - \sum_j y_{jg}(\mathbf{p}) \Big), \text{ where}$$

$$J(\mathbf{p}) = \begin{bmatrix} \dfrac{\partial(\sum_i (x_{i1}(\mathbf{p}) - e_{i1}) - \sum_j y_{j1}(\mathbf{p}))}{\partial p_1} & \cdots & \dfrac{\partial(\sum_i (x_{i1}(\mathbf{p}) - e_{i1}) - \sum_j y_{j1}(\mathbf{p}))}{\partial p_n} \\ \vdots & & \vdots \\ \dfrac{\partial(\sum_i (x_{in}(\mathbf{p}) - e_{in}) - \sum_j y_{jn}(\mathbf{p}))}{\partial p_1} & \cdots & \dfrac{\partial(\sum_i (x_{in}(\mathbf{p}) - e_{in}) - \sum_j y_{jn}(\mathbf{p}))}{\partial p_n} \end{bmatrix}$$

The Newton method often requires fewer iterations than steepest descent, but each iteration is computationally more intensive for the adjustor, and requires the computation and communication of the derivative information by the consumers and producers. One could conceptually take this information communication to the limit by having the producers and consumers submit their entire production and consumption functions (plans as a function of the possible price vectors), and the price adjustor could run a centralized search—with known efficient algorithms— for an equilibrium. However, this conflicts with one of the original motivations of market mechanisms: decentralization.

The tâtonnement process used in the WALRAS simulation [82] differs from Algorithm 5.2. WALRAS uses asynchronous declarations by the agents, i.e. an agent might only change its plan regarding a subset of goods at a time. Similarly, agents might take arbitrary turns in making new declarations. Under certain conditions, this process still converges to a general equilibrium [10]. As in tâtonnement, trades in WALRAS only occur after the market process has arrived (close) to a general equilibrium.

In addition to price-based market mechanisms, quantity-based (commodity-based, resource-based) mechanisms exist for reaching the general equilibrium [39]. In those mechanisms, the adjustor announces production and consumption plans, and the producers and consumers announce willingness to pay in terms of prices or marginal utilities. Unlike price-based algorithms, quantity-based algorithms maintain a feasible solution (once—e.g. up front—a feasible solution has been found) where markets clear at every iteration. This constitutes an interruptible anytime algorithm. Also, quantity-based algorithms offer the choice of carrying out the actual exchanges at every iteration or only at the end as in price-based algorithms. These advantages come at the cost of increased information centralization (communication). For example, the adjustor needs to know the production possibilities sets.

Most treatments of market-based search only discuss the complexity of finding an equilibrium once the agent's supply and demand functions are known. However, it may be computationally complex for each agent to generate its optimal supply/demand decision given the current prices. For example, if the agent is a manufacturer, it may need to solve several planning and scheduling problems just to construct its production possibilities set from which it has to choose the profit maximizing production plan. Furthermore, each agent has to go through this local deliberation at every iteration of the market protocol because prices change, and that affects what the optimal plan for each agent is.

### 5.6.3   Speculative Strategies in Equilibrium Markets

In general equilibrium markets, the agents are assumed to act *competitively*: they treat prices as exogenous. This means that each agent makes and reveals its demand (supply) decisions truthfully so as to maximize its utility (profit) given the market prices—assuming that it has no impact on those prices. The idea behind this *price-taking assumption* is that the market is so large that no single agent's actions affect the prices. However, this is paradoxical since the agents' declarations completely determine the prices. The price-taking assumption becomes valid as the number of agents approaches infinity: with infinitely many agents (of comparable size), each agent is best off acting competitively since it will not affect the prices.

However, in markets with a finite number of agents, an agent can act strategically, and potentially achieve higher utility by over/under representing [69], [38, pp. 220-223], [27]. In doing so, the agent has to speculate how its misrepresentation affects the market prices, which are simultaneously affected by how other agents respond to the prices which changed due to the first agent's strategic actions. In other words, general equilibria do not in general correspond to strictly rational, strategic equilibria of game theory.

This section is based on [69]. We analyze how much an agent can gain by speculation. Standard lies are also presented via which an agent can drive the market to a solution that maximizes the agent's gains from speculation, and looks like a general equilibrium to the other agents and the adjustor. These results are independent of the market algorithm as long as actual exchanges take place only after the market has reached (close to) an equilibrium.

#### Case A: Speculating Consumer

The goal of a self-interested consumer is to find the consumption bundle that maximizes its utility. To find the optimal bundle when acting in an equilibrium market, the consumer must speculate how other agents respond to prices. This is because its demand decisions affect the prices, which affect the demand and supply decisions of others, which again affect the prices that the consumer faces. Using the model of other agents, the consumer computes its optimal demand decisions. Note that other agents might also be speculating (in the same way or some other, suboptimal way). That is included in the agent's model of the other agents. A solution to the following maximization problem gives the highest utility that a speculating consumer $s$ can possibly obtain.

$$\max_{\mathbf{p}} \ u_s(\mathbf{x_s}(\mathbf{p})) \ \text{ s.t.} \tag{5.1}$$

$x_{sg}(\mathbf{p}) \geq 0$ (consumer does not produce)

$$x_{sg}(\mathbf{p}) = e_{sg} - \Big( \sum_{i \in \text{Consumers}-\{s\}} (x_{ig} - e_{ig}) - \sum_j y_{jg} \Big) \ \text{ (supply meets demand)}$$

$$\mathbf{p} \cdot (\mathbf{x_s} - \mathbf{e_s}) \leq \sum_j \theta_{sj} \ \mathbf{p} \cdot \mathbf{y_j}(\mathbf{p}) \ \text{ (budget constraint)}$$

### Case B: Speculating Producer

The goal of a self-interested producer is to find the production vector that maximizes its profits. Again, this requires a model of how others react to prices because the producer's production decisions affect the prices, which affect the demand and supply decisions of others, which again affect the prices that the producer faces. A solution to the following maximization problem gives the highest profit that a speculating producer $s$ can possibly obtain.

$$\max_{\mathbf{p}} \ \mathbf{p} \cdot \mathbf{y}_s(\mathbf{p}) \ \text{ s.t.} \tag{5.2}$$

$\mathbf{y}_s(\mathbf{p}) \in Y_s$ (feasible production plan)

$$y_{sg} = \sum_i (x_{ig} - e_{ig}) - \sum_{j \in \text{Producers}-\{s\}} y_{jg} \ \text{ (supply meets demand)}$$

The last equality turns into $\geq$ if free disposal for both inputs and outputs is possible.

The solution to the applicable optimization problem above (depending on whether the speculator is a producer or a consumer) is denoted $\mathbf{p}^{**}$. The equilibrium at $p^{**}$ is not Pareto efficient in general. This does not violate Theorem. 5.10 because that result only applies to true general equilibria where agents act competitively.

### Reaching Equilibrium under Speculation: Driving the Market

The discussion above focused on the prices that a speculating agent would like to drive the market to. However, there is a risk for the speculator that even though such an equilibrium exists, the market algorithm would not find it. A speculating agent's best strategy is to declare demand plans $\mathbf{x_s}(\mathbf{p})$ (or production plans $\mathbf{y_s}(\mathbf{p})$) such that the market clears at the desired prices $\mathbf{p}^{**}$ (an equilibrium exists), and the market process will find it. Formally, the market clears at $\mathbf{p}^{**}$ if for each good $g$,

$$x_{sg}(\mathbf{p}^{**}) = e_{sg} - ( \sum_{i \in \text{Consumers} - \{s\}} (x_{ig}(\mathbf{p}^{**}) - e_{ig}) - \sum_j y_{jg}(\mathbf{p}^{**})) \text{ if } s \text{ is a consumer, and}$$

$$y_{sg}(\mathbf{p}^{**}) = \sum_i (x_{ig}(\mathbf{p}^{**}) - e_{ig}) - \sum_{j \in \text{Producers} - \{s\}} y_{jg}(\mathbf{p}^{**}) \text{ if } s \text{ is a producer.}$$

What remains to be analyzed is whether the particular market algorithms finds the equilibrium even if the speculator acts strategically. Many standard market algorithms, e.g. price tâtonnement, Newtonian price tâtonnement, and WALRAS, are guaranteed to find the equilibrium if $\partial(\sum_i(x_{ig}(\mathbf{p}) - e_{ig}) - \sum_j y_{jg}(\mathbf{p}))/\partial p_g < 0$ (society-wide demand decreases as price increases), and $\partial(\sum_i(x_{ig}(\mathbf{p}) - e_{ig}) - \sum_j y_{jg}(\mathbf{p}))/\partial p_h \geq 0$, for goods $g \neq h$ (goods are gross substitutes). Let us assume that these two conditions would hold in the market if the speculator were not present. Now, if the speculating agent uses a strategy that satisfies

- Eq. 5.6.3, and
- $\partial(x_{sg}(\mathbf{p}) - e_{sg})/\partial p_g \leq 0$ if $s$ is a consumer, and $\partial y_{sg}(\mathbf{p})/\partial p_g \geq 0$ if $s$ is a producer, and
- for goods $g \neq h$, $\partial(x_{sg}(\mathbf{p}) - e_{sg})/\partial p_h \geq 0$ if $s$ is a consumer, and $\partial y_{sg}(\mathbf{p})/\partial p_h \leq 0$ if $s$ is a producer,

the market is guaranteed to converge to the unique equilibrium prices $\mathbf{p}^{**}$ that maximize the speculator's gain.

It turns out that simple generic strategies exist for the speculator that guarantee that these three conditions are met, i.e. that the speculator will be able to drive the market to an equilibrium where his maximal gain from speculation materializes [69]. For example, the following linear strategy is viable for a consumer:

$$\mathbf{x_s}(\mathbf{p}) = -\mathbf{e_s} + \mathbf{p}^{**} - \mathbf{p} - ( \sum_{i \in \text{Consumers} - \{s\}} (x_{ig}(\mathbf{p}^{**}) - e_{ig}) - \sum_j y_{jg}(\mathbf{p}^{**}))$$

and so is the constant strategy

$$\mathbf{x_s}(\mathbf{p}) = -\mathbf{e_s} - ( \sum_{i \in \text{Consumers} - \{s\}} (x_{ig}(\mathbf{p}^{**}) - e_{ig}) - \sum_j y_{jg}(\mathbf{p}^{**})).$$

The corresponding strategies for a speculating producer are

$$\mathbf{y_s}(\mathbf{p}) = \mathbf{p} - \mathbf{p}^{**} + \sum_i (x_{ig}(\mathbf{p}^{**}) - e_{ig}) - \sum_{j \in \text{Producers} - \{s\}} y_{jg}(\mathbf{p}^{**})$$

and

$$\mathbf{y_s}(\mathbf{p}) = \sum_i (x_{ig}(\mathbf{p}^{**}) - e_{ig}) - \sum_{j \in \text{Producers} - \{s\}} y_{jg}(\mathbf{p}^{**}).$$

The last consideration is the speed of convergence to equilibrium. In any particular market setting, it may be that the market converges slower or faster when an agent acts strategically than when he acts competitively.

### Strategic Behavior by Multiple Agents

In the analysis so far, one agent designed its speculative strategy while the others' strategies were fixed. However, the others would like to tailor their strategies to the specific strategy that the agent chooses. For this reason, we argue that strategic solution concepts from game theory should be used to design market protocols. The strategies are in Nash equilibrium if each agent's strategy is its best response to the others' strategies. This can be viewed as a necessary condition for system stability in settings where all agents act strategically.

A stronger condition is to require dominant strategy equilibrium, i.e. that each agent's strategy is optimal for that agent no matter what strategies others choose. Market protocols have been studied using dominant strategy equilibrium in [6]. The results are negative in the sense that the agents need to be given price ratios for trading in advance by the protocol designer, and the designer does not know the agents' preferences and capabilities. Therefore, not all beneficial trades can occur, and thus the solution is usually not Pareto efficient.

In sequential protocols, one can also strengthen the Nash equilibrium solution concept in multiple ways by requiring that the strategies stay in equilibrium at every step of the game [39, 35]. Unlike the market speculation analysis presented in this section so far, the Nash equilibrium outcome is specific to the market protocol. Important factors impacting the outcome are the order in which bids are submitted (see e.g. Stackleberg vs. Cournot models [39]), whether the bids are sealed or open [61], whether the protocol is iterative (the agents can change their excess demand between iterations) or not, whether the agents can decommit from their agreements by paying a penalty [67, 62], *etc.*

In some games, no Nash equilibrium exists for the market in pure (non-randomized) strategies. The following simple example illustrates this. Let there be two consumer agents, A and B, that engage in a market where they reveal their excess demand functions simultaneously and in a single round. Agent A can choose between two strategies (A1 and A2), and B can choose between B1 and B2. Provided that A knows that B will choose B1, A will choose A2, and A1 if B chooses B2. Provided that B knows that A will choose A2, B will choose B2, and B1 if A chooses A1. Now, from every possible pair of strategies, one agent would be motivated to deviate to another strategy, i.e. no Nash equilibrium exists. In general, existence and uniqueness of a general equilibrium (where agents act competitively) for a market does not imply existence and uniqueness of a Nash equilibrium.

Some market protocols may be difficult to analyze game theoretically. For example, in WALRAS, the agents might change their demand functions during the computation of the equilibrium. Then some agents may deliberately send false bids to generate more iterations of the market process in order to learn more about other agents' excess demand/supply functions. If many agents are involved in such probing, it seems that time becomes an important factor. Some agents might reveal progressively more of their competitive demands in order to speed up the convergence (as it might be urgent for them to get the resources traded), while others might extend the probing in order to maximize their benefit from the trade.[6]

While the game theoretic approach is clearly to be preferred (when it is viable) over the general equilibrium approach for designing interaction mechanisms for self-interested agents, the general equilibrium approach may still allow one to build reasonably nonmanipulable multiagent systems. For example, as the number of—comparably sized—agents increases, the gains from strategic acting decrease, approaching zero as the number of agents approaches infinity [55, 69]. Secondly, lack of knowledge about the others may make speculation unprofitable. If there is even minor uncertainty in the speculator's estimates about the others' strategies, the speculator's expected payoff may be significantly higher by acting competitively than by acting speculatively [69]. Finally, although beneficial lies are easy to compute once the others' strategies are known, it may be computationally complex to deduce the others' strategies even if the speculator knows the others' physical characteristics completely. For example, the speculator would need to solve a manufacturer's planning and scheduling problems in order to be able to deduce what the production possibilities sets of the manufacturer are, and what the manufacturer's (competitive) strategy will be. Sometimes the potential gains from speculation are not great enough to warrant such costly computation that may be required for speculation.

## 5.7   Contract Nets

General equilibrium market mechanisms use global prices, and—at least in the implementations up to now—use a single centralized mediator. The mediator might become a communication and computation bottleneck or a potential point of failure for the whole system. Also, in some settings the agents want to have direct control of who receives their sensitive information instead of posting the information to a mediator who controls its dissemination. Furthermore, sometimes it is unrealistic to assume that prices are global because there may be market frictions, costs to propagate information to all agents, *etc.* In such settings, a more distributed negotiation may be warranted.

The contract net protocol (see Chapter 2) was an early variant of such distributed

---

6. Some work has addressed non-competitive behavior in WALRAS [24], although there was only one speculating agent in the experiments, and this agent was limited to simple linear price prediction about how its actions affect the prices. Further analysis is required to determine whether its optimal strategy can be captured in this model. This need not be the case because the optimal strategy may involve some more "aggressive" behavior, e.g. the probing described above.

negotiation in a task allocation domain [77]. This section discusses some of the recent improvements to the contract net protocol. The new methods lead to better results, and they are viable among self-interested agents as well—unlike the original contract net protocol which was for cooperative agents only.

### 5.7.1   Task Allocation Negotiation

The capability of (re)allocating tasks among agents is a key feature in automated negotiation systems. In many domains, significant savings can be achieved by reallocating tasks among agents. Some tasks are inherently synergic, and should therefore be handled by the same agent. On the other hand, some tasks have negative interactions, in which case it is better to allocate them to different agents. Furthermore, different agents may have different resources which leads to different capabilities and costs for handling tasks. This section discusses task allocation among self-interested agents in the following model which captures the above considerations.

### Definition 5.1 [64]

A *task allocation problem* is defined by a set of tasks $T$, a set of agents $A$, a cost function $c_i : 2^T \rightarrow \Re \cup \{\infty\}$ (which states the cost that agent $i$ incurs by handling a particular subset of tasks), and the initial allocation of tasks among agents $\langle T_1^{init}, ..., T_{|A|}^{init} \rangle$, where $\bigcup_{i \in A} T_i^{init} = T$, and $T_i^{init} \cap T_j^{init} = \emptyset$ for all $i \neq j$. [7]

The original contract net and many of its later variants lacked a formal model for making bidding and awarding decisions. More recently, such a formal model was introduced which gives rise to a negotiation protocol that provably leads to desirable task allocations among agents [60, 62, 64]. In that model, contracting decisions are based on marginal cost calculations, i.e. that model invokes the concept of *individual rationality* on a per contract basis (which implies individual rationality of sequences of contracts). A contract is individually rational (IR) to an agent if that agent is better off with the contract than without it.

Specifically, a contractee $q$ accepts a contract if it gets paid more than its marginal cost

$$MC^{add}(T^{contract}|T_q) = c_q(T^{contract} \cup T_q) - c_q(T_q)$$

of handling the tasks $T^{contract}$ of the contract. The marginal cost is dynamic in the sense that it depends on the other tasks $T_q$ that the contractee already has.

Similarly, a contractor $r$ is willing to allocate the tasks $T^{contract}$ from its current task set $T_r$ to the contractee if it has to pay the contractee less than it saves by not

---

7. Although a static version of the problem is discussed, the contracting scheme works even if tasks and resources (resources affect the cost functions) are added and removed dynamically.

handling the tasks $T^{contract}$ itself:

$$MC^{remove}(T^{contract}|T_r) = c_r(T_r) - c_r(T_r - T^{contract}).$$

In the protocol, agents then suggest contracts to each other, and make their accepting/rejecting decisions based on these marginal cost calculations. An agent can take on both contractor and contractee roles. It can also recontract out tasks that it received earlier via another contract. The scheme does not assume that agents know the tasks or cost functions of others.

With this domain independent contracting scheme, the task allocation can only improve at each step. This corresponds to hill-climbing in the space of task allocations where the height-metric of the hill is social welfare $(-\sum_{i \in A} c_i(T_i))$. The fact that the contractor pays the contractee some amount between their marginal costs (e.g. half way between) causes the benefit from the improved task allocation to be divided so that no agent is worse off with a contract than without it.

The scheme is an *anytime algorithm*: contracting can be terminated at any time, and the worth (payments received from others minus cost of handling tasks) of each agent's solution increases monotonically. It follows that social welfare increases monotonically. Details on an asynchronous distributed implementation based on marginal costs can be found in [60, 62, 66].

### Convergence to the Globally Optimal Task Allocation

In most contract net implementations, each contract regards only one task , i.e. one task is moved from one agent to another against a payment [77, 72, 22]. Such an *original (O) contract* can be understood as a particular search operator in the global hill-climbing contracting algorithm that is used for task reallocation. When the contracting protocol is equipped with O-contracts only, it may get stuck in a local optimum where no contract is individually rational but the task allocation is not globally optimal.

To solve this problem, several new contract types have recently been introduced: *cluster (C) contracts* where a set of tasks is atomically contracted from one agent to another, *swap (S) contracts* where a pair of agents swaps a pair of tasks, and *multiagent (M) contracts* where more than two agents are involved in an atomic exchange of tasks [64, 62, 60]. Each of the four contract types avoids some of the local optima that the other three do not:

### Theorem 5.15

For each of the four contract types (O, C, S, and M), there exist task allocations where no IR contract with the other three contract types is possible, but an IR contract with the fourth type is [64].

Unfortunately, even if the contracting protocol is equipped with all four of the contract types, the globally optimal task allocation may not be reached via IR contracts—even if there were an oracle for choosing the sequence of contracts:

### Theorem 5.16

There are instances of the task allocation problem where no IR sequence from the initial task allocation to the optimal one exists using O-, C-, S- and M-contracts [64].

Clearly, no subset of the contract types suffices either. Another problem is that without an oracle, contracting may get stuck in a local optimum even if some IR sequence exists because the agents may choose some other IR sequence.

To address this shortcoming, a new contract type, *OCSM-contract*, has been defined, which combines the characteristics of O-, C-, S-, and M-contracts into one contract type—where the ideas of the four earlier contract types can be applied simultaneously (atomically):

### Definition 5.2 [64, 62]

An *OCSM-contract* is defined by a pair $\langle \mathbf{T}, \boldsymbol{\rho} \rangle$ of $|A| \times |A|$ matrices. An element $T_{i,j}$ is the set of tasks that agent $i$ gives to agent $j$, and an element $\rho_{i,j}$ is the amount that $i$ pays to $j$.

So OCSM contracts allow moving from a task allocation to any other task allocation with a single contract.

It could be shown that an IR sequence always exists from any task allocation to the optimal one if the contracting protocol incorporates OCSM-contracts. However, a stronger claim is now made. The following theorem states that OCSM-contracts are sufficient for reaching the global task allocation optimum in a finite number of contracts. The result holds for any sequence of IR OCSM-contracts, i.e. for any hill-climbing algorithm that uses OCSM-contracts: an oracle is not needed for choosing the sequence. This means that from the perspectives of social welfare maximization and of individual rationality, agents can accept IR contracts as they are offered. They need not wait for more profitable ones, and they need not worry that a current contract may make a more profitable future contract unprofitable. Neither do they need to accept contracts that are not IR in anticipation of future contracts that make the combination beneficial. Furthermore, these hill-climbing algorithms do not need to backtrack.

### Theorem 5.17

Let $|A|$ and $|T|$ be finite. If the contracting protocol allows OCSM-contracts, any hill-climbing algorithm (i.e. any sequence of IR contracts) finds the globally optimal task allocation in a finite number of steps (without backtracking) [64, 62].

***Proof*** With OCSM-contracts there are no local optima (that are not global optima) since the global optimum can be reached from any task allocation in a single contract. This last contract will be IR because moving to the optimum from some suboptimal allocation improves welfare, and this gain can be arbitrarily divided among the contract parties. Thus the algorithm will not run out of IR contracts before the optimum has been reached. With finite $|A|$ and $|T|$, there are only a finite number of task allocations. Since the algorithm hill-climbs, no task allocation will be repeated. Therefore, the optimum is reached in a finite number of contracts. ∎

OCSM-contracts are also necessary: no weaker set of contract types suffices—even if there were an oracle to choose the order in which to apply them:

### Theorem 5.18

If there is some OCSM-contract that the protocol does not allow, there are instances of the task allocation problem where no IR sequence exists from the initial allocation to the optimal one [64].

While OCSM-contracts are necessary in the general case, there may well be cost functions $c_i(\cdot)$ with special structure that guarantees that the global optimum is reached even with less powerful contract types.

Theorem 5.17 gives a powerful tool for problem instances where the number of possible task allocations is relatively small. On the other hand, for large problem instances, the number of contracts made before the optimal task allocation is reached may be impractically large—albeit finite. For example on a large-scale real-world distributed vehicle routing problem instance, the TRACONET [60] (marginal cost based) contracting system never reached even a local optimum even with just O-contracts—with multiple hours of negotiation on five Unix machines. Another problem is that although any OCSM-contract can be represented in $O(|A|^2 + |T|)$ space, the identification of welfare increasing contracts may be complex—especially in a distributed setting—because there are $\frac{v^2 - v}{2} = \frac{|A|^{2|T|} - |A|^{|T|}}{2}$ possible OCSM-contracts, and the evaluation of just one contract requires each contract party to compute the cost of handling its current tasks and the tasks allocated to it via the contract. With such large problem instances, one cannot expect to reach the global optimum in practice. Instead, the contracting should occur as long as there is time, and then have a solution ready: the anytime character of this contracting scheme becomes more important.

### Insincere Agents in Task Allocation

So far in this section on contracting it was assumed that agents act based on individual rationality. This differs from payoff maximizing agents of game theory. Such an agent may reject an IR contract e.g. if it believes that it could be better off by waiting for a more beneficial contract that cannot be accepted if the former contract is accepted (e.g. due to limited resources). Similarly, such an agent may accept a non-IR contract in anticipation of a synergic later contract that will make the combination beneficial. Furthermore, strategic agents can also speculate on the order of accepting contracts because different sequences of (IR) contracts may have different payoff to the agent. The IR approach is sometimes more practical than the full game theoretic analysis because each contract can be made by evaluating just a single contract (each contract party evaluating one new task set) instead of doing exponential lookahead into the future. The deviation from game theory comes at the cost of not being able to normatively guarantee that a self-interested agent is best off by following the strategy of accepting any IR contracts.

In this section on contracting it was also assumed that agents truthfully bid their marginal costs. However, an agent can benefit more in the contract payment by exaggerating its marginal cost. On the other hand, too much lying may cause some IR contracts to be perceived non-IR, and to be rejected. This issue of lying about the valuation was discussed in Section 5.4 on auctions.

Agents could also lie about what tasks they have. This type of lying has been thoroughly analyzed in a 2-agent task allocation setting [56]. The "Task Oriented Domains (TODs)" in that work are a strict subset of the task allocation problems presented here. Specifically, they assume that agents have symmetric cost functions ($c_i(T') = c_j(T')$) and that every agent is capable of handling all tasks of all agents, i.e. that the cost functions are always finite. The analysis is specific to a protocol where all agents reveal their costs for all possible task sets up front, the social welfare maximizing allocation is chosen, and then payoff is divided according to the Nash bargaining solution (Section 5.5.1). So their protocol is not an anytime algorithm: all task allocations have to be evaluated before any agreement is made.

How truthfully do agents reveal tasks to each other when each agent only knows about its own tasks? The domain class of TODs includes subclasses with very different properties regarding insincere task revelation. *Subadditive TODs* are TODs where $c_i(T' \cup T'') \leq c_i(T') + c_i(T'')$. A subclass of Subadditive TODs, *Concave TODs* are TODs where $c_i(T' \cup T''') - c_i(T') \geq c_i(T'' \cup T''') - c_i(T'')$. Finally, a subclass of Concave TODs, *Modular TODs* are TODs where $c_i(T' \cup T'') = c_i(T') + c_i(T'') - c_i(T' \cap T'')$.

Three alternative types of deals are analyzed. In *pure deals*, agents are deterministically allocated exhaustive, disjoint task sets. *Mixed deals* specify a probability distribution over such partitions. *All-or-nothing* deals are mixed deals where the alternatives only include partitions where one agent handles the tasks of all agents.

Three forms of lying are analyzed. First, an agent may *hide tasks* by not revealing them. Second, it may declare *phantom tasks* which do not exist and cannot be generated if another agent wants to see them. Finally, it may announce *decoy tasks*, which really did not exist, but which can be generated on demand. The forms of lying that are possible in different domain classes and with different deal types are summarized in Table 5.6. With more general TODs, many different lying methods can be profitable.

The analysis shows that even in the restricted settings, lying is often beneficial under the three variants of this protocol. Because these restricted domains are subproblems of more complex task allocation domains, the negative results carry over directly to the more complex settings. The results leave open the possibility that other protocols would demote lying more (while leading to Pareto efficient IR outcomes).

| Deal type | General TOD | | | SubadditiveTOD | | | Concave TOD | | | Modular TOD | | |
|---|---|---|---|---|---|---|---|---|---|---|---|---|
| | Hid | Pha | Dec | Hid | Pha | Dec | Hid | Pha | Dec | Hid | Pha | Dec |
| Pure | L | L | L | L | L | L | L | L | L | L | | |
| Mixed | L | | L | L | | L | L | | | L | | |
| All-or-nothing | - | - | - | | | L | | | | | | |

**Table 5.6**  Results on lying in task revelation. An 'L' indicates that lying of the specified type is profitable in some problem instances within the given domain class using the deal type. In general TODs using all-or-nothing deals, the negotiation set (set of individually rational Pareto efficient deals) may be empty.

### 5.7.2  Contingency Contracts and Leveled Commitment Contracts

In traditional multiagent negotiation protocols among self-interested agents, once a contract is made, it is binding, i.e. neither party can back out [56, 60, 64, 1, 14, 34, 69, 10]. Once an agent agrees to a contract, it has to follow through with it no matter how future events unravel. Although a contract may be profitable to an agent when viewed *ex ante*, it need not be profitable when viewed after some future events have occurred, i.e. *ex post*. Similarly, a contract may have too low expected payoff *ex ante*, but in some realizations of the future events, the same contract may be desirable when viewed *ex post*. Normal full commitment contracts are unable to efficiently take advantage of the possibilities that such—probabilistically known— future events provide.

On the other hand, many multiagent systems consisting of cooperative agents incorporate some form of decommitment possibility in order to allow the agents to accommodate new events. For example, in the original contract net protocol, the agent that had contracted out a task could send a termination message to cancel the contract even when the contractee had already partially fulfilled the contract. This was possible because the agents were not self-interested: the contractee did not mind losing part of its effort without a monetary compensation. Similarly, the role of decommitment possibilities among cooperative agents has been studied in meeting scheduling using a contracting approach [73]. Again, the agents did not require a monetary compensation for their efforts: an agent agreed to cancel a contract merely based on the fact that some other agent wanted to decommit. In such multiagent systems consisting of cooperative agents, each agent can be trusted to use such an externally imposed strategy even though using that strategy might not be in the agent's self-interest.

Some research in game theory has focused on utilizing the potential provided by probabilistically known future events by *contingency contracts* among self-interested agents. The obligations of the contract are made contingent on future events. There are games in which this method provides an expected payoff increase to both parties of the contract compared to any full commitment contract [53]. Also, some deals are enabled by contingency contracts in the sense that there is no full commitment contract that both agents prefer over their fallback positions, but there is a contingency contract that each agent prefers over its fallback.

There are at least three problems regarding the use of contingency contracts in automated negotiation among self-interested agents. Though useful in anticipating a small number of key events, contingency contracts get cumbersome as the number of relevant events to monitor from the future increases. In the limit, all domain events (changes in the domain problem, e.g. new tasks arriving or resources breaking down) and all negotiation events—contracts from other negotiations—can affect the value of the obligations of the original contract, and should therefore be conditioned on. Furthermore, these future events may not only affect the value of the original contract independently: the value of the original contract may depend on combinations of the future events [66, 60, 56]. Thus there is a potential combinatorial explosion of items to be conditioned on. Second, even if it were feasible to use such cumbersome contingency contracts among the computerized agents, it is often impossible to enumerate all possible relevant future events in advance. The third problem is that of verifying the unraveling of the events. Sometimes an event is only observable by one of the agents. This agent may have an incentive to lie to the other party of the contract about the event in case the event is associated with a disadvantageous contingency to the directly observing agent. Thus, to be viable, contingency contracts would require an event verification mechanism that is not manipulable and not prohibitively complicated or costly.

*Leveled commitment contracts* are another method for taking advantage of the possibilities provided by probabilistically known future events [67, 62, 2, 3]. Instead of conditioning the contract on future events, a mechanism is built into the contract that allows unilateral decommitting at any point in time. This is achieved by specifying in the contract decommitment penalties, one for each agent. If an agent wants to decommit—i.e. to be freed from the obligations of the contract—it can do so simply by paying the decommitment penalty to the other party. Such contracts are called leveled commitment contracts because the decommitment penalties can be used to choose a level of commitment. The method requires no explicit conditioning on future events: each agent can do its own conditioning dynamically. Therefore no event verification mechanism is required either.

While the leveled commitment contracting protocol has intuitive appeal and several practical advantages [62], it is not obvious that it is beneficial. First, the breacher's gain may be smaller than the breach victim's loss. Second, agents might decommit insincerely. A truthful agent would decommit whenever its best outside offer plus the decommitting penalty is better than the current contract. However, a rational self-interested agent would be more reluctant in decommitting. It can take into account the chance that the other party will decommit, in which case the former agent gets freed from the contract obligations, does not have to pay a decommitting penalty, and will collect a decommitting penalty from the other party. Due to such reluctant decommitting, contracts may end up being kept even though breaking them would be best from the social welfare perspective.

This issue was recently analyzed formally [67, 62]. A Nash equilibrium analysis was carried out where both contract parties' decommitting strategies (characterized by how good an agent's outside offer has to be to induce the agent to decommit) were best responses to each other. Both agents were decommitting insincerely but neither was motivated to change the extent of his lie given that the other did not change. It was shown that even under such insincere decommitting, the leveled commitment protocol outperforms the full commitment protocol. First, it enables contracts by making them IR in settings where no full commitment contract is IR (the reverse cannot happen). Second, leveled commitment contracts increase both contract parties' expected payoffs over any full commitment contracts.

## 5.8  Coalition Formation

In many domains, self-interested real world parties—e.g., companies or individual people—can save costs by coordinating their activities with other parties. For example when the planning activities are automated, it can be useful to automate the coordination activities as well. This can be done via a negotiating software agent representing each party.

The most general approach would be to state the coalition formation protocol as a normal form game (see e.g. Table 5.1) or an extensive form (i.e. sequential) game, and then analyze the Nash equilibria to see how the game would be played and how efficient the outcomes would be. To rigorously incorporate computation in the analysis, one could treat computational actions as part of each agent's strategy—just like physical actions.

However, the Nash equilibrium is often too weak because subgroups of agents can deviate in a coordinated manner. The *Strong Nash equilibrium* is a solution concept that guarantees more stability [5]. It requires that there is no subgroup that can deviate by changing strategies jointly in a manner that increases the payoff of all of its members given that nonmembers do not deviate from the original solution. The Strong Nash equilibrium is often too strong a solution concept because in many games no such equilibria exist.

The *Coalition-Proof Nash equilibrium* has been suggested as a partial remedy to the nonexistence problem of the Strong Nash equilibrium [7, 8]. It requires that there is no subgroup that can make a mutually beneficial deviation (keeping the strategies of nonmembers fixed) *in a way that the deviation itself is stable according to the same criterion*. A conceptual problem with this solution concept is that the deviation may be stable within the deviating group, but the solution concept ignores the possibility that some of the agents that deviated may prefer to deviate again with agents that did not originally deviate. Furthermore, even these kinds of solutions do not exist in all games.

Instead of the strategic approach that uses equilibrium analysis, coalition formation is often studied in a more abstract setting called a *characteristic function game*

*(CFG)*. The rest of this section will be restricted to coalition formation in CFGs. In such games, the value of each coalition $S$ is given by a characteristic function $v_S$. In other words, each coalition's value is independent of nonmembers' actions. However, in general the value of a coalition may depend on nonmembers' actions due to positive and negative externalities (interactions of the agents' solutions). Negative externalities between a coalition and nonmembers are often caused by shared resources. Once nonmembers are using the resource to a certain extent, not enough of that resource is available to agents in the coalition to carry out the planned solution at the minimum cost. Negative externalities can also be caused by conflicting goals. In satisfying their goals, nonmembers may actually move the world further from the coalition's goal state(s). Positive externalities are often caused by partially overlapping goals. In satisfying their goals, nonmembers may actually move the world closer to the coalition's goal state(s). From there the coalition can reach its goals less expensively than it could have without the actions of nonmembers. Settings with externalities between coalitions and nonmembers can be modeled e.g. as normal form games. CFGs are a strict subset of them. However, many real-world multiagent problems happen to be CFGs [68].

Coalition formation in CFGs includes three activities:

1.  *Coalition structure generation*: formation of coalitions by the agents such that agents within each coalition coordinate their activities, but agents do not coordinate between coalitions. Precisely this means partitioning the set of agents into exhaustive and disjoint coalitions. This partition is called a *coalition structure (CS)*. For example, in a game with three agents, there are seven possible coalitions: {1}, {2}, {3}, {1,2}, {2,3}, {3,1}, {1,2,3} and five possible coalition structures: {{1}, {2}, {3}}, {{1}, {2,3}}, {{2}, {1,3}}, {{3}, {1,2}}, {{1,2,3}}.

2.  *Solving the optimization problem* of each coalition. This means pooling the tasks and resources of the agents in the coalition, and solving this joint problem. The coalition's objective is to maximize monetary value: money received from outside the system for accomplishing tasks minus the cost of using resources. (In some problems, not all tasks have to be handled. This can be incorporated by associating a cost with each omitted task.)

3.  *Dividing the value* of the generated solution among agents. This value may be negative because agents incur costs for using their resources.

These activities may be interleaved, and they are not independent. For example, the coalition that an agent wants to join depends on the portion of the value that the agent would be allocated in each potential coalition.

### 5.8.1   Coalition Formation Activity 1: Coalition Structure Generation

Classically, coalition formation research has mostly focused on the payoff division activity. Coalition structure generation and optimization within a coalition have not previously received as much attention. Research has focused [29, 86] on super-additive games, i.e. games where $v_{S \cup T} \geq v_S + v_T$ for all disjoint coalitions $S, T \subseteq A$. In such games, coalition structure generation is trivial because the agents are best off by forming the grand coalition where all agents operate together.

Superadditivity means that any pair of coalitions is best off by merging into one. Classically it is argued that almost all games are superadditive because, at worst, the agents in a composite coalition can use solutions that they had when they were in separate coalitions.

However, many games are not superadditive because there is some cost to the coalition formation process itself. For example, there might be coordination overhead like communication costs, or possible anti-trust penalties. Similarly, solving the optimization problem of a composite coalition may be more complex than solving the optimization problems of component coalitions. Therefore, under costly computation, component coalitions may be better off by not forming the composite coalition [68]. Also, if time is limited, the agents may not have time to carry out the communications and computations required to coordinate effectively within a composite coalition, so component coalitions may be more advantageous.

In games that are not superadditive, some coalitions are best off merging while others are not. In such settings, the social welfare maximizing coalition structure varies, and coalition structure generation becomes highly nontrivial. The goal is to maximize the social welfare of the agents $A$ by finding a coalition structure

$$CS^* = \arg \max_{CS \in \text{partitions of A}} V(CS),$$

where

$$V(CS) = \sum_{S \in CS} v_S$$

The problem is that the number of coalition structures is large $(\Omega(|A|^{|A|/2}))$, so not all coalition structures can be enumerated unless the number of agents is extremely small—in practice about 15 or fewer. Instead, one would like to search through a subset ($N \subset$ partitions of A) of coalition structures, and pick the best coalition structure seen so far:

$$CS_N^* = \arg \max_{CS \in N} V(CS)$$

Taking an outsider's view, the coalition structure generation process can be viewed as search in a *coalition structure graph*, Figure 5.3. Now, how should such a graph be searched if there are too many nodes to search it completely?

One desideratum is to be able to guarantee that this coalition structure is within a worst case bound from optimal, i.e. that

$$k \geq \frac{V(CS^*)}{V(CS_N^*)}$$

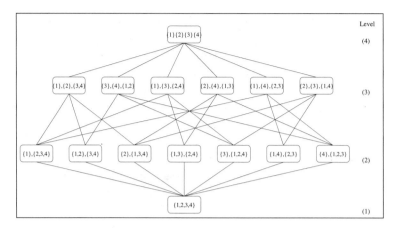

**Figure 5.3**  Coalition structure graph for a 4-agent game. The nodes represent coalition structures. The arcs represent mergers of two coalition when followed downward, and splits of a coalition into two coalitions when followed upward.

is finite, and as small as possible. Let us define $n_{min}$ to be the smallest size of $N$ that allows us to establish such a bound $k$.

### *Theorem 5.19 Minimal search to establish a bound*

To bound $k$, it suffices to search the lowest two levels of the coalition structure graph (Figure 5.3). With this search, the bound $k = |A|$, this bound is tight, and the number of nodes searched is $n = 2^{|A|-1}$. No other search algorithm (than the one that searches the bottom two levels) can establish a bound $k$ while searching only $n = 2^{|A|-1}$ nodes or fewer [65].

Interpreted positively, this means that—somewhat unintuitively—a worst case bound from optimum can be guaranteed without seeing all CSs. Moreover, as the number of agents grows, the fraction of coalition structures needed to be searched approaches zero, i.e. $\frac{n_{min}}{|\text{partitions of A}|} \to 0$ as $|A| \to \infty$. This is because the algorithm needs to see only $2^{|A|-1}$ coalition structures while the total number of coalition structures is $\Omega(|A|^{|A|/2})$.

Interpreted negatively, the theorem shows that exponentially many coalition structures have to be searched before a bound can be established. This may be prohibitively complex if the number of agents is large—albeit significantly better than attempting to enumerate all coalition structures. Viewed as a general impossibility result, the theorem states that no algorithm for coalition structure generation can establish a bound in general characteristic function games without trying at least $2^{|A|-1}$ coalition structures.[8] This sheds light on earlier algorithms. Specifi-

---

8. In restricted domains where the $v_S$ values have special structure, it may be possible to establish a bound $k$ with less search. Shehory and Kraus have analyzed coalition structure generation in one such setting [75]. However, the bound that they compute is not a bound

1. Search the **bottom** two levels of the coalition structure graph.

2. Continue with a breadth-first search from the **top** of the graph as long as there is time left, or until the entire graph has been searched.

3. Return the coalition structure that has the highest welfare among those seen so far.

**Algorithm 5.3**   COALITION-STRUCTURE-SEARCH-1 [Sandholm et al.]

cally, all prior coalition structure generation algorithms for general characteristic function games [76, 32]—which we know of—fail to establish such a bound. In other words, the coalition structure that they find may be arbitrarily far from optimal.

On the other hand, the following algorithm will establish a bound in the minimal amount of search, and then rapidly reduce the bound further if there is time for more search. If the domain happens to be superadditive, the algorithm finds the optimal coalition structure immediately.

The next theorem shows how this algorithm reduces the worst case bound, $k$, as more of the graph is searched. For convenience, we introduce the notation $h = \lfloor \frac{|A|-l}{2} \rfloor + 2$.

### Theorem 5.20  Lowering the bound with further search

After searching level $l$ with Algorithm 5.3, the bound $k$ is $\lceil \frac{|A|}{h} \rceil$ if $|A| \equiv h-1 \pmod{h}$ and $|A| \equiv l \pmod 2$. Otherwise the bound is $\lfloor \frac{|A|}{h} \rfloor$. The bound is tight [65].

As was discussed earlier, before $2^{|A|-1}$ nodes have been searched, no bound can be established, and at $n = 2^{|A|-1}$ the bound $k = |A|$. The surprising fact is that by seeing just one additional node, i.e. the top node, the bound drops in half ($k = \frac{|A|}{2}$). Then, to drop $k$ to about $\frac{|A|}{3}$, two more levels need to be searched. Roughly speaking, the divisor in the bound increases by one every time two more levels are searched. So, the anytime phase (step 2) of Algorithm 5.3 has the desirable feature that the bound drops rapidly early on, and there are overall diminishing returns to further search, Figure 5.4.

### Comparison to Other Algorithms

All previous coalition structure generation algorithms for general CFGs [76, 32]— that we know of—fail to establish any worst case bound because they search fewer than $2^{a-1}$ coalition structures. Therefore, we compare Algorithm 5.3 to two other obvious candidates:

- **Merging algorithm**, i.e. breadth first search from the top of the coalition structure graph. This algorithm cannot establish any bound before it has searched the

---

from optimum, but from a benchmark (best that is achievable given a preset limit on the size of coalitions) which itself may be arbitrarily far from optimum.

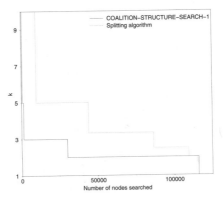

**Figure 5.4**  Ratio bound $k$ as a function of search size in a 10-agent game.

entire graph. This is because, to establish a bound, the algorithm needs to see every coalition, and the grand coalition only occurs in the bottom node. Visiting the grand coalition as a special case would not help much since at least part of level 2 needs to be searched as well: coalitions of size $a - 2$ only occur there.

- **Splitting algorithm**, i.e. breadth first search from the bottom of the graph. This is identical to Algorithm 5.3 up to the point where $2^{a-1}$ nodes have been searched, and a bound $k = a$ has been established. After that, the splitting algorithm reduces the bound much slower than Algorithm 5.3. This can be shown by constructing bad cases for the splitting algorithm: the worst case may be even worse. To construct a bad case, set $v_S = 1$ if $|S| = 1$, and $v_S = 0$ otherwise. Now, $CS^* = \{\{1\}, ..., \{a\}\}$, $V(CS^*) = a$, and $V(CS_N^*) = l - 1$, where $l$ is the level that the algorithm has completed (because the number of unit coalitions in a $CS$ never exceeds $l - 1$). So, $\frac{V(CS^*)}{V(CS_N^*)} = \frac{a}{l-1}$,[9] Figure 5.4. In other words the divisor drops by one every time a level is searched. However, the levels that this algorithm searches first have many more nodes than the levels that Algorithm 5.3 searches first.

### Variants of the Coalition Structure Generation Problem

One would like to construct an anytime algorithm that establishes a lower $k$ for any amount of search $n$, compared to any other anytime algorithm. However, such an algorithm might not exist. It is conceivable that the search which establishes the minimal $k$ while searching $n'$ nodes ($n' > n$) does not include all nodes of the search which establishes the minimal $k$ while searching $n$ nodes. This hypothesis is supported by the fact that the curves in Figure 5.4 cross in the end. However, this is not conclusive because Algorithm 5.3 might not be the optimal anytime algorithm,

---

9. The only exception comes when the algorithm completes the last (top) level, i.e $l = a$. Then $\frac{V(CS^*)}{V(CS_N^*)} = 1$.

and because the bad cases for the splitting algorithm might not be the worst cases.

If it turns out that no anytime algorithm is best for all $n$, one could use information (e.g. exact, probabilistic, or bounds) about the termination time to construct a *design-to-time algorithm* which establishes the lowest possible $k$ for the specified amount of search.

So far we have discussed algorithms that have an *off-line search control* policy, i.e. the nodes to be searched have to be selected without using information accrued from the search so far. With *on-line search control*, one could perhaps establish a lower $k$ with less search because the search can be redirected based on the values observed in the nodes so far. With on-line search control, it might make a difference whether the search observes only values of coalition structures, $V(CS)$, or values of individual coalitions, $v_S$, in those structures. The latter gives more information.

None of these variants (anytime vs. design-to-time, and off-line vs. on-line search control) would affect the result that searching the bottom two levels of the coalition structure graph is the unique minimal way to establish a worst case bound, and that the bound is tight. However, the results on searching further might vary in these different settings.

### Parallelizing Coalition Structure Search among Insincere Agents

This section discusses the parallelizing of coalition structure search—or any other search for that matter—across agents because the search can be done more efficiently in parallel, and the agents will share the burden of computation. Self-interested agents prefer greater personal payoffs, so they will search for coalition structures that maximize personal payoffs, ignoring $k$. Algorithm 5.4 can be used to motivate self-interested agents to exactly follow the socially desirable search. The randomizations in that algorithm can be done without a trusted third party by using a distributed nonmanipulable protocol for randomly permuting the agents, discussed at the end of Section 5.8.3.

### 5.8.2 Coalition Formation Activity 2: Optimization within a Coalition

Under unlimited and costless computation, each coalition would solve its optimization problem, which would define the value of that coalition. However, in practice, in many domains it is too complex from a combinatorial viewpoint to solve the problem exactly. Instead, only an approximate solution can be found. In such settings, self-interested agents would want to strike the optimal tradeoff between solution quality and the cost of the associated computation. This will affect the values of coalitions, which in turn will affect which coalition structure gives the highest welfare. This issue and several related questions are studied in detail in [68].

### 5.8.3 Coalition Formation Activity 3: Payoff Division

Payoff division strives to divide the value of the chosen coalition structure among agents in a fair and stable way so that the agents are motivated to stay with the

1. **Deciding what part of the coalition structure graph to search**. This can be decided in advance, or be dictated by a central authority or a randomly chosen agent, or be decided using some form of negotiation.

2. **Partitioning the search space among agents**. Each agent is assigned some part of the coalition structure graph to search. The enforcement mechanism in step 4 will motivate the agents to search exactly what they are assigned, no matter how unfairly the assignment is done. One way of achieving *ex ante* fairness is to randomly allocate the set search space portions to the agents. In this way, each agent searches equally on an expected value basis, although *ex post*, some may search more than others. Another option is to distribute the space equally among agents, or have some agents pay others to compensate for unequal amounts of search.

3. **Actual search**. Each agent searches its part of the search space, and tells the others which $CS$ maximized $V(CS)$ in its search space.

4. **Enforcement**. Two agents, $i$ and $j$, will be selected at random. Agent $i$ will re-search the search space of $j$ to verify that $j$ has performed its search. Agent $j$ gets caught of mis-searching (or misrepresenting) if $i$ finds a better $CS$ in $j$'s space than $j$ reported (or $i$ sees that the $CS$ that $j$ reported does not belong to $j$'s space at all). If $j$ gets caught, it has to pay a penalty $P$. To motivate $i$ to conduct this additional search, we make $i$ the claimant of $P$. There is no pure strategy Nash equilibrium in this protocol. (If $i$ searches and the penalty is high enough, then $j$ is motivated to search sincerely. But then $i$ is not motivated to search since it cannot receive $P$.) Instead, there will be a mixed strategy Nash equilibrium where $i$ and $j$ search truthfully with some probabilities. By increasing $P$, the probability that $j$ searches can be made arbitrarily close to one. The probability that $i$ searches approaches zero, which minimizes enforcement overhead.

5. **Additional search**. The previous steps can be repeated if more time to search remains. For example, the agents could first do step 1 of Algorithm 5.3. Then, they could repeatedly search more and more as time allows.

6. **Payoff division**. Many alternative methods for payoff division among agents could be used here. The only concern is that the division of $V(CS)$ may affect what $CS$ an agent wants to report as a result of its search since different $CS$s may give the agent different payoffs—depending on the payoff division scheme. However, by making $P$ high enough compared to $V(CS)$s, this consideration can be made negligible compared to the risk of getting caught.

**Algorithm 5.4**   Parallel search for self-interested agents [Sandholm et al.]

---

Repeat:
    Choose a coalition T
    For every agent $i \in T$, $x_i^{new} = x_i + \dfrac{v_T - \sum_{j \in T} x_j}{|T|}$, and $x_i^{new} = x_i$ for $i \notin T$
    Maintain feasibility: For every agent $i \in A$, $x_i = x_i^{new} - \dfrac{\sum_{j \in A} x_j^{new} - \sum_{S \in CS} v_S}{|A|}$

---

**Algorithm 5.5**  A transfer scheme for reaching the core [84].

coalition structure rather than move out of it. Several ways of dividing payoffs have been proposed in the literature [29]. This section discusses only two of them: the *core*, and the *Shapley value*.

### *Payoff Division According to the Core*

The *core* of a CFG with transferable payoffs is a set of *payoff configurations* $(\vec{x}, CS)$, where each $\vec{x}$ is a vector of payoffs to the agents in such a manner that no subgroup is motivated to depart from the coalition structure $CS$:

### *Definition 5.3*
Core = $\{(\vec{x}, CS) | \forall S \subset A, \sum_{i \in S} x_i \geq v_S$ and $\sum_{i \in A} x_i = \sum_{S \in CS} v_S\}$

Clearly, only coalition structures that maximize social welfare can be stable in the sense of the core because from any other coalition structure, the group of all agents would prefer to switch to a social welfare maximizing one.

The core is the strongest of the classical solution concepts in coalition formation. It is often too strong: in many cases it is empty [29, 78, 53, 86]. In such games there is no way to divide the social good so that the coalition structure becomes stable: any payoff configuration is prone to deviation by some subgroup of agents. The new solution that is acquired by the deviation is again prone to deviation and so on. There will be an infinite sequence of steps from one payoff configuration to another. To avoid this, explicit mechanisms such as limits on negotiation rounds, contract costs, or some social norms need to be in place in the negotiation setting.

Another problem is that the core may include multiple payoff vectors and the agents have to agree on one of them. An often used solution is to pick the *nucleolus* which, intuitively speaking, corresponds to a payoff vector that is in the center of the set of payoff vectors in the core [29, 78, 53].

A further problem with the core is that the constraints in the definition become numerous as the number of agents increases. This is due to the combinatorial subset operator in the definition. To reduce the associated cognitive burden of the agents that try to reach a payoff division in the core, Algorithm 5.5 can be used for payoff division. It stays within the given $CS$, and iteratively changes the payoff division. If the core is nonempty, Algorithm 5.5 will converge to a solution in the core starting from any initial payoff division. The choice of $T$ can be made at random, or largest $v_T - \sum_{j \in T} x_j$ first. The latter variant tends to converge faster. There is no guarantee that a self-interested agent is motivated to follow the transfer scheme truthfully.

### Payoff Division according to the Shapley Value

The *Shapley value* is another policy for dividing payoff in CFGs. It will first be characterized axiomatically. Agent $i$ is called a *dummy* if $v_{S \cup \{i\}} - v_S = v_{\{i\}}$ for every coalition $S$ that does not include $i$. Agents $i$ and $j$ are called *interchangeable* if $v_{(S \setminus \{i\}) \cup \{j\}} = v_S$ for every coalition $S$ that includes $i$ but not $j$. The axioms of the Shapley value are:

- Symmetry: If $i$ and $j$ are interchangeable then $x_i = x_j$.

- Dummies: If $i$ is a dummy then $x_i = v_{\{i\}}$.

- Additivity: For any two games $v$ and $w$, $x_i$ in $v + w$ equals $x_i$ in $v$ plus $x_i$ in $w$, where $v + w$ is the game defined by $(v + w)_S = v_S + w_S$.

### Theorem 5.21
The following is the only payoff division scheme that satisfies these three axioms [74]:

$$x_i = \sum_{S \subseteq A} \frac{(|A| - |S|)!(|S| - 1)!}{|A|!}[v_S - v_{S - \{i\}}]$$

This payoff is called the Shapley value of agent $i$. It can be interpreted as the marginal contribution of agent $i$ to the coalition structure, averaged over all possible joining orders. The joining order matters since the perceived contribution of agent $i$ varies based on which agents have joined before it.

The Shapley value always exists and is unique, while the core guarantees neither of these desirable properties. Like the core, the Shapley value is also Pareto efficient: the entire value of the coalition structure gets distributed among the agents. Like the core, the Shapley value guarantees that individual agents and the grand coalition are motivated to stay with the coalition structure. However, unlike the core, it does not guarantee that all subgroups of agents are better off in the coalition structure than by breaking off into a coalition of their own. This is not guaranteed by the Shapley value even in games where such a solution exists, i.e. the core is nonempty.

Another problem with the Shapley value is that the marginal contribution of each agent has to be computed over all joining orders, and there are $|A|!$ of them. One can guarantee each agent an *expected* payoff equal to its Shapley value by randomizing the joining order. This allows one to focus on one joining order only. A trusted third party needs to carry out the randomization since each agent has strong preferences over different joining orders because these orders lead to different payoffs for the agent.

The need for a trusted third party randomizer can be overcome via Zlotkin and Rosenschein's recent distributed nonmanipulable protocol for finding a randomized joining order [86]. First, every agent constructs a random permutation of the agents, encrypts it, and sends it to all others. Once an agent has received an encrypted permutation from every other agent, it broadcasts its key. These keys are then used to decrypt the permutations. The overall joining order is determined by sequentially permuting the results. For example, say that in a game of three agents, agent one's permutation is 3, 1, 2, agent two's permutation is 1, 3, 2, and agent three's permutation is 2, 3, 1. Applying agent one's permutation gives 3, 1, 2. Applying two's permutation to that gives 3, 2, 1. Applying three's permutation to that results in a joining order of 2, 1, 3.

An agent can do no better than randomize its permutation—assuming that at least one other agent randomizes its permutation (if the former agent knew exactly what all other agents' permutations are, that agent could tailor its permutation and do better). This assumes that the agent cannot change the interpretation of its permutation by changing its key after receiving the keys from others and decrypting their permutations. Changing the key so as to customize the interpretation of the permutation at that point may be difficult, and it can be made more difficult by enhancing Zlotkin and Rosenschein's protocol by requiring that every agent prefixes its permutation by a common string, e.g. "Hello world". Now manipulation would require the agent to construct a key that will change the interpretation of the agent's permutation in a desirable way while not changing the prefix.

## 5.9 Conclusions

Multiagent systems consisting of self-interested agents are becoming ubiquitous. Such agents cannot be coordinated by externally imposing the agent's strategies. Instead the interaction protocols have to be designed so that each agent really is motivated to follow the strategies that the protocol designer wants it to follow. This chapter discussed these issues under different types of protocols and different settings. Substantial knowledge exists of impossibility results and of constructive possibility demonstrations [39, 35]. This chapter only touched on some of it.

The implications of computational limitations were given special emphasis as a topic that has not traditionally received adequate attention. It is clear that such limitations have fundamental impact on what strategies agents want to use, and therefore also on what protocols are desirable, and what is (im)possible. This is one area where microeconomics and computer science fruitfully blend. Another area of substantial current and potential future cross-fertilization is the relaxation of the common knowledge assumption that underlies the Nash equilibrium solution concept and its refinements [16, 20].

In the future, systems will increasingly be designed, built, and operated in a distributed manner. A larger number of systems will be used by multiple real-world parties. The problem of coordinating these parties and avoiding manipulation cannot be tackled by technological or economic methods alone. Instead, the successful solutions are likely to emerge from a deep understanding and careful hybridization of both.

## 5.10    Exercises

1. *[Level 1]* The Gibbard-Satterthwaite theorem states that it is impossible to devise a truthpromoting voting mechanism for insincere agents. On the other hand, the Clarke tax mechanism is such a voting mechanism. Explain why this is not a contradiction.

2. *[Level 2]* Let there be a salesman located at each one of the following three coordinates: $(0,0)$, $(0,5)$, and $(5,0)$. Let there be a customer at each one of the following five locations: $(1,4)$, $(1.5,0)$, $(2,2)$, $(3,2)$, $(5,2)$. Each customer has to be assigned to exactly one salesman who will visit the customer. After visiting all of the customers assigned to him, the salesman has to return to his initial location. The domain cost that the salesman incurs from his travel is the Euclidean length of the trip. The tasks (locations of customers) are known to all salesmen. Write a program which uses the Clarke tax voting mechanism to solve this problem, i.e. tax is levied in a way that each salesman is motivated to reveal his preferences (over task allocations among agents) truthfully.

   (a)   How many possible task allocations are there?

   (b)   List each agent's preference (numeric value) for each of these.

   (c)   Which task allocation will be chosen?

   (d)   List the route of each salesman.

   (e)   How much domain (travel) cost does each salesman incur?

   (f)   How much tax does each agent pay/receive?

   (g)   What is the budget balance/deficit?

   (h)   Demonstrate a way—if one exists—how some agents can beneficially collude by revealing their preferences untruthfully. How would this changes answers (c)-(g)?

3. *[Level 3]* Program an example general equilibrium market economy that satisfies the gross substitutes property. Compare the convergence of the price tâtonnement algorithm and the Newtonian price tâtonnement algorithm. Then, experiment with how much one agent can gain by acting strategically (speculatively) instead of acting competitively as a price taker.

4. *[Level 1]* Discuss how the revelation principle relates the Vickrey auction to the English auction. How does this relate to the "agent" that bids on the human's behalf at http://www.webauction.com?

5. *[Level 2]* Prove Theorem 5.5.

6. *[Level 2]* Show an example where an agent is best off bidding insincerely if the second-price auction is implemented as open-cry instead of sealed-bid.

7. *[Level 2]* Construct an example where O-contracts lead to a local optimum (when agents use per contract individual rationality as their decision criterion)

that is not globally optimal.

8. *[Level 4]* How should agents look ahead in contracting and in auctions of interrelated items? The extremes are no lookahead (IR contracts), and full (game theoretic) lookahead. In practice something in between these extremes is likely to be best since there is a tradeoff between the computational cost of looking ahead and the domain cost savings that lookahead may provide.

9. *[Level 3]* Construct a 2-agent task allocation problem instance where an agent benefits from a decoy lie. The protocol should make every agent reveal its tasks at once (cost functions over tasks may be assumed common knowledge), should use pure deals, and should divide payoffs according to the Nash bargaining solution.

10. *[Level 1]* Program the transfer scheme for the core. Run it on an example problem instance where the core is nonempty. What happens when you run it on a problem instance where the core is empty?

11. *[Level 2]* This question is based on [68]. Let there be three agents. Let the unit cost of computation be \$200 (e.g. for a day of supercomputer time). Let the algorithms' performance profiles be:

$$c_{\{1\}}(t_{CPU}) = \$100 \cdot e^{-t_{CPU}} + \$300$$
$$c_{\{2\}}(t_{CPU}) = \$80 \cdot e^{-t_{CPU}} + \$200$$
$$c_{\{3\}}(t_{CPU}) = \$65 \cdot e^{-t_{CPU}} + \$200$$
$$c_{\{1,2\}}(t_{CPU}) = \$240 \cdot e^{-t_{CPU}} + \$400$$
$$c_{\{2,3\}}(t_{CPU}) = \$175 \cdot e^{-t_{CPU}} + \$419$$
$$c_{\{1,3\}}(t_{CPU}) = \$190 \cdot e^{-t_{CPU}} + \$400$$
$$c_{\{1,2,3\}}(t_{CPU}) = \$500 \cdot e^{-t_{CPU}} + \$595$$

Note that different coalitions might use different amounts of computation. What is the social welfare maximizing coalition structure? Is it stable according to the core (justify your answer)? How would these answers change if computation were free?

## 5.11 References

1. Martin R Andersson and Tuomas W Sandholm. Contract types for satisficing task allocation: II experimental results. In *AAAI Spring Symposium Series: Satisficing Models*, pages 1–7, Stanford University, CA, March 1998.

2. Martin R Andersson and Tuomas W Sandholm. Leveled commitment contracting among myopic individually rational agents. In *Proceedings of the Third International Conference on Multi-Agent Systems (ICMAS)*, Paris, France, July 1998.

3. Martin R Andersson and Tuomas W Sandholm. Leveled commitment contracts

with myopic and strategic agents. In *Proceedings of the National Conference on Artificial Intelligence*, Madison, WI, July 1998.

4. Kenneth Arrow. *Social choice and individual values*. New Haven: Cowles Foundation, 2nd edition, 1963. 1st edition 1951.

5. R Aumann. Acceptable points in general cooperative n-person games. volume IV of *Contributions to the Theory of Games*. Princeton University Press, 1959.

6. Salvador Barbera and Matthew O Jackson. Strategy-proof exchange. *Econometrica*, 63(1):51–87, 1995.

7. B Douglas Bernheim, Bezalel Peleg, and Michael D Whinston. Coalition-proof Nash equilibria: I concepts. *Journal of Economic Theory*, 42(1):1–12, June 1987.

8. B Douglas Bernheim and Michael D Whinston. Coalition-proof Nash equilibria: II applications. *Journal of Economic Theory*, 42(1):13–29, June 1987.

9. Alan H. Bond and Les Gasser. *Readings in Distributed Artificial Intelligence*. Morgan Kaufmann Publishers, San Mateo, CA, 1988.

10. John Q. Cheng and Michael P. Wellman. The WALRAS algorithm: A convergent distributed implementation of general equilibrium outcomes. *Computational Economics*, 1997.

11. E H Clarke. Multipart pricing of public goods. *Public Choice*, 11:17–33, 1971.

12. E Durfee, V Lesser, and D Corkill. Cooperative distributed problem solving. In A Barr, P Cohen, and E Feigenbaum, editors, *The Handbook of Artificial Intelligence*, volume IV, pages 83–147. Addison Wesley, 1989.

13. Eithan Ephrati. A non-manipulable meeting scheduling system. In *Proc. 13th International Distributed Artificial Intelligence Workshop*, Lake Quinalt, Washington, July 1994. AAAI Press Technical Report WS-94-02.

14. Eithan Ephrati and Jeffrey S Rosenschein. The Clarke tax as a consensus mechanism among automated agents. In *Proceedings of the National Conference on Artificial Intelligence*, pages 173–178, Anaheim, CA, 1991.

15. Eithan Ephrati and Jeffrey S Rosenschein. Multi-agent planning as a dynamic search for social consensus. In *Proceedings of the Thirteenth International Joint Conference on Artificial Intelligence*, pages 423–429, Chambery, France, 1993.

16. Ronald Fagin, Joseph Y. Halpern, Yoram Moses, and Moshe Y. Vardi. *Reasoning About Knowledge*. MIT Press, 1995.

17. Drew Fudenberg and Jean Tirole. *Game Theory*. MIT Press, 1991.

18. A Gibbard. Manipulation of voting schemes. *Econometrica*, 41:587–602, 1973.

19. Natalie S. Glance and Tad Hogg. Dilemmas in computational societies. In *Proceedings of the First International Conference on Multi-Agent Systems (ICMAS)*, pages 117–124, San Francisco, CA, 1995.

20. P. J. Gmytrasiewicz and E. H. Durfee. A rigorous, operational formalization of recursive modeling. In *Proceedings of the First International Conference on Multi-Agent Systems (ICMAS)*, pages 125–132, San Francisco, CA, June 1995.

21. Theodore Groves. Incentives in teams. *Econometrica*, 41:617–631, 1973.

22. Cheng Gu and Toru Ishida. A quantitative analysis of the contract net protocol. In *Proceedings of the First International Conference on Multi-Agent Systems (ICMAS)*, page 449, San Francisco, CA, June 1995. In the poster collection.

23. Tad Hogg. Social dilemmas in computational ecosystems. In *Proceedings of the Fourteenth International Joint Conference on Artificial Intelligence*, pages 711–716,

Montreal, Canada, 1995.

24. J. Hu and M. P. Wellman. Self-fulfilling bias in multiagent learning. In *Proceedings of the Second International Conference on Multi-Agent Systems (ICMAS)*, pages 118–125, Keihanna Plaza, Kyoto, Japan, December 1996.

25. Bernardo Huberman and Scott H Clearwater. A multi-agent system for controlling building environments. In *Proceedings of the First International Conference on Multi-Agent Systems (ICMAS)*, pages 171–176, San Francisco, CA, June 1995.

26. Bernardo A. Huberman and Tad Hogg. The behavior of computational ecologies. In B. A. Huberman, editor, *The Ecology of Computation*. North-Holland, 1988.

27. L. Hurwicz. On informationally decentralized systems. In C.B McGuire and R. Radner, editors, *Decision and Organization*, chapter 14, pages 297–336. University of Minnesota Press, 1986. Second edition.

28. Matthew Jackson and James Peck. Speculation and price fluctuations with private, extrinsic signals. *Journal of Economic Theory*, 55:274–295, 1991.

29. James P Kahan and Amnon Rapoport. *Theories of Coalition Formation*. Lawrence Erlbaum Associates Publishers, 1984.

30. Ehud Kalai. Solutions to the bargaining problem. In Leonid Hurwicz, David Schmeidler, and Hugo Sonnenschein, editors, *Social goals and social organization: Essays in memory of Elisha Pazner*, chapter 3, pages 77–106. Cambridge University Press, 1985.

31. Ravi Kalakota and Andrew B. Whinston. *Frontiers of Electronic Commerce*. Addison-Wesley Publishing Company, Inc, 1996.

32. Steven Ketchpel. Forming coalitions in the face of uncertain rewards. In *Proceedings of the National Conference on Artificial Intelligence*, pages 414–419, Seattle, WA, July 1994.

33. Richard E. Korf. Real-time heuristic search. *Artificial Intelligence*, 42(2-3):189–211, March 1990.

34. Sarit Kraus, Jonathan Wilkenfeld, and Gilad Zlotkin. Multiagent negotiation under time constraints. *Artificial Intelligence*, 75:297–345, 1995.

35. David M Kreps. *A Course in Microeconomic Theory*. Princeton University Press, 1990.

36. Jacques Lenting and Peter Braspenning. An all-pay auction approach to reallocation. In *Proceedings of the 11th European Conference on Artificial Intelligence*, pages 259–263, August 1994.

37. Jeffrey K. MacKie-Mason and Hal R. Varian. Pricing the Internet. In *Proceedings of the Public Access to the Internet Conference*. JFK School of Government, May 1993.

38. E. Malinvaud. *Lectures on Microeconomic Theory*. North-Holland, 1985.

39. Andreu Mas-Colell, Michael Whinston, and Jerry R. Green. *Microeconomic Theory*. Oxford University Press, 1995.

40. Eric S Maskin. The theory of implementation in Nash equilibrium: a survey. In Leonid Hurwicz, David Schmeidler, and Hugo Sonnenschein, editors, *Social goals and social organization: Essays in memory of Elisha Pazner*, chapter 6, pages 173–204. Cambridge University Press, 1985.

41. R Preston McAfee and John McMillan. Analyzing the airwaves auction. *Journal of Economic Perspectives*, 10(1):159–175, 1996.

42. Paul R Milgrom. The economics of competitive bidding: a selective survey. In

Leonid Hurwicz, David Schmeidler, and Hugo Sonnenschein, editors, *Social goals and social organization: Essays in memory of Elisha Pazner*, chapter 9, pages 261–292. Cambridge University Press, 1985.

43. Mark S. Miller and K. Eric Drexler. Comparative ecology: A computational perspective. In B. A. Huberman, editor, *The Ecology of Computation*. North-Holland, 1988.

44. Tracy Mullen and Michael P Wellman. A simple computational market for network information services. In *Proceedings of the First International Conference on Multi-Agent Systems (ICMAS)*, pages 283–289, San Francisco, CA, June 1995.

45. Eithan Muller and Mark A Satterwaithe. Strategy-proofness: the existence of dominant strategy mechanisms. In Leonid Hurwicz, David Schmeidler, and Hugo Sonnenschein, editors, *Social goals and social organization: Essays in memory of Elisha Pazner*, chapter 5, pages 131–172. Cambridge University Press, 1985.

46. Roger B Myerson. Bayesian equilibrium and incentive compatibility: an introduction. In Leonid Hurwicz, David Schmeidler, and Hugo Sonnenschein, editors, *Social goals and social organization: Essays in memory of Elisha Pazner*, chapter 8, pages 229–260. Cambridge University Press, 1985.

47. John Nash. The bargaining problem. *Econometrica*, 18:155–162, 1950.

48. John Nash. Equilibrium points in n-person games. *Proc. of the National Academy of Sciences*, 36:48–49, 1950.

49. Peter C Ordeshook. *Game theory and political theory*. Cambridge University Press, 1986.

50. Martin J Osborne and Ariel Rubinstein. *Bargaining and Markets*. Academic Press, Inc., 1990.

51. Martin J Osborne and Ariel Rubinstein. *A Course in Game Theory*. MIT Press, 1994.

52. Andrew Postlewaite. Implementation via Nash equilibria in economic environments. In Leonid Hurwicz, David Schmeidler, and Hugo Sonnenschein, editors, *Social goals and social organization: Essays in memory of Elisha Pazner*, chapter 7, pages 205–228. Cambridge University Press, 1985.

53. H. Raiffa. *The Art and Science of Negotiation*. Harvard Univ. Press, Cambridge, Mass., 1982.

54. Eric Rasmusen. *Games and Information*. Basil Blackwell, 1989.

55. Donald John Roberts and Andrew Postlewaite. The incentives for price-taking behavior in large exchange economies. *Econometrica*, 44(1):115–127, 1976.

56. Jeffrey S Rosenschein and Gilad Zlotkin. *Rules of Encounter*. MIT Press, 1994.

57. Michael H Rothkopf and Ronald M Harstad. Two models of bid-taker cheating in Vickrey auctions. *Journal of Business*, 68(2):257–267, 1995.

58. Michael H Rothkopf, Thomas J Teisberg, and Edward P Kahn. Why are Vickrey auctions rare? *Journal of Political Economy*, 98(1):94–109, 1990.

59. Ariel Rubinstein. Perfect equilibrium in a bargaining model. *Econometrica*, 50, 1982.

60. Tuomas W Sandholm. An implementation of the contract net protocol based on marginal cost calculations. In *Proceedings of the National Conference on Artificial Intelligence*, pages 256–262, Washington, D.C., July 1993.

61. Tuomas W Sandholm. Limitations of the Vickrey auction in computational multiagent systems. In *Proceedings of the Second International Conference on*

*Multi-Agent Systems (ICMAS)*, pages 299–306, Keihanna Plaza, Kyoto, Japan, December 1996.

62. Tuomas W Sandholm. *Negotiation among Self-Interested Computationally Limited Agents*. PhD thesis, University of Massachusetts, Amherst, 1996. Available at http://www.cs.wustl.edu/~sandholm/dissertation.ps.

63. Tuomas W Sandholm. Unenforced E-commerce transactions. *IEEE Internet Computing*, 1(6):47–54, Nov–Dec 1997. Special issue on Electronic Commerce.

64. Tuomas W. Sandholm. Contract types for satisficing task allocation: I theoretical results. In *AAAI Spring Symposium Series: Satisficing Models*, pages 68–75, Stanford University, CA, March 1998.

65. Tuomas W Sandholm, Kate S Larson, Martin R Andersson, Onn Shehory, and Fernando Tohmé. Anytime coalition structure generation with worst case guarantees. In *Proceedings of the National Conference on Artificial Intelligence*, Madison, WI, July 1998.

66. Tuomas W Sandholm and Victor R Lesser. Issues in automated negotiation and electronic commerce: Extending the contract net framework. In *Proceedings of the First International Conference on Multi-Agent Systems (ICMAS)*, pages 328–335, San Francisco, CA, June 1995. Reprinted in *Readings in Agents*, Huhns and Singh, eds., pp. 66–73, 1997.

67. Tuomas W Sandholm and Victor R Lesser. Advantages of a leveled commitment contracting protocol. In *Proceedings of the National Conference on Artificial Intelligence*, pages 126–133, Portland, OR, August 1996.

68. Tuomas W Sandholm and Victor R Lesser. Coalitions among computationally bounded agents. *Artificial Intelligence*, 94(1):99–137, 1997. Special issue on Economic Principles of Multiagent Systems.

69. Tuomas W Sandholm and Fredrik Ygge. On the gains and losses of speculation in equilibrium markets. In *Proceedings of the Fifteenth International Joint Conference on Artificial Intelligence*, pages 632–638, Nagoya, Japan, August 1997.

70. M A Satterthwaite. Strategy-proofness and Arrow's conditions: existence and correspondence theorems for voting procedures and social welfare functions. *Journal of Economic Theory*, 10:187–217, 1975.

71. R Selten. Spieltheoretische behandlung eines oligopolmodells mit nachfrageträgheit. *Zeitschrift für die gesamte Staatswissenschaft*, 12:301–324, 1965.

72. Sandip Sen. *Tradeoffs in Contract-Based Distributed Scheduling*. PhD thesis, Univ. of Michigan, 1993.

73. Sandip Sen and Edmund Durfee. The role of commitment in cooperative negotiation. *International Journal on Intelligent Cooperative Information Systems*, 3(1):67–81, 1994.

74. Lloyd S Shapley. A value for n-person games. In H. W. Kuhn and A. W. Tucker, editors, *Contributions to the Theory of Games*, volume 2 of *Annals of Mathematics Studies, 28*, pages 307–317. Princeton University Press, 1953.

75. Onn Shehory and Sarit Kraus. Task allocation via coalition formation among autonomous agents. In *Proceedings of the Fourteenth International Joint Conference on Artificial Intelligence*, pages 655–661, Montreal, Canada, August 1995.

76. Onn Shehory and Sarit Kraus. A kernel-oriented model for coalition-formation in general environments: Implemetation and results. In *Proceedings of the National Conference on Artificial Intelligence*, pages 134–140, Portland, OR, August 1996.

77. Reid G. Smith. The contract net protocol: High-level communication and control in a distributed problem solver. *IEEE Transactions on Computers*, C-29(12):1104–1113, December 1980.

78. Wim J van der Linden and Albert Verbeek. Coalition formation: A game-theoretic approach. In Henk A M Wilke, editor, *Coalition Formation*, volume 24 of *Advances in Psychology*. North Holland, 1985.

79. Hal R Varian. *Microeconomic analysis*. New York: W. W. Norton, 1992.

80. W Vickrey. Counterspeculation, auctions, and competitive sealed tenders. *Journal of Finance*, 16:8–37, 1961.

81. Carl A Waldspurger, Tad Hogg, Bernardo Huberman, Jeffrey O Kephart, and W Scott Stornetta. Spawn: A distributed computational economy. *IEEE Transactions on Software Engineering*, 18(2):103–117, 1992.

82. Michael Wellman. A market-oriented programming environment and its application to distributed multicommodity flow problems. *Journal of Artificial Intelligence Research*, 1:1–23, 1993.

83. Michael Wellman. A computational market model for distributed configuration design. In *Proc. 12th National Conference on Artificial Intelligence (AAAI-94)*, pages 401–407, Seattle, WA, July 1994.

84. L. S. Wu. A dynamic theory for the class of games with nonempty cores. *SIAM Journal of Applied Mathematics*, 32:328–338, 1977.

85. F. Ygge and J. M. Akkermans. Power load management as a computational market. In *Proceedings of the Second International Conference on Multi-Agent Systems (ICMAS)*, pages 393–400, Keihanna Plaza, Kyoto, Japan, December 1996.

86. Gilad Zlotkin and Jeffrey S Rosenschein. Coalition, cryptography and stability: Mechanisms for coalition formation in task oriented domains. In *Proceedings of the National Conference on Artificial Intelligence*, pages 432–437, Seattle, WA, July 1994.

# 6    Learning in Multiagent Systems

Sandip Sen and Gerhard Weiss

## 6.1    Introduction

Learning and intelligence are intimately related to each other. It is usually agreed that a system capable of learning deserves to be called intelligent; and conversely, a system being considered as intelligent is, among other things, usually expected to be able to learn. Learning always has to do with the self-improvement of future behavior based on past experience. More precisely, according to the standard artificial intelligence (AI) point of view learning can be informally defined as follows:

*The acquisition of new knowledge and motor and cognitive skills and the incorporation of the acquired knowledge and skills in future system activities, provided that this acquisition and incorporation is conducted by the system itself and leads to an improvement in its performance.*

This definition also serves as a basis for this chapter. Machine learning (ML), as one of the core fields of AI, is concerned with the computational aspects of learning in natural as well as technical systems. It is beyond the scope and intention of this chapter to offer an introduction to the broad and well developed field of ML. Instead, it introduces the reader into learning in multiagent systems and, with that, into a subfield of both ML and distributed AI (DAI). The chapter is written such that it can be understood without requiring familiarity with ML.

The intersection of DAI and ML constitutes a young but important area of research and application. The DAI and the ML communities largely ignored this area for a long time (there are exceptions on both sides, but they just prove the rule). On the one hand, work in DAI was mainly concerned with multiagent systems whose structural organization and functional behavior typically were determined in detail and therefore were more or less fixed. On the other hand, work in ML primarily dealt with learning as a centralized and isolated process that occurs in intelligent stand-alone systems. In the past this mutual ignorance of DAI and ML has disappeared, and today the area of learning in multiagent systems receives broad and steadily increasing attention. This is also reflected by the growing number of publications in this area; see [23, 24, 43, 45, 64, 66, 68] for collections of papers related to learning in multiagent systems. There are two major reasons for this attention, both showing the importance of bringing DAI and ML together:

- there is a strong need to equip multiagent systems with learning abilities; and

- an extended view of ML that captures not only single-agent learning but also multiagent learning can lead to an improved understanding of the general principles underlying learning in both computational and natural systems.

The first reason is grounded in the insight that multiagent systems typically are intended to act in complex—large, open, dynamic, and unpredictable—environments. For such environments it is extremely difficult and sometimes even impossible to correctly and completely specify these systems a priori, that is, at the time of their design and prior to their use. This would require, for instance, that it is known a priori which environmental conditions will emerge in the future, which agents will be available at the time of emergence, and how the available agents will have to react and interact in response to these conditions. The only feasible way to cope with this difficulty is to endow the individual agents with the ability to improve their own and the overall system performance. The second reason reflects the insight that learning in multiagent systems is not just a magnification of learning in stand-alone systems, and not just the sum of isolated learning activities of several agents. Learning in multiagent systems comprises learning in stand-alone systems because an agent may learn in a solitary way and completely independent of other agents. Moreover, learning in multiagent systems extends learning in stand-alone systems. This is because the learning activities of an individual agent may be considerably influenced (e.g., delayed, accelerated, redirected, or made possible at all) by other agents and because several agents may learn in a distributed and interactive way as a single coherent whole. Such an extended view of learning is qualitatively different from the view traditionally taken in ML, and has the capacity to provoke valuable research impulses that lead to novel machine learning techniques and algorithms.

The chapter is organized as follows. First, Section 6.2 presents a general characterization of learning in multiagent systems. Next, Sections 6.3 to 6.5 describe several concrete learning approaches in detail. These sections offer three major, overlapping perspectives of learning in multiagent systems, each reflecting a different focus of attention: learning and activity coordination; learning about and from other agents; and learning and communication. Section 6.6 shows open directions for future research, and gives some further references to related work in ML, economics, and psychology.

## 6.2   A General Characterization

Learning in multiagent systems is a many-faceted phenomenon, and it is therefore not surprising that many terms can be found in the literature that all refer to this kind of learning while stressing different facets. Examples of such terms are: mutual learning, cooperative learning, collaborative learning, co-learning, team learning, social learning, shared learning, pluralistic learning, and organizational learning. The purpose of this section is to make the different facets more explicit by offering a general characterization of learning in multiagent systems. This is done by describing, from the point of view of multiagent systems, principal categories of learning, basic features in which learning approaches may differ, and the fundamental learning problem known as the credit-assignment problem. The intention of this section is to enable the reader to basically characterize algorithms for learning in multiagent systems, and to get an understanding of what makes this kind of learning different from learning in stand-alone systems. (Further considerations of how to characterize learning in multiagent systems can be found in [63].)

### 6.2.1   Principal Categories

It is useful to distinguish two principal categories of learning in multiagent systems:

- *centralized learning* (or isolated learning) and
- *decentralized learning* (or interactive learning).

In order to make clear what kinds of learning are covered by these two categories we introduce the notion of a *learning process*:

> *The term learning process refers to all activities (e.g., planning, inference or decision steps) that are executed with the intention to achieve a particular learning goal.*

Learning is said to be centralized if the learning process is executed in all its parts by a single agent and does not require any interaction with other agents. With that, centralized learning takes place through an agent completely independent of other agents—in conducting centralized learning the learner acts as if it were alone. Learning is said to be decentralized if several agents are engaged in the same learning process. This means that in decentralized learning the activities constituting the learning process are executed by different agents. In contrast to centralized learning, decentralized learning relies on, or even requires, the presence of several agents capable of carrying out particular activities.

In a multiagent system several centralized learners that try to obtain different or even the same learning goals may be active at the same time. Similarly, there may be several groups of agents that are involved in different decentralized learning processes. Moreover, the learning goals pursued by such groups may be different or identical. It is also important to see that a single agent may be involved in several centralized and/or distributed learning processes at the same time. Centralized and decentralized learning are best interpreted as two appearances of learning in multiagent systems that span a broad range of possible forms of learning. Learning features that can be applied to structure this broad range are shown in the next subsection.

### 6.2.2 Differencing Features

The two learning categories described above are of a rather general nature, and they cover a broad variety of forms of learning that can occur in multiagent systems. In the following, several differencing features are described that are useful for structuring this variety. The last two features, which are well known in the field of ML (see, e.g., [6] where several other features are described), are equally well suited for characterizing centralized and decentralized learning approaches. The others are particularly or even exclusively useful for characterizing decentralized learning.

**(1) The degree of decentralization.** The decentralization of a learning process concerns its

- distributedness and
- parallelism.

One extreme is that a single agent carries out all learning activities sequentially. The other extreme is that the learning activities are distributed over and parallelized through all agents in a multiagent system.

**(2) Interaction-specific features.** There is a number of features that can be applied to classifying the interactions required for realizing a decentralized learning process. Here are some examples:

- the level of interaction (ranging from pure observation over simple signal passing and sophisticated information exchange to complex dialogues and negotiations);
- the persistence of interaction (ranging from short-term to long-term);
- the frequency of interaction (ranging from low to high);
- the pattern of interaction (ranging from completely unstructured to strictly hierarchical); and
- the variability of interaction (ranging from fixed to changeable).

There may be situations in which learning requires only "minimal interaction" (e.g., the observation of another agent for a short time interval), whereas other learning situations require "maximal interaction" (e.g., iterated negotiation over a long time period).

**(3) Involvement-specific features.** Examples of features that can be used for characterizing the involvement of an agent into a learning process are

- the relevance of involvement and
- role played during involvement.

With respect to relevance, two extremes can be distinguished: the involvement of an agent is not a condition for goal attainment because its learning activities could be executed by another available agent as well; and to the contrary, the learning goal could not be achieved without the involvement of exactly this agent. With respect to the role an agent plays in learning, an agent may act as a "generalist" in so far as it performs all learning activities (in the case of centralized learning), or it may act as a "specialist" in so far as it is specialized in a particular activity (in the case of decentralized learning).

**(4) Goal-specific features.** Two examples of features that characterize learning in multiagent systems with respect to the learning goals are

- the type of improvement that is tried to be achieved by learning and
- the compatibility of the learning goals pursued by the agents.

The first feature leads to the important distinction between learning that aims at an improvement with respect to a single agent (e.g., its motor skills or inference abilities) and learning that aims at an improvement with respect to several agents acting as a group (e.g., their communication and negotiation abilities or their degree of coordination and coherence). The second feature leads to the important distinction between conflicting and complementary learning goals.

**(5) The learning method.** The following learning methods or strategies used by an agent are usually distinguished:

- rote learning (i.e., direct implantation of knowledge and skills without requiring further inference or transformation from the learner);
- learning from instruction and by advice taking (i.e., operationalization—transformation into an internal representation and integration with prior knowledge and skills—of new information like an instruction or advice that is not directly executable by the learner);
- learning from examples and by practice (i.e., extraction and refinement of knowledge and skills like a general concept or a standardized pattern of motion from positive and negative examples or from practical experience);
- learning by analogy (i.e., solution-preserving transformation of knowledge and skills from a solved to a similar but unsolved problem);
- learning by discovery (i.e., gathering new knowledge and skills by making observations, conducting experiments, and generating and testing hypotheses or theories on the basis of the observational and experimental results).

A major difference between these methods lies in the amount of learning efforts required by them (increasing from top to bottom).

**(6) The learning feedback.** The learning feedback indicates the performance level achieved so far. This feature leads to the following distinction:

- supervised learning (i.e., the feedback specifies the desired activity of the learner and the objective of learning is to match this desired action as closely as possible);
- reinforcement learning (i.e., the feedback only specifies the utility of the actual activity of the learner and the objective is to maximize this utility);

- unsupervised learning (i.e., no explicit feedback is provided and the objective is to find out useful and desired activities on the basis of trial-and-error and self-organization processes).

In all three cases the learning feedback is assumed to be provided by the system environment or the agents themselves. This means that the environment or an agent providing feedback acts as a "teacher" in the case of supervised learning, as a "critic" in the case of reinforcement learning, and just as a passive "observer" in the case of unsupervised learning.

These features characterize learning in multiagent systems from different points of view and at different levels. In particular, they have a significant impact on the requirements on the abilities of the agents involved in learning. Numerous combinations of different values for these features are possible. It is recommended that the reader thinks about concrete learning scenarios (e.g., ones known from everyday life), their characterizing features, and how easy or difficult it would be to implement them.

### 6.2.3  The Credit-Assignment Problem

The basic problem any learning system is confronted with is the credit-assignment problem (CAP), that is, the problem of properly assigning feedback—credit or blame—for an overall performance change (increase or decrease) to each of the system activities that contributed to that change. This problem has been traditionally considered in the context of stand-alone systems, but it also exists in the context of multiagent systems. Taking the standard AI view according to which the activities of an intelligent system are given by the external actions carried out by it and its internal inferences and decisions implying these actions, the credit-assignment problem for multiagent systems can be usefully decomposed into two subproblems:

- the *inter-agent CAP*, that is, the assignment of credit or blame for an overall performance change to the external actions of the agents; and

- the *intra-agent CAP*, that is, the assignment of credit or blame for a particular external action of an agent to its underlying internal inferences and decisions.

Figures 6.1 and 6.2 illustrate these subproblems. The inter-agent CAP is particularly difficult for multiagent systems, because here an overall performance change may be caused by external actions of different spatial and/or logically distributed agents. Solving this subproblem necessitates to operate on the level of the overall system, and to answer the question of *what action carried out by what agent contributed to what extent to the performance change.* The second subproblem is equally difficult in single-agent and multiagent systems. Solving this sub-problem necessitates to operate on the level of the individual agent, and to answer the question of *what knowledge, what inferences and what decisions led to an action.* How difficult it is to answer these questions and, with that, to solve the CAP, depends on the concrete learning situation.

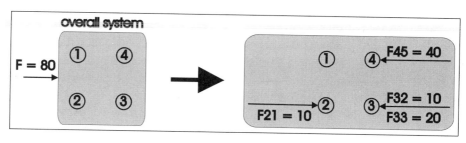

**Figure 6.1**   Inter-agent CAP. The overall system consists of four agents. The $i$th agent is represented by $(i)$. A feedback F for an overall performance change is "decomposed" into action-specific portions $F_{ij}$, where $F_{ij}$ indicates to what degree the $j$th external action carried out by the $i$th agent contributes to F.

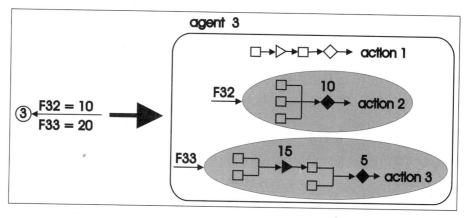

**Figure 6.2**   Intra-agent CAP. Agent 3 carried out three actions, each based on internal knowledge ($\square$), inferences ($\triangleright$) and decisions ($\diamond$). The feedback $F_{33}$ for action 3, for instance, is divided among an inference and a decision step. Action 1 is assumed to have no influence on the overall performance change.

The above description of the CAP is of a conceptual nature, and aims at a clear distinction between the inter-agent and intra-agent subproblems. In practice this distinction is not always obvious. Moreover, typically the available approaches to learning in multiagent systems do not explicitly differ between the two subproblems, or just focus on one of them while strongly simplifying the other. In any case, it is useful to be aware of both subproblems when attacking a multiagent learning problem.

## 6.3  Learning and Activity Coordination

This section is centered around the question of how multiple agents can learn to appropriately coordinate their activities (e.g., in order to optimally share resources or to maximize one own's profit). Appropriate activity coordination is much concerned with the development and adaptation of data-flow and control patterns that improve the interactions among multiple agents (see also Chapters 2, 3, and 7). Whereas previous research on developing agent coordination mechanisms focused on off-line design of agent organizations, behavioral rules, negotiation protocols, etc., it was recognized that agents operating in open, dynamic environments must be able to adapt to changing demands and opportunities [29, 44, 68]. In particular, individual agents are forced to engage with other agents that have varying goals, abilities, composition, and lifespan. To effectively utilize opportunities presented and avoid pitfalls, agents need to learn about other agents and adapt local behavior based on group composition and dynamics. To represent the basic problems and approaches used for developing coordination through learning, two of the earliest research efforts in the area of multiagent learning will be described below. The first is work by Sen and his students [47] on the use of reinforcement learning techniques for the purpose of achieving coordination in multiagent situations in which the individual agents are not aware of each another. The second approach is work by Weiss on optimization of environmental reinforcement by a group of cooperating learners [62]. (Both approaches were developed in the first half of the 1990s, and thus at a time of intensified interest in reinforcement learning techniques. It is stressed that several other reinforcement learning methods were described in the literature that could be also used to demonstrate the scope and benefits of learning to coordinate in multiagent settings; we choose the two approaches mentioned above because we are particular familiar with them.) To enable the reader to follow the discussion of the use of reinforcement learning techniques, a brief overview of the reinforcement learning problem and a couple of widely used techniques for this problem class is presented.

### 6.3.1  Reinforcement Learning

In reinforcement learning problems [3, 26] reactive and adaptive agents are given a description of the current state and have to choose the next action from a set of possible actions so as to maximize a scalar *reinforcement* or *feedback* received after each action. The learner's environment can be modeled by a discrete time, finite state, Markov decision process that can be represented by a 4-tuple $\langle S, A, P, r \rangle$ where $S$ is a set of states, $A$ is a set of actions, $P : S \times S \times A \mapsto [0,1]$ gives the probability of moving from state $s_1$ to $s_2$ on performing action $a$, and $r : S \times A \mapsto \Re$ is a scalar reward function. Each agent maintains a policy, $\pi$, that maps the current state into the desirable action(s) to be performed in that state. The expected value of a discounted sum of future rewards of a policy $\pi$ at a state $x$ is given by $V_\gamma^\pi \stackrel{\text{def}}{=} E\{\sum_{t=0}^{\infty} \gamma^t r_{s,t}^\pi\}$, where $r_{s,t}^\pi$ is the random variable corresponding to the reward received by the learning agent $t$ time steps after if starts using the policy $\pi$ in state $s$, and $\gamma$ is a discount rate ($0 \leq \gamma < 1$).

### Q-Learning

Various reinforcement learning strategies have been proposed that can be used by agents to develop a policy for maximizing rewards accumulated over time. For evaluating the classifier system paradigm for multiagent reinforcement learning described below, it is compared with the Q-learning [59] algorithm, which is designed to find a policy $\pi^*$ that maximizes $V_\gamma^\pi(s)$ for all states $s \in S$. The decision policy is represented by a function, $Q : S \times A \mapsto \Re$, which estimates long-term discounted rewards for each state-action pair. The $Q$ values are defined as $Q_\gamma^\pi(s,a) = V_\gamma^{a;\pi}(s)$, where $a; \pi$ denotes the event sequence of choosing action $a$ at the current state, followed by choosing actions based on policy $\pi$. The action, $a$, to perform in a state $s$ is chosen such that it is expected to maximize the reward,

$$V_\gamma^{\pi^*}(s) = \max_{a \in A} Q_\gamma^{\pi^*}(s,a) \text{ for all } s \in S.$$

If an action $a$ in state $s$ produces a *reinforcement* of $R$ and a transition to state $s'$, then the corresponding $Q$ value is modified as follows:

$$Q(s,a) \leftarrow (1 - \beta)\, Q(s,a) + \beta\, (R + \gamma \max_{a' \in A} Q(s',a')) \quad,$$

where $\beta$ is a small constant called *learning rate*.

### Learning Classifier Systems

Classifier systems are rule based systems that learn by adjusting rule strengths from environmental feedback and by discovering better rules using genetic algorithms. In the following a simplified classifier system is used where all possible message action pairs are explicitly stored and classifiers have one condition and one action. These assumptions are similar to those made by Dorigo and Bersini [15]. Following their notation, a classifier $i$ is described by $(c_i, a_i)$, where $c_i$ and $a_i$ are respectively the condition and action parts of the classifier. $S_t(c_i, a_i)$ gives the strength of classifier $i$ at time step $t$.

   All classifiers are initialized to some default strength. At each time step of problem solving, an input message is received from the environment and matched with the classifier rules to form a matchset, $\mathcal{M}$. One of these classifiers is chosen to fire and, based on its action, a feedback may be received from the environment. Then the strengths of the classifier rules are adjusted. This cycle is repeated for a given number of time steps. A series of cycles constitute a *trial* of the classifier system. In the bucket brigade algorithm (BBA) for credit allocation, when a classifier is chosen to fire, its strength is increased by the environmental feedback. But before that, a fraction $\alpha$ of its strength is removed and added to the strength of the classifier that fired in the last time cycle. So, if *(i)* the firing of classifier $i$ at time step $t$ results in an external feedback $R$ and *(ii)* classifier $j$ fires at the next time step, the following equation gives the strength update of classifier $i$:

$$S_{t+1}(c_i, a_i) = (1 - \alpha) * S_t(c_i, a_i) + \alpha * (R + S_{t+1}(c_j, a_j)) \quad .$$

It is instructive to note that the BBA and Q-learning credit allocation schemes are similar in nature.

### 6.3.2 Isolated, Concurrent Reinforcement Learners

Reinforcement learning techniques can be used by agents to develop action selection policies to optimize environmental feedback by forming a mapping between perceptions and actions. A particular advantage of these techniques is the fact that they can be used in domains in which agents have little or no pre-existing domain expertise, and have little information about the capabilities and goals of other agents. The lack of this useful information makes the coordination problem particularly hard. Almost all currently used coordination mechanisms rely heavily on domain knowledge and shared information between agents. The position espoused here is that reinforcement learning approaches can be used as new coordination techniques for domains where currently available coordination schemes are ineffective.

A related question is: should agents choose not to use communication while learning to coordinate (see 6.5)? Though communication is often helpful and indispensable as an aid to group activity, it does not guarantee coordinated behavior [20], is time-consuming, and can detract from other problem-solving activity if not carefully controlled [16]. Also, agents overly reliant on communication will be severely affected if the quality of communication is compromised (broken communication channels, incorrect or deliberately misleading information, etc.). At other times, communication can be risky or even fatal (as in some combat situations where the adversary can intercept communicated messages). Even when communication is feasible and safe, it is prudent to use it only when absolutely necessary. Such a design philosophy produces systems where agents do not flood communication channels with unwarranted information. As a result, agents do not have to shift through a maze of useless data to locate necessary and time-critical information.

In the isolated, concurrent form of learning discussed here, each agent learns to optimize its reinforcement from the environment. Other agents in the environment are not explicitly modeled. As such, an interesting research question is whether it is feasible for such an agent to use the same learning mechanism in both cooperative and non-cooperative environments.

An underlying assumption of most reinforcement learning techniques is that the dynamics of the environment is not affected by other agencies. This assumption is invalid in domains with multiple, concurrent learners. A valid concern, therefore, is whether standard reinforcement learning techniques will be adequate for concurrent, isolated learning of coordination. More generally, the following dimensions were identified to characterize domains amenable to concurrent, isolated, reinforcement learning (referred to as CIRL henceforth) approach:

**Agent coupling:** In some domains the actions of one agent strongly and frequently affect the plans of other agents (tightly coupled system), whereas in other domains the actions of one agent only weakly and infrequently affect the plans of other agents (loosely coupled system).

**Agent relationships:** Agents in a multiagent system can have different kinds of mutual relationships:

- they may act in a group to solve a common problem (cooperative agents),
- they may not have any preset disposition towards each other but interact because they use common resources (indifferent agents),
- they may have opposing interests (adversarial agents).

For the discussions in this chapter, the latter two classes of domains are grouped as non-cooperative domains.

**Feedback timing:** In some domains, the agents may have immediate knowledge of the effects of their actions, whereas in others they may get the feedback for their actions only after a period of delay.

**Optimal behavior combinations:** How many behavior combinations of participating agents will optimally solve the task at hand? This value varies from one to infinity for different domains.

To evaluate these questions, both Q-learning and classifier systems were used in three different domains:

**Block pushing:** Two agents individually learn to push a box from a starting location to a goal location along a given trajectory. Both cooperative (two agents have same goal location) and competitive (two agents have distinct goal locations) situations are studied. Feedback is based on the deviation of box location from desired path. Domain characteristics are: concurrent learning by two agents with immediate environmental feedback; strongly coupled system; multiple optimal behaviors.

**Resource sharing:** Given individual task loads, two agents have to learn to share a resource over a time period. Domain characteristics are: delayed environmental feedback; strongly coupled system; single optimal behavior.

**Robot navigation:** Two robots learn to navigate intersecting paths on a grid without colliding. Domain characteristics: immediate environmental feedback; variable coupling; multiple optimal behaviors.

The basic conclusion from these series of experiments is that CIRL provides a novel paradigm for multiagent systems through which both friends and foes can concurrently acquire useful coordination knowledge. Neither prior knowledge about domain characteristics nor an explicit model about capabilities of other agents is required. The limitation of this approach lies in the inability of CIRL to develop effective coordination when agent actions are strongly coupled, feedback is delayed, and there is one or only a few optimal behavior combinations. A possible partial fix to this problem would be to use some form of staggered or lock-step learning. In this approach, each agent can learn for a period of time, then execute its current policy without modification for some time, then switch back to learning, etc. Two agents can synchronize their behavior so that one is learning while the other is following a fixed policy and vice versa. Even if perfect synchronization is infeasible, the staggered learning mode is likely to be more effective than the concurrent learning mode.

Other interesting observations include the following:

- In cooperative situations, agents can learn complimentary policies to solve the problem. This amounts to role specialization rather than developing identical behavior. This phenomenon has been observed by other researchers when global reinforcement is used [1].

- Agents can transfer learning to similar situations, i.e., once agents learn to coordinate for a given problem, they can learn to coordinate quickly for a similar problem.

### 6.3.3   Interactive Reinforcement Learning of Coordination

In contrast to the above-mentioned work, Weiss [62] investigates agents explicitly communicating to decide on individual and group actions. The learning approach used is a modification of the BBA scheme for classifier systems. In this approach, agents can observe the set of actions being considered by other agents, and accordingly can eliminate incompatible actions from its local choices. Two variants of the BBA algorithm, the Action Estimation (ACE) and Action Group Estimation (AGE) algorithms, are investigated that requires varying degree of involvement and coordination effort on the part of the group members. The underlying assumption of this work is that the agents are working to optimize a group goal. Below simplified versions of the ACE and AGE algorithms are presented. An algorithm called Dissolution and Formation of Groups (DFG), which is based on these two algorithms but explicitly models group development processes, is described in [61].

**Action Estimation Algorithm (ACE):** Given its perception, $S_i$, of the current environmental state, $S$, each agent, $a_i$, in a group first calculates the set of actions, $A_i(S)$, it can execute in that state. For each such executable action, $A_i^j \in A_i(S)$, an agent calculates the goal relevance, $E_i^j(S)$, of that action. For all actions whose estimated goal relevance is above a threshold, the agent calculates and announces to other agents a bid that is proportional to its goal relevance plus a noise term, $\beta$ (to prevent convergence to local minima):

$$B_i^j(S) = (\alpha + \beta)E_i^j(S)   ,$$

where $\alpha$ is a small constant *risk factor*.

The action with the highest bid is selected for execution, and incompatible actions are eliminated from consideration. This process is repeated until all actions for which bids were submitted are either selected or eliminated. Selected actions form the *activity context*, $\mathcal{A}$. Then a BBA type mechanism is used to reduce the estimates of the selected action, with the total reduced amount being distributed among actions in the previous activity context. If upon the execution of actions in the current activity context the system receives external payoff, the latter is equally distributed among the executed actions. The goal of this estimate reassignment is to enable successful action sequences to increase in estimate over time and to suppress the estimates of ineffective actions. The net estimate update for any action selected for execution is as follows:

$$E_i^j(S) \leftarrow E_i^j(S) - B_i^j(S) + \frac{R}{|\mathcal{A}|} \quad ,$$

where $R$ is the external rewards received. The bid values paid out are then summed up and redistributed equally between all actions $A_k^l$ executed in the immediately previous activity context, $\mathcal{B}$, corresponding the previous state $S'$:

$$E_k^l(S') \leftarrow E_k^l(S') + \frac{\sum_{A_i^j \in \mathcal{A}} B_i^j(S)}{|\mathcal{B}|} \quad .$$

**Action Group Estimation Algorithm (AGE):** In the AGE algorithm, first the applicable actions from all agents in a given environmental state are collected. From these action sets, the set of all activity contexts, $\mathcal{A}(S)$ is calculated where an activity context, $\mathcal{A}$, consists of any set of mutually compatible actions:

$$\mathcal{A}(S) = \{\mathcal{A} : \forall A_k^l, A_i^j \in \mathcal{A}, \ A_k^l \text{ and } A_i^j \text{ are compatible } \} \quad .$$

Then, for each activity context, bids are collected from each agent for all of its actions in that activity context:

$$B_i^j(S, \mathcal{A}) = (\alpha + \beta)E_i^j(S, \mathcal{A}) \quad ,$$

where $E_i^j(S, \mathcal{A})$ is $a_i$'s estimate of goal relevance of action $A_i^j$ given its perception $S_i$ of state $S$ and the activity context $\mathcal{A}$. The activity context with the highest sum of bids for the actions contained is selected, and all the actions contained in it are executed by respective agents.

Let $\mathcal{A}$ be the activity context selected as above. Then for each $A_i^j \in \mathcal{A}$ agent $a_i$ modifies its estimate as follows:

$$E_i^j(S, \mathcal{A}) \leftarrow E_i^j(S, \mathcal{A}) - B_i^j(S, \mathcal{A}) + \frac{R}{|\mathcal{A}|} \quad .$$

The total bid paid out in the current activity activity context is distributed among actions executed in the previous activity context in a manner analogous to the ACE algorithm:

$$E_k^l(S', \mathcal{B}) \leftarrow E_k^l(S', \mathcal{B}) + \frac{\sum_{A_i^j \in \mathcal{A}} B_i^j(S, \mathcal{A})}{|\mathcal{B}|} \quad .$$

From the above descriptions, it is clear that the AGE algorithm requires more computational effort. The possible gain is the use of a global view in selecting the activity context. The conjecture is that this will lead to better system performance. To test this conjecture, a multiagent blocks world domain is used, where each agent is capable of performing only some of the necessary operations in the environment.

Experiments demonstrated that both the ACE and AGE algorithms enabled agents to learn coordinated behavior in the sense that the agents were able to much more effectively solve problems compared to random action selection. AGE produced more effective coordination compared to ACE but at the cost of increased higher space and computation costs. Globally optimal performance, however, was not attained because of the limited local perception and the inability to distinguish some distinct global states. Though fairly simple in design, ACE and AGE represent potent designs that can be extended and augmented to enable the use of additional agent knowledge and reasoning abilities.

Recent work on theoretical and experimental issues in multiagent reinforcement learning promises new frameworks for isolated and interactive learning of coordination (e.g., [1, 11, 19, 42, 64]).

## 6.4    Learning about and from Other Agents

In the last section, scenarios are discussed where agents learned to coordinate their actions. The primary emphasis there was on learning to better cooperate to achieve common tasks. In this section scenarios are considered where agents learn to improve their individual performance. At times such improvement in performance or increase in environmental reward has to come at the expense of other agents in the environment. The emphasis in the learning scenarios presented in this section is on agents trying to learn about other agents in order to better capitalize on available opportunities, and on the question of how learning conducted by an agent can be influenced by other agents. This focus is much concerned with the prediction of the behavior of other agents (including their preferences, strategies, intentions, etc.), with the improvement and refinement of an agent's behavior by interacting with and observing other agents, and with the development of a common view of the world.

Since space restrictions preclude the possibility of discussing all published research in this area, a few representative samples from literature were chosen for illustration:

**Learning organizational roles:** Agents in groups need to learn role assignments to effectively complement each other. Adapting group structure and individual member activities in a situation-dependent manner enables a group to enhance system performance and meet unforeseen challenges. Nagendra Prasad, Lesser, and Lander [35] present a formalism that combines memory-based reasoning and reinforcement learning to enable group members to adaptively select organizational roles.

**Learning to benefit from market conditions:** Information agents selling and buying information units in an electronic marketplace need to be adaptive to their environmental conditions. Vidal and Durfee investigate the advantages of learning agents that learn models of other agents [58]. They empirically characterize situations when it is beneficial for agents selling information to model other sellers and prospective buyers.

**Learning to play better against an opponent:** In adversarial domains like board games, classical maximin strategy provides a conservative approach to playing games. If the strategy used by the opponent to choose moves can be approximated, exploitation of weaknesses in the strategy can lead to better results when playing against that particular opponent [7, 46].

All of the domains discussed below involve isolated learning in a distributed sense. One or more agents may be concurrently learning in the environment. The agents interact frequently, and information from such interactions is used by agents to develop models about other agents. Since each agent learns separately, every agent has to execute all learning activities. Most of the learning mechanisms used are variants of reinforcement learning approaches discussed before.

### 6.4.1  Learning Organizational Roles

Nagendra Prasad, Lesser, and Lander [35] address the important multiagent learning problem of agents learning to adopt situation-specific roles in a cooperative problem-solving domain. Each agent is assumed to have the capability of playing one of several roles in a situation. The learning goal is for an agent to be able to select the most appropriate role to play in a problem-solving state that is likely to lead to better problem solving with less cost.

The basic framework includes the use of Utility, Probability and Cost (UPC) estimates of a role adopted at a particular situation. World states, $\mathcal{S}$, are mapped into a smaller set of situations. Utility represents an agent's estimate of a desired final state's worth if the agent adopted the given role in the current situation. Probability represents the likelihood of reaching a successful final state given the agent plays the adopted role in the current situation, and cost is the associated computational cost incurred. In addition, potentials for roles are maintained, which estimate the usefulness of a role in discovering pertinent global information and constraints. This measure can be orthogonal to the utility measure.

Let $S_k$ and $R_k$ be the sets of situation vectors and roles for agent $k$ respectively. An agent maintains up to $|S_k| * |R_k|$ vectors of UPC and potential values describing the estimates of different roles in different situations. During the learning phase, the probability of selecting a given role $r$ in a situation $s$ is given by

$$Pr(r) = \frac{f(U_{rs}, P_{rs}, C_{rs}, Potential_{rs})}{\sum_{j \in R_k} f(U_{js}, P_{js}, C_{js}, Potential_{js})} \quad,$$

where $f$ is an objective function used to rate a role by combining the different component measures mentioned before. After the learning phase is over, the role to be played in situation $s$ is chosen deterministically as follows:

$$r = \arg\max_{j \in R_k} f(U_{js}, P_{js}, C_{js}, Potential_{js}) \quad.$$

The abstracting of states to situations, and selecting the highest rated role for the situation is suggestive of a memory based approach. The estimation of role UPC and potential values, however, is learned using a reinforcement learning framework. Repeated problem solving is used to incrementally update estimates of these values. Let $\hat{U}^n_{rs}$, $\hat{P}^n_{rs}$, $\widehat{Potential}^n_{rs}$, represent estimates of the utility, probability, and potential of role $r$ in situation $s$ after $n$ updates. Let $S$ be the situations encountered between the time of adopting role $r$ in situation $s$ and reaching a final state $F$. A learning rate of $0 \leq \alpha \leq 1$ is used for updating estimates.

If $U_F$ is the utility of the final state reached, then the utility values are updated as follows:

$$\hat{U}^{n+1}_{rs} \leftarrow (1-\alpha)\hat{U}^n_{rs} + \alpha U_F \quad.$$

This and other updates shown below are performed for all roles chosen in each of the situations, $S$, that are encountered on the path to the final state.

Let $O : S \rightarrow [0,1]$, be a function which returns 1 if the given state is successful and 0 otherwise. Then the update rule for probability is as follows:

$$\hat{P}^{n+1}_{rs} \leftarrow (1-\alpha)\hat{P}^n_{rs} + \alpha O(F) \quad.$$

Let $Conf(S)$ be a function which returns 1 if in the path to the final state, conflicts between agents are detected followed by information exchange to resolve these conflicts. $Conf(S)$ returns 0 otherwise. Then the update rule for potential is

$$\widehat{Potential}^{n+1}_{rs} \leftarrow (1-\alpha)\widehat{Potential}^n_{rs} + \alpha Conf(S) \quad.$$

The update rules for cost are domain dependent as is the nature of the function $f$. Prasad, Lesser, and Lander have successfully used this learning organization role approach in a steam condenser design domain. The evaluation function used by them ignores the cost metric: $f(U, P, C, Potential) = U * P + Potential$.

### Related Approaches to Learning Organizational Roles

In a related approach, Haynes and Sen [22] present a multiagent case-based learning (MCBL) algorithm by which agents can learn complementary behaviors to improve group performance. The domain of experimentation is the predator-prey domain [57]. Agents are initialized with hand-crafted behavioral strategies which are modified based on their interaction with the world. Failures to successfully execute actions suggested by default rules trigger learning of negative cases. These negative cases alter the agent policies, and with experience, team members are shown to improve problem-solving performance.

Stone and Veloso [55] investigate the effectiveness of teammates learning to coordinate their actions against opponent teams. The domain of study is a simulated robotic soccer game. Their approach is interesting in the novel use of a layered learning methodology, where learning of low-level skills is followed by learning of higher-level decision making. For example, a neural network–based approach is used to learn how to shoot the ball towards a chosen direction. After this skill is acquired, a decision tree–based method is used to select a teammate to pass the ball to. Higher-level decision making in the context of a team of agents, such as moving into open positions expecting a pass from the teammate with the ball, is possible in such a layered learning approach.

### 6.4.2   Learning in Market Environments

Vidal and Durfee [58] investigate the use of agents to buy and sell information in electronic marketplaces like digital libraries. They assume such environments are open in nature as new agents (either buyers or sellers of information) can enter or leave the marketplace at will. A practical approach to implementing such systems would be to consider each agent as a self-interested entity with the goal of maximizing local utility. A market mechanism is used to control the transfer of information units between agents that can supply the information and agents that need it. Quality of information available to different sellers may not be the same, and the pricing and buying decisions are left to individual sellers and buyers respectively.

It is assumed that information can be reproduced arbitrarily at negligible cost and agents have uniform access to all other agents in the marketplace. In such scenarios, a seller needs to provide value-added services to differentiate its products from other sellers. In such a market, a buyer announces for a good it needs. Sellers bid with prices for delivering such goods. The buyer then selects from these bids and pays the corresponding seller the bid price. This seller then provides the good to the buyer. The buyer can assess the quality of the received good only after it receives it from the seller, i.e., it cannot examine the quality of the good before buying. The profit of a seller $s$ in selling a good $g$ at price $p$ is $p - c_s^g$, where $c_s^g$ is its cost of producing that good. If this good was of quality $q$, its value to a buyer $b$ is $V_b^g(p, q)$. In a transaction, the goal of the buyer and the seller is to maximize value and profit respectively.

Three types of agents are investigated in such a market economy:

**0-level agents:** These are agents that do not model the behavior of other agents. They set their buying and selling prices based on aggregate past experience.

**1-level agents:** These are agents that analyze the past behavior of other agents and try to predict their buying or selling price preferences. Other agents, however, are just modeled as 0-level agents or agents with no model of other agents. That is, if an 1-level agent A is modeling a 0-level agent B, A does not consider the fact that B is also modeling A. Note that 1-level agents have information about individual agents in the environment, where 0-level agents just use their aggregate past experience.

**2-level agents:** These are agents that model other agents as 1-level agents. That is, these agents view other agents as agents which are modeling others as 0-level agents or agents having no models of others.

In the following the strategies of 0-level and 1-level agents are only described concisely. The performance comparison of such agents will be presented next.

### Strategy of 0-level Agents

A 0-level buyer chooses the seller $s^*$ for supplying a good $g$, such that

$$s^* = \arg \max_{s \in S} f^g(p_s^g) \quad ,$$

where $S$ is the set of sellers and the function $f^g(p)$ returns the expected value to the buyer of buying $g$ at price $p$. This value function is incrementally learned in a reinforcement learning framework:

$$f_{t+1}^g = (1 - \alpha) f_t^g(p) + \alpha V_b^g(p, q) \quad ,$$

where $\alpha$ is the learning rate which is decreased over time from a starting value of 1 to a final value close to $\alpha_{min}$. The buyer also explores randomly (picks a random seller) with probability $\epsilon$, with this probability also decreased over time in a manner similar to that of $\alpha$.

A seller $s$ has to sell a good $g$ at a price greater than or equal to its cost, i.e., $p_s^g \geq c_s^g$. The actual price $p_s^*$ is chosen to maximize expected profit:

$$p_s^* = \arg \max_{p \in P \& p \geq c_s^g} h_s^g(p) \quad ,$$

where $P$ is the set of prices and the function $h_s^g(p)$ returns the expected profit for the seller if it offers good $g$ at a price $p$. This expected profit function is learned as

$$h_{t+1}^g(p) = (1 - \alpha) h_t^g(p) + \alpha Profit_s^g(p) \quad ,$$

where $Profit_s^g(p) = p - c_s^g$ if it wins the auction and is 0 otherwise.

### Strategy of 1-level Agents

A 1-level buyer models each seller by a probability density function, $q_s^g(x)$ over the qualities $x$ returned by $s$ when providing good $g$ in the past. Such a buyer chooses the seller $s^*$ for supplying a good $g$ to obtain the highest expected value:

$$s^* = \arg\max_{s \in S} E(V_b^g(p_s^g, q_s^g(x)))$$

$$= \arg\max_{s \in S} \frac{1}{|Q|} \sum_{x \in Q} q_s^g(x) V_b^g(p_s^g, x),$$

where $Q$ is the set of possible quality levels. The 1-level buyer does not model other buyers.

The 1-level seller models each buyer $b$ for good $g$ by a probability density function $m_b^g(p)$ that returns the probability that $b$ will choose price $p$ for good $g$. It also models every seller $s$ for good $g$ by a probability density function $n_s^g(y)$, which gives the probability that $s$ will bid $y$ for good $g$. With these information, the 1-level seller can determine its bid to maximize expected profits as

$$p^* = \arg\max_{p \in P}(p - c_s^g) \prod_{s' \in \bar{s}} \sum_{p'} N(g, b, s, s', p, p') \quad ,$$

where $\bar{s} = S - \{s\}$, and $N(g, b, s, s', p, p') = n_{s'}^g(p')$ if $m_b^g(p') \leq m_b^g(p)$ and is $0$ otherwise. The function chooses the best bid by calculating for each possible bid the product of the probability of winning the auction with that bid and the profit from that bid. The probability of winning a bid is obtained by multiplying the probabilities of bidding lower than each of the other sellers. The probability of bidding lower than a given seller is calculated by summing the probabilities corresponding to all bids by that seller for which the buyer will prefer the bid of the learning agent.

Vidal and Durfee [58] simulated different artificial economies with 5 buyers and 8 sellers with the value function used by buyers being $V_b(p, q) = 3q - p$ for all goods. The following list shows the major conclusions from the observed behavior of learning mechanisms described above:

- In a group consisting of 0-level agents only, isolated learning produced equilibrium prices when all seller agents offered goods of the same quality. If the latter condition was violated, price fluctuations prevent equilibrium.

- If buyers are 0-level agents, 1-level sellers can benefit based on price volatility as the buyers try to figure out the price-quality correlation. The 1-level sellers can pretend to be high-quality goods sellers by bidding high prices and thus obtain substantial profits at the expense of the buyer.

- If the buyers are 1-level agents, they learn to buy from sellers who can provide them with the highest value. Interestingly enough, 1-level sellers suffer, because they assume buyers are 0-level agents and hence try to over-price their goods.

The above observations suggest that if the model of the other agents is accurate, an agent can gain substantially from it. But if the model underestimates the true capability of the other agent, the modeling agent can also lose out.

### 6.4.3   Learning to Exploit an Opponent

Two player zero-sum games have been studied widely within both the game theory and artificial intelligence communities. The most prominent approach in AI for developing game playing programs has been the use of the minimax algorithm (developed from the maximin strategy espoused in the game theory literature). In the absence of any knowledge of the opponent's strategy, the maximin approach assumes that the opponent will chose a move that is the worst from the player's viewpoint.

If an accurate model of the opponent is available, such a model can be used to predict the exact move the opponent is going to play corresponding to each of the moves that the player can play from the current board configuration. Carmel and Markovitch [7] present an $M^*$ algorithm, a generalization of minimax, that can use an opponent model to choose a more appropriate move to play against that player. Given the set of possible game states $S$, a successor function $\sigma : S \to 2^S$, an opponent model to specify opponent's move from any given state, $\varphi : S \to S$, from a given state $s$ and for a search depth $d$, the $M^*$ algorithm returns the following value:

$$M(s, d, f, \varphi) = \begin{cases} f(s) & d \leq 0 \\ \max s' \in \sigma(s)(f(s')) & d = 1 \\ \max s' \in \sigma(s)(M(\varphi(s'), d - 2, f, \varphi)) & d > 1 \end{cases} .$$

If the player is using an evaluation function of $f_0$, the standard minimax algorithm can be written as a special form of $M$ as

$$M^0_{(\langle f_0 \rangle, d)}(s) = M(s, d, f_0, M^0_{(\langle -f_0 \rangle, d-1)})$$

which denotes the fact that minimax assumes the opponent is minimizing the player's payoff by searching up to a depth of $d - 1$.

If the player was using an evaluation of $f_1$ and the actual evaluation function, $f_0$, used by the opponent was known, then another special case of $M$, the $M^1$ algorithm, can be defined as

$$M^1_{(\langle f_1, f_0 \rangle, d)}(s) = M(s, d, f_1, M^0_{(\langle f_0 \rangle, d-1)}) .$$

The $M^1$ algorithm first finds the opponents choice move by performing the opponent's minimax search to depth $d-1$. It then evaluates the selected moves by calling itself recursively to depth $d - 2$.

In the general case, it is possible to define the $M^n$ algorithm to be the $M$ algorithm for which $\varphi = M^{n-1}$:

$$M^n_{(\langle f_n,\ldots,f_0\rangle,d)}(s) = M(s, f_n, d, M^{n-1}_{(\langle f_{n-1},\ldots,f_0\rangle,d-1)})  .$$

For example, The player with the $M^1$ algorithm assumes that its opponent is a $M^0$ or minimax player, the $M^2$ player assumes that its opponent is a $M^1$ player, and so on.

Carmel and Markovitch use the domain of checkers to show that the $M^1$ player performs better than $M^0$ or minimax player against different opponents when the model of the opponent is accurately known. The problem in approaches like this is how one gets to know about the evaluation function of the opponent.

In a related work Carmel and Markovitch have developed a learning approach to approximating the opponent model [8]. Given a set of opponent moves from specific board configurations, they first present an algorithm to calculate the depth of search being used by the opponent. If the assumed function model is accurate then few examples suffice to induce the depth of search.

They also present an algorithm to learn the opponent's game-playing strategy. The assumptions made are the following: the opponent's evaluation function is a linear combination of known board features, and the opponent does not change its function while playing (because this would eliminate the possibility of concurrent learning). A hill-climbing approach is used to select the weight vector on the features and depth of search. They also experimentally demonstrate the effectiveness of this learning approach for different opponent strategies.

### Related Approaches to Opponent Modeling

In a similar approach to developing game players that can exploit weaknesses of a particular opponent, Sen and Arora [46] have used a Maximum Expected Utility (MEU) principle approach to exploiting learned opponent models. In their approach, conditional probabilities for different opponent moves corresponding to all moves from the current state are used to compute expected utilities of each of the possible moves. The move with the maximum expected utility is then played. A probabilistic model of the opponent strategy is developed by observing moves played by the opponent in different discrepancy ranges as measured by the evaluation function of the player.

Let the player and the opponent be required to choose from move sets $\{\alpha_1, \alpha_2, \ldots\} = \alpha$ and $\{\beta_1, \beta_2, \ldots\} = \beta$ respectively, and the utility received by A for a $(\alpha_i, \beta_j)$ pair of moves be $u(\alpha_i, \beta_j)$. The MEU principle can be used to choose a move as follows:

$$\arg\max_{\alpha_i \in \alpha} \sum_{\beta_j \in \beta} p(\beta_j | \alpha_i)\, u(\alpha_i, \beta_j)  ,$$

where $p(\beta_j | \alpha_i)$ is the conditional probability that the opponent chooses the move

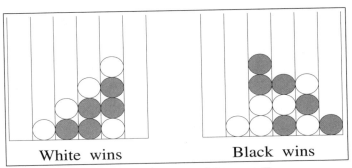

**Figure 6.3**  Winning scenarios in the game of Connect-Four.

$\beta_j$ given that the agent plays its move $\alpha_i$. The maximin strategy can be shown to be a special case of the MEU strategy. If the opponent strategy can be accurately modeled by the learning mechanism, the MEU player will be able to exploit the opponent's weaknesses.

The initial domain of application of this approach involves the two-player zero-sum game of Connect-Four. Connect-Four is a popular two-player board game. Each player has several round tokens of a specific color (black or white). The board is placed vertically and is divided into six slots (the actual game sold in the market has seven slots, but most of the AI programs use the six-slot version of the game). Each slot has room for six tokens. Players alternate in making moves. A player wins if it is able to line up four tokens horizontally, vertically, or diagonally. The game ends in a draw if the board fills up with neither player winning. Examples of winning and losing scenarios are shown in Figure 6.3. In this board game, the MEU player is shown to be able to beat a simple opponent in fewer moves compared to the maximin player.

Other related work worthy of mention include Carmel and Markovitch's work on modeling opponent strategies with a finite automaton [9]; Bui, Kieronska and Venkatesh's work on learning probabilistic models of the preferences of other agents in the meeting scheduling domain [5]; and Zeng and Sycara's work on using Bayesian updating by bargainers to learn opponent preferences in sequential decision making situations [69].

### Explanation-Based Learning

Sugawara and Lesser [56] present an explanation-based learning [17] approach to improving cooperative problem-solving behavior. Their proposed learning framework contains a collection of heuristics for recognizing inefficiencies in coordinated behavior, identifying control decisions causing such inefficiencies, and rectifying these decisions.

The general procedure is to record problem-solving traces including tasks and operations executed, relationships existing between tasks, messages communicated between agents, resource usage logs, domain data, and knowledge and control knowledge used for problem solving. Local traces and models of problem-solving activities are exchanged by agents when a coordination inefficiency is detected. This information is used to construct a global model and to review the problem-solving activities. A *lack-of-information* problem is solved by choosing alternative tasks to satisfy certain goals. An *incorrect-control* problem requires more elaborate processing and coordination strategies need to be altered in such cases.

To identify the type of problem confronting the system, agents analyze traces to identify mainstream tasks and messages. Based on this identification, *learning analysis problem* (LAPs) situations are identified which include execution of unnecessary actions, task processing delays, longer task durations, redundant task processing, etc. After some LAP is detected, agents try to locally generate the existing task relationships that may have caused the LAP. Information is exchanged incrementally to form a more comprehensive description of the problem. The purpose of this analysis is to identify whether the LAP is of *lack-of-control* or *incorrect control* problem type. Problems of the former type can normally be resolved in a relatively straightforward manner. For incorrect-control problems, the following solution methods are applied: changing the rating of specific goals and messages, changing the order of operations and communications, allocating tasks to idle agents, and using results calculated by other agents. For both types encountered, the system learns to avoid similar problems in the future. To accomplish this, the system learns situation-specific rules using an inductive learning scheme.

The learning approach discussed above relies extensively on domain models and sophisticated diagnostic reasoning. In contrast, most of the other multiagent learning approaches that have been studied in literature rely very little on prior domain knowledge.

## 6.5 Learning and Communication

The focus of this section is on how learning and communication are related to each other. This relationship is mainly concerned with requirements on the agents' ability to effectively exchange useful information. The available work on learning in multiagent systems allows us to identify two major relationships and research lines:

- *Learning to communicate*: Learning is viewed as a method for reducing the load of communication among individual agents.

- *Communication as learning*: Communication is viewed as a method for exchanging information that allows agents to continue or refine their learning activities.

Work along the former line starts from the fact that communication usually is very slow and expensive, and therefore should be avoided or at least reduced whenever this is possible (see also 6.3.2). Work along the latter line starts from the fact that learning (as well as, e.g., planning and decision making) is inherently limited in its potential effects by the information that is available to and can be processed by an agent. Both lines of research have to do with improving communication and learning in multiagent systems, and are related to the following issues:

- What to communicate (e.g., what information is of interest to the others).

- When to communicate (e.g., what efforts should an agent investigate in solving a problem before asking others for support).

- With whom to communicate (e.g., what agent is interested in this information, what agent should be asked for support).

- How to communicate (e.g., at what level should the agents communicate, what language and protocol should be used, should the exchange of information occur directly—point-to-point and broadcast—or via a blackboard mechanism).

These issues have to be addressed by the system designer or derived by the system itself. The following two subsections illustrate the two lines of research by describing representative approaches to "learning to communicate" and "communication as learning."

There is another aspect that is worth stressing when talking about learning and communication in multiagent systems. A necessary condition for a useful exchange of information is the existence of a common ontology. Obviously, communication is not possible if the agents assign different meanings to the same symbols without being aware of the differences (or without being able to detect and handle them). The development of a common and shared meaning of symbols therefore can be considered as an essential learning task in multiagent systems (see [18] for further considerations). This "shared meaning problem" is closely related to (or may be considered as the DAI variant of) the symbol grounding problem [21], that is, the problem of grounding the meaning of symbols in the real world. According to the physical grounding hypothesis [4], which has received particular attention in behavior-oriented AI and robotics, the grounding of symbols in the physical world is a necessary condition for building a system that is intelligent. This hypothesis was formulated as a counterpart to the symbol system hypothesis [36] upon which classical knowledge-oriented AI is based and which states that the ability to handle, manipulate, and operate on symbols is a necessary and sufficient condition for general intelligence (independent of the symbols' grounding).

### 6.5.1   Reducing Communication by Learning

Consider the contract-net approach (e.g., [54]) as described in Chapter 2. According to this approach the process of task distribution consists of three elementary activities: announcement of tasks by *managers* (i.e., agents that want to allocate tasks to other agents); submission of bids by potential *contractors* (i.e., agents that could execute announced tasks); and conclusion of contracts among managers and contractors. In the basic form of the contract net a broadcasting of task announcements is assumed. This works well in small problem environments, but runs into problems as the problem size—the number of communicating agents and the number of tasks announced by them—increases. What therefore is needed in more complex environments are mechanisms for reducing the communication load resulting from broadcasting. Smith [53] proposed several such mechanisms like focused addressing and direct contracting which aim at substituting point-to-point communication for broadcasting. A drawback of these mechanisms is, however, that direct communication paths must be known in advance by the system designer, and that the resulting communication patterns therefore may be too inflexible in non-static environments. In the following, an alternative and more flexible learning-based mechanism called addressee learning [37] is described (in a slightly simplified form).

The primary idea underlying addressee learning is to reduce the communication efforts for task announcement by enabling the individual agents to acquire and refine knowledge about the other agents' task solving abilities. With the help of the acquired knowledge, tasks can be assign more directly without the need of broadcasting their announcements to all agents. Case-based reasoning (e.g., [27, 60]) is employed as an experience-based mechanism for knowledge acquisition and refinement. Case-based reasoning is based on the observation that humans often solve a problem on the basis of solutions that worked well for similar problems in the past. Case-based reasoning aims at constructing cases, that is, problem-solution pairs. Whenever a new problem arises, it is checked whether it is completely unknown or similar to an already known problem (case retrieval). If it is unknown, a solution must be generated from scratch. If there is some similarity to a known problem, the solution of this problem can be used as a starting point for solving the new one (case adaptation). All problems encountered so far, together with their solutions, are stored as cases in the case base (case storage). This mechanism can be applied to communication reduction in a contract net as follows. Each agent maintains its own case base. A case is assumed to consist of *(i)* a task specification and *(ii)* information about which agent already solved this task in the past and how good or bad the solution was. The specification of a task $T_i$ is of the form

$$T_i = \{A_{i1}V_{i1}, \ldots, A_{im_i}V_{im_i}\} \quad ,$$

where $A_{ij}$ is an attribute of $T_i$ and $V_{ij}$ is the attribute's value. What is needed in order to apply case-based reasoning is a measure for the similarity between the tasks. In the case of addressee learning, this measure is reduced to the similarity between attributes and attribute values. More precisely, for each two attributes $A_{ir}$ and $A_{js}$ the distance between them is defined as

$$\text{DIST}(A_{ir}, A_{js}) = \text{SIMILAR-ATT}(A_{ir}, A_{js}) \cdot \text{SIMILAR-VAL}(V_{ir}, V_{js}) \quad,$$

where SIMILAR-ATT and SIMILAR-VAL express the similarity between the attributes and the attribute values, respectively. How these two measures are defined depends on the application domain and on the available knowledge about the task attributes and their values. In the most simplest form, they are defined as

$$\text{SIMILAR-ATT}(x, y) = \text{SIMILAR-VAL}(x, y) = \begin{cases} 1 & \text{if } x = y \\ 0 & \text{otherwise} \end{cases} \quad,$$

which means that similarity is equal to identity. With the help of the distance DIST between attributes, now the similarity between two tasks $T_i$ and $T_j$ can be defined in an intuitively clear and straightforward way as

$$\text{SIMILAR}(T_i, T_j) = \sum_r \sum_s \text{DIST}(A_{ir}, A_{js}) \quad.$$

For every task, $T_i$, a set of similar tasks, $S(T_i)$, can be defined by specifying the demands on the similarity between tasks. An example of such a specification is

$$S(T_i) = \{T_j : \text{SIMILAR}(T_i, T_j) \geq 0.85\} \quad,$$

where the tasks $T_j$ are contained in the case base of the agent searching for similar cases. Now consider the situation in which a agent $N$ has to decide about assigning some task $T_i$ to another agent. Instead of broadcasting the announcement of $T_i$, $N$ tries to preselect one or several agents which it considers as appropriate for solving $T_i$ by calculating for each agent $M$ the suitability

$$\text{SUIT}(M, T_i) = \frac{1}{|S(T_i)|} \sum_{T_j \in S(T_i)} \text{PERFORM}(M, T_j) \quad,$$

where $\text{PERFORM}(M, T_j)$ is an experience-based measure indicating how good or bad $T_j$ has been performed by $M$ in the past. (The specification of PERFORM again depends on the application domain.) With that, agent $N$ just sends the announcement of $T_i$ to the most appropriate agent(s), instead of all agents.

## 6.5.2   Improving Learning by Communication

As an agent usually can not be assumed to be omnipotent, in most problem domains it also can not be assumed to be omniscient without violating realistic assumptions. The lack of information an agent suffers from may concern

- the environment in which it is embedded (e.g., the location of obstacles) and the problem to be solved (e.g., the specification of the goal state to be reached);

- other agents (e.g., their abilities, strategies, and knowledge);

- the dependencies among different activities and the effects of one own's and other agents' activities on the environment and on potential future activities (e.g., an action $a$ carried out by an agent $A$ may prevent an agent $B$ from carrying out action $b$ and enable an agent $C$ to carry out action $c$).

Agents having a limited access to relevant information run the risk of failing in solving a given learning task. This risk may be reduced by enabling the agents to explicitly exchange information, that is, to communicate with each other. Generally, the following two forms of improving learning by communication may be distinguished:

- learning based on low-level communication, that is, relatively simple query-and-answer interactions for the purpose of exchanging missing pieces of information (knowledge and belief); and

- learning based on high-level communication, that is, more complex communicative interactions like negotiation and mutual explanation for the purpose of combining and synthesizing pieces of information.

Whereas the first form of communicative learning results in shared information, the second form results in shared understanding. Below two communication-based learning approaches are described which illustrate these two forms.

In both forms communication is used as a means for improving learning. Aside from this "assisting view" of communication, the reader should keep in mind that communication as such can be viewed as learning, because it is a multiagent-specific realization of knowledge acquisition. Whether learning should be enriched by communication is a very difficult question. In the light of the standard evaluation criteria for learning algorithms—speed, quality, and complexity—this question can be decomposed into the following three subquestions:

- How fast are the learning results achieved with/without communication?

- Are the learning results achieved with/without communication of sufficient quality?

- How complex is the overall learning process with/without communication?

The above considerations should make clear that communication offers numerous possibilities to improve learning, but that it is not a panacea for solving learning problems in multiagent systems. Combining them therefore has to be done very carefully. In particular, it is important to see that communication itself may bring in incomplete and false information into an agent's information base (e.g., because of transmission errors) which then makes it even more difficult to solve a learning task.

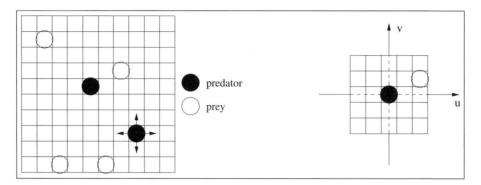

**Figure 6.4**  Predator-prey domain: a 10 by 10 grid world (left) and a visual field of depth 2 (right).

### *Illustration 1: Let's Hunt Together!*

Many attempts have been made to improve learning in multiagent systems by allowing low-level communication among the learners. Among them is the work by Tan [57] which is also well suited for illustrating this form of learning. Related work that focuses on multirobot learning was presented, e.g., by Matarić [31, 32] and Parker [38, 39].

Tan investigated learning based on low-level communication in the context of the predator-prey domain shown in Figure 6.4. The left part of this figure shows a two-dimensional world in which two types of agents, predators and prey, act and live. The task to be solved by the predators is to catch a prey by occupying the same position. Each agent has four possible actions $a$ to choose from: *moving up, moving down, moving left,* and *moving right*. On each time step each prey randomly moves around and each predator chooses its next move according to the decision policy it has gained through Q-learning (see Section 6.3.1). Each predator has a limited visual field of some predefined depth. The sensation of a predator is represented by $s = [u, v]$, where $u$ and $v$ describe the relative distance to the closest prey within its visual field. This is illustrated by the right part of Figure 6.4; here the perceptual state is represented by $[2, 1]$. Tan identified two kinds of information that the learners could exchange in order to support each other in their learning:

- *Sensor data.* Here the predators inform each other about their visual input. If the predators know their relative positions (e.g., by continuously informing each other about their moves), then they can draw inferences about the prey's actual positions. This corresponds to a pooling of sensory resources, and thus aims at a more centralized control of distributed sensors.

- *Decision/Activity policies.* Here the predators inform each other about what they have learned so far w.r.t. their decisions/activities (i.e., the values $Q(s, a)$ in the case of Q-learning). This corresponds to a pooling of motor resources, and thus aims at a more centralized control of distributed effectors.

The experimental investigations reported by Tan show that these kinds of information exchange clearly lead to improved learning results. The fact that these two kinds of information exchange are applicable in most problem domains makes them essential. It is stressed that it is an important but still unanswered question how closely a centralized control of sensors and effectors should be approached. It is obvious, however, that an optimal degree of centralization of control depends on the problem domain under consideration and on the abilities of the individual agents.

### Illustration 2: What Will a Cup of Coffee Cost?

Learning based on high-level communication—which is a characteristic of human-human learning—is rather complex, and so it is not surprising that not many approaches to this form of learning are available so far. In the following, an idea of this form of learning is given by describing the approach by Sian [48, 49] called consensus learning (details omitted and slightly simplified). According to this approach a number of agents is assumed to interact through a blackboard. The agents use a simple language for communication that consists of the following nine operators for hypotheses:

- *Introduction and removal of hypotheses* to/from the blackboard

  $ASSERT(H)$      – Introduction of a non-modifiable hypothesis $H$.

  $PROPOSE(H, C)$ – Proposal of a new hypothesis $H$ with confidence value $C$.

  $WITHDRAW(H)$ – Rejection of a hypothesis $H$.

- *Evaluation of hypotheses*

  $CONFIRM(H, C)$ – Indication of confirmatory evidence for a hypothesis $H$ with confidence value $C$.

  $DISAGREE(H, C)$– Indication of disagreement with a hypothesis $H$ with confidence value $C$.

  $NOOPINION(H)$ – Indication that no opinion is available with regards to a hypothesis $H$.

  $MODIFY(H, G, C)$– Generation of a modified version $G$ (hence, of a new hypothesis) of $H$ with confidence value $C$.

- *Modification of the status of hypotheses and acceptance*

  $AGREED(H, T)$    – Change of status of a hypothesis $H$ from "proposed" to "agreed" with the resultant confidence value $T$ (see below).

  $ACCEPT(H)$      – Acceptance of a previously agreed hypothesis $H$.

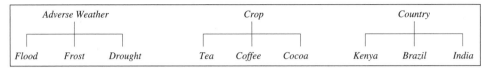

**Figure 6.5**  Taxonomies available to the agents.

After an agent introduced a hypothesis $H$ (by means of $PROPOSE$) and the other agents responded (by means of $CONFIRM$, $DISAGREE$, $NOOPINION$, or $MODIFY$), the introducing agent can determine the resultant confidence value $T$ of $H$. Let $\{C_1^+, \ldots, C_m^+\}$ be the confidence values associated with the $CONFIRM$ and $MODIFY$ responses of the other agents, and $\{C_1^-, \ldots, C_n^-\}$ the confidence values associated with the $DISAGREE$ responses of the other agents. Then

$$T = SUPPORT(H) \cdot [1 - AGAINST(H)]$$

where $SUPPORT(\mathrm{H}) = V(C_m^+)$ and $AGAINST(H) = V(C_n^-)$ with

$$V(C_m^+) = \begin{cases} V(C_{m-1}^+) + C_m^+ \cdot [1 - V(C_{m-1}^+)] & if \quad m \geq 1 \\ 0 & if \quad m = 0 \end{cases}$$

and

$$V(C_n^-) = \begin{cases} V(C_{n-1}^-) + C_n^- \cdot [1 - V(C_{n-1}^-)] & if \quad n \geq 1 \\ 0 & if \quad n = 0 \end{cases}.$$

For instance, $V(C_3^+) = C_1^+ + C_2^+ + C_3^+ - C_1^+ C_2^+ - C_1^+ C_3^+ - C_2^+ C_3^+ + C_1^+ C_2^+ C_3^+$. The definition of $V$ aims at adding confidence values (which represent a measure of belief on the part of an agent) and, at the same time, taking their potential overlaps into consideration.

For an illustration of consensus learning, consider the case of three agents who want to find out how the prices for coffee, tea, and cocoa will develop. The common knowledge available to the three agents is shown in Figure 6.5. In addition, the agents have the following local domain knowledge:

Agent 1:     *Major-Producer(Kenya, Coffee)*
             *Major-Producer(Kenya, Tea)*

Agent 2:     *Major-Producer(Brazil, Coffee)*
             *Major-Producer(Brazil, Cocoa)*

Agent 3:     *Major-Producer(India, Tea)*

Assume that after a period of time the agents observed the following data and have constructed the following generalizations:

Agent 1:     *Weather(Kenya, Drought)*, *Price(Tea, Rising)*
             *Weather(Kenya, Drought)*, *Price(Cocoa, Steady)*

$$Weather(Kenya, Frost), Price(Coffee, Rising)$$
$$\text{GEN: } Weather(Kenya, Adverse) \text{ and}$$
$$Major\text{-}Producer(Kenya, Crop) \rightarrow Price(Crop, Rising)$$

Agent 2:  $Weather(Brazil, Frost), Price(Coffee, Rising)$
$$Weather(Brazil, Flood), Price(Cocoa, Rising)$$
$$\text{GEN: } Weather(Brazil, Adverse) \rightarrow Price(Crop, Rising)$$

Agent 3:  $Weather(India, Flood), Price(Tea, Rising)$
$$\text{GEN: } Weather(India, Flood) \rightarrow Price(Tea, Rising)$$

Figure 6.6 shows a potential interaction sequence. The Agent 3 has enough confidence in its generalization, and starts the interaction with the hypothesis $H1$. The other agents respond to $H1$. Agent 2 has no direct evidence for H1, but its generalization totally subsumes $H1$. It therefore proposes its generalization as a modification of $H1$, leading to the hypothesis $H2$. The situation is similar with Agent 3, and this agent proposes the hypothesis $H3$. At this point, Agent 3 can calculate the resultant confidence value for its hypothesis $H1$. In the sequel, the non-proposing agents respond to the hypotheses $H2$ and $H3$, and the proposing agents calculate the resultant confidence values. Based on the confidence values Agent 2 and Agent 3 withdraw their hypotheses. After Agent 1 has agreed, the others accept $H3$. What has been gained is the broad acceptance of the hypothesis $H3$ which is less specific than $H1$ and less general than $H2$.

## 6.6   Conclusions

**Summary.** This chapter concentrated on the area of learning in multiagent systems. It was argued that this area is of particular interest to DAI as well as ML. Two principal categories of learning—centralized and decentralized learning—were distinguished and characterized from a more general point of view. Several concrete learning approaches were described that illustrate the current stage of development in this area. They were chosen because they reflect very well the current methodological main streams and research foci in this area: learning and activity coordination; learning about and from other agents; and learning and communication. It is very important to see that these foci are not orthogonal, but complementary to each other. For instance, agents may learn to cooperate by learning about each other's abilities, and in order to learn from one another the agents may communicate with each other. It is stressed that several interesting and elaborated approaches to learning in multiagent systems other than those described here are available. Space did not allow us to treat them all, and the reader therefore is referred to the literature mentioned thoughout this chapter.

**Open research issues.** Learning in multiagent systems constitutes a relatively young area that brings up many open questions. The following areas of research are of particular interest:

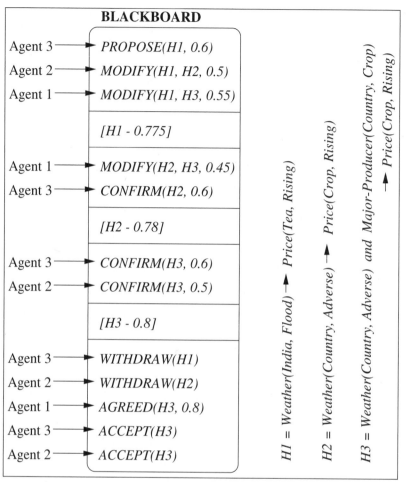

**Figure 6.6**   An example of an interaction sequence.

- The identification of general principles and concepts of multiagent learning. Along this direction questions arise like *What are the unique requirements and conditions of multiagent learning?* and *Are there general guidelines for the design of multiagent learning algorithms?*

- The investigation of the relationships between single-agent and multiagent learning. This necessitates to answer questions like *Do centralized and decentralized learning qualitatively differ from each other?* and *How and under what conditions can a single-agent learning algorithm be applied in multiagent contexts?*

- The application of multiagent learning in complex real-world environments. Going in this direction helps to further improve our understanding of the benefits and limitations of this form of learning.

- The development of theoretical foundations of decentralized learning. This ranges from convergence proofs for particular algorithms to general formal models of decentralized learning.

An overview of challenges for ML in cooperative information systems is presented in [51]. In this overview a useful distinction is made between requirements for learning about passive components (e.g., databases), learning about active components (e.g., workflows and agents), and learning about interactive components (e.g., roles and organizational structures).

**Pointers to relevant related work.** As already mentioned, this chapter is restricted to learning in multiagent systems. The reader interested in textbooks on single-agent learning is referred to [28] and [34]. There is a number of approaches to distributed reinforcement learning that are not covered by this chapter; see, e.g., [12, 30, 41, 65]. Moreover, there is much work in ML that does not directly deal with learning in multiagent systems, but is closely related to it. There are three lines of ML research that are of particular interest from the point of view of DAI:

- *Parallel and distributed inductive learning* (e.g., [10, 40, 50]). Here the focus is on inductive learning algorithms that cope with massive amounts of data.

- *Multistrategy learning* (e.g., [33]). Here the focus is on the development of learning systems that employ and synthesize different learning strategies (e.g., inductive and analogical, or empirical and analytical).

- *Theory of team learning* (e.g., [25, 52]). Here the focus is on teams of independent machines that learn to identify functions or languages, and on the theoretical characterization—the limitations and the complexity—of this kind of learning.

Research along these lines is much concerned with the decentralization of learning processes, and with combining learning results obtained at different times and/or locations.

Apart from ML, there is a considerable amount of related work in economics. Learning in organizations like business companies and large-scale institutions constitutes a traditional and well-established subject of study. Organizational learning is considered as a fundamental requirement for an organization's competitiveness, productivity, and innovativeness in uncertain and changing technological and market circumstances. With that, organizational learning is essential to the flexibility and sustained existence of an organization. Part II of the Bibliography provided in [63] offers a number of pointers to this work.

There is also a large amount of related work in psychology. Whereas economics mainly concentrates on organizational aspects, psychology mainly focuses on the cognitive aspects underlying the collaborative learning processes in human groups. The reader interested in related psychological research is referred to [2] and, in particular, to [13]. A guide to research on collaborative learning can be found in [14]. Interdisciplinary research that, among other things, is aimed at identifying essential differences between available approaches to multiagent learning and collaborative human-human learning is described in [67].

These pointers to related work in ML, economics, and psychology are also intended to give an idea of the broad spectrum of learning in multiagent systems. In attacking the open questions and problems sketched above it is likely to be helpful and inspiring to take this related work into consideration.

## 6.7   Exercises

1.  *[Level 1]* Consider a group of students who agreed to work together in preparing an examination in DAI. Their goal is to share the load of learning. Identify possible forms of interactive learning. How do the forms differ from each other (e.g., w.r.t. efficiency and robustness) and what are their advantages and disadvantages? What abilities must the students have in order to be able to participate in the different forms of learning? Do you think it is possible to apply the different forms in (technical) multiagent contexts? What are the main difficulties in such an application?

2.  *[Level 2]* Design domains with varying agent couplings, feedback delays, and optimal strategy combinations, and run experiments with isolated reinforcement learners. Summarize and explain the success and failures of developing coordinated behaviors using isolated, concurrent reinforcement learners in the domains that you have investigated.

3.  Consider the algorithms ACE and AGE.

    (a)  *[Level 2]* Calculate and compare the computational complexities per action selection cycle of both algorithms.

    (b)  *[Level 2]* Evaluate the scale up in speed of both algorithms with increasing number of agents in the group.

    (c)  *[Level 3]* How could the complexity be reduced? Do you see any possibility to reduce the number of activity contexts to be considered by the agents? Implement and test your solution.

4.  *[Level 2/3]* Implement and experiment with 0, 1, and 2-level agents in an information economy. How does 2-level buyer agent benefit compare to 1-level buyer agents when the seller agents are 0-level agents? How does 2-level buyer agent benefit compare to 1-level buyer agents when the seller agents are 1-level agents?

5.  Consider the problem of learning an opponent strategy.

    (a)  *[Level 2]* Formulate this problem in a two player zero-sum game as a reinforcement learning problem.

    (b)  *[Level 3]* Implement a reinforcement learning algorithm to learn the opponent strategy in a simple two-player zero-sum game. Show how the learned opponent model can be used to exploit weaknesses in the strategies of a weaker player.

6.   A popular multiagent learning task is block pushing. As described in this chapter, this task requires that (at least) two agents learn to work together in pushing a box from a start to a goal position, where the box chosen is large enough so that none of the agents can solve this problem alone. This learning task becomes especially challenging under two reasonable assumptions: each agent is limited in its sensory abilities (i.e., its sensors provide incomplete and noisy data), and learning feedback is provided only when the agents are successful in moving the block into the goal position (i.e., no intermediate feedback is provided).

   (a)  *[Level 2/3]* Assume that both agents are capable of Q-learning and that they select and perform their actions simultaneously. Furthermore, assume that *(i)* the agents do not communicate and *(ii)* that at each time each of the agents knows only its own position, the goal position, and the position of the block. Implement this learning scenario and run some experiments. What can be observed?

   (b)  *[Level 3/4]* Now assume that the agents are able to communicate with each other. What information should they exchange in order to improve their overall performance? Implement your ideas and compare the results with those gained for non-communicating learning agents. Do your ideas result in faster learning? What about the quality of the learning results and the complexity of learning?

7.   Another popular learning task is multiagent foraging. This task requires that multiple agents learn to collect food in a confined area (their "living environment") and take it to a predefined region (their "home"). An agent receives positive learning feedback whenever it arrived at home with some food (each agent is able to collect food without requiring help from the others).

   (a)  *[Level 1]* What are the essential differences between this learning task and the block pushing task?

   (b)  *[Level 2/3]* Assume that the agents are capable of Q-learning. Implement this learning scenario and run some experiments.

   (c)  *[Level 3/4]* Additionally assume that that there are two different types of food: food of type A can be carried by a single agent, while food of type B must be carried by two agents. Furthermore assume that the learning feedback for collecting food of type B is four times higher than for type A, and that some agents are better (e.g., faster) in collecting food of type A while others are better in collecting (together with others) food of type B. What information should the agents exchange and what communication and coordination mechanisms should they use in order to collect both type-A and type-B food as fast as possible? Think about equipping the individual agents with the ability to learn about other agents. Implement your ideas, and compare the results with those achieved by the more primitive non-communicating agents (i.e., agents that do neither communicate nor learn about each other).

8.  *[Level 3/4]* Consider Exercise 14 of Chapter 1 (vacuum world example). Instead of implementing chains of sample passing agents, the agents themselves could learn to form appropriate chains. (Alternatively, the agents could learn to appropriately divide the vacuum world into smaller sections that are then occupied by fixed sets or teams of agents.) Identify criteria according to which the agents can decide when and how to form chains. Run experiments with the learning agents and analyze, e.g., the orientation and the position of the chains learned. Identify criteria according to which the agents can decide when and how to dissolve chains. Again run experiments. Give particular attention to the learning feedback (immediate vs. delayed) and the communication and negotiation abilities of the agents.

9.  *[Level 3/4]* Consider Exercise 11 of Chapter 2 (package-moving robots). How could the robots learn to build appropriate roadways and drop-off points? (What exactly does appropriate mean in this example? What communication and negotiation abilities should the robots possess?) Implement your ideas, and compare the results achieved by learning and non-learning robots.

10. *[Level 3/4]* Consider Exercise 8 of Chapter 4 (multiagent LRTA* algorithm). How could the agents learn to coordinate their activities? What activities should be coordinated at all? What information must be exchanged by the agents in order to achieve a higher degree of coordination? Choose one of the search problems described in Chapter 4, and run some experiments.

11. *[Level 3/4]* Consider Exercise 8 of Chapter 5 (lookahead in contracting). Choose one of the contracting scenarios described in that chapter; alternatively, you may choose the multiagent foraging scenario (see Exercise 7 above), the vacuum world scenario (Exercise 8), or the package-moving domain (Exercise 9). Give examples of criteria for deciding about the depth of lookahead in contracting. Implement an algorithm for lookahead contracting, where the depth of lookahead is adapted by the agents themselves.

## 6.8   References

1.  T. Balch. Learning roles: Behavioral diversity in robot teams. In *Collected Papers from the AAAI-97 Workshop on Multiagent Learning*, pages 7–12. AAAI, 1997.

2.  A. Bandura. *Social learning theory*. Prentice-Hall, Englewood Cliffs, NJ, 1977.

3.  A.B. Barto, R.S. Sutton, and C. Watkins. Sequential decision problems and neural networks. In *Proceedings of 1989 Conference on Neural Information Processing*, 1989.

4.  R.A. Brooks. Elephants don't play chess. *Robotics and Autonomous Systems*,

6:3–15, 1990.

5.   H.H. Bui, D. Kieronska, and S. Venkatesh. Learning other agents' preferences in multiagent negotiation. In *Proceedings of the Thirteenth National Conference on Artificial Intelligence*, pages 114–119, Menlo Park, CA, 1996. AAAI Press.

6.   J.G. Carbonell, R.S. Michalski, and T.M. Mitchell. An overview of machine learning. In J.G. Carbonell and T.M. Mitchell, editors, *Machine learning – An artificial intelligence approach*, pages 3–23. Springer-Verlag, Berlin, 1994.

7.   D. Carmel and S. Markovitch. Incorporating opponent models into adversary search. In *Thirteenth National Conference on Artificial Intelligence*, pages 120–125, Menlo Park, CA, 1996. AAAI Press/MIT Press.

8.   D. Carmel and S. Markovitch. Learning and using opponent models in adversary search. Technical Report Technical Report 9609, Technion, 1996.

9.   D. Carmel and S. Markovitch. Learning models of intelligent agents. In *Thirteenth National Conference on Artificial Intelligence*, pages 62–67, Menlo Park, CA, 1996. AAAI Press/MIT Press.

10.   P.K. Chan and S.J. Stolfo. Toward parallel and distributed learning by meta-learning. In *Working Notes of the AAAI Workshop on Know. Disc. Databases*, pages 227–240, 1993.

11.   C. Claus and C. Boutilier. The dynamics of reinforcement learning in cooperative multiagent systems. In *Collected papers from the AAAI-97 Workshop on Multiagent Learning*, pages 13–18. AAAI, 1997.

12.   R.H. Crites and A.G. Barto. Improving elevator performances using reinforcement learning. In D.S. Touretzky, M.C. Mozer, and M.E. Hasselmo, editors, *Advances in neural information processing systems 8*. MIT Press, Cambridge, MA, 1996.

13.   P. Dillenbourg, editor. *Collaborative learning: Cognitive and computational approaches*. Pergamon Press, 1998.

14.   P. Dillenbourg, M. Baker, A. Blaye, and C. O'Malley. The evolution of research on collaborative learning. In H. Spada and P. Reimann, editors, *Learning in humans and machines*. Elsevier Science Publ., Amsterdam, 1996.

15.   M. Dorigo and H. Bersini. A comparison of Q-learning and classifier systems. In *Proceedings of From Animals to Animats, Third International Conference on Simulation of Adaptive Behavior*, 1994.

16.   E.H. Durfee, V.R. Lesser, and D.D. Corkill. Coherent cooperation among communicating problem solvers. *IEEE Transactions on Computers*, C-36(11):1275–1291, 1987.

17.   T. Ellman. Explanation-based learning: A survey of programs and perspectives. *ACM Computing Surveys*, 21(2):163–221, 1989.

18.   H. Friedrich, M. Kaiser, O. Rogalla, and R. Dillmann. Learning and communication in multi-agent systems. In G. Weiß, editor, *Distributed artificial intelligence meets machine learning*, Lecture Notes in Artificial in Artificial Intelligence, Vol. 1221, pages 259–275. Springer-Verlag, Berlin, 1997.

19.   P. Gu and A.B. Maddox. A framework for distributed reinforcement learning. In Gerhard Weiß and Sandip Sen, editors, *Adaptation and Learning in Multi–Agent Systems*, Lecture Notes in Artificial Intelligence, pages 97–112. Springer Verlag, Berlin, 1996.

20.   J. Halpern and Y. Moses. Knowledge and common knowledge in a distributed environment. *Journal of the ACM*, 37(3):549–587, 1990. A preliminary version

appeared in *Proc. 3rd ACM Symposium on Principles of Distributed Computing*, 1984.

21. S. Harnad. The symbol grounding problem. *Physica D*, 42:335–346, 1990.

22. T. Haynes and S. Sen. Learning cases to compliment rules for conflict resolutions in multiagent systems. *International Journal of Human-Computer Studies*, to appear, 1998.

23. M. Huhns and G. Weiß, editors. Special Issue on Multiagent Learning of the *Machine Learning Journal*. Vol. 33(2-3), 1998.

24. I.F. Imam. Intelligent adaptive agents. Papers from the 1996 AAAI Workshop. Technical Report WS-96-04, AAAI Press, 1996.

25. S. Jain and A. Sharma. On aggregating teams of learning machines. *Theoretical Computer Science A*, 137(1):85–105, 1982.

26. L.P. Kaelbling, Michael L. Littman, and Andrew W. Moore. Reinforcement learning: A survey. *Journal of AI Research*, 4:237–285, 1996.

27. J.L. Kolonder. *Case-based reasoning*. Morgan Kaufmann, San Francisco, 1993.

28. P. Langley. *Elements of machine learning*. Morgan Kaufmann, San Francisco, 1995.

29. V.R. Lesser. Multiagent systems: An emerging subdiscipline of AI. *ACM Computing Surveys*, 27(3):340–342, 1995.

30. M.L. Littmann and J.A. Boyan. A distributed reinforcement learning scheme for network routing. Report CMU-CS-93-165, School of Computer Science, Carnegie Mellon University, 1993.

31. M. Matarić. Learning in multi-robot systems. In G. Weiß and S. Sen, editors, *Adaption and learning in multi-agent systems*, Lecture Notes in Artificial in Artificial Intelligence, Vol. 1042, pages 152–163. Springer-Verlag, Berlin, 1996.

32. M. Matarić. Using communication to reduce locality in distributed multi-agent learning. *Journal of Experimental and Theoretical Artificial Intelligence*, to appear, 1998.

33. R. Michalski and G. Tecuci, editors. *Machine learning. A multistrategy approach*. Morgan-Kaufmann, San Francisco, CA, 1995.

34. T. Mitchell. *Machine learning*. McGraw-Hill, New York, 1997.

35. M.V. Nagendra Prasad, V.R. Lesser, and S.E. Lander. Learning organizational roles in a heterogeneous multi-agent system. In *Proceedings of the Second International Conference on Multiagent Systems*, pages 291–298, 1996.

36. A. Newell and H.A. Simon. Computer science as empirical inquiry: Symbols and search. *Communications of the ACM*, 19(3):113–126, 1976.

37. T. Ohko, K. Hiraki, and Y. Anzai. Addressee learning and message interception for communication load reduction in multiple robot environments. In G. Weiß, editor, *Distributed artificial intelligence meets machine learning*, Lecture Notes in Artificial in Artificial Intelligence, Vol. 1221, pages 242–258. Springer-Verlag, Berlin, 1997.

38. L.E. Parker. Task-oriented multi-robot learning in behavior-based systems. In *Proceedings of the 1996 IEEE/RSJ International Conference on Intelligent Robots and Systems*, pages 1478–1487, 1996.

39. L.E. Parker. L-alliance: Task-oriented multi-robot learning in behavior-based systems. *Journal of Advanced Robotics*, to appear, 1997.

40. F.J. Provost and J.M. Aronis. Scaling up inductive learning with massive parallelism. *Machine Learning*, 23:33f, 1996.

41. A. Schaerf, Y. Shoham, and M. Tennenholtz. Adaptive load balancing: a study in multi-agent learning. *Journal of Artificial Intelligence Research*, 2:475–500, 1995.

42. J. Schmidhuber. A general method for multi-agent reinforcement learning in unrestricted environments. In Sandip Sen, editor, *Working Notes for the AAAI Symposium on Adaptation, Co-evolution and Learning in Multiagent Systems*, pages 84–87, Stanford University, CA, 1996.

43. S. Sen. Adaptation, coevolution and learning in multiagent systems. Papers from the 1996 Spring Symposium. Technical Report SS-96-01, AAAI Press, 1996.

44. S. Sen. IJCAI-95 workshop on adaptation and learning in multiagent systems. *AI Magazine*, 17(1):87–89, Spring 1996.

45. S. Sen, editor. Special Issue on Evolution and Learning in Multiagent Systems of the *International Journal of Human-Computer Studies*. Vol. 48(1), 1998.

46. S. Sen and N. Arora. Learning to take risks. In *Collected papers from AAAI-97 workshop on Multiagent Learning*, pages 59–64. AAAI, 1997.

47. S. Sen, M. Sekaran, and J. Hale. Learning to coordinate without sharing information. In *National Conference on Artificial Intelligence*, pages 426–431, 1994.

48. S.S. Sian. Adaptation based on cooperative learning in multi-agent systems. In Y. Demazeau and J.-P. Müller, editors, *Decentralised AI (Vol. 2)*, pages 257–272. Elsevier Science Publ., Amsterdam, 1991.

49. S.S. Sian. Extending learning to multiple agents: Issues and a model for multi-agent machine learning (ma-ml). In Y. Kodratoff, editor, *Machine learning – EWSL-91*, pages 440–456. Springer-Verlag, Berlin, 1991.

50. R. Sikora and M.J. Shaw. A distributed problem-solving approach to inductive learning. Faculty Working Paper 91-0109, College of Commerce and Business Administration, University of Illinois at Urbana-Champaign, 1991.

51. M.P. Singh and M.N. Huhns. Challenges for machine learning in cooperative information systems. In G. Weiß, editor, *Distributed artificial intelligence meets machine learning*, Lecture Notes in Artificial in Artificial Intelligence, Vol. 1221, pages 11–24. Springer-Verlag, Berlin, 1997.

52. C. Smith. The power of pluralism for automatic program synthesis. *Journal of the ACM*, 29:1144–1165, 1982.

53. R.G. Smith. A framework for problem solving in a distributed processing environment. Stanford Memo STAN-CS-78-700, Department of Computer Science, Stanford University, 1978.

54. R.G. Smith. The contract-net protocol: High-level communication and control in a distributed problem solver. *IEEE Transactions on Computers*, C-29(12):1104–1113, 1980.

55. P. Stone and M. Veloso. A layered approach to learning client behaviors in the robocup soccer. *Applied Artificial Intelligence*, to appear, 1998.

56. T. Sugawara and V. Lesser. On-line learning of coordination plans. In *Working Papers of the 12th International Workshop on Distributed Artificial Intelligence*, 1993.

57. M. Tan. Multi-agent reinforcement learning: Independent vs. cooperative agents. In *Proceedings of the Tenth International Conference on Machine Learning*, pages 330–337, 1993.

58. J.M. Vidal and E.H. Durfee. The impact of nested agent models in an information economy. In *Proceedings of the Second International Conference on Multiagent*

*Systems*, pages 377–384, Menlo Park, CA, 1996. AAAI Press.

59. C.J.C.H. Watkins. *Learning from Delayed Rewards*. PhD thesis, King's College, Cambridge University, 1989.

60. I. Watson and F. Marir. Case-based reasoning: A review. *The Knowledge Engineering Review*, 9(4):327–354, 1994.

61. G. Weiß. Action selection and learning in multi-agent environments. In *From animals to animats 2 – Proceedings of the Second International Conference on Simulation of Adaptive Behavior*, pages 502–510, 1993.

62. G. Weiß. Learning to coordinate actions in multi-agent systems. In *Proceedings of the 13th International Joint Conference on Artificial Intelligence*, pages 311–316, 1993.

63. G. Weiß. Adaptation and learning in multi-agent systems: Some remarks and a bibliography. In G. Weiß and S. Sen, editors, *Adaption and learning in multiagent systems*, Lecture Notes in Artificial in Artificial Intelligence, Vol. 1042. Springer-Verlag, Berlin, 1996.

64. G. Weiß, editor. *Distributed artificial intelligence meets machine learning*. Lecture Notes in Artificial in Artificial Intelligence, Vol. 1221. Springer-Verlag, Berlin, 1997.

65. G. Weiß. A multiagent perspective of parallel and distributed machine learning. In *Proceedings of the 2nd International Conference on Autonomous Agents*, pages 226–230, 1998.

66. G. Weiß, editor. Special Issue on Learning in Distributed Artificial Intelligence Systems of the *Journal of Experimental and Theoretical Artificial Intelligence*. Vol. 10(3), 1998.

67. G. Weiß and P. Dillenbourg. What is "multi" in multiagent learning? In P. Dillenbourg, editor, *Collaborative learning: Cognitive and computational approaches*. Pergamon Press, 1998.

68. G. Weiß and S. Sen, editors. *Adaption and learning in multiagent systems*. Lecture Notes in Artificial in Artificial Intelligence, Vol. 1042. Springer-Verlag, Berin, 1996.

69. D. Zeng and K. Sycara. Bayesian learning in negotiation. International Journal of Human Computer Studies (to appear), 1998.

# 7 Computational Organization Theory

**Kathleen M. Carley and Les Gasser**

## 7.1 Introduction

From the hospital, to the schoolroom, to the boardroom people find that the actions they take affect and are affected by various organizations, and the norms, procedures, culture, and members of those organizations. In order to navigate through an organizational world, agents (human and artificial) need social and organizational intelligence. This organizational intelligence comprises many dimensions, including communication capabilities, knowledge about who knows what, knowledge about norms, procedures, and culture of the organization, and more.

The ability of an organization to act is certainly dependent on the intelligence of the agents within it. However, organizations, and multiagent systems in general, often show an intelligence and a set of capabilities that are distinct from the intelligence and capabilities of the agents within them. It is not difficult to find multiagent systems that display non-random and repeated patterns and processes of action, communication, knowledge, and memory (beyond the lifetime of a single agent) regardless of whether or not the agents are human. Said another way, many multiagent systems exhibit characteristics of organization, and sometimes of intentional organization design. Organization designs may emerge spontaneously or be imposed, and they can can structure activities and attention within a system or control the actions of a system as a corporate entity.

From country to country, culture to culture, task to task, and agent type to agent type, we find both differences and commonalties in the patterns and processes connecting individual agents and in the forms organizations take. In order to navigate through environments and achieve results not achievable by individual agents, or to exhibit capabilities not held by individual agents, organizations (and indeed all multiagent systems) need to act as intelligent information processors, capable of responding as a single corporate entity, and to coordinate individual agents using organizing principles or designs. Research in the computational organization area employs computational techniques to theorize about and analyze organizations and the processes of organizing.

The goal of this chapter is to describe what can be done and what others have done in this area: the underlying principles, assumptions, concerns, and the major streams of work. After reading this chapter you will have gained insight into the aims, findings and new possibilities of this field. Further, after reading this chapter you should have developed a preliminary understanding of the nature of computational organizational models and developed some of your own ideas about how to construct virtual experiments using such models.

### 7.1.1   What Is an Organization?

A classic response to the question "What is an organization?" is "I know it when I see it." Indeed, every text book in organizational theory provides a definition of organizations. Unfortunately, there is no wide consensus on the definition of "organization," and indeed as theorists reason about organizations trying to answer fundamentally different questions, they construct different definitions of the basic phenomenon. While there is no single definition of organizations that is uniformly agreed to, there are general tenets that are more or less shared. In general, organizations are characterized as:

- large-scale problem solving technologies
- comprised of multiple agents (human, artificial, or both)
- engaged in one or more tasks; organizations are systems of activity
- goal directed (however, goals can change, may not be articulable, and may not be shared by all organizational members)
- able to affect and be affected by their environment
- having knowledge, culture, memories, history, and capabilities distinct from any single agent
- having legal standing distinct from that of individual agents

One rationale for the existence of organizations qua organizations is that they exist to overcome the limitations of individual agency.[1] From this viewpoint, there are four basic limitations: cognitive, physical, temporal, and institutional.

1.  Cognitive Limitations – Agents as boundedly rational actors have cognitive limitations and therefore must join together to achieve higher-levels of performance.
2.  Physical Limitations – Agents are limited physically, both because of their physiology and because of the resources available to them, and therefore must coordinate their actions, e.g., to achieve higher-levels of productivity. All action takes place situated in specific space-time locations, and agents are limited (e.g. by relativity limits) in their access to other space-time locations; this fundamental locality means that distributed action is fundamentally a

---

1. Other rationales include human needs for social affiliation, and the simple non-teleological emergence of patterns of activity in complex environments. However, in this chapter the focus is on the standard information processing approach.

multiagent—and hence potentially organized—phenomenon.

3.    Temporal Limitations – Agents are temporally limited and therefore must join together to achieve goals which transcend the lifetime of any one agent.

4.    Institutional Limitations – Agents are legally or politically limited and therefore must attain organizational status to act as a corporate actor rather than as an individual actor.

There is a plethora of ways in which organizations are constituted to overcome limitations of individual agency. Researchers in various areas refer to the way in which an organization is organized as the form, structure, architecture or design of that organization. Decades of research in this area have repeatedly shown that there is no single correct or proper organizational design. Field and survey research on actual human organizations, laboratory experiments on human groups, virtual experiments using computational models, and analyses using mathematical models all point to the same conclusion. There is no single organizational design that yields the optimal performance under all conditions. Which organizational design is optimal depends on a variety of factors including the specific task or tasks being performed, the intelligence, cognitive capabilities, or training of the agents, the volatility of the environment, legal or political constraints on organizational design, and the type of outcome desired (e.g., efficiency, effectiveness, accuracy, or minimal costs). The recognition by researchers of how organizational performance differentially depends upon multiple factors has led to the development of "contingency theories" of organization. From an organizational engineering perspective, locating an optimal organizational design for a specific, multidimensional situation is key. Whereas, from a theoretical perspective locating the general principles and tradeoffs underlying organizational design in a multidimensional space is key.

Consequently, research in this area has often focused on the search for general principles of organizing and the conditions under which these principles do or do not apply. For example, two such linked principles are specialization and the division of labor. Specialization of task or occupation refers to the principle that individuals can become more effective when they are expert in particular activities requiring particular and limited types of knowledge. Division of labor refers to the principle that appropriate division of tasks, knowledge, and skills among agents in an organization can improve organizational performance; e.g., by limiting task and knowledge dependencies. In general, organizations which employ specific and productive instances of these principles are able to overcome the limitations of individual agency, coordinate individual actions, and leverage training costs, skill development, and resources in such a way that the organization as a whole achieves higher levels of performance than are otherwise achievable. However, over-specialization and excessive division can reduce performance and flexibility by de-skilling individuals, decreasing attention due to boredom, and increasing decision making time, and by actually increasing coordination costs in situations of uncertainty or failure.

### 7.1.2   What Is Computational Organization Theory?

Researchers in the field of Computational Organization Theory (COT) use mathematical and computational methods to study both human and automated organizations as computational entities. Human organizations can be viewed as inherently computational because many of their activities transform information from one form to another, and because organizational activity is frequently information-driven.

COT attempts to understand and model two distinct but complementary types of organization. The first is the natural or human organization which continually acquires, manipulates, and produces information (and possibly other material goods) through the joint, interlocked activities of people and automated information technologies. Second, COT studies artificial computational organizations generally comprised of multiple distributed agents which exhibit collective organizational properties (such as the need to act collectively, an assignment of tasks, the distribution of knowledge and ability across agents, and constraints on the connections and communication among agents). Researchers use computational analysis to develop a better understanding of the fundamental principles of organizing multiple information processing agents and the nature of organizations as computational entities. The general aims of research in this area is to build new concepts, theories, and knowledge about organizing and organization in the abstract, to develop tools and procedures for the validation and analysis of computational organizational models, and to reflect these computational abstractions back to actual organizational practice through both tools and knowledge.

Research in this area has resulted in a large number of models, each with its own special characteristics. Many of these models focus on specific aspects of organizational behavior. Some research projects with particular illustrative models are listed in Table 7.1. These models differ in the way in which individual cognition is modeled. For example, in the Organizational Consultant there are no individual cognitive agents; in Sugarscape, the agents have physical positions and follow simple rules to respond to each other and their environment; in VDT agents are modeled as simple processors with in- and out-boxes; in CORP a simple model of experiential learning is used; in ORGAHEAD both experiential learning and annealing are used to model the decision process; and in Plural-Soar and TAC Air Soar a fully articulated model of human cognition is used. Further, differences in these models are effected by whether or not the agents within them can learn (see also Chapter 6). These models differ in the degree to which the organizational design is captured; e.g., in Sugarscape organizational design is not considered, but emergent patterns and structures of activity are an outcome of the model; the Organizational Consultant covers design in terms of a set of features; the Garbage Can model, AAIS, the CORP model, and the Cultural Transmission model all consider only a small set of designs; whereas HITOP-A, ACTION, ORGAHEAD, and VDT admit a wide range of explicitly parameterized designs. Models also differ on the extent to which specific features of tasks are modeled. In the Garbage Can model the task is generic and simply requires energy, in the Cultural Transition

| Model | Author |
|---|---|
| Garbage Can | Cohen, March and Olsen (1972) |
| AAIS | Masuch and LaPotin (1989) |
| CORP | Carley (1992) |
| HITOP-A | Majchrzak and Gasser (1992) |
| Plural-Soar | Carley et al. (1992) |
| VDT | Cohen (1992), Levitt et al. (1994) |
| TAC Air Soar | Tambe (1997) |
| Organizational Consultant | Baligh, Burton and Obel (1990, 1994) |
| ACTION | Gasser, Majchrzak, et al., (1993,94) |
| ORGAHEAD | Carley and Svoboda (1996) |
| TAEMS | Decker (1995,1996) |
| Sugarscape | Epstein and Axtell (1996) |
| Cultural Transmission | Harrison and Carrol (1991) |

**Table 7.1**  Illustrative Models

model shared knowledge rather than the task itself is considered, in CORP and ORGAHEAD a detailed classification task is used as a generic simulation activity; ACTION captures features of 141 generic manufacturing tasks; In VDT specific features of routine design tasks in which the precedent ordering among subtasks and needed skills can be explored, and TAEMS extends this to non-routine tasks as well.

Research in this area has also resulted in several "generalist" models that can be used in a number of applications in addition to their use in organizational theory. For example, one useful general model of information-seeking, decision making, and problem-solving activity in organizations is distributed search. Since formal computational models of search are well understood, modeling organizational activity as search can provide a clear and tractable explanatory framework (see Chapter 4). New approaches to control or task allocation in distributed search frameworks can, by analogy, provide suggestive new approaches to these problems in human organizations, e.g., in the development of new organizational forms or for reasoning about the effects of alternative strategic decisions. In the end, distributed search models provide just one type of abstraction that is useful for reasoning about problems of both human organizations and computational ones, and so help to unify thinking about both types.

Computational organization theories are most often grounded in existing cognitive, knowledge-based, information-processing theories of individual behavior. However, COT extends this to an organizational level [60, for example] and gives precision to the notion of bounded rationality by specifying the nature of the boundaries [7]. The original information processing perspective basically argued simply that agents were boundedly rational, that information is ubiquitous in the organization, and that the organization itself becomes a computational system. Today there is a neo-information processing perspective on organizational behavior that extends and refines this early view. The basic tenets of this neo-information processing perspective on organizations are:

- Bounded rationality: Organizational agents are boundedly rational. There are two types of bounds—limits to capabilities and limits to knowledge. Capabilities depend on the agents' cognitive, computational, and/or physical architecture. Knowledge depends on the agents' ability to learn and the agents' intellectual history. The agents' position in an organization influences to which information an agent has access. Thus, an agents' knowledge of how to do specific tasks, of how its specific organization operates, and indeed of how organizations operate in general, is a function of what positions the agent has held.

- Information ubiquity: Within organizations large quantities of information in many different forms are widely distributed across multiple agents. The information may not necessarily be correct.

- Task orientation: Organizations and the agents within them are continually engaged in performing tasks. The tasks in which an organization and its constituent agents are engaged require these agents to communicate, build on, analyze, adapt or otherwise process organizational information using various technologies, and to search out new information and new solutions.

- Distributional constraints: Organizational performance is a function of what information is shared by whom, when, and of the process of searching for that information. An organization's culture is the distribution of the knowledge and processes across the agents within it. This distribution affects the extent and character of socially shared cognition, team mental models, group information processing, and concurrent information analysis.

- Uncertainty: Uncertainty about task outcomes, environmental conditions, and about many other aspects of organizational life influences organizational activity. Distributed computational models such as distributed search or distributed constraint satisfaction pose distribution itself as a source of uncertainty: distribution can render critical uncertainty-reducing information less available because of the cost of seeking, transmitting, or assimilating it, and because of the overhead of coordinating information needs across agents.

- Organizational intelligence: Organizational intelligence resides in the distribution of knowledge, processes, procedures across agents and the linkages among agents. Organizations redesign themselves and their vision of their environments on the basis of the information available to them, with the aim of enabling them to better search for or process information. Such redesign is part of organizational learning processes. It can alter an organization's intelligence, and may or may not improve organizational performance.

- Irrevocable change (path dependence): As agents and organizations learn, their intelligence is irrevocably restructured. This one-directional evolution means that the kind and order in which things are learned—particular histories—can have dramatic consequences.

- Necessity of communication: In order to function as a corporate unit, agents within an organization need to communicate. This communication may take place explicitly by sending and receiving messages or implicitly by perceiving the actions of others.

In addition to this neo-information-processing view of organizations researchers in this area share a series of implicit background assumptions. These are:

- Modelability: Organizational phenomena are modelable.

- Performance differential: It is possible to distinguish differences in organizational performance.

- Manipulability: Organization are entities that can be manipulated and transformed.

- Designability: Organizations are entities that can be designed. This is not to say that organizations do not evolve, nor that they cannot be found in nature, for assuredly both events occur. However, they can also be consciously designed and redesigned: organizational transformations can be purposeful and principled.

- Practicality: Organizational transformations (based on the design or manipulation of models) can be transferred into and implemented in actual practice.

- Pragmatism: The costs of modeling and researching organizations using computational methods are relatively lower than the costs of manipulating or researching similar aspects of actual organizations in vivo, and the benefits gained outweigh the costs.

These assumptions that underlie the research in computational organization theory are the result of a fundamentally interdisciplinary intellectual history. Research in this area draws on work in distributed artificial intelligence (DAI), multiagent systems, adaptive agents, organizational theory, communication theory, social networks, and information diffusion. One of the foundational works in this area is The Behavioral Theory of the Firm [13] in which a simple information processing model of an organization is used to address issues of design and performance. While the strongest roots are in the information processing [60, 48, 64, 19, 13]. and social information processing [59], tradition, current models also have roots in the areas of resource dependency [54], institutionalism [56], population ecology [31], and symbolic interaction [21]. Formalisms and specific measures of organizational design are drawn from the work in the areas of coordination [45], social networks [65], and distributed control [12, 16, 41].

### 7.1.3   Why Take a Computational Approach?

Organizations are heterogeneous, complex, dynamic nonlinear adaptive and evolving systems. Organizational action results from interactions among adaptive systems (both human and artificial), emergent structuration in response to non-linear processes, and detailed interactions among hundreds of factors. As such, they are poor candidates for analytical models. Because of the natural complexity of the object of study, existing models and theories of organization are often vague, intuitive, and under-specified. Scientific progress will be more readily achievable if the theories are more explicit and well defined. Computational theorizing helps to achieve this.

Computational analysis is an invaluable tool for theory building and examining issues of organizational dynamics as it enables the researcher to generate a set of precise, consistent and complete set of theoretical propositions from basic principles even when there are complex interactions among the relevant factors. Computational models allow researchers to show proofs of concept and to demonstrate whether or not completely modelable factors can generate certain phenomena. In this way, computational models can be used to show the potential legitimacy of various theoretical claims in organization science.

Theoretical computational models can be used to demonstrate lower bounds or tractability of organizational information processing phenomena (e.g., minimal information necessary to reach distributed agreement or awareness [29], or the tractability of an organizational decision or negotiation processes [57]. Experimental and empirically-based models can also provide computationally-plausible accounts of organizational activity [36, 15].

## 7.2   Organizational Concepts Useful in Modeling Organizations

In order to model an organization the following factors are generally modeled at

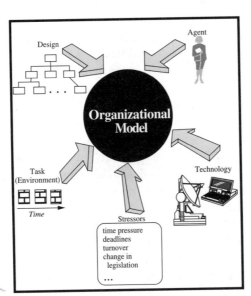

**Figure 7.1**   Necessary elements in an organizational model.

some level of detail: agents comprising the organization, the organization's design or structure, tasks the organization carries out, any environment of the organization, the organization's material transformation and/or information processing technology, and any stressors on the organization (see Figure 7.1). Organizations can use different configurations of agents, designs, tasks, and technology to accomplish the same goal—this is the concept of "equifinality." In fact, one of the major issues in the computational organization area is determining what organizational designs make sense when and what are the relative costs and benefits of these various configurations that exhibit degrees of equifinality.

Models in the COT area vary dramatically in the level of detail in which agents, designs, tasks, and technology are modeled. The better or more detailed these underlying models, the more precise the predictions possible, but the greater the computational and modeling resources required. Models run the gamut from simple abstract models of generic decision making behavior (such as the Garbage Can Model and CORP) to detailed models of specific organizational decisions or decision making processes (such as VDT, HITOP-A and ACTION). For example, ACTION represents literally tens of thousands of organizational relationships among 14 different categories of organizational elements [23]. The simpler more abstract models are typically referred to as "intellective" models. These simpler models allow the researcher to use the model to simulate the general behavior of classes of organizations, policies, technologies, tasks or agents. For these models a central research goal is theory building: to discover general principles underlying organizational behavior.

The more detailed models are often referred to as "emulation" or "engineering" models. These detailed models may allow the researcher to use the model to emulate specific organizations by entering specific detailed parameters such as authority structures, detailed organizational procedures, or specific skill requirements. For these models a key research goal is organizational engineering: to examine whether or not the performance of a specific organization will be affected by making some specific change such as re-engineering the task in a particular way or adding a new technology.

### 7.2.1  Agent and Agency

In most COT models, organizations are composed of agents.[2] These agents may be human, artificial, or both. Agents take action, are constrained by their organizational role, and agents can make decisions. The actions of which the agents are capable, and the decisions that they make, depend on their capabilities and knowledge, the situation in which they are embedded, and the task(s) they are performing (see Figure 7.2).

Figure 7.2 is an adaptation of a scheme provided by Carley and Newell (1994) for thinking through the nature of agents and models employing such agents. In organizations, agents have some level of cognitive capability and occupy at a position in their organization. This position defines what task(s) the agent performs, with whom the agent must communicate, to whom the agent reports, who reports to the agent, and so forth. Agents have specific knowledge, skills, and capabilities. Classes of agents can be defined on the basis of differences in position, knowledge, skills, capabilities, or organizational roles. For example, one class of agents are

---

2. This need not be the case in general, and other approaches are being investigated. Most models take agents as the starting point, and compose organizations out of them. Some models, however, treat agents themselves as the emergent outcome of organizing processes. This is a conceptual necessary step to handle hierarchies of organizations and dynamic-organizations-as-agents. See further discussion below, and, e.g., [25, 33].

manager agents, another might be worker agents. Importantly, an agent's knowledge is potentially comprised not just of task-based or technical knowledge but also of social or organizational knowledge. Classes of agents, differing in their cognitive architecture and/or knowledge, would be capable of different actions.

From an artificial agent standpoint, what actions an agent can take is a function of the agent's cognitive capabilities and knowledge. Figure 7.2 is based on Carley and Newell's (1994) argument that the cognitive architecture serves to constrain what the agent can know and when the agent can know what and so constrains what types of actions are needed. Knowledge about the social and organizational world constrains what types of actions are possible. In Figure 7.2 as you move down each column the cognitive architecture becomes increasingly well specified and creates increasing need for more types of actions. As you move across each row the context becomes increasingly realistic and increasingly knowledge rich. An agent, in a particular cell, should be capable of taking all the actions to the left and up of its position. The MODEL SOCIAL AGENT, which is capable of all human actions, would be in the bottom right corner. Computational organizational models can be contrasted one with the other in terms of where they are at in this matrix of possibilities. For example, all models mentioned in Table 1 are positioned in the relevant cell in Figure 7.2.

Today, advances in the computational organization area are being achieved through the use of multiagent modeling techniques (see Chapters 1 and 2). In most organizational models, these multiple agents are viewed as cooperating together to achieve some collective goal such as producing more widgets, finding the best path through a maze, filling orders, or classifying objects (see Chapters 3 and 4). However, organizational agents need not be cooperative. Competition among agents may emerge for a variety of reasons. One of the most common examples is that of an organizational accounting system that reimburses individuals on the basis of individual contribution or performance and rather than on the overall organization performance. Moreover, competition among agents may even improve overall organizational performance on some tasks. Similarly, in most organizational models agents are viewed as essentially honest and as not knowingly communicating incorrect information or decisions. However, this need not be the case, particularly in organizations of people or in cases of information warfare. Ironically, for many organizational tasks, the task itself may be so ambiguous, that the agent may not be able to detect whether or not other agents are lying. Or, the task may be so constraining that lying is immediately obvious. MAS/DAI researchers have begun to investigate incentive models that link the rationality of truthfulness to the task structure of the domain and the constraints of the environment [57] but to date these models have not been incorporated into COT models.

Models of organizations have represented organizations as single decision makers and as collections of decision makers. Within the multiagent organizational models agents have been modeled in a variety of ways. For example, in the Garbage Can Model agents are characterized by a small set of parameters and vectors such as their energy, what problems they consider salient, what problems they can act on,

**Knowledge**
Increasingly Rich Situation

| Cognitive Architecture<br>Increasingly Limited Capabilities | Nonsocial Task | Multiple Agents | Real Interaction | Social Structural | Social Goals | Cultural Historical |
|---|---|---|---|---|---|---|
| Omniscient Agent | goal directed<br>produces goods<br>uses tools<br>uses language | models of others<br>turn taking<br>exchange | face-to-face | class differences | organizational goals | historically situated |
| Rational Agent | reasons<br>acquires<br>learns | learns from others<br>education<br>negotiation | mis-communication | promotion<br>social mobility | competition<br>cooperation<br>social cognition | emergent norms<br><br>*Cultural Transmission* |
| Boundedly Rational Agent | satisfices<br>task planning<br>adaptation | group making | social planning<br>coercion<br>priority disputes | altruism<br>uses networks<br>for information<br>boundary spanners<br>*Garbage Can Model*<br>*Sugarscape, AAIS* | delays gratification<br>moral obligation<br><br>*VDT*<br>*TAEMS* | gate keeping<br>role emergence<br>*CORP, HITOP-A,*<br>*ACTION, ORGAHEAD,*<br>*Organizational Consultant* |
| Cognitive Agent | compulsiveness<br>lack of awareness<br>multi-tasking | group think | spontaneous exchange<br>social interactions | automatic response to status cues | group conflict<br>power struggles<br><br>*TAC Air Soar*<br>*Plural-Soar* | develop language<br>institutional change |
| Emotional Cognitive Agent | habituation<br>variable performance | protesting<br>trust | play<br>rapid emotional responce<br>cons | campaining | team player | norm maintenance<br>ritual maintenance<br>advertising<br>**MODEL SOCIAL AGENT** |

**Figure 7.2**  Relating Cognitive Architecture and Knowledge to the Organizational Agent's Actions

and so forth. In this case the agent's abilities are represented as numerical arrays or values. For example, what problems are salient to an agent is represented by which cells in an agent by problem matrix are ones, and agent energy is simply a numeric value. In VDT the agent is modeled as an in-box, an out-box, a set of preferences for how to handle information, a set of skills, and so forth. In Plural-Soar each agent is modeled as a separate Soar agent. In this case the agent's knowledge is a set of rules in a series of problem spaces. In very sophisticated models, such as TAC Air Soar and Plural-Soar, agents are represented as complex, multilevel search processes, which have several interleaved levels and timescales of reasoning, and include both strategic and tactical modes.

## 7.2.2   Organizational Design

An organization's design can be conceptualized as a specific configuration of parameters that control the organization's behavior. The types of parameters generally considered include all of the configuration elements noted above (tasks, roles, organization structure, etc) as well as specific model-dependent parameters (inbox-sizes and delays for VDT, critical process variances for ACTION, etc.) Taken together, the parameters with their ranges of potential values define a parameter space, which in turn defines a space of potential organization designs. The process of designing an organization is in essence a process of refining and constraining that space to a single point (or to a set of points for a dynamically-restructurable organization).

Other commonly modeled design-oriented parameters include procedures and rules that embody organizational knowledge and the set of connections linking agents and tasks. Typical procedures and rules range from task-based rules, to accounting procedures, to procedures for hiring, firing, promoting, and moving agents about. The set of linkages among agents and tasks are often described as structures or networks. There can be many such structures in the organization. The structure perhaps most familiar to people who have worked organizations is the authority and communications structure. This is often represented in specific terms by an organization chart. However, the organization chart is most often simply the formal representation structure. In addition, there is a myriad of other interlinked structures that constrain and provide opportunities for action, and which are typically not perceived by those who work in the organization. One set of additional structures is the informal structure: the networks of interactions among agents such as friendship networks, and advice networks. In addition to these structures is are task structures (hierarchical and precedence ordering among subtasks, see also Chapter 3), task-resource structures (defining which resources are needed for which task), task-skill structures (defining what skills are needed for which task), resource access structures (defining which agent has access to which resources), skill structures (defining which agent has which skills), task assignment structures (defining which agent is assigned or is allowed to work on which subtasks), and so on. Modeling these structures in concert so as to account for and explain their interactions is a daunting and complex task for COT models.

Within the COT area the two most typical ways of conceptualizing the organization's design is as a set of attributes (such as centralized or decentralized communication, authority, skill, or other structures, or density of communication ties) or as a set of matrices. The attribute approach is used in HITOP-A, the Organizational Consultant, and AAIS. The matrix approach is used in the Garbage Can Model, CORP, VDT and ACTION. Illustrative structures in both their matrix and graphical network form are shown in Figure 7.3.

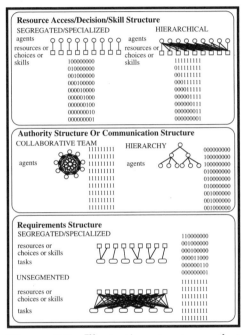

**Figure 7.3**  Illustrative structures that comprise an organization's design.

In Figure 7.3 two examples of each of three of the types of structures that comprise the overall design of an organization are shown. The resource access structure (top) links agents to resources; the decision access links agents to possible decision choices, and the skill structure links agents to their skills. Such structures show what is possible for each agent. A segregated or specialized structure implies that each agent is unique. This can imply little or no overlap in their mental models. A hierarchical structure at this level implies that there is one agent who has comprehensive access to, or knowledge about, the items in question. The authority and/or communication structures (middle) link agents to agents. In the authority structure the links show who has authority over whom and thus who reports to whom. In the communication structure the links show who talks to whom. In a collaborative structure all links are possible, in a hierarchy there is a central or apex agent. Finally, the requirements structure (bottom) links resources or skills with tasks. This structure shows what is needed to meet a certain task based goal. In the segregated or specialized structure each task has different requirements. In the unsegmented structure each task potentially requires all resources or skills. The structures shown are illustrative. Many other types of structures are possible. By thinking in terms of agents, resources (decisions or skills), tasks, and the linkages between them it is possible to describe analytically the set of possible designs and the designs as enacted by an organization.

Over time, researchers have begun to embed knowledge about organizations' structures in the agents so that it constrains the sharing of results and other information among organizational agents (see Chapter 3). In early organization design experiments with the Distributed Vehicle Monitoring Testbed (DVMT) [16] structure was embedded in each agent by (1) temporarily restricting its problem-solving capabilities (i.e., "skills") to a subset of its full set of available capabilities by "shutting off" some—this established a specialized "role"; (2) providing communication and reasoning mechanisms that linked current problem-solving capabilities (the current role) to agents and thus drove communications dynamically, and (3) providing strategic-level mechanisms for dynamically reconfiguring agent roles and role-to-agent maps (selectively activating and deactivating agent skills), thus implementing changes in the organization structure simply by changing the knowledge and skills of the agents.

In other cases, an organization's structure is represented as a series of rules for when to communicate what to whom and how to structure the communication. Representing organization's structure as a series of procedures or rules also facilitates linking up models of structure with models of intelligent agents. This approach is taken in the team (or multiagent) Soar work [37, 62, 63, 6]. In much of this work, organizational structure changes in response to changes in the environment because built into the agent's knowledge base are a set of standard operating procedures for how to restructure the communication under various conditions.

### 7.2.3   Task

The organization and its members are engaged in one or more tasks at any point in time. Further, over time, the organization repeatedly engages in a sequence of often quite similar tasks. These tasks may be composed of subtasks which may themselves be further subdivided. These tasks may have dependencies among them. Thompson identified three such dependencies—pooled (the results from two or more tasks are jointly needed to perform a different task), sequential (two or more subtasks must be performed in a specified sequence), and reciprocal (two tasks depend jointly on each other). Organizations are expected to improve their performance if they match the rest of their structures to the underlying task structure. (This concept of high performance as structural alignment is a characteristic explicitly represented in the mutual alignment approach of the ACTION model.)

The set of tasks faced by the organization can be thought of as its environment (or problem space). For example, in the car industry, the task can be viewed as a repeated design task. Each year, the industry generates new models that are more or less similar to the year before through a process of design and redesign. Task environments vary in many dimensions. Among the most important of these dimensions are degree of repetition, volatility, bias, and complexity. Some of these concepts are illustrated graphically in Figure 7.4.

Repetition: whether the set of tasks are repetitive (agents do the same thing over and over), quasi-repetitive (agents do the same type of thing repeatedly but the specific instances or details are different), or non-repetitive (each task is unique). This is shown graphically in Figure 7.4 by each task being composed of a set of bricks, and the pattern of bricks being different for each task.

Volatility: the rapidity with which the task environment changes. For example, in

Figure 7.4 when the task environment oscillates between two types of tasks (such as selling swimming pools in the summer and selling Christmas goods in the winter), this oscillation can be rapid (high volatility) or slow (low volatility).

Bias: the extent to which all possible tasks, regardless of task features, have the same outcome or solution. For example, in the binary choice task, a biased environment would be one where most outcomes were to choose 1 (as opposed to an unbiased environment where 1's and 0's would be equally likely).

Complexity: the amount of information that needs to be processed to do the task. For example, in the warehouse task, as the number of items on the order, the number of stacks, and the number of items per stack increases the complexity of the task increases.

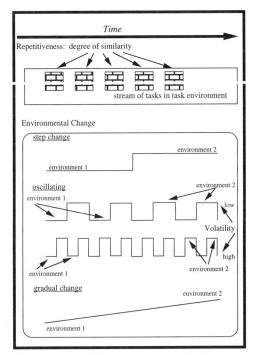

**Figure 7.4**  Characteristics of the task environment.

Typical task environment changes are step change, oscillating, and gradual (see Figure 7.4). In a "step change" environment, a discontinuity caused by legislation or technology alters the environment faced by the organization. For example, when a new manufacturing technology is introduced firms change from one task to another that is quite different. In an "oscillating" environment tasks or sets of tasks are chosen alternately from two different sets. Seasonal firms, for example, face oscillating environments. One such seasonal firm is the firm which sells swimming pools in the summer and Christmas goods in the winters. In an environment of gradual change, minor changes result in a gradual shift in the types of tasks faced by the organization. For example, the gradual aging and learning of students results in gradual changes in the types of problem sets the teachers must devise.

The performance of an organization can be measured with respect to the task or tasks it is performing. Three types of performance measures are commonly employed: effectiveness (is the task being performed well), efficiency (is the task being performed in such as way that output is maximized relative to some input), and perceived effectiveness (is the organization perceived as performing well by one or more stakeholders such as the general public, the government, the board of directors, or the media). For many tasks in which the product is generated by the group as a whole, while it might be possible to measure an organization's overall performance, in real human groups it is often impossible to objectively measure the actual contribution of any one member. Three aspects of effectiveness are: relative performance (how well is the organization performing compared to other organizations), accuracy (how many decisions are being made correctly), and timeliness (how rapidly are decisions begin made). For particular tasks or industries there are often entire literatures on how specifically to measure performance in specific situations. In general, for most models, multiple measures of performance are be gathered.

Within the COT area there are two strands of research on tasks. Some models, such as VDT, offer the capability of modeling a wide variety of organizational tasks, focusing on dependencies among subtasks but leaving the specific content of what is done in any particular subtask otherwise unspecified. In contrast, other models such as CORP are constrained to highly stylized and specific experimental tasks that, although retaining key features of actual tasks, differ in detail and complexity from those done in actual organizations. These highly stylized tasks are often referred to as canonical tasks, and they are valuable as research vehicles because researchers can share them among different modeling systems and environments and can more easily compare results. A set of such tasks is emerging for COT research. This set includes: the sugar-production task, the maze task, the binary classification task, the radar task, the warehouse task, the PTC task (production, transportation, and consumption), and the meeting scheduling task. In Figure 7.5 the binary choice task [5] and the warehouse task [6] are illustrated.

The warehouse task (Figure 7.5 top) is a simplified version of the more general search task. The key element of a search task is that there are a set of things being searched for, a set of locations where those things might be, and the organization must find all of the items. Organizational performance is based on the rapidity with which items are found and the effort spent in locating them. If the items cannot be depleted and the rule linking items to location does not change, then this problem, for a single agent, is simply a matter of remembering where things

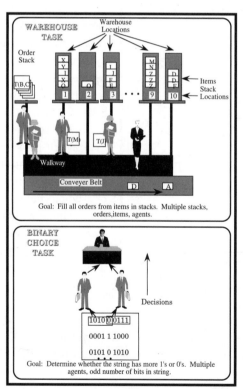

**Figure 7.5**  Illustrative tasks.

are. The task is complicated by agents being too boundedly rational to remember where things are or to act rapidly enough, by items being depleted or moved, and by information errors in what items are asked for and how items are represented at the various locations.

The binary choice task (Figure 7.5 bottom) is a simplified version of the more general classification choice task. The key element of a classification choice task is that there is a set of incoming information, a set of possible outcomes, and the organization must classify the incoming information to determine which outcome is most likely to be correct, and then the organization is told what was the correct classification. Organizational performance is based on the rapidity and accuracy with which a problem is classified. If the rule linking incoming information to choice does not change dynamically, then this problem for a single agent, is simply a matter of remembering what outcome is associated with which incoming pattern of information. This task is complicated by agents being too boundedly rational to be able to handle all of the information, by information errors or incomplete information, and by errors or latency in the feedback.

For both tasks, the goal is not to find the optimal way of solving this task. Rather, the goal of a computational organization theory model is to do the task as an organization would and to show the relative tradeoffs between different types of organizational designs, the relative impact of various communication technologies, or the relative benefits of different mixtures of agents.

From an organizational perspective, the question is how to structure a group of agents (what resource structure, what authority structure, what task structure, etc...) so that the organization as a whole exhibits high performance despite these, and other, types of complications (or stressors).

### 7.2.4  Technology

Research on organizational behavior needs to account for the role of information and telecommunication technologies. Most COT models ignore issues of technology within the organization. In a few cases, researchers have begun to look at how different technologies for processing, storing, retrieving, or communicating information might affect the actions of the individuals within the organization and/or the organization's overall performance. Two different approaches to examining the impact of technologies have appeared: technology as tool and technology as agent.

One approach to modeling technology is to treat it as a tool and to differentiate tools in terms of the attributes such as access, speed, synchronicity, and recordability. This approach is taken in the Virtual Design Team (VDT) [42, 35]. Within VDT, the organizational agents have a suite of communication technologies available to them like telephone, face-to-face meetings, and email. The agent also has a preference to send certain information via certain technologies. Using VDT the researcher can begin to examine how altering the way in which memos are sent, e.g., by paper or email, may affect the speed with which the organization solves a task and the amount of rework that needs to be done.

A second approach to modeling technology is to treat it as an artificial agent (and as altering the information processing capabilities of existing human agents who have access to the technology). This approach is taken in the constructural model

[36]. Within the constructural model the agents have an information processing or communication technology available to them which affects how many other agents they can simultaneously communicate with, whether the communicated message must be the same to all receivers, how much information the agent can retain, and so on. The technology itself may act as an agent with particular information processing and communicative capabilities. For example, a book as an artificial agent can interact with many other agents at the same time, send a different message to each receiver, can survive longer in the population than human agents, and, unlike human agents, cannot learn. As another example, a website as an artificial agent can interact with many other agents at the same time, send a different message to each receiver, has a shorter lifespan than its creator, and can "learn" by a specific subset of interactants adding information to the site. Within a computational model of an organization, such artificial agents can be represented simply as a separate class of agents with capabilities and knowledge that differ from humans and each other in systematic ways.

## 7.3   Dynamics

Many of the key issues in the COT area center around organizational dynamics. How do organizations learn? How do organizations evolve? What new organizational designs will emerge in the next decade or century? To examine such issues researchers use many tools, ranging from empirical observation and explanation of the behavior of complex agent-based models such as the DVMT, TAEMS, or Plural-Soar on dynamically-evolving tasks, to complex adaptive approaches or optimization approaches, such as genetic algorithms, genetic programming, neural networks, and simulated annealing. This work demonstrates that interactions between agent architecture, the way agents are coordinated, and the way the agents and the coordination structure adapt and change over time affect organizational behavior. Another common result is that for collections of even minimally intelligent agents organization often spontaneously emerges. Indeed, many studies show how structures that can be characterized as hierarchies sometimes spontaneously emerge.

Organizations are seen to be potentially dynamic in many ways. Organizations are capable of being redesigned or re-engineered moving the organization in a configuration space, making changes such as what agent reports to what other agent, or which agent handles what tasks. Agents within an organization are capable of changing; e.g., by learning or, in the case of artificial agents, by reconfiguring themselves or acquiring new knowledge. The processes, communications, or types of interactions can change, and so forth. There is a variety of processes that affect an organization's ability to adapt. For example, in order to achieve new levels of performance organizations often need to engage in an exploration process where they examine new technologies, new ways of doing business, new designs, and so on. However, organizations can also improve performance by exploiting current knowledge and technologies and getting better at what they do best. Exploration and exploitation are somewhat at odds with each other and organizations need to balance these two forces for change [46]. Organizational change is not guaranteed to improve performance. Organizations are typically more likely to redesign themselves when they are new and such changes may in turn cause the organization to fail. Such early failure is referred to as the liability of newness.

A variety of different approaches to organizational dynamics has been taken. To illustrate some of the issues involved two different approaches to will be briefly described. The first approach is based on the idea of flexible agents—agents which can restructure themselves in response to changes in the environment. The second approach is based on the idea of dual-level learning—organizations in which agent level and structural level learning occur in response to changes in the environment.

Ishida, Gasser and Yokoo [33, 34] (see also [25]) demonstrated the potential for flexible organizational structures to emerge from flexible agents. The basic idea underlying their approach is that the agents are flexible entities and knowledge interactions are the stable foundation of social grouping. Agents were modeled as sets of problem-solving production rules; i.e. mappings of individual rules to rule-collections. These mappings were flexible—rules could migrate from collection to collection (from agent to agent). Knowledge interactions were modeled as individual production rules. That is, an individual production rule is a way of saying that under certain meta-level control (rule-firing) conditions, certain particular knowledge (modeled as a LHS clause or input) interacts with certain other knowledge (another specific LHS clause or input) to produce specific additional knowledge (a particular RHS clause). This new RHS clause maps into (interacts to produce) an LHS clause for another rule or to an output. These production rules never changed. Agents flexibly emerged out of a fabric of interactions—production rules—which got mapped and re-mapped to rule collections. Agents re-configured their local knowledge and the structure or pattern of interactions among themselves, in response to changes in the environment. The actual number and character of agents changed over time as did the organizational structure. Which agents reported to which other agents was clearly not fixed, since the content and boundaries of agents themselves were not fixed. Experimental simulations showed that highly effective organizations tended to learn adaptations over time; i.e., on repeated exposure to similar (oscillating) environmental changes these organizations went through fewer adaptations over time. In this sense the organizations of agents learned how to learn.

Carley and Svoboda [9] used the ORGAHEAD model of organizational change to demonstrate the importance of learning histories and that organizations in which both the agents and the structure were flexible and could learn over time were not guaranteed to improve their performance. The ORGAHEAD model is based on the social conception of organizations as inherently complex, computational and adaptive in which knowledge and learning occurs at multiple levels. Within ORGA-HEAD organizational action results from both the behavior of multiple agents and the structure (or network) connecting these agents and the way in which knowledge is distributed among these agents. Agents learn through gaining new knowledge through experience. This is implemented using a standard experiential learning model in which agents add new knowledge to old knowledge and continually update the probability with which they take certain actions based on the likelihood that the proposed action led to the desired outcome in the past. Learning occurs at the structural level—by altering procedures and linkages among the agents and tasks (such as who reports to whom and who does what)—as the organization redesigns and restructures itself. This strategic learning is implemented as a simulated annealing algorithm. In this case there is a chief executive officer (the annealer) that proposes a change, evaluates the potential impact of this change on the organization by trying to anticipate what will happen in the future, and then decides whether or not to accept the change according to the Metropolis criteria. According to the Metropolis criteria the change is always accepted if it is anticipated to improve performance and is accepted but with decreasing likelihood over time if the change is risky and is anticipated to decrease performance. The results from these studies show that not all change is advantageous. Individual and structural learning clash; e.g., organizations re-engineer themselves for better performance only to lose the lessons of experience learned by various agents as those new agents are moved to different tasks or leave the organization. Because of such learning clashes change often results in maladaptation. The history of how and when the organization changes is as much a determinant of the organization's performance as the organization's design. And, truly adaptive organizations, those whose performance actually improves over time are those organizations which engage in a meta-learning to balance change due to learning at the structural level with change due to gathering new experiences at the individual agent level.

## 7.4  Methodological Issues

There are numerous methodological issues involved in the development and testing of computational models of organizations and organizing. There are three, however, that require special mention. The first, is the use of virtual experiments to examine the implications of the computational model. The second, has to do with validation, verification and the relation of the computational models to data on organizations. The third, has to do with the role of development tools and frameworks to mitigate the costs of developing these models.

### 7.4.1  Virtual Experiments and Data Collection

Unlike early models in this area, such as the Garbage Can Model, today's computational models of organizations are often sufficiently complex that they cannot be completely analyzed. For example, the parameter space of set of options is frequently so extensive that the researcher cannot explore all possible input combinations to determine the performance of the system. Nevertheless, a large number of combinations need to be explored as the performance of the system may change drastically for different combinations of inputs. One of the reasons that modern models are so complex is that organizations themselves are complex. Another, is that models are often designed by representing process. As such, the same model can be used to address a number of questions about organizations and organizing.

To address this problem, researchers in this area run virtual experiments. A virtual experiment is an experiment in which the results are gathered via simulation. In running a virtual experiment the researcher sets up a series of simulations to address a specific question. For the virtual experiment the researcher chooses a small set of parameters—perhaps three—and then varies these systematically over some range. All other parameters are typically held constant or allowed to vary randomly in classic Monte Carlo fashion. Statistical procedures for designing and analyzing the resulting data can be used for virtual experiments just as they can for experiments using humans in the laboratory.

For example, imagine that the computational organizational model allows the researcher to control the number of agents, the way agents make decisions (following standard operating procedures or based on experience, how the agents can send messages (such as face-to-face one-on-one or group meetings, email to one other agent or to all other agents), the complexity of the task, the complexity of the organization's authority and communication structure, and a variety of other parameters or options. Such a model could be used to address a number of research questions including: (1) How large does the organization need to be to reap the benefits of email? And (2) for the same task are there different combinations of technology, authority structure, and communication structure that lead to the same level of performance? To address the first question the researcher might vary the size of the organization from say 2 to 200 in increments of 20 (11 cells) and may consider all four communication technologies. This would by a 11x4 experimental design. To address the second question the researcher might consider all four communication technologies, two different authority structures (e.g., team and hierarchy), and two different communication structures (e.g., a completely connected structure like everyone-to- everyone and one that follows the authority structure (only communication is to or from manager). This would be a 4x2x2 design. In each case some number of simulations would be needed to be run for each cell, with the number chosen based on the required power of the test.

### 7.4.2   Validation and Verification

Computational organization theory is a type of grounded theory [28]. That is, the models that embody the theory are informed by and tested against empirical data. This grounding is done using various validation and verification procedures. In the COT area three types of validation are particularly important: theoretical, external, and cross-model. Theoretical verification has to do with determining whether the model is an adequate conceptualization of the real world for assessing the key issue being addressed. The adequacy of the conceptualization is often determined on the basis of whether or not a set of situation experts consider the model to have captured the main factors that they observe in organizations. External validation has to do with determining whether or not the results from the virtual experiments match the results from the real world. Finally, cross-model validation has to do with determining whether or not the results from one computational model map on to, and/or extend, the results of another model.[3]

For both theoretical and external validation the real world may be a human organization, a laboratory experiment, or an organization of artificial agents, and so on. Organizations leave "traces" of their activities such as accounting records, stockholder reports, technical connections among parts, operating procedures, web pages, etc. These can be analyzed using computational methods. Such data can also be captured, mapped, analyzed, and linked to other computational models either as input or as data against which to validate the computational models. Such data helps to form and test computational theories of organization and organizing.

### 7.4.3 Computational Frameworks

One of the pressing issues in the COT area is the development of a general testbed or framework that has the appropriate building blocks to minimize the time required to develop organizational and social models. A variety of tools are beginning to appear; as yet, however, no one tool dominates. Among the existing tools are: MACE, SDML, Multiagent Soar, and SWARM.

### *MACE*

MACE [20, 21] was one of the first general (domain-independent) testbeds for modeling multiagent systems. It was one of the first truly concurrent distributed object systems built. MACE introduced the idea of using agents for all phases of system construction, user interaction, and management of experiments, as well as for the basis of the modeled system itself. For example, "user interface agents" were used as actual asynchronous user-to-system and system-to-user representatives, interpreters, translators, displayers, managers, and so forth. This feature meant that the testbed and the experiment were an integrated multiagent organization for interacting with the experimenter and for testing ideas about the structure of organizations of artificial agents.

MACE also included explicit social modeling concepts drawn from sociological theory. One such idea was the notion of recursive composition of agents so that a group can itself be treated as an agent with distributed internal structure. In other words, agents, groups and groups of groups all have "agency"; i.e., a

---

3. Cross-model validation is also called docking [2].

set of specialized knowledge and a set of possible actions that can be taken. The second idea is that of the "social worlds." Herbert Blumer, Anselm Strauss, and other symbolic interactionists introduced the notion that individual people negotiate their lives by operating within social worlds which constrain both what they need to know and with whom they interact. In MACE, social worlds were operationalized as knowledge-based agent boundaries. Each agent defined a set of "acquaintances." This acquaintanceship knowledge, rather than explicit constraints, laws or testbed programming structures, defined the boundaries of communication and interaction, and hence the social structure. This concept provides a clean semantic model for flexible agent organizations. Finally, MACE used "modeling other agents" as its foundation of social knowledge and social structure, drawing on the ideas of G.H. Mead and the symbolic interactionists. Here the concept of 'taking the role of the other' served as a unifying principle for mind, self, and society over time. Acquaintances were also based on Hewitt's [32] ideas of Actor acquaintances (which were a much simpler notion, basically just message addresses for actors). MACE included specific facilities to model a number of features of other agents (including goals, roles, skills, etc.) in special a acquaintance database, and it used these to structure individual interactions and thus to establish social structure defined as patterns of interaction over time. This idea of modeling others and acquaintances has now become commonplace within MAS and DAI research; however, few researchers recognize the link they are making to social theory.

### SDML

SDML (Strictly Declarative Modeling Language) [53, 17, 52] is a multiagent object-oriented language for modeling organizations. SDML is particularly suited for modeling multiagent systems in which the agents interact in a team (flat) or hierarchical organizational structure. SDML is effectively theory-neutral with respect to the cognitive capabilities of the agent. It is flexible enough to represent both simple agents and more sophisticated agents as well as the linkages among them. SDML currently includes various libraries for alternate architectures such as genetic programming and Soar. These libraries facilitate exploring the interaction between agent cognition and organizational design.

Key social ideas are captured in the SDML architecture. For example, social agents are capable of distinguishing between explanation and action. The declarative representation within SDML makes this possible. Within SDML agents in the same class can be represented by sharing rules between them. Another key idea in organizations is that within the organization there are predefined linkages among agents and predefined roles in which knowledge is embedded and that constrain behavior. From this perspective, structure is patterns of positions or roles over time. This notion of structure is integral to SDML as within SDML the structure of the multiagent system is represented as a container hierarchy. For example, agents may be contained within divisions which are contained within organizations. Containers and their associated agents are also linked by an inheritance hierarchy. Change in agents and in the linkages among them is made possible by controlling the time levels associated with agent and container data bases.

### *Multiagent Soar*

Soar is a computational architecture for general intelligence [38]. Agents are goal directed and can be characterized in terms of their goals, problem spaces, states, operators, and associated preferences. Preferences can be used to represent shared norms or cultural choices about the existence of, acceptability of, or relative ranking of goals, states, problem spaces and operators. The agent's goals need not be articulable and can be automatically generated or consciously selected by the agent as deliberation ensues. The agent's long term knowledge base is a set of rules. The agent's short term memory is the set of information currently in working memory. Soar was designed as a specification of key psychological ideas such as bounded rationality. As such, Soar can be thought of as a unified theory of cognition. Indeed, empirical research on Soar suggests that in many instances its behavior is comparable to that of humans both in how well it does and in what errors are made.

Multiagent Soar is an approach to modeling teams as collections of Soar agents [37, 62, 63, 6]. The current Soar system facilitates inter-agent communication and does not require each agent to be a separate processor. Multiagent soar is built around three core social ideas: internal models of other agents, cognitive social structures, and communication. In multiagent Soar models, each team member is a Soar agent with a mental model of what other agents either know or will do in certain circumstances. This knowledge may include expectations about the other agents' goals, preferences, and so forth and allows the agent to anticipate what it thinks others will do. Further, each Soar agent in the team has embedded in its knowledge (its set of rules) a cognitive social structure. A cognitive social structure is an agent's perception of who interacts with whom, how, and about what. Finally, each Soar agent in the team has knowledge about how to communicate and what to communicate when and to whom, and how to compose and parse messages. Communication in these models is handled by passing communique's with specific task-related content. Within the multiagent Soar models, agent's typically monitor their environment and so can be interrupted by communications from other agents, changes in the environment, or changes in what other agents are present.

### *SWARM*

SWARM is a multiagent simulation language for modeling collections of concurrently interacting agents in a dynamic environment [61, 51, 1]. SWARM emerged from of work in computational biology. As such, SWARM is particularly suited to exploring complex systems composed of large numbers of relatively simple agents which interact as they seek to optimize some function. Within SWARM the agents can, to an extent, dynamically restructure themselves to accommodate changes in the input data and the objective function. In a SWARM model it must be possible to define the objective function. SWARM agents can act either synchronously and asynchronously. Consequently, many different technological or biological constraints on communication and adaptation can be modeled within SWARM. One of the intended applications of SWARM is to artificial life applications. That is, one of the goals of SWARM models is to demonstrate that certain complex group level behaviors can emerge from concurrent interactions between agents who by themselves are not capable of exhibiting that complex behavior. One of the intents of a SWARM model is to "grow" realistic looking social behaviors. Todate, there has been little attempt to empirically validate whether the behaviors grown in SWARM models are comparable to those seen in human systems.

The key social idea that is captured in SWARM is the logic of collective intelligence. That is, over time systems of SWARM agents come to exhibit collective intelligence over and above the simple aggregation of agent knowledge. This notion of emergent intelligence is central to the science of complexity. A second key idea that is captured in SWARM is evolution. That is, there are large populations of agents who can engage in reproductive activities and cease to exist.

## 7.5   Conclusions

Computational organization theory (COT) is the study of organizations as computational entities. As noted, the computational organization is seen as taking two complementary forms: [1] the natural or human organization which is replete with information and the need to process it and [2] computational systems composed of multiple distributed agents which have organizational properties. Computational analysis is used to develop a better understanding of organizing and organizations.

Organization is seen to arise from the need to overcome the various limitations on individual agency—cognitive, physical, temporal, and institutional. Organizations, however, are complex entities in which one or more agents are engaged in one or more tasks and where knowledge, capabilities and semantics are distributed. Thus, each organization has a design, a set of networks and procedures linking agents, tasks, resources, and skills that describes these various distributions.

Computational organizational models are grounded operational theories. In other words, unlike traditional DAI or multiagent models COT models draw on and have integrated into them empirical knowledge from organization science about how human organizations operate and about basic principles for organizing. Much of this work follows in the information processing tradition. Many of the COT models are models composed of other embedded models. In these multi-level models, the traditional distinction between normative and descriptive often becomes blurred. For example, the models may be descriptive at the individual level—describing individuals as boundedly rational, with various built in cognitive biases—but normative at the structural level—finding the best organizational design subject to a set of task based or procedural constraints.

Computational analysis is not simply a service to organizational theorizing; rather, computational organizational theorizing is actually pushing the research envelope in terms of computational tools and techniques. COT makes contributions to mainstream AI and CS, including fostering progress on such issues as: large scale qualitative simulation, comparison and extension of optimization procedures (particularly procedures suited to extremely complex and possibly changing performance surfaces); aggregation/disaggregation of distributed objects; on-line/off-line coordination algorithms; organizational and multiagent learning; semantic heterogeneity; and understanding/managing the tradeoff between agent quantity and computational complexity. Research in this area requires further development of the scientific infrastructure including developing: easy-to-use cost-effective computational tool kits for designing and building computational models of organizations, teams, and social systems (e.g., a multiagent oriented language with built in task objects and communication); multiagent logics; intelligent tools for analyzing computational models; validation procedures, protocols, and canonical data sets; managerial decision aids based on computational organization models; and protocols and standards for inter-agent communication. Key theoretical concerns in this area center around determining: what coordination structures are best for what types of agents and tasks; whether hybrid models (such as a joint annealer and genetic programming model) are better models for exploring organizational issues and for locating new organizational designs; representations for, and management of, uncertainty in organizational systems; the interactions among, and the relative advantages and disadvantages of various types of adaptation, evolution, learning, and flexibility; measures of organizational design; the existence of, or limitations of, fundamental principles of organizing; the tradeoffs for system performance of task-based, agent-based, and structure-based coordination schemes; representations for information and communication technology in computational models; and the relation between distributed semantics and knowledge on teamwork, organizational culture and performance.

Three directions that are particularly important for future research are organizational design, organizational dynamics and organizational cognition. The key issue under organizational design is not what is the appropriate division of labor, nor is it how should agents be coordinated. Rather, there is a growing understanding that there is a complex interaction among task, agent cognition or capabilities, and the other structural and procedural elements of organizational design. As such, the issue is finding what combinations of types of agents, structures (patterns of interactions among agents), and ways of organizing the task are most likely to meet the organization's goal. The key issue for organizational dynamics is not whether or not organizations adapt. Rather, the issues center on how to encourage effective learning, how to change to improve performance, how to retain capabilities and knowledge as the organization changes to address changes in the environment, and what new designs are possible. As to organizational cognition (perception, memory) there are a variety of issues ranging from how to represent organizational knowledge, to what level of sharing (of knowledge, procedures, or semantics) is necessary and by which agents to ensure effective organizational performance.

## 7.6 Exercises

1. *[Level 1]* Provide a critical discussion of the following statement. You do not need to know organizational theory to create good models of organizations. Anyone who has ever worked in an organization can develop such models.

2. *[Level 1]* Provide a critical discussion of the following questions. How does the organizational design and the task bound the agent? What are typical constraints and opportunities afforded the agent by the design and task? Provide at least five examples for both design and task.

3. *[Level 1]* For an organization that you are familiar what types of agents exist in that organization, what are their limitations.

4. *[Level 1]* Develop a measure of coordination based on structures like those shown in Figure 7.3.

5. *[Level 2]* Develop a simple model of a small group of agents (1,2 or 3) trying to collectively solve a simple canonical task such as the binary choice task or the maze task. What additional issues are involved, and what extra features does the model need, as you move from 1 to 2 to 3 agents working together to do the task? How is performance affected by the increase in the number of agents?

6. *[Level 3]* Reimplement and extend in one or more ways the garbage can model of organizational choice [11]. There are many possible extensions, some of which have been discussed in the literature. Possible extensions include, but are not limited to the following: adding a formal organization authority structure, having agents work on multiple tasks simultaneously, altering the task so that it requires specific skills and not just energy to be completed, and allowing agent turnover. Show that your model can replicate the original results reported by Cohen, March and Olsen (i.e., dock the models [2]). Then show which results are altered, or what additional results are possible, given your extension.

7. *[Level 3]* Reimplement and extend in one or more ways the CORP model of organizational performance [43]. There are many possible extensions, some of which have been discussed in the literature. Possible extensions include, but are not limited to the following: adding an informal communication structure, having agents work on multiple tasks simultaneously, allowing agents to be promoted, altering incoming information so that it is potentially incomplete or erroneous, altering the nature of the feedback (e.g., by delaying it or making it more ambiguous), and making the agents competitive (e.g., make agents try to maximize the performance relative to other's performance). Show that your

model can replicate the original results reported by Lin and Carley (i.e., dock the models). Then show which results are altered, or what additional results are possible, given your extension.

8. *[Level 3]* For a small organization (5 to 30 people) develop a description of its design. What is the formal organization chart? What is the informal advice network (who goes to whom for work related advice)? What are the main tasks and subtasks being accomplished? Develop a task dependency graph matrix. What are the skills or resources needed to do those tasks? Develop a resource/skill access matrix and a resource/skill requirements matrix. What were the major difficulties you encountered in locating this information for an actual organization?

9. *[Level 4]* Develop a comprehensive representation scheme for task or a multi-agent language for doing task based models of organizations. Consider how task is represented in various organizational models. What are the limitations or features of the various representation schemes? What features should be built into your approach? Demonstrate the strength of your approach by reimplementing one or more existing COT models.

10. *[Level 4]* Develop a general purpose approach for modeling telecommunication and information processing technologies in the organization. What are the critical features or components of these technologies that must be modeled? How does your approach contrast with the technology as agent approach and the technology as feature approach? What are the limitations and advantages of your approach?

## 7.7 References

1. R. Axelrod. Advancing the art of simulation in the social sciences. Working Paper 97-05-048, Santa Fe Institute, 1997.

2. R. Axtell, R. Axelrod, J. M. Epstein, and M. D. Cohen. Aligning simulation models: A case study and results. *Computational and Mathematical Organization Theory*, 1(2): 123–142, 1996.

3. H. H. Baligh, R. M. Burton and B. Obel. Devising expert systems in organization theory: The organizational consultant. In M. Masuch, editor, *Organization, Management, and Expert Systems*, pages 35–57. Walter De Gruyter, Berlin, 1990.

4. H. H. Baligh, R. M. Burton and B. Obel. Validating the organizational consultant on the fly. In K. M. Carley and M. J. Prietula, editors, *Computational Organization Theory*, pages 179–194. Lawrence Erlbaum Associates, Hillsdale, NJ, 1994.

5. K. M. Carley. Organizational learning and personnel turnover. *Organization Science*, 3(1): 2–46, 1992.

6. K. M. Carley, J. Kjaer-Hansen, M. Prietula and A. Newell. Plural-Soar: A prolegomenon to Artificial Agents and Organizational Behavior. In M. Masuch and M. Warglien, editors, *Distributed Intelligence: Applications in Human*

*Organizations*, pages 87–118. Elsevier Science Publications, Amsterdam, The Netherlands. 1992.

7.  K. M. Carley and A. Newell. The nature of the social agent. *Journal of Mathematical Sociology*, 19(4): 221–262, 1994.

8.  K. M. Carley and M. J. Prietula, editors. *Computational Organization Theory*. Lawrence Erlbaum Associates. Hillsdale, NJ, 1994.

9.  K. M. Carley and D. M. Svoboda, Modeling organizational adaptation as a simulated annealing process. *Sociological Methods and Research*, 25(1): 138-168, 1996.

10. G. P. Cohen. *The Virtual Design Team: An Information Processing Model of Coordination in Project Design Teams*. PhD thesis, Stanford University, Department of Civil Engineering. Stanford, CA, 1992.

11. M. D. Cohen, J. G. March and J. P. Olsen. A garbage can model of organizational choice, *Administrative Sciences Quarterly* 17(1): 1–25, 1972.

12. D. D. Corkill. *A Framework for organizational self- design in distributed problem solving networks*. PhD Thesis, University of Massachusetts, Dept. of Computer and Information Science, Amherst, MA, 1982.

13. R. Cyert and J. G. March. *A Behavioral Theory of the Firm*. 2nd Edition. Blackwell Publishers, Cambridge, MA, 1992[1963].

14. K. Decker, 1995 A framework for modeling task environment. Chapter 5 in Environment-Centered Analysis and Design of Coordination Mechanisms. Ph.D. Dissertation, University of Massachusetts.

15. K. Decker, 1996, TAEMS: A framework for environment centered analysis and design of coordination mechanisms. In *Foundations of Distributed Artificial Intelligence*, G.M.P. O'Hare and N.R. Jennings, eds. New York: John Wiley and Sons.

16. E. H. Durfee, V. R. Lesser and D. D. Corkill. Coherent cooperations among communicating problem solvers. *IEEE Transactions on Computers*, C-36: 1275-1291, 1987.

17. B. Edmonds, M. Scott and S. Wallis. Logic, reasoning and a programming language for simulating economic and business processes with artificially intelligent agents. In P. Ein-Dor, editor, *Artificial Intelligence in Economics and Management*, pages 221–230. Kluwer Academic Publishers, Boston, MA, 1996.

18. J. M. Epstein and R. Axtell. *Growing Artificial Societies*. MIT Press, Cambridge, MA, 1997.

19. J. R. Galbraith, *Designing Complex Organizations*, Addison-Wesley Publishing Company, 1973.

20. L. Gasser, C. Braganza and N. Herman. MACE: A flexible testbed for distributed AI research. In M. N. Huhns, editor, *Distributed Artificial Intelligence*, pages 119-152. Pitman Publishers, 1987a.

21. L. Gasser, C. Braganza and N. Herman, Implementing distributed AI systems using MACE. In *Proceedings of the 3rd IEEE Conference on Artificial Intelligence Applications*, pages 315–320. Orlando, FL, February, 1987b. (Also in Readings in DAI).

22. L. Gasser and A. Majchrzak. ACTION Integrates manufacturing strategy, design, and planning. In P. Kidd and W. Karwowski, editors, *Ergonomics of Hybrid Automated Systems IV*, IOS Press, Netherlands, 1994.

23. L. Gasser, I. Hulthage, B. Leverich, J. Lieb, and A. Majchrzak, "Organizations as Complex, Dynamic Design Problems", in M. Filgueiras and L. Damas, eds. *Progress in Artificial Intelligence.* Lecture Notes in Artificial Intelligence 727, Springer Verlag, 1993.

24. L. Gasser and A. Majchrzak. HITOP-A: Coordination, infrastructure, and enterprise integration. In em Proceedings of the First International Conference on Enterprise Integration, Hilton Head, South Carolina: MIT Press, Cambridge, MA, 1992.

25. L. Gasser and T. Ishida. A dynamic organizational architecture for adaptive problem solving, In *Proceedings of the National Conference on AI*, pages 52-58. July, 1991.

26. N. S. Glance and B. A. Huberman. The outbreak of cooperation. *Journal of Mathematical Sociology*, 17(4): 281–302, 1993.

27. N. S. Glance and B. Huberman. Social dilemmas and fluid organizations. In K. M. Carley and M. J. Prietula, editors, *Computational Organization Theory*, pages 217–240.Lawrence Erlbaum Associates. Hillsdale, NJ, 1994.

28. B. Glaser and A. L. Strauss, *The Discovery of Grounded Theory: Strategies for Qualitative Research*, Walter de Gruyter, 1967.

29. R. Fagin, J. Y. Halpern, and Y. Moses, *Reasoning About Knowledge*, MIT Press, Cambridge, MA, 1995.

30. J. R. Harrison and G. R. Carrol. Keeping the faith: A model of cultural transmission in formal organizations. *Administrative Science Quarterly*, 36: 552–582, 1991.

31. M. T. Hannan. and J. Freeman. *Organizational Ecology.* Harvard University Press, Cambridge, MA, 1989.

32. C. E. Hewitt, "Viewing Control Structures as Patterns of Passing Messages," *Artificial Intelligence*, 8(3): 323–364, 1977.

33. T. Ishida, L. Gasser and M. Yokoo. Organization self-design of distributed production systems. *IEEE Transactions on Data and Knowledge Engineering*, 4(2): 123–134, 1992a.

34. T. Ishida, L. Gasser and M. Yokoo. An organizational approach to real-time continuous problem solving. *Japanese Society of Artificial Intelligence Journal*, 7(2): 300–308, 1992b (In Japanese).

35. Y. Jin and R. Levitt. The Virtual Design Team: A computational model of project organizations. *Computational and Mathematical Organization Theory*, 2(3): 171–196, 1996.

36. D. S. Kaufer and K. M. Carley. *Communication at a Distance: The Effect of Print on Socio-Cultural Organization and Change.* Lawrence Erlbaum Associates, Hillsdale, NJ, 1993.

37. J. E. Laird, Jones, and Nielsen. Knowledge-based multi-agent coordination. *Presence,* in press.

38. J. E. Laird, A. Newell, and P. S. Rosenbloom. Soar: An architecture for general intelligence. *Artificial Intelligence,* 33:(1): 1-64, 1987.

39. J. E. Laird, P. S. Rosenbloom, and A. Newell. *Universal Subgoaling and Chunking: The Automatic Generation and Learning of Goal Hierarchies.* Boston, Massachusetts: Kluwer Academic Publishers. 1986.

40. T. K. Lant and S. J. Mezias. Managing discontinuous change: A simulation study of organizational learning and entrepreneurial strategies, *Strategic Management Journal*, 11: 147–179, 1990.

41. V. R. Lesser and D. D. Corkill. Functionally accurate. cooperative distributed systems. In A. H. Bond and L. Gasser, editors, *Readings in Distributed Artificial Intelligence*, Morgan Kaufmann, Inc., San Mateo, CA, 1988.

42. R. E. Levitt, G. P. Cohen, J. C. Kunz, C. I. Nass, T. Christiansen and Y. Jin. The 'Virtual Design Team': simulating how organization structure and information processing tools affect team performance. In K. M. Carley and M. J. Prietula, editors, *Computational Organization Theory* pages 1–18. Lawrence Erlbaum Associates, Hillsdale, NJ, 1994.

43. Z. Lin, and KM. Carley. Organizational response: The cost performance tradeoff. *Management Science,* 43(2): 217–234, 1997.

44. A. Majchrzak and L. Gasser, HITOP-A: A tool to facilitate interdisciplinary manufacturing systems design, *International Journal of Human Factors in Manufacturing*, 2(3): 255–276, 1992.

45. T. W. Malone. Modeling coordination in organizations and markets. *Management Science*, 33: 1317–1332, 1986.

46. J. G. March. Exploration and exploitation in organizational learning. In M. D. Cohen and L. S. Sproull, editors, *Organizational Learning*. Sage, Thousand Oaks, CA, 1996.

47. J. G. March and R. Weissinger-Baylon, editors. *Ambiguity and Command: Organizational Perspectives on Military Decision Making*. Pitman, Boston, MA,1996.

48. J. G. March and H. A. Simon. *Organizations*. Wiley, 1958.

49. M. Masuch and M. Warglien. *Artificial Intelligence in Organization and Management Theory* Elsevier Science Publishers, Amsterdam, The Netherlands,1992.

50. M. Masuch and P. LaPotin (1989). Beyond Garbage Cans: An AI Model of Organizational Choice. *Administrative Science Quarterly*, 34: 38–67.

51. N. Minar, R. Burkhart, C. Langton, M. Askenazi. The Swarm simulation system: A toolkit for building multi-agent simulations. Working Paper 96-06-042. Santa Fe Institute.1996.

52. S. Moss and O. Kuznetsova. Modelling the process of market emergence. In J. W. Owsinski and Z. Nahorski, editors, *Modelling and analysing economies in transition,* pages 125–138. MODEST, Warsaw. 1996.

53. S. Moss and B. Edmonds. A formal preference-state model with qualitative market judgements. *Omega—the international journal of management science*, 25(2): 155–169, 1997.

54. J. Pfeffer and G. R. Salancik. *The external control of organizations : a resource dependence perspective*. Harper and Row, New York, 1978.

55. J. F. Padgett. Managing garbage can hierarchies. *Administrative Science Quarterly,* 25(4): 583-604, 1980.

56. W. W. Powell and P. J. DiMaggio. *The New Institutionalism in Organizational Analysis*. The University of Chicago Press, Chicago, IL, 1991.

57. J. SRosenschein and G. Zlotkin. *Rules of Encounter: Designing Conventions for Automated Negotiation Among Computers*, MIT Press, Cambridge, MA, 1994.

58. G. R. Salancik and H. Leblebici. Variety and form in organizing transactions: A generative grammar of organization. *Research in the Sociology of Organizations*, 6:1–31, 1988.

59. G. R. Salancik and J. Pfeffer. A social information professing approach to job attitudes and task design. *Administrative Science Quarterly*, 23:224–253. 1978.

60. H. A. Simon, *Administrative Behavior*. Free Press, New York, 1947.

61. J. Stites. Complexity. *Omni*, 16(8):42–52. 1994.

62. M. Tambe. Teamwork in real-world, dynamic environments. In *Proceedings of the International Conference on Multi-agent Systems*, 1996.

63. M. Tambe. Agent Architectures for flexible, practical teamwork. In Proceedings of the AAAI American Association of Artificial Intelligence, 1997.

64. J. Thompson. *Organizations in Action*. McGraw- Hill, New York, NY, 1967.

65. S. Wasserman and K. Faust. *Social Network Analysis: Methods and Applications*. Cambridge University Press, New York, NY, 1994.

# 8    Formal Methods in DAI: Logic-Based Representation and Reasoning

Munindar P. Singh, Anand S. Rao, and Michael P. Georgeff

## 8.1   Introduction

It is clear from a reading of the other chapters that agent applications are becoming ever more important. Agents are being deployed in increasingly complex production environments, where the failure or misbehavior of an agent might easily cause loss of life or property. Accordingly, a major challenge is to develop techniques for ensuring that agents will behave as we expect them to—or at least, will not behave in ways that are unacceptable or undesirable.

Of course, ensuring correctness is a challenge for all of computer science. Previous work in computer science has studied formal methods as a good basis for creating systems with minimal errors. These methods have found useful application, but much remains to be understood in terms of specifying complex systems in the first place. Agents are desirable for the very reason that they provide higher-level abstractions for complex systems. These abstractions can lead to simpler techniques for design and development, because they offer an approach to sidestep the complexity inherent in the larger applications.

Formal methods in DAI and elsewhere offer an understanding of the systems being designed at a level higher than their specific implementation. They can provide a way to help debug specifications and to validate system implementations with respect to precise specifications. However, the role of formal methods in DAI—like in the rest of computer science—is somewhat controversial. Despite the above potential advantages, some practitioners believe that formal methods do not assist them in their efforts. This might indeed be true in many cases. Formal methods, because of their call for precision, naturally lag the *ad hoc*, quick-and-dirty approaches to system construction, which are often effective in the short run. Although several powerful formalisms exist, finding the right formalism is a nontrivial challenge. Such a formalism would provide a level of expressiveness that suffices for the practical problems at hand, but would nevertheless be tractable. Also, formal methods are the most effective when included in tools and used by specially trained designers. For that reason, just as software engineers have discovered, there is no substitute for good tools nor for education in formal methods.

Despite the above controversy, there is general agreement that formal methods do help in the long run, in helping developing a clearer understanding of problems and solutions. Indeed, over the years, a number of formal techniques developed in DAI have found their way into practical systems. They usually do not constitute the entire system, but provide key functionality.

This chapter covers the major approaches to formal methods for describing and reasoning about agents and their behavior. It puts a special emphasis on how these methods may be realized in practical systems. It discusses the state of the art in theory and practice, and outlines some promising directions for future research. This chapter is primarily focused on formalizations that involve variants of symbolic logic. Some other mathematical techniques are discussed in Chapters 5 and 12. Although this chapter is self-contained, some familiarity with logic would help the reader.

## 8.2 Logical Background

In general, formalizations of agent systems can be, and have been, used for two quite distinct purposes:

- as internal specification languages to be used by the agent in its reasoning or action; and

- as external metalanguages to be used by the designer to specify, design, and verify certain behavioral properties of agent(s) situated in a dynamic environment.

The first class of approaches is more traditional in DAI. It presupposes that the agents have the capability to reason explicitly. Such agents are commonly referred to as *cognitive, rational, deliberative,* or *heavyweight*—some of this terminology is introduced in Chapter 1. The second class of approaches is more recent in the study of agents, although it is more traditional in the rest of computer science. This is to use the formalism to enable a designer to reason about the agent. The agent may or may not be able to reason itself when it is deployed in the field.

Fortunately, although the conceptual basis of the two approaches is radically different, the underlying mathematics is not always as different. We exploit this similarity by presenting most ideas in terms of what reasoning is required and how it may be performed, and only secondarily treating its actual realization as a component for the agent, or as a tool for its designer. Ideally, one would like to have the same logical language serve both of the above purposes. However, the trade-off between expressiveness and computability makes this ideal somewhat infeasible in general. The real-time constraints on agents situated in dynamic environments require the internal language to be computationally efficient, while the variety of complex behaviors that are possible in a system of distributed autonomous agents requires the external language to be more expressive.

We begin with the formalizations of distributed agents from the designer's perspective. We then move on to describe some of the practical tools and systems that have been built by reducing the expressive power of these languages to make them more feasible for direct execution by distributed agents.

### 8.2.1   Basic Concepts

The techniques used in formalizing DAI concepts make extensive use of propositional, modal, temporal, and dynamic logics. We now review these logics, which have been used in classical computer science to give the semantics of concurrent programs. For reasons of space, we avoid many details of the logics, instead accreting concepts that are of special value to DAI. We combine these into a single logic, which we study in somewhat more detail.

Simply put, there are three aspects to a logic. The *well-formed formulas* of the logic are the statements that can be made in it. These are specified as a formal language that underlies a given logic. The *proof-theory* includes the axioms and rules of inference, which state entailment relationships among well-formed formulas. The *model-theory* gives the formal meaning of the well-formed formulas. The language and proof-theory are called the syntax; the model-theory is also called the semantics.

An important practical consideration is to make the semantics natural. Since logic is used to formalize our intuitions about computational systems, their interactions with each other, or with the environments in which they exist, it is crucial that the formulas refer to the meaning that we wish to formalize.

The purpose of the semantics is to relate formulas to some simplified representation of the reality that interests us. This simplified version of reality corresponds to the nontechnical term "model." However, in logic, a *model* means more than just any simplified version of reality—it is one that is closely related to the formal language that underlies the given logic. Fundamentally, logic can handle only one kind of meaning, namely, the truth or falsity of a given formula. Since models are often quite large and structured, we often need to specify a suitable component of a model with respect to which the truth or falsity of a formula would carry the intuitive meaning one seeks to formalize. We use the term *index* to refer to any such component, be it a piece of the world, a spatial location, a moment or period in time, a potential course of events, or whatever is appropriate.

A formula is *satisfied* at a model and some index into it if and only if it is given the meaning true there. For a model $M$, index $i$, and formula $p$, this is written as $M \models_i p$. A formula is *valid* in a model $M$ if and only if it is satisfied at all indices in the model; this is written as $M \models p$.

The following exposition defines a series of formal languages to capture some pretheoretic intuitions about concepts such as truth, possibility, action, time, beliefs, desires, and intentions. The typical formal languages of interest are context-free, and hence can be specified in the traditional Backus-Naur Form (BNF) [1, chapter 4]. However, for simplicity, and in keeping with most works on logic, we specify their syntax as a set of informal rules. Also, for most of the logics we present, syntactic variants are possible, but it won't be worth our while to discuss them here.

Along with each language, we will define a class of formal models that have the requisite amount of detail. Further, we will give *meaning postulates* or *semantic conditions* defining exactly where in the model (i.e., at what indices) a formula is true. A well-known caveat about logic in general is that the informal meanings of different terms may not be fully captured by the formalization. Sometimes this is because the informal meanings are not mutually consistent, and the formalization helps remove harmful ambiguity. However, sometimes this is because certain nuances of meaning are difficult to capture. If these nuances are not worth the trouble, then nothing is lost; otherwise, one should to consider an alternative formalization.

### 8.2.2  Propositional and Predicate Logic

Propositional logic is the simplest and one of the most widely used logics to represent factual information, often about the agents' environment. Formulas in this language are built up from *atomic propositions*, which intuitively express atomic facts about the world and *truth-functional connectives*. The connectives $\wedge$, $\vee$, $\neg$, and $\rightarrow$ denote "and," "or," "not," and "implies," respectively. The reader may consult a textbook, such as [26] for additional details.

**Example 8.1**
The facts "it rains" and "road is wet" can be captured as atomic propositions `rains` and `wet-road`, respectively. The implication that "if it rains, then the road is wet" can be captured by the propositional formula `rain` $\rightarrow$`wet-road`.

$\mathcal{L}_P$ is the language of propositional logic. It is given by the following rules. Here we assume that a set $\Phi$ of atomic propositions is given.

SYN-1.   $\psi \in \Phi$ implies that $\psi \in \mathcal{L}_P$

SYN-2.   $p, q \in \mathcal{L}_P$ implies that $p \wedge q$, $\neg p \in \mathcal{L}_P$

Let $M_0 \stackrel{\text{def}}{=} \langle L \rangle$ be the formal model for $\mathcal{L}_P$. We use $\langle\,\rangle$ brackets around $L$ to highlight similarities with the later development. Here $L \subseteq \Phi$ is an *interpretation* or *label*. $L$ identifies the set of atomic propositions that are *true*. This gives us the base case; the meanings of the nonatomic formulas are recursively defined.

SEM-1.   $M_0 \models \psi$ iff $\psi \in L$, where $\psi \in \Phi$

SEM-2.   $M_0 \models p \wedge q$ iff $M_0 \models p$ and $M_0 \models q$

SEM-3.   $M_0 \models \neg p$ iff $M_0 \not\models p$

The atomic propositions and boolean combinations of them are used to describe states of the system. They do not consider how the system may evolve or has been evolving. Two useful abbreviations are false $\equiv (p \wedge \neg p)$, for any $p \in \Phi$, and true $\equiv \neg$false. As is customary, we define $p \vee q$ as $\neg(\neg p \wedge \neg q)$, and $p \rightarrow q$ as $\neg p \vee q$.

With reference to the caveat mentioned above, the logic operators and their natural language counterparts are different notions. For example, $p \rightarrow q$ is *true* if

$p$ is *false* irrespective of $q$—thus it identifies potentially irrelevant connections. Alternative, more faithful, formalizations of "implies" do exist, e.g., in *relevance* logic [2]. We will refer to a simple variant in Section 8.2.3. However, most current research in logic and computer science ignores the subtlety and uses the above definition.

Although we do not use predicate logic in the specification languages, we do use it in the metalanguage, which is used in the semantic conditions. The universal ($\forall$) and existential ($\exists$) quantifiers are used to *bind* variables and make claims, respectively, about all or some of their possible values. A variable that is not bound is *free*. Let $Q(x)$ be some expression involving a free variable $x$, e.g., $x < y$. $(\forall x : Q(x))$ holds if $Q(l)$ holds for each possible object $l$ that may be substituted for $x$ in the entire expression $Q$. $(\exists x : Q(x))$ holds if $Q(l)$ holds for some possible object $l$ substituted throughout for $x$.

### 8.2.3  Modal Logic

Recall the remark in Section 8.2.1 that logic treats truth or falsity of a formula as its exclusive notion of meaning. Modal logic has been used extensively in artificial intelligence to refer to other kinds of meaning of formulas. In its general form, modal logic was used by philosophers to investigate different *modes* of truth, such as *possibly* true and *necessarily* true. In the study of agents, it is used to give meaning to concepts such as belief and knowledge. In modal languages, classical propositional logic is extended with two *modal operators*: $\Diamond$ (for possibility) and $\Box$ (for necessity). The modal language $\mathcal{L}_M$ is defined as follows:

SYN-3.  the rules for $\mathcal{L}_P$ (with "$\mathcal{L}_M$" substituted for "$\mathcal{L}_P$")

SYN-4.  $p \in \mathcal{L}_P$ implies that $\Diamond p, \Box p \in \mathcal{L}_M$

**Example 8.2**
We can capture "it is possible that it rains" as $\Diamond$`rain`, and "it is necessary that the sun rises in the east" as $\Box$`sun-rises-in-the-east`.

Models for modal logic require additional structure beyond $M_0$. The semantics of modal logics is traditionally given in terms of sets of the so-called *possible worlds*. A world can be thought of in several different ways. A simple idea is that a world is a possible state of affairs, corresponding roughly to an interpretation, as in the semantics for $\mathcal{L}_P$. However, a world can also be treated as a history, i.e., a sequence of states of affairs. It can even be treated as a set of all possible histories starting from a given state. The above views—as a history or set of histories—are more common in the philosophical literature. However, in this chapter, we treat a world (in the technical sense) usually as a state of affairs, and sometimes corresponding to a possible history.

With sets of worlds as primitive, the structure of the model is captured by relating the different worlds via a binary *accessibility relation* [54]. Intuitively, this relation tells us what worlds are within the realm of possibility from the standpoint of a given world. A condition is possible if it is true somewhere in the realm of possibility; a condition is necessary if it is true everywhere in the realm of possibility.

Let $M_1 \stackrel{\text{def}}{=} \langle W, L, R \rangle$, where $W$ is the set of worlds, $L : W \mapsto 2^\Phi$ gives the set of formulas true at a world, and $R \subseteq W \times W$ is an accessibility relation. Here, since the model is structured, the relevant index is the possible world with respect to which we evaluate a formula.

SEM-4. $M_1 \models_w \psi$ iff $\psi \in L(w)$, where $\psi \in \Phi$

SEM-5. $M_1 \models_w p \wedge q$ iff $M_1 \models_w q$ and $M_1 \models_w q$

SEM-6. $M_1 \models_w \neg p$ iff $M_1 \not\models_w p$

SEM-7. $M_1 \models_w \Diamond p$ iff $(\exists w' : R(w, w') \,\& \, M_1 \models_{w'} p)$

SEM-8. $M_1 \models_w \Box p$ iff $(\forall w' : R(w, w') \Rightarrow M_1 \models_{w'} p)$

## Example 8.3

Modal logics enable us to represent *strict conditionals*, which offer a more accurate formalization of natural language implication than the propositional operator. $\Box(p \rightarrow q)$ holds not merely when $p$ is *false*, but if $p$ and $q$ are appropriately related at all possible worlds.

Importantly, algebraic properties of the accessibility relation translate into entailment properties of the logic. Some common algebraic properties are the following.

- $R$ is *reflexive* iff $(\forall w : (w, w) \in R)$
- $R$ is *serial* iff $(\forall w : (\exists w' : (w, w') \in R))$
- $R$ is *transitive* iff $(\forall w_1, w_2, w_3 : (w_1, w_2) \in R \,\&\, (w_2, w_3) \in R \Rightarrow (w_1, w_3) \in R)$
- $R$ is *symmetric* iff $(\forall w_1, w_2 : (w_1, w_2) \in R \Rightarrow (w_2, w_1) \in R)$
- $R$ is *euclidean* iff $(\forall w_1, w_2, w_3 : (w_1, w_2) \in R \,\&\, (w_1, w_3) \in R \Rightarrow (w_2, w_3) \in R)$

We leave it to the reader to verify that models that satisfy the above properties validate the following formulas, respectively.

- $\Box p \rightarrow p$
- $\Box p \rightarrow \Diamond p$
- $\Box p \rightarrow \Box \Box p$
- $p \rightarrow \Box \Diamond p$
- $\Diamond p \rightarrow \Box \Diamond p$

Since the above formulas do not depend on $p$, they are properly viewed as *schemas* that apply to any condition. In the literature, these are termed the $T$, $D$, $4$, $B$, and $5$ schemas, respectively [12].

### 8.2.4 Deontic Logic

Deontic logic is about what ought to be the case or what an agent is obliged to do. Traditional deontic logic introduces an operator Obl for obliged, whose dual is Per for permitted. Deontic logic is specified as a modal logic with the main axiom that Obl$p$→¬Obl¬$p$, i.e., the agent is obliged to bring about $p$ only if it is not obliged to bring about ¬$p$. The rest of the logic is fairly straightforward. Unfortunately, this formulation suffers from a number of paradoxes. We shall not study it in detail here, nor the more sophisticated approaches of dyadic deontic logic and logics of directed obligation. Instead, we refer the reader to some important collections of essays on this subject [40, 41, 62].

### 8.2.5   Dynamic Logic

Dynamic logic can be thought of as the modal logic of action [53]. Unlike traditional modal logics, however, the necessity and possibility operators of dynamic logic are based upon the kinds of actions available. As a consequence of this flexibility, it has found use in a number of areas of DAI.

We consider the propositional dynamic logic of regular programs, which is the most common variant. This logic has a sublanguage based on regular expressions for defining action expressions—these composite actions correspond to Algol-60 programs, hence the name *regular programs*. We define $\mathcal{L}_D$ along with $\mathcal{L}_R$ as an auxiliary definition. Here, $\mathcal{B}$ is a set of atomic action symbols.

SYN-5.   the rules for $\mathcal{L}_P$ applied to $\mathcal{L}_D$

SYN-6.   $\beta \in \mathcal{B}$ implies that $\beta \in \mathcal{L}_R$

SYN-7.   $a, b \in \mathcal{L}_R$ implies that $a; b, (a + b), a* \in \mathcal{L}_R$

SYN-8.   $p \in \mathcal{L}_D$ implies that $p? \in \mathcal{L}_R$

SYN-9.   $a \in \mathcal{L}_R$ and $p \in \mathcal{L}_D$ implies that $[a]p, \langle a \rangle p \in \mathcal{L}_R$

Intuitively, the atomic actions are what the agent can perform directly. The program $a; b$ means doing $a$ and $b$ in sequence. The program $a + b$ means doing either $a$ or $b$, whichever works. This is nondeterministic choice—although it might sound a little unintuitive at first, it is logically clean and one gets to appreciate it after some experience. However, a nondeterministic program may not be physically executable, because it can require arbitrary lookahead to infer which branch is really taken. The program $p?$ is an action based on confirming the truth value of proposition $p$. If $p$ is true, this action succeeds as a noop, i.e., without affecting the state of the world. If $p$ is false, it fails, and the branch of the action of which it is part is terminated in failure—it is as if the branch did not exist. The program $a*$ means 0 or more (but finitely many) iterations of $a$.

### *Example 8.4*
The Algol-60 program `if q then a else b endif` is translated as $((q?; a) + ((\neg q)?; b))$. If $q$ holds, the $(\neg q)?$ branch fails, so $a$ must be performed. Otherwise $b$ must be performed.

The semantics of dynamic logic is given with respect to a model that includes a set of states (or worlds) related by possible transitions based on the actions in $\mathcal{B}$.

Let $M_2 \stackrel{\text{def}}{=} \langle W, L, \delta \rangle$, where $W$ and $L$ are as before. $\delta \subseteq W \times \mathcal{B} \times W$ is a transition relation. It is convenient to define a class of accessibility relations based on $\mathcal{L}_R$.

RP-1.   $R_\beta(w, w')$ iff $\delta(w, \beta, w')$

RP-2.   $R_{a;b}(w, w')$ iff $(\exists w'' : R_a(w, w'') \& R_b(w'', w'))$

RP-3.   $R_{a+b}(w, w')$ iff $R_a(w, w')$ or $R_b(w, w')$

RP-4.   $R_{a*}(w, w')$ iff $(\exists w_0, \ldots, w_n : (w = w_0) \& (w' = w_n) \& (\forall i : 0 \leq i < n \Rightarrow R_a(w_i, w_{i+1})))$

SEM-9.   $M_2 \models_w \langle a \rangle p$ iff $(\exists w' : R_a(w, w') \& M_2 \models_{w'} p)$

SEM-10.   $M_2 \models_w [a]p$ iff $(\forall w' : R_a(w, w') \Rightarrow M_2 \models_{w'} p)$

We refer the reader to the survey by Kozen & Tiurzyn [53] for additional details.

### 8.2.6   Temporal Logic

Temporal logic is, naturally enough, the logic of time. There are several variants. Of these, the most important distinctions are the following:

- *Linear versus Branching:* whether time is viewed as a single course of history or as multiple possible courses of history. The branching can be in the past, in the future, or both.

- *Discrete versus Dense:* whether time is viewed as consisting of discrete steps (like the natural numbers) or as always having intermediate states (like the rationals or reals).

- *Moment-Based versus Period-Based:* whether the atoms of time are points or intervals.

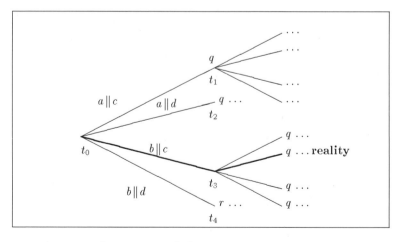

**Figure 8.1**   An example structure of time.

Although there are advantages to each of the above variants, we will concentrate on discrete moment-based models with linear past, but consider both linear and branching futures. Let us consider an informal view of time before we enter into a formalization. This view is based on a set of *moments* with a strict partial order, which denotes temporal precedence. Each moment is associated with a possible state of the world, identified by the atomic conditions or propositions that hold at that moment. A *path* at a moment is any maximal set of moments containing the given moment, and all moments in its future along some particular branch of $<$. Thus a path is a possible course of events. It is useful for capturing many intuitions about the choices and abilities of agents to identify one of the paths beginning at a moment as the *real* one. This is the path on which the world progresses, assuming it was in the state denoted by the given moment. Constraints on what should or will happen can naturally be formulated in terms of the real path. Figure 8.1 has a schematic picture of this view of time.

### Example 8.5

Figure 8.1 is labeled with the actions of two agents. Each agent influences the future by acting, but the outcome also depends on other events. For example, in Figure 8.1, the first agent can constrain the future to some extent by choosing to do action $a$ or action $b$. If it does action $a$, then the world progresses along one of the top two branches out of $t_0$; if it does action $b$, then it progresses along one of the bottom two branches.

The important intuition about actions is that they correspond to the granularity at which an agent can make its choices. The agent cannot control what exactly transpires, but it can influence it to some extent through its actions.

### Example 8.6

In Figure 8.1, the first agent can choose between $t_1$ and $t_2$, on the one hand, and between $t_3$ and $t_4$, on the other hand. However, it can choose neither between $t_1$ and $t_2$, nor between $t_3$ and $t_4$.

### Linear Temporal Logic

$\mathcal{L}_L$ is a linear-time temporal language.

SYN-10.   the rules for $\mathcal{L}_P$

SYN-11.   $p, q \in \mathcal{L}_L$ implies that $p\mathsf{U}q$, $\mathsf{X}p$, $\mathsf{P}p \in \mathcal{L}$

$p\mathsf{U}q$ is true at a moment $t$ on a path, if and only if $q$ holds at a future moment on the given path and $p$ holds on all moments between $t$ and the selected occurrence of $q$. $\mathsf{F}p$ means that $p$ holds sometimes in the future on the given path and abbreviates $\mathsf{true}\mathsf{U}p$. $\mathsf{G}p$ means that $p$ always holds in the future on the given path; it abbreviates $\neg\mathsf{F}\neg p$. $\mathsf{X}p$ means that $p$ holds in the next moment. $\mathsf{P}q$ means that $q$ held in a past moment.

The semantics is given with respect to a model $M_3 \stackrel{\text{def}}{=} \langle \mathbf{T}, <, [\![\,]\!] \rangle$, where $\mathbf{T}$ is the set of moments, $<$ the temporal ordering relation, and $[\![\,]\!]$ gives the denotations of the atomic propositions. It is convenient to use $[\![\,]\!]$, which is the dual of the interpretation $L$: $w \in [\![\psi]\!]$ iff $\psi \in L(w)$.

SEM-11.   $M_3 \models_t \mathsf{P}p$ iff ($\exists t' : t' < t$ and $M_3 \models_{t'} p$)

SEM-12.   $M_3 \models_t \mathsf{X}p$ iff $M_3 \models_{t+1} p$

SEM-13.   $M_3 \models_t p\mathsf{U}q$ iff ($\exists t' : t \leq t'$ and $M_3 \models_{t'} q$ and ($\forall t'' : t \leq t'' \leq t' \Rightarrow M_3 \models_{t''} p$))

For the later formal development, it is useful to keep in mind that $M_3$ is linear, i.e., $<$ here is a total ordering.

### Branching Temporal and Action Logic

$\mathcal{L}_B$ is a branching-time temporal and action language. It builds on top of $\mathcal{L}_L$ and $\mathcal{L}_D$, and especially uses the ideas of the well-known language CTL* [24]. $\mathcal{L}_B$ captures the essential properties of actions and time that are of value in specifying agents.

Formally, $\mathcal{L}$ is the minimal set closed under the rules given below. Here $\mathcal{L}_s$ is the set of "path-formulas," which is used as an auxiliary definition. Here $\mathcal{X}$ is a set of variables and $\mathcal{A}$ is a set of agent symbols. We give intuitive meanings of the constructs of this formal language after the following syntactic definitions.

SYN-12.   the rules of $\mathcal{L}_P$

SYN-13.   $p, q \in \mathcal{L}_B$ and implies that $\mathsf{P}p$, $(\bigvee a : p) \in \mathcal{L}_B$

SYN-14.   $\mathcal{L}_B \subseteq \mathcal{L}_s$

SYN-15.   $p, q \in \mathcal{L}_s$, $x \in \mathcal{A}$, and $a \in \mathcal{B}$ implies that $p \wedge q$, $\neg p$, $p\mathsf{U}q$, $\mathsf{X}p$, $x[a]p$, $x\langle a\rangle p$ $\in \mathcal{L}_s$

SYN-16.   $p \in \mathcal{L}_s$ implies that $\mathsf{A}p$, $\mathsf{R}p \in \mathcal{L}_B$

SYN-17.   $p \in (\mathcal{L}_s \setminus \mathcal{L}_B)$ and $a \in \mathcal{X}$ implies that $(\bigvee a : p) \in \mathcal{L}_s$

The formulas in $\mathcal{L}_B$ refer to moments. The formulas in $\mathcal{L}_s$ refer to paths as in the models of $\mathcal{L}_L$. Although $\mathcal{L}_B \subseteq \mathcal{L}_s$, the formulas in $\mathcal{L}_B$ get a unique semantics.

The branching-time operator, $\mathsf{A}$, denotes "in *all* paths at the present moment." Here "the present moment" refers to the moment at which a given formula is evaluated. A useful abbreviation is $\mathsf{E}$, which denotes "in *some* path at the present moment." In other words, $\mathsf{E}p \equiv \neg\mathsf{A}\neg p$.

### Example 8.7
In Figure 8.1, $\mathsf{EF}r$ and $\mathsf{AF}(q \vee r)$ hold at $t_0$, since $r$ holds on some moment on some path at $t_0$ and $q$ holds on some moment on each path.

The *reality* operator, $\mathsf{R}$, denotes "in the *real* path at the present moment." $\mathsf{R}$ is not included in traditional temporal logics, but here helps tie together intuitions about what may and what will happen.

### Example 8.8
In Figure 8.1, $\mathsf{RF}q$ holds at $t_0$, since $q$ holds on some moment on the real path identified at $t_0$.

$\mathcal{L}_B$ also contains operators on actions. These are adapted and generalized from $\mathcal{L}_D$, in which the action operators essentially yield state-formulas, whereas in $\mathcal{L}_B$ they yield path-formulas. The operators in $\mathcal{L}_B$ capture the operators of $\mathcal{L}_D$. $x[a]p$ holds on a given path $S$ and a moment $t$ on it, if and only if, if $x$ performs $a$ on $S$ starting at $t$, then $p$ holds along $S$ at the moment where $a$ ends. The formula $x\langle a \rangle p$ holds on a given path $S$ and a moment $t$ on it, if and only if, $x$ performs $a$ on $S$ starting at $t$ and $p$ holds at the moment where $a$ ends.

### Example 8.9
In Figure 8.1, $\mathsf{E}\langle b\rangle r$ and $\mathsf{A}[a]q$ hold at $t_0$, since $r$ holds at the end of $b$ on one path, and $q$ holds at the end of $a$ on each path. Similarly, $\mathsf{A}[d](q \vee r)$ also holds at $t_0$. Also, $\mathsf{A}[e]\mathsf{true}$ holds at $t_0$, because action $e$ does not occur at $t_0$.

The construct $(\bigvee a : p)$ means that there is an action under which $p$ becomes true. The action symbol $a$ typically would occur in $p$ and would be replaced by the specific action which makes $p$ true.

### Example 8.10
In Figure 8.1, $(\bigvee e : \mathsf{E}x\langle e\rangle\mathsf{true} \wedge \mathsf{A}x[e]q)$ holds at $t_0$. This means there is an action, namely, $a$, such that $x$ performs it on some path starting at $t_0$ and on all paths on which it is performed, it results in $q$ being true. In other words, some action is possible that always leads to $q$. This paradigm is used in formalizing know-how.

Let $M_4 \overset{\text{def}}{=} \langle \mathbf{T}, <, [\![\ ]\!], \mathbf{R}\rangle$ be a formal model for $\mathcal{L}_B$. Unlike $M_3$, $M_4$ is branching, and its $[\![\ ]\!]$ also applies to actions. In other words, $<$ is branching. It might partition $\mathbf{T}$ into a number of connected components, each of which would then correspond to worlds as traditionally understood. For an atomic proposition, $p$, $[\![p]\!]$ is the set of moments where $p$ holds; for an action $a$ and an agent $x$, $[\![a]\!]^x$ is the set of periods over which $a$ is performed by $x$. These periods are notated as $[S; t, t']$ such that $a$ begins at $t$ and ends at $t'$, where $t, t' \in S$. $\mathbf{R}$ picks out at each moment the *real* path at that moment. This is the notion of relativized reality alluded to above, and which is highlighted by a bold line in Figure 8.1.

For simplicity, we assume that each action symbol is quantified over at most once in any formula. Below, $p\vert_b^a$ is the formula resulting from the substitution of all occurrences of $a$ in $p$ by $b$. We also assume that agent symbols are mapped to unique agents throughout the model. Formally, we have:

SEM-14.　$M_4 \models_t \psi$ iff $t \in [\![\psi]\!]$, where $\psi \in \Phi$

SEM-15.　$M_4 \models_t p \wedge q$ iff $M_4 \models_t p$ and $M_4 \models_t q$

SEM-16.　$M_4 \models_t \neg p$ iff $M_4 \not\models_t p$

SEM-17.　$M_4 \models_t \mathsf{A}p$ iff $(\forall S : S \in \mathbf{S}_t \Rightarrow M_4 \models_{S,t} p)$

SEM-18.　$M_4 \models_t \mathsf{R}p$ iff $M_4 \models_{\mathbf{R}(t),t} p$

SEM-19.   $M_4 \models_t \mathsf{P}p$ iff $(\exists t' : t' < t$ and $M_4 \models_{t'} p)$

SEM-20.   $M_4 \models_{s,t} \mathsf{X}p$ iff $M_4 \models_{s,t+1} p)$

SEM-21.   $M_4 \models_t (\bigvee a : p)$ iff $(\exists b : b \in \mathcal{B}$ and $M_4 \models_t p|_b^a)$, where $p \in \mathcal{L}$

SEM-22.   $M_4 \models_{s,t} (\bigvee a : p)$ iff $(\exists b : b \in \mathcal{B}$ and $M_4 \models_{s,t} p|_b^a)$, where $p \in (\mathcal{L}_s \setminus \mathcal{L})$

SEM-23.   $M_4 \models_{s,t} p\mathsf{U}q$ iff $(\exists t' : t \leq t'$ and $M_4 \models_{s,t'} q$ and $(\forall t'' : t \leq t'' \leq t' \Rightarrow M_4 \models_{s,t''} p))$

SEM-24.   $M_4 \models_{s,t} x[a]p$ iff $(\forall t' \in S : [S;t,t'] \in [\![a]\!]^x \Rightarrow M_4 \models_{s,t'} p)$

SEM-25.   $M_4 \models_{s,t} x\langle a\rangle p$ iff $(\exists t' \in S : [S;t,t'] \in [\![a]\!]^x \& M_4 \models_{s,t'} p)$

SEM-26.   $M_4 \models_{s,t} p \wedge q$ iff $M_4 \models_{s,t} p$ and $M_4 \models_{s,t} q$

SEM-27.   $M_4 \models_{s,t} \neg p$ iff $M_4 \not\models_{s,t} p$

SEM-28.   $M_4 \models_{s,t} p$ iff $M_4 \models_t p$, where $p \in \mathcal{L}$

## 8.3   Cognitive Primitives

As discussed in Chapter 1, in many cases of interest, the agent metaphor is most useful when the agents are given high-level cognitive specifications. This is described as taking an *intentional stance* toward agents [60] or viewing agents at the *knowledge level* [63]. There is sometimes disagreement as to the similarity of the two doctrines, but for our purposes, they are essentially interchangeable. The high-level cognitive specifications involve concepts such as beliefs, knowledge, desires, and intentions (the terms *intentional stance* and *knowledge level* apply to more than just intentions and knowledge). They are high-level, because they enable us to define the current state of an agent, what the agent might do, and how the agent might behave in different situations without regard to how the agent is implemented. Specifications derived from cognitive notions are perhaps the most significant of the AI contributions to agents.

Such high-level specifications serve as natural scientific abstractions for agents. However, to be used effectively, cognitive notions must be given rigorous definitions in general models of action and time. If they are to find broad application, DAI approaches must meet the standards of traditional disciplines such as distributed computing. Much of the material we discussed in Section 8.2 originated in concurrent or distributed computing. Here we build on it by including the concepts of belief, desire, and intention (BDI), and giving them formal definitions. The resulting logics can then be used to reason about agents and the way in which their beliefs, intentions, and actions bring about the satisfaction of their desires. To this end, we introduce the modal operators $\mathsf{Bel}$ (belief), $\mathsf{Des}$ (desire), $\mathsf{K_h}$ (know-how), and $\mathsf{Int}$ (intention). The language $\mathcal{L}_I$ is based on $\mathcal{L}_B$.

SYN-18.   $p \in \mathcal{L}_s$ and $x \in \mathcal{A}$ implies that $(x\mathsf{Int}p), (x\mathsf{K_h}p), (x\mathsf{K_t}p), (x\mathsf{Des}p) \in \mathcal{L}_I$

The semantics for $\mathcal{L}_I$ is given with respect to $M_5 \stackrel{\text{def}}{=} \langle \mathbf{T}, <, [\![\,]\!], \mathbf{R}, \mathbf{B}, \mathbf{D}, \mathbf{I} \rangle$. The semantics for the part of $\mathcal{L}_I$ that uses the constructs of $\mathcal{L}_B$ is as given using $M_4$.

**Example 8.11**

Consider an agent who has the desire to win a lottery eventually and intends to buy a lottery ticket sometime, but does not believe that he will ever win the lottery. The mental state of this agent can be represented by the following formula: `DesAFwin` $\wedge$ `IntEFbuy` $\wedge$ `¬BelAFwin`.

### 8.3.1  Knowledge and Beliefs

**B**, a *belief accessibility* relation, is introduced to give the semantics of the belief operator, which behaves as a modal necessity operator, such as $\square$ above. **B** assigns to each agent at each moment the set of moments that the agent believes possible at that moment. Knowledge (know-that) is customarily defined as a true belief. Traditionally, to model belief, **B** is assumed to be serial, symmetric, and euclidean (as defined in Section 8.2.3). To model knowledge, it is in addition also assumed to be reflexive. In that case, it becomes an equivalence relation, resulting in $\mathsf{K_t}$ being an S5 modal logic operator [12].

When $\square$ is treated as belief (or knowledge), the schemas 4 and 5 of Section 8.2.3 have an interesting interpretation. The former means that if an agent believes a condition, it believes that it believes it. The latter means that if an agent does not believe a condition, it believes that it does not believe it. Therefore, these schemas are referred to as *positive* and *negative introspection*, respectively. Negative introspection is a particularly strong assumption for limited agents.

SEM-29.  $M_5 \models_t x\mathsf{Bel}p$ iff $(\forall t' : (t, t') \in \mathbf{B}(x, t) \Rightarrow M_5 \models_{t'} p)$

**B** depends on the given moment. Thus the agent can change its beliefs over time.

### 8.3.2  Desires and Goals

**D** associates with each moment a set of moments to represent the desires of the agent. The agent has a desire $\phi$ in a given moment if and only if $\phi$ is true in all the **D**-accessible worlds of the agent in that moment.

SEM-30.  $M_5 \models_t x\mathsf{Des}p$ iff $(\forall t' : (t, t') \in \mathbf{D}(x, t) \Rightarrow M_5 \models_{t'} p)$

In the philosophical literature, desires can be inconsistent and the agent need not know the means of achieving these desires. Desires have the tendency to 'tug' the agent in different directions. They are inputs to the agent's deliberation process, which results in the agent choosing a subset of desires that are both consistent and achievable. Such consistent achievable desires are usually called *goals*. As a great simplification, the desires as presented here are logically consistent.

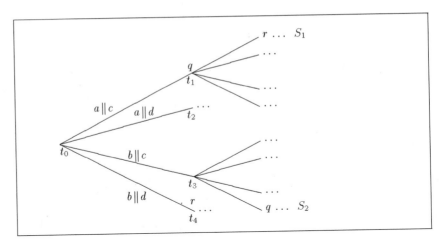

**Figure 8.2**   Intentions.

### 8.3.3   Intentions

At each moment in the model, **I** assigns to each agent a set of paths that the agent is interpreted as having selected or preferred. Roughly, intentions are defined as *the conditions that inevitably hold on each of the selected paths*. Here we consider achievement intentions in that these intentions are about achieving various conditions. However, intentions can be defined for maintaining certain conditions as well. Whereas achievement intentions are useful for liveness reasoning, maintenance intentions are useful for safety reasoning. For reasons of space, we will not discuss the latter in this chapter. We now turn to the fairly simple formal definition of achievement intentions:

SEM-31.   $M \models_t x\mathsf{Int}p$ iff $(\forall S : S \in \mathbf{I}(x,t) \Rightarrow M \models_{S,t} \mathsf{F}p)$

### *Example 8.12*

Consider Figure 8.2. Assume that $\neg r$ and $\neg q$ hold everywhere other than as shown. Let the agent $x$ (whose actions are written first in the figure) at moment $t_0$ prefer the paths $S_1$ and $S_2$. Then, by the informal definition given above, we have that $x$ intends $q$ (because it occurs eventually on both the preferred paths) and does not intend $r$ (because it never occurs on $S_2$).

The above definition validates several useful properties of intentions. Some of these were obtained with an entirely different formal structure in [76]—the present development uses fewer conceptual primitives but ignores certain abstraction issues.

IC1.   **Satisfiability:**

$x\mathsf{Int}p \rightarrow \mathsf{EF}p$

This says that if $p$ is intended by $x$, then it occurs eventually on some path. That is, the given intention is satisfiable. This does not hold in general, since the sets of paths assigned by **I** may be empty. We must additionally constrain the models so that $\mathbf{I}(x,t) \neq \emptyset$.

IC2. **Temporal Consistency:**

$(x\mathsf{Int}p \wedge x\mathsf{Int}q) \rightarrow x\mathsf{Int}(\mathsf{F}p \wedge \mathsf{F}q)$

This says that if an agent intends $p$ and intends $q$, then it (implicitly) intends achieving them in some undetermined temporal order: $p$ before $q$, $q$ before $p$, or both simultaneously. This holds because the function **I** assigns exactly one set of paths to each agent at each moment. Thus if both $p$ and $q$, which are path-formulas, occur on all selected paths, then they occur in some temporal order on each of those paths. The formula $(\mathsf{F}p \wedge \mathsf{F}q)$ is true at a moment on a path precisely when $p$ and $q$ are true at (possibly distinct) future moments on the given path.

IC3. **Persistence does not entail success:**

$\mathsf{EG}((x\mathsf{Int}p) \wedge \neg p)$ is satisfiable

This is quite intuitive: just because an agent persists with an intention does not mean that it will succeed. Technically, two main ingredients are missing. The agent must know how to achieve the intended condition and must act on its intentions. We include this here to point out that in the theory of [15], persistence is sufficient for success (p. 233). This is a major conceptual weakness, since it violates the usual understanding that intentions do not entail know-how [75]. The need to state the conditions under which an agent can succeed with its intentions is one of the motivations for the concept of know-how.

Other important constraints on intentions include (a) the absence of closure of intentions under beliefs, (b) the consistency of intentions with beliefs about reality, and (c) the non-entailment of beliefs about reality. Of these, (a) and (b) are jointly termed the *asymmetry thesis* by Bratman [5, p. 38]. He argues that they are among the more basic constraints on the intentions and beliefs of rational agents.

### 8.3.4 Commitments

As presented, goals and intentions are quite similar in their semantic structure. The difference in these modalities arises in their relationships with other modalities and in terms of how they may evolve over time. One of the properties that separates them is *commitment*.

An agent is typically treated as being committed to its intentions [5]. Such commitments apply within a given individual agent, and are accordingly also termed *psychological commitments* [10, 74]. An agent's commitment governs whether it will persist with its intentions and if so, for how long. There is general agreement that commitment be treated as constraining how intentions are revised and updated, and resides in their processing rather than in their core semantics [36, 65, 76]. A contrasting approach is to include commitment in the core semantical definition of intentions [15]; this approach is criticized by [65, 73, 75]. Constraint IC4 shows how commitment may be expressed in the present framework. This version of commitment is purely qualitative.

IC4.   **Persist while succeeding:**

This constraint requires that agents desist from revising their intentions as long as they are able to proceed properly. If an agent selects some paths, then at future moments on those paths, it selects from among the future components of those paths:

$(S \in \mathbf{I}(x,t)$ and $[S;t,t'] \in [\![a]\!]^x) \Rightarrow (\forall S' \in \mathbf{I}(x,t') \Rightarrow (\exists S'' \in \mathbf{I}(x,t)$ and $S' \subseteq S''))$

However, it is believed that handling commitment and the update of intentions will involve greater subtlety than the above, e.g., see [34, 81] for logic-based and probabilistic approaches, respectively.

### 8.3.5   Know-How

Intentions have an obvious connection with actions—agents act to satisfy their intentions. However, intentions do not ensure success; IC3 above showed that even persistence is not sufficient for success. A key ingredient is know-how, which we now formalize.

***Example 8.13***

Consider Figure 8.2. At $t_0$, $x$ may do either action $a$ or action $b$, since both can potentially lead to one of the preferred paths being realized. However, if the other agent does action $d$, then no matter which action $x$ chooses, $x$ will not succeed with its intentions, because none of its preferred paths will be realized.

We propose that an agent, $x$, knows how to achieve $p$, if it is able to bring about $p$ through its actions, i.e., force $p$ to occur. The agent's beliefs or knowledge must be explicitly considered, since these influence its decision. For example, if an agent is able to dial all possible combinations of a safe, then it is able to open that safe: for, surely, the correct combination is among those that it can dial. On the other hand, for an agent to really know how to open a safe, it must not only have the basic skills to dial different combinations on it, but also know which combination to dial.

A tree of actions consists of an action, called its *radix*, and a set of subtrees. The idea is that the agent does the radix action initially and, then, picks out one of the available subtrees to pursue further. In other words, a tree of actions for an agent is a projection to the agent's actions of a fragment of **T**. Thus a tree includes *some* of the possible actions of the given agent, chosen to force a given condition. Let $\Upsilon$ be the set of trees. Then $\Upsilon$ is defined as follows.

T1.   $\emptyset \in \Upsilon$ ($\emptyset$ is the empty tree)

T2.   $a \in \mathcal{B}$ implies that $a \in \Upsilon$

T3.   $\{\tau_1, \ldots, \tau_m\} \subseteq \Upsilon$, $\tau_1, \ldots, \tau_m$ have different radices, and $a \in \mathcal{B}$ implies that $\langle a; \tau_1, \ldots, \tau_m \rangle \in \Upsilon$

Now we extend the formal language with an auxiliary construct. This extension is only meant to simplify the definitions.

SYN-19.   $\tau \in \Upsilon$, $x \in \mathcal{A}$, and $p \in \mathcal{L}_I$ implies that $x[\![\tau]\!]p \in \mathcal{L}_I$

$x[\![\tau]\!]p$ denotes that agent $x$ knows how to achieve $p$ relative to tree $\tau$. As usual, the agent symbol can be omitted when it is obvious from the context. To simplify notation, we extend $\bigvee$ to apply to a given range of trees. Since distinct trees in each such range have distinct radix actions, the extension of $\bigvee$ from actions to trees is not a major step.

SEM-32.   $M \models_t [\![\emptyset]\!]p$ iff $M \models_t \mathsf{K_t}p$

SEM-33.   $M \models_t [\![a]\!]p$ iff $M \models_t \mathsf{K_t}(\mathsf{E}\langle a \rangle \mathsf{true} \wedge \mathsf{A}[a]\mathsf{K_t}p)$

SEM-34.   $M \models_t [\![\langle a; \tau_1, \ldots, \tau_m \rangle]\!]p$ iff
$M \models_t \mathsf{K_t}(\mathsf{E}\langle a \rangle \mathsf{true} \wedge \mathsf{A}[a](\bigvee_{1 \leq i \leq m} \tau_i : ([\![\tau_i]\!]p)))$

Thus an agent knows how to achieve $p$ by following the empty tree, i.e., by doing nothing, if it knows that $p$ already holds. As a consequence of this knowledge, the agent will undertake no specific action to achieve $p$. The nontrivial base case is when the agent knows how to achieve $p$ by doing a single action: this would be the last action that the agent performs to achieve $p$. In this case, the agent has to know that it will know $p$ immediately after the given action.

It is important to require knowledge in the state in which the agent finally achieves the given condition, because it helps limit the actions selected by the agent. If $p$ holds, but the agent does not know this, then it might select still more actions in order to achieve $p$.

Lastly, an agent knows how to achieve $p$ by following a nested tree if it knows that it must choose the radix of this tree first and, when it is done, that it would know how to achieve $p$ by following one of its subtrees. Thus know-how presupposes knowledge to choose the next action and confidence that one would know what to do when that action has been performed.

SEM-35.   $M \models_t x\mathsf{K_h}p$ iff $(\exists \tau : M \models_t x[\![\tau]\!]p)$

### Example 8.14

Consider Figure 8.3. Let $x$ be the agent whose actions are written first there. Assume for simplicity that each moment is its own unique alternative for $x$ (this is tantamount to assuming that $x$ has perfect knowledge—the above definition does not make this assumption). Then, by the above definitions, $x\mathsf{K_t}q$ holds at $t_3$ and $t_4$. Also, $x\mathsf{K_h}q$ holds at $t_1$ (using a tree with the single action $a$) and at $t_2$ (using the empty tree). As a result, at moment $t_0$, $x$ knows that if it performs $a$, then it will know how to achieve $q$ at each moment where $a$ ends. In other words, we can

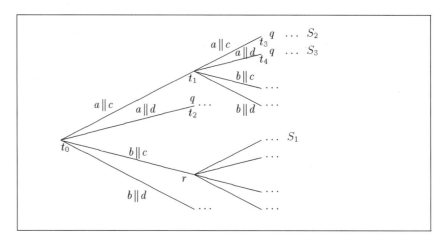

**Figure 8.3**   Know-how.

define a tree, $\langle a; a, \emptyset \rangle$, such that $x$ can achieve $q$ by properly executing that tree. Therefore, $x$ knows how to achieve $q$ at $t_0$.

A number of technical approaches to concepts of the know-how family exist. Some of the leading ones are Segerberg's *bringing it about* [68] and Belnap & Perloff's *seeing to it that (STIT)* [4] theories.

### 8.3.6   Sentential and Hybrid Approaches

The above approaches have used modal logics to formalize various cognitive concepts. Although technically intuitive and elegant, modal approaches have the undesirable feature that they over-estimate the reasoning capabilities of an agent. For example, an agent who knows (or intends) $p$ is automatically assumed to know (or intend) all logical consequences of $p$. For knowledge, this is termed the problem of *logical omniscience* [42]. Real-life agents cannot be logical omniscient. Consequently, alternative approaches have been proposed to formalizing the cognitive concepts. These approaches include the explicit representations that an agent has for its beliefs or intentions, e.g., [50, 51]. Unfortunately, although these approaches solve the problem of logical omniscience, they do not naturally support any inferences among the cognitive concepts. This too is undesirable, and has accounted for the lack of attention paid to these approaches. Some hybrid approaches the give a possible worlds semantics, but restrict it via some representational mechanism have also been developed, e.g., [27, 82], but these two have not been intensively pursued in the literature.

One way to understand the above issue is as a natural consequence of the knowledge level [63]. Newell observed that the knowledge level (corresponding to the modal approaches) would be inherently inaccurate, whereas the more accurate *symbol* level (corresponding to the representational approaches) would be more accurate, but only as a lower-level, procedural level of discourse.

### 8.3.7   Reasoning with Cognitive Concepts

Section 8.2 described two main roles for formal methods in DAI. The concepts introduced above may be used in each of those roles. In either case, there is need for efficient reasoning techniques. In the first use, the agent itself applies the logic, and needs methods such as *theorem proving* to decide its actions. In the second use, the designer applies the logic to specify and validate the design of an agent, and needs methods such as theorem proving and *model checking* to relate logical specifications to the construction of the agent. The two uses differ in their complexity requirements. Although both benefit from improved techniques, the first use is by far the more demanding, because it requires an answer in less time than the agent has to respond to its environment or to other agents. For this reason, the second use is the more practical one, at least when the logic is expressive.

There are two main approaches for reasoning with a logic. The more traditional one in logic and AI is theorem proving, which essentially involves establishing that a given formula (the purported theorem) follows through a finite sequence of applications of axioms and inferences rules of a given logic [26]. The other approach, which was invented in logics of programs and is finding increasing application in AI, is model checking. This involves checking if a given formula is satisfied at a given model and index. For certain logics, model checking can be a lot more tractable than theorem proving [24, 14]. However, model checking requires additional inputs in the form of the model and index. This does not prove to be a problem in several cases, where one if trying to validate a given agent design in a given environment. The model can be derived given knowledge of the agent and its environment.

Temporal logics and modal logics of knowledge have been studied for some time, and their complexity issues are well-understood. We lack the space to discuss complexity issues in much detail here, and refer the reader to [24, 28, 53] for details. The $\mu$-calculus is a logical language that has explicit operators for computing greatest and least fixpoints [24, 52]. This can be used to specify various modal and temporal logics in uniform framework, which can be naturally used for model checking [9, 14].

Both of the above classes of techniques are now being extended and applied in DAI. Rao has developed some tableau-based decision procedures for variants of the above BDI logics [64]. The $\mu$-calculus is recently being applied to reasoning about the actions of agents [17, 79].

## 8.4   BDI Implementations

We now consider some possible ways to realize the above theories of BDI concepts in a computational system.

### 8.4.1    Abstract Architecture

We first characterize a BDI architecture abstractly and then show how a concrete practical instantiation may be obtained.

#### *A Basic Interpreter*

We now describe a basic abstract interpreter for situated systems. The architecture makes use of the underlying concepts of BDI architectures, but implements the entities defined by the modal operators directly as data structures.

The inputs to the system are *events*, received via an *event queue*. The system can recognize (on its event queue) both *external* (environmental) and *internal* events. External events may directly generate particular internal events, such as updating some component of the system state. We assume that the events are atomic and are recognized upon completion (and not during occurrence).

The outputs of the system are atomic *actions*, which are performed by an *execute* function. The system may, but is not required to, recognize events corresponding to the successful or unsuccessful execution of actions. Based on its current state and the events in its queue, the system selects and executes *options*, which correspond to subroutines, production rules, tasks, plans, finite automata, or circuit networks. Correspondingly, the option-invoking events would be subroutine calls or the assertion of antecedents of a production rule.

The abstract interpreter is given below. We assume the procedures and functions appearing in the interpreter operate on the system state, denoted by S. The interpreter continually performs the following. First, it determines the available options. Next, it deliberates to commit to some options. It then updates its state and executes appropriate atomic actions. Finally, the event queue is updated to contain all those recognizable events that have occurred during the cycle. Since events are recognized (and thus acted upon) only once per cycle, the system's reaction time is bounded from below by the time taken to perform a cycle.

**basic-interpreter**
initialize-state();
**do**
    options := option-generator(event-queue, S);
    selected-options := deliberate(options, S);
    update-state(selected-options, S);
    execute(S);
    event-queue := get-new-events();
**until** quit.

This abstract interpreter can be used as a basis for different situated systems, including those in which most of the deliberation is precompiled [67].

### An Abstract BDI Interpreter

We now consider the special case of a BDI architecture by refining both the system state and interpreter. The system state comprises three dynamic data structures representing the agent's beliefs, desires, and intentions. For simplicity, we assume that the agent's desires are mutually consistent, although not necessarily all achievable. Such mutually consistent desires are called *goals*. The data structures support query and update operations, which include `b-add`, `b-remove`, `g-add`, `g-remove`, `i-add`, and `i-remove`. The update operations are subject to compatibility requirements, captured in the functions `b-compatible`, `g-compatible`, and `i-compatible`. These functions are critical in enforcing the constraints on the agent's mental attitudes.

The interpreter is refined as follows. Here `get-new-external-events` returns the external events that have occurred since its last invocation. At the beginning of a cycle, the option generator reads the event queue. It returns a list of the best options for further deliberation and possible execution. Next, the deliberator selects a subset of options and adds them to the intention structure. If there is an intention to perform an atomic action now, the agent executes it. Any external events that have occurred during the interpreter cycle are then added to the event queue. Internal events are added as they occur. Next, the agent modifies the intention and goal structures by dropping all successful goals and satisfied intentions, as well as impossible goals and unrealizable intentions.

**BDI-interpreter**
initialize-state();
**do**
    options := option-generator(event-queue,B,G,I);
    selected-options := deliberate(options,B,G,I);
    update-intentions(selected-options,I);
    execute(I);
    get-new-external-events();
    drop-successful-attitudes(B,G,I);
    drop-impossible-attitudes(B,G,I);
**until** quit.

This interpreter extends the basic interpreter mainly in the last three procedures, which eliminate a number of options that would otherwise be carried over to the next cycle.

### 8.4.2   Practical System

The above abstract architecture is a useful abstraction of the preceding theoretical model. It illustrates the main components of practical reasoning: option generation, deliberation, execution, and intention handling [5].

However, it is not practical. The architecture assumes a (logically) closed set of beliefs, goals, and intentions. It is not specified how the option generator and deliberation procedures can be made sufficiently fast to satisfy the real-time demands placed upon the system. We now make a number of additional representational choices which, while constraining expressive power, provide a more practical system. The resulting system is a simplified version of the Procedural Reasoning System (PRS) [46].

### Beliefs and Goals

The system operates only on *explicit* beliefs and goals and not on their consequential closure. Further, we identify a subset of the agent's beliefs and goals, which we call *current*. These are taken to be ground literals (rather like atomic propositions, but actually predicates applied to constants). Ground literals can be negated, but do not include any binary operators such as disjunction or implication. Intuitively, they represent beliefs and goals that are currently held, but which can be expected to change over time.

It may seem that such a language is too simple to be of practical use. However, implications and variables can be introduced through the plan constructs, resulting in little loss of expressiveness, but for a substantial gain in control.

### Plans

The above abstract interpreter represents information about means and options as beliefs. These can be more directly represented as *plans*. A plan has a name or *type*. The *body* of a plan is the method for executing it, and is specified by a *plan graph*, which is a rooted, directed, acyclic graph whose edges are labeled with simple plan expressions. A simple plan expression is either an atomic action or a subgoal. The *invocation condition* (a triggering event) and *precondition* specify when the plan may be selected. The *add list* and *delete list* of a plan respectively specify the atomic propositions to be believed or not believed upon its successful execution.

Plans represent a number of beliefs corresponding to complex modal formulas. Having a plan means that its body is believed to be an option whenever its invocation condition and precondition are satisfied. A plan represents the belief that, whenever its invocation condition and precondition are satisfied and its body successfully executed, the propositions in the add list will become true. Since the preconditions are conditions on the agent's beliefs, the agent can execute plans to compute new consequences. These consequences can trigger further plans to infer further consequences. This gives the agent greater control as to when to compute consequences of its current beliefs, goals, and intentions.

### Example 8.15

Suppose John acquires a goal to quench his thirst. He believes he has two ways to satsify it. One, perform a sequence of two atomic actions: open the tap and drink water from the tap. Two, satsify a subgoal (obtain a soda bottle) and then perform an atomic action (drink soda from the bottle). The subgoal can be satisfied

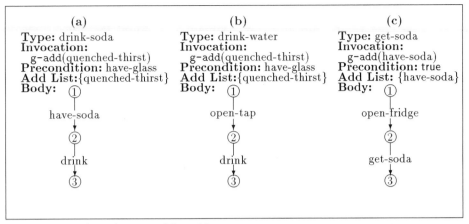

**Figure 8.4**   Plans for quenching thirst.

by opening the refrigerator and removing a soda bottle. These plans are shown in Figure 8.4.

## Intentions

Plans provide a hierarchical structure and allow tractable real-time option generation and means-end reasoning. The options are, in fact, plans. As they are adopted, they are added to the intention structure. Thus, intentions are represented as sets of hierarchically related plans.

To achieve an intended end, the agent forms an intention towards a means for this end; namely, the plan body of an appropriate plan. This means-end pair, together with information about variable bindings and control points, is called an *intention frame*. An intention towards a means results in the agent adopting another end (subgoal) and the means for achieving this end, thus creating another intention frame. This process continues until the subgoal can be directly executed as an atomic action. The next subgoal in the plan is then attempted.

An *intention stack* is used to keep track of variable bindings and control points. Each intention stack represents a separate process or task. These intention stacks are organized into an *intention structure*, which places various ordering constraints on them. Intention stacks can also be created for any event that appears in the invocation condition of a plan. This enables the system to be responsive to external events without mediating everything through goals.

## A Practical Interpreter

A practical interpreter can be derived from the above. The main loop for this interpreter is as above. However, as the system is embedded in a dynamic environment, the procedures appearing in the interpreter must be fast enough to satisfy the real-time demands of the appropriate applications.

Given a set of trigger events from the event queue, the option generator iterates through the plan library and returns those plans whose invocation condition matches the trigger event and whose preconditions are believed by the agent. The provability procedure involves simple unification with the beliefs.

**option-generator(trigger-events)**
options := {};
**for** trigger-event ∈ trigger-events **do**
    **for** plan ∈ *plan-library* **do**
        **if** matches(invocation(plan),trigger-event) **then**
            **if** provable(precondition(plan),B) **then**
                options := options ∪ {plan};
**return**(options).

The **deliberate** procedure's execution time should conform with the time constraints of the environment. Under certain circumstances, random choice may be appropriate. Sometimes, however, it is necessary to carry out lengthy deliberation. Such deliberation can be achieved by including metalevel plans in the plan library. Thus the **deliberate** procedure may select, and thus form an intention towards, metalevel plans for performing more complex deliberation than it itself is capable. We give a simplified version of the procedure implemented in PRS [32].

**deliberate(options)**
**if** length(options) ≤ 1 **then** **return**(options);
**else** metalevel-options := option-generator(**b-add**(option-set(options)));
    selected-options := deliberate(metalevel-options);
    **if** null(selected-options) **then**
      **return**(random-choice(options));
**else** **return**(selected-options).

Note that there can be more than one metalevel option, which results in the procedure being called recursively until at most one option remains. If no metalevel options are available, the deliberator chooses randomly.

Option generation can be simplified by inserting **post-intention-status** at the end of the loop. This procedure delays posting events on the queue to avoid the work caused by spurious changes otherwise sent to the event queue. In the abstract interpreter, commitment is achieved by reducing the options generated. Since the options depend on the events in the queue, **post-intention-status** determines the elements of the intention structure that are carried forward. Thus, **post-intention-status** can yield various notions of commitment, which result in different behaviors of the agent. One variant is given next.

**post-intention-status()**
**if** null(I) **then**
  **for** goal ∈ G **do**
    event-queue := event-queue ∪ **g-add**(goal);

**else for** stack $\in$ I **do**

event-queue := event-queue $\cup$ **g-add**(means(top(stack))).

| Bel | Goal | Int | *done* | *succeeded* |
|---|---|---|---|---|
| glass | – | – | – | – |
| unchanged | quench | – | – | g-add(quench) |
| unchanged | unchanged | { soda; drink} | – | g-add(soda) |
| ¬ remove-soda | unchanged | – | fridge | fridge, |
| | | | | g-add(quench) |
| unchanged | unchanged | { drink} | tap | tap |
| quench | – | – | drink | drink |

**Table 8.1**   Trace of practical BDI interpreter.

### *Example 8.16*

Consider Example 8.15 with plans as shown in Figure 8.4. Assume that the event **g-add**(quench) has just been added to the event queue. As the invocation conditions of **drink-soda** and **drink-water** match with the trigger event and their context conditions are believed, the option generator returns both these plans as suitable options.

Assume that the deliberator first selects the **drink-soda** option. As this option is to satisfy a new goal, rather than a subgoal of a previous intention, a new intention stack is created. The end (goal) for the top intention frame of the stack is **quench** and the means are given by the **drink-soda** plan. Since the first action in this plan is not atomic, no action is executed. Assume that no external events occur on this cycle. Thus the event queue contains only the internal event corresponding to the creation of the intention for the chosen option. As the system has not succeeded in any of its goals nor discovered that any intentions are impossible, it posts the current intention status. This results in **g-add**(soda) being added to the event queue.

In the next cycle, the option generator selects the plan for getting soda. This is adopted, and its frame added to the intention stack. The agent opens the refrigerator door, but at the next moment discovers that no soda is present. It is thus forced to drop its intention. Finally, the initial goal is reposted by **post-intention-status**.

On the next cycle, the option to drink water is selected, and the plan is completed successfully over further cycles. Table 8.1 shows the trace.

In the above we showed how the logics of the BDI concepts can be mapped into realistic implementations of systems. Although we didn't discuss the interactional aspects in the above, those can be worked in as well [36, 66]. We now our attention to some direct ways of capturing the interactional aspects of multiagent systems.

## 8.5   Coordination

Coordination is one of the key functionalities needed to implement a multiagent system. This is especially so when the component agents are *heterogeneous*, i.e., of diverse constructions and internal structures, and *autonomous*, i.e., making decisions without regard to the other agents.

A number of techniques for coordination have been developed in DAI. These are discussed in Chapter 3. A thorough logical account of these techniques, however, remains to be developed. A logical account would have the usual benefits of formal methods: a declarative, high-level specification independent of its ultimate realization, and the possibility of rigorously validating the implementations with respect to the specifications.

One formal approach to coordination was developed by Singh [77]. This approach represents each agent as a small *skeleton*, which includes only the *events* or *transitions* made by the agent that are significant for coordination. Coordination requirements are stated as temporal logic formulas involving the events. Formulas have been obtained that can capture the coordination requirements that arise in the literature.

The specific approach uses a temporal logic that is a variant of the linear temporal logic of Section 8.2.6. For that logic, it is possible to compile the specification in such a way as to localize most decision-making information on the individual agents. Effectively, the agents relinquish part of their autonomy (or their designers do it for them) when they decide to be coordinated. This leads to constraints on some of their events. If the agents respect these constraints, then the system as a whole behaves in the desired coordinated manner.

Sometimes, the term *coordination* is taken to mean a bit more than the above. In such cases, coordination involves the agents' beliefs and intentions. We discuss such cases under *collaboration* below.

### 8.5.1   Architecture

We now discuss the architecture that underlies a distributed coordination scheme based on temporal logic. We assume that agents are designed autonomously, and their internal details may be inaccessible. Also, that agents act autonomously and may unilaterally perform certain actions within their purview. However, in order to be able to coordinate the agents at all, the designer of the multiagent system must have some limited knowledge of the designs of the individual agents. This knowledge is in terms of their externally visible actions, which are potentially significant for coordination. We call these the significant *events* of the agent. In other words, the only events we speak of are those publicly known—the rest are of no concern to the coordination service. These events are organized into *skeletons* that characterize the coordination behavior of the agents. The idea of using events and skeletons is well-known from logics of programs [25].

### Event Classes

We allow four classes of events, which have different properties with respect to coordination. Events may be

- *flexible*, which the agent is willing to delay or omit
- *inevitable*, which the agent is willing only to delay
- *immediate*, which the agent performs unilaterally, that is, is willing neither to delay nor to omit
- *triggerable*, which the agent is willing to perform based on external request.

The first three classes are mutually exclusive; each can be conjoined with triggerability. We do not have a category where an agent will entertain omitting an event, but not delaying it, because unless the agent performs the event unilaterally, there must be some delay in receiving a response from the coordination service.

### Agent Skeletons

It is useful to view the events as organized into a *skeleton* to provide a simple representation of an agent for coordination purposes. This representation is typically a finite state automaton. Although the automaton is not used explicitly by the coordination service during execution, it can be used to validate specified coordination requirements. The set of events, their properties, and the skeleton of an agent depends on the agent, and is application-specific. The coordination service is independent of the exact skeletons or events used in a multiagent system. Examples 8.17 and 8.18 discuss two common skeletons in information search.

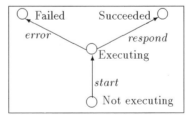

**Figure 8.5**   Skeleton for a simple querying agent.

### Example 8.17

Figure 8.5 shows a skeleton that is suited for agents who perform one-shot queries. Its significant events are *start* (accept an input and begin), *error*, and *respond* (produce an answer and terminate). The application-specific computation takes place in the node labeled "Executing." We must also specify the classes of the different events. For instance, we may state that *error* and *respond* are immediate, and *start* is flexible and triggerable.

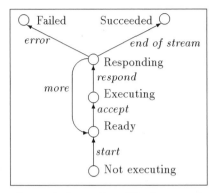

**Figure 8.6**   Skeleton for an information filtering agent.

### Example 8.18

Figure 8.6 shows a skeleton that is suited for agents who filter a stream, monitor a database, or perform any activity iteratively. Its significant events are *start* (accept an input, if necessary, and begin), *error*, *end of stream*, *accept* (accept an input, if necessary), *respond* (produce an answer), *more* (loop back to expecting more input). Here, too, the application-specific computation takes place in the node labeled "Executing." The events *error*, *end of stream*, and *respond* are immediate, and all other events are flexible, and *start* is in addition triggerable.

### 8.5.2   Specification Language

$\mathcal{L}_C$ is a language for specifying coordinations. It is a variant of $\mathcal{L}_L$, the linear-time language, with some restrictions. $\mathcal{L}_C$ is $\mathcal{L}_P$ augmented with the *before* (·) temporal operator. Before is related to the until operator of $\mathcal{L}_L$: it is used because it is easier to process symbolically for the purpose at hand. The literals denote event types, and can have parameters. Here we only consider the nonparameterized case, for simplicity. Also, in $\mathcal{L}_C$ negation applies only on the atoms, and is written as a ⁻ (bar) to highlight this fact. Further, the atoms are interpreted as events, such as are listed in the agent skeletons.

SYN-20.   $\psi \in \Phi$ implies that $\psi, \overline{\psi} \in \mathcal{L}_C$

SYN-21.   $p, q \in \mathcal{L}_C$ implies that $p \wedge q,\ p \vee p,\ p \cdot q \in \mathcal{L}_C$

The semantics of $\mathcal{L}_C$ is given with respect to a model $M_6 \stackrel{\text{def}}{=} \langle \mathbf{T}, <, [\![\,]\!] \rangle$. $M_6$ has the same structure as $M_3$. However, we restrict $M_6$ further so that it consists of paths or traces, which are *consistent*. By a consistent trace, we mean one on which no event is repeated and an event and its complement do not both occur. The following semantic definitions take as their index a given trace, $\tau$, not a specific moment on it, as for the previous semantic definitions. The motivation for this is that in giving a specification we only care about the behavior of the system as given by a trace, not by what may or may not have transpired at a given moment. When we execute the coordinations, we do care about the specific moments, of course, but that is not the concern of the specifier. The operator $\odot$ denotes concatenation of two traces, the first of which is finite. The following semantics looks at specific indices of a trace (as in $\tau_i$). This substitutes for the labeling function or $[\![\,]\!]$ used previously, and emphasizes the fact that each event happens at a particular moment.

SEM-36.   $M_6 \models_\tau \psi$ iff $(\exists i : \tau_i = \psi)$, where $\psi \in \Phi$

SEM-37.   $M_6 \models_\tau \overline{\psi}$ iff $(\exists i : \tau_i = \overline{\psi})$, where $\psi \in \Phi$

SEM-38.   $M_6 \models_\tau p \wedge q$ iff $M_6 \models_\tau p$ and $M_6 \models_\tau q$

SEM-39.   $M_6 \models_\tau p \vee q$ iff $M_6 \models_\tau p$ or $M_6 \models_\tau q$

SEM-40.   $M_6 \models_\tau p \cdot q$ iff $(\exists \sigma, \gamma : (\tau = \sigma \odot \gamma) \& M_6 \models_\sigma p \& M_6 \models_\gamma q)$

$\overline{\psi}$ refers to the complement of $\psi$. From the above, it is possible that a trace $\tau$ may satisfy neither $\psi$ nor $\overline{\psi}$. In this way, negation in $\mathcal{L}_C$ is stronger than in traditional logics. $\overline{\psi}$ means that it is definite that $\psi$ will never occur. Consequently, maximal traces will satisfy $\psi \vee \overline{\psi}$.

Singh [77] presents a set of equations that enable symbolic reasoning on $\mathcal{L}_C$ to determine when a certain event may be permitted, prevented, or triggered.

### 8.5.3   Common Coordination Relationships

Coordinations are specified by expressing appropriate relationships among the events of different agents. $\mathcal{L}_C$ allows a variety of relationships to be captured.

Table 8.2 presents some common relationships. Some of the relationships involve coordinating multiple events. For example, R8 captures requirements such as that

|    | Name | Description | Formal notation |
|----|------|-------------|-----------------|
| R1 | $e$ is required by $f$ | If $f$ occurs, $e$ must occur before or after $f$ | $e \vee \overline{f}$ |
| R2 | $e$ disables $f$ | If $e$ occurs, then $f$ must occur before $e$ | $\overline{e} \vee \overline{f} \vee f \cdot e$ |
| R3 | $e$ feeds or enables $f$ | $f$ requires $e$ to occur before | $e \cdot f \vee \overline{f}$ |
| R4 | $e$ conditionally feeds $f$ | If $e$ occurs, it feeds $f$ | $\overline{e} \vee e \cdot f \vee \overline{f}$ |
| R5 | Guaranteeing $e$ enables $f$ | $f$ can occur only if $e$ has occurred or will occur | $e \wedge f \vee \overline{e} \wedge \overline{f}$ |
| R6 | $e$ initiates $f$ | $f$ occurs iff $e$ precedes it | $\overline{e} \wedge \overline{f} \vee e \cdot f$ |
| R7 | $e$ and $f$ jointly require $g$ | If $e$ and $f$ occur in any order, then $g$ must also occur (in any order) | $\overline{e} \vee \overline{f} \vee g$ |
| R8 | $g$ compensates for $e$ failing $f$ | if $e$ happens and $f$ does not, then perform $g$ | $(\overline{e} \vee f \vee g) \wedge (\overline{g} \vee e) \wedge (\overline{g} \vee \overline{f})$ |

**Table 8.2**   Example relationships.

if an agent does something ($e$), but another agent does not match it with something else ($f$), then a third agent can perform $g$. This is a typical pattern in applications with data updates, where $g$ corresponds to an action to restore the consistency of the information (potentially) violated by the success of $e$ and the failure of $f$. Hence the name *compensation*.

## 8.6    Communications

Communications are a natural way in which the agents in a DAI system may interact with one another other than through incidental interactions through the environment. Communications is discussed in detail in Chapter 2.

Speech act theory, which originated in the philosophy of language, gives the basis for communications. Speech act theory is founded on the idea that with language you not only make statements, but also *perform actions* [3]. For example, when you request something you do not just report on a request, but you actually effect the request; when a justice of the peace declares a couple man and wife, she is not reporting on their marital status, but changing it. The stylized syntactic form for speech acts that begins "I hereby request ..." or "I hereby declare ..." is called a *performative*. With a performative, literally, saying it makes it so! [3, p. 7]. Interestingly, verbs that cannot be put in this form are not speech acts. For example, "solve" is not a performative, because "I hereby solve this problem" just does not work out—or Math students would be a much happier lot! For most computing purposes, speech acts are classified into assertives (informing), directives (requesting or querying), commissives (promising), permissives, prohibitives, declaratives (causing events in themselves, e.g., what the justice of the peace does in a marriage ceremony), expressives (expressing emotions and evaluations).

Austin identified three main aspects of a speech act. The *locution* refers to the lowest level of the speech act, namely, the string that is transmitted. The *illocution* refers to the intrinsic meaning of the speech act. The *perlocution* refers to the possible effects of the speech act on the recipients. The locution can be varied and the perlocutions depend on the recipient. However, the illocution tells us the meaning that is conveyed. For this reason, studies of communication in DAI focus primarily on the illocutions.

### 8.6.1    Semantics

Formalizing the semantics of communications has proved a longstanding challenge. This is partly because more than one view of what can be formalized is possible. The earliest work was carried out in computational linguistics, and sought to determine the conditions under which the intended meaning of a speech act might be inferred. For example, given a locution in the form of a question (e.g., "can you pass the salt?"), one might infer an illocution that is a request (e.g., "please pass the salt").

There is considerable subtlety involved in this reasoning, but for the most part, it is specific to human languages and can be avoided in DAI.

A different approach was developed by Singh [78]. This approach sought to give the objective criteria under which speech acts of different illocutionary forces could be said to be satisfied. The idea was to identify the conditions in a framework that highlighted the proof-obligations of a designer in showing that different speech acts were satisfied. Following Hamblin [38], Singh defined a notion of *whole-hearted satisfaction*. This was formalized using a modal operator; truth conditions for this operator corresponded to satisfaction conditions for the corresponding speech acts. An example condition is that a directive for $p$ is whole-heartedly satisfied if and only if the recipient adopts and intention to satisfy $p$, has the know-how to achieve $p$, and acts resulting in $p$.

Recently, Labrou & Finin have developed a formal semantics for communications and *conversations* (consisting of a series of communications) that considers the preconditions and postconditions for each speech act. These conditions are stated in terms of the beliefs and wants of the participating agents.

Fundamentally, communication is a social phenomenon. Although this fact is noted in informal discussions, existing approaches have not recognized it in their theoretical development. We believe that the study of social primitives (discussed below) has advanced enough that directly social semantics of communications can now be explored. We leave the development as a significant open research problem in DAI.

### 8.6.2 Ontologies

An ontology is a representation of some part of the world. Ontologies are thus of interest to knowledge representation. Although ontologies in themselves are not a social concept, they can provide a shared "virtual world" that can serve as the basis for communications [44]. In fact, when many people talk of the "semantics" of a communication, they mean understanding the concepts and terms used in it. Ontologies provide a natural, declarative way of identifying concepts and terms. If two agents agree on the upper nodes of a taxonomy, they can jointly traverse the taxonomy till they find the location of a newly introduced concept. Thus, they can build a shared understanding of their content language. It is this fact that makes ontologies interesting. They found much application in DAI systems, especially those involving access to, or interactions among, information systems and databases [22, 90]. Consequently, ontologies are included in several multiagent architectures.

Ontologies are amenable to formal methods in two main places. One place is in the algorithms for processing ontologies, which exploit the connection between lattice theory and taxonomies [43]. Another place is in approaches to help interlink ontologies developed by different vendors, or incorporated by different agents, who must reconcile them in order to communicate. An interesting class of approaches may be based on algebraic techniques [89]; however, this work is still in its infancy.

## 8.7   Social Primitives

Arguably, it is the active use of social concepts in its design and implementation that distinguish a DAI system from a traditional distributed computing system [31]. We lump into the category of social primitives those that concern societies of agents as well as those that concern smaller and more heavily structured organizations. Some related social concepts are introduced in Chapter 2, and organizational concepts in Chapter 7.

### 8.7.1   Teams and Organizational Structure

A *group* or multiagent system is a system of agents that are somehow constrained in their mutual interactions. Typically, these constraints arise because the agents play different *roles* in the group, and their roles impose requirements on how they are to behave and interact with others. A *team* is a group in which the agents are restricted to having a common goal of some sort. Typically, team-members cooperate and assist each other in achieving their common goals. Groups and teams prove to be a fertile ground for the development of formal theories in DAI, especially theories that are unlike the theories in traditional AI or computer science. We emphasize, however, that some of this work is still in an early stage, and the descriptions below, although moderately stable, should not be taken as final.

Some good work has focused on formalizing cooperative problem solving [92], and the representations needed for effective cooperation [21].

### 8.7.2   Mutual Beliefs and Joint Intentions

One of the oldest ways of lifting single-agent concepts to multiagent concepts is through the use of *mutual beliefs*. A set of agents is said to have a mutual belief that $p$ if they each (a) believe $p$, (b) believe that condition (a) holds of the others (that they believe $p$), (c) believe that condition (b) holds of the others, and so on. Mutual belief thus provides a means to achieve the effect of a perfectly shared mental state. It has been argued the mutual beliefs can account for various aspects of human communication [13, 39] and social conventions [58].

Levesque & Cohen developed an approach that generalizes the notion of intentions to *joint intentions* [57]. This theory is extremely complicated, and our presentation can at best be thought of an intuitive approximation of the original. A joint intention for $p$ exists among a group of agents if they (a) each have a goal that $p$, (b) each will persist with this goal until it is mutually believed that $p$ has been achieved or that $p$ cannot be achieved, (c) conditions (a) and (b) are mutually believed.

Grosz & Kraus develop a formal theory of shared plans [35]. This theory relates the cooperative activities of agents via their individual and shared plans. A distinction is sometimes made between an agent intending to achieve something and an agent intending that some condition be obtained. Usually, actions and propositions are closely related, although they are often treated differently in human languages. Grosz & Kraus adapt this idea to develop a framework in which the agent is itself committed to performing the intentions toward actions, but depending on the situation can act on the intentions for propositions that are held by its team-members (and, similarly, can expect others to take on the propositions it intends).

On the one hand, mutual beliefs play a role in several theories; on the other hand, it is well-known that if communications among the agents are not reliable (in terms of delivery and delay), then mutual beliefs cannot be attained [11, 37]. In other words, the mutual beliefs are limited to the beliefs that the designer hard-wires into the agents at the start, but additional mutual beliefs cannot be attained.

This conflict between some theoretically appealing properties of mutual beliefs and their infeasibility in practical situations has led some researchers to explore alternative ways to achieve the same effect. It has been suggested that social primitives, appropriately formalized, might provide a more direct means to capture the social aspects of multiagent systems, which apparently are the ones that mutual beliefs seek to capture.

### 8.7.3 Social Commitments

Section 8.3.4 introduced psychological commitments. Here we consider social commitments, which are the commitments that an agent toward another agent [10, 74]. Such commitments related to directed obligations [55] as studied in deontic logic (see Section 8.2.4). Social commitments are a genuinely multiagent concept, since they have no analog in a single-agent system. Social commitments can potentially be used to give clear specifications at the social level of how the agents in a multiagent system ought to interact; such specifications will not delve into implementational details, and give maximal freedom to diverse designers to implement agents that can behave together cohesively.

Although concepts such as social commitments have long been identified, this topic has drawn much interest recently [10, 16, 23, 66, 80]. Castelfranchi introduced the idea of a *witness* of a commitment, which certifies to its creation [10]. Singh generalizes notion to a *context group*, which is usually the multiagent system within which the given commitment exists [80]. The formalization of social commitments involves defining an independent primitive. They also involve the description of associated notions such as the *roles* that may exist in the given multiagent system, and what capabilities and authorities (or authorizations) agents would need to play specific roles. This work is still in its infancy, but we encourage the reader to peruse the cited works for some open research problems.

### 8.7.4 Group Know-How and Intentions

There is a view that multiagent systems can themselves be treated as agents. These are then referred to as *groups* and distinguished from ordinary *individual* agents.

In many interesting cases, when an agent interacts with another entity, it may have no knowledge or concern that the other entity is an individual or a group. It may have expectations about the other entities as usual, and may enter into social commitments with it. Thus the other entity is justifiably treated as an agent.

A natural question is how may we define the beliefs, knowledge, know-how, and intentions of groups. Some conventional approaches were mentioned in Section 8.7.2. An alternative approach is to define the structure of a group explicitly, and define the intentions and know-how of the group as based on its structure and the intentions and know-how of its members. The structure may itself be formalized in several ways. One way is through a combination of the *reactive* and the *strategic* interactions among the members that are called for by the group [71, 72].

For reasons of space, we only consider group intentions below. Recall the scenarios selected by the model component **I** in formalizing intentions. With reactive interactions, the selected scenarios are restricted to those that satisfy some additionally specified temporal (path) formulas, which intuitively correspond to the habits of interaction of the different members. Similarly, strategic interactions restrict the selected scenarios to those in which the specified communications among the members are satisfied. For example, a group could require that all directives issued by an agent playing the role of leader must be satisfied, or that all commitments created through explicit promises must be discharged. These requirements eliminate unacceptable scenarios, leading to a stronger notion of intentions than if we considered the agents individually. However, this notion is potentially weaker than traditional notions, which always require some form of mutual belief among the members.

Interestingly, when formalized, the above definitions lead to some algebraic properties of group intentions that relate to the underlying structure of the given groups [71].

## 8.8 Tools and Systems

Now we present a variety of implemented tools and systems for DAI that bear some significant connection with the formal techniques introduced above. We have three categories of these tools and systems: those that follow the above approaches closely; those that are essentially traditional techniques applied to DAI, and those that were informally influenced by the DAI approaches.

### 8.8.1 Direct Implementations

We now review some of the popular systems that are fairly directly based on the above ideas.

### PRS and dMARS

The Procedural Reasoning System (PRS) [33] was one of the first implemented systems to be based on a BDI architecture. As described in the foregoing, PRS provides goal-oriented as well as reactive behavior. It was implemented in LISP and has been used for a wide range of applications in problem diagnosis for the Space Shuttle [46], air-traffic management [59], and network management [46].

dMARS is a faster, more robust reimplementation of PRS in C++. It has been used in a variety of operational environments, including paint shop scheduling in car manufacturing, air combat simulation, resource exploration, malfunction handling on NASA's space shuttle, and management of business processes in Internet and call center applications [49].

### COSY

COSY is also a BDI architecture, and bears several similarities to PRS and dMARS [36]. It involves the same concepts, and uses plans as its core representation. However, in addition, COSY has gives importance to both psychological and social commitments. COSY has a strong component of cooperation, which is based on formal protocols built on top of an agent communication language. The formation of commitments is declaratively captured in various rules. The above protocols involve commitments among the agents, and include rules through which tasks may be delegated to and adopted by different agents.

### Agent-Oriented Languages

The concepts discussed in the chapter are also finding their way into programming language constructs. Shoham [69] in his proposal for an agent-oriented language called AGENT0 made extensive use of notions such as beliefs, commitments, and know-how. The language was subsequently extended by Thomas [88] to include planning capability similar to that of BDI architectures.

Agent-oriented languages based on alternative formalisms are also gaining ground. Golog and ConGolog [56] are logic programming languages that allow explicit reasoning about actions. The system is based on situation calculus to represent and reason about change [61]. As the Golog interpreter can reason about actions it can avoid "dead paths" that the BDI interpreter cannot. However, it does not offer the reactivity offered by the BDI architecture because of its inability to indirectly invoke the execution of plans.

### Concurrent MetateM

An alternative approach uses temporal logic to specify the behavior of agents. A Concurrent MetateM system [29] consists of a set of objects each executing temporal specifications. A rule in this language is of the form "past and present formula" implies "present or future formula." As a result, execution of this rule involves matching the antecedent of these rules against the history of incoming messages and then executing the present and future-time consequents. Enhancements with explicit BDI operators are beginning to be developed [30].

### *ARTIMIS*

Breiter & Sadek have implemented a formal theory of beliefs and intentions in the ARTIMIS system [7]. The ARTIMIS system carries out intelligent dialogue with a user in assisting the user in tasks such as information access. This system, being designed as a user interface, applies the Gricean maxims, whereby the computer attempts to infer the user's intentions and act accordingly. It also uses an agent communication language, Arcol, to carry out a dialogue with the user.

### *DEPNET*

DEPNET is an interpreter for agents who can perform social reasoning [70]. Agents in DEPNET represent knowledge about one another to determine their relative autonomy or dependence for various goals. Dependence leads to joint plans for achieving the intended goals. The underlying theory is based on dependence rather than social commitments. Thus it is more amenable to processing by the agents individually, but is also more limited because it cannot easily capture the normative aspects of social interaction among agents. However, this tool shows how social notions can be realized in tools for simulating and analyzing multiagent systems.

### *TFM-CAA: Coordinating Autonomous Agents*

TFM-CAA is an implementation of a customizable coordination service based on the approach described in Section 8.5. This service (a) takes declarative specifications of the desired interactions, and (b) automatically enacts them. This approach enacts the coordination requirements in a distributed manner with minimal intrusion into the design of the agents being coordinated.

### 8.8.2   Partial Implementations

These are systems that do not involve a full implementation of the theoretical concepts, but were influenced by the theories and used them in designing their solutions. They are, however, full systems in their own right.

### *STEAM*

STEAM is an architecture for teamwork by agents [87]. STEAM offers abstractions for teams, based on the work on joint intentions and shared plans. STEAM also uses some coordination abstractions. One of STEAM's features is the specification of team plan operators in terms of *role operators*—that is, plan operators for member agents. Three *role-monitoring constraints* are defined, through which STEAM can infer the potential achievability of a team operator. If a team operator becomes unachievable because of a role-monitoring failure, it can be repaired by examining the roles that caused the failure. STEAM is being enhanced with functionality using which an agent can compare its behavior to that of its peers and thereby determine if a failure has occurred. STEAM has been applied in domains such as military helicopter missions and simulated soccer.

### Carnot

Carnot was a research project primarily focused on accessing and updating information from heterogeneous databases, such as are common in large enterprises [91]. Carnot was applied on accessing information from legacy databases, automating workflow for service-order processing, and retrieving related information from structured and text databases [83]. In these applications, Carnot adapted formal techniques for ontology management [43] and transaction management [84]. The latter were a precursor of the formal theory later extended to coordinating autonomous agents, as described in Section 8.5.

### ARCHON

The ARCHON project developed a domain-independent architecture of multiagent systems, which was applied in an electricity transportation management system and a particle accelerator [48]. This architecture emphasized the role of cooperation among agents through a declarative representation of cooperation, which was reasoned about explicitly. The agents autonomously detected the need to cooperate— this generalizes distributed problem solving, and enhances the autonomy of the agents. The agents maintain *self models* and *acquaintance models* to effectively decide when and how to cooperate. This system adapted the notion of joint intentions mentioned above. It also included a framework for information access similar to Carnot's.

### maDes

Ishizaki develops maDes, a *multiagent model of dynamic design*. Design is understood as the creative activity in which a designer constructs a suitable representation for a message [47]. Ishizaki's model is interesting to the design community, because it emphasizes the dynamic or active aspects of modern media, such as computers. It is interesting to the agent community, because it finds a novel application of agents. It considers a number of agents with different abilities who come together to create a composite design. This model uses the theory of group ability as its basis for defining the reactive interaction among design agents [72].

### 8.8.3 Traditional Approaches

This section reviews some formal approaches that initially were designed for traditional software engineering, but which are being applied to DAI systems. We include these here, because as we have maintained in this Chapter, DAI requires the careful synthesis of traditional and new techniques.

### *DESIRE*

Design and Specification of Interacting Reasoning Components, better known as DESIRE, is a framework for the design and specification of multiagent systems [6]. DESIRE can be thought of as an object modeling framework with enhancements for DAI. The primary unit of representation in DESIRE is a task. The user can specify task composition, sequencing of tasks, and task delegation, in addition to the information exchanged between agents and the knowledge structures that capture the domain knowledge. Tasks are similar to PRS plans, except that when it comes to execution plans are executed indirectly by posting an event to achieve a goal, rather than directly. This has the advantage that any external events can be handled *during* the execution of a plan.

### *The Z Specification Language*

The Z language was developed for the formal specification of software systems [86]. It has found application in DAI as well. One class of uses of Z involves formally specifying properties such as the autonomy and dependence of agents in multiagent systems, as well as the cognitive concepts discussed above [20]. Another use involves formalizing existing systems after the fact to give a mathematical characterization of their behavior that may be more faithful than a pure knowledge-level BDI treatment [19].

## 8.9 Conclusions

As DAI matures and its applications expand into increasingly critical settings, we will need sophisticated approaches for engineering DAI systems. As in other branches of computer science, these approaches will involve a combination of tools and methodologies. Effective tools and methodologies must not only support a rich variety of powerful abstractions, but also be founded on and respect rigorous treatments of the abstractions they support.

DAI systems involve a variety of concepts. Some of these are the BDI concepts that have been studied for the longest time in DAI. Other relevant concepts involve communications among agents as well as a wide range of coordination and social primitives. Consequently, formal methods in DAI inherently involve mathematical structures that explicate these notions. Although formal methods in DAI are still in their infancy, some interesting results have been obtained. The formal techniques have also been used to influence a variety of practical systems.

However, an important caveat is that most of the present-generation systems that "implement" various theories have only limited fidelity to those theories. They need to go beyond the theories to a significant extent. This deviation is essential because current theories tend to be incomplete in their coverage and somewhat simplistic and top-heavy. Consequently, more than in traditional systems, DAI systems require a greater contribution of insights from their developers. Although the insights are valuable, their insertion detracts from the formal underpinnings of the work, because the insights are typically *ad hoc*, and do not facilitate establishing the kinds of properties that make formal methods attractive.

This speaks to the need for carefully engineered, tractable logics that may not be expressive in general, but have the power needed for a specific class of tasks. Full automation may not be essential, especially at design time, if the insights a human may offer are from a well-understood set of patterns. But, of course, that is what tools and methodologies are all about. Consequently, a range of future challenges is to develop well-honed formal theories that cover the phenomena that emerge in practice, are more accurate in their treatment of real systems, and can be used to analyze and design them.

## 8.10   Exercises

1.  *[Level 1]* Formalize the following conditions in propositional logic:

    (a)   it is cold

    (b)   it is cold in room 1344

    (c)   room 1344 has an air conditioner

    (d)   the agent $x$ feels cold

    (e)   if it is raining, it is cold

2.  *[Level 1]* Formalize the following conditions in temporal logic:

    (a)   room 1344 will always be cold

    (b)   if room 1344 gets cold, it will stay cold forever

    (c)   room 1344 will repeatedly be getting cold and hot

3.  *[Level 1]* Formalize the following conditions in dynamic logic:

    (a)   turning on the air conditioner makes room 1344 cold

    (b)   turning off the air conditioner does not make room 1344 hot

4.  *[Level 2]* Formalize the following conditions in predicate logic [26] (requires extra reading):

    (a)   every room with an air conditioner is cold

    (b)   the agent $x$ feels cold in every room that has an air conditioner

    (c)   some agent feels cold in every room that has an air conditioner

5. *[Level 2]* Verify the correspondence between the properties on accessibility relations and inferences in modal logic, as mentioned in Section 8.2.3.

6. *[Level 2]* Translate `while` loops from Algol-60 into regular programs.

7. *[Level 2]* Relate *partial* and *total* correctness of programs (as defined in any introductory text on analysis of programs) with the dynamic logic operators.

8. *[Level 2]* Prove or disprove the following properties about $\mathcal{L}_L$:

   - $\mathsf{FF}p \rightarrow \mathsf{F}p$
   - $\mathsf{G}p \rightarrow \mathsf{F}p$
   - $\mathsf{GG}p \rightarrow \mathsf{G}p$
   - $\mathsf{GG}p \rightarrow \mathsf{GF}p$
   - $\mathsf{GF}p \rightarrow \mathsf{FG}p$
   - $\mathsf{FG}p \rightarrow \mathsf{GF}p$
   - $\mathsf{FGF}p \equiv \mathsf{GF}p$

9. *[Level 2]* Prove or disprove the following properties about $\mathcal{L}_B$:

   - $\mathsf{EX}\mathsf{true}$
   - $\mathsf{AGAG}p \rightarrow \mathsf{AGAF}p$
   - $\mathsf{E}(p\mathsf{U}q) \rightarrow (q \vee p \wedge \mathsf{EX}(\mathsf{E}(p\mathsf{U}q)))$
   - $(q \vee p \wedge \mathsf{EX}(\mathsf{E}(p\mathsf{U}q))) \rightarrow \mathsf{E}(p\mathsf{U}q)$

10. *[Level 2]* Establish the results mentioned in the context of Constraints cons-i-sat, IC2, and IC3 in Section 8.3.3.

11. *[Level 2]* Prove or disprove the following properties about know-how (the agent is omitted):

    - $\mathsf{K}_h p \rightarrow \mathsf{K}_h \mathsf{K}_h p$
    - $\mathsf{K}_h p \rightarrow (\mathsf{K}_t p \vee (\bigvee a : \mathsf{E}\langle a \rangle \mathsf{true} \wedge \mathsf{A}[a]\mathsf{K}_h p))$
    - $(\mathsf{K}_t p \vee (\bigvee a : \mathsf{E}\langle a \rangle \mathsf{true} \wedge \mathsf{A}[a]\mathsf{K}_h p)) \rightarrow \mathsf{K}_h p$

12. *[Level 3]* Implement a BDI interpreter based on the architecture described above.

    (a)   Make turning on the air conditioner makes room 1344 cold

    (b)   turning off the air conditioner does not make room 1344 hot

13. *[Level 3]* Implement a deliberation component of a BDI interpreter based on heuristic graph search.

14. *[Level 4]* What might be the nature of a social-level semantics for agent communication languages? Give such a semantics.

    (a)   reconcile it with conventional approaches based on the BDI notions

(b) develop a scheme for testing compliance with your semantics of implementations by different vendors.

# References

1. Alfred V. Aho and Jeffrey D. Ullman. *Principles of Compiler Design.* Addison-Wesley, Reading, MA, 1977.

2. Alan Ross Anderson and Nuel D. Belnap. *Entailment: The Logic of Relevance and Necessity.* Princeton University Press, Princeton, 1975.

3. John L. Austin. *How to Do Things with Words.* Clarendon Press, Oxford, 1962.

4. Nuel Belnap and Michael Perloff. Seeing to it that: A canonical form for agentives. *Theoria*, 54(3):175–199, 1988.

5. Michael E. Bratman. *Intention, Plans, and Practical Reason.* Harvard University Press, Cambridge, MA, 1987.

6. Frances M. T. Brazier, Barbara M. Dunin-Kęplicz, Nick Jennings, and Jan Treur. Desire: Modelling multi-agent systems in a compositional formal framework. *International Journal of Cooperative Information Systems*, 6(1):67–94, 1997.

7. Phillipe Breiter and M. David Sadek. A rational agent as a kernel of a cooperative dialogue system: Implementing a logical theory of interaction. In *ECAI-96 Workshop on Agent Theories, Architectures, and Languages*, pages 261–276. Springer-Verlag, 1996.

8. Omran A. Bukhres and Ahmed K. Elmagarmid, editors. *Object-Oriented Multidatabase Systems: A Solution for Advanced Applications.* Prentice-Hall, 1996.

9. J. R. Burch, E. C. Clarke, K. L. McMillan, D. L. Dill, and L. J. Hwang. Symbolic model checking: $10^{20}$ states and beyond. In *Proceedings of the 5th International Symposium on Logic in Computer Science*, pages 428–439, 1990.

10. Cristiano Castelfranchi. Commitments: From individual intentions to groups and organizations. In *Proceedings of the International Conference on Multiagent Systems*, pages 41–48, 1995.

11. K. M. Chandy and Jayadev Misra. How processes learn. *Distributed Computing*, 1:40–52, 1986.

12. Brian F. Chellas. *Modal Logic.* Cambridge University Press, New York, 1980.

13. Herbert H. Clark and Thomas B. Carlson. Speech acts and hearer's beliefs. In *[85]*, pages 1–36. 1982.

14. E. Clarke, O. Grumberg, and D. Long. Model checking. In *Proceedings of the International Summer School on Deductive Program Design*, pages 428–439, 1990.

15. Philip R. Cohen and Hector J. Levesque. Intention is choice with commitment. *Artificial Intelligence*, 42:213–261, 1990.

16. Rosaria Conte and Cristiano Castelfranchi. *Cognitive and Social Action.* UCL Press, London, 1995.

17. Giuseppe De Giacomo and Xiao Jun Chen. Reasoning about nondeterministic and concurrent actions: A process algebra approach. In *Proceedings of the National Conference on Artificial Intelligence*, pages 658–663, 1996.

18. Yves Demazeau and Jean-Pierre Müller, editors. *Decentralized Artificial Intelligence, Volume 2*. Elsevier/North-Holland, Amsterdam, 1991.

19. Mark d'Inverno, David Kinny, Michael Luck, and Michael Wooldridge. A formal specification of dMARS. In *Intelligent Agents IV: Agent Theories, Architectures, and Languages*, 1998.

20. Mark d'Inverno and Michael Luck. Understanding autonomous interaction. In *Proceedings of the European Conference on Artificial Intelligence*, 1996.

21. Mark d'Inverno, Michael Luck, and Michael Wooldridge. Cooperation structures. In *Proceedings of the International Joint Conference on Artificial Intelligence*, pages 600–605, 1997.

22. Michael L. Dowell, Larry M. Stephens, and Ronald D. Bonnell. Using a domain-knowledge ontology as a semantic gateway among information resources. In *[45]*, pages 255–260. 1997. (*Reprinted from* Proceedings of the IJCAI Workshop on Basic Ontological Issues in Knowledge Sharing, 1995).

23. Barbara Dunin-Kęplicz and Rineke Verbrugge. Collective commitments. In *Proceedings of the International Conference on Multiagent Systems*, pages 56–63, 1996.

24. E. Allen Emerson. Temporal and modal logic. In Jan van Leeuwen, editor, *Handbook of Theoretical Computer Science*, volume B, pages 995–1072. North-Holland, Amsterdam, 1990.

25. E. Allen Emerson and Edmund C. Clarke. Using branching time temporal logic to synthesize synchronization skeletons. *Science of Computer Programming*, 2:241–266, 1982.

26. Herbert B. Enderton. *A Mathematical Introduction to Logic*. Academic Press, San Diego, 1972.

27. Ronald Fagin and Joseph Y. Halpern. Belief, awareness, and limited reasoning. *Artificial Intelligence*, 34:39–76, 1988.

28. Ronald Fagin, Joseph Y. Halpern, Yoram Moses, and Moshe Y. Vardi. *Reasoning About Knowledge*. MIT Press, Cambridge, MA, 1995.

29. Michael Fisher. A survey of concurrent MetateM - the language and its applications. In *Proceedings of the 1st International Conference on Temporal Logic (ICTL)*, 1994.

30. Michael Fisher and Michael Wooldridge. On the formal specification and verification of multi-agent systems. *International Journal of Intelligent and Cooperative Information Systems*, 6(1):37–65, 1997.

31. Les Gasser. Social conceptions of knowledge and action: DAI foundations and open systems semantics. In *[45]*, pages 389–404. 1997. (*Reprinted from* Artificial Intelligence, 1991).

32. Michael P. Georgeff and F. Felix Ingrand. Decision-making in an embedded reasoning system. In *Proceedings of the International Joint Conference on Artificial Intelligence (IJCAI)*, 1989.

33. Michael P. Georgeff and Amy L. Lansky. Procedural knowledge. *Proceedings of the IEEE*, 74:1383–1398, 1986.

34. Michael P. Georgeff and Anand S. Rao. The semantics of intention maintenance for rational agents. In *Proceedings of the International Joint Conference on Artificial Intelligence (IJCAI)*, pages 704–710, 1995.

35.  Barbara J. Grosz and Sarit Kraus. Collaborative plans for complex group action. *Artificial Intelligence*, 86(2):269–357, October 1996.

36.  Afsaneh Haddadi. *Communication and Cooperation in Agent Systems : A Pragmatic Theory*. Springer-Verlag, Heidelberg, 1996.

37.  Joseph Y. Halpern and Yoram O. Moses. Knowledge and common knowledge in a distributed environment. *Journal of the Association for Computing Machinery*, 37:549–587, 1990.

38.  C. L. Hamblin. *Imperatives*. Basil Blackwell, Oxford, 1987.

39.  Gilbert Harman. Review of Jonathan Bennett's *Linguistic Behaviour*. *Language*, 53(2):417–424, 1977.

40.  Risto Hilpinen, editor. *Deontic Logic: Introductory and Systematic Readings*, volume 33 of *Synthese Library*. D. Reidel, Dordrecht, Holland, 1971.

41.  Risto Hilpinen, editor. *New Studies in Deontic Logic: Norms, Actions, and the Foundations of Ethics*, volume 152 of *Synthese Library*. D. Reidel, Dordrecht, Holland, 1981.

42.  Jaakko Hintikka. *Knowledge and Belief: An Introduction to the Logic of the Two Notions*. Cornell University Press, Ithaca, 1962.

43.  Michael N. Huhns, Christine Collet, and Wei-Min Shen. Resource integration using a large knowledge base in Carnot. *IEEE Computer*, 24(12):55–62, December 1991.

44.  Michael N. Huhns and Munindar P. Singh. Ontologies for agents. *IEEE Internet Computing*, 1(6):81–83, December 1997. Instance of the column *Agents on the Web*.

45.  Michael N. Huhns and Munindar P. Singh, editors. *Readings in Agents*. Morgan Kaufmann, San Francisco, 1997.

46.  F. Felix Ingrand, Michael P. Georgeff, and Anand S. Rao. An architecture for real-time reasoning and system control. *IEEE Expert*, 7(6), 1992.

47.  Suguru Ishizaki. Multiagent model of dynamic design: Visualization as an emergent behavior of active design agents. In *[45]*, pages 172–179. 1997. (*Reprinted from* Proceedings of the ACM Conference on Computer Human Interaction, 1996).

48.  Nick R. Jennings, E. H. Mamdani, Jose Manuel Corera, Inaki Laresgoiti, Fabien Perriollat, Paul Skarek, and Laszlo Zsolt Varga. Using Archon to develop real-world DAI applications, part 1. *IEEE Expert*, 11(6):64–70, December 1996.

49.  David Kinny and Michael P. Georgeff. Modelling and design of multi-agent systems. In *Intelligent Agents III: Agent Theories, Architectures, and Languages*, pages 1–20, 1997.

50.  Kurt Konolige. *A Deduction Model of Belief*. Morgan Kaufmann, 1986.

51.  Kurt G. Konolige and Martha E. Pollack. A representationalist theory of intentions. In *Proceedings of the International Joint Conference on Artificial Intelligence (IJCAI)*, 1989.

52.  Dexter Kozen. Results on the propositional $\mu$-calculus. *Theoretical Computer Science*, 27:333–354, 1983.

53.  Dexter Kozen and Jerzy Tiurzyn. Logics of program. In Jan van Leeuwen, editor, *Handbook of Theoretical Computer Science*, volume B, pages 789–840. North-Holland, Amsterdam, 1990.

54.  Saul A. Kripke. Semantic analysis of modal logic I: Normal modal propositional calculi. *Zeitschrift für Mathematische Logik und Grundlagen der Mathematik*, 9:67–96, 1963.

55. Christen Krogh and Henning Herrestad. Getting personal – some notes on the relationship between personal and impersonal obligation. In *Proceedings of the 3rd International Workshop on Deontic Logic in Computer Science (DEON)*, 1996.

56. Yves Lespérance, Hector J. Levesque, Fangzhen Lin, Daniel Marcu, Raymond Reiter, and Richard B. Scherl. Foundations of a logical approach to agent programming. In *Intelligent Agents II: Agent Theories, Architectures, and Languages*, pages 331–346, 1996.

57. H. J. Levesque, P. R. Cohen, and J. T. Nunes. On acting together. In *Proceedings of the National Conference on Artificial Intelligence*, pages 94–99, 1990.

58. David K. Lewis. *Convention: A Philosophical Study.* Harvard University Press, Cambridge, MA, 1969.

59. Magnus Ljungberg and Andrew Lucas. The OASIS air-traffic management system. In *Proceedings of the 2nd Pacific Rim International Conference on Artificial Intelligence (PRICAI)*, 1992.

60. John McCarthy. Ascribing mental qualities to machines. In Martin Ringle, editor, *Philosophical Perspectives in Artificial Intelligence*. Harvester Press, 1979.

61. John McCarthy and Patrick J. Hayes. Some philosophical problems from the standpoint of artificial intelligence. In *Machine Intelligence 4*. American Elsevier, 1969.

62. John-Jules Ch. Meyer and Roel J. Wieringa, editors. *Deontic Logic in Computer Science: Normative System Specification*. Wiley, Chichester, UK, 1993.

63. Allen Newell. The knowledge level. *Artificial Intelligence*, 18(1):87–127, 1982.

64. Anand S. Rao. Decision procedures for propositional linear-time belief-desire-intention logics. In *Intelligent Agents II: Agent Theories, Architectures, and Languages*, pages 33–48. Springer-Verlag, 1995.

65. Anand S. Rao and Michael P. Georgeff. Modeling rational agents within a BDI-architecture. In *[45]*, pages 317–328. 1997. (*Reprinted from* Proceedings of the International Conference on Principles of Knowledge Representation and Reasoning, 1991).

66. Anand S. Rao, Michael P. Georgeff, and Elizabeth Sonenberg. Social plans: A preliminary report. In *Proceedings of the 3rd European Workshop on Modelling Autonomous Agents in a Multi-Agent World (MAAMAW)*, pages 57–76, Amsterdam, 1992. Elsevier.

67. Stanley J. Rosenschein and Leslie Pack Kaelbling. A situated view of representation and control. *Artificial Intelligence*, 7, 1995.

68. Krister Segerberg. Bringing it about. *Journal of Philosophical Logic*, 18:327–347, 1989.

69. Yoav Shoham. Agent-oriented programming. In *[45]*, pages 329–349. 1997. (*Reprinted from* Artificial Intelligence, 1993).

70. Jaime Simão Sichman, Rosaria Conte, Yves Demazeau, and Cristiano Castelfranchi. A social reasoning mechanism based on dependence networks. In *[45]*, pages 416–420. 1997. (*Reprinted from* Proceedings of the 11th European Conference on Artificial Intelligence, 1994).

71. Munindar P. Singh. Group intentions. In *Proceedings of the 10th Workshop on Distributed Artificial Intelligence*, October 1990.

72. Munindar P. Singh. Group ability and structure. In *[18]*, pages 127–145. 1991.

73. Munindar P. Singh. Intentions, commitments and rationality. In *Proceedings of the 13th Annual Conference of the Cognitive Science Society*, pages 493–498, August 1991.

74. Munindar P. Singh. Social and psychological commitments in multiagent systems. In *AAAI Fall Symposium on Knowledge and Action at Social and Organizational Levels*, pages 104–106, 1991.

75. Munindar P. Singh. A critical examination of the Cohen-Levesque theory of intentions. In *Proceedings of the 10th European Conference on Artificial Intelligence*, pages 364–368, August 1992.

76. Munindar P. Singh. *Multiagent Systems: A Theoretical Framework for Intentions, Know-How, and Communications*. Springer-Verlag, Heidelberg, 1994.

77. Munindar P. Singh. A customizable coordination service for autonomous agents. In *Proceedings of the 4th International Workshop on Agent Theories, Architectures, and Languages (ATAL)*, July 1997.

78. Munindar P. Singh. A semantics for speech acts. In *[45]*, pages 458–470. 1997. (*Reprinted from* Annals of Mathematics and Artificial Intelligence, 1993).

79. Munindar P. Singh. Applying the mu-calculus in planning and reasoning about action. *Journal of Logic and Computation*, 1998. In press.

80. Munindar P. Singh. An ontology for commitments in multiagent systems: Toward a unification of normative concepts. *Artificial Intelligence and Law*, 1998. In press.

81. Munindar P. Singh. Semantical considerations on intention dynamics for BDI agents. *Journal of Experimental and Theoretical Artificial Intelligence*, 1998. In press.

82. Munindar P. Singh and Nicholas M. Asher. A logic of intentions and beliefs. *Journal of Philosophical Logic*, 22(5):513–544, October 1993.

83. Munindar P. Singh, Philip E. Cannata, Michael N. Huhns, Nigel Jacobs, Tomasz Ksiezyk, Kayliang Ong, Amit P. Sheth, Christine Tomlinson, and Darrell Woelk. The Carnot heterogeneous database project: Implemented applications. *Distributed and Parallel Databases: An International Journal*, 5(2):207–225, April 1997.

84. Munindar P. Singh and Michael N. Huhns. Automating workflows for service provisioning: Integrating AI and database technologies. *IEEE Expert*, 9(5):19–23, October 1994.

85. N. V. Smith, editor. *Mutual Knowledge*. Academic Press, London, 1982.

86. J. M. Spivey. *The Z Notation*. Prentice-Hall International, Hemel Hempstead, UK, 2nd edition, 1992.

87. Milind Tambe. Agent architectures for flexible, practical teamwork. In *Proceedings of the National Conference on Artificial Intelligence*, pages 22–28, 1997.

88. S. Rebecca Thomas. The PLACA agent programming language. In *Intelligent Agents: Agent Theories, Architectures, and Languages*, pages 355–370, 1995.

89. Gio Wiederhold. Value-added mediation. In *Proceedings of the IFIP TC2/WG2.6 Conference on Database Application Semantics (DS-6)*. Chapman and Hall, 1995.

90. Gio Wiederhold. Mediators in the architecture of future information systems. In *[45]*, pages 185–196. 1997. (*Reprinted from* IEEE Computer, 1992).

91. Darrell Woelk, Philip Cannata, Michael Huhns, Nigel Jacobs, Tomasz Ksiezyk, Greg Lavender, Greg Meredith, Kayliang Ong, Wei-Min Shen, Munindar Singh, and Christine Tomlinson. Carnot prototype. In *[8]*, chapter 18, pages 621–648. 1996.

92. Michael Wooldridge and Nick Jennings. Formalizing the cooperative problem solving process. In *[45]*, pages 430–440. 1997. (*Reprinted from* Proceedings of the 13th International Workshop on Distributed Artificial Intelligence, 1994).

# 9    Industrial and Practical Applications of DAI

H. Van Dyke Parunak

## 9.1    Introduction

Successful application of agents (as of any technology) must reconcile two perspectives. The researcher (exemplified in the preceding chapters) focuses on a particular capability (e.g., communication, planning, learning), and seeks practical problems to demonstrate the usefulness of this capability (and justify further funding). The industrial practitioner has a practical problem to solve, and cares much more about the speed and cost-effectiveness of the solution than about its elegance or sophistication. This chapter attempts to bridge these perspectives. To the agent researcher, it offers an overview of the kinds of problems that industrialists face, and some examples of agent technologies that have made their way into practical application. To the industrialist, it explains why agents are not just the latest technical fad, but a natural match to the characteristics of a broad class of real problems.

This chapter is both broader and narrower than its title suggests. It is broader because it includes selected development projects that are not yet industrial strength, but embody industrially important concepts or are being conducted in a way likely to lead to deployable technology. It is narrower in that it emphasizes agent applications in manufacturing and physical control over other fielded industrial applications such as Web-based information-gathering agents ([50]; Appendix G of [12]), network management, or business planning agents (e.g., the ADEPT project [45, 47, 48, 60]). This focus has three motivations: I am better acquainted with the domain of manufacturing and control, the problems of interfacing agents to the environment are more challenging, and the evidence of success or failure is clearer when a system must directly confront the laws of physics.

Section 9.2 describes the main industrial motivations for choosing an agent architecture for a particular problem. Section 9.3 describes the concept of a system life cycle. Section 9.4 and uses this concept to organize case studies of industrial agent-based systems, and Section 9.5 uses it to examine the process of constructing an industrial system. Section 9.6 reviews some development tools that will hasten deployment of agent technology in industry. Section 9.7 summarizes some basic insights.

## 9.2   Why Use DAI in Industry?

Agents are not a panacea for industrial software. Like any other technology, they are best used for problems whose characteristics require their particular capabilities. Agents are appropriate for applications that are modular, decentralized, changeable, ill-structured, and complex [44]. In some cases, a problem may naturally exhibit or lack these characteristics, but many industrial problems can be formulated in different ways. In these cases, attention to these characteristics during problem formulation and analysis can yield a solution that is more robust and adaptable than one supported by other technologies.

**Modular.** As defined in more detail in Chapter 1, agents are pro-active objects, and share the benefits of modularity enjoyed by object technology. They are best suited to applications that fall into natural modules. An agent has its own set of state variables, distinct from those of the environment. Some subset of the agent's state variables is coupled to some subset of the environment's state variables to provide input and output. An industrial entity is a good candidate for agent-hood if it has a well-defined set of state variables that are distinct from those of its environment, and if its interfaces with that environment can be clearly identified.

The state-based view of the distinction between an agent and its environment suggests that functional decompositions are less well suited to agent-based systems than are physical decompositions. Functional decompositions tend to share many state variables across different functions. Separate agents must share many state variables, leading to problems of consistency and unintended interaction. A physical decomposition naturally defines distinct sets of state variables that can be managed efficiently by individual agents with limited interactions. The choice between functional and physical decomposition is often up to the system analyst. Emphasizing the physical dimension enables more modular software. Because the agent characterizes a physical entity, that entity can be redeployed with minimal changes to the agent's code. As a result, the cost of software reconfiguration drops dramatically, and reusability increases.

**Decentralized.** An agent is more than an object; it is a pro-active object, a bounded process. It does not need to be invoked externally, but autonomously monitors its own environment and takes action as it deems appropriate. This characteristic of agents makes them particularly suited for applications that can be decomposed into stand-alone processes, each capable of doing useful things without continuous direction by some other process.

Many industrial processes can be organized in either a centralized or a decentralized fashion. Centralized organizations go back to the imperial governments of ancient Egypt, Assyria, China, and Babylon, with their focus on a central demigod and an elaborate bureaucracy to manage the flow of control down and information back up. The popularity of this structure can be traced through the army of

Alexander the Great, the Roman legions, and the rival empires of pre-modern Europe down to the structure of modern Fortune 500 companies and industrial control architectures [2].

There is an alternative approach. The power of decentralization has been made clear in recent years in the contrast in performance between a centralized economic system (the former Soviet Union) and a decentralized one (free-market capitalism). In fact, a European observer suggests that one of the forces leading to the growing popularity of multiagent systems is "the rise of the American style of liberalism and individualism" [80].

Modern industrial strategists seek to eliminate excessive layers of management and push decision-making down to the very lowest level, and are developing the vision of the "virtual enterprise," formed for a particular market opportunity from a collection of independent firms with well-defined core competencies [58]. It is increasingly common for the manufacturer of a complex product to purchase half or even more of the content in the product from other companies. For example, an automotive manufacturer might buy seats from one company, brake systems from another, air conditioning from a third, and electrical systems from a fourth, and manufacture only the chassis, body, and powertrain in its own facilities. The suppliers of major subsystems (such as seats) in turn purchase much of their content from still other companies. As a result, the "production line" that turns raw materials into a vehicle is a network, or "supply chain," of many different firms. Agent-based architectures are an ideal fit to such an organizational strategy.

**Changeable.** Agents are well suited to modular problems because they are objects. They are well suited to decentralized problems because they are pro-active objects. These two characteristics combine to make them especially valuable when a problem is likely to change frequently. Modularity permits the system to be modified one piece at a time. Decentralization minimizes the impact that changing one module has on the behavior of other modules.

Modularization alone is not sufficient to permit frequent changes. As Figure 9.1 suggests, in a system with a single thread of control, changes to a single module can cause later modules, those it invokes, to malfunction. Decentralization decouples the individual modules from one another, so that errors in one module impact only those modules that interact with it, leaving the rest of the system unaffected. (The original version of this figure was created by Seiichi Yaskawa of Yaskawa Electric Corporation, Tokyo, Japan, and is used with his kind permission.)

From an industrial perspective, the ability to change a system quickly, frequently, and without damaging side effects is increasingly important to competitiveness. In manufacturing, the product that pleases the most customers has a tremendous advantage. One of the most effective means to determine the features that customers like is to turn out as many different product variations as quickly as possible, sampling customer response and adjusting new offerings accordingly. This strategy is responsible for the precipitous drop in the time-to-market for many products. The time from product concept to first production in automotive used to be 60

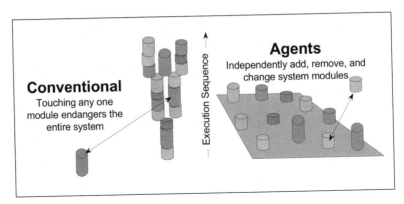

**Figure 9.1**   Modularity + Decentralization → Changeability

months. Now world-class performance requires 30 months, and some vehicles have been produced in even less time. Much of the cost of a new manufacturing facility is in its software. Agent-based architectures permit reuse of much existing code and self-configuration of large portions of the system, reducing both the cost and the time needed to bring up a new factory.

**Ill-structured.** An early deliverable in traditional systems design is an architecture of the application, showing which entities interact with which other entities and specifying the interfaces among them. For example, installation of a conventional system for electronic data interchange (EDI) among trading partners requires that one know the providers and consumers of the various goods and services being traded, so that orders can be sent to the appropriate parties. Sometimes, determining this information in advance is extremely difficult or even impossible. Consider an electronic system to support open trading, where orders are made available to any qualified bidder. Requiring the system designer to specify the sender and recipient of each transaction would quickly lead to "paralysis by analysis." From a traditional point of view, this application is ill structured. That is, not all of the necessary structural information is available when the system is designed.

Agents naturally support such an application. The fundamental distinction in an agent's view of the world is between "self" and "environment." "Self" is known and predictable, while "environment" can change on its own within limits. Other agents are part of this dynamic, changing environment. Depending on the complexity of individual agents, they may or may not model one another explicitly. Instead of specifying the individual entities to be interconnected and their interfaces with one another, an agent-based design need identify only the classes of entities in the system and their impact on the environment. Because each agent is designed to interact with the environment rather than with specific other agents, it can interact appropriately with any other agent that modifies the environment within the range of variation with which other agents are prepared to deal.

Some applications are intrinsically under-specified and thus ill structured, and agents offer the only realistic approach to managing them. Even where more detailed structural information is available, the wiser course may be to pretend that it isn't. A system that is designed to a specific domain structure will require modification if that structure changes. Agent technology permits the analyst to design a system to the classes that generate a given domain structure rather than to that structure itself, thus extending the useful life of the resulting system and reducing the cost of maintenance and reconfiguration.

**Complex.** One measure of the complexity of a system is the number of different behaviors it must exhibit. For example, a manufacturing job shop might produce a given part in several different ways, depending on which machines are used and in which order. The number of possible behaviors in this simple example depends exponentially on the number of different machines in the shop. For a shop with only a few machines, one might code a separate subroutine for each possible routing, but this approach quickly becomes prohibitive as the shop grows.

This example shows combinatorial complexity. The number of different interactions among a set of elements increases much faster than does the number of elements in the set. By mapping individual agents to the interacting elements, agent architectures can replace explicit coding of this large set of interactions with generation of them at run-time. Consider 100 agents, each with ten behaviors, each behavior requiring 20 lines of code. The total amount of software that has to be produced to instantiate this system is 20,000 lines of code, an extremely modest undertaking. But the total number of behaviors in the repertoire of the resulting system is on the order of ten for the first agent, times ten for the second, times ten for the third, and so forth, or $10^{100}$, an overwhelmingly large number. Naturally, not all of these will be useful behaviors, and one can imagine pathological agent designs in which none of the generated behaviors will be appropriate. However, appropriately designed agent architectures can move the generation of combinatorial behavior spaces from design-time to run-time, drastically reducing the amount of software that must be generated and thus the cost of the system to be constructed.

Modification of a system during its life can increase its complexity as well as making it ill structured. By adopting an agent approach at the outset, systems engineers can provide a much more robust and adaptable solution that will grow naturally to meet business needs.

## 9.3  Overview of the Industrial Life-Cycle

Industrial people tend to view what they do in terms of a life cycle, made up of a series of stages: requirements analysis, design, implementation and deployment, operation, logistics and maintenance, and decommissioning. Any industrial activity follows such a pattern, whether it be building a product, putting in place the process for making a product, supplying a service, or creating a piece of infrastructure.

The life cycle perspective raises two questions about industrial multiagent systems. First, to what stages in the life cycle of an industrial activity (say, an automobile) have agents been applied? Second, since an industrial agent-based system will itself be constructed according to a life cycle, what constraints does the industrial environment place on each of the life-cycle phases of such a system?

In this exposition, the term "project" represents a specific system or activity. Two projects are discussed: a physical system (a new automobile), and a software system (a new factory scheduling system). Figure 9.2 shows how the physical system bifurcates at the design phase into two systems, one concerned with the product itself, the other concerned with the process that manufactures the product. A generic life cycle has eight phases, some of which may not be appropriate in a given project.

**Requirements Definition** defines the set of needs or requirements that the project must satisfy. The focus is on why an effort is needed in the first place, not on *what* the project will do or *how* it will do it.

- Physical: Market analysis reveals that we are losing sales to competitors who are offering sport utility vehicles, a niche in which we currently have no product offering.

- Software: We have benchmarked our production facilities against world class performance, and found that we are below the 75% level in every major category, including throughput, machine utilization, order tardiness, and work-in-process levels.

**Positioning** defines the project's relationship to other projects in the enterprise. This phase identifies potential overlaps, synergies, or conflicts among different projects early enough that their impact can be managed.

- Physical: Our current product divisions are luxury auto, economy auto, minivan, and light truck. The minivan and light truck divisions seem the best candidates to host the new offering. Further study shows that we are aiming for a consumer market, not an industrial one, so the new vehicle is positioned as a new product in the minivan division.

- Software: Shop-floor control can be approached from the perspective either of controls (a bottom-up view) or of manufacturing information systems (a top-down view). In our company, the information department is notoriously insensitive to plant needs, and their data is usually wrong, so we have no confidence that a scheduling project that grows out of our existing information systems will solve the requirements. However, the controls group has been remarkably successful in solving a wide range of integration problems, so we will try to address our problems from the controls perspective.

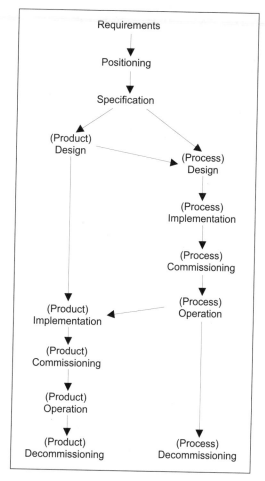

**Figure 9.2**   The life cycle for physical products bifurcates.

**Specification** spells out the functions that the project will support. The specification tells what the project will do, but not how it does it. The functions in a successful specification will satisfy the needs identified in Requirements Definition and interface appropriately with other relevant components of the enterprise identified in Positioning.

- Physical: We benchmark the performance of our competitors' offerings to determine what customers do and do not like, and to identify features we can add to differentiate our product in the marketplace. The result is a list of the features and performance characteristics of the new vehicle.

- Software: A collection of shop-floor war stories highlights a set of issues that can explain the poor performance, including no way to schedule preventive maintenance (leading in turn to reduced maintenance and increased machine failure), operating policies that permit upstream workstations to produce parts for which there is no downstream demand, release of jobs to the floor before both raw materials and tooling are available, and job classifications that prevent operators from helping one another as demands shift across the factory.

**Design** maps the functions ("what") identified in Specification to implementation strategies that tell how the project will be executed to provide those functions.

- Physical: The product engineering department develops a design for the new vehicle, including chassis, seating system, powertrain, suspension, climate control, sound system, and beverage cooler. Concurrently, the process engineering department designs the factory that will manufacture the new vehicle. At this point the automotive project actually becomes two projects: one to produce the vehicle, the other to produce the process that will make the vehicle.
- Software: The manufacturing systems group decides to adopt an agent-based approach to shop scheduling. It identifies the classes of agents that will be required, and refines these classes and their interactions through role-playing and simulation.

**Implementation** is the phase of the life cycle in which the system is actually constructed. If the project is an activity rather than a system, it may move directly form Design to Commissioning without an intervening Implementation.

- Physical (Process): Purchasing negotiates contracts for the equipment needed to construct the new vehicle. A plant is selected to house the new line, the old equipment is removed, and the new equipment is installed.
- Physical (Product): Purchasing negotiates contracts for the raw materials and preassembled subsystems that will be purchased from vendors
- Software: The systems group codes the agents that will make up the new scheduling system. The modular decentralized nature of agent-based software makes it possible to extend some design activities, such as system simulation, into implementation by running newly coded real agents against a simulation of the part of the system not yet implemented. The emergent nature of agent-based systems makes this approach necessary to avoid unexpected global behaviors.

In **Commissioning**, the project is placed into use. Commissioning usually includes system shakedown, training activities, and transition of operations from previous systems or methods.

- Physical (Process): The factory produces its first sports utility vehicle.
- Physical (Product): Each unit of the product is commissioned when a dealer sells it to a customer.
- Software: The scheduling agents are released onto the shop floor.

**Operation** maintains the project in regular productive use. It is during this phase that the project actually satisfies the needs identified during Requirements Definition. Operation includes three specific activities: routine operation, maintenance and repair, and incremental upgrading. In the life cycle of a product, this phase also includes customer support and maintenance.

- Physical (Process): The factory continues to produce vehicles.

- Physical (Product): The dealer network services the vehicles already in the field.

- Software: The systems group adjusts the behavior of individual agents based on feedback from the operators and changes in the firm's business environment.

**Decommissioning** removes the project from service, either because the needs it satisfied no longer exist or because a replacement project is about to be commissioned. The growing importance of ecologically friendly or "green" manufacturing is placing increasing emphasis on this phase as the point at which reuse or recycling is applied.

- Physical (Process): After about ten years, this model is phased out, and the factory and equipment that produced it are reconfigured for a new product.

- Physical (Product): Vehicles that have completed their useful life are recycled.

- Software: Because the scheduling system is agent-based, there is no sharp line when it is decommissioned as a system. Individual agents are replaced over the years as equipment changes and new functionality is required, but the changes are incremental.

## 9.4   Where in the Life Cycle Are Agents Used?

In principle, agents can support many different stages in the life cycle of a system or product. For example, agents might help design a new vehicle, operate the plant that manufactures it, and maintain it when it fails. This section begins by outlining a series of questions that are useful in comparing different agent applications. Then it describes three areas in which agents have been used effectively: product design, process operation at the planning and scheduling level, and process operation at the lower level of real-time equipment control.

### 9.4.1   Questions that Matter

When comparing different agent-based applications, some questions arise repeatedly. This section groups these questions in three categories: those that pertain to individual agents, those that concern the community of agents, and a single question dealing with the maturity of the application.

The building blocks of agent-based systems are the individual agents. Three questions are important here. Chapter 1 explores a number of these details in greater depth.

**What in a system becomes an agent?** Classical software engineering techniques lead many systems designers toward "functional decomposition." For example, manufacturing information systems typically contain modules dedicated to functions such as "scheduling," "material management," and "maintenance," suggesting that these functions should be assigned to distinct agents [6, 32]. The functional approach is well suited to centralized systems, but unprecedented in naturally occurring distributed systems, which divide agents on the basis of distinct entities in the physical world rather than functional abstractions in the mind of the designer [71]. Experience with agent-based prototypes supports this principle, with two exceptions. Most industrial agent applications are additions to existing systems, and functionally oriented *legacy systems* may be most easily attached by encapsulating them as (functional) agents. A *watchdog agent* may usefully monitor the behavior of a population of physical agents for important system states that local agents cannot perceive.

**How Does each agent model the world?** Any agent that functions in a changing world must model that world internally [40]. However, agents differ in the sophistication of the knowledge representation and reasoning they use for this task. Some agents model aspects of their world explicitly, so that they can reason about the model. In other agents, these models are hard-wired and often distributed throughout the agent's architecture [26]. In addition to the implicit-explicit distinction, agents differ in the scope of what they model (for instance, whether they individuate other agents or not) and whether they model the world as it is now, or as the agent wishes the world to be. The BDI architecture discussed in Chapter 1 recommends explicit models that include both the present (beliefs) and the future (desires).

**How are agents structured internally?** The different agents in a system may be identical, heterogeneous, or sharing some common modules and differing in others. They may or may not remember past states, and their internal code may or may not change over time.

The next five questions have to do with the community that the agents form. Chapter 2 discusses many of these issues in more detail.

**How many agents are there?** Both the number of different agent species and the total number of individual agents are important characteristics of a given system, as well as whether the agent population can change while the system is running.

**What communication channels do agents use?** The channels through which information moves from one agent to another can differ in medium (the shared physical environment vs. a digital network), addressing (broadcast, subject-based, agent-to-agent), whether messages persist after being sent, and locality (whether agents need to move "close" to one another in order to exchange messages).

**What communications protocols do agents use?** A communications protocol determines how conversations among agents are structured. Some agents simply give orders to one another and expect them to be received. Others vote, negotiate, or engage in more complex dialogues based on speech-act theory.

**How is the configuration of agents relative to one another established?** The configuration of an agent community describes the immediate acquaintances of each agent and the resulting topology over which information and material move among them. This topology may be set in advance by the system implementer and remain unchanged as the system operates, or the agents may be able to discover new relationships and reconfigure themselves while running.

**How do agents coordinate their actions?** Agents are autonomous in that they do not have to be invoked in order to execute. However, in a useful system they are not anarchical, but coordinate with one another. In hierarchical coordination, commands flow down from higher levels and status information flows back up. In egalitarian or heterarchical coordination [37], coordination emerges from the dynamics of agent interaction, through mechanisms such as dissipative fields (currency-based markets [15], pheromones in insect societies) or constraint propagation.

The final question is **"How mature is the application?"** It is useful to distinguish six levels of maturity:

1. Modeled: The system exists as an architecture or a theoretical model.
2. Emulated: The system has been demonstrated against a simulation of its intended domain environment.
3. Prototype: The system has been demonstrated on real domain hardware, but in a controlled laboratory environment.
4. Pilot: The system has been demonstrated in a commercial environment.
5. Production: The system is used in regular commercial practice.
6. Product: The system is sold and supported as a commercial product.

### 9.4.2   Agents in Product Design

Design systems help teams of designers, often in different locations and working for different companies, to design the components and subsystems of a complex product, using many different analysis tools. As suppliers take increasing responsibility for the detailed design of the subsystems they supply, design becomes increasingly decentralized.

Designers begin with a picture of what is required but no details on how it is to be produced. Often the "what" that is desired turns out to be prohibitively

| System | What is an Agent? | Noteworthy Technology |
|---|---|---|
| ACDS (Automated Configuration Design Service) [19] | Catalogs of pre-defined parts; constraints among components; the overall system; a bid monitor. | Distributed constraint management |
| PACT (Palo Alto Collaborative Testbed) [18] | Pre-existing design tools; facilitators to translate between tools and a common language | A common language between agents |
| RAPPID (Responsible Agents for Product-Process Integrated Design) [72, 76] | Designers (representing components and subsystems of the product); design variables | Set-based reasoning and market protocols among designers |

**Table 9.1**  Design systems.

expensive when the "how" is understood in more detail, leading to frequent changes in the design. The more ambitious the product vision, the less well its structure is understood at the outset, and the more valuable reconfigurable agents are to represent the various components, designers, and tools. The increased complexity embodied in modern products also favors the combinatorial benefits of an agent-based system. State-of-the-art agent concepts have been demonstrated in three design systems at the prototype level of maturity. Each of these systems decomposes the world into agents in a different way, as summarized in Table 9.1.

RAPPID illustrates how agents can help human designers coordinate their work more effectively. Figure 9.3 illustrates how different people are responsible for the components and subsystems that make up a product. Conflicts arise when different teams disagree on the relation between the characteristics of their own functional pieces and the characteristics of the entire product. Some conflicts are within the design team: How much of a mechanism's total power budget should be available to the sensor circuitry, and how much to the actuator? Other conflicts set design against other manufacturing functions: How should one balance the functional desirability of an unusual machined shape against the increased manufacturing expense of creating that shape?

It is easy to represent how much a mechanism weighs or how much power it consumes, but there is seldom a disciplined way to trade off (say) weight and power consumption against one another. The more characteristics are involved in a design compromise, the more difficult the trade-off becomes. The problem is the classic dilemma of multivariate optimization. Analytical solutions are available only in specialized and limited niches. In current practice such trade-offs are sometimes supported by processes such as Quality Functional Deployment [38] or resolved politically, rather than in a way that optimizes the overall design and its manufacturability. The problem is compounded when design teams are distributed across different companies.

RAPPID explores two innovative techniques for coordinating the actions of

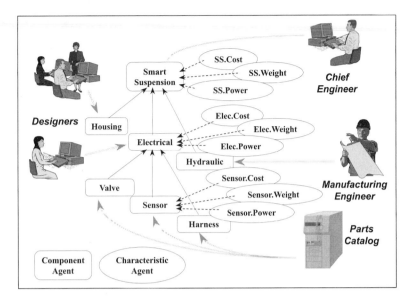

**Figure 9.3**  The RAPPID ecosystem includes both components and characteristics.

different agents (designers): *market dynamics* and *set-based reasoning* [77, 78].

In RAPPID, designers buy and sell the various characteristics of a design. Each characteristic agent is a computerized agent that maintains a marketplace in that characteristic. In the current implementation, the agents representing components are interfaces for human designers, who bid in these markets to buy and sell units of the characteristics. A component that needs more latitude in a given characteristic (say, more weight) can purchase increments of that characteristic from another component, but may need to sell another characteristic to raise resources for this purchase. In some cases, analytical models of the dependencies between characteristics help designers estimate their relative costs, but even where such models are clumsy or nonexistent, prices set in the marketplace define the coupling among characteristics.

To drive the design process toward convergence, RAPPID uses set-based reasoning. Most design in industry today follows a point-based approach, in which the participating designers repeatedly propose specific solutions to their component or subsystem. The chief engineer is expected to envision the final product at the outset, specifying to the designers what volume in design space it should occupy and challenging them to fit something into that space. Inevitably, as illustrated in Figure 9.4, some of the chief engineer's assumptions turn out to be wrong, requiring designers to reconsider previous decisions and compromise the original vision. This approach is analogous to constraint optimization by backtracking. Because mechanisms for disciplined backtracking are not well developed in design methodology, this approach usually terminates through fatigue or the arrival of a critical market deadline, rather than through convergence to an optimal solution.

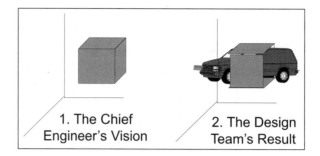

**Figure 9.4**   Point-based design requires backtracking.

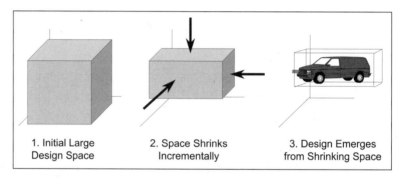

**Figure 9.5**   Set-based design converges to the solution.

Toyota has pioneered another approach, set-based design [89]. In this approach, illustrated in Figure 9.5, the chief engineer's task is not to guess the product's location in design space, but to guide the design team in a process of progressively shrinking the design space until it collapses around the product. Each designer shrinks the space of options for one component in concert with the other members of the team, all the while communicating about their common dependencies. This approach directly reflects consistency algorithms for solving constraint problems. If the communications among team members are managed appropriately, the shrinking design space drives the team to convergence.

Here is how RAPPID answers the questions introduced earlier in this section.

*Agent Mapping and Modeling:* Component agents are computer-assisted humans and thus maintain extensive as-is and to-be models of the other agents and the non-agented environment. Characteristic agents model the component agents that have an interest in them, and use these models to recommend future action.

*Agent Structure:* Characteristic agents are structurally identical to one another. Their code does not change over time, but they do aggregate information from recent bids as a guide to future activity. Component agents vary as widely as the humans they represent. If a component is to be selected from a catalog, RAPPID

| | **Planning & Scheduling** | **Control** |
|---|---|---|
| **Time Constants** | Human-scale (minutes and longer) | Electronic-scale (seconds and shorter) |
| **Kind of Information** | Includes symbols; involves semantics | Mostly numerical |

**Table 9.2** Comparing planning and control.

provides a catalog module that automates much of the problem of selecting the appropriate offering, and thus subsumes some of the functionality of ACDS. If a component is to be designed from the ground up, the RAPPID interface hides the idiosyncrasies of the various tools the human may use in the design process, and thus subsumes some of the functionality of PACT.

*Population:* A realistic application of RAPPID will have one or two dozen component agents and on the order of a hundred characteristic agents. In the current implementation, agents are not created, destroyed, divided, or fused during operation, but as the system matures, designers will need a way to add both component and characteristics agents to the community as a design is refined.

*Communication Channels and Protocols:* Agents communicate digitally, and currently use point addressing. Messages do not persist outside of agents, and agents do not move over the network. RAPPID uses a fixed market protocol, but also provides for the humans behind component agents to communicate directly with one another using Standard Legacy-Oriented Work Habits (SLOWH mechanisms).

*Configuration:* The initial configuration of component agents and characteristic agents is defined when the system is initialized, but component agents can engage in markets for other characteristics as the system runs.

*Coordination:* RAPPID combines dissipative and constraint-based egalitarian coordination.

*Maturity:* RAPPID has been piloted in the high-level design of a military vehicle at the U.S. Army's Tank and Automotive Command (TACOM) at Warren, MI.

### 9.4.3 Agents in Planning and Scheduling

Both this section and the next deal with the problem of monitoring a system's trajectory through state space over time and adjusting operating parameters to make that trajectory satisfy some overall criterion. The difference between the two is one of time constants and the kind of information manipulated, as summarized in Table 9.2. Planning and scheduling is longer-term, usually on a scale that humans can handle, and involves the manipulation of concepts through semantically-grounded symbols. Control handles the detailed real-time interface with the world, and usually happens too fast for direct human supervision.

The fundamental challenge in applying agents to both planning and control is satisfying a global criterion on the basis of parallel local decisions. In spite of the natural benefit that centralization has in dealing with control criteria, the cases in these two sections show that many users have found agents an even better approach. Operational systems must be maintained, and it is much easier and safer to maintain a set of well-bounded modules than to make changes to a large monolithic program. The move toward supply chains means that the manufacturing system is geographically distributed, and agent decentralization reduces communication bottlenecks and permits local parts of the enterprise to continue operation during temporary lapses in connectivity. Competitiveness increasingly depends on adjusting a system's operation frequently to track customer requirements, benefiting from the changeability of agent systems. The ability of agents to deal with ill-structured systems is less important in the operation of an engineered system than in its design. However, the ability of agents to deal with dynamically changing structures means that computers can now be applied to manage systems (such as networks of trading partners) that formerly required extensive manual attention. The increased complexity that agents can manage also extends the scope of operational problems to which they can be applied.

Table 9.3 summarizes four examples of planning and scheduling systems. The Daewoo scheduling system produced by Metra Corp. is a mature example (in regular production use) of the most promising approach to agent-based scheduling and control. It schedules the press shop at Daewoo Motors' integrated automobile production facility in Korea.

Most of the exterior components of an automobile, and many structural components as well, are manufactured by stamping sheet metal between shaped metal dies in hydraulic presses exerting hundreds or thousands of tons of pressure. The process of setting up and running such a press is daunting. Sheet metal arrives in coils that must be unrolled and cut into blanks before being stamped. Different parts require different kinds of sheet metal, from different coils. The dies weigh thousands of pounds, and must be transported from a storage area and aligned precisely with the press before parts can be made. Dies wear with use, requiring periodic refurbishing. The type of part being produced (and thus the setup) must change frequently to provide the vehicle assembly operation with the right components for the vehicles currently being manufactured.

The Daewoo shop supplies all stamped body parts for five different car models, as well as parts for several off-site assembly plants. The shop operates three shifts per day and produces more than 500 different parts, using more than 2000 dies. Efficient operation requires careful scheduling of the presses, sheet metal stock, and dies.

*Agent Mapping:* Research on agent-based factory planning and scheduling differs widely on what is represented as an agent. ISCM assigns an agent to each traditional manufacturing function (such as Order Acquisition, Logistics, Scheduling, Resource Management, Dispatching, Transportation, and Plant Management). Evidence from

| System | What is an Agent? | Noteworthy Technology |
|---|---|---|
| AARIA (Autonomous Agents for Rock Island Arsenal) [4, 73] | Resources (e.g., machines, tooling, and operators), part types, unit processes, management, parts, and engagements between a unit process and its resources | Market-driven inter-agent coordination; density-based least-commitment scheduling of resources |
| Daewoo [14] | Task agents (work orders), resource agents (machines), service agents (per community: bidding, constraint propagation, meta-agent) | Market-driven coordination; hierarchical aggregation of agents into communities |
| ISCM (Integrated Supply Chain Management) [31] | Functional agents: Logistics, Order Acquisition, and Transportation agents at enterprise level; Plant Manager, Resource Management, Dispatching, and Scheduler agents at plant level | Traditional AI within individual functional agents |
| LMS (Logistics Management System) [29, 30] | A critic for each production characteristic (Serviceability, Daily Planned Output, Downstream Pull, and Tool Charge, Characteristics, & Utilization); and a judge to combine votes | The judge combines votes from critics based on their individual objectives. |

**Table 9.3** Planning and scheduling systems.

natural systems suggests that it may be more effective to assign agents to physical entities in the system. Even here there is considerable variation. Agents have represented levels in a hierarchical decomposition of the factory [11, 67, 87], resources [3, 39, 74, 84], and parts [20, 53]. AARIA has developed a comprehensive ontology, summarized in Figure 9.6. It includes both agents that persist from one operation to another (such as part types, unit processes, and resources) and agents with much shorter lifetime (including individual parts and engagements between a unit process and the resources it requires). In terms of this ontology, manufacturing processes occur when the flow of parts and the flow of resources intersect at a unit process.

Daewoo uses a subset of the AARIA ontology. Task agents (corresponding to sets of unit processes) represent individual work orders, and resource agents

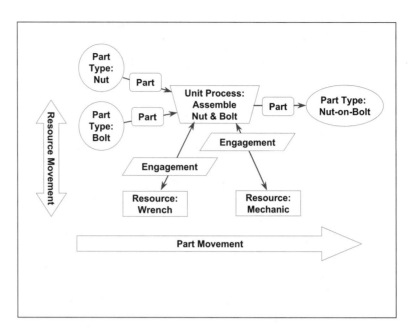

**Figure 9.6**   AARIA agents represent entities in the shop.

represent manufacturing resources such as machines. These domain-oriented agents are clustered into communities, and each community has several service agents: a bidding agent that handles all transactions among domain agents, a constraint propagation agent that propagates task dependencies and does some constraint satisfaction, and a meta agent that registers the skills of the domain agents in the community.

*Agent Modeling:* Critical information in manufacturing is usually organized by physical entities. Agents that represent these entities are the natural locus for maintaining this information. At Daewoo a resource agent caches information regarding previous bidding and the utilization of other compatible machines to guide subsequent bidding in directions that maximize overall goals and minimize later backtracking. In AARIA, resource agents also store maintenance and reliability information, while part type agents model the supply and demand of their parts over time. At Daewoo, each domain agent has a friend module in which it caches information about its colleagues that it obtains in the course of interaction. Each agent also has access to information about its community indirectly through the meta agent, and directly through a community-wide blackboard. The community information includes both present state and future objectives.

*Agent Structure:* All agents of a given class are the same. There are some shared modules (e.g., the friend module to store information about acquaintances). Agents do not change as they run, but do maintain state information.

*Population:* The Daewoo application has 30 machine agents and 700 task agents, together with the community's three service agents. Machine agents join the community when they are on-line and leave it when they go off-line. Task agents join the community when they are released to the shop, and leave it when they are completed.

*Communication Channels:* Agents communicate with one another electronically in two ways. The meta-agent provides a publish and subscribe service that agents can use to identify potential collaborators. Once one agent knows the identity of another, it communicates directly on the basis of information it has cached in its friend module. At Dæwoo, messages do not persist, and agents do not travel. AARIA does use traveling agents to model parts as they move between part type agents and unit processes, and engagements as they move between resources and unit processes.

*Communication Protocols:* Daewoo uses a contract net negotiation protocol.

*Configuration:* Relations among agents are defined dynamically as a result of negotiation.

*Coordination:* The bidding process propagates constraints among the agents. Market interactions among agents generate a dissipative flow of currency to which the agents orient themselves, making efficient use of scarce resources.

*Maturity:* This system is in production use at Daewoo Motors in Korea.

### 9.4.4   Agents in Real-Time Control

Control systems operate faster and with more semantically constrained information than do planning and scheduling systems. They must provide real-time response, which is discussed further in Chapter 11.

Current technology for industrial process control offers many examples of coordinated pro-active objects that can usefully be viewed as agent-based systems. A typical chemical plant contains hundreds of PID control loops. PID stands for "proportional, integral, derivative," and describes the three functions that the agent can apply to the stream of data from a sensor. Each loop is a separate computer that adjusts some actuator as a function of various sensors. Because the action of one such loop changes physical quantities that will affect the behavior of other loops in the system, these loops can be viewed as (analog) agents that communicate through a shared environment. Table 9.4 summarizes six control systems that use digital agents.

The Zone Logic system applies agents to real-time control. Complicated manufactured parts such as engine blocks are often manufactured on a machine called a transfer line. Such a machine moves workpieces sequentially through a series of stations. At each position, individual mechanisms perform some specific task. For

| System | Domain | What is an Agent? | Noteworthy Technology |
|---|---|---|---|
| ADS [43, 55, 56] | Steel Production | Group of related functions on a single processor | Subject-Based Addressing of messages; Hot swapping of running agents |
| AMROSE [65] | Robotic Control in Shipbuilding | One link in a segmented robot arm | Exploitation of locality of inter-agent communications |
| ARCHON [46, 49] | Electrical power grids [17]; Particle Accelerators [79] | Pre-existing expert system | Modeling partner agents |
| GM Paint Shop [23, 57] | Automotive paint shop control | Individual devices in the paint system (humidifiers, burners, chillers, steam) | Communication through the environment |
| Market-Based Climate Control [17, 18] | Building climate control | Office thermostats; air duct dampers | Market-based resource allocation |
| Zone Logic [81] | Handling and machining of complex mechanical parts | A single mechanism in a transfer line | Communication through the environment |

**Table 9.4**   Real-time control systems.

example, the first station might bore a hole, the second might thread the hole, and the third might screw a hardened insert into the threaded hole.

A transfer line permits higher processing rates than discrete machines served by separate material transport systems. It contains a large number of mechanisms that must be controlled and coordinated. A typical transfer line may be a hundred meters long and contain dozens of stations with hundreds of mechanisms and more than 1500 degrees of freedom in movement overall. Traditional control schemes for such systems require the software engineer to understand the relations among all these mechanisms. When the system fails, identifying the responsible mechanism and the reason for the failure can be very time consuming. As a result, transfer lines often are down for maintenance more than half of the time. When the system is restarted after a failure, the various stations must be reset to a standard initial state, often requiring the scrapping or manual reprocessing of parts in process at the time of the failure. Because of the complex interactions among their mechanisms, transfer lines are notoriously difficult to keep operating. In many environments, 50% productivity is the most that can be achieved. By giving mechanisms autonomy, a

| | | State Variables | | | | | | |
|---|---|---|---|---|---|---|---|---|
| | **Zone # & Name** | **A** | **B** | **C** | **D** | **E** | **F** | **G** |
| **1** | **Initializing** | X | X | 0 | 0 | 0.1 | | 2, 5, 8 |
| **2** | **Returned** | 0 | 1 | 0 | 0 | | | 3 |
| **3** | **Advancing from Returned** | 0 | 1 | 1 | 0 | 1.0 | 9 | 4, 2 |
| **4** | **Advancing Between** | 0 | 0 | 1 | 0 | 5.0 | 9 | 5, 8 |
| **5** | **Advanced** | 1 | 0 | 0 | 0 | | | 6 |
| **6** | **Returning from Advanced** | 1 | 0 | 0 | 1 | 1.0 | 9 | 7, 5 |
| **7** | **Returned Between** | 0 | 0 | 0 | 1 | 5.0 | 9 | 4, 8 |
| **8** | **Stopped Between** | 0 | 0 | 0 | 0 | | | 4, 7 |
| **9** | **Error Default** | X | X | 0 | 0 | | | 1 |

0 = off; 1 = on; X = ignore     A = Advanced Limit Switch
B = Returned Limit Switch     C = Advance Motor Power
D = Return Motor Power     E = Max. Time in Zone (sec.)
F = Next Zone on Time-Out     G = Allowed Next Zones

**Table 9.5**   Rules for Zone Logic slide agent.

Zone Logic-controlled machine can readily achieve 90% productivity.

*Agent Mapping:* Zone Logic makes each mechanism in the transfer line (e.g., clamp, slide, transfer bar, probe) an agent that expects a certain range of conditions and knows what to do in each. This same mapping of agents onto basic physical entities in the control system is a common strategy for agent-based control, and appears also in AMROSE (where each link in a segmented robot arm is an agent), the GM Paint Booth system, and Xerox PARC's market-based climate control. These fine-grained agents that represent physical entities contrast with coarse-grained functional agents in the ARCHON and ADS systems. ADS is an older system, and probably owes its functional orientation to traditional methods of software design. ARCHON's functional structure reflects its mission to integrate pre-existing functional expert systems. In both cases, the functional approach reflects the transition from traditional software architectures, while physical decomposition seems to be the most direct approach to a new design.

*Agent Modeling and Structure:* Each mechanism maintains a rule base listing the state conditions it recognizes and what action it should take in each case, illustrated in Table 9.5. There are no explicit models of other agents and no explicit goals. For example, a slide mechanism includes two power switches (one to energize the motor that advances the slide, another to energize the motor that returns it) and two limit switches (one at the fully advanced position, the other at the fully returned position). The slide's state space thus includes $2^4 = 16$ possible states, only nine of which are physically possible. The other seven states reflect an error condition. For example, if both motors are energized or both limit switches are on, the mechanism has entered an error state and requires attention from an operator. For each allowed state or "zone," the mechanism's rule table lists the maximum amount of time the mechanism can spend in that zone and the allowable next zones it can enter. If the mechanism exhausts its time in a zone or if one of its state variables changes, it searches the list of next zones for one that it can enter by changing an output variable (e.g., actuating a motor), and makes the transition. If no specified next zone is accessible, it enters the error state and requests operator attention.

For example, if the slide is Advancing from Returned (state 3), the Returned limit switch should go off within one second. If it does not, the mechanism enters the error state and turns off both motors. Otherwise, it should next be found either in state 4 (Advancing Between) or state 2 (Returned), in case the advance motor shuts off before the slide leaves the Returned limit switch), and any other state defaults to Error.

*Population:* Each mechanism has its own agent, so a typical transfer line consists of hundreds of agents.

*Communication Channels:* Zone Logic agents communicate both physically and electronically. Individual mechanisms use physical sensors to determine the state and location of the part, thus adapting their behavior to what did or did not happen at earlier stations. Point-to-point non-persistent electronic communication between mechanisms guards against interference between mechanisms that may need access to the same physical space. The preferred design for agent-based control is to maximize interaction through the physical environment and minimize such explicitly coded dependencies between mechanisms, because explicit linkages make systems susceptible to failure when one mechanism is modified. Zone Logic agents are assigned to specific physical mechanisms installed at fixed locations on the line, and so do not need to migrate over a network.

*Communication Protocols:* Agent interaction in Zone Logic is directive. Both sensor information and interference signals are conditions in agent rules that lead reactively to action. Reactive protocols are especially well suited to low-level control environments, in which the digital logic must keep pace with physical events in the real world. At higher levels of control, exemplified by ARCHON, more complex protocols are useful.

*Configuration:* Agents are assigned to mechanisms when the transfer line is constructed. Which agents are active on a given part depends on an electronic processing file that accompanies the part through the system.

*Coordination:* one Logic agents coordinate their activity by propagating constraints. Market mechanisms are another candidate for real-time control, as seen in the Xerox market-based climate-control system.

*Maturity:* Zone Logic is deployed as a commercial product in several automotive manufacturing facilities.

## 9.5  How Does Industry Constrain the Life Cycle of an Agent-Based System?

The industrial life cycle poses restrictions and constraints on developing an agent-based system that are not present in most research environments. The cases in this section deal more with the tools and techniques used in constructing agent-based systems and less with the characteristics of the agent-based systems themselves.

The role of tools and methods defines an important distinction between industrial and academic projects. Academic laboratories often construct their own tools and methods, for two reasons.

1.  Tools and methods may not exist to meet the challenges they explore.

2.  Their educational mission is advanced by having students design and build tools.

In an industrial setting, a technology without supporting tools and methods has little hope of deployment, again for two reasons.

1.  An industrial system is a means to an end, not an end in itself, and will be approved only if the firm can estimate its cost in advance and justify that cost against expected benefits. Well-defined tools and methods are the cornerstone of such a cost justification exercise.

2.  The designers and implementers of industrial systems are first of all experts in the problems these systems are intended to solve, not in agent-based technology, and rely on tools and methods that package best practice in a way that they can use without becoming agent experts.

### 9.5.1  Requirements, Positioning, and Specification

The classical view of these phases of the life cycle is that they concern only *why* a system is needed and *what* it must do, not *how* its objectives are accomplished. On this view, the fact that the system will be implemented with agents is irrelevant, and firms should feel comfortable using traditional techniques for these phases. Thus little thought has been given to agent-specific mechanisms. Two caveats are in order.

1.  Agents permit application of computers to highly-distributed, ill-structured problems that previously would not have been candidates for automation. Requirements can now be drafted for problems that would not have been addressed before. Engineers need to understand the benefits of agent-based systems over centralized monolithic systems, at least at a high level, to appreciate what kinds of problems such systems can address.

2.  Agents establish a new paradigm for human-computer interaction that is less like the traditional master-slave relationship and more like a partnership. As

a result, the kinds of system-level behaviors that need to be specified will look more like specifications for a business process among people than does a traditional information system specification.

System behavior is one issue that needs to be determined in the requirements and specification phase. Others include interface constraints, performance constraints, operating constraints, life-cycle constraints (e.g., maintainability), economic constraints, and political constraints [82]. A complete design method for agent-based systems must take account of all these issues. This chapter focuses on the requirements that concern the behavior of the system.

At a high level, desired system behavior may be of several kinds. The system may maintain some set of state variables in a specified relationship with one another, thus exhibiting *homeostasis*. The system may be a *transducer* that converts specified stimuli into corresponding responses. Or the system may *learn* over time in response to its experience. At least two criteria are involved in a good behavioral specification.

- It should be specific enough to know if it has been achieved. A qualitative specification is usually adequate for role-playing, but we need a quantitative one to support simulation. For example, in a process control environment, "homeostasis" by itself is too vague. "Balance temperature and pressure" is OK for role-playing. Simulation requires specifying the quantitative link desired between pressure and temperature.

- It should be amenable to solution by architectural decisions. For example, the behavior "Have tooling available when needed" might be satisfied better by buying more tools than by expecting magic from agents. A better specification might be "Get high-value parts through the system first," "Identify relative scarcity of tool types," or "Reduce overall tool idleness."

The design team needs a concise statement of the problem to be solved and the constraints that must be observed. For example:

- What is the desired overall system behavior?
- What can be varied in the effort to achieve this behavior?
- What must not be touched?
- What approach is currently taken to solving the problem?
- Why is a new solution being contemplated? (Are there obvious shortcomings of the current solution? Is a change needed that is beyond the scope of the current solution?)

These questions are not exhaustive, but illustrate the kind of information that the requirements and specification process should produce.

| The Agent Community (Social Level) | Protocols (dynamics of communication and coordination) |
|---|---|
| | Organization (roles or services of each agent with respect to the others) |
| The Individual Agent (Knowledge Level) | Local Planning (capabilities and plans) |
| | Local Behavior (reactivity, routine tasks) |
| | Local Knowledge (The agent's beliefs) |

**Table 9.6**   What needs to be designed?

### 9.5.2   Design: The Conceptual Context

Design of an engineered artifact (such as an agent-based system) is a *process* that takes place within a conceptual *context*. In the agent research community, the "conceptual context" is often called an "agent architecture," and this subject has received considerable attention. Relatively less attention has been paid to the important question of the processes that designers go through. Industrial users will use agents more readily if basic principles and guidelines are available in both areas.

There is growing agreement among agent researchers on the set of issues that need to be resolved in order to design an agent-based system. Chapters 1 and 2 summarize a number of these. The common insight of all these proposals is that design must address both the individual agent and the community of which it is a part. Table 9.6 summarizes the various subcategories distinguished by one or another of these approaches.

### 9.5.3   Design: The Process

An iterative refinement approach is useful in designing agent-based systems [75]. The four stages outlined in Table 9.7 lead from a rough initial sketch of the community and its interactions to the point that software engineers can begin implementation. The stages are not strictly linear. Role-playing may show the need to rethink what agents are needed and what they should do individually; formal analysis may uncover a need for a revised organizational structure that requires more role-playing; and implementation design may raise further questions that require additional simulation. Still, there is a rough time ordering of these activities, in that conceptual analysis is the first to begin and implementation design is the last to complete.

#### *Conceptual Analysis*

The specification phase has defined what the system as a whole will do. Conceptual analysis gives an initial vision of what agents will be involved and how they will behave.

One widely-used technique for identifying objects in an object-oriented systems

| Stage | Focus | Supporting Analysis | Answers |
|---|---|---|---|
| Conceptual Analysis | Components | Case Grammar | What system-level behavior is needed? |
| | | | What kinds of agents might we need to get it? |
| | | | How should they behave? |
| Role-Playing | Architecture (Kinematics) | Speech Acts & Dooley Graphs | How do the proposed agents interact with one another in an organization? |
| | | | What low-level behaviors are needed? |
| Formal Analysis | Behavior (Dynamics) | Formal Modeling, Simulation & Nonlinear mathematics | Are the descriptions logically consistent and complete? |
| | | | What kind of behavior emerges from realistic numbers of agents and interchanges? |
| Implementation Design | Platforms & Tools | Simulation | How can this design become a deployable system? |

**Table 9.7** Stages in designing multiagent systems.

analysis [83] is to extract the nouns from a narrative description of the desired system behavior. A refinement of this approach is based on linguistic case theory [16, 27, 68]. Each verb has a set of named slots that can be filled by other items, typically nouns. Each slot describes the semantic role of its filler with respect to the verb. Thus the case role of a noun captures basic behavioral differences among entities in the domain, and is a candidate for an agent class.

To complete the preliminary decomposition, these categories are reviewed and possibly revised against overall system requirements and general principles of agent-based systems. Naturally occurring agent systems have proven remarkably robust and adaptable, and suggest a set of useful engineering principles [71].

**Thing vs. Function.** This chapter has repeatedly emphasized the natural precedents and practical benefits of physical rather than functional decomposition in agent-based systems. In most cases, deriving agents from the nouns in a narrative description of the problem to be solved yields things rather than functions. Legacy systems and watchdogs (agents that monitor the overall system for emergent behaviors) are two exceptions to this principle.

**Small in Size.** Natural systems like insect colonies and market economies are characterized by many agents, each small in comparison with the whole system. Such agents are easier to construct and understand than large ones, and the impact of the failure of any single agent will be minimal. In addition, a large population of agents gives the system a richer overall space of possible behaviors. (Very roughly, system state space is exponential in the number of agents.) The same benefits apply to artificial systems. Keeping agents small often means favoring specialized agents over more general ones, using appropriate aggregation techniques. For example, rather than writing a single agent to represent a complete manufacturing cell, consider an agent for each mechanism in the cell (e.g., one for the fixture, one for the tool, one for the load-unload mechanism, one for the gauging station).

**Decentralized.** Natural systems are not centralized as artificial systems often are. There are several reasons for imitating this tendency. A central agent is a single point of failure that makes the system vulnerable to accident. It can easily become a performance bottleneck. More subtly, it tends to attract functionality and code as the system develops, pulling the design away from the benefits of agents and regressing to a large software artifact that is difficult to understand and maintain. Centralization can sometimes creep in when designers confuse a class of agents with individual agents. For example, one might be tempted to represent a bank of paint booths as "the paint agent," because "they all do the same thing." Certainly, one would develop a single class for paint-booth agents, but each paint booth should be a separate instance of that class.

**Diversity and Generalization.** Natural communities of agents balance diversity (which enables them to monitor an environment much larger than any single agent) with generalized mechanisms (enhancing their interaction with one another and reducing the need for task-specific processing). For example, pheromones enable insects not only to map out paths to food sources, but also to coordinate nest construction. Conventional class inheritance mechanisms support generalization across agents, but the hard part is identifying appropriate generalizations in the first place. Early designs typically multiply differences among agents, while later refinements make more effective use of inheritance.

With a candidate set of agents in hand, the next step is to hypothesize their individual behaviors and the classes of messages they can exchange, keeping in mind the desired overall system behavior. This process is intuitive, not algorithmic. Some behaviors may be obvious, but there will always be subsystems where only simulation of example agent behaviors (first in role-playing, later on a computer) can verify the right behaviors. At this point, the main concern is to identify the decisions each agent needs to make and the other agents with which it needs to make them rather than on the details of each agent's internal reasoning. Again, principles observed in naturally occurring systems help evaluate candidate agent dynamics and interactions.

**Concurrent Planning and Execution.** Traditional systems alternate planning and execution. For example, a firm develops a schedule each night for its manufacturing operations the next day. The real world tends to change in ways that invalidate advance plans. Natural systems do not plan in advance, but adjust their operations on a time scale comparable to the environment's rate of change. Watch out for behaviors that involve extensive up-front planning.

**Currency.** Naturally occurring multiagent systems often use a flow field, such as the flow of money in a market economy and the evaporation of pheromones in insect communities. These mechanisms accomplish two purposes. They provide an "entropy leak" that permits self-organization (reduction of entropy) at the macro level without violating the second law of thermodynamics overall, and they generate a gradient field that agents perceive and reinforce and to which they can orient their actions, thus becoming more organized [51]. Wherever possible, artificial agent communities should include such a flow.

**Local Communication.** Agents need to limit the recipients of their messages [86]. Wherever possible, instead of "broadcast X," define more precisely the audience that needs to receive the message.

**Information Sharing.** Agents often need to share information across both time and space. ("Learning" thus becomes a special case of information sharing.) Phylogenetic learning is not nearly as demanding as the ontogenetic mechanisms developed in classical AI, and sociogenetic mechanisms can be even simpler

### Role-Playing

With agents identified and tentative behaviors described, the emergent behavior of selected subsystems can be explored by having people play the roles of the various agents. Such a rehearsal does not show the full dynamic behavior expected from a complete population of agents operating at computer speed, but does validate the basic behaviors needed and provides a basis for defining some internal details of computerized agents. Where computer agents supplement the activity of human operators, the role-playing exercise also helps capture the techniques, knowledge, and rules that the humans have been using to ensure that the computer agent augments this behavior appropriately [8].

Many of the individual behaviors for most of the agents will be fairly obvious. This situation is fortunate, since role-playing a complete system as small as 50 or 100 agents can be slow, tedious, and inconclusive. To explore the emergent behaviors of the system in regions that are not obvious, analysis focuses on subsystems of a dozen or so agents where there are significant questions about the match between individual and system behaviors.

Role-playing requires both identified subsystems and several scripts of the desired system behavior. For example, role-playing a system with homeostasis requires a list of the state variables that can independently change, the range of variation that they can expect, and the corresponding corrections needed in other variables. These scripts guide the role-playing activities. Because of the time and effort constraints of role-playing, they will sample the overall space of desired system behaviors only sparsely, and should be chosen to explore widely separated regions of this space.

A separate person should represent each agent in the subsystem identified in the conceptual analysis phase. When there are many more agents than people available, a single person may handle a complete class of agents. In this case one must distinguish carefully between the behavior of the agent class and what a single agent of that class can know. Agents, even those of the same class, do not have direct access to one another's variables, and people representing them in a role-play need to be careful not to "leak" information among them.

The environment in which agents live is not necessarily passive, but may have state and processes associated with it. In addition to the agents proposed for the system being engineered (the "system agents"), someone should play the role of the environment. This person raises external conditions as called for in the script, receives actuator outputs from the system agents, and integrates these outputs into their overall effect on the environment, thus monitoring the system's ability to achieve the required changes. The facilitator can represent a simple environment. When the environment is more complicated, its representative may need to do more extensive reasoning, and should be separate from the facilitator.

The primary responsibility of participants in role-playing is to figure out the rules that should guide the behavior of the agent for which they are responsible. The structure of the conversation among agents will emerge naturally from the interaction, and can be retrieved by post-hoc analysis, but the internal rules need to be developed by the participants themselves. A stochastic process (such as rolling a die or flipping a coin) is used to choose among internal agent decisions that later will be the subject of detailed computation. (By treating a penny, a dime, a nickel, and a quarter as successively higher bit positions, up to $2^4$ alternatives can be represented.)

All actions among role-players are recorded for later analysis. These actions may be either speech acts (messages to other agents) or non-speech acts (influences on the environment). The agents record these actions on cards that are then given to the participant representing the receiving agent (for a message) or the environment (for a physical action). Each card records five pieces of information, in addition to the actual content of the message:

1. The identity of the sending agent
2. The identity of the receiving agent
3. The time the card is sent
4. The identity of the agent whose card stimulated this one
5. The time that the card stimulating this one was sent

This information enables reconstruction of the thread of conversation among the agents. The time entries capture the order in which messages are generated. Ideally, one could assign a unique sequence number to all cards, but the task of maintaining such a number across all participants is burdensome and prone to error. By placing a digital desk clock in full view, it is easy to maintain an unambiguous ordering of the cards.

A facilitator who is not one of the agents oversees the execution of each script. There are three phases in this responsibility.

1.  *Initiate:* The facilitator announces that a new script is starting. If the facilitator and environment are not the same person, the facilitator makes sure the correct script drives the environment.

2.  *Run:* While the participants are running the script, the facilitator carries message cards between agents, watches for possible cross-talk ("Isn't your action based partly on what B said a few moments ago to C? Should you have been included on the distribution for that message?"), and (if also serving as the environment) simulates exogenous inputs to the system and accounts for the effect of outputs.

3.  *Debrief:* After completing a script, the facilitator helps participants synthesize important conclusions from the session. For example: What operational decisions could not be resolved locally? What state information does each agent need to maintain? How complex do agents need to be? Are participants conscious of internal state shifts?

Enhanced Dooley Graphs [69] can help analyze conversations in agent-based systems. Each node in the graph represents an agent in a role. A given agent may appear at different nodes if it changes roles in the course of the conversation. These roles suggest units of behavior that can often be reused across an agent community. Thus they provide a first-level decomposition of individual agents into behaviors, and guide the initial coding of the system.

### Formal Analysis

Brainstorming and role-playing are flexible, creative ways to explore possible agent designs, but their results need to be checked more formally before implementation begins. Two important tools are formal modeling and simulation. With a rudimentary design in place, a logician can develop a formal model of the individual agents and their interactions over time. Logical manipulation of this model can then test for consistency and completeness against project requirements. The research program of the DESIRE team [22] is one example among many of this approach. Like the "correctness proof" approach to program development, formal analysis of an agent design is complex and expensive, and should be used selectively. Simulation is a more broadly used tool, and a more necessary one. It enables the designer to observe and evaluate the emergent behavior of the entire community, and to test how the behavior seen in a role-play scales up to a full population. The growing acceptance of genetic methods in industry opens the door for using simulation to grow agents, avoiding the need to program them manually. The code of the simulated agents can serve as a detailed design for the final implementation.

### Implementation Design

In preparation for implementation, the designer selects the deployment platforms and tools that will be used in the fielded system. Sometimes these choices are known at the outset. In other cases, the results of the earlier steps of design may guide implementation design, as when simulation studies show that the required level of performance requires agents to execute on separate processors.

### 9.5.4  System Implementation

The various tools described in this section vary widely in their functionality and capabilities. Often the tool needed for a given application will depend on the details of the design that has been developed using the methods of the last section.

### Hardware

General-purpose computers dominate agent research, but many industrial applications are better served by parallel architectures that can assign a single processor to each agent. Such an architecture supports real-time control applications much better than do general-purpose operating systems such as UNIX or Windows, and most of the examples here permit processors to be distributed physically so that software agents can be embedded in physical devices.

The simplest products in this category are single-chip or single-board microcomputers, such as the Basic Stamp [66] or Z-World's C-based offerings [94], with a dozen or so I/O points and a supporting PC-based development environment. Such platforms require additional peripheral support for inter-agent communication over any significant distance. The next level of sophistication is represented by LonWorks [21], which is built around a single-chip computer that includes LonTalk, a complete 7-layer OSI protocol. The product line includes a wide variety of transceivers for a variety of interconnections among individual chips, and interfaces to other networks.

An example of the high end of dedicated agent hardware for industrial applications is the Flavors PIM (Parallel Inference Machine) [25], a centralized parallel computer that is available either as a board for a Macintosh with four powerPC604e processors, or in a VME format with up to 125 68040 processors. Each processor supports 125 virtual "cells" or virtual processors, in a real-time operating environment.

### Standards

Broadly accepted standards bring users and developers together into a critical mass. If the requirements of various users differ widely from one another, developers will not have a large enough market for any single technology to justify the expense of bringing it to commercial status. If the offerings of different developers do not work together, users will not be able to assemble the full suite of tools that they require. To the extent that agent standards agree with standards currently deployed in the pre-agent environment, they enable incremental introduction of agents, an approach that is less painful and more likely to be accepted by management than requiring a wholesale redesign of the factory to accommodate agents.

Two organizations are devoted specifically to the definition and promulgation of standards for agent-based systems. The National Industrial Information Infrastructure Protocols program (NIIIP) [59] is a consortium of U.S. companies addressing the problem of enabling manufacturers and their suppliers to interoperate as effectively as if they were part of the same enterprise. FIPA [13], the Foundation for Intelligent Physical Agents, is a world-wide consortium devoted to agent standards in general.

Commercial developers of agent tools draw on a wide variety of standards for distributed systems and networking. The following examples begin with the lowest levels of agent communication and extending to the high-level definition of agent behavior.

Physically moving bytes around can be a problem in an industrial environment. Electromagnetic interference from arc welders, induction furnaces, and motor starters can overwhelm many network structures that are completely adequate for laboratory work. Until recently, industrial control relied on point-to-point wiring of I/O between a controller and the devices being controlled, with separate conductors for each device. Control-area networks such as DeviceNet [63] replace these unwieldy tangles with multiplexed communications, and are engineered to cope with potential interference.

Once an electronic pathway exists between agents, they need to be able to find one another. Heterogeneous platforms are the rule rather than the exception in many factories: a shop-floor server running on a DEC machine may support machine controllers from Fanuc, Rockwell Automation, and Modicon, and a number of applications built on an industrially-hardened personal computer platform. CORBA [64], the Common Object Request Broker Architecture, defines a standard mechanism by which objects written in different languages and executing in a distributed environment can make requests of, and respond to, one another.

After finding one another, agents need to be able to exchange information and express themselves about it. Chapter 2 discusses in detail two important standards that support inter-agent communication: KIF [34], the Knowledge Interchange Format, and. KQML [28], the Knowledge Query and Manipulation Language. KIF expresses the content of a proposition, while KQML expresses the agent's attitude toward the proposition.

Sometimes it is not enough for agents to talk to one another over the network. If their interactions are intensive, they should share the same processor. A part agent may need to move from one machine agent to another during its residency in the shop. Java [85] enables agent behavior to travel from one processor to another, and thus provides a way for agents themselves to travel over networks and execute on diverse platforms.

These standards provide interoperability between different computer systems. Another category of standards enables people to communicate effectively with agents. Industrial engineers have evolved their own conventions for specifying and implementing systems, and they will accept agent technologies more readily if an agent system supports these conventions. For example, Grafcet [9] is an international standard (IEC 848) for a graphical control language based on Petri nets. Petri nets are a powerful mechanism for representing the internal logic of an agent [26], and Grafcet enjoys widespread industrial use as a representation for control logic, making it a good candidate for implementing industrial agents.

### Tools

A growing array of software tools is available for developers of agent-based systems. Section 9.6 discusses several examples.

### 9.5.5   System Operation

Little specific case information is available at this time concerning the operation of industrial agent-based systems, but the nature of agent technology suggests two important issues that will make the difference between successful and unsuccessful systems.

**Agent Dynamics.** One of the great benefits of agent-based systems is their ability to generate complex system-level performance from relatively simple individual agents. This system-level behavior often cannot be predicted analytically from the descriptions of individual agents, but must be observed in simulation or real-life. As a result, the detailed behavior of an implemented system may not be known in advance, and individual agent behaviors may need to be modified in real time as the system runs. The tools to support the monitoring, analysis, and adjustment of an agent-based system in operation are the same ones needed to design the system in the first place. Thus one expects that the more successful development tools discussed in the previous section will take on more and more features of operational interfaces, such as simplicity for use by non-programmers, alarm and emergency management, and data logging and archiving.

**Humans and Agents.** Agent-based systems require closer interaction between human and computer than do traditional systems, even as they enable automation of many tasks that previously required human attention. The reason for this paradox is that the autonomy of agents, one of their main strengths, moves them from a position of an obedient slave to that of a cooperating partner. One can tolerate bad manners on the part of a slave, but people who relinquish decision-making ability to a silicon peer expect a certain level of etiquette on the part of their new associates. The problem is more complex because people can learn to recognize their own bad habits and modify their behavior accordingly, but at the present state of technology, acceptable demeanor must be programmed into computer agents. Successful operations requires systems that embody not only advanced computational science but also sophisticated psychological understanding of how people work together and what makes teams successful.

## 9.6   Development Tools

Development tools are one of the most powerful ways to move a new technology into widespread use. Object-oriented programming was possible before the advent of specific object-oriented languages, but each team had to define its own conventions and rely on the expertise of individual developers to enforce them. Wide-spread industrial acceptance came only with languages such as Smalltalk, C++, and Objective C that package an agent model and enforce a set of best practices about how to use it. The lack of commercially supported development environments has been a major roadblock to wider agent deployment in industry [70].

Several products have recently emerged to address this need. Since one function of a tool is to enforce best practice, it is not surprising that each of these tools emphasizes its own view of what an agent is and what kind of resources agent developers need. This section groups example tools under five such views, ordered roughly from simplest to most complex. Unless otherwise noted, the tools described in this section are commercially available and supported. Chapter 1 discusses several tools that are more oriented toward research.

**An Agent as a Single Reactive Process.** IBM's Agent Building Environment [41] is an extensible C++ library for constructing rule-based forward chaining agents, and is designed for applications such as monitoring a network information source and informing a human when certain conditions are satisfied. ABE represents its facts and rules in KIF. The core reasoning engine can be attached to procedures external to itself. These procedures, which can be written in C++ or Java, provide the means of sensing conditions in the environment, taking action in the environment, and triggering inferencing activity in the underlying engine. Attached procedures are packaged into "adapters," and the ABE distribution includes a number of predefined examples: an alarm clock that can trigger time-based events, a USENET News monitor, an HTTP monitor, an adapter that can observe and manipulate files, an Email sender, and an example of an adapter that fetches stock quotes from a WWW site. ABE is designed to support isolated intelligent agents rather than multiagent systems.

**Agents as Capitalists.** Dissipative mechanisms such as currency flows are a powerful way to coordinate a decentralized system. Agorics is a software development company that applies market mechanisms to real-world problems. Agorics is developing Joule, a programming language for distributed concurrent asynchronous systems, that supports market-based computing with the encapsulation of resources and the management of access to them [1]. Joule raises the communication channel between agents to first-class status as a "channel," a unidirectional route with two "ports." Agents (called "servers" in Joule) place messages into a channel's acceptor port and read them from a distributor port. These ports can be passed from one agent to another, thus controlling access to the services provided by a given server. The message objects themselves handle authentication and other security concerns. Currently, Joule is not distributed externally, but is used within Agorics on industrial projects for its clients.

**Agents as Travelers.** Some agents can migrate from one processor to another. This capability permits agents that must conduct a high-bandwidth conversation to move to a common processor so that the network as a whole is not burdened with the traffic between them. It also permits local communities of agents to interact with one another even when the processor on which they are located is disconnected from the rest of the network. The earliest widely publicized tool for mobile agents is General Magic's proprietary Telescript language [90-92], which models the world as places (processors) and agents (processes). Several firms are implementing these concepts in Java to avoid the need for a proprietary language interpreter on each processor that an agent might wish to visit. IBM's Aglets [42] are Java objects that can move from one host to another. The Java Aglet API (J-AAPI) defines the methods necessary to create aglets, handle messages, and manage the course of the aglet's life. Danny Lange, the lead developer of Aglets, has joined General Magic, and is now a member of the Odyssey team that is producing a Java version of Telescript [33]. ObjectSpace's Voyager [62] provides a Java-based Object Request Broker (ORB) designed for mobile agents. ObjectSpace offers a detailed comparison of Aglets, Odyssey, and Voyager [61]. All three tools are available free for noncommercial use, and Voyager is freely available for commercial use as well.

**Agents as Members of a Community.** The next level of sophistication in agent tools provides explicit support at the level of the community, with special emphasis on communication mechanisms. As functionality is added to the Java-based frameworks discussed in the previous section, they will come to look more like these tools as well.

Gensym's Agent Development Environment (ADE) [35] builds on its widely accepted G2 object-oriented environment, a robust real-time platform for industrial deployment of AI techniques. The ADE provides a predefined class hierarchy of agents and agent parts, agent communications "middleware," a graphical specification and programming language for agent behavior based on the Grafcet standard for industrial-strength Petri nets, and a simulation tool for performing simulations of (distributed) agent-based applications. ADE supports agents running on a distributed network of computers as well as on a single machine. Each agent has a network-wide unique identifier, and agents can be grouped into nested "environments," each of which is also an agent. ADE itself provides a basic direct addressing message service, to which users can add additional functionality (such as guaranteed delivery or subject-based addressing). An agent uses messages not only to communicate with other agents but also to queue up events for its own subsequent activity.

In support of the AARIA project described in Section 9.4.3, Intelligent Automation, Inc., the AARIA prime contractor, created the first version of Cybele, a NeXT-based agent infrastructure [24]. Based on the requirements analyzed in [52], Cybele supports agent creation and deployment over a network of varied platforms, a message addressing scheme for agent communication that is independent of the location of a sending or receiving agent, the accumulation of messages intended for a currently busy recipient agent, the proper conversion of message data across platforms, multicasting, broadcasting, and peer-to-peer messaging, and the migration of agents across processors for performance optimization and/or fault tolerance. Building on the lessons learned in the initial implementation, Cybele is currently being reimplemented in Java.

Metra's UNITY_Agent [54] is a Java-based agent environment that builds on the three-level "tactical, operational, strategic" agent hierarchy of [10]. Agents are grouped into communities, themselves agents, each with a Meta Agent that monitors the identity and capabilities of agents in the community. The framework supports communication via direct addressing, subject-based addressing, and blackboards. The base agent class includes capabilities for modeling self and other agents, performing situation assessment, managing local tasks, negotiating for resources, and competitive bidding to resolve conflicts. Users configure a new agent by specifying the agent's attributes, defining trigger events, writing actions to be taken on a trigger event in Java, and binding trigger events and actions in rules. The interface to the external world is CORBA-based and supports standard database access. UNITY_Agent is the environment underlying the Daewoo scheduling system described in Section 9.4.3.

**Agents as Intelligent Processes.** Much agent research grows out of the Artificial Intelligence community, and assumes that individual agents aspire to some level of intelligence. The tools described thus far do not provide any explicit support for individually intelligent agents, and are appropriate for systems of relatively simply agents whose interactions produce intelligent system-level behavior. The tools in this section embody specific models of individual intelligence, and illustrate how a well-crafted tool can make complex techniques accessible to a wide range of users.

dMARS [36], a descendant of SRI's Procedural Reasoning System, is an instantiation of the BDI model of agents, according to which agents should explicitly model their Beliefs, Desires, and Intentions. Each dMARS agent includes a Belief Database of current beliefs about the world, a Goal Database of objectives or desires to be realized, a Plan Library of context-sensitive procedures that the agent can use to achieve goals and react to situations, an Intention Structure of tasks to be performed, and a Task Manager that repeatedly selects a Plan based on the agent's Beliefs and Goals, places it in the Intention Structure, and manages its execution. Plans can be conditioned either on external conditions or on the state of the agent's internal databases, and so can support reflective planning and dynamic reprogramming of the agent.

D-Muse [93] is a distributed version of an earlier commercial AI toolkit, MUSE. Based on the PopTalk object language, MUSE offers a complete frame representation system with forward and backward chaining that supports real-time operation. D-Muse provides a layered set of communication capabilities that enable the interaction of individual MUSE-based agents. Agents interact mainly through mirrored objects. One agent (the publisher) creates a master object that is then made visible to one or more subscriber agents by being copied as a slave object within the subscriber. Whenever the publisher modifies the master object, D-Muse synchronizes the slaves. A subscriber cannot modify a slave object, but can attach demons or relations to it, match rule patterns to it, or manipulate it in any other way that would be possible within the native MUSE environment.

The Agent Building Shell (ABS) [5, 7] at the University of Toronto is a set of object classes and supporting tools that implement a four-layer architecture for coarse-grained agents. The *knowledge management layer* provides general-purpose representation and inference mechanisms that agents can use to model their knowledge and beliefs about the problem domain, the environment (including other agents), and themselves. The *ontology layer* uses the knowledge management layer to construct the specific models that an agent maintains of its domain, its environment, and itself. The *cooperation and conflict layer* supports two services to manage shared knowledge between agents: a subscription-based information service that enables agents to be notified automatically when information of interest to them is posted, and mechanisms for managing an agent's beliefs when it receives contradictory information from other agents. The *coordination and communication layer* is supported by the Coordination Language (COOL) and provides inter-agent communication using a superset of KQML, definition of arbitrary inter-agent protocols, and integration of legacy applications. While the Agent Building Shell is not offered commercially, it embodies techniques of knowledge representation and automated inferencing that have been deployed commercially in expert system shells such as KnowledgeCraft and KEE, and shows how classical AI methods are migrating into agent tools.

## 9.7  Conclusions

This brief survey of industrial agent systems suggests two ways in which such systems differ from research systems: the systems must be practical, and the tools used to develop them must be packaged.

Industrial systems are driven by the need to solve a practical problem, rather than curiosity about the possibility of some technology. The criterion for success in an industrial project is not how clever the technology is, or what one has learned about that technology, but how well the system solves the problem that it addresses. The entire life cycle of an industrial system is shaped by this unrelenting pressure to make a difference to the firm's effectiveness. At first glance this focus on profit and practical results strikes some researchers as confining and unimaginative. In fact, the complexity of real-world problems offers intellectual challenges every bit as stimulating as the more theoretical challenges of the research laboratory, and the unforgiving nature of the business environment provides a much clearer sense of success or failure than can be achieved in a more abstract domain.

The methods of designing, building, operating, and maintaining agent-based systems must be packaged if they are ever to find wide-spread deployment in the industrial world. The orientation to practical problems means that engineers in industry must be first of all experts in the products they manufacture, the processes they control, or the services they render. Agent technology is for them a means to an end, a tool. The more the tool fades into the background and lets them concentrate on the requirements of the problem at hand, the more likely they are to use it.

The PAAM (Practical Application of Intelligent Agents and Multiagent Technology) conferences [88] are more oriented toward applications than other agent conferences, and their proceedings are a good source of further readings. As with other technologies, detailed application issues are more likely to be discussed in venues associated with the application domain than in those dedicated to the underlying technology, and as a result the best case studies will be scattered throughout a wide range of conference proceedings and journals. Ultimately, application expertise is best communicated by hands-on experience rather than by papers, and readers eager to learn more about this area should establish joint projects with industrial partners around application problems of industrial scope and complexity, where the objective is to improve the industrial partner's operations rather than to generate research reports.

The big open issue in applications of DAI is the instantiation of the techniques that researchers develop in standards and development tools that make them accessible to industrial users. The best techniques will not be widely used unless they are embedded in commercially supported tools. Now that multiple products are becoming available, market forces will join technical excellence in determining the platforms on which industry will build in the future. Researchers who are alert to these market forces and who pay special attention to packaging and deployment of their results will see their work have the most lasting impact on the field.

## 9.8   Exercises

1. *[Level 3]* The deployed agent-based systems described in this chapter focus on the design and operation phases of the life cycle. Why is this the case? Make friends with some industrialists, identify the main challenges in each phase of the life cycle of some process or product of interest to them, and see if you can propose an application for agents in some of the neglected phases.

2. *[Level 4]* Formulate a project proposal to do an agent application in one of these neglected phases, in partnership with your industrial acquaintance. Obtain funding for the project and execute it.

3. *[Level 2]* Analyze a recent or upcoming research project in your laboratory according to the life cycle pattern outlined in this chapter. To which steps do you usually devote attention? Which ones are novel or unusual in your environment? For each of these steps that is not part of your usual project cycle, identify the difference between an industrial setting and your own that makes it important to an industrial user.

4. Software packages that support an industrial team as they work their way through the life cycle are called "work flow" packages, and research concerning them is centered in the discipline of computer-supported collaborative work.

   (a) *[Level 1]* Conduct a literature review on workflow packages. Compare and contrast the ways different solutions decompose the problem.

   (b) *[Level 2]* Design an agent-based workflow program. Explain how your decomposition into agents supports the industrial requirements outlined in Section 9.2.

   (c) *[Level 3]* Implement your program.

   (d) *[Level 4]* Field-test your program with an industrial partner. If the test is successful, start a company to market it.

5. *[Level 1]* Compare the agent architecture used in your work with that discussed in Section 9.4.2 above. Which categories do you design explicitly, and which are left implicit? Are there other categories, not discussed here, which industrial agent designers should consider?

6. *[Level 2]* Itemize the development tools that you use in your projects. For each tool that is developed in your own laboratory, answer the following questions:

   - What philosophy of agents does this tool impose on your work?

   - What functionality does it provide that is not yet available in the market?

   - What functionality of more widely available tools does it duplicate?

   - How does the capability of this tool, and the availability (or lack of availability) of commercial sources for this capability, impact the prospect for transferring your discovers to industrial practice?

7.   *[Level 4]* Implement your next project in a commercial development environment that meets as many of your requirements as possible. Explore ways to package the additional functionality you require as extensions to this environment. Transfer these extensions to the vendor of the development environment for them to make available in the next release of their product.

## 9.9   References

1.   Agorics. *Joule: Distributed Application Foundations*. Agorics Technical Report ADd003.4P, http://www.webcom.com/~agorics/joule.html, Agorics, Inc., Los Altos, CA, 1995.

2.   J. S. Albus, H. G. McCain, and R. Lumia. *NASA/NBS Standard Reference Model for Telerobot Control System Architecture (NASREM)*. NBS Technical Note 1235, National Bureau of Standards, Gaithersburg, MD, 1987.

3.   A.D. Baker. *Manufacturing Control with a Market Driven Contract Net*. Ph.D. thesis, Rensselaer Polytechnic Institute, Electrical Engineering, 1991.

4.   A. D. Baker, H. V. D. Parunak, and K. Erol. *Manufacturing over the Internet and into Your Living Room: Perspectives from the AARIA Project*. http://www.aaria.uc.edu/cybermfg.ps, Department of Electrical & Computer Engineering and Computer Science, University of Cincinnati, Cincinnati, OH, 1997.

5.   M. Barbuceanu. The Agent Building Shell: Programming Cooperative Enterprise Agents. http://www.ie.utoronto.ca/EIL/ABS-page/ABS-intro.html, 1997.

6.   M. Barbuceanu and M. S. Fox. The Architecture of an Agent Based Infrastructure for Agile Manufacturing. In *Proceedings of IJCAI-95*, 1995.

7.   M. Barbuceanu and M. S. Fox. The Architecture of an Agent Building Shell. In *Proceedings of Agent Theories, Architectures, and Languages*, pages 235-250, Springer, 1995.

8.   D. Bellin and S. S. Simone. *The CRC Card Book*. Addison-Wesley, 1997.

9.   E. Bierel and J.-M. Roussel. "Welcome to the GRAFCET Home Page". http://www.lurpa.ens-cachan.fr/grafcet.html, 1995.

10.   P. Burke and P. Prosser. The Distributed Asynchronous Scheduler. In M. B. Morgan, editor, *Intelligent Scheduling*, pages 309-339. Morgan Kaufman Publishers, Inc., San Francisco, 1994.

11.   J. Butler and H. Ohtsubo. ADDYMS: Architecture for Distributed DYnamic Manufacturing Scheduling. In A. Famili, D. S. Nau, and S. H. Kim, editors, *Artificial Intelligence Applications in Manufacturing*, pages 199-214. AAAI Press/The MIT Press, Menlo Park, CA, 1992.

12.   F.-C. Cheong. *Internet Agents: Spiders, Wanderers, Brokers, and Bots*. Indianapolis, IN, New Riders, 1996.

13.   L. Chiariglione. Foundation for Intelligent Physical Agents. http://drogo.cselt.stet.it/fipa/, 1987.

14.   K. T. Chung and C.-H. Wu. *Dynamic Scheduling with Intelligent Agents: An Application Note*. Metra Application Note 105, Metra, Palo Alto, CA, 1997.

15.   S. H. Clearwater, editor. *Market-Based Control: A Paradigm for Distributed*

*Resource Allocation*. Singapore, World Scientific, 1996.

16. W. A. Cook. *Case Grammar: Development of the Matrix Model*. Washington, Georgetown University, 1979.

17. J. M. Corera, I. Laresgoiti, and N. R. Jennings. Using ARCHON, Part 2: Electricity Transportation Management. *IEEE Expert*, 11(6):71-79, 1996.

18. M. R. Cutkosky, R. S. Englemore, R. E. Fikes, T. R. Gruber, M. R. Genesereth, W. S. Mark, J. M. Tenenbaum, and J. C. Weber. PACT: An Experiment in Integrating Concurrent Engineering Systems. *IEEE Computer*, 26 (January)(1):28-37, 1993.

19. T. P. Darr and W. P. Birmingham. An Attribute-Space Representation and Algorithm for Concurrent Engineering. *AI EDAM*, 10(1):21-35, 1996.

20. N. A. Duffie, R. Chitturi, and J. I. Mou. Fault-tolerant Heterarchical Control of Heterogeneous Manufacturing System Entities. *Journal of Manufacturing Systems*, 7(4):315-28, 1988.

21. Echelon. Welcome to Echelon. http://www.lonworks.echelon.com, 1997.

22. P. v. Eck. The DESIRE Research Programme. http://www.cs.vu.nl/vakgroepen/ai/projects/desire/, 1996.

23. G. Ekberg. Benefits of Autonomous Agent Approach to Manufacturing Systems Control. In *Proceedings of Third Annual Chaos East Technical Conference*, R. Morley, Inc., 1997.

24. K. Erol. Cybele: An Infrastructure for Autonomous Agents. http://www.i-a-i.com/projects/cybele/index.html, 1996.

25. P. Fandel, R. DeSimone, and H. Mitchell. Paracell/PIM Product Summary Preface. http://www.flavors.com/docn/ppps/index.html, 1996.

26. J. Ferber. *Les systèmes multi-agents: vers une intelligence collective*. Paris, France, InterEditions, 1995.

27. C. J. Fillmore. The Case for Case Reopened. *Studies in Syntax and Semantics*, (8):59-81, 1977.

28. T. Finin. UMBC KQML Web. http://www.cs.umbc.edu/kqml/, 1997.

29. K. Fordyce, R. Dunki-Jacobs, B. Gerard, R. Sell, and G. Sullivan. Logistics Management System: An Advanced Decision Support System for the Fourth Decision Tier Dispatch or Short-Interval Scheduling. *Production and Operations Management*, 1(1):70-86, 1992.

30. K. Fordyce and G. G. Sullivan. Logistics Management System (LMS): Integrating Decision Technologies for Dispatch Scheduling in Semiconductor Manufacturing. In M. B. Morgan, editor, *Intelligent Scheduling*, pages 473-516. Morgan Kaufman Publishers, Inc., San Francisco, 1994.

31. M. S. Fox. The Integrated Supply Chain Management Project. http://www.ie.utoronto.ca/EIL/iscm-descr.html, 1996.

32. M. S. Fox, J. F. Chionglo, and M. Barbuceanu. The Integrated Supply Chain Management System. http://www.ie.utoronto.ca/EIL/public/iscm-intro.ps, Department of Industrial Engineering, University of Toronto, Toronto, Ontario, 1993.

33. General Magic. General Magic: Odyssey. http://www.genmagic.com/agents/odyssey.html, 1997.

34. M. R. Genesereth. Knowledge Interchange Format (KIF). http://logic.stanford.edu/kif/, 1996.

35.  Gensym. Agent Development Environment (ADE) Overview. Gensym, Inc., Cambridge, MA, 1997.

36.  M. Georgeff. dMARS Technical Overview. http://www.aaii.oz.au/proj/dmars_tech_overview/dMARS-1.html, 1996.

37.  J. Hatvany. Intelligence and Cooperation in Heterarchic Manufacturing Systems. *Robotics & Computer-Integrated Manufacturing*, 2(2):101-104, 1985.

38.  R. Hauser and D. Clausing. The House of Quality. *Harvard Business Review*, 66(May-June):63-73, 1988.

39.  J. Heaton. *Agent Architecture Distributes Decisions for the Agile Manufacturer: Reengineering at AlliedSignal Automotive Safety Restraint Systems*. AMR Report, (June):8-13, 1994.

40.  J. H. Holland. *Hidden Order: How Adaptation Builds Complexity*. Reading, MA, Addison-Wesley, 1995.

41.  IBM. IBM Agent Building Environment (ABE) – A toolkit for building intelligent agent applications. http://www.networking.ibm.com/iag/iagsoft.htm, 1997.

42.  IBM. IBM Aglets Workbench-Home Page. http://www.trl.ibm.co.jp/aglets/, 1997.

43.  H. Ihara and K. Mori. Autonomous Decentralized Computer Control Systems. *IEEE Computer*, 17(8):57-66, 1984.

44.  N. Jennings. Applying Agent Technology. Plenary presentation at PAAM'96. 1996.

45.  N. R. Jennings. ADEPT: Advanced Decision Environment for Process Tasks. http://www.elec.qmw.ac.uk/dai/projects/adept/, 1997.

46.  N. R. Jennings, J. Corera, and I. Laresgoiti. Developing Industrial Multi-Agent Systems. In *Proceedings of 1st Int. Conf. on Multi-Agent Systems*, pages 423-430, AAAI Press, 1995.

47.  N. R. Jennings, P. Faratin, M. J. Johnson, T. J. Norman, P. O'Brien, and M. E. Wiegand. Agent-based business process management. *International Journal of Cooperative Information Systems, Forthcoming*, 1997. Available at ftp://ftp.elec.qmw.ac.uk/pub/isag/distributed-ai/publications/IJCIS96.ps.gz.

48.  N. R. Jennings, P. Faratin, M. J. Johnson, P. O'Brien, and M. E. Wiegand. Using Intelligent Agents to Manage Business Processes. In *Proceedings of The First International Conference and Exhibition on The Practical Application of Intelligent Agents and Multi-Agent Technology*, pages 345-360, The Practical Application Company Ltd, 1996.

49.  N. R. Jennings, E. H. Mamdani, J. M. Corera, I. Laresgoiti, F. Perriolat, P. Skarek, and L. Z. Varga. Using ARCHON to develop real-word DAI applications, Part 1. *IEEE Expert*, 11(6):64-70, 1996.

50.  M. Koster. The Web Robots Pages. http://info.webcrawler.com/mak/projects/robots/robots.html, 1996.

51.  P. N. Kugler and M. T. Turvey. *Information, Natural Law, and the Self-Assembly of Rhythmic Movement*. Lawrence Erlbaum, 1987.

52.  R. Levy, K. Erol, and J. J. Howell Mitchell. A Study of Infrastructure Requirements and Software Platforms for Autonomous Agents. In *Proceedings of iCSE'96*, 1996.

53.  J. Maley. Managing the Flow of Intelligent Parts. *Robotics and Computer-Integrated Manufacturing*, 4(3/4):525-30, 1988.

54.  Metra. *Agent Technology: UNITY_Agent: An Agent Enabler*. Metra Corporation, San Jose, CA, 1997.

55. J. Mori, H. Torikoshi, K. Nakai, K. Mori, and T. Masuda. Computer Control System for Iron and Steel Plants. *Hitachi Review*, 37(4):251-8, 1988.

56. K. Mori, H. Ihara, Y. Suzuki, K. Kawano, M. Koizumi, M. Orimo, K. Nakai, and H. Nakanishi. Autonomous Decentralized Software Structure and its Application. In *Proceedings of Fall Joint Computer Conference*, pages 1056-63, 1986.

57. D. Morley. Painting Trucks at General Motors: The Effectiveness of a Complexity-Bsed Approach. In Ernst & Young, editors, *Embracing Complexity*, pages 53-58. Ernst & Young, Boston, MA, 1996.

58. R. N. Nagel and R. Dove. 21st Century Manufacturing Enterprise Strategy. Bethlehem, PA, Agility Forum, 1991.

59. NIIIP. Mother NIIIP Homepage. http://www.niiip.org, 1996.

60. T. J. Norman, N. R. Jennings, P. Faratin, and E. H. Mamdani. Designing and implementing a multi-agent architecture for business process management. In J. P. Müller, M. J. Wooldridge, and N. R. Jennings, editors, *Intelligent Agents III: ECAI'96 Workshop on Agent Theories, Architectures, and Languages*, vol. 1193, Lecture Notes in Artificial Intelligence, pages 261-275. Springer, Berlin, 1996.

61. ObjectSpace. *ObjectSpace Voyager, General Magic Odyssey, IBM Aglets: A Comparison*. ObjectSpace, Inc., Dallas, TX, http://www.objectspace.com/voyager/VoyagerAgentComparisons.PDF, 1997.

62. ObjectSpace. Voyager(tm) Core Package Technical Overview. http://www.objectspace.com/Voyager/VoyagerTechOviewOnlineVersion.PDF, ObjectSpace, Inc., Dallas, TX, 1997.

63. ODVA. Learn About DeviceNet. http://www.industry.net/c/orgunpro/odva/dev-net, 1997.

64. OMG. *The Common Object Request Broker: Architecture and Specification, Revision 2*. OMG Technical Document formal/97-02-25, http://www.omg.org/corba/corbiiop.htm, Object Management Group, 1996.

65. L. Overgaard, H. G. Petersen, and J. W. Perram. Motion Planning for an Articulated Robot: A Multi-Agent Approach. In *Proceedings of Modelling Autonomous Agent in a Multi-Agent World*, pages 171-182, Odense University, 1994.

66. Parallax. BASIC Stamp FAQs. Parallax, Inc., ftp://ftp.parallaxinc.com/pub/acrobat/stamp_faqs.pdf, 1997.

67. H. V. D. Parunak. Manufacturing Experience with the Contract Net. In M. N. Huhns, editor, *Distributed Artificial Intelligence*, pages 285-310. Pitman, London, 1987.

68. H. V. D. Parunak. *Case Grammar: A Linguistic Tool for Engineering Agent-Based Systems*. ITI Technical Memorandum, http://www.iti.org/~van/casegram.ps, Industrial Technology Institute, Ann Arbor, 1995.

69. H. V. D. Parunak. Visualizing Agent Conversations: Using Enhanced Dooley Graphs for Agent Design and Analysis. In *Proceedings of ICMAS'96*, pages 275-282, 1996.

70. H. V. D. Parunak. Workshop Report: Implementing Manufacturing Agents. *In Proceedings of PAAM'96*, 1996.

71. H. V. D. Parunak. 'Go to the Ant': Engineering Principles from Natural Agent Systems. *Annals of Operations Research*, 75:69-101, 1997. Available at http://www.iti.org/~van/gotoant.ps.

72. H. V. D. Parunak. RAPPID Project Index Page. http://www.iti.org/cec/rappid/, 1997.

73. H. V. D. Parunak, A. D. Baker, and S. J. Clark. The AARIA Agent Architecture: An Example of Requirements-Driven Agent-Based System Design. In *Proceedings of First International Conference on Autonomous Agents (ICAA-97)*, 1997.

74. H. V. D. Parunak, J. Kindrick, and B. Irish. Material Handling: A Conservative Domain for Neural Connectivity and Propagation. In *Proceedings of Sixth National Conference on Artificial Intelligence*, pages 307-311, American Association for Artificial Intelligence, 1987.

75. H. V. D. Parunak, J. Sauter, and S. J. Clark. Specification and Design of Industrial Synthetic Ecosystems. In *Proceedings of Fourth International Workshop on Agent Theories, Architectures, and Languages (ATAL)*, Springer, 1997.

76. H. V. D. Parunak, A. Ward, M. Fleischer, and J. Sauter. A Marketplace of Design Agents for Distributed Concurrent Set-Based Design. In *Proceedings of ISPE/CE97: Fourth ISPE International Conference on Concurrent Engineering: Research and Applications*, 1997.

77. H. V. D. Parunak, A. Ward, M. Fleischer, J. Sauter, and T.-C. Chang. Distributed Component-Centered Design as Agent-Based Distributed Constraint Optimization. In *Proceedings of AAAI Workshop on Constraints and Agents*, pages 93-99, American Association for Artificial Intelligence, 1997.

78. H. V. D. Parunak, A. Ward, and J. Sauter. A Systematic Market Approach To Distributed Constraint Problems. In *Proceedings of International Conference on Multi-Agent Systems*, pages (submitted), AAAI, 1998.

79. F. Perriolat, P. Skarek, L. Z. Varga, and N. R. Jennings. Using ARCHON, Part 3: Particle Accelerator Control. *IEEE Expert*, 11(6):80-86, 1996.

80. J.-F. Perrot. Preface. In J. Ferber, editor, *Les Systèmes Multi-Agents: Vers une intelligence collective*, pages xiii-xiv. InterEditions, Paris, 1995.

81. R. Roberts. *Zone Logic: A Unique Method of Practical Artificial Intelligence*. Radnor, PA, Compute! Books, 1989.

82. G. C. Roman. A Taxonomy of Current Issues in Requirements Engineering. *IEEE Computer*, (April):14-22, 1985.

83. J. Rumbaugh, M. Blaha, W. Premerlani, F. Eddy, and W. Lorensen. *Object-Oriented Modeling and Design*. Englewood Cliffs, Prentice Hall, 1991.

84. M. J. Shaw and A. B. Whinston. Task Bidding and Distributed Planning in Flexible Manufacturing. In *Proceedings of IEEE Int. Conf. on AI Applications*, pages 184-89, 1985.

85. Sun. JavaSoft Home Page. http://java.sun.com, 1997.

86. T. Takashina and S. Watanabe. The Locality of Information Gathering in Multiagent Systems. In *Proceedings of Second International Conference on Multi-Agent Systems (ICMAS-96)*, pages 461, 1996.

87. K. J. Tilley and D. J. Williams. Modelling of Communications and Control in an Auction-based Manufacturing Control System. In *Proceedings of IEEE International Conference on Robotics and Automation*, pages 962-967, IEEE, 1992.

88. TPAC. The Practical Application Company. http://www.demon.co.uk/ar/TPAC/index.html, 1997.

89. A. Ward, J. K. Liker, J. J. Cristiano, and D. K. S. II. The Second Toyota Paradox: How Delaying Decisions Can Make Better Cars Faster. *Sloan Management Review*, (Spring):43-61, 1995.

90. J. E. White. *Telescript Technology: The Foundation for the Electronic Marketplace.*

1994.

91. J. E. White. Telescript: Transportable Agent Systems.
    http://www.genmagic.com/Telescript/, 1996.

92. J. E. White, C. S. Helgeson, and D. A. Steedman. *System and method for distributed computation based upon the movement, execution, and interaction of processes in a network*. General Magic, Inc., U.S.A., 1997.

93. R. Zanconato. An inter-agent communication model for real-time Distributed AI Applications. In *Proceedings of PAAM-96: First International Conference on the Practical Application of Intelligent Agents and Multi-Agent Technology*, pages 755-771, The Practical Application Company, 1996.

94. Z-World. About Z-World. http://www.zworld.com/about.html, 1997

# Part II:

# Related Themes

# 10  Groupware and Computer Supported Cooperative Work

Clarence Ellis and Jacques Wainer

## 10.1  Introduction

Groupware is hardware and software technology to assist interacting groups. Computer Supported Cooperative Work (CSCW) is the study of how groups work, and how we can implement technology to enhance group interaction and collaboration. This chapter presents definitions, concepts, examples, and issues related to groupware and CSCW. It is written as an overview for the non-specialist, and primarily emphasizes the technical perspective. The material is presented and discussed in the context of a functional 4-part groupware classification. The four categories described within the classification are keepers, coordinators, communicators, and team-agents. This classification is also convenient for the investigation of middleware, and of low level issues of groupware. It also facilitates a discussion of social and organizational implications.

### 10.1.1  Well-Known Groupware Examples

One way to answer the question of what is groupware is via examples. Groupware comes in many shapes and styles. Most everyone is familiar with electronic mail, and understands that this is a technology used at different times, and different places by its participants. The sender does not expect an immediate reply from the receiver. This can be contrasted with face-to-face electronic meeting room technology, sometimes called group decision support systems (GDSS.) These systems typically consist of the following networked technology in a single room:

- presentation technology (large screen projector, or electronic whiteboard), and
- computation technology (a workstation or portable PC for each participant), and
- group process technology (voting tools, brainstorming tools, etc.)

Notice that in contrast to electronic mail, a GDSS is designed to support real-time face-to-face interaction among people, so it is called same time, same place technology.

Another well-known groupware example is video conferencing, which allows participants in different locations to see and hear each other for a same time, different place collaboration. There are many systems and products of this type available. For example, MBone [40] tools are available and free to allow meeting attendees in different locations to have a distributed meeting over the Internet. Participants in various locations can see (VIC), and hear (VAT) each other, and share a group window on their screens (Whiteboard.) This same time, different place technology is in the same category as MUDs and MOOs (chat rooms,) and group virtual realities.

Our final groupware example is workflow. A workflow management system is a networked control system that assists in analyzing, coordinating, and executing business processes. A workflow management system typically has two sub-systems: (1) A modeling subsystem which allows organizational administrators and analysts to construct a procedural models of the flow of work among people and tasks. This model is embedded in the network system to drive the enactment subsystem. (2) An enactment subsystem which uses the model to coordinate task executions by various participants at various workstations connected to a network. It initiates tasks in their correct order, and keeps track of completed work. Since a workflow system has a representation of work procedures, and knows which actors at which workstations are assigned to do what, it is called "organizationally aware groupware." This is a potentially powerful system which can download appropriate programs and data to users' workstations as needed; assist in task execution; send reminders when and if a user misses a deadline; automatically fill out electronic forms when needed; and generally act as coordinator, historian, and process overseer.

The above groupware examples suggest that there is a wide variety of systems. Some are same time, same place; some are different time, different place like workflow; and some fall in between these. But we see that all of these groupware systems aim to assist people in their communication, coordination, and collaboration.

## 10.2   Basic Definitions

### 10.2.1   Groupware

As stated above, groupware is technology to assist groups. Before presenting our elaborated definition of groupware, we discuss the notion of group. In this document, we define groups very generally as collaborating communities of participants. A group may be very small (e.g. two designers working via an electronic whiteboard,) or very large (e.g. all citizens of a large country participating in electronic voting.) A group may be very close knit, sharing goals and tasks and common knowledge and preferences and etc; or it may be a very amorphous group with no knowledge of other group members and no explicit shared goals. This latter type of group is of interest because it is commonly found on the Internet. Terms such as teams, organizations, corporations, communities and societies all fall within our notion of groups; thus groupware may be applicable to these quite varied entities.

When one thinks about typical groupware, electronic mail and video conferencing come to mind as typical examples. In fact, there are many single user tools which have been upgraded to be "group enabled." For example, a single user text editor which has an add-on electronic mail feature integrated into its latest release is groupware, or at least it has a groupware aspect. Thus, when examining the utility of groupware, we must specify which aspects of it we are focusing upon. This chapter suggests a four part classification of groupware according to its aspects.

It is clear that some groupware are much more useful to groups than others. For example, ordinary electronic mail is not as useful as enhanced electronic mail that filters, sorts into various mailboxes, and is multimedia. The filtering helps prevent information overload, the sorting helps to categorize messages into conversations— thereby providing context for messages, and the multimedia allows much more of the group spirit, emphases, and social background to be captured. This document therefore suggests that the question of "Is that technology groupware?" may not have a simple YES or NO answer, but depends upon the aspect of the technology that we are focusing upon, and is best represented by a spectrum. Some technological tools are high on this spectrum, meaning that they incorporate powerful and appropriate aids for group work. Others are considered low on the spectrum because they provide weak or inappropriate aids for group work. Ordinary email is much lower on the spectrum than enhanced email. Fax is also groupware, but it is quite low on the scale. Many group enabled systems tend to be lower on the scale than systems which were initially designed as group support systems.

We are now ready to state our definition of groupware: *Groupware* (also sometimes called *collaboration technology*) is defined as computing and communications technology based systems that assist groups of participants, and help to support a shared environment.

### 10.2.2  Computer Supported Cooperative Work (CSCW)

*CSCW* is the name of the research area that studies the use of computing and communications technologies to support group activities. Associated with this are are questions such as "How do people interact and collaborate?" and "How can technology facilitate and enhance this interaction and collaboration?" The emerging new focus on groupware presents opportunities for new paradigms, new types of systems, and new ways of working. Along with these opportunities come new problems and new intellectual challenges. Research methodologies utilized in this area include field studies, laboratory experiments, ethnographic studies, systems prototyping, simulation, and conceptual modeling. There have been a large number of studies, utilizing a wide variety of techniques. The techniques, technologies, and findings in this area have been useful to enhance interactions ranging from real time face to face meetings, to asynchronous organizational workflows.

In this area, it has been the case that technology tends to change and progress at a much faster rate than our understanding of human interaction phenomena. We need a much deeper understanding of the social and organizational factors, and their interaction with technology, than currently exists. There is an important component of the CSCW area concerned with theories, frameworks, and mathematical models. Thus, CSCW includes the theoretical development of models of teams, organizations, and social systems. This effort supports the analysis, prediction, and design of social structures taking into account the participants' information, communication possibilities, objectives, relationships, and incentive mechanisms. In constructing such theories, the area draws upon diverse disciplines including social psychology, organizational design, economics, computer science, and management science. As information technologies drive the underlying factors such as communication possibilities, the theoretical models provide a means to evaluate the effects of alternate designs, and a guide to shaping both the technology and the social systems for beneficial outcomes.

## 10.3   Aspects of Groupware

In this section we propose a classification of groupware systems that, we believe, is more interesting than previous taxonomies both in terms of its pedagogical advantages and in terms of its ability to direct future research in the area.

Other researchers have proposed taxonomies of groupware systems based upon a same/different time/space distinction [31], based upon areas of application [17], and based upon other criteria such as group size. We propose a classification based upon underlying functionalities of groupware. We introduce four classes, which we call *aspects*. Briefly, the first aspect, *keeper*, groups functionalities that are related to storage and access to share data; the second aspect, *coordinator*, is related to the ordering and synchronization of individual activities that make up the whole process; the third aspect, *communicator*, groups functionalities related to unconstrained and explicit communication among the participants; and finally the forth aspect, *team-agent*, refers to intelligent or semi-intelligent software components that perform specialized functions and help the dynamic of a group.

This classification is neither complete, in the sense that not all functionalities fall within one of such aspects, nor it is categorical, in the sense that it is always possible to say when a functionality falls within one or other aspect. In fact there will be functionalities that seem to lay on the intersection of different aspects. But despite these problems, we believe that the aspect taxonomy is helpful to understand the past and present of the field, and to suggest directions for the future.

It turns out that most current groupware systems have functionalities that fall overwhelmingly within one of the first three aspects. In this sense, we will talk about typical keeper systems, typical coordinator systems and typical communicator systems.

### 10.3.1  Keepers

Sometimes the collaboration among a group of people is centered on the access and change of a shared set of data. Sometimes the goal of the collaboration is the construction of this shared data, which we will call the *artifact*. The keeper of the artifact, or keeper for short, is the set of functionalities related to the storage and manipulation of the artifact.

Two examples of non computer-mediated keepers are the white board in a brainstorming session in which three engineers are drafting a new circuit, and the draft of a business contract that is circulating among some executives who write their comments about the contract on the margins.

These two examples reflect an important distinction among keepers: there are keepers that allow for more than one user at the same time to alter the artifact, such as the white board, whereas some other keepers do not.

In groupware systems some typical keepers are:

- systems that allow for revision of documents [41]. In such systems, a single person writes a document and then submits it to be reviewed by others. The reviewers may attach comments to segments of the document, or propose changes to it. Then the original author receives the comments, proposals of change, and so on, and changes the document, which may be again submitted to more reviews.

- concurrent editors [16], that allow more than one user to change the same file/document at the same time.

- computer aided design (CAD) and computer aided software engineering (CASE) tools [6].

Functionalities that fall within the keeper are:

- control access rights to the objects. Not all participants have the same rights to the objects that make up the artifact or the same rights to perform certain operations onto these objects. For example in a document reviewing groupware, the reviewers do not have the right to change the real document, they only have the right to attach comments and substitutions to it. In some systems one reviewer do not have the right to read other reviewer's comments, whereas in others, the reviewers can both read and comment each other's contributions.

- control of simultaneous access to the artifact. Some groupware allow for simultaneous changes to the artifact. This poses the problem of maintaining the consistency of the artifact: if two simultaneous and contradictory changes are submitted to the keeper, how will it perform them?

- versioning of the artifact. In some applications it is important to store stable situations of the artifact during the process and to allow the artifact to be restored to such stable situations.

- storage of time stamp and author information on objects of the artifact. Some groupware allow a user to view just the changes performed since she last logged on, or the changes made by another participant.

■ floor control. Some groupware systems use a mechanism of floor control to avoid simultaneous access to the artifact, for example a classroom blackboard. At each time only one user has the right to change the artifact (the participant that has control of the floor). Other users may request the floor which will be granted by the system as soon as the participant that has the floor relinquishes it.

### Ontological Model — Model for Keepers

The ontological model is a description of the objects and operations that can be used to construct and manipulate the artifact; the semantics of such objects and how they should be used.

Sometimes, a precise description of how the objects should be used is the essence of a groupware system. That is the case of QuestMap [44]. QuestMap product evolved from the experimental gIBIS [11] system, and as with the other members in the IBIS family it supports decision making by structuring the discussions. It implements the IBIS model of discussion and decision developed during the early 1970 [35]. The IBIS model proposes that decision making about "wicked problems" should be performed in three phases: *divergence*, when solutions to the problems are creatively suggested, *convergence* when after listing all alternatives the group converges to a few of them, and *decision* when all in the group are convinced of the solution to be adopted. Of these three phases the IBIS model considers the first as the most important and proposes that in that phase the participants make a clear distinction between the questions, the solution for those questions, and the arguments in favor or against those proposed solutions. Questions are named *issues* in IBIS and solution are named *positions*.

QuestMap is a tool to support the divergence phase: the discussion is the collective construction of a graphical map that contains nodes to represent issues, positions and arguments; and different links connecting these nodes. By clicking on a node, the user accesses the content of the node: the statement of an issue, position, or argument. Each user can add new objects to the discussion and can delete objects created by herself. All users can access and change the map simultaneously, and their changes will be transmitted to all other participants, or they can access and change the map asynchronously.

Another component of the ontological model is its *concurrency control*: how are simultaneous access and change requests to the artifact dealt with. Some systems would not allow for concurrent change to the artifact because either their collaboration model does not allow for concurrent activities that may access the artifact, or because their mechanism of floor control is restrictive. There are many varieties of floor control. Many systems implement a floor control mechanism in which only one participant at a time has the right to perform changes to the artifact or artifact attributes. Those changes may occur in a fashion that is immediately visible to all group members. A common feature of concurrent systems is the existence of a group window (for example GROVE, a concurrent group editor [16]) in which the same view is displayed to all participants. The region of the artifact that is being viewed in all group windows is controlled by one of many possible floor control mechanisms.

In some other systems, there is no floor mechanism but there is some form of locking: a participant protects a region of the artifact by placing a lock that prevents other users from making changes within that region (for example REDUCE [10]). Some other systems accept all operations from the participants and deal with inconsistent ones in an application dependent way.

Another component of the ontological model is *currency*: how up-to-date are the views that each participant has of the artifact. Depending on the implementation, some systems may present an out-of-date view of the artifact to the participants. In such cases the model may specify a mechanism allowing a participant to request the current version of the artifact, or if this is done automatically, how frequent is the update. Also the model has to specify what happens with changes that are performed on out-of-date views of the artifact. Many options exist. For example, they may remain local, they may be later merged into the current version of the artifact, or they may be sent to the current version immediately. Another issues is how are inconsistencies due to the lack of currency dealt with.

### 10.3.2   Coordinators

Sometimes collaborating is each participant of the group performing some activity, possibly but not necessarily an individual activity, in a previously defined order. The coordinator of activities, or coordinator for short is the set of functionalities related to this temporal evolution of the system, the enabling of an activity after all its preceding activities are terminated.

A prototypical non-computer-mediated coordinator is the production line in a factory. In the production line, the process of constructing, say a car, was carefully and previously divided into a set of individually performed and temporally ordered activities. This example also shows one of the limits of our aspect model: in a line of production, the point is the construction of the artifact, that is the car. In fact there is almost always some data involved in a coordinator system: people frequently perform their activity upon some data that is passed along to the person that will perform the next activity in line. But we claim that in most coordinators this data is not really shared, the data flows overwhelmingly in one direction, that is, as soon as someone has terminated her activity and performed all the changes in the data, that person will not receive that data again in the process. Keepers to store and control such data are simple (or uninteresting) because the changes to the data are linear and predictable. We claim that for such systems, the coordinator aspect is much more interesting than the keeper aspect, and thus we call them coordinators.

Other non-computer mediated coordinators are techniques for meeting management such as the Delphi method [37].

Some typical groupware with strong coordinator components are:

- workflow management systems [30]
- software process management systems [19, 22].
- some examples of meeting coordinators and group decision support systems [51]

The basic functionalities of a coordinator are centered on the execution (or enactment) of a *plan*, or a sequence of activities (sometimes called a procedure or a process). The coordinator is responsible for insuring that an instance of a process follows its predefined plan. This is also referred as *enacting* the plan or model for that process. Some functionalities related to enactment are:

- enabling an activity once its preceding activities have terminated.
- notification to the users that they may start a particular activity or that a particular activity is late.
- inspecting the current stage of a process. Some systems allow privileged users to obtain various information about the process state, such as which activities have been completed, and when, and by who, and which activities are being carried on.
- dynamic alteration of a process description to cope with surprises. Very few of the existing coordinators allow for changes on the plan of a process. Changes to the plan are important in dealing with unexpected situations, that were not taken into consideration when the plan was conceived.
- helping participants to manage their work. Some systems, such as workflow systems, deal with more than one process at a time. For example, John's purchase order and Bill's travel reimbursement may both be processed under the control of the same workflow system although they are instances of different processes. In such cases there will usually be many activities attributed to a single actor, and the workflow management system may help that actor by displaying the list of activities to be performed by that actor, displaying the deadlines, and allowing the user to choose which activity she wants to perform.

Another important group of functionalities of coordinators centers on defining the plan itself. This is also referred as *modeling*. In general terms, the plan or model is a description of the sequence of activities that should be performed, who will perform them, when they must terminate, and so on. Most coordinators allow for some form of definition of the plan. Meeting support systems sometimes have a predefined sequence of activities, but allow the users to define who will perform them and when should they be finished. Workflow systems and software process management systems allow for the definition of not only who will perform the activities and when, but also what activities will be performed, which supporting tools and environment will be available for each activity, and in what order the activities should be executed.

### Coordination Model

The main concept of the coordination model is that of an *activity*. Other important concepts are *role* and *actor*. An activity is a potential set of operations (and the corresponding objects) that an actor playing a particular role can perform, with a defined goal. In general, an actor may be a user, a computer system, or a group. The actor carrying out the activity is called the performer of the activity. A set of activities and the ordering among them make up a *procedure*. Some coordinators are designed for a single procedure, for example software inspection, others, such as workflow systems deal with multiple processes, such as "order processing procedure" and "travel reimbursement procedure" for example.

More than one instance of each procedure may be "executing" at the same time: there may be many order processing jobs being carried out simultaneously in a company for many different customers. Each of this instances of the procedure will be called an *endeavor*.

The coordination model has two components, as indicated above: a component that deals with the modeling of the process and one that deals with the enactment. The plan is a predefined specification on how an endeavor will or should proceed. The plan specifies the activities and their goals, who perform them, the objects and operations available in each activity, the order in which the activities should be performed, when should the activities end, etc. We will call the part of the plan that defines which activities should be performed and in what sequence as the *activity plan*. The component that describes who will perform what activity is the *actor assignment*, and the component that defines deadlines as the *temporal plan*.

The coordination model has to specify which of these components are fixed and which can be set by the user. Some systems have a fixed activity plan, but both the actor assignment and temporal plan can be set by the user. In such systems, the fixed activity plan reflects a methodology that is embedded into the system. Document reviewing systems is an example of a coordination model with fixed activity plan. Other coordinators that have a fixed activity plan are meeting management systems.

Other coordinators allow for all parameters of a plan to be defined by the user. Workflows and software process management systems are examples in this category. Such systems are limited by the language used to define the activity plans, the actor assignment and so on.

The enactment component of the coordination model defines the relationship between the plan and the execution of an endeavor: is the plan a specification of what will happen with the endeavor, or just a suggestion. In other words, is it possible, at enactment time, to change the plan for a particular endeavor or not. This replanning for a particular endeavor may be important to deal with unplanned, unexpected, or exceptional situations. In a workflow system, the order processing endeavor for a particular case may have to follow a different plan than the one predefined because, for example, that customer, which is the most important customer of the company, needs to receive the goods ordered in a very short time.

In this case, the plan for that endeavor may be altered to skip some activities.

Another aspect at the enactment level is whether the system controls/monitors more than one endeavor at the same time. For example a document review system may not be designed to monitor more than one endeavor. In this case, although many documents can be reviewed at the same time, each document is being controlled by a separate instance of the document reviewing system, and each instance does not know about the others. In such a case, the system (or better an instance of the system) cannot know that a particular reviewer is overburdened with five other reviews.

Multiple-endeavor systems may also help users manage their work. Since the system knows about all activities that are assigned to a particular actor, it can provide the actor with information such as which activities are urgent, and which are late.

### 10.3.3   Communicators

Communication is a basic aspect of any collaborative endeavor. In a mainly keeper application there is (implicit) communication when one participant changes the artifact, and that is known to the others. Also, in a mainly coordinator application there is (implicit) communication when one participant finishes an activity and that enables another participant to start the next activity. But many times there is need for explicit communication among people. The communicator aspect groups the functionalities that allow different users to communicate explicitly among themselves.

Two non-computer mediated examples of communicator are telephone and letters. These two examples also illustrate an interesting distinction among communicators: whether they are same time (real-time) or different time (off-line).

Typical groupware communicators are:

- e-mail.

- desktop conferencing systems (for example [43, 46]). These systems allow a group of people to communicate through audio and/or video from their desktop computers. Some systems allow for all users to both transmit and receive, while others allow only one person to transmit while the others only receive.

- chat and muds/moos (for example [36]). These systems allow for a group of people to interact mainly through text. Participants send their contributions either to the whole group or privately to some subset of the whole group, and each participant sees all messages sent to the group or to her privately.

- white-boards (for example [46, 40]).

Typical functionalities of communicators are:

- sending and receiving a message.

- joining and leaving a conference.

- management help functions and abbreviations, such as mailing lists, alias, and so on.

### Conference and Conversational Models

The conference and conversational models are the underlying models of communicators. The conference model describes whether only two or more people can communicate and how that communication is initiated, and if more than two party conferences are allowed, how new people join the conversation, whether it is possible within a multi-party conversation to talk privately to some subset of the group, and so on. The conference model must also specify whether all participants can transmit/receive, and if not how one switches from transmitting to receiving.

The conversational model describes what are the conversational moves allowed in the communication, how participants take turns in performing these conversational moves, what are appropriate conversational replies to the moves, how the groupware can help the user manage each conversation, and manage multiple conversations.

In real time communicators the emphasis is on the conference model. It is assumed that the participants themselves will manage the conversation. For example, in a video-conference system once the participants "get together" in a conference (following the system's particular conference model) it is assumed that the participants will understand when someone's contribution is a question, for example, because the participants will use the group/culture/language appropriate markers and intonations to convey the question. In other words, it is usually left to the participants, and not to the system, to interpret the conversational moves and follow (or not) the appropriate cultural/group protocols for such moves.

In some video-conference systems, such as IVS [29] all participants transmit video but only one transmits sound, while the others listen. Once the participant terminates her contribution she releases the sound control to others. In CU-SeeMe [14] all participants can transmit video and sound, and each participant chooses which video and sound transmissions to receive.

In off-line communicators, the emphasis is on the conversational model. Because there may be a long period between one conversational message and its reply, the groupware system, if it incorporates an appropriate conversational model, may provide help to its users. It may help a user that just received a message to figure out its context, that is, what are the other conversational messages that preceded this one, and what are the appropriate replies to it. The system may help the user by listing all messages that need reply, and what kind of reply is appropriate for each of them, list all conversations that have not yet reached a final state, list all previous conversations, and so on.

Furthermore the conversational model may state that some types of messages need no reply but should be processed automatically. For example, let us assume that the conversation model specifies that a message of acknowledgment of receipt should be sent in response for a message in which the field "acknowledge-receipt" is set. The communicator not only can send this acknowledgment upon receiving an incoming message with the field set, but can also process incoming acknowledgments and alert the user of messages that the user sent more that 2 days ago and for which there has been no acknowledgment.

An communication system that has an elaborate and explicit conversation model is The Coordinator [52, 21]. The Coordinator implements Winograd and Flores' model of conversation for actions. In the model a conversation is started by a request (to do something, before some time). The recipient may accept the request, may refuse it, or may negotiate. If the request is accepted, maybe after negotiations, and performed, the recipient of the request declares it completed, which is accepted or not by the original sender. Each message identifies itself as a particular message type called a "conversational move" in an ongoing conversation. For example the user would understand that a particular message is user B's modified request after a first round of negotiations and that this user appropriate response would be to accept, reject, or re-negotiate this new request. Furthermore, The Coordinator would assist the user to manage her obligations: the user would be able to list which requests from others she has accepted and still has to perform, and when are they due, which request the user has not answered yet, which of her requests has not been performed until now and so on.

The clarity of the Coordinator's conversational model has caused a large impact in groupware research, and there has been much discussion, debate and study about the usage of this type of system [49, 15].

### 10.3.4   Team-Agents

Team agents are artificial participants that perform specialized functions within a group setting. Besides groupware modules which must be concerned with the operation of the entire groupware system, there are frequently modules which are built to perform specific non-global subtasks. These frequently involve specialized domain knowledge; we call these modules team agents. Examples include the "performance specialist" within a software engineering team, and the "social mediator" within an electronic meeting. Neither of these examples is concerned with the overall workings of the system, but each contributes useful functionality in a specialized domain as part of a group. Thus each is a team agent. Ideally, team agents act as if they were full fledged, actively participating members of the group.

An important distinction within the category of team agents is *autonomous agents* versus *single user agents* versus *group agents*. Autonomous agents primarily work alone on an independent subtask; single user agents (e.g. user interface agents) interact with, and work for a single participant within the group; group agents interact and collaborate with the various members of the group as a true colleague. Group agents thus need a good understanding of the goals, structures, and personalities of the group, and of their role within the group.

### Group Critic

Some (single-ware) computer aided design (CAD) systems have critics that comment or check the user's designs. Critics are AI programs that tap into an artifact being developed and reports problems with the design. For example, the critic described in [20] warns the designer of problems in kitchen design such as a stove too close to a window and so on. Although at the time of the writing of this chapter there was no group-CAD that incorporated critics, it is conceivable that they will in the short future. Such critics would be good examples of team-agents.

As a team agent, and more specifically as a group agent, a group critic must be aware that the problems it find in the design are the result of different users acting on different goals and all are responsible for the problem. For example, if the critic detects that the stove is too close to the window it must warn the user that placed the window and the user that placed the stove, even if placing the stove was done last.

### Appointment Scheduler

A popular groupware application is group calendaring and scheduling of meetings [50]. Such softwares allow one to schedule a meeting among a group of people by selecting a free time slot for all meeting participants. In order to do that, the scheduler must have access to each participant's individual calendar. An interesting scheduler would also know about peoples' preferences for meeting hours, and in case of a cancellation of a meeting this system could re-arrange some of the meetings so the participants would be happier with their times.

The appointment scheduler, specially the implemented ones are mainly autonomous agents. But depending on the functionalities it may also be a single user agent. An appointment scheduler that knows about its user's preferences and pro-actively tries to satisfy those preferences is certainly acting on behalf of its user.

### 10.3.5   Agent Models

It is important to notice that the use of the term agent in this chapter is broader than its use in most of the other chapters in this book. Agent is any automatic process; it does not need to be "intelligent" or "autonomous" in the sense used in other chapters.

In particular, for the purposes of this chapter, an autonomous agent is a program that runs independently, and has no interaction with any user. An autonomous agent may tally the votes in a decision meeting, it may compile a program in a software development workflow, it may print an acceptance letter based on a template and data available in a database, and so on. None of these activities are considered intelligent. But an autonomous agent may choose a particular methodology and tool for a meeting, based on the problem [1], or another agent may plan the sequence of activities to be performed based on the goals to be achieved

[12]; these are more "intelligent" activities.

A model of an autonomous agent will not be developed in this chapter. The theories and models put forth in the other chapters are all relevant to define, classify and model autonomous agents.

Group agents are programs that interacts with all participants and thus "should behave like a participant" therefore group agents should incorporate a model that at least describes what is "to behave like a participant." But there are no implemented group agent and thus there is not enough experience to abstract into a group-agent model.

### *User Agent Models*

Groupware reflects a change in emphasis from using the computer to solve problems to using the computer to facilitate human interaction. Users can best take advantage of this changed emphasis via systems with user-interfaces especially designed for groupware. We call these group user-interfaces. The issues that designers of group user-interfaces face are challenging and are significant extensions of the usual issues of interfaces for single-user systems. Thus the user interface conceptual model is highly concerned with representation of human-human interaction, and significantly transcends single user interface models. The model has four components:

- views of information objects and operators
- views of process and communication;
- views of participants;
- views of shared context.

Firstly, the user interface for a participant in a groupware session must be capable of presentation of the objects and operations embodied in the ontological model as previously defined in this chapter. Since different participants may have different abilities (or different perspectives), the user interface model includes the concept of multiple views of objects and the concept of local operations which are typically not present in single user models.

Besides the ontological model data, the user interface in a groupware system may have to deal with other "meta objects". Examples include telepointers and group windows [16]. For example, on systems that allow for inspection of the stage, the user-interface has to display this information.

Views of objects derives from the fact that different participants may want to have different views of the same objects of the system. For example, in a GDSS, an object may be semantically an array of numbers, but one participant may opt to view it as a bar chart, another may prefer to see it as a pie graph, or as a table. All these different representations are views of the same object, and in principle it should be an issue related to the user interface. Furthermore, if one of the operations allowed upon this generic array object is to alter the values of its elements, the operation has to be translated appropriately to each view of the object. In the bar chart view of the table, one could change the corresponding element by stretching the height of the bar corresponding to the element. In a table view, one could type the element index and change its value using the keyboard.

Similarly, in an IBIS one participant may want to view the network of issues, positions and arguments as a graphic network of connected nodes. Another may want to view it as linearized text, indented appropriately to differentiate issues from positions from arguments.

The concept of local operations derives from the observation that group editing is a common and necessary operation in many groupware systems, but all edits need not be seen immediately by all participants. There are decisions or options that must be built into each groupware system concerning granularity of edits and locality and when to transmit to others. If an edit operation is part of a real time synchronous interaction, then a WYSIWIS ("what-you-see-is-what-I-see") system may transmit the edit immediately to all participants. Alternatively, within an asynchronous system, edits may not be transmitted to other participants until a save operation is executed. For many existing systems, when entering data through the keyboard, the system considers all key presses as local operations until the return key is pressed. Thus composing a line is an atomic operation. Finally, it should be pointed out that in some systems, operations on meta objects, e.g. pointer movement, are permanently local operations which are never transmitted to other participants.

In a group editor system, for example, if the participant realizes that he mistyped the last character, he would press the backspace key and erase it. If we were to consider that within a real time interaction, it might be transmitted immediately. In GROVE and the Unix talk program, backspace key presses are object level operations, and are transmitted immediately. Clearly the level of granularity of operations depends upon the application and the group environment.

In a synchronous system, understanding who is simultaneously doing what is useful, and should be presented to users. In an asynchronous system, it is useful to understand who did what since the user last signed on. This leads to the notion of "view of the process." Workflow systems are a clear example where it is useful to have answers to questions of what step preceded mine, and what follows. The user should be able to see upon demand, a simple view of which workcases are in which stages. As exceptions arise in processing, formal and informal communication ought to be facilitated. Maps of who holds which positions, and who talks to whom help to make communication visible.

Groupware is much more concerned with assisting people to people communication than single-user systems. Providing some convenient means of knowing other participants, and what they are doing is an important aspect of our model. The identity of a participant is not directly related to the completion of the endeavor, but this information can be extremely helpful to the other participants in evaluating the situation of the group dynamics. For example, knowing that Smith is in a group long-distance discussion mediated by an IBIS, may lead the other participants to formulate their contributions in different ways than if Smith was absent.

GROVE, for instance, provides this context information by displaying the pictures of the participants at the bottom of each group window. Systems of video windows, video walls, virtual rooms, and virtual realities may display the real time video images of participants which helps with the evaluation of everybody's attention and mood during the session. ClearBoard, for example, allows shared video drawing, while super-imposing the image of the collaborating colleague [28]. This allows eye contact and gaze awareness, while still focusing on the work artifact.

In addition to displaying participants, it is possible to present, in an unobtrusive manner, relevant status, background, and preferences of participants. Benford discusses concepts of auras, nimbus, focus, and adapters [3], all of which are within the scope of the group user interface model. Group information such as the social network of who talks to whom can be presented, and the view of this can be tailored to the viewing participant. For example, if there is a relevant and significant shared previous experience between Smith and me, then I would like to be reminded, and associate this with Smith.

Other possible forms of participant context information are: group opinion on relevant issues, extent to which participants know each other, status of the communications technology, how are the participants geographically distributed; information from a database on relevant aspects of each participant; etc. The information on the geographical distribution of participants may help long distance participants to realize that the subgroups that are in the same place may have developed other protocols of communication besides the one enforced by the collaboration model of the system. Remote response time information may help the division of labor among the group members so that the tasks of a long-distance participant should not depend on high currency. Finally, information about other participants may help a user to place the context of the other participants contributions.

Another area of presentation that should be dealt with by a group user interface is all of the useful background material that we call context. The choice of what and how to present contextual information is a challenge, and that context may include items as diverse as the time of the next meeting, the current weather, and the presence of new mail messages from other participants.

We categorize contextual information as structural, social, or organizational, Structural context includes what and where data, such as the set of interactions in which I am currently participating, and temporal information such as what data has changed since I last accessed this hypertext web. Within a software engineering project, useful context may include languages and case tools used, status of various code and documentation files, and future milestones.

Social context includes items such as group norms, group metrics, and social history of the group. One proposed metaphor of shared virtual reality is that different projects would take place in dramatically different virtual rooms. Thus, the group's difficult design project would take place in a Tahitian hut, and the formal election processes always takes place in a London House of Lords; just the act of re-entering these contexts might trigger much useful contextual information in the heads of the participants. The research work on GroupAnalyzer [38] explored the efficacy of providing an electronic meeting barometer for groups in face to face interaction. This is an excellent example of the utility of graphical context presentation.

Organizational context can apply to small groups, large corporations, countries, or international organizations. It potentially includes formal reporting and responsibility structures of the group such as the organization chart. Also included are other items such as rules of the organization (procedures manuals, etc.,) and inter-organizational data (competitive edge, mergers, etc.) In general, it must be understood that a meeting or any interaction is not an event in isolation, so these contextual clues provided by the user-interface can make the difference between a successful interaction versus a failure.

Finally, we note that participants are not context! Context connotes objects and conditions that are in the background. A primary function of groupware is support of communication and collaboration among participants, so participants are in the foreground.

### 10.3.6   An Example of Aspect Analysis of a Groupware

Let us discuss some different possible implementations of whiteboards which mix aspects from communicators and keepers. Whiteboards are group drawing tools, somewhat like a group Paint. Whiteboards have a strong communicator component, specially the conference model. People may join and leave a ongoing whiteboard session.

The simpler whiteboard has one cursor for each participant. The participant by moving the cursor around sets some pixels to, say, black, and each participant sees the composition of all contributions. The canvas can be seen as a keeper, but a trivial one. The objects maintained buy the keeper are pixels and the only operation available is to set them on. There is no problem of concurrent access to the same pixel, and the currency of each participant's view is not critical.

In a more elaborate whiteboard, each participant still has her own cursor but each cursor paints the canvas in a different color. The objects maintained by the keeper are a little more complex, pixels with colors, but still very simple. An even more elaborate whiteboard in terms of its keeper model would be one in which each participant paints on her own transparent canvas, and each participant can choose whose canvas or canvases she wants to see. Now the ontology model is yet more complex. Finally, let us assume that the system is also used asynchronously, and that each participant can choose to see only the changes made by some particular participants since she last logged into the system. Now the ontology model includes objects like canvas, time and author stamps, and so on. But all these versions of a whiteboard are simple in regard to object coordination, or concurrency control.

A whiteboard system that is more complex in terms of concurrency control, even though it has a very simple ontological model, is the first whiteboard modified so that there is only one cursor for the whole group. The cursor is the resource that needs to be controlled by the keeper, and some way of passing this control must be planned. It could be a first come first serve floor control with explicit release (the one that holds the cursor must explicitly release it, and control will pass to the first one waiting in line for it), or release by timeout (after a period of inactivity the cursor goes to the next in line). Or the cursor may be owned by some privileged participant that may pass temporarily the control of the cursor to one participant, but may regain its control any time she wants.

## 10.4    Multi-Aspect Groupware

The aspects model of groupware is interesting because not only does it serve as a guide to the designers and users of groupware systems but it also allows for a perspective on the past research on groupware and we believe can point the way to future research in the field.

Most Groupware research done until the 90's were single-aspect systems, that is, a system in which functionalities within one aspect overwhelm the functionalities within other aspects. But there are some exceptions, such as document reviewing systems (for example [42]) which mix keepers with coordinators. Another such system is The Coordinator [52, 21], which mixes communicators with coordinators.

We will describe below the Chautauqua workflow system, which mixes all the four aspects described above.

### 10.4.1    Chautauqua — A Multi-Aspect System

Chautauqua is an Internet based collaboration management system designed and implemented within the Collaboration Technology Research Group [13] at the University of Colorado, USA, and the Center for Informatics (ZID) at the University of Arts, Austria. This exploratory prototype, which has been in test usage since 1995, illustrates the possibilities and advantages of tight integration of coordinator, keeper, communicator, and agents. At its base, this system is a workflow management system. However, unlike conventional workflow systems, this system carefully incorporates functionality for goal based reasoning, for real time interaction, and for flexible, human controlled dynamic change [18].

The history of workflow products in corporate America has been mixed; more systems have silently died than been successful [24]. Workflow has been heavily criticized because of its typically inflexible and dictatorial nature compared to the way that office workers really accomplish tasks. Chautauqua attempts to address these criticisms by being strictly a subservient system—it incorporates novels features including flexible exception handling mechanisms, representation of inconsistent concurrently updated information, assistance for simultaneous group editing, and powerful, verifiable dynamic change capability. All of these features are accessible to any and all users with appropriate access rights.

Thus, the information concerning procedural specifications associated with the coordination aspect, which we call organizational awareness, is the artifact maintained by the sophisticated Chautauqua keeper. This information is available (in graphical, easy to use form) to all users for seeing and understanding the procedures, and also for making changes to the procedures. The keeper must support simultaneous editing of this information, and must be capable of mediating and merging inconsistent information entered by different users. The keeper is thus integrally integrated with the coordinator.

Techniques implemented by Chautauqua for assisting with the above mediation include the concept of "town meetings" and "group decision sessions". Clearly some of the tasks such as problem solving and decision making can be facilitated if the system can schedule and initiate real time video conferences. Being organizationally aware, the workflow system is in a good position to do this. Thus, Chautauqua integrally integrates a communicator.

The dynamic change feature goes far beyond application data update capability to allow open change to control flow and to organizational structures. Furthermore this change can take place in the midst of system enactment without stopping and restarting, or aborting work cases in progress. This feature is implemented via "Change Agents" that have certain global knowledge about the state of the executing system and which work cases are where. Consider a procedure in which task A is specified to execute before task B. If the dynamic structural change is to re-specify that A and B should be done in parallel, then work that is "inside of task A" at the time of change (the change taking effect immediately and instantaneously) may accidentally never execute task B. This is a simple example of potentially complex inconsistencies that can occur if dynamic change is not carefully managed.

In general, the change agent can work with the users and utilize its global knowledge to analyze changes for potential problems. Note that a change can be permanent, or a temporary one time change. Thus, exception handling falls within the dynamic change category. The change agent in Chautauqua is integrally woven into the design of the Chautauqua system, and uses an analytic method based upon graph grammar rules applied to Petri nets to do this change analysis efficiently and effectively. This is yet another example of the importance of designing in the multiple aspects of a groupware system rather than attempting to add on an agent or a keeper as an after-thought.

## 10.5   Social and Group Issues in Designing Groupware Systems

On designing a groupware system, one has to be aware of multiple levels of issues. At the top most level, one has to be aware that because groupware systems deals with groups, intuitions and experiences appropriate for singe-ware may not be appropriate for groupware.

For example, [23] discusses that group appointment schedulers are used in real work situations far less than the intuitions of someone that had to schedule a meeting among a couple of people would suggest. Grudin suggests that the explanation for that is that in real, hierarchic work situations there is a strong separation between the people that benefit from the existence of the system (the ones that can call a meeting) and the people that, because of the system, has to do extra work (the ones that have to enter their schedules into the system). If someone fails to mark all her appointments in the system she risks the possibility that the system will schedule a meeting during those unmarked but otherwise busy time slots. On the other hand, it is very to sabotage the system by blocking all time slots; by marking all time slots as busy, one will not have to enter one's detailed schedule, nor risk having a meeting scheduled at a busy time slot.

Thus for such a system to be successful the users have to have an incentive to use the scheduler by itself, despite its group benefits. Thus the real issue on the success of failure of a group scheduler is not centered in the group part: finding a free time slot, communication protocols that would allow users in different computer to schedule a meeting and so on. The central issue is providing functionality that pleases the user when using the system as a single-ware. If that is resolved, then the designer has to deal with the next level of issues, in this case the ones that relates to the group functionalities. If the user decides to use the system as his calendar tool, then this user will probably not be happy if his daily appointments were made known to other users when they try to schedule a meeting with her. Thus the issue of privacy, which is a very important issue when dealing with groups, becomes relevant at this level.

Because groupware systems have to be used by all participants, there is an all/nothing or sometimes critical-mass characteristic to the adoption of such systems. Using the scheduler example above, if one of the team members decides not to use the scheduler, either because she does not like the user-interface or the functionalities, the whole team cannot use system as intended.

In other cases the issue is not whether a whole team adopts or not a groupware system, but whether a single user decides to adopt a new technology that would allow her to participate in some collaboration. This shows a critical mass characteristics: it is only attractive to adopt a new communication technology, say voice electronic mail, if enough of the people one wants to talk has voice electronic mail.

In order for a groupware systems to be adopted and accepted its designer must be aware of the issues above, but even more important, he must be aware of how the people for whom the system is being build really work. There is a difficult and moving line between wanting to improve how people work together by means of a groupware system and not violating how the work is done without such system [15].

More and more research reported in Groupware conferences are analysis of work practices, the influence of technology in these practices, the influence of a particular groupware system on a team, aspects of the adoption (or not) of a groupware system, and so on. For example [5] describes the use of anthropology to understand the work practices of a group as part of the methodology to design a particular groupware system. [47] describes the two distinct views about work in organizations and its impacts on the design of groupware systems.

## 10.6   Supporting Technologies and Theories

We believe that the espoused taxonomy of keepers, coordinators, communicators, and agents is not only useful at the application level, but also at the middleware (resource managers, protocols, etc.) level and at the underware (hardware, basic resource providers, etc.) level. In this section, we discuss supporting technologies, where technology is interpreted in the broad sense to include hardware underpinnings, software underpinnings, and conceptual underpinnings. Thus, communications hardware, software construction kits, toolboxes, protocols, and underlying theories are included.

We also note in passing that any lower level category of technology may be useful for the implementation of several different categories at higher levels. Thus, for example, low level technology such as Ethernet, which is in the communicator category, is very useful and important to implement higher level communicators, but also to implement items in the high level coordinator category. Otherwise there is no vehicle for synchronization signals to get from one module to another.

### 10.6.1   Keepers

At the bottom underware level there are numerous examples such as RAID disks and CD-ROM technologies that form data storage underpinnings for groupware applications. At the middleware level, examples include file and database systems, particularly distributed ones. We should also mention conceptual middleware such as object oriented and relational database schema technology. All of these technologies help to support generic application level groupware such as organizational memory and electronic librarians; also groupware in the keeper category targeted toward a specific application, such as group CAD systems.

### 10.6.2   Coordinators

Coordinators may range from workflow systems to GDSS to the UNIX Make software. Middleware that greatly facilitates the construction of this includes the ISIS synchronizer [7], workflow meta-systems such as ADONIS [33], and at a lower level, network operating systems. At the lowest levels, we find interrupt hardware as a primitive that handles coordination at the lowest level. Kernel schedulers are software just above the interrupt hardware that would also be categorized as coordination underware. Although ATM transmission technology is within the communicator category, the ATM switch is a sophisticated technology that is strictly concerned with synchronization—it is within the coordination underware category.

Some of the conceptual underpinnings for coordination seem to fall close to the boundary between middleware and underware. We feel that the speech act primitives [48] are indeed conceptual primitives and fall within the underware category. On the other hand, process description languages such as ICNs, and fundamental models of coordination such as Petri nets seem to fall within the middleware category because they are really concerned with the description and management of coordination.

### 10.6.3 Communicators

Communicators at the application level may range from generic email and video conferencing systems to very application specific systems. Increasingly more and more remote collaboration is performed over the Internet using the MBone technology [34, 40], and modern successors to it [46]. On the one hand, the specific tools for MBone video, audio, and whiteboard are at the application level. On the other hand, the underlying multicast protocols are middleware, and the hardware systems which allow implementation of efficient MBone multicast protocol are underware. At the communication underware level, many examples such as Ethernet exist. And below this there is much work on wireless transmission, and on satellite transmission, and etc. As previously mentioned we definitely consider conceptual technologies within our categories. Thus, there are many communication protocols which fall within the communication middleware category. The well-known ISO seven layer communication protocol is an example. Of course the lowest layer of this is clearly underware, and the highest, 7th layer, is clearly and strictly at the application level, but all other layers are middleware. Finally, we remark that the Internet and the WWW when viewed from our taxonomy, are not synonymous with groupware (contrary to some vendors claims.) In fact the Internet is simply one of many possible communication vehicles, and the various parts of this technology need to be placed in various sub-categories. Thus, HTTP, the hypertext transport protocol, is simply one of many choices of middleware for implementation of groupware. This needs to be clearly distinguished from HTML, the hypertext markup language, which is not concerned with communication but with presentation to the user. It thus falls in the category of user agent technology which is discussed next.

### 10.6.4 Team-Agents

As previously described, we divide agents into categories of autonomous agents, (single) user agents, and group agents. The other chapters in this book describe both technological and conceptual underpinning of the agents. In the domain of agents supporting users, UIMS's (user interface management systems) and user interface implementation toolkits have been well used to construct sophisticated user agents.

An interesting category which is much less visible is the group agent category. However, one domain where rapid progress is being made is virtual reality for groups of participants. These systems allow multiple participants connected via a network to a virtual reality system to also see (or sense) and interact with each other. These systems sometimes implement the metaphor of a room, a shared desktop, or perhaps a castle or dungeon with dragons. New middleware that can be used to implement these types of systems includes NetEffect, a distributed server based toolkit for multi-user virtual worlds on the Internet [8]. As conceptual middleware, HTML and VRML (virtual reality markup language) are available. At the underware level, multimedia hardware and virtual reality hardware are proliferating. We see this team agents category as an under-represented one where exciting research and development is now happening.

## 10.7  Other Taxonomies of Groupware

### 10.7.1  Space/Time Matrix

[32] classifies groupware systems based on the same space, different space, same time, different time distinction. GROVE and IVS for example, would be both same-time, different-space groupware. Sometimes this distinction is more profitable applied to certain activities or functions within particular groupware rather than to the system as a whole. Let us consider a software inspection system which supports a single programmer writing the code, supports the simultaneous and concurrent inspection of the code by three reviewers that attach comments to segments of the code, and supports the programmer changing the code to suit the reviewers' comments, or discussing with that reviewer why the code is correct as it is, and finally supports the reviewers verification that all their concerns were addressed by the programmer. Is this system same-time or different-time? In fact, its both! But at different stages. This is becoming more prevalent as the needs of groups are becoming better understood.

Furthermore the distinction of whether the activities were performed at the same time or at different times is sometimes not appropriate. In the example above, one could assume that the system would also support that the review activities were performed at different times. What is important is whether the system necessarily requires some activities to be performed at different times, or necessarily require that they are performed at the same time. In the example above, the activity of reviewing and the activity of changing the code had to be performed at different times. That may be because limitations on the keeper component of the application, or it may be because the coordination model so requires: it is reasonable to require that the programmer should not have access to the reviews until they are done, in order to avoid unnecessary argumentation and confusion.

### 10.7.2  Application Area

It is also reasonable to classify groupware systems according to application domains [17]: group editing and reviewing, workflow, group decision support, real-time communication, distance learning, etc. It turns out that groupware systems for some of these application areas fall clearly within one or another aspect. Group editing and reviewing, for example, are typical keeper systems. Workflow systems are typically coordinators.

The application area in which there is some interesting diversity in terms of aspects and models is group decision support, or meeting support. In this area the goal is to provide methodological and technological support for meetings.

In some way meetings can be seen as the most unstructured form of collaboration; however activities within meetings, such as voting, are frequently very rigid and structured. Some systems propose to support meeting by temporally structuring well defined activities, and thus are mainly coordinators with fixed activity plans. Each activity has some predefined goals and need some specific tools, which may be communicators or keepers. For example, many meeting methodologies propose at least an activity of brainstorming [25], in which all participants are encourage to contribute many possible solutions to the problem at hand. An appropriate tool for such activity is a backboard-like communicator, to which the participants submit contributions, usually anonymously [43]. A few other systems, such as those in the IBIS tradition, choose to structure the meeting "spatially" and thus are mainly keepers.

## 10.8   Groupware and Internet

At the time of the writing of this chapter, the word Groupware is frequently accompanied with the word Internet especially in the non academic press. This section tries to elicit the relationship between these two concepts.

In order to do that, we need to model the architecture of a typical groupware system/application. The user will interface with the system through a software component that we will call *user software component* (*USC*). The USC runs in the user's computer, but its functionalities are varied: the USC may include all or just part of the user interface, it may host part, or the whole, or a version of that artifact if the system is mainly a keeper, and so on. The USC must communicate/exchange information with other software components that are, typically, in other computers. Thus if the groupware is a teleconference system, each USC needs to communicate with other USCs and there may be a server component.

In order for the USC to communicate with components in other computers it must make use of services provided by another software components, the *network software component* (*NSC*). It is unimportant whether the NSC is part of the operating system of the user's computer, or if it is implemented explicit as part of the USC. The relevant issue is that the NSC runs in the user machine and it is either provided by that machine or implemented in the USC itself.

Given this abstract architecture of a groupware system, one can elucidate two possible relations between Groupware and the Internet. The first relation, which we call *Internet as infrastructure*, the Internet implements the NSC. In the second relation, which we call *Internet as presumed user software*, the Internet implements the USC.

### 10.8.1   Internet as Infrastructure

The idea behind the Internet as infrastructure is that computers that are on the Internet must have software that allows for some/all of the functionalities required from the NSC. A computer is "connected" to the Internet when it is able to send and receive information according to the many standard protocols (UDP, TCP, FTP, SMTP, NNTP, HTTP, and so on).

Thus, by using the user's computer's own Internet software as NSC, the designer of the groupware avoids having to design the groupware's own NSC (which may be extremely difficult since the services provided by the NSC must necessarily interact with the computer's low level software and hardware), or avoids having to assume that the user's computer has a particular non-standard NSC incorporated into the operating system.

First, it is important to notice that using the Internet as NSC is not the only option available for the designer: computers in a local network may use other protocols that are not available in the Internet; even if the computers are not in a local network, the designed has the option of having one computer phone the other and use non-standard protocols over this phone connection, or the distant computers may be part of a private non-Internet network with its own protocols. But in all these alternatives, the designer has to assume that the user computer will be on the local network, or will have access to a phone line, or will be part of the private wide-area network, and in many of the cases the designer will have to write the NSC herself.

The Internet has some peculiarities that must be taken into account by the groupware designer: it is unreliable, that is messages may not get to their recipients, and it is insecure. Furthermore, at the time of the writing of this chapter, the Internet is still weak concerning protocols for real-time transmissions, and multicasting.

### 10.8.2   Internet as Presumed Software

The second frequent relation between Internet and groupware is that the Internet implements the USC altogether. One Internet software popular for this task is the WWW browser; at the time of the writing of this chapter, to "be in the Internet" is to have access to a WWW browser. By implementing the USC by a WWW browser, all Internet members are potential participants in the groupware. By pointing the browser toward the server in which the applications runs, one becomes a participant in that system.

The advantages of implementing the USC by a WWW browsers are many for the user: there is no need to buy/install a separate USC to become a participant in a system; the user has to deal with a single interface, the same software (WWW browser) can be used for many applications.

But using a WWW browser as the USC has some problems and limitations. The limitations can be separated into three categories: user interface, client-server architecture, and system interface limitations [4].

The WWW browser can display a large variety of information in different media: text, different picture formats and so on. Furthermore for most browsers it is possible to define external programs that will display media types that are not internally dealt with by the browser. These media types include many audio and video formats and also application specific formats, such as postscript, and text editors internal formats. But as an input device, the WWW browser is very limited; it accepts text typed into the fill-in fields, selection of radio buttons and predefined lists, and mouse click on predefined regions of text and on predefined images. No other gestures, such as mouse movement, and single and double clicks are supported. This poses some severe limitations for some applications; it is not possible to write an application in which the users freely draw a diagram, or changes a diagram by dragging some of its components, or build a diagram by placing predefined shapes onto a canvas.

The client-server limitation is also central for the designer of groupware systems. WWW was designed as a typical client-server protocol: it is stateless, that is the server does not remember any of the previous history of communication with the client, and only the client can initiate communication. The first limitation has been long solved in the WWW community either by using cookies [45] or by encoding the state of the communication in the information sent by the client to the server. When the client requests new information, the encoded state is also transmitted and used by the server.

The real problem is the fact that the WWW server was originally designed as "pull" technology. This means that the server cannot initiate communication with the client. This limits applications in which the currency must be high. In a keeper application, for example, if other participants change the artifact, the server cannot warn the client that the artifact has changed unless the server is "push" technology.

The user system limitations are less severe. They refer to the browsers ability to communicate and operate changes into the user's system. WWW browsers typically allow for files to be downloaded, from server to browsers, but not uploaded.

If the user has locally made changes onto the artifact, using software that runs on the user environment, it may not be possible to easily upload it to a central repository or to the other users

The use of JAVA seems to be a solution for all this problems, but at a price. By writing a JAVA program (or applet) that runs on the user's environment the groupware designer is able to overcome the three problems mentioned above. For example the designer may write a program that accepts user's gestures as inputs, or a program that communicates with other components of the system using its own protocol, instead of using the client-server model underlying HTTP. But in the first case the designer will have to write at least the interface components of the USC, and in the latter case, the NSC. The advantage is that the designer does not need to make presuppositions about the user's environment; if JAVA indeed becomes a widely accepted standard then the designer may assume that the user's WWW browser will both be able to run the program and serve as interface to the user's environment. Thus the same USC program will run in different hardware, operating systems and network environments.

## 10.9  Conclusions

The authors believe that future research on groupware will be centered on agents and multi-aspect groupware. There are many forms of mixing aspects into a single system. Let us discuss some.

### 10.9.1  Incorporating Communicators into Keepers

Sometimes participants working in a keeper must communicate to each other directly to understand points of view, to synchronize actions and so on. Some of these communications will be about the artifact and for these communications it would be important to be able to refer to parts of the artifact within the communication, in similar ways that pronouns such as *this*, and *that* are used in conversation to refer to outside entities.

This could be accomplished, for instance, by incorporating a video conference tool within a keeper that would allow synchronous communication among participants, plus some form of telepointer, which would allow the participants to make references to parts of the artifact. The solution is less clear if one also wants to provide off-line communication among the designers.

### 10.9.2  Incorporating Keepers and Communicators into Coordinators

There is a very common view associated with coordinators that the whole process should be decomposed into sub-processes and so on, until one reaches an "atomic" sub-process, usually called a task or an activity, which cannot (or need not) be further decomposed and which is to be performed by a single actor. The model of the production line is a good example of this "decomposition until the individual task" idea. But there are activities which should not be further decomposed and are not individual. In a workflow system, one may have, for example, a "write proposal" activity which is to be performed by a team. This activity should not be further decomposed into smaller activities because that would constrain too much the team creativity to write the proposal.

To support these collective activities within a coordinator, one needs an appropriate keeper. For example in the "write proposal" activity one needs a keeper that would allow all the actors to work on the proposal. Probably one would also need communicators so that the participants can interact beyond the limits of the ontological model of the keeper for that activity.

### 10.9.3   Future Research on Agents

Future research in agents in groupware will follow two directions: (autonomous or group) agents to act on the domain and agents that act on the interaction. Domain agents are similar to the group critic described above: they know about the domain of the collaboration. The kitchen group critic knows about kitchens and stoves and so on. A group critic on bridge building may know about material strength and stress; a group critic on software development may know about coding and naming conventions, or about proving a program correct in relation to its specification, and so on.

An interaction agent does not need to know about the domain of the collaboration but knows about interaction/collaboration itself. These agents could play a role similar to human facilitators in meetings. Such facilitators do not necessarily know about the topic that will be discussed in the meeting but they understand meetings, they know when the discussion is becoming too polarized, when an intermission is appropriate, when there are people and views that could not be expressed because of the dynamics of the meeting, and so on.

An interaction agent would analyze the state of the interaction and propose activities for the participants. For example, given the number of alternatives to answer an issue, an interaction agent may propose one of many voting procedures. Or given the statistics of the messages being exchanged (mainly from a few participants), the agent may propose a different methodology for the discussion. More ellaborate interaction agents may understand some aspects of the messages being exchanged and help to categorize the group in terms of its group dynamics [2].

### 10.9.4   Future Research on Keepers

Another area in which future development would be interesting are the specifiable keepers. Keepers embed an ontology model that is usually fixed, and defined a priori by the groupware designer. But it would be interesting if the users themselves could define or adapt the ontology of the keeper. In the same way that workflow systems are specifiable coordinators, there is a need for specifiable keepers.

In fact Lotus Notes [39], is a specifiable keeper. In a simplistic view, Lotus Notes is a free form database; users (or the system administrators) can define and provide semantics (attach programs) for particular fields of the documents and thus adapt Lotus Notes to particular applications. However, it is not at all easy for naive users to define and adopt.

There is very little research on the languages and primitives appropriate to specify or parameterize an ontology model.

## 10.10   Exercises

1. *[Level 2]* CSCW and Groupware typically complement and help each other. However, sometimes CSCW studies technological mismatch in which certain groupware is inappropriate for certain work situations. Concoct a work situation, and a groupware technology in which this mismatch might occur. Explain why you think that the groupware technology is inappropriate for your concocted work situation.

2. *[Level 2]* Define the terms collaboration, cooperation, and coordination in a way which you feel is clear and useful for the CSCW community. Justify your definitions, and compare / contrast the three terms.

3. *[Level 2]* This chapter also introduced a time-space taxonomy. Criticize this taxonomy. Should there be any further cells than the four which are presented? Are there any further dimensions which should be added to the simple 2X2 matrix?

4. *[Level 2]* Two family of applications were not mentioned in the aspect section. They are multi-user action games, such as DOOM and QUAKE [26], and shared window [53]. Discuss if these systems fall overwhelmingly into one aspect or another, of if they are multi-aspect systems, of if they show that the aspect classification is not complete because it does not capture what is essential in these two softwares.

5. *[Level 2]* There are a few WWW-based chat services available. In most of them, the user fills a form with her utterance and after submitting it, she receives back a page with all recent interactions in the chat. Thus a user cannot "lurk" at the chat, that is, listen to the other conversations without making herself a contribution. But some chat pages allow for real-time chat, in the sense that the page will change to reflect the recent interactions even though the user has not send her contribution. Which non standard WWW technology does these pages use, and what is the network impact of using them.

6. *[Level 2]* Besides WWW-based chats there are many other examples of Groupware applications that use WWW as infrastructure. In particular INOTE [27] is an image annotation system, and BSCS [9] is a central repository of artifacts. Discuss which of the problems mentioned in section 10.8.2 these systems faced and how did they solve them.

7. *[Level 2]* There is a view that the collection of WWW pages available in the Internet is a Groupware system. Discuss this view. If that is true, what are the main aspects of this system? Describe the model underlying this of these aspects? Is it an elaborate model or a trivial one?

8. *[Level 3]* In some places in this chapter we mentioned virtual reality. Investigate if there are groupware applications that use virtual reality as a way

of interfacing with the user. Doesn't current technology VR has some of the problems discussed in using WWW as the underlying infrastructure of groupware? Is VRML, for example, an appropriate technology for non-client-server applications?

9. *[Level 3]* In engineering design there is a strong movement towards "Concurrent Engineering," which state that many specialists in areas such as as marketing, manufacturing, cost, materials, maintenance, and so on, must take part in the design of engineering artifacts. Investigate what groupware tools are being used by concurrent engineering practitioners, specially what multi-user support does CAD systems provide.

10. *[Level 4]* In the writing of this chapter, the authors did not use very elaborated groupware. We divided the chapter into sections and for each section one of us had the writing role, while the other had the reviewing and commenting role. In the beginning we would take turns, once a section was written the author would wait for the reviewers changes and comments before working on that section again. By the end of the writing the interaction became more intense and there times when an author would make changes in a section before receiving the comments, and thus the comments and changes would be out-of-date. We use e-mail to send the LaTeX file from one to the other, that is we used a communicator as the means of our collaboration. Specify a keeper that would be appropriate for the task and for our mode of working. Take into consideration that each of us have different preferences as to which text editor to use, that Internet connection between us was slow and unreliable. The keeper should be appropriate for both the turn-taking and the "closer-to-deadline" working patterns.

11. *[Level 4]* Design a group spreadsheet in which the four aspects described in this chapter are carefully taken into account and articulated. Create a design specification that includes description of spreadsheet operations, multi-user features, group user interface, centralized versus distributed implementation, access control, and concurrency control. Emphasis of your design should be on the groupware aspects and features that allow a group to all use the spreadsheet at the same time, and also at different times. Do not spend much effort on the single user features that are identical to those of single user spreadsheets. State clearly any assumptions or extensions that you make; feel free to suggest creative ideas and innovative designs.

## 10.11   References

1.  P. Antunes, N. Guimaraes, J. Segovia, and J. Cardenosa.  Beyond formal processes: Augmenting workflow with group interaction techniques. In *Conference on Organizational Computing Systems*, pages 1–9. ACM Press, 1995.

2.  R. F. Bales and S. P. Cohen. *SYMLOG: A System for Multiple Level Observation of Groups*. The Free Press, 1979.

3.  S. D. Benford and L. E. Fahlen. A spatial model of interaction in virtual environments. In *Proceedings of The Third European Conference on Computer Supported Cooperative Work (ECSCW'93)*, pages 109–124, 1993.

4.  R. Bentley, U. Busbach, D. Kerr, and K. Sikkel, editors. *Computer Supported Cooeprative Work: The Journal of Collaborative Computing*, volume 6. Kluwer Academic Press, 1997. Special issue on Groupware and the World Wide Web.

5.  R. Bentley, J. A. Hughes, D. Randall, T. Rodden, P. Sawyer, D. Shapiro, and I. Sommerville. Ethnographically-informed systems design for air traffic control. In *Proceedings of the ACM Conference on Computer Supported Cooperative Work (CSCW'92)*, pages 123–129, Toronto, Ontario, 1992. ACM Press.

6.  S. Bharwani. The MIT design studio of the future. Videotape presentation at the ACM CSCW'96 Conference, 1996.

7.  K. Birman. The process group approach to reliable distributed computing. *Communications of the ACM*, 36(12):37–53, 1993.

8.  R. Braham and R. Comerford. Sharing virtual worlds. In *IEEE Spectrum*, volume 34, pages 18–20, 1997.

9.  BSCS. http://bscw.gmd.de/.

10. S. Chengzheng et al. A generic operation transformation scheme for cooperative editing systems. In *Proceedings of the 1997 ACM SIGGROUP Conference on Supporting Group Work*, pages 425–434. ACM Press, 1997.

11. J. Conklin and M. Begeman. gIBIS: An hypertext tool for exploring policy discussion. In *Proceedings of the Second Conference on Computer Supported Cooperative Work*, Portland, OR, September 26–28 1998.

12. W. Croft and L. Lefkowitz. Using a planner to support office work. In *Proceedings of the ACM COIS*, pages 55–62. ACM Press, 1988.

13. CTRG. http://www.cs.colorado.edu/s̆kip/ctrg.html.

14. CU-SeeMe. http://cu-seeme.cornell.edu/W̄CW/.

15. J. Dietz et al. Speech acts or communicative action? In *Proceedings of The 1991 European Conference on Computer Supported Cooperative Work*, pages 235–248, 1991.

16. C. Ellis, S. J. Gibbs, and G. Rein. Design and use of a group editor. In G. Cockton, editor, *Engineering for Human Computer Interaction*. North Holland, 1990.

17. C. Ellis, S. J. Gibbs, and G. Rein. Groupware: Some issues and experiences. *Communications of the ACM*, 34(1):38–58, 1991.

18. C. Ellis and C. Maltzahn. Chautauqua: Merging workflow and groupware. In *Proceedings of the HICSS'96 Conference (Hawaii International Conference on Systems Science)*, 1996.

19. C. Fernstrom. Process Weaver: Adding process support to UNIX. In *2nd*

*International Conference on the Software Process*, pages 12–26. IEEE Computer Society Press, 1993.

20. G. Fischer, K. Nakakoji, J. Oswald, G. Stahl, and T. Sumner. Embedding computer-based critics in the context of design. In *Human Factors in Computing Systems, INTERCHI'93 Conference Proceedings*, pages 157–164. ACM, 1993.

21. F. Flores, M. Graves, B. Hartfield, and T. Winograd. Computer systems and the design of organizational interaction. *ACM Trans. Office Information Systems*, 6(2):153–172, 1988.

22. R. Grinter. Using a configuration management tool to coordinate software development. In *Proceedings of the 1995 ACM SIGOIS Conference on Organizational Computing Systems*, pages 168–177. ACM Press, 1995.

23. J. Grudin. Groupware and social dynamics: eight challenges for developers. *Communications of the ACM*, 37(1):92–105, 1994.

24. W. F. Heitman. The Business Improvement Lab: 1997 Summary of Best Practices, 1997.

25. C. Hwang and M. Lin. *Group Descision Making under Multiple Criteria: Methods and Applications*. Srpinger Verlag, 1987.

26. id Software. http://ww.idsoftware.com/.

27. INOTE. http://jefferson.village.virginia.edu/mar4g/index.html.

28. H. Ishii et al. Clearface: Translucent multi-user interface for teamworkstation. In *Proceedings of The 1991 European Conference on Computer Supported Cooperative Work*, pages 163–174, 1991.

29. IVS. http://www.inria.fr/rodeo/personnel/Thierry.Turletti/ivs.html.

30. S. Jablonski and C. Bussler. *Workflow Management Systems: Modeling, Architecture, and Implementation*. International Thomson Computer Press, 1996.

31. R. Johansen. *Groupware: Computer Support for Business Teams*. The Free Press, New York, 1988.

32. R. Johansen. *Leading Buisness Teams*. Addison-Wesley, Reading, Mass., 1991.

33. D. Karagianis. The adonis workflow system. In *Proceedings of the 1996 Linz Workshop on Workflow Systems*,, Linz, Austria, 1996.

34. V. Kumar. *MBone: Interactive Multimedia On The Internet*. Macmillan Publishing, 1995.

35. W. Kunz and H. Rittel. Issues as elements of information systems. Technical report, Working paper No. 131, Institute of Urban and Regional Development, Univ. of California, Berkeley, 1970.

36. W. Lehnet. *Internte 101*. Addison-Wesley, 1998.

37. H. Linstone and M. Turoff. *The Delphi Method: Techniques and Applications*. Addison-Wsley Publishing Co., 1975.

38. M. Losada and S. Markovitch. Groupanalyzer: A system for dynamic analysis of group interaction. In *Proceedings of the 23rd Hawaii International Conference on Systems Science*, 1990.

39. Lotus. Lotus notes. http://www.lotus.com.

40. Mbone. http://www.mbone.com/.

41. J. H. Morris. Issues in the design of computer support for co-authoring and commenting. In *Proceedings of ACM CSCW'90*, pages 183–195, 1990.

42. C. M. Neuwirt, D. S. Kaufer, R. Chandhok, and J. H. Morris. Issues in the design of computer support for co-authoring and commenting. In *Proceedings of the Third Conference on Computer Supported Cooperative Work*, pages 183–195. ACM, Los Angeles, CA October 7–10 1990.

43. J. Nunamaker, A. Dennis, J. Valacich, D. Vogel, and J. George. Electonic meeting systems to support group work. *Communications of the ACM*, 34(7), 1991.

44. QuestMap. http://www.cmsi.com/business/info/.

45. RFC2109. HTTP state management mechanism. http://www.cis.ohio-state.edu/htbin/rfc/rfc2109.html.

46. M. Roseman and S. Greenberg. Teamrooms: Network places for collaboration. In *Proceedings of the 1996 ACM CSCW Conference*, pages 325–333. ACM Press, 1996.

47. P. Sachs. Transforming work: Collaboration, learning and design. *Communications of the ACM*, 38(9):36–44, 1995.

48. J. R. Searle. *Speech Acts*. Cambridge University Press, 1969.

49. L. Suchman. Do categories have politics? the language/action perspective reconsidered. In *Proceedings of the Third European Conference on Computer-Supported Cooperative Work*, pages 1–14, 1993.

50. ON Technologies. Meetingmaker. http://www.on.com/mmxp/.

51. M. Turoff. Computer-mediated communication requirements for group support. *Journal of Organizational Computing*, 1(1):85–113, 1991.

52. T. Winograd and F. Flores. *Understanding Computers and Cognition*. Addison Wesley, 1987.

53. XTV. http://www.visc.vt.edu/succeed/xtv.html.

# 11 Distributed Models for Decision Support

**Jose Cuena and Sascha Ossowski**

---

## 11.1 Introduction

The outside world is full of systems which are governed by complex laws of behavior. Independently of whether these systems are made of unanimated entities, governed by the laws of physics, organizations of humans with predefined artificial process rules or a mixture of both, often there is a need to influence their dynamics and to bias their evolution into a desired direction. The consequences of natural disasters, such as floods, can be alleviated if the spill gates of dams are managed to distribute the water volume in the watershed basin, keeping rivers and channels from overflowing. In industrial plants the production processes need to be monitored and adapted in order to ensure the quality of the final product, economic efficiency and security. Faults in chemical industries require actions that restore normal conditions and prevent the formation of toxic clouds. Computer networks have to be managed in order to maintain a certain quality of service to the users, which requires upper bounds on message delays etc. In much the same way, companies are interested in maintaining their business processes effective and robust. The flow of work in an office is to be kept smooth despite the illness of employees; material flow on car assembly lines should not be disrupted by any kind of contingencies. Traffic domains comprise a mixture of natural and artificial laws of behavior: road traffic flows have to be influenced so as to avoid traffic jams, to reduce travel times etc. In air traffic control, the primary concern is to influence the planes' routes so as to avoid accidents. This list could be extended easily.

The above examples motivate that it is a major challenge—for both economic and social reasons—to take the adequate control decisions to maximize the efficiency of the systems and to minimize the negative impact of faults. Sometimes one single person, but usually a group of *control personnel* is in charge of taking such decisions and is responsible for their effects. This implies to monitor continuously the system to be managed and requires to take decisions respecting changes in control variables, usually in *real time*. The increasing data volume and the decreasing time horizon within which control decisions have to be taken, have generated a need for computer applications that support the responsible persons in this task. These *decision support systems (DSS)* acquire data about the system state either directly or through a (real-time) database, on top of which they device an intelligent monitoring system that warns the control personnel of undesired evolution and answers their questions concerning potential reasons, effects and therapies. For instance, DSSs assist hydrology engineers to decide upon actions on spill gates, chemical engineers to manage modifications on valves etc. and network administrators on configuring routers, leasing lines and identifying faulty equipment; support to business managers is rendered by suggesting modifications in the usual work process, e.g. by reassigning work tasks or by modifying the route of some product through a jobshop; advice for traffic engineers may consist in suggesting which road traffic signals should be set or which air corridors should be assigned to certain flights.

This chapter is concerned with the principled construction of such DSSs. In particular, it points out how distributed artificial intelligence (DAI) models and architectures can be applied to the domain of Decision Support (DS). In addition, some reflections on the adequacy of DAI models for DS problems are presented: do DAI models and multiagent architectures really produce an "added value" for DSSs; or can everything that DAI systems contribute to the design and implementation of DSS be achieved better and cheaper by carefully engineered systems which are based on a conventional centralized approach?

Section 11.2 characterizes DS problems formally and informally and motivates the potential role of multiagent DS architectures in this domain. Section 11.3 presents a model for distributed DSS and a simple but powerful architecture for the agents that constitute it. The main body of this chapter is section 11.4, where this multiagent architecture is applied to the domains of environmental emergency management, energy management and traffic management. For any of these cases the characteristic domain features are highlighted first, then the generic agent architecture is instantiated to the domain, and finally the dynamics of the distributed DSS is illustrated by "simulating" the agent interactions that an example problem scenario generates. Section 11.5 summarizes the conclusions that can be drawn from these case studies.

## 11.2   Decision Support Systems

This section provides a model of the DS problem and introduces the knowledge-based approach to DSS design. Finally, the adequacy of a distributed approach to DS, based on a multiagent architecture, is discussed.

### 11.2.1   The Decision Support Problem

DSSs render support to the personnel that is in charge of managing natural or artificial systems, each governed by its particular physical and/or organizational behavior laws. So, the "area of interest" of DSS designers spreads from Control

Theory for industrial installations up to Computer Supported Cooperative Work (CSCW) in organizations and groups. Given this diverse nature of the DS domains, it does not surprise that the requirements for DS applications are as manifold as there are complex systems to control. Still, the core of the problem faced by DSS is captured by the following simple model:

- A set of *world states* $S$
  The relevant state of the world with respect to a DS problem is given by the values of the state and control variables of the managed system.

- A set of *ideal states* $S^+$ and/or a set of *undesired states* $S^-$, where $S^+, S^- \subset S$
  Ideal and undesired states determine configurations of values for state and control variables that shall be achieved or are to be avoided respectively.

- A notion of *preference* $\prec$ on states
  The notion of preference expresses "how close" one state is to another. It can be expressed either in qualitative (e.g. a partial order) or in quantitative (e.g. a metric) fashion.

- A set $\Pi$ of *control actions*
  Control actions can be performed on the system to be controlled which change the values of certain control variables directly. State variables are modified indirectly during the evolution of the system as implied by its behavior laws.

In real-world DS applications ideal states are almost never fully achievable. Instead, the objective of a DSS is to generate sets or sequences of control plans $\pi$ so as to transform the current world state $s$ into a state $s'$ that is "as close as possible" with respect to $\prec$ to some ideal state $s_i^+$ and "as far away as possible" with respect to $\prec$ from any undesired state $s_i^-$.

The above semi-formal model is useful to characterize the problem that DSSs face in a less ambiguous way. Still, a whole bunch of quite different domains could be described by a similar formalism. This is because certain characteristic features of DS problems cannot be expressed easily in a formal fashion:

- Critical domains: some of the complex systems to be monitored are sensitive with respect to failures: wrong management decisions may have disastrous economic or environmental consequences.

- Understandable results and explanations: the responsible persons must assume the impact of the management actions that are taken on the system. They will be more inclined to accept suggestions from a DSS that explains its proposals using reasoning schemes and concepts that it is familiar with.

- Heterogeneous information and knowledge sources: The data, that the system needs to cope with, usually ranges from huge amounts of numeric data streams arriving in real time from a variety of different sensors, over visual information from video cameras, to quite informal messages such as telephone calls: incomplete, erroneous or even contradictory data may arrive. In much the same way, a DSS needs to integrate the different and even partially contradictory knowledge and reasoning methods, elicited from several different experts.

- Environmental contingencies: DSSs are embedded in dynamic domains, whose state changes due to events that cannot be anticipated. As a result, a DSS continuously needs to monitor its predictions and plans in order to maintain them in line with the current world state.

Although the degree of automation in the area is increasing, DSSs—as the name indicates—rarely *implement* control actions, in the sense that they seldom manipulate the world directly. Rather, they are expected to interact with the control personnel which is finally in charge of taking certain actions. Though a DSS needs to generate warnings proactively, its main functionality is to assist in the development of an adequate set of control actions and this is done on request of the control personnel. In consequence, the functionality of DSSs is greatly determined by the questions that can be put to a system and the kind of answers that they are able to supply. Crucial questions in the area of DS include [15]:

- *What is happening?*
  The system needs to analyze a situation and "understand" it by identifying advantageous and problematic aspects.

- *What may happen?*
  In many domains, there has to be an ability to reason about the evolution of the systems if no intervention takes place, i.e. in case that no management actions are performed. The main objective of this question is to foresee the decay of the present circumstances into an undesirable future situation, in order to be given the possibility to undertake appropriate counteractions. A variant of this type of question is *what may happen if...* some decision scenarios are undertaken.

- *What should be done?*
  The final aim of a DSS is to answer the questions respecting which are the most convenient actions to improve the results of system operation.

### 11.2.2   Knowledge-Based Decision Support

Keeping in mind the above peculiarities of DS, it becomes clear that the design of such systems actually "calls for" a knowledge-based approach. Knowledge-based systems model the expertise of the control engineers and explicitly represent it in a declarative fashion. By this, the system is not just capable of generating understandable explanations, but it also allows the designer to incrementally improve the expertise model, which has shown to be crucial in complex real world domains. Simulating the control personnel's reasoning process, which has proved to work well in the domain at hand, the system manages to cope with heterogeneous information and knowledge sources and to react adequately to environmental contingencies.

Modern methodologies for the construction of large-scale knowledge systems suggest that the expertise is organized in accordance with some structuring principle, in order to facilitate knowledge acquisition and the maintenance of knowledge mod-

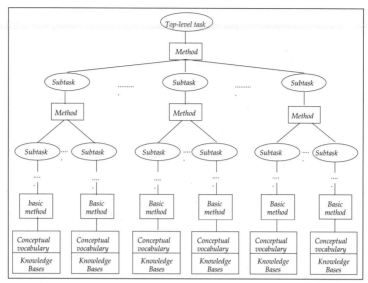

**Figure 11.1**   An example of a task-methods-subtasks tree.

els on the basis of a "divide and conquer" strategy[1]. The task-oriented stance is a way to express the result of such knowledge structuring. A *task* is an abstract description of how the world (or the "mental model" that the intelligent system maintains of it) needs to be transformed in order to achieve a desired behavior or functionality. Obviously, the top-level task of a DSS is to manage a complex system, answering any of the aforementioned questions that the control personnel might pose to it. *Problem solving methods* are used to cope with the tasks. They indicate *how* a task is achieved, by describing the different steps by which its inputs are transformed into its outputs. Simple tasks can be attained directly by means of *basic methods.* They rely on a *conceptual vocabulary* (or "ontology"), which defines the entities that the methods deal with, together with a *knowledge base* modeling the declarative domain knowledge, that describes how these entities are related. The method enactment uses these relations to solve elementary tasks. Still, the complexity of the DS task requires *compound problem-solving methods* that decompose the task into subtasks. These subtasks may again be decomposed by some method etc., giving rise to a task-methods-substasks (TMST) tree, whose leaves are given by basic methods. Figure 11.1 illustrates this approach, which is widely accepted as a general knowledge structure description. [7] [5]

---

1. The resulting structural model is often called a knowledge-level model, based on the idea of the *knowledge level*, as introduced by Newell [21]. A knowledge-level model of intelligent behavior does not focus on *how* it is achieved, but rather on *what* knowledge a system needs to be endowed with, so as to be able to reproduce that behavior, given that the knowledge is applied in a "rational way". The actual representation of the model and its "mechanization" through reasoning procedures is done at the *symbol level.*

When modeling a knowledge-based DSS from a task-oriented stance, the following set of tasks can usually be identified:

- The *classification* task takes as an input all available data about the state of the world and classifies the situation with respect to its desirability (i.e. its distance to $S^-$ resp. $S^+$ with respect to $\prec$). Its output comprises the set of problematic features of the current situation. For instance, a traffic management system will receive numerical data from road sensors, on the basis of which it may classify situations as "fluid", "slight delays at junction x" or "medium congestion in area $\Lambda$".

- On the basis of the problematic features, the "symptoms" that indicate that something is going wrong in the modelled system, the *diagnosis* task comes up with an explanation that identifies the causes of such undesirable behavior. For instance, diagnosis might explain the "medium congestion in area $\Lambda$" by an incident at the outlets of that area.

- The *prediction* task evaluates how the state $s$ of the modelled system will evolve into a state $s'$ given certain values for the control variables. For instance, this task might conclude that if no actions are taken, the congestion in area $\Lambda$ will become heavy, or that a change in the traffic light cycles will lighten the problem.

- The *option generation* task generates a set of plans (i.e. sequences of actions out of $\Pi$) that are considered to be adequate to overcome the problems identified previously. In the example, this will be the different plans' traffic guidance that deviate traffic from area $\Lambda$.

- The *action selection* task decides which of the potential plans proposed previously will be the outcome of the management process.

A major research line in the knowledge-based systems community is concerned with building up libraries of generic problem-solving methods (e.g. the European KADS project [5]). Ideally, for any concise task description, the library should contain methods to cope with it. So, the design process for a traditional "monolithic" knowledge-based DSS can be sketched as follows: first, the fundamental tasks for a specific domain are identified; subsequently, adequate problem-solving methods are selected; then, the knowledge types necessary for defining the functionality of the basic methods are elicited; and finally the knowledge is represented and the reasoning procedures of the basic methods operationalized.

### 11.2.3  Distributed Decision Support Models

So far, the use of a knowledge-based approach to DS has been motivated and a formalism to express the structure of the knowledge of the resulting DSSs has been introduced. Still, it remains to be shown where this structure comes from. In order to design complex DSSs there needs to be a *decomposition criterion*, that determines the shape of the TMST tree. The traditional solution is a hierarchical decomposition of the tasks via methods which require other tasks to be performed by other methods, etc. until a basic level is attained where the modules are simple enough. This is a version of the traditional *functional* decomposition standard in AI for many years.

When distributed models were considered, taking into account the low efficiency of the available hardware, this hierarchical organization was adapted in structures specialized in different tasks that may be computed in parallel. In some cases, however, this functional organization may not be easily understandable, which makes the process of knowledge modeling difficult, because the analogy between the agents' contents and the commonsense understanding of the expert is insufficient.

The search for a good modular structure in the applications is traditional in computer science. The first approach was a hierarchical functional decomposition with the already commented drawbacks. In order to improve the integration of different functionalities in understandable and maintainable entities, the following step towards modularization was the concept of *object*, where a collection of functions sharing data structures were integrated in a module. Still, although the organization in objects is an adequate organization for conventional software units, in many cases it turned out not to be intuitive enough from the point of view of knowledge models .

### Multiagent Decision Support

Agent-based structuring introduces a more complex notion of modularity to computer science. This idea has evolved from Hewitt's actors concept [19] to the modern concept of agents which integrates a collection of functionalities, achieved by the interplay of both knowledge about certain problem types and about the environment in which the agent operates. By this, the agent can react to the environment situation and can interact with other agents to look for solution to its problems. The notion of agents allows a design of modules that balance two aspects:

- Level of *specialty*
  it is possible to model a detailed functional decomposition by designing agents that specialized in basic functions.

- Level of *autonomy*
  it is possible to integrate in an agent a significant set of the functions required for the whole application but limited in scope (for instance, in time if the agent performs in specific periods or in space if the agent acts on a reduced spatial environment).

In fact, the idea of agents represents the highest level in *modularity* that is used in computer science so far. It gives rise to a new generation of application structures, with a high degree of *antropomorphy* and, hence, *understandability* by the users. Additionally, the fact that agents embody a collection of functions that may serve in different societies is a design principle supporting the potential *reuse* of these advanced modules. Moreover, the generality of the agent concept allows to use human principles for structuring organizations as design criteria: an agent is an

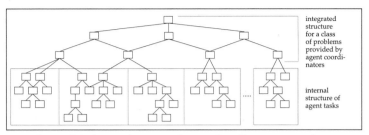

**Figure 11.2**   Centralized coordination: hierarchically integrated agent structure.

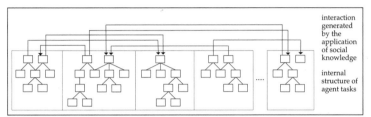

**Figure 11.3**   Decentralized coordination: dynamic agent interaction by social knowledge.

entity specialized in playing a social role in an organization which is a new basis for design provided by the social science area.

The experience with DSSs build so far prove that it is feasible to design the local problem-solving capabilities of agents by means of TMST trees in a principled fashion. Still, methods for modeling the interaction between agents, in order to ensure an intelligent global response of the whole society for certain tasks, are still maturing. This is the challenge of this type of models: to achieve intelligence by means of an adequate level of coordination.

### The Coordination Problem

As shown in Figure 11.2, to achieve intelligent coordination a special coordinator agent can be designed, that is responsible for detecting interdependencies between the local agents' activities at successive levels of abstraction. This approach is contrasted by a decentralized stance, depicted in Figure 11.3, where no such special agent exists and agents interact laterally: agents are endowed with the knowledge to discover inconsistencies between their intended actions and interchange messages to mutually adapt their local decisions, so as to converge on one or several sets of consistent local control plans. The former coordination model leads to a hierarchical integration of control plans as determined by the upper level functions, while in the latter this integration emerges from agent interactions as implied by the agents' social knowledge. From an abstract point of view both approaches seem feasible. However, the first seems more reliable with respect to operation, while the second appears more adequate from a design perspective.

Once the knowledge to reason at the upper levels is elicited, the centralized approach provides a model of predictable behavior where all possible cases of inconsistencies are all analyzed a priori and are taken into account by the upper level modules. However, the bottleneck of this type of models is precisely the knowledge elicitation of the different inconsistencies: in many cases it is difficult to identify the precise way in which methods and domain models need to be integrated in order to solve a problem. In addition, once such a centralized model is built, the maintenance process is complex because, if additional lower level models are introduced, a sequence of changes has to be produced in the upper level models to take into account the potential modification of the situations produced by the new element.

The decentralized approach promises systems that are easier to build, because the model needs to be defined very accurately only at the local level, where it is more feasible to elicitate the knowledge to solve the specific problems of each agent. Normative coexistence knowledge for coordination may be defined in a more abstract way. Once both elements are sufficiently tuned to cope with the problems, the system may be maintained easily because the norms of coexistence are stable and independent of the number of agents in society and, if a new agent is introduced in the society, the only thing to be done is to include norms as a part of the external world model for the agent. No problems of propagation to upper levels appear. The problem of this decentralized approach is the quality of the intelligence of the whole society of agents, as it is difficult to identify the impact of normative knowledge in the quality of the global task achievement.

## 11.3   An Agent Architecture for Distributed DSSs

This section outlines an architecture for distributed DSSs. In particular, it is concerned with an "anatomy" of agents which, as in society, are capable of solving DS problems. The architecture does not pay special attention to computational and efficiency considerations, but comprises just features that are necessary to describe the different case studies, that will be presented in section 11.4, from a unifying view [2]. In line with the recommendations concerning design structures for agent architectures that are presented in chapter 1 of this book, the architecture is built around three major components, which are summarized in Figure 11.4.

- a *perception subsystem* allows the agent to be situated in the environment by data acquisition and in the society by perceiving agent messages. It implements the function *see*, described in chapter 1.

---

2. We assume that the reader is familiar with basic knowledge representation techniques and reasoning methods from symbolic AI, such as rules used by forward and backward chaining or frames used by pattern matching. An introduction to these issues is given in [26] and [27] .

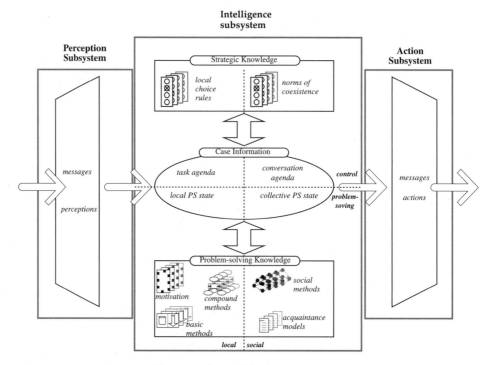

**Figure 11.4**   Agent architecture for a DS agent.

- an *intelligence subsystem* manages the different aspects of information processing as well as individual and social problem-solving. It implements functionality similar to chapter 1's function *next*.

- an *action subsystem* enacts the plans produced by the intelligence subsystem, displaying messages to the control personnel, sending messages to other agents or activating robotic effectors. In terms of chapter 1, it models the function *action*.

The subsequent description of the architecture focuses on the *intelligence* subsystem. First, the knowledge requirements of the DS agent will be presented. Subsequently, the structure of its information model is sketched, and finally the control model that makes the above components operational is described.

### 11.3.1   Information Model

The agents' dynamic beliefs about the world itself and the others are stored in the information model. The perception subsystem writes data on it according to perceptions and received messages, when the intelligence subsystem's knowledge is enacted, the information model is modified, while the action subsystem reads from it. We can distinguish two types of information in this model:

- *Problem-solving information* refers to inputs, outputs and intermediate results of tasks. Depending on whether the information refers to tasks pursued by the agent itself or by members of the society, *local* problem-solving tasks information and *social* problem-solving information can be distinguished.

- The second important part of the model contains *control information*, specifying in an *agenda* what is "intended" to be done. Respecting the agent itself there is a *task agenda* that keeps track of the tasks that are to be achieved locally. The *conversation agenda* keeps track of the "conversations" (see below) that the agent participates in, i.e. the social method in which it is involved somehow.

### 11.3.2 Knowledge Model

Agent knowledge can be classified from two perspectives. On the one hand, *problem-solving* knowledge, which is used to determine which actions to take, *is* distinguished from *strategic* knowledge that helps to choose among different options (the tasks or conversations, see below) that the intelligence subsystem is to process next. This knowledge may also be classified according to its role: there is *individual* agent knowledge, modeling the capacity of an agent to propose decisions and *social* knowledge, modeling the interaction knowledge framework representing the regulation of the society of agents.

For the DS problem, the individual knowledge comprises the following areas of knowledge:

- *Motivation* knowledge. It will be described by a collection of patterns modeling different classes of events considered by the agent as relevant in the external world. They are formulated by a collection of frames where the slots are classes of values of the information variables provided by the perception subsystem. When the perceptions have modified the information model in a way that some motivation frame can be matched against it, then this frame is activated. It represents an undesirable scenario in the world from the point of view of the agent. The difference between this undesirable situation and some no problem scenario, defines the task that the agent creates.

- *Local problem-solving knowledge.* The agent is endowed with the knowledge necessary to enact problem-solving methods so as to achieve tasks. This will be organized in the following form:

  - *Basic methods* perform elementary functions which are implemented either by specific algorithms or in terms of some knowledge representation and reasoning formalism as rules, frames or constraints. In addition, conceptual vocabularies model the entities that are manipulated by basic methods. A domain ontology, which comprises the different conceptual vocabularies together with the declarative relations between concepts, supports the inference operation of the different simple and composed methods.

  - *Compound methods* describe how a task is coped with by solving its subtasks. Thus, they establish a task-methods relations which, for each problem to be solved, gives rise to a TMST tree of the type shown in Figure 11.1. Compound methods can be represented as rules, where the antecedent represents some intermediate state of task execution (e.g. the result of a previously executed subtask) and the consequent a sequence of subtasks to be executed in consequence, and relations that establish how the inputs and outputs of subtasks are related. As an alternative, this procedure might just be hard-coded in a simple algorithm.

- *Local Strategic knowledge.* This type of knowledge has as main goal to guide the process of generation of the TMST tree by selecting at every level and for every task the adequate method to be used for its performance. Then, it will be organized by a priority list of methods for the different types of tasks. The method of reasoning will recommend at a given level of the TMST tree to select the adequate options to continue tree formation.

*Social knowledge* comprises all expertise respecting the interaction between agents. Its components are:

- *Acquaintance models.* Knowledge about other agents is stored in these models, which can be supported by a *frame base*. Each frame comprises what is known about others in a collection of slots. Most important, such slots will represent features of every method known of a given agent (every agent models its acquaintances by its problem-solving capacity, i.e. in terms of characteristics such as levels of inference of the methods, the classes of subtasks that require to be supported, the kind of domain models supporting the basic methods, etc.). By application of a *pattern matching method* it can be deduced whether and up to which degree some acquaintance provides some desired characteristics. For instance, some task can be matched against the method slots of some acquaintance's frame, in order to evaluate its adequacy to perform that task.

- *Social methods.* These methods constitute the social problem-solving knowledge of the agent. As in the case of compound individual methods, a social method copes with a task by solving its subtasks (which will usually be handled by different agents). Still, social methods just specify at a very high level how these subtasks are to be integrated. Essentially, they configure an interaction protocol, which determines a set of meaningful *conversations* between agents [31]. A simple way of specifying such conversations is by means of a finite state automaton, whose nodes determine conversation states (in which some agents are supposed to perform tasks) and whose transitions are labelled with messages. Still, usually more flexible and more powerful techniques are used [25] [4].

  Social methods usually need to specify which agent has to solve a certain subtask, when and to whom to send task-related information and how to integrate the outcomes of tasks. So, social methods usually comprise three "meta tasks":

  - Task assignment. Through the individual selection of an agent, when several of them may be available to perform the same task. This may be done in different ways: by direct order, when one agent is endowed with acquaintance knowledge to choose the most suitable agent; by a "contract net," where one agent asks all potential executors of a task for their adequacy and then grants the task to the best agent etc. In the remaining part of this chapter, it is assumed that tasks are assigned directly.

- □ Task synchronization. Once tasks are assigned, the flow of information between them needs to be configured and constraints on their execution posed. For instance, it needs to be specified what information needs to be present in order to initiate a tasks, and to which other tasks the result of one task are to be sent.

- □ Solution integration. Contrary to compound methods, whose subtasks have been defined in a way that their solutions neatly fit together and make up a solution for the task, the results of subtasks of a social method often need to be adapted to each other in order to constitute a consistent whole. As this adaptation usually leads to different alternatives, some choice mechanism needs to be present. Again this can be done in different ways: one agent can impose its preference in a dictatorial fashion, or a process of group decision making can be initiated (e.g. voting or negotiation).

- ∎ *Social strategic knowledge.* If there are several conversations in course, this knowledge determines the next one to work on. Again, this type of knowledge has as main goal to guide the process of generation of the TMST tree that, when several agents are involved, integrates methods of different agents integrated as a result of the conversation among agents.

### 11.3.3  Control Model

The mode of operation of the agent model is given by a simple reasoning cycle. It contains the following steps:

1. the perception subsystem captures percepts and messages from other agents, and updates the information model accordingly;

2. the conversation agenda is updated and reordered in accordance with the social strategic knowledge. As a result of the selection of some conversation, new tasks are added to the task agenda;

3. the motivation is matched against the information model and eventually more new tasks are created on the task agenda;

4. Using the local strategic knowledge the task agenda is reordered and some tasks are chosen for execution;

5. for every task two approaches are to be followed:

   (a) the local problem-solving approach where, using the knowledge about relation between tasks and methods, a method is chosen for execution. Usually, basic methods are preferred to compound methods, and the latter are given priority over social methods;

(b)   the delegation approach, if in the previous process no method is available in the internal problem-solving knowledge to cope with a task. In this case, the agent consults its acquaintance models and identifies a collection of agents that may perform the required tasks. The agent then assigns the task to the most adequate agent;

6.   the action subsystem performs actions and sends messages as indicated by the intelligence subsystem in the information model.

This pattern of operation will be simulated and illustrated in the following examples.

## 11.4   Application Case Studies

The objective of this section is to illustrate the possibilities of the distributed approach for DSS design. Three examples of distributed DS in the domains of environmental emergency management, energy management and traffic management are provided, instantiating the previously described agent architecture to the particular domain and illustrating the modes of operation of the resulting multiagent DSS. You might see the agent and interaction model as the result of some multiagent design methodology, as discussed in chapter 9 of this book. This chapter also gives an overview of the architecture and operation of other industrial DAI applications.

The examples to be presented in the sequel go back to real-world designs and systems: they try to capture the "spirit" of the applications that they are based on. The reader be warned, however, that the presented models and modes of operation need not be identical with the original systems, due to lack of published information on the one hand and for educational purposes on the other.

### 11.4.1   Environmental Emergency Management

#### *The Problem*

Environmental emergency management is concerned with events that alter the usual mode of operation of an installation, having a negative impact on its environment. Often, even human and material damages and losses may be produced. Examples of such events are forest fires, river floods or gas dispersions from chemical plants.

The current state of sensor and communication technology allows for a dramatic change in the mode of management of these catastrophic events. Today it is possible to get on-line information about the wind state, temperatures and smoke in a forest data grid for fire control purposes, or to obtain directly data respecting rainfall and water levels in a watershed where floods may happen. On this basis, a decision-maker can evaluate the current situation (*what is happening?*) as well as its short term evolution (*what may happen if... ?*) within different scenarios, and elaborate potential action plans to apply (*what to do?*), so that an adequate *real-time* risk management is performed. So, in summary, the emergency management problem consists in generating an "understanding" of a potentially problematic situation and in elaborating consistent action proposals *in time*, so as to avoid damages when this is possible and to reduce their effects when no control action is applicable to eliminate them.

The nature of the problem comprises centralized aspects (the services to support large areas are usually located in a central place) and distributed aspects (the impacts of problems are spatially distributed, as in the case of floods).

Advanced systems can greatly improve the efficiency of environmental emergency management. In [10] the application of AI models to flood management is proposed, which have been developed along the sixties [1] [11]. Current advances in knowledge modeling promise to improve these techniques, as they support a better structuring. The European Union has promoted this line of applications in several projects such as ARTEMIS [17] in the area of Telematics for Environment, which is concerned with the management of heavy gas dispersions and river floods. In [2] a cooperation architecture for chemical plant emergencies is proposed.

A simple architecture is proposed in the following paragraph taking into account both features.

### The Agent Architecture

Setting out from this problem description, the following types of agents can be identified:

- The Local Emergency Management Agent (LEMA), responsible for understanding the problem situation in a predefined area, and for proposing local decisions respecting initial management plans on this basis.

- The Dam Management Agent (DMA), responsible for taking decisions about dam control, on the basis of the needs of other agents as well as the situation of the dam and its water resources.

- The Fire Brigade Management Agent (FBMA), responsible for population evacuation as well as for the provision of manpower and other resources for protection works.

- Transport and Ambulance Management Agent (TAMA), responsible for the viability in the road transport network and ambulance resources management.

In line with these concepts an intelligent system for emergency management is designed by defining an instance of the Local Emergency Management Agent for every area where damages may be done to the population and the surrounding region where floods may impact. Furthermore, there is one agent of each of the above types, i.e. one Dam Management Agent, one Fire Brigade Management Agent and one Transport and Ambulance Management Agent (i.e. if there are nine endangered areas, a model of 12 agents is required).

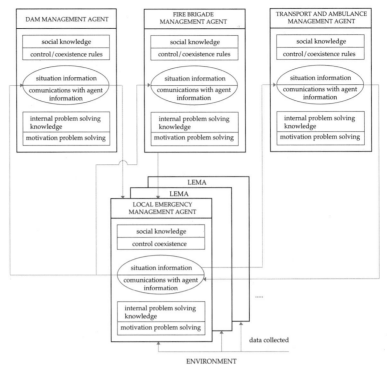

**Figure 11.5**   Summary of agent interactions in emergency management.

The society configuration is a simple one (summarized in Figure 11.5): every LEMA maintains two-way communications with any of the FBMA, TAMA and DMA agents. In general, no communication is designed between the latter three agents.

According with these design criteria the strategic knowledge will be based on:

- Local choice rules at the LEMA where the tasks to be provided by every general agent will be defined (given the degree of specialization of the general agents this knowledge will be expressed by statements of assignment of tasks to general agents).

- Local choice rules at the level of general agents where the preferences between the different LEMAs are established for sending messages according with general considerations of the agents and types of messages to be communicated.

- Norms of coexistence establish the preferences of some agents for task performance. In this case, given the specialty of every agent by function and by location, there are no doubts respecting which agent will perform a task.

The social methods in this case are also general enough:

- Task assignment, will be based on the specialty of every agent defined by the corresponding rule set.

- Task synchronization and solution integration. As will be commented later the general agents perform a task of activity integration constrained by the limitation of resources of the corresponding agent. A dialogue will be established between the LEMAs and the general agents where some proposed tasks by the LEMAs may be proposed to modify (see Figure 11.5).

In the following paragraphs the internal knowledge structure for every type of agent will be commented. Finally, an example of LEMA agent reasoning integrated in the society may serve to clarify the proposed specifications outline.

Every agent will receive total or partial information from the environment and from the society of agents. In the following paragraphs some features of information and knowledge operating in every agent will be described:

- Local Emergency Management Agent (LEMA):
  - The information received by the agent about the situation is the state of a collection of variables of rainfall and water levels that may influence the area controlled by the agent.
  - The motivation knowledge is used to detect if a current situation is problematic for the area. This knowledge may be described by a domain model of frames of situations describing patterns of potential damages together with a pattern matching method to infer the potentially activated problem frames for a given situation.
  - The local problem solving knowledge will propose local action plans to solve the detected problems:
    * Diagnosis knowledge. Once a subset of frames is activated by a given situation, the knowledge of diagnosis is based on a method of simulation and a rule base proposing potential causes in such a way that a procedure of generate and test supported by the simulator is applicable until a collection of explanatory factors is identified as likely enough.
    * Repair knowledge. Once a collection of causes has been identified this area of knowledge defines plans of actions. The objective is to eliminate the causes or, if this cannot be achieved entirely on the basis of local actions, to alleviate the effects through protection actions such as building flood walls or evacuating people.

The domain model will be described by a library of plans together with a rule base for plan selection and a method of progressive plan refinement such as proposed by [6]. The kind of basic actions to be included in the plan are protection works to retain the water or transport actions using some available resources such as vans and ambulances to send people to hospital. To perform a transport action of this type requires an answer from the transport and ambulance agent about the accessibility between the desired origin and destination.

□ Social knowledge. This knowledge has to be built based on the unsolved task resulting from the planning phase in the problem solving knowledge. In fact, when the agent tries to look for a solution using its own knowledge, it tries to build a task method tree to act on the causes of problems. Still, when this is not feasible there will be unsolved task nodes, so there is a need the help of other specialized agents such as the dam control agent, the transport ambulance or fire brigade. To cope with this type of problems a domain model will describe for every unsolved task which messages will be sent to these three types of agents. For instance, if there is a problem of evacuation that cannot be solved by the local resources transport, there will be a message to the fire brigade establishing the conditions of the task to be performed.

□ In this case the knowledge will be very simple because the only task to be performed is the preference attribution to the possible agent of the same task.

■ The Fire Brigade Management Agent and Transport and Ambulance Management Agent. Both agents have a similar structure so the general description of their contents will be the following:

□ Information:

* Receives data about the state of its resources in terms of machinery vehicles and manpower.

* Receives from the LEMA demands on manpower or transport according with the resulting needs in the local analysis.

□ Knowledge:

* Motivation knowledge. After the reception of the environment situation and the other agent demands it may happen that a major complex event is inferred (if many demands come from one area it may be inferred that some catastrophe is happening). Accordingly, domain knowledge defining this type of global events may be included.It will be used by a method of pattern matching to detect its occurrence in a given situation.

* Problem solving knowledge. The domain model will be described by a constraint set representing the condition of resource application for every local task (or for the more global task inferred as major event). The reasoning method will infer possible answers to the questions compatible with the constraint base. After this first step of reasoning it may happen that no feasible solution exists capable of giving a compatible answer to the current demand of the different agents. In these cases, the reasoning method will be able to propose alternative options by introducing adequate delays. To decide these delays the knowledge about control and social knowledge will be applied to reformulate the constraint base until some solutions are found (i.e. it may happen that the model answers in terms of no provision of a task now but is positive for the same task after some predefined delay). The type of constraint modification will be the object

of the conversation with the corresponding LEMA agents in a loop that will end up in an acceptable and feasible solution.

* Social knowledge. This knowledge will model the preferences between the LEMA agents' demands to perform the delay generation described before.

* Control knowledge. This knowledge will select options to guide the process of constraint reformulation.

- The Dam Management Agent:
  - Information. Receives data about the state in the dam system of the water levels and spill flows in every dam. Receives from LEMA limitations of the outflows from dams proposed by the LEMA according with its flooding problems.
  - Knowledge.
    * Motivation knowledge. As with the other agents, it may happen that some major event such as a dam break or a local flood must be detected, so a collection of frames with the corresponding pattern matching methods will be designed modeling this type of events.
    * Problem solving knowledge. The main task to be performed by this agent is to decide the outflows from every dam including the case of spill null. The way of performing this task will be similar at the previous agent by defining a domain model using constraint and rules representing the exploitation conditions of the dam system in such a way that if there is a solution according with the demands of the different agents the reasoning method will produce it or if there is not a solution guided by the control knowledge or social knowledge there will be a process of constraint relaxation introducing modifications in the demands of the LEMAagents according with their category until a solution is met.

### Example of Operation

Figure 11.6 summarizes the mode of operation of a LEMA agent. As commented before, this agent is primarily concerned with management tasks for its area: (1) *what is happening*, (2) *why it happens* and (3) *what to do*.

The *what is happening* task may be performed by the event detection method of the agent supported by the domain model of a collection of predefined event patterns. The explanation of the detected events is also obtained using the internal knowledge of the agent based on a generate and test method supported by a production rule base and a simulator. The *what to do* task is to be performed by a more complex method using social and individual resources. Two options for action are considered:

- The *damage suppression* option where it is possible by applying actions from the agent and the society to eliminate the causes of damage. The figure shows the option of the LEMA problem solving method and the option to call DMA to help

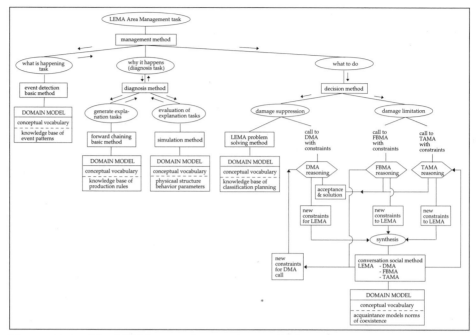

**Figure 11.6**    The LEMA general reasoning method.

by providing dam control actions. Two results are possible: (1) the DMA actions are sufficient to suppress damage; in this case the process is finished, (2) the DMA cannot attend totally the needs of the LEMA and proposes actions which solve the problem partially. In this case a conversation between both agents is started as commented previously in the DMA description, where several proposals are interchanged in terms of constraint size and delay until a balanced situation is obtained according with the LEMA social method.

■ The *damage limitation* option where an estimate of damages and the needs to support its effects is provided by LEMA to the FBMA and TAMA agents. As in the previous case a dialogue is established depending on the available resources in FBMA and TAMA together with the norms of coexistence with LEMA (both agents propose reduced answers in time and size and the LEMA proposes alternative options).

In Figure 11.6 the conversation effect has been represented by loops of arrows derived from the LEMA synthesis task execution by using the conversation social method.

In this section, a simple model of agent interaction has been considered for illustration purposes. In the following case studies more complex interactions will be considered.

### 11.4.2 Energy Management

Energy management aims to assure a permanent and high quality supply of electrical energy. It is a crucial factor for the maintenance and success of modern economies.

Electricity is generated at power plants, as the result of the transformation of (thermal, nuclear, solar etc.) raw energy. For a variety technical, economical and political reasons, power plants have grown in size and generation capacity, so that the final electricity consumption takes place rather far away from the place of its production. In consequence, in nowadays electricity infrastructure, producer and consumers may be separated by several thousands of kilometers, so there is a need for an electricity network that connects the end users to the generation sites. Two types of such networks may be distinguished:

- Electricity transport networks
  Transport networks cover wide areas and assure that all regions of a country are connected to electricity supply. These networks are run at high-voltage (132 kV or more) in order to minimize losses during transportation. At transmission substations different high-voltage lines may be joined and electricity is fed from the transport network to the regional low voltage electricity distribution networks.

- Electricity distribution networks
  Distribution networks cover a much smaller geographical area than the transport network, but are more dense, as it needs to deliver electricity to all customers. They are usually run at lower voltage levels for security reasons and to reduce installation costs (lower voltages allows for "thinner" lines and thus save copper). Furthermore, as different classes of customers need different voltage levels, the network comprises a series of transformers that sustain a variety of different voltages on the net. For instance, in the UK large industries are connected to 33 kV lines, commercials and smaller industries are fed by 11 kV, while domestic customers are connected to a 240 V part [30].

Generation, transportation and distribution of electrical energy to industrial and domestic customers needs must be saved from damages due to equipment damage due to wind icing, lightning and other disasters, which are unpredictable and thus have to be coped with in real-time when they occur, there are quite frequent factors that might unbalance the network state and which allow for an extenuation of their effects well in advance [30]: fluctuations of temperature may cause changes of load; the overall demand changes according to the time of the day and of the week, to the season and the weather; *maintenance work* requires to check, exchange and install equipment safely etc.

Some of the above circumstances just affect the quality of supply (voltage peaks etc.), but others may imply real emergency situations, where problematic areas need to be isolated from the rest of the net as soon as possible: short circuits, for instance, may produce a chain reaction: an overload in a certain line increases the load in neighboring lines, giving rise to a new overload situation etc.; the situation deteriorates even more if power stations become disconnected, as this will cause an imbalance in the network's power. Still, it also has to be assured that the corresponding black-out area is minimal, that is, that as few customers as possible are affected by the incident.

Electricity networks are usually managed from a control room. High voltage distribution networks are usually telemetered so that the control engineers are provided with on-line information. They are endowed with protection equipment that can be operated remotely from the control room. In low voltage networks, this is often too expensive. So, information respecting deviant network states is usually obtained by observations from a field engineer and by telephone call of customers, reporting loss of supply. Work on the network is also performed "manually" by the field engineer. Distributed DSSs have been developed for both high-voltage and low-voltage networks [9].

### The Problem: Fault Management in Electricity Transport Networks

This section is concerned with an almost fully telecontroled high-voltage electricity transport network. The model of such a network, that will be developed in the sequel, sets out from a set of *substations*. Each such substation hosts one or several *busbars*. Two busbars can be connected either by a *switch* or by a conductor *line*. For security reasons, in the latter case both edges of the line are to be connected to circuit *breakers*, that interrupt electricity flow on the line when opened. Breakers usually come with a *protection* (relay), which automatically opens the breaker in case of a short circuit. Such a distribution of breakers makes it possible to disconnect every single line or busbar from the rest of the network and, in theory, this isolation is done automatically through the protections. The firing of breakers and protections causes alarm messages to be sent to a control room. From there, control engineers have the possibility to control the state of breakers remotely.

Figure 11.7 shows a transport network modelled in these terms. It actually represents a part of the high voltage distribution network of the Iberdrola company, which supplies large regions of northern and central Spain with electricity. This network with a generation capacity of 16.715 MW and a maximum demand of 10.000 MW is managed from the control room, located in Bilbao in the Basque Country. The transport network comprises three voltage levels and amounts to 401 busbars, 296 lines, 294 transformers, 939 breakers and 2322 switches. [20]

Emergency situations in this network are usually caused by a short circuit in a line or busbar, which is coped with immediately by isolating the affected area as soon as possible. The effects of such an incident can become worse in case of equipment malfunctioning: if a breaker fails to open, the affected area out of service is much bigger. The final objective of fault management is to restore supply for a maximum number of customers as fast as possible. As there are different "routes" along which electricity may be delivered, according to current network topology (which is determined by the state of breakers and switches), this is done

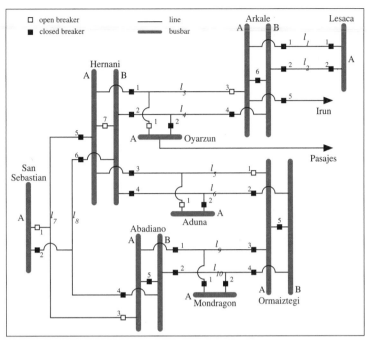

**Figure 11.7**   A snapshot of a high-voltage transport network in the Basque Country (adapted from [3]).

by establishing alternative routes (by operating breakers and switches) that skip the faulty devices. More specifically, the tasks comprise:

- to identify malfunctioning in switches and protective relays;
- to generate a fault diagnosis that explains all received alarm messages;
- to generate an efficient and *safe* switching plan, i.e. to restore supply for a maximum number of customers under the condition that the network is always in a consistent state (in all intermediate states the load on equipment is within acceptable ranges etc.).

The available information sources for this enterprise are also twofold. While *snapshots* provide a comprehensive picture of the current state of all components in the network, the *alarm messages* indicate how the state of the components changes over time, i.e. they describe the network's transition from one state to another. The former can be produced quickly, whereas it may take minutes until the latter arrive at the control room.

### The Multiagent Architecture

In the frame of the ARCHON project [20] the distributed power transportation DSS has been built for parts of electricity distribution network as described above. The preexisting management infrastructure of Iberdrola had a crucial influence in the final shape of the multiagent system that has been developed. The assumptions made in this section are similar to those encountered by the ARCHON project. There are essentially two design constraints [20]:

- The supplier company was using stand-alone DS tools to ease the workload of the control engineers. The functionality of DS should be augmented on the basis of these *preexisting systems*, but without modifying them, as they have evolved to work efficiently and reliably in the Iberdrola network. Instead, preexisting applications should interact with new functionality in the frame of a distribution intelligent system.

- the current *configuration of the data transmission network* had to be maintained. In particular, this configuration assigns a low priority to messages containing temporal information, giving rise to two different classes of alarm messages:

  - *Non-chronological alarm messages (NAM)* contain abstracted information about the state changes in the network and are timestamped at the time of arrival at the control center. Thus, NAMs arrive at the control center rather fast, but important information respecting the sequence of events is lost.

  - By contrast, *chronological alarm messages (CAM)* receive their timestamp at the substations. So, they contain precise chronological information at the cost of a greater delay in their availability at the control center and a higher error probability due to synchronization problems between the substations' clocks.

The design of an agent society for the electricity transport network management DSS sets out from the definition of the constituting agents. In the sequel, the six agents that have been identified will be described, but with simplified knowledge and services for illustrative purposes.

The preexisting applications have been "wrapped" into two agents:

- *Alarm Analysis Agent (AAA)*
  On the basis of NAMs, the *AAA* detects the occurrence of a disturbance, determines the type of fault and establishes hypotheses respecting the malfunctioning equipment. The *AAA* to provides the following basic methods:

  - on the basis of the NAMs the basic method *simple classify* of the *AAA* detects new disturbances and classifies them into categories such as short circuit, overload etc. The conceptual vocabulary on which this process is based will minimally contain a list of possible NAMs as well as of classes of situations (e.g. short circuit, overload and manoeuvre). The knowledge can be given in terms of rules that directly associate sets of NAMs with these classes.

  - *cover NAMs* takes NAMs and their classification in order to output a set of hypotheses about faults that "explain" them. As conceptual vocabulary the domain's NAMs, network elements and fault types need to be given. A rule base uses these concepts for a shallow hypothesis generation.

The only compound method is *cover and differentiate by NAMs*. It specifies that first a fault hypothesis needs to be generated that explains all symptoms. Then, the *determine BOA* subtask is set up, that determines what would have been the detected symptoms if the hypothesis were true. The fault hypothesis is refined until real and simulated symptoms are consistent.

- *Control System Interface (CSI)*
  The *CSI* constitutes the application's front end to the control system computers. Besides serving as an interface to the conventional management system application programs, its main objective is to acquire and distribute network data to other agents. It offers two basic methods:

  □ *acquire data* detects, preprocesses and formats NAMs and CAMs for their future use within the system; this is done by a fast hard-wired formatting algorithm.

  □ *simulate effects* calculates the power distribution in the system given a certain state of devices (breakers etc.). For this, a numerical simulator applies knowledge about the physics of load distribution in electrical installations to the distribution network which is described on the basis of a conceptual vocabulary defining the network lines, busbars, breakers and their characteristics.

  The compound method *classify situation* specifies that in order to cope with the *disturbance detection* task, it is necessary first to perform *alarm detection* and then to do *alarm classification*. In addition, it offers the social method *coordinate classification*, which determines where the results of the CAM and NAM classifications should be sent to, and that no integration of the different classifications is necessary.
  The CSI's motivation detects situations in which logical coherent sequences of alarm messages have arrived (probably all messages that have been caused by one network event). In this case, it sets up a *disturbance detection* task.

In addition to the above preexisting applications, four new agents have been developed to cover all tasks that the system specification requires.

- *Blackout Area Identifier (BAI)*
  The *BAI* uses NAM in order to identify which network elements are initially out of service. It offers just one basic method: *determine BOA*. Given a network state and faults, a rule base that constitutes a causal model of the network determines what the results of such a scenario would be. The conceptual vocabulary necessary for this will minimally contain a list of faults and alarms.

- *Breakers and Relays Supervisor (BRS)*
  The *BRS* is a new alarm analysis expert system that works on the basis of CAMs. It detects the occurrence of a disturbance, determines the type of fault and establishes hypotheses respecting the malfunctioning equipment. The following basic methods are provided:

□ on the basis of CAMs the basic method *simply classify* of the *BRS* detects new disturbances and classifies them into categories such as short circuit, overload, manoeuvre etc. As in the case of the *AAA*, the conceptual vocabulary on which this process is based will minimally contain a list of possible CAMs as well as of classes of situations. The declarative domain model can be given in terms of rules that directly associate sets of CAMs with these classes.

□ *cover CAMs* takes CAMs and their classification uses a rule base in order to provide a shallow fault hypothesis that explains all received CAMs.

The only compound methods is *cover and differentiate by CAMs*, which specifies that first a fault hypothesis needs to be generated that explains all symptoms and then it is simulated which symptoms would have been produced if the hypothesis were true. The fault hypothesis is refined until real and simulated symptoms are consistent.

- *Service Restauration Agent (SRA)*
  The objective of the SRA is the elaboration of a safe service restauration plan after a blackout has taken place. On the basis a snapshot of the current network state and information about malfunctioning equipment, it offers the following basic methods:

  □ *propose switching plan* devises an initial service restauration plan given the alarm messages and the results of the diagnosis process. On the basis of network model as described by the conceptual vocabulary, heuristic knowledge is used to construct a sequence of operations that finally make up a switching plan.

  □ *modify switching plan* uses rules that, depending on plan critique, indicate how a certain plan is to be modified. Again, this is done on the basis of a vocabulary that expresses the network model.

- *User Interface Agent (UIA)*
  The *UIA* serves as an interface between the users of the multiagent system and the agent society for presenting data (e.g. to browse through the list of alarm messages), the result of the different tasks that are resolved within the system (e.g. to display the results of diagnosis together with an explanation) and the effect of control actions (e.g. the simulated effect of the enactment of a certain service restauration plan). In addition, the *UIA* provides compound methods *propose and revise* for service restauration, by means of which the user controls how long the cycle of proposal generation, critique and revision should be run. In addition, the social method *coordinate diagnosis* sets up guidelines for the coordination of the *diagnose by CAM* and *diagnose by NAM* tasks.

  The motivation of the *UIA* specifies that no disturbance classified as "short circuit" should be kept untreated and generates a *diagnosis* task in consequence. In much the same way, it requires that a diagnose fault should be overcome, so that a *service restauration* task is set up.

| Agent | Simple Methods | Compound Methods | Social Methods |
|---|---|---|---|
| CSI | acquire data | classify situation | coordinate classification |
|  | simulate effects |  |  |
| BRS | classify CAMs | cover & differentiate |  |
|  | cover CAMs |  |  |
| AAA | classify NAMs | cover & differentiate |  |
|  | cover NAMs |  |  |
| BAI | determine BOA |  |  |
| SRA | propose switching plan |  |  |
|  | revise switching plan |  |  |
| UIA |  | propose & revise | coordinate diagnosis |

**Table 11.1** Overview of Methods for Energy Management

The methods of the agents are summarized in table 11.1. For the purpose of this example, it is assumed that each agent is endowed with a model of any other acquaintance (although this is not necessary for the model to work well). So, in each agent this model comprises six frames, that contain the methods shown in table 11.1. Besides the method *type* (simple, compound or social), the acquaintance model contains information about the competence with which the method can be applied. For instance, the *cover and differentiate* method of the *BRS* can diagnose breaker, busbar and clock faults, while the *AAA*'s *cover and differentiate* method is just competent to diagnose breaker and busbar failures. Control knowledge is not specified in this example, as the characteristics of tasks and agents imply a certain determinism in the problem-solving process.

### An Example Operation

Consider the situation shown in Figure 11.7. The following CAMs and NAMs have occurred.

```
10:10:10 BRK OYA 1        10:10:09.34 PRT ADU 1
10:10:10 PRT OYA 1        10:10:09.36 BRK ADU 1
10:10:10 BRK ADU 1        10:10:09.41 PRT ORM 1
10:10:10 PRT ADU 1        10:10:09.43 BRK ORM 1
10:10:10 BRK ORM 1        10:10:09.43 PRT HER 7
10:10:10 PRT ORM 1        10:10:09.45 BRK HER 7
10:10:10 BRK ARK 3        10:10:09.46 PRT OYA 1
10:10:10 PRT ARK 3        10:10:09.46 BRK OYA 1
10:10:10 BRK HER 7        10:10:09.49 PRT ARK 3
10:10:10 PRT HER 7        10:10:09.51 BRK ARK 3
10:10:12 BRK ABA 3        10:10:09.54 PRT SSE 1
10:10:12 PRT ABA 3        10:10:09.56 BRK SSE 1
10:10:12 BRK SSE 1        10:10:10.04 PRT ABA 3
10:10:12 PRT SSE 1        10:10:10.07 BRK ABA 3
```

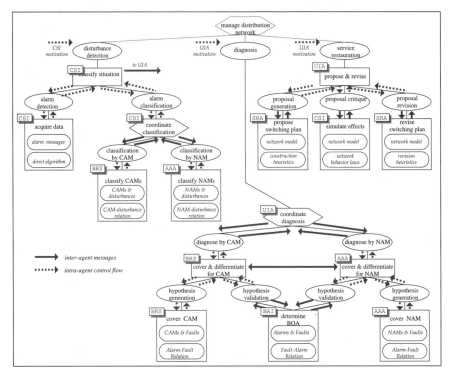

**Figure 11.8**  Task structure generated by the society of energy management agents.

Figure 11.8 shows the TMST tree that is generated when these alarms arrive at the *CSI*. In the sequel, we illustrate how this tree is constructed following the general control method.

The *CSI*'s motivation frames match the representation of these messages in the information model, and a *disturbance detection* task is generated and put on the agenda. The agent notices that it is endowed with the *classify situation* method, and puts the resulting subtasks on its agenda. In a next cycle, it notices that the *alarm detection* task can be coped with by the basic method *acquire data*, which formats alarm messages. The resulting alarm strings are passed upwards, until the *classify situation* method specifies that they serve as input to the *alarm classification* task. The *alarm classification* task is coped with by the social method *coordinate classification* of the *CSI*. It requires direct task assignment and, according to the agent's capabilities contained in the acquaintance models, messages are sent to *BRS* and *AAA*, assigning the tasks *classification by CAM* to the former and *classification by NAM* to the latter. Once any of these tasks have finished, the results of the classification of alarm messages are passed upwards to the *classify situation* task. A message with the resulting classification (a short circuit occurred) is sent to the *UIA*.

As a result, the UIA's information model is modified in such a way that it matches a motivation frame. So, a *diagnose* task is activated and put on the *UIA*'s agenda. The agent copes with it by activating the social *coordinate diagnosis* method, which directly assigns the tasks *diagnose by CAM* and *diagnose by NAM* to the *BRS* and the *AAA* respectively. Furthermore it specifies that in case of differing resulting diagnosis, the "more knowledgeable" diagnosis should be given preference. The *AAA* chooses this task and assigns the compound *cover and differentiate by NAM* method to it, giving rise to the subtasks *hypothesis creation* and *hypothesis validation*. First, the *AAA* generates its hypothesis on the basis of the NAM. The rule base assigned to the simple *cover CAM* method, makes it initially suspect that each firing of a protection has been caused by a fault in the adjacent lines and busbars, which leads to the following list of hypotheses respecting faulty devices:

$$\text{fault}(\{l_7, \text{Her}_A, l_3, l_5\})$$

As the *AAA* is not capable of resolving the hypothesis validation task, the control cycle looks for an acquaintance frame with a method slot that matches that task. The BAI does and so it asssigns this task to the *BAI*.

The *BAI* tackles this task by the *determine BOA* method, which infers what the effects of the occurrence of the hypothesis would have been: given the initial situation, it concludes that the following events would have occurred in case of the faults:

$$l_7 \Rightarrow (\{\text{SSe}_1, \text{Aba}_3, \text{Her}_5\}),$$
$$l_3 \Rightarrow (\{\text{Her}_1, \text{Ark}_3, \text{Oya}_1\}),$$
$$l_5 \Rightarrow (\{\text{Orm}_1, \text{Adu}_1, \text{Her}_3\})$$
$$\text{Her}_A \Rightarrow (\text{Her}_7, \text{Oya}_1, \text{Adu}_1, \text{Ark}_3, \text{Orm}_1, \text{SSe}_1, \text{Aba}_3)$$

The *AAA* receives this answer and reconsiders its hypothesis. By default, the *AAA* suspects that breaker failures are more likely than simultaneous faults in different devices, so it refines its initial hypothesis, giving rise to the following list which is ordered by decreasing confidence in them

$$\text{fault}(\{\text{Her}_A\}), \text{fault}(\{l_5, \text{Her}_3\}, \text{fault}(\{l_3, \text{Her}_1\}), \text{fault}(\{l_7, \text{Her}_5\}).$$

Again, each of these fault hypotheses covers all alarm mesasages. It sends these hypotheses to the *BAI* and receives the answer that each of them explains the received NAM.

Suppose that the *BRS* generates its initial hypothesis in the same way as the *AAA*, but on the basis of the CAMs, so it arrives at the same fault hypothesis. A *hypothesis validation* task is created and passed to the *BAI*. As in the case of the *AAA*, the *BRS* receives the differentiating information from the *BAI* and starts to reconsider its hypothesis. As clock severe synchronization failures are rather rare, the *BRS* reorders its list of validated hypothesis in the following way:

$$\text{fault}(\{l_5, \text{Her}_3\}), \text{fault}(\{\text{Her}_A, \text{Adu}_{clock}, \text{Orm}_{clock}\}),$$

The *BAI* confirms that each of these faults covers all received alarms. Still, it has also received the diagnosis from the *AAA* and notices a difference of opinions. As indicated by the social *coordinate diagnosis* method, the *BRS* does its part in the solution integration searching its acquaintance models and discovering that the *AAA* does not know about clock failures, which means that it is not competent to reject the *BRS*'s diagnosis. So, it maintains its diagnosis and sends it to the *AAA* and the *UIA*. The *AAA*, after receiving that diagnosis, performs a similar reasoning with its acquaintance models and, as a result, adapts its own by integrating the clock fault hypothesis. Finally, it also sends this adapted diagnosis (which is now consistent with the diagnosis of the *BRS*) to the *UIA*.

Again, these messages modify the *UIA*'s information model, a motivation frame applies and a *service restauration* task is created. The *UIA* assigns the *propose and revise* method to cope with it, which results in the *proposal generation*, *proposal critique* and *proposal revision* subtasks. The *UIA* has no method for any of them, so after consulting its acquaintance model, the first task that the method requires to be executed, *proposal generation*, is assigned to the *SRA*. The *SRA* generates the following switching plan

plan(open(Her$_3$), close(Ark$_3$), close(Oya$_1$), close(Her$_7$) , close(SSe$_1$), close(Aba$_3$))

which it returns to the *UIA*. The *proposal critique* subtask is delegated to the CSI, which applies the *simulate effects* methods, returning characterizations of all intermediate states of the potential switching plan to the *UIA*. As the last intermediate state is not considered to be safe, the *UIA* delegates the *revise switching plan* task to the *SRA*, which revises it by exchanging the last two actions:

plan(open(Her$_3$), close(Ark$_3$), close(Oya$_1$), close(Her$_7$) , close(Aba$_3$), close(SSe$_1$))

Again, the *UIA* sends the revised plan to the *CSI*. Its simulation proves that the modified switching plan is acceptable, and the *propose and revise* method returns it as a result.

The above example describes a complete reasoning cycle of the energy management multiagent DSS. The functionality of a fictitious top-level task *manage distribution network* has been generated "bottom-up" by communication among agents and their adequate motivations. Other types of events may lead to other task distributions between agents. Note that every agent decision may be explained to the responsible engineers using the trace of the reasoning methods.

### 11.4.3   Road Traffic Management

The increasing popularity of road transport and the incessant rise of the number of vehicles have caused a tremendous growth of the magnitude of traffic flows on public roads. Especially in urban areas, where the road network is dense and the traffic volume in peak situations is enormous, significant economic losses are produced by enduring and recurrent congestions. Still, it is precisely in these urban areas where there are severe obstacles to the expansion of traditional infrastructure, due to the scarcity of space and resources as well as for environmental reasons. As a consequence, urban road traffic management has become an increasingly important task: strategies to guide traffic flows are essential in order to avoid collapses of individual transport and the corresponding losses for the local economy.

In big cities, traffic control centres (TCC) are in charge of managing urban transport. A TCC's responsibilities cover a wide range of different tasks. In particular, traffic engineers within a TCC are to supervise the current road traffic situation, detect problems and take actions to overcome them, so as to maintain and restore flows of vehicles adequate for the network capacity. Information about the current traffic state is obtained from many different sources, the most important of which include:

- messages transmitted from human *observers*, which constitute a classical source of information for traffic control centres. In most cases, such information is provided by urban police or members of related public organisms;

- visual control of certain problematic areas is possible by means of *TV cameras*. They are especially useful to assess unusual and emergency situations, such as the gravity of accidents etc.;

- *sensors*, which are installed in strategic parts of the network and generate a continuous flow of numerical data about traffic conditions at a certain point. There are different types of sensors with different costs and capabilities. One of the classical sensors are loop detectors that usually provide information about speed (mean velocity of the vehicles detected by the sensor), flow (average number of vehicles that pass through a certain road section per time unit) and occupancy (the average time that vehicles are spotted by the sensor).

On the basis of such heterogeneous traffic information (informal, visual and numeric data) a traffic control engineer identifies potential problems and decides upon signal plans to overcome them. Such signal plans comprise a coherent set of uses of control devices that the TCC can act upon. The most popular devices for urban road traffic management are the following:

- *Variable Message Signs (VMS)*, that allow to influence traffic behavior by dynamically setting, modifying or deleting traffic signals. The most advanced VMS are panels which are installed above the road. They allow to display arbitrary messages that inform drivers about the network situation downstream. In addition to this, they can display pictograms and traffic signs, thereby announcing warnings, speed limits, prohibitions to overtake etc. Older types of VMS support just a small collection of different traffic signs or constrain the set of messages that can be displayed due to technical limitations;

- *traffic lights*, by means of which the access of vehicles to certain parts of a road network, typically junctions, is controlled. Different features of traffic light signaling can be modified: the relative amount of green time can be increased or decreased, the overall length of a cycle may be changed and the time offset between different cycles is modified. Ramp meters are special traffic lights that are positioned on the entry ramps of motorways. They enable the traffic controller to regulate the amount of vehicles entering the motorway.

Figure 11.9 depicts a typical traffic management installation. The task of traffic management performed in the TCC is to generate *signal plans* for control devices in order to alleviate traffic problems that have been identified on the basis of the collected traffic information.

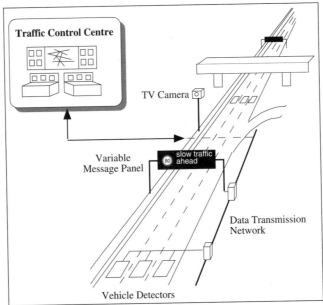

**Figure 11.9**  A typical traffic control infrastructure: traffic information from vehicle detectors and TV cameras is transmitted to the Traffic Control Center, which acts upon road traffic by displaying messages on Variable Message Panels.

### The Problem: Urban Highway Traffic Control

This section is concerned with road traffic management of the urban highway network around Madrid. It consists of two beltways and 8 adjacent highways is endowed with about 100 VMS panels, 50 cameras and over 300 loop detectors. These devices are connected to the Madrid traffic control center via fiber optics communication links. Certain parts of the network support peak load of over 6.000 vehicles per hour.

Figure 11.10 depicts part of the highway network of eastern Madrid. It shows the eastern part of the two beltways *M30* and *M40* as well as the three adjacent highways *NII*, *NIII* and *NIV*. Data sources such as loop detectors are not shown, but the figure indicates the location of the nine VMS that are installed in this area.

The objective of traffic management is to ensure the "smooth flow of traffic" which can be expressed along measures such as travel times or "length" of congestions etc. It is pursued by enacting signal plans, which—in the example of Figure 11.10—coincide with coherent sets of messages to be displayed on the different VMS. These messages inform drivers about the traffic situation downstream. This guidance influences the "size" of traffic flows in the network (thereby reducing the traffic load in congested areas), as some drivers will choose a different "route" from their origin to their destination. More specifically, traffic management comprises the following tasks:

- to identify problematic situations, classifying their type (incident congestion,

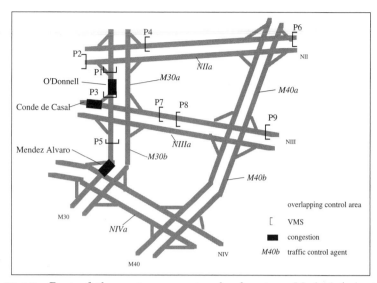

**Figure 11.10**   Part of the motorway network of eastern Madrid (adapted from [12].)

overload congestion etc.) and location;

- to diagnose the *causes* of the problems in terms of the traffic flows that contribute to it;

- to generate a legal signal plan proposal on such a way that the causes of problems be eliminated or alleviated enough to improve the traffic conditions.

### The Multiagent Architecture

In the frame of the European KITS [12] and the Spanish TRYS projects [13] [14] agent-based traffic management systems have been built for the road network of different towns. The structure of the systems was crucially determined by the fact that the human operators, from which traffic management knowledge had to be elicited, analyzed traffic flows in terms of *problem areas*. Problem areas usually reflect special characteristics of the network topology, but also comprises empirical behavior rules for certain parts of the town. In consequence, one traffic control agent was built for each problem area. Agents are homogeneous, in the sense that they share the architecture and the reasoning structure, but the knowledge they are endowed with is pertinent to the specific problem area they are responsible for (e.g. empiric knowledge about area behavior rules).

In the example of Figure 11.10 there are seven traffic control agents—*M30a, M40a, M30b, M40b, NIIa, NIIIa* and *NIVa* —whose problem areas comprise the highway section between two highway junctions, including all entries and exits that connect this section with the ordinary road network. Each of them is to generate local signal plan proposals that help to overcome traffic problems in their area. For this. it is endowed with the following basic methods:

- *data abstraction* takes as input raw sensor data, filters out noisy data, calculates aggregate values such as temporal and spatial gradients and finally determines qualitative measures for different system variables (e.g. the average speed may be high, medium, or low).

- *problem type identification* takes all the data generated through data abstraction in order to identify problems, such as incident congestions, overload congestions etc. This is done by matching the data against problem scenario frames. Each such frame characterizes a specific problem situation by relating the type of problem to patterns of abstracted traffic data.

- *solution refinement* specifies the identified problem in further details.

- *demand estimation* determines the traffic demand between some arbitrary origin and some arbitrary destination in the network. Obviously, this varies temporally (peak hours etc), so that this basic method uses a frame base that associates temporal patterns (hour, day of the week etc) with demands for the different origin/destination pairs.

- *effect estimation* determines the effect that certain traffic flows have on a problem. This is done by means of distribution scenario frames that relate three types of information: traffic problems, the state of control devices and the contribution of certain routes to the problem. By matching the current state of control devices and the traffic problem against these frames, the "final causes" of the problem are found in the traffic flows that contribute to it.

- *signal plan selection* aims to generate a proposal of how a problem can be overcome. It also uses the distribution scenario frames, but in another way. All scenarios that match the traffic problem are potential signal plans.

- *short term prediction* estimates the result of a change in traffic flows within the network. It uses a simple assignment algorithm to do this.

These are used by the following compound methods:

- *heuristic classification* is a classical problem-solving method [8], which comprises three subtasks, which are executed sequentially: *abstract state* determines relevant aggregate information for the classification, which is done by the *match problem* subtask. The result is refined in the following *refine problem* subtask.

- *contributor differentiation* determines how much each of a set of potential causes contributes to a problem. In order do assure this, it first generates the subtask *find contributors* and then *estimate contribution*. This is repeated until all contributors are evaluated.

- *generate and test* first sets up a generate proposal subtask, which produces a set of tentative signal plans. These are judged subsequently within the test proposal subtask. If a plan is not considered to be sufficiently adequate, a now proposal is generated.

- *local management* just indicates that traffic control of the local area consists of first identifying traffic problems, then diagnosing its causes in order to finally

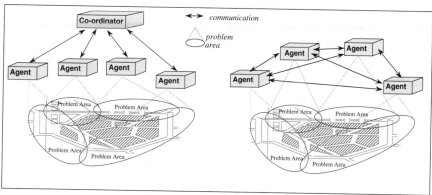

**Figure 11.11** Centralized and decentralized multiagent traffic control architectures: in the former there is a special coordinator agent in charge of harmonizing local control proposals of the traffic control agents, while in the latter this functionality emerges among traffic agent interaction in the frame of a social method.

configure signal plans to overcome them.

Still, the subdivision of the road network is made on the basis of empirical (logical) criteria, so the spatial division of the network is not perfect, i.e. the areas are not disjointed, but rather constitute a set of overlapping zones. So, local signal plan proposals use to be interdependent. There may be either *physical* conflicts between them, when the proposals of two agents require to display different messages on the same panel, or *logical* conflicts when one agent's signal plan proposal hinders or even cancels the effectiveness of another. In consequence, the agents' proposals need to be coordinated. As Figure 11.11 depicts this can be either done by means of a dedicated coordinator agent, or laterally through peer-to-peer communication. It has shown to be difficult to elicit explicit coordination knowledge, so in the sequel the second option will be discussed.

In this domain, the *acquaintance models* are also given by frames. Still, such a frame does directly represent information concerning methods that another agent can perform or tasks that it can cope with (as the agents are, in principle, self-sufficient for the management of their local area). Rather it describes the actions that the acquaintance can take, specifying which resources they require (causing potential physical conflicts), and which effects they may have (causing potential logical conflicts).

An agent's *motivation* matches the information model once complete sequences of new data have arrived. In consequence, it generates *manage 'local area'* task. This task is similar to those generated by a social method. Although no synchronization with the acquaintance's tasks is necessary, it is required that local signal plans be sent to those agents with which there might be a conflict (e.g. those with overlapping problem areas). In case of conflicts, the agent with the most *severe* problem will be allowed to maintain its signal plan.

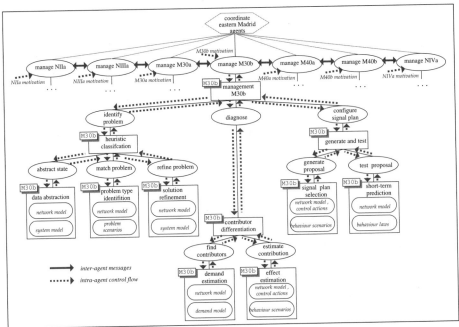

**Figure 11.12**  Task structure generated by the society of traffic management agents.

### An Example

Consider the traffic situation shown in Figure 11.10. There are three problems: in the area of *M30a* at O'Donell, in the area of *M30b* at Mendez Alvaro and in the *NIII* area at Conde de Casal. Figure 11.12 shows the TMST tree that the society of traffic control agents generates from this situation.

The reasoning process of the *M30b* agent will be described as an example. The arrival of new data makes its motivation create the *manage M30b* task. The *management M30b* method is found to be an adequate means to cope with it. Its first subtask, *identify problem*, is solved by *heuristic classification*, which first performs *data abstraction* by completing possibly erroneous sensor data and calculating temporal and spatial gradients etc. The *M30b* then agent matches this information against its frames, representing typical problem scenarios, and identifies that there is an overload problem at Mendez Alvaro. In a *solution refinement* step, it detects that the overload problem manifests itself in a saturated off ramp.[3]

The *management* method then requires a *diagnosis* task to be solved, which is done by the *contributor differentiation* method. First, the current traffic demand between entry and exit points in the network is determined (*demand estimation* method), in order to estimate then by means of pattern matching (*effect estimation* method) how much each flow between each origin and destination contributes to

---

3. Note that this problem identification already comprises certain aspects of diagnosis.

| VMS | M30a | M30b | NIII |
|-----|------|------|------|
| P1 | C. at O'Donell | C. at Mendez Alvaro | |
| P2 | C. in M30 at O'Donell | | |
| P3 | | C. at Mendez Alvaro | |
| P4 | C. in M30 at O'Donell | | |
| P5 | | C. at Mendez Alvaro | |
| P7 | | | C. at Conde de Casal |
| P8 | | | C. at Conde de Casal |

**Table 11.2**  Local signal plan proposals ("C." stands for "Congestion").

the problem.

Once this has been done the *configure signal plan* task is set up, which is coped with by a generate and test method. First, a proposal is generated by matching distribution scenario frames against the problem situation, deducing a potential signal plan and the corresponding change in traffic flows. The subtask *test proposal* gives rise to the execution of a short term prediction method, which estimates the effectiveness of the potential signal plan. It is selected or rejected accordingly.

Other agents perform similar local reasoning. As a result of this reasoning process, just the agents *M30a*, *M30b* and *NIII* have identified problems and generated signal plan proposals shown in table 11.2.

The agent *M30b* detects a physical conflict with *M30a*, because the latter proposes to display a message on the panel *P1*, which *M30b* already wants to access with a different message. The agent *NIII* detects a logical conflict with *M30a*, as the message shown on *P3* will make drivers on *M30* leave this beltway and turn into Madrid by *NIII*, aggravating the problem at Conde de Casal. In much the same way, agent *M30a* detects the physical conflict with *M30b* as well as a logical conflict with *NIII*, as the message on *P7* induces drivers on *NIII* heading towards downtown Madrid to use alternative entrances, thereby worsening the problem at Mendez Alvaro.

The agents notice that the physical conflict at *P1* can be solved by merging the proposals to a "Congestion from O'Donnell to Mendez Alvaro" message. In addition, the agents *M30a* and *NIII* interchange information about the gravity of their problems. As a result, and according to the distributed *coordinate* method, *M30a* gets preference, as its problem is more severe: Panel *P3* will show as proposed "Congestion at Mendez Alvaro," while *P7* will be switched off. This final proposal is presented to the control personnel.

As in the electricity management domain, the agents' motivations have been designed in a way that is equivalent to a hypothetic social method *coordinate eastern Madrid agents*. Still, the way in which solution integration is performed relies on knowledge about a "preference ordering" (the more severe problem is given precedence) which all agents share. But this is precisely that kind of knowledge that a fictitious central coordinator agent (see Figure 11.11) would be endowed with; it is just replicated among many agents.

Other, more decentralized modes of coordination can be achieved by augmenting the *degree of autonomy* of the traffic control agents. For instance, the designer can set out from the notion of self-interested agents, whose autonomy to manage the traffic in their area is only bounded by the existence of its acquaintances. In such a design, agents behave selfish and, in principle, are only interested in the traffic state of their problem area. Still, the interactions between their local signal plans makes it rational from them to coordinate with others.

However, although the agents may benefit from coordinating their signal plans, they have a conflict of interest respecting which global plan should be agreed upon. The compromise that is reached in such situations of mutual dependence will certainly depend on the agents' "social position," i.e. as to how far an agent can help or harm others, and up to which degree others may influence in the effectivity of an agent's local signal plan proposals.

One way of modeling decentralized coordination in such a scenario is to see the compromise reached (or: the social equilibrium) as being biased towards the less dependent agent: the "stronger" an agent is, the more "weight" will have its individual preferences in a potential compromise. The designer can influence this social equilibrium by means of prescriptions, which prohibit or permit certain agents to use certain control panels, thereby increasing or decreasing their degree of dependence [24], [22].

The formal representation and operationalization of such models will most probably be based on some model of distributed rational decision making, which are discussed in detail in chapter 5 of this book. Cooperative bargaining models, for instance, are strong candidates for this enterprise [23]. An example of the application of these ideas is given by the decentrally coordinated traffic management system which has been built on top of the ProsA$_2$ architecture described in [24]. Such approaches, however, are still an area of research and their potentials and drawbacks in different real-world applications have to be tested.

## 11.5    Conclusions

This chapter has outlined the potential of DAI models for decision support. The DS problem has been described by means of a semi-formal model and the knowledge-based approach to DSS design explained. The application of DAI techniques to DS problems has been motivated, and the design and operation of such distributed DSSs has been illustrated by presenting an abstract agent architecture and by simulating the reasoning and interaction processes within problem-solving societies of such DS agents in different domains.

From an abstract point of view, the concept of an agent has been used as modularization principle for the DSSs' software and knowledge. The principle by which agents were formed reflected an *a priori* distribution in the domain. Emergency management agents were built in line with preestablished organizational entities. In the electricity distribution example, agents were created around preexisting expert systems. In the road traffic management example, the agentification was implied by the control engineer's understanding of a town's traffic behavior in terms of problem areas which, to a certain degree, reflect a logical distribution of the domain.

It has been argued, that such a non-functional distribution implies a need for additional coordination that standard problem-solving methods cannot cope with in a natural way. The notion of a social method has been introduced in order to cope with coordination problems.

The intersection of the areas of Knowledge Modeling and DAI is a busy and exciting research area. Once the concept as well as structuring and enactment principles of social knowledge have further evoluted, libraries of distributed interaction methods might be developed that will greatly ease the development of distributed DSSs.

## 11.6   Exercises

In this section two example scenarios for decision support are presented. Each such scenario constitutes the basis for several exercises. Do not be driven back by the large introductory texts; they will help you to cope with the subsequent exercises.

1.   Consider the following emergency management scenario for flood prevention. There is an area with a high risk of flooding, whose structure is shown in Figure 11.13. Six watershed basins collect rainfall and produce a runoff to four major water streams, which lead into two reservoirs created by dams located downstream the rainfall collection areas. The dams are endowed with spill gates and discharge pipes by means of which the water retention capacity of the dams can be controlled. Consider the relation between discharge capacity, water level and the state of spill gates to be given in a table.

Downstream the dams there are two villages within floodable areas, where damage can potentially be done to people. In every such area civil protection works can be performed (e.g. to reinforce flood walls), in order to improve the security against floods. Three levels of civil protection can be planned: "low," "medium," and "high." For every level of protection different amounts of human resources are required, which are available either locally or from the next main town which is located within a secure area. Furthermore, the availability of resources changes with the time of the year.

According to the situation, it is possible to infer a relation between the acceptable outflow from the reservoirs and the level of protection works to be performed in every village. The following two extreme emergency management strategies are possible:

  - minimum flow limitation in dams (i.e. wide opening of spill gates) together with maximum protection works;

- maximum flow limitation in dams with minimum protection works;

Eventually, these plans need to go in line with evacuation actions, which are to be provided by the village transport resources and additional central services from the main town (e.g. given a situation where defenses have a limited capacity it may happen that some subset of population requires evacuation). Local emergency management may be supported through the help of the following organisms:

- the water management authority, which determines the amount of flow to be discharged from dams within the next hours, given the current remaining capacity of the reservoir and the predicted inflows.

- the fire brigade which manages manpower to provide capacity for protection works. Limited resources will be defined in terms of available vehicles of known capacity and available human resources.

- the sanitary and ambulance authority that is responsible for population evacuation and medical treatment where also a limited number of ambulance vehicles and persons are available.

Any of the above organisms receives requests for support from the endangered areas and determines as to how far to grant help on the basis of a predefined policy of preferences.

The aim of the exercise is to design an agent-based DSS for this domain. It is recommended to define the following agents:

- two LEMA agents, which perform local emergency management in the endangered areas, i.e. LEMA-P for area P and LEMA-Q for area Q,

- one DMA agent, responsible for dam control on reservoirs A and B;

- one FBMA and one TAMA agent for central resource management concerning protection and evacuation works respectively.

In the sequel we will provide descriptions of two types of these agents, leaving the design of the remaining agents to the reader. The following knowledge components of a LEMA agent can be identified:

- The motivation knowledge must be applied to react to the meteorology conditions. A classification method will be applied supported by a domain model, which is based on predefined patterns which consist of two parts. The first part is defined by slots representing the current state and the recent trend in the variables. For instance, for area P the slots will include the measures of the state of the rainfall basins 1,2 and 5 as well as the situation in reservoir A; for area Q the patterns include slots for all six rainfall basins and both reservoirs. Either on the basis of available expertise or through simulation, different emergency situations are characterized by assigning characteristic values to the slots. The second part includes slots that characterize the estimated impact in floodable areas in terms of waterlevel excess and overflows entering the area. So, the patterns relate meteorology situations with their potential impacts. In consequence, a pattern matching

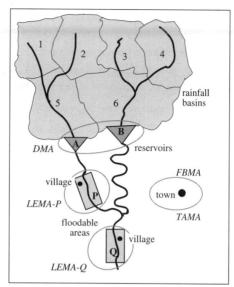

**Figure 11.13**  A Flood Management Scenario.

method can be used to generate hypotheses about potential impacts, whose negative effects need to be avoided.

- The local problem-solving methods are used to repair or to alleviate the potential damages predicted previously. Essentially two local problem-solving methods are enacted sequentially:

  - on the basis of water-level excess and overflows entering the area the impact specification deduces the affected area and the number of affected persons using a rule based classification.

  - the impact alleviation knowledge estimates the protection actions in terms of dam control actions, the level of protection works or the magnitude of population evacuation. First, a sequence of actions leading to impact alleviation is constructed. This is a planning problem, which may be coped with by a hierarchical classificative planner as proposed by Brown and Chandrasekaran [6] for routine design. Local resources are assigned to the plan on the basis of a rule base. External resources are assigned using social methods.

- The acquaintance models for DMA, FBMA and TAMA contain slots describing the kind of help that any of these agents can supply together with an estimation of its maximal amount.

- The social methods used by the LEMA are of quite simple structure. Depending on the type of resource required, the task of determining the help to be granted to a LEMA is assigned to DMA, FBMA or TAMA. After accomplishing the task its results are sent to the LEMA.

- The norms of coexistence determine the order in which the LEMA's acquaintances are asked for help. They can be modelled by rules, e.g.:

```
IF rainfall in basins 1,2,5 = very high AND
   rainfall in basins 3,4,6 = medium THEN
   preference = (DMA, LEMA, FBMA)
```

In consequence, the following sequence of conversations may arise:

- the LEMA asks the DMA to reduce water level excess totally;
- the DMA answers with an alternative, expressed by a range of admissible reductions;
- the LEMA estimates the civil protection works necessary for any of these options. If external help is required it asks the FBMA for additional manpower;
- the FBMA responds with the range of possibilities to satisfy the LEMA's help request, specifying the amount of manpower and the required waiting time;
- finally, in accordance with the previous answer, the LEMA infers evacuation needs and asks the TAMA to provide the necessary resources;

The knowledge contents of the remaining agents determines their behavior within these conversations. Concerning the DMA agent the following observations can be made:

- As in the case of the LEMA agent, the DMA's motivation knowledge is expressed in terms of a frame base of patterns, which characterize storms that act on rainfall areas and relate them to possible undesirable impacts that have to be avoided.

- The problem-solving knowledge aims to find reasonable values for the opening of spill gates and discharge pipes at the dams so as to avoid the aforementioned undesirable impacts of meteorology conditions, taking into account the limiting criteria on water storage and the maximum waterflow downstream that the reservoir's outlets may produce. To meet this goal a generate-and-test method is applied:

  □ a rule knowledge base generates reasonable values for openings on the basis of the current data and the default impact estimation that the motivation frame base provided;
  
    * a simulator determines the impact of this decision, using an artificially generated rainfall series and the structure of the drainage network (knowledge for the operationalization of a simulator can be derived from flow routing methods in hydrology engineering);
    * in an evaluation step it is determined whether the short-term effects of dam management actions as estimated by the simulator satisfy the safety constraints mentioned above. If this is not the case, another action proposal is generated and the generate-and-test cycle reinitiated.

- The behavior of the DMA in social interactions with a LEMA agent is based on its current situation and a priority evaluation of the different LEMAs. It determines the amount of help that can be granted in the current situation (negative impacts of rainfall as determined by the motivation knowledge in relation to security constraints). The amount of help that is granted to each LEMA agent in response to its request is determined by a priority rule base.

The reader may proceed by the following steps:

(a) *[Level 2]* Specify knowledge models—analogous to those presented for LEMA agents—for DMA, TAMA and FBMA.

(b) *[Level 3]* Propose a detailed contents of the knowledge bases for the four types of agents.

(c) *[Level 1]* Perform a "manual" simulation of agent reasoning and agent interaction.

2. Consider the urban traffic management domain as described in section 11.4.3. A fictitious road-network is given, consisting of one beltway and three adjacent highways as shown in Figure 11.14. Highways hit the beltway at junctions J1, J2 and J3 respectively, and meet each other in the center of the town at junction J4. The entry and exit points to the network are labelled by E1, E2 and E3. There are three traffic management agents, A-I to A-III, each responsible for the swift flow of traffic in a different beltway section. The agents act upon the traffic by means of messages to be displayed on any of the nine VMS P1 to P9.

The different VMS messages and their effects are as follows:

- switch off
  all drivers take the shortest path to their destination. For instance, if the amount of vehicles going from E1 to E2 increases by 500 veh/h, the beltway area of A-I will support an additional load of 500 veh/h.

- "to <exit> on beltway by <junction>"
  80% of the drivers follow the recommended route, while 20% still try the shortest path. In the above example, the message "to E2 on beltway by J3" will result in an additional load of 100 veh/h for the A-I and 400 veh/h for the A-II and A-III areas.

- "to <exit> by center"
  just half of the drivers will obey the message and pass through the center, while the rest still tries the direct path. In the above example, the message "to E2 by center" will result in an additional load of 250 veh/h in the A-I area and another 250 veh/h in the center.

If one agent wants to display some messages M on a VMS while another would like the same panel to be switched off, message M will be displayed. Messages "to X by Z" and "to Y by Z" can be merged into a message "to X and Y by Z." All other combinations of messages on the same panel are incompatible.

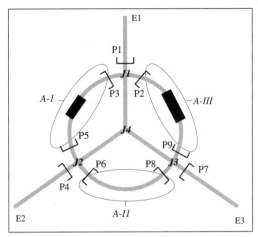

**Figure 11.14** Traffic scenario.

Consider a scenario with a medium size congestion in the area of A-I and a severe congestion in the area of A-III as shown in Figure 11.14. In the downtown and A-II areas there is only light traffic; these areas can absorb further traffic load without generating problems.

(a) *[Level 1]* Which are the different alternative local signal plans generated by the agents A-I and A-III? They should be ordered by their effectivity in the eyes of A-I and A-III.

(b) *[Level 3]* Develop knowledge models for the A-I and A-III agents based on the agent architecture presented in this chapter. Enacting this knowledge agents should come up with the local signal plans mentioned above.

(c) *[Level 1]* Simulate the social method *coordination* performing "severity-based" integration of local signal plans as in section 11.4.3. What is the resulting global signal plan?

(d) *[Level 2]* What "compromise solutions" are possible as global signal plans. What criteria could a social method use so as to ensure that its outcome is such a compromise solution?

(e) *[Level 4]* Develop a formal framework by means of which you specify the precise meaning of your notion of a "compromise solution." How can such solutions be computed in a distributed fashion? You may want to borrow from part one of this book (especially the chapters 4 and 5) to accomplish this.

## 11.7   References

1.  Alonso, M.; Cuena, J.; Molina, M.: SIRAH: An Architecture for a Professional Intelligence. In *9th Europ. Conf. on Artificial Intelligence (ECAI-90)*. Pitman, 1990.

2.  Avouris, N.: Cooperating Knowledge-based Systems for Environmental Decision Support. *Knowledge-based Systems* 8 (1): 39-54, 1995.

3.  Barandiaran, J.; Laresgoiti, I; Perez, J.; Echavarri, J.; Corera, J.: Solucion de Problemas Complejos utilizando diversos puntos de vista. In *Proc. Spanish Conf. on Artificial Intelligence(CAEPIA-91)*, pages 413-421, 1991.

4.  Barbuceanu, M.; Fox, S.: COOL: A Language for Describing Coordination in Multi Agent Systems. In *Proc. 1st Int. Conf. on Multiagent Systems (ICMAS-95)*, pages 17-24. AAAI/MIT Press, 1995.

5.  Breuker, J., van de Velde, W.: *CommonKADS Library for Expertise Modelling*. IOS Press, 1994.

6.  Brown, D.; Chandrasekaran, B.: *Design Problem Solving*. Morgan Kaufmann, 1989.

7.  Chandrasekaran, B.; Johnson, T.; Smith, J.: Task-Structure Analysis for Knowledge Modelling. *Communications of the ACM 35 (9)*. 1992.

8.  Clancey, W.: Heuristic Classification. *Artificial Intelligence 27*. 1985.

9.  Correra, J.; Laresgoiti, I.; Cockburn, D.; Cross, A.: A Co-operative Approach Towards the Solution of Complex Decision Problems in Energy Management and Electricity Networks. In *Proc. Int. Conf. on Electricity Distribution*, pages 4.19.1-4.19.6, 1994.

10. Cuena, J.: The Use of Simulation Models and Human Advice to Build an Expert System for the Defense and Control of River Floods. In *Int. Joint Conf. on Artificial Intelligence (IJCAI-83)*. Morgan Kaufmann, 1983.

11. Cuena, J.; Molina, M.; Garrote, L.: An Architecture for Cooperation of Knowledge Bases and Quantitative Models: The CYRAH Environment. In *11th Int. Workshop on Expert Systems. Special Conference on Second Generation Expert Systems (Avignon-91)*. EC2, 1991.

12. Cuena, J.; Hernandez, J.; Molina, M.: Case Presentation for the Use of Knowledge-based Models for Traffic Management – Madrid. In *Proc. 1st World Congress on Applications of Transport Telematics and Intelligent Vehicle-Highway Systems*, pages 564-571, 1994.

13. Cuena, J.; Hernandez, J.; Molina, M.: Knowledge-based Models for Adaptive Traffic Management. *Transportation Research* 3 (5): 311-337, 1995.

14. Cuena, J.; Hernandez, J.; Molina, M.: Knowledge Oriented Design of an Application for Real Time Traffic Management. In *Proc. 12th Europ. Conf. on Artificial Intelligence (ECAI-96)*, pages 308-312. Wiley, 1996.

15. Cuena, J., Hernandez, J.: An Exercise of Knowledge Oriented Design: Architecture for Real Time Decision Support Systems. In S. Tzafestas, editor, *Knowledge-Based Systems. Advanced Concepts, Techniques and Applications*. World Scientific, 1997.

16. Emaldi, M.; Fernandez, J.; Laresgoiti, I; Perez, J.; Amantegui, J.; Echavarri, J.: Design and Operation of an Expert System Prototype for Fault Analysis in Electrical Nets. In J. Campbell and J. Cuena, editors, *Perspectives in Artificial Intelligence Vol. 1*, pages 145-152. Ellis Horwood, 1989.

17. European Commission: Telematics Applications Programme (1994-1998). In *Guide to the 1995-1996 Telematics Projects*. European Commission, Directorate-General XIII, Telecommunications, Information Market and Exploitation of Research, 1996.

18. Haugeneder, H.; Steiner, D.: A Multi-agent Approach to Co-operation in Urban Traffic. In *Proc. Co-operative Knowledge-based Systems SIG Workshop*, pages 83-99, 1993.

19. Hewitt, C.: Viewing Control Structures as Patterns of Message Passing. *Artificial Intelligence* 8: 323-364, 1977.

20. Jennings, N.; Corera, J., Laresgoiti, Y.; Mamdani, E.; Perriollat, F.; Skarek, P.; Varga, L.: Using ARCHON to Develop Real-world DAI Applications for Electricity Transportation Management and Particle Accelerator Control. In *IEEE Expert Special Issue on Real World Applications of DAI systems*, 1996.

21. Newell, A.: The Knowledge Level. *Artificial Intelligence* 18: 87-127, 1982.

22. Ossowski, S.; Garcia-Serrano, A.; Cuena, J.: Emergent Co-ordination of Flow Control Actions Through Functional Co-operation of Social Agents. In *Proc. 12th Europ. Conf. on Artificial Intelligence (ECAI-96)*, pages 539-543. Wiley, 1996.

23. Ossowski, S.; Garcia-Serrano, A.: Social Co-ordination Among Autonomous Problem-solving Agents. In *Proc. 3rd Australian Workshop on Distributed Artificial Intelligence (DAI-97)*, 1997.

24. Ossowski, S.: *On the Functionality of Social Structure in Artificial Agent Societies—Emergent Co-ordination of Autonomous Problem-solving Agents*. Ph.D. Thesis, TU Madrid, School of Computer Science, AI Dpt., 1997.

25. Parunak, H.: Visualizing Agent Conversations: Using Enhanced Dooley Graphs for Agent Design and Analysis. In *Proc. 2nd Int. Conf. on Multiagent Systems (ICMAS-96)*, pages 275-282. AAAI/MIT Press, 1996.

26. Puppe, F.: *Systematic Introduction to Expert Systems*. Springer, 1993.

27. Russell, S.; Norvig, P.: *Artificial Intelligence—A Modern Approach*. Prentice Hall, 1995.

28. Sichman, J.; Demazeau, Y.; Conte, R.; Castelfranchi, C.: A Social Reasoning Mechanism Based on Dependence Networks. In *Proc. 11th Europ. Conf. on Artificial Intelligence (ECAI-94)*, pages 188-192. Wiley,1994.

29. van de Velde, W.: Issues in Knowledge-level Modelling. In J. David, J. Krivine and R. Simmons, editors, *Second Generation Expert Systems*, pages 211-231. Springer, 1993.

30. Varga, L.; Jennings, N.; Cockburn, D.: Integrating Intelligent Systems into a Cooperating Community for Electricity Distribution Management. In *Proc. Int. Journal of Expert Systems* 7 (4): 168-179, 1994.

31. Winograd, T.; Flores, F.: *Understanding Computers and Cognition*. Ablex, 1986.

32. Zhang, M.; Zhang, C.: Analysis and Methodologies of Synthesis of Solutions in Distributed Expert Systems. In *Proc. 2nd Int. Conf. on Multiagent Systems (ICMAS-96)*, pages 417-424. AAAI/MIT Press, 1996.

# 12 Concurrent Programming for DAI

Gul A. Agha and Nadeem Jamali

## 12.1 Introduction

The increasing performance and decreasing cost of processors and computer networks have continued to fuel an explosion of interest in solving larger problems using concurrent computing. In particular, agent-based programming has emerged as a promising paradigm which may help realize Artificial Intelligence through distributed problem solving. Agents are persistent and goal directed entities that may move between hosts in response to changes in requirements such as security and efficiency, and that would normally be limited in the computational resources they may employ in pursuing their goals. Such resources include processor time, memory, and network bandwidth.

A key challenge in concurrent computing is the difficulty of programming parallel and distributed architectures. Many models of concurrency are rather low-level. For example, shared variable models often violate data encapsulation, an essential feature for modular software development. A promising approach to address this difficulty is the use of concurrent objects in a reflective architecture. In particular, *actors* provide a formal model for building and representing the behavior of concurrent objects and thus serve as a foundation for concurrent object-oriented programming.

The definition of actors corresponds to that of agents given in Chapter 1. Actors are autonomous, interacting computing elements, which encapsulate a behavior (data and procedure) as well as a process. Different actors carry out their actions asynchronously and communicate with each other by sending messages. The basic mechanism for communication is also asynchronous and buffered; however, other forms of message passing can be defined in the context of the model. Finally, actors may be dynamically created and reconfigured, which provides considerable flexibility in organizing concurrent activity.

Actors are a model for specifying coordination in a distributed system. Because the internal behavior of an actor is encapsulated and cannot be observed directly, the Actor model supports heterogeneous, variable grained objects. Specifically, the behavior of individual actors may be defined using any programming language.

There are two advantages to using actors for building multiagent systems. First, actors provide a logically distributed programming model which allows systems to be decomposed into autonomous, interacting components without the need for managing the concurrency explicitly. Second, by using actor implementations on parallel and distributed architectures, performance gains will allow larger problems to be solved.

In this chapter, we discuss a powerful concurrent programming paradigm for DAI; the paradigm is based on abstractions built using extensions of the basic Actor model.

## 12.2    Defining Multiagent Systems

Defining agents has been an elusive problem. A common type of agent is the various personal assistants that have recently become commercially available; such agents perform a large number of light weight queries in search of some information. Personal assistants perform functions such as finding the best travel fares, monitoring product or stock prices, or searching academic articles related to a certain area of research. Often these agents have the decision making authority to make binding contracts on behalf of a user, such as by purchasing something using a credit card number. Another type of agent uses a variety of filtering mechanisms to make the huge amount of information available over (say) the Internet more manageable for human consumption. All these can be seen as examples of personal agents that act for or on behalf of a user.

A study of personal agents is limited in a fundamental way. Because there is a 1-to-1 correspondence between *interests* and agents, each agent competes or cooperates with others on the basis of its own interest. Although some notion of a "cooperation instinct" can be coded into the interests of agents, it may come at the cost of reduced code re-usability.

A common limitation comes from either not addressing the issue of *mobility*, or not doing so in the context of an open system. In an open system, mobile agents would be able to migrate from one node to another looking for desired computation environments at affordable costs, and to spawn child agents to pursue subtasks. There is no interesting model available to help control the *resources* that such mobile agents serving some particular interest could use. Even in the case of a single node, there is no way of preventing agents pursuing a particular task from monopolizing the entire system's resources.

Let us consider the example of a system of mobile agents spread over a large network, related to the construction industry. There will be agents for clients looking for contractors, agents for contractors looking for potential clients, and agents for smaller sub-contractors at different levels. Each agent shops around and tries to negotiate the best deal for its own interest. But, unless controlled, any number of overly aggressive (say) contractor agents could spawn hundreds of child agents looking for potential clients in parallel, potentially bringing the entire system down. Worse, even well-meaning agents do not have the means to decide what is a reasonable use of the available resources.

Similarly, there is a possibility of multiple child agents working for the same agent (i.e. serving the same interest) to take competing postures. Even if means are provided for some sort of coordination to emerge at a higher level, such agents may still be competing for computational resources at the scheduler level.

These reasons make it important to study ways of controlling ensembles of agents. On the one hand, we need a *bounded resources* model to control the amount of computational resources consumed by agents serving an interest; on the other, we need a *bounded autonomy* model for allowing coordination among agents. In the following sections, we will develop a model for studying systems of such agents, that addresses these issues.

We represent agents as actors; specifically, we extend the actor model to explicitly model the location of agents on location on particular *hosts* and the fact that agents have *bounded computational resources*. Hosts are actors that manage physical and logical resources and offer them to agents interested in paying for them. A *uniform currency* is used to pay for the cost of these resources. The behavior of an actor may be interpreted in a suitable framework for agents, e.g., the belief, desire, intent model [28]. In any event, agents are persistent, have relatively long-lived goals describing the functional aspect of what they are doing, and have computational engines which serve as mechanisms for achieving these goals. These computational engines include a resource utilization strategy. Of course, all these aspects of an agent may evolve dynamically.

Although the description of goals and procedures falls largely in the domain of conventional AI, explicit resource modeling is a need specific to multiagent systems. Control is not based solely on programming structures, as agents may create or invoke other autonomous agents. The resource consumption model provides the basis for an economic model that is needed to provide mechanisms to bound use of computational and network resources.

An agent which has a model of its own behavior and that of the environments in which it may be executed, may improve its resource consumption by using mobility. Moreover, because an agent may execute in new contexts which do not satisfy its requirements, the agent may need to systematically customize behavior of the underlying execution environment. Such agent requirements include security, rendering software, device drivers, etc.

A model of *computational reflection* [22] provides a formal basis for an agent to have a representation of its own behavior. In general, reflection models enable interaction of higher level operations, such as real-time constraint enforcement, and lower level information about the execution environment, such as load distribution over a group of processors, available network bandwidth, etc. Specifically, reflection allows an agent to have a continuous interaction with its environment in order to determine available resources and relate such resources to the agents' own state; thus the use of reflection can support evolving resource utilization strategies.

## 12.3   Actors

Actors are self-contained, interactive, autonomous components of a computing system that communicate by asynchronous message passing [1, 5]. The basic actor primitives are:

- send($a, v$) creates a new message:
  - □ with receiver $a$, and
  - □ contents $v$
- newactor($e$) creates a new actor:
  - □ which is evaluating the expression $e$, and
  - □ returns its address
- ready($b$) captures local state change:
  - □ alters the behavior of the actor executing the ready expression to $b$
  - □ frees that actor to accept another message.

These primitives form a simple but powerful set upon which to build further abstractions. Thus actors are a natural basis for a low-level language that supports a wide range of higher level abstractions and concurrent programming paradigms.

The actor newactor primitive extends the dynamic data creation capability in sequential programming languages by allowing creation of processes. The ready primitive gives actors a history-sensitive behavior necessary for shared data objects, by delineating a group of actions as atomic. This is in contrast to a purely functional programming model and generalizes the Lisp/Scheme/ML style sharing to concurrent computation. The send primitive is the asynchronous analog of function application. It is the basic communication primitive, causing a message to be put in an actor's mailbox (message queue).

Using the three basic actor primitives, actor systems can be dynamically configured. New actors can be created and connections between actors can be made and broken as computation proceeds. Thus the model does not require that the structure or shape of a computational problem be completely determined, or that the execution resources be fixed, before work on solving it can be initiated.

Actors provide a natural extension of the object-oriented paradigm to concurrent and distributed computation. They support encapsulation, description as behavior templates, and re-usability via libraries accessed using message-passing protocols. The locality properties of actors guarantee that changes of representation and elaborations can be made independent of the interaction with, and behavior of, other actors. Thus actors can support local instrumentation and monitoring which provide important tools for analysis and debugging.

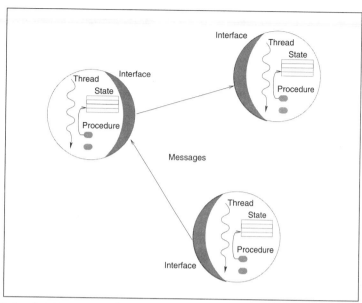

**Figure 12.1**   Actors encapsulate a thread and state. The interface is comprised of public methods which operate on the state.

### Example 12.1  Filtered Search

Consider the problem of a parallel multi-ary tree search, where we want to use a function `filter` to determine what subset of a set of results obtained is useful, before sending them on to the client. There are two different behaviors being defined. FILTERSEARCH has a single method (hence, not named) that takes two parameters, the identity of the customer `cust` and the tree to be searched `tree`. Assume that the number of subtrees and a list of the subtrees can be obtained by using functions `num-children` and `children` respectively; `content` returns the content of the root. After checking for the base case, the behavior FILTERSEARCH creates a *join continuation* actor jc with behavior COLLECT with its client's identity `cust` and the number of subtrees `num-children tree` as acquaintances. Next, the actor creates a new actor with its own behavior for each of the tree's subtrees, and sends each new actor the identity of the join continuation actor as its client, and one of the subtrees to search. Once this is done, it gets ready to service another request.

```
(defActor FILTERSEARCH ()
  (let ((filter (lambda (list)
                   ... )))
    (method (cust tree)
      (if (= (num-children tree) 0)
          (send cust (content tree))
          (let ((jc (newActor COLLECT
```

```
                        (cust (num-children tree)
                          (list (content tree)) filter))))
              (map (lambda (x)
                      (let ((f (newActor FILTERSEARCH ())))
                           (send f jc x)))
                    (children tree))
              (ready FILTERSEARCH ()))))))
```

An actor with behavior COLLECT is created with acquaintances `cust`, `n`, and `results` to represent the customer, the number of values to expect, and the list of results collected so far, respectively. After receipt of each new result, the actor gets ready to receive more results with the same behavior acquaintances modified to represent state change. When all results have been received, it uses the function `filter` to eliminate unwanted results, and sends the remaining to its client. Finally, the actor changes into a SINK which ignores all messages.

```
(defActor COLLECT (cust n results filter)
  (method (res)
    (cond ((> n 1)
            (ready COLLECT (cust (- n 1) (append res results))))
          ((= n 1)
            (send cust (filter (append res results)))
            (ready SINK ())))))
```

Here is how a typical FILTERSEARCH actor would be created and invoked.

```
(let ((FS (newActor FILTERSEARCH ())))
     (send FS self tree))                                          □
```

### 12.3.1   Semantics of Actors

It is possible to extend any sequential language with the actor constructs described above. For example, the call-by-value $\lambda$-calculus is extended in [4].

Instantaneous snapshots of actor systems are called *configurations*; actor computation is defined by a transition relation on configurations. The notion of open systems is captured by defining a dynamic interface to a configuration, i.e. by explicitly representing a set of *receptionists* which may receive messages from actors outside a configuration and a set of actors *external* to a configuration which may receive messages from the actors within.

**Definition (Actor Configurations):**   An *actor configuration* with actor map, $\alpha$, multi-set of messages, $\mu$, receptionists, $\rho$, and external actors, $\chi$, is written

$$\langle\, \alpha \mid \mu \,\rangle_\chi^\rho$$

where $\rho, \chi$ are finite sets of actor addresses, $\alpha$ maps a finite set of addresses to their behaviors, $\mu$ is a finite multi-set of (pending) messages. Let $A = \mathrm{Dom}(\alpha)$, i.e., the domain of $\alpha$, then:

(0)   $\rho \subseteq A$ and $A \cap \chi = \emptyset$,
(1)   if $a \in A$, then $\mathrm{FV}(\alpha(a)) \subseteq A \cup \chi$, where $\mathrm{FV}(\alpha(a))$ represents the free variables of $\alpha(a)$; and if $<v_0 \Leftarrow v_1>$ is a message with content $v_1$ to actor address $v_0$, then $\mathrm{FV}(v_i) \subseteq A \cup \chi$ for $i < 2$.

For an actor with address $a$, we indicate its state as $[e]_a$, where it is busy executing $e$; $e$ represents the actor's current (local) processing state.

We can extend the local transitions defined for a sequential language ($\overset{\lambda}{\mapsto}$), by providing labeled transitions for the actor program as follows (assume that $R$ is the reduction context in which the expression currently being evaluated occurs). For brevity, we skip writing the labels corresponding to each transition unless needed.

**Definition ($\mapsto$):**

$$e \overset{\lambda}{\mapsto}_{\mathrm{Dom}(\alpha) \cup \{a\}} e' \Rightarrow \big\langle \alpha, [e]_a \mid \mu \big\rangle_\chi^\rho \mapsto \big\langle \alpha, [e']_a \mid \mu \big\rangle_\chi^\rho$$

$$\big\langle \alpha, [R[\![\mathtt{newactor}(e)]\!]]_a \mid \mu \big\rangle_\chi^\rho \mapsto \big\langle \alpha, [R[\![a']\!]]_a, [e]_{a'} \mid \mu \big\rangle_\chi^\rho \qquad a' \text{ fresh}$$

$$\big\langle \alpha, [R[\![\mathtt{ready}(v)]\!]]_a \mid \mu, <a \Leftarrow v> \big\rangle_\chi^\rho \mapsto \big\langle \alpha, [\mathtt{app}(v, v)]_a \mid \mu \big\rangle_\chi^\rho$$

$$\big\langle \alpha, [R[\![\mathtt{send}(v_0, v_1)]\!]]_a \mid \mu \big\rangle_\chi^\rho \mapsto \big\langle \alpha, [R[\![\mathtt{nil}]\!]]_a \mid \mu, <v_0 \Leftarrow v_1> \big\rangle_\chi^\rho$$

$$\big\langle \alpha \mid \mu, m \big\rangle_\chi^\rho \mapsto \big\langle \alpha \mid \mu \big\rangle_\chi^{\rho'}$$
$$\text{if } m = <a \Leftarrow v>, \ a \in \chi, \text{ and } \rho' = \rho \cup (\mathrm{FV}(v) \cap \mathrm{Dom}(\alpha))$$

$$\big\langle \alpha \mid \mu \big\rangle_\chi^\rho \mapsto \big\langle \alpha \mid \mu, m \big\rangle_{\chi \cup (\mathrm{FV}(v) - \mathrm{Dom}(\alpha))}^\rho$$
$$\text{if } m = <a \Leftarrow v>, \ a \in \rho \text{ and } \mathrm{FV}(v) \cap \mathrm{Dom}(\alpha) \subseteq \rho$$

### 12.3.2   Equivalence of Actor Systems

Based on a slight variant of the transition system described above, a rigorous theory of actor systems is developed in [4]. Specifically, various notions of testing equivalence on actor expressions and configurations are designed and studied. The model provides fairness, namely that any enabled transition eventually fires. Thus fairness implies three things. First, every busy actor eventually makes progress. Second, every actor that is ready to receive a message will eventually receive a message, provided there is a message pending for it. Finally, if an actor does not become "stuck," i.e. is ready infinitely often, it will eventually process every message sent to it. Fairness is an important requirement for reasoning about eventuality properties. It is particularly relevant in supporting modular reasoning: if we compose one configuration with another which has a nonterminating computation, computation in the first configuration may nevertheless proceed as before, for example, if actors in the two configurations do not interact.

The notion of equivalence is defined by adding an observable distinguished *event* to the set of transitions. This technique is a variant of operational equivalence defined in [23]. Two actor expressions may be plugged into a context to see if the event occurs in one or the other case. Two expressions are considered equivalent if they have the same observations over all possible contexts.

The nondeterminism in the arrival order of the messages in an actor computation gives rise to three notions of observation over a computation tree. Notice there are many computational paths in the tree. Now it is possible that the event occurs in every computational path (*must* happen); occurs in some but not all computational paths (*may* happen), or never occurs.

Three distinct well-known equivalence relations may now be defined. In *may* equivalence, *always occurs* is as good as *sometimes occurs* (that is, either is a sufficient condition for proving equivalence); in *must* equivalence *never occurs* is as good as *only sometimes occurs*. *Convex* equivalence requires the two sets to coincide (the intersection of the two equivalences). An important result is that, in the presence of fairness, the three forms of equivalence collapse to two, namely, *may* and *convex*. Thus, while fairness makes some aspects of reasoning harder—we cannot simply use co-induction in proofs—it simplifies others.

Methods for proving laws of equivalence and proof techniques that simplify reasoning about actor systems have been developed. Finally, the composition of configurations defines an algebra.

Note that the model we have defined thus far does not capture mobility of code. Specifically, $\lambda$-abstractions cannot be communicated. Since behaviors are modeled as $\lambda$-abstractions, this implies that remote creation and migration cannot be explicitly modeled.

### 12.3.3   Actors and Concurrent Programming

In addition to the asynchronous message passing paradigm used by the Actor model, other paradigms have also been used for implementing concurrent systems. A detailed treatment of these can be found in [6]. In the *shared variable* paradigm, processes communicate by writing to and reading from memory locations shared by them. Although the apparent simplicity of this paradigm is appealing, it violates principles of abstraction and encapsulation, making it difficult to implement large systems reliably. Among the issues such implementations have to address include support for *mutual exclusion*, the ability to disallow all but one process to access a set of shared variables, and *condition synchronization*, requiring that a piece of code in some process be not executed until some condition is met.

A classic problem in concurrent programming is called the *critical section problem*, in which $n$ processes execute indefinitely long alternating between sections of code that do and those that do not access some shared variables. The part of code that does access these variables is called the *critical section*. The objective is to provide mutual exclusion, while preventing deadlock/livelock or an unnecessary delay, and ensuring that every process attempting to enter its critical section does eventually do so.

A construct that can be used to solve the critical section problem and many other synchronization problems for shared variable systems is *semaphores*. Semaphores provide a disciplined way for supporting condition synchronization by using values of shared counters to control whether a section of code can or cannot be executed. *Conditional critical regions* are an abstraction that groups together shared resources and allows only conditional access to such groups. *Monitors* abstract this further by limiting access to shared variables strictly through use of a fixed set of procedures.

The actor model abstracts over issues of low-level synchronization by encapsulating the state of an object and its execution thread, and limiting communication to asynchronous message passing. Actors thus provide an abstract level at which to program and reason about agents. Synchronous communication and other more complex communication mechanisms can be built on top of the basic asynchronous communication mechanism [5]. Moreover, as we will see later in this chapter, high-level commit protocols can be used for agent-level synchronization.

## 12.4   Representing Agents as Actors

In developing multi-agent systems, a key issue to be addressed is *mobility*. Mobility allows an agent to migrate from one node in the distributed system to another, seeking a "better" execution environment. The increased flexibility raises some other important issues.

It may be desirable for an agent to migrate to a different physical location for a variety of reasons. These reasons may include lower cost of execution compared to the current location, or improved quality of service. The need to migrate can also be task specific. For example, if an agent needs to access huge amounts of data at different locations, it may make sense to migrate to those locations in order to exploit better locality.

The above examples essentially assume that mobile agents are clients. On the other hand, it is also possible to have server agents that roam around the network looking for hospitable execution environments attempting to sell their services. This may even take the shape of a partnership whereby server agents are allowed to exist on nodes, and the nodes can advertise the additional services thus made available to attract other clients.

To support a system where agents can use resources available "elsewhere" in a satisfactory way, it is important to have some notion of an economy. Such an economy would provide the basis on which nodes would allow agents to use their resources, and would serve as an environment that would enable nodes and agents to get into binding contracts about the services needed.

A complementary issue to limiting the resources consumed by an agent is that of supporting an agent or an ensemble of agents in pursuit of their goals. The system must provide means for agents serving the same interest to cooperate, or otherwise not impede each other's progress.

### 12.4.1   Mobility of Actors

Because Actor semantics is location transparent, systems based on the model (e.g., [18]), do not allow actors to reason about their locations. This limits the use of migration to system level decisions where only system level goals such as load balancing can be considered. To take advantage of agents' ability to autonomously decide whether, when and where they want to migrate, we need to extend the Actor model with notions of location and mobility.

A precursor to true migration is the ability to create an actor at a remote site. The Actor programming language Hal [3] uses annotations to govern actor placement at creation.

*Example 12.2 Distributed Filtered Search*

Consider a variation of the Filtered Search example we saw earlier, where the tree is distributed over many nodes. New actors for searching the subtrees are created at nodes hosting the roots of the respective subtrees. We assume that the tree is non-empty.

```
(defActor FILTERSEARCH ()
  (let ((filter (lambda (list)
                  ... )))
    (method (cust tree)
      (if (= (num-children tree) 0)
          (send cust (content tree))
          (let ((jc (newActor COLLECT
                      (cust (num-children tree)
                        (list (content tree)) filter))))
            (map
              (lambda (x)
                (let ((f (newActor FILTERSEARCH ())
                         @ (host-of x)))
                  (send f jc x)))
              (children tree))
            (ready FILTERSEARCH ()))))))
```
                                                                    □

A similar construct, called `trojan-multisend`, sends new actors to a collection of remote locations, along with the first messages that each will process [3].

True migration must allow an actor to migrate to a different node while it is in the middle of its execution. We will describe a specific way of providing this functionality.

First, we define some important changes in the actor naming scheme that is used, to allow migration to be represented. Because actors can migrate, we need to identify an actor's current location. Specifically, we change the naming scheme for identifying individual actors for the purpose of sending messages: an actor name is now $h.a$, where $a$ is a globally unique identifier for any actor, and $h$ identifies the node at which it currently resides. The important implication is that a name $a$ at any node in the system corresponds to the same actor. Practical implications of the new name representation will be discussed shortly.

The message send that simply resulted in creation of a message from the standard Actor semantics, now creates such a message locally in the host node's queue, necessitating keeping track of which node a message is physically located at, at any time. The transfer of a message from its current location to the target actor's node is handled separately.

Migration can be represented in two ways: the agent language can provide a migration primitive, or it could provide an agent with a way to grab its own state and send it over (inside a message) to a remote node to create a duplicate with that state; the original actor can then become a forwarder. Because a migration primitive introduces greater semantic complexity, we choose to study the latter. A `ccf` primitive can be introduced to grab the local state of an actor by enclosing the actor's reduction context inside a $\lambda$-abstraction. Using this primitive, we can represent higher level operations as macros.

### *Example 12.3  Migration*

A construct for migration, called `migrate@h`, may be defined as a macro. Without loss of generality, assume that each host also has a manager actor $h.m$ that acts on behalf of the host and manages the host's resources. The `ccf` primitive is used for grabbing the current continuation of the actor. Unlike Lisp/Scheme, here continuations are local to a single actor; in Scheme, the continuation represents the state of the entire sequential program—typically a much larger object. The function given to `ccf` first sends a `move` request to the remote host's manager `h.m` to create a new actor with the same personal name as the actor requesting migration, using the reduction context enclosed in `y` as its behavior. It then changes the requesting actor's behavior to WAIT-ACK. Assume we have a procedure `getkey` to generate a new key every time it is invoked; `personal-name` returns the name of an actor minus the host's identifier.

```
(let ((k (getkey)))
  (ccf (lambda (y)
         (seq (send h.m move self y k (personal-name self))
              (ready WAIT-ACK (h m k (personal-name self)))))))
```

Assuming that a `move` method is a part of `h.m`'s behavior, it would accept the message, create a new duplicate actor, and return an acknowledgment. The behavior WAIT-ACK waits for an acknowledgment from the remote host manager, containing identities of the host and its manager, and a copy of the key sent with the request.

```
(defActor WAIT-ACK (h m k a)
  (lambda (ret-h ret-m ret-k)
    (if (and (= h ret-h) (= m ret-m) (= k ret-k))
        (ready FORWARDER (h.a))))))
```

To avoid the blocking semantics, the actor may add the method WAIT-ACK to its current behavior rather than replacing with it. In such a case, until the acknowledgment message is received the actor would keep acting as usual. Once the message is received, it would change its behavior into that of a FORWARDER.

Note that because actor names are globally unique, there is no need to transmit the complete name of the new actor. If a particular name is in use at multiple nodes, only one of them corresponds to an actual actor; others have to be forwarders. An important implication of this is that if an actor migrates to a node where the name is already in use, it must be in use as a forwarder which can be safely overwritten by the actual actor. □

### Example 12.4  Remote Creation

A construct for remote creation, `remote-actor(e)@h`, may similarly be defined as a macro. As above, assume that `h.m` is the manager actor for the host `h`. Here, the function given to `ccf` sends a `newactor` request to the remote host's manager `h.m` to create a new actor with name `a` and behavior `e`, and changes the requesting actor's behavior to WAIT-ADDR.

```
(let ((k (getkey)))
  (ccf (lambda (y)
         (seq (send h.m newactor self e k)
              (ready WAIT-ADDR (h m y k))))))
```

Behavior WAIT-ADDR waits for the address of the new actor created remotely, and after verifying all the information, it inserts the new address in the reduction context contained in y.

```
(defActor WAIT-ADDR (h m y k)
  (lambda (ret-h ret-m ret-k a)
    (if (and (= h ret-h) (= m ret-m) (= k ret-k))
        (ready (y h.a)))))
```

To avoid the blocking semantics in this case, the actor could perform a local `newactor` to create a local actor with a migrate expression preceding rest of the desired behavior. This would be facilitated by the fact that actor names do not change as actors move from node to node. □

### Semantics of Mobile Actors

Transitions presented in Section 12.3.1 can now be modified to address support for migration. To identify an actor's current location, a superscript is added to the actor state representation that identifies the host; recall that the subscript identifies the actor itself.

**Definition ($\mapsto$):**

$$e \overset{\lambda}{\mapsto}_{\text{Dom}(\alpha) \cup \{a\}} e' \Rightarrow \Big\langle \alpha, [e]_a^h \mid \mu \Big\rangle_\chi^\rho \mapsto \Big\langle \alpha, [e']_a^h \mid \mu \Big\rangle_\chi^\rho$$

We assume that all creation is local and that only messages co-located on the same host as an actor are consumed. Remote messages, actor migration, and remote creation will be dealt with separately.

We keep track of which node a message is physically located at by attaching a superscript to each message, identifying the host of the intended recipient. A separate transition is added to represent the transfer of a message from its current location to the target node.

$$\Big\langle \alpha, [R[\![\text{newactor}(e)]\!]]_a^h \mid \mu \Big\rangle_\chi^\rho \mapsto \Big\langle \alpha, [R[\![h.a']\!]]_a^h, [e]_{a'}^h \mid \mu \Big\rangle_\chi^\rho \qquad a' \text{ fresh}$$

$$\Big\langle \alpha, [R[\![\text{ready}(e)]\!]]_a^h \mid \mu, {<}a \Leftarrow v{>}^h \Big\rangle_\chi^\rho \mapsto \Big\langle \alpha, [\text{app}(e, v)]_a^h \mid \mu \Big\rangle_\chi^\rho$$

$$\Big\langle \alpha, [R[\![\text{send}(h_2.a_2, v)]\!]]_{a_1}^{h_1} \mid \mu \Big\rangle_\chi^\rho \mapsto \Big\langle \alpha, [R[\![\text{nil}]\!]]_{a_1}^{h_1} \mid \mu, {<}h_2.a_2 \Leftarrow v{>}^{h_1} \Big\rangle_\chi^\rho$$

$$\Big\langle \alpha \mid \mu, {<}h_2.a \Leftarrow v{>}^{h_1} \Big\rangle_\chi^\rho \mapsto \Big\langle \alpha \mid \mu, {<}h_2.a \Leftarrow v{>}^{h_2} \Big\rangle_\chi^\rho$$

The two transitions for interaction with actors outside the system remain unchanged, except for the fact that the receptionists $\rho$ and the external actors $\chi$ now contain actors as well as host managers.

The following last transition provides access to the local state of an actor, which is needed to support migration. It introduces the primitive ccf, which grabs the continuation by putting the reduction context $R$ inside a $\lambda$-abstraction, and applying it to the given function $v$.

$$\Big\langle \alpha, [R[\![\text{ccf}(v)]\!]]_a^h \mid \mu \Big\rangle_\chi^\rho \mapsto \Big\langle \alpha, [\text{app}(v, \lambda x.R[\![x]\!])]_a^h \mid \mu \Big\rangle_\chi^\rho$$

$$x \notin \text{FV}(R[\![\text{nil}]\!])$$

Although these semantics explain the process of migration, note that to establish the need to migrate, an agent must be able to observe its own state. The model of *computational reflection* provides a formal basis for an agent to have a representation of its own behavior. We will discuss reflection in Section 12.5.1.

## 12.4.2   Resource Model

Resource allocation in multiagent systems is a problem that raises issues of reciprocity as well as performance and security concerns. Nodes in a multiagent system over the worldwide web, for instance, may be willing to be part of a multiagent system if they receive something in return for allowing foreign agents to use their resources. From the performance and security perspective, agents migrating to a node may exhibit undesirable resource consumptive behaviors, either individually, or as ensembles. Similarly, network channels are a scarce resource requiring controls on how they may be used.

We may use an economic model to protect against resource consumptive behavior of agents in a multiagent system. Recall that control in agent systems is not based solely on programming structures, as agents may create or invoke other autonomous agents. Such autonomy makes it important to devise explicit mechanisms for controlling the extent to which an expanding group of agents, working on a single task, can utilize a system's resources. In an open distributed system, the problem is compounded by the ability of agents to exist in a resource space not entirely dedicated to their computations alone. We need mechanisms to support bounding the resource utilization of individual agents, or ensembles of agents working together, according to the terms under which they are allowed access to those resources.

### Example 12.5  Bounded Distributed Filtered Search

Consider a variation of the Distributed Filtered Search application described earlier, where we want to control the amount of resources that can be consumed in pursuit of the goal. The typical message send to an actor with behavior FILTERSEARCH will contain a value `res` representing the resources allocated for the task:

```
(let ((FS (newActor FILTERSEARCH ())))
    (send FS self tree res))
```

The system will strip the value `res` from the message, and keep track of the resources remaining at any time. The agent would have read access to the current value of this quantity by asking the system.

The application keeps creating new agents to search subtrees as long as it has resources, and stops when only `delta` remains. We assume that `delta` represents sufficient resources for transmitting results to the client. `part` represents the agent's consumption strategy that tells it what portion of the available resources may be allocated to a sub-task.

Because there isn't a way to know how many messages `jc` should expect at the time of its creation, its initial behavior is set to TELLCOLLECT, which waits for a count of the number of responses to expect. After receiving that message, a TELLCOLLECT actor uses the value in replacing its behavior with COLLECT.

```
(defActor FILTERSEARCH ()
  (let ((filter (lambda (list)
                    ... )))
    (method (cust tree)
      (if (= (num-children tree) 0)
          (send cust (content tree))
          (let ((jc (newActor TELLCOLLECT ()))
                (count 0))
            (map
              (lambda (x)
```

```
(if (> (my-resources) delta)
    (let ((f (newActor FILTERSEARCH ())
                            @ (host-of x)))
        (send f jc x (part (my-resources)))
        (setf count (+ count 1)))))
    (children tree))
    (send jc cust count (content tree)
        (part (my-resource)) filter)
    (ready FILTERSEARCH ()))))))
```

This example does not account for resources needed for agents to survive on a node while they are inactive.

Note that an agent's resource consumption strategy is independent of the system's ability to *pull the plug* when the resources run out. Needless to add, any attempt to send more resources to another agent than it possesses, would be trapped by the run-time system.  □

To implement an economic model, we will use the notion of a universal currency. Specifically, resource allocation will be measured in a common currency called GCU (for *global currency unit*). Every computational activity would be allocated some GCU's which can be used in completing the task. Because activity in message-based systems is triggered by a message send, these GCU's can be allocated at message send time. But note that what is counted as resources is the physical and logical computational resources needed to service a message. This is not the only use of resources; agents residing at a host waiting for something to happen, for instance, also use resources such as memory. Thus, the notion of computational resources must be broad enough to include all entities in the system whose use by one agent can affect the performance of rest of the system. The amount of time devoted to an agent by the processors, the memories, the disks and the channels, are all resources which need to be paid for. The analog of renting resources seems to apply more accurately than that of purchasing.

In addition to the resources consumed while progressing towards accomplishing their goals, individual agents may sometimes be waiting for information from elsewhere, or for reasons of coordination. Such waiting consumes memory resources which must be accounted for. At the same time, an agent should not have to pay if the idle wait is increased by the host's scheduling choices. Thus, it is important to represent resources both in terms of individual agents as well as in terms of the larger application they are serving at a particular hosting node. Only the delays caused by co-agents in an application should be charged.

Similarly, it is important to distinguish between economic boundaries in an open distributed system and the physical boundaries between computational nodes. Although resources such as network bandwidth usage depend on physical boundaries, costs of other resources would more logically vary as one crosses economic boundaries.

### Semantics of Resource Bounded Agents

In developing the semantics for representing resource allocation, we add a value $r$ to the agent state (we now use the term *agent* instead of actor), to represent the units of universal currency (GCU's) available to the agent. The configuration also includes $\beta$ to represent the system map, which includes all the *host agents* representing the nodes, and the network connecting these nodes. $[s]_h$ says that the host agent $h$ has state $s$. We treat the host agents separately because they are not mobile, and because the fact that a host's state may determine the cost of its computational resources, makes it important to keep track of its state changes.

We are also introducing two new functions. $T_{st}$ is a function that takes the current state of a host and the transition being applied, to give the next state. This function is applied to all members of $\beta$ being effected by a transition. $T_{res(a,h)}$ is a function that represents a contract between an agent $a$ and the node $h$ hosting it, and determines the cost (in GCU's) of performing a transition $t$ when the host is in state $s$ ( $\overset{t}{\mapsto}$ will be used to represent transitions, where $t$ is a variable representing the specific transition taking place). Such a contract would be reached at after a process of negotiation between the agent and the host. Note that this function is very general because it allows the cost of the services to vary as the host's state changes.

**Definition ($\mapsto$):**

$$e \overset{\lambda}{\mapsto}_{\text{Dom}(\alpha) \cup \{a\}} e' \Rightarrow$$

$$\left\langle \alpha, [e, r]_a^h \mid \beta, [s]_h \mid \mu \right\rangle_\chi^\rho \overset{t}{\mapsto}$$

$$\left\langle \alpha, [e', r - T_{res(a,h)}(t, s)]_a^h \mid \beta, [T_{st}(t, s)]_h \mid \mu \right\rangle_\chi^\rho$$

$$\text{if } r \geq T_{res(a,h)}(t, s)$$

The transitions for `newactor` and `ccf` expressions remain identical to those for mobile actors, except that the actor is charged for the cost of performing the transitions.

Because it is the `send` primitive that initiates a new activity, a certain number of GCU's has to be sent along with the message for pursuing the activity. So, in addition to the cost of the transition, the wealth of the sending actor is also reduced by $r'$. As the activity is entirely local, only the local host's state changes.

The complementary activity of transferring a message from one node to another represents change in states of both the nodes as well as the state of the network $s_n$. We make a convention that the cost of this transfer is always incurred by the sender. Because of this, it is important to identify the sender of the message, for which we add a subscript to the messages to represent the sender's identity. The only amount charged for transferring a message is the network cost $T_{net}(h_1, h_2, \mid v \mid, s_n)$ of transferring a message of size $\mid v \mid$. We assume that any cost of handling the message at both ends of the channel is negligible in comparison and can be ignored.

$$\langle\, \alpha,\, [R[\![\text{send}(h_2.a_2, v, r')]\!], r]_{a_1}^{h_1} \mid \beta,\, [s]_{h_1} \mid \mu \,\rangle_{\chi}^{\rho} \overset{t}{\mapsto}$$

$$\langle\, \alpha,\, [R[\![\text{nil}]\!], r - r' - T_{res(a,h)}(t, s)]_{a_1}^{h_1} \mid \beta,\, [T_{st}(t, s)]_{h_1} \mid \mu, m \,\rangle_{\chi}^{\rho}$$

$$m = <h_2.a_2 \Leftarrow [v, r']>_{h_1.a_1}^{h_1}$$

$$\langle\, \alpha,\, [e, r]_{a_1}^{h_1} \mid \beta,\, [s_1]_{h_1},\, [s_2]_{h_2},\, [s_n]_{net} \mid \mu, <h_2.a_2 \Leftarrow [v, r']>_{h_1.a_1}^{h_1} \,\rangle_{\chi}^{\rho} \overset{t}{\mapsto}$$

$$\langle\, \alpha,\, [e, r - T_{net}(h_1, h_2, |\, v\, |, s_n)]_{a_1}^{h_1} \mid \beta,\, [T_{st}(t, s_1)]_{h_1},\, [T_{st}(t, s_2)]_{h_2},$$

$$[T_{st}(t, s_n)]_{net} \mid \mu, <h_2.a_2 \Leftarrow [v, r']>_{h_1.a_1}^{h_2} \,\rangle_{\chi}^{\rho}$$

Receipt of a message simply results in addition of the GCU's sent in the message to the wealth of the receiving agent.

$$\langle\, \alpha,\, [R[\![\text{ready}(e)]\!], r]_{a}^{h} \mid \beta,\, [s]_{h_1} \mid \mu, <h_1.a_1. \Leftarrow [v, r']>_{h_2.a_2}^{h} \,\rangle_{\chi}^{\rho} \overset{t}{\mapsto}$$

$$\langle\, \alpha,\, [\text{app}(e, v), r + r' - T_{res(a_1, h_1)}(t, s)]_{a_1}^{h} \mid \beta,\, [T_{st}(t, s)]_{h_1} \mid \mu \,\rangle_{\chi}^{\rho}$$

Following are the two transitions representing communication with the outside world in the form of transfer of a message to or from the system. Because the cost of such a transfer is to be incurred by the sender, there is no need to represent a cost in the transition when a message is received from outside the system. Transferring a message out of the system does result in a cost that will be incurred by the sending agent. The host state changes occur in the network, the local host $h_1$, and in the host $h_2$ of the external actor, but because the external host is itself not included in $\beta$, its state change is not represented in the transition.

$$\langle\, \alpha,\, [e, r]_{a_1}^{h_1} \mid \beta,\, [s]_{h_1},\, [s_n]_{net} \mid \mu, <h_2.a_2 \Leftarrow [v, r']>_{h_1.a_1}^{h_1} \,\rangle_{\chi}^{\rho} \overset{t}{\mapsto}$$

$$\langle\, \alpha,\, [e, r - T_{net}(h_1, h_2, v, s_n)]_{a_1}^{h_1} \mid \beta,\, [T_{st}(t, s)]_{h_1},\, [T_{st}(t, s_n)]_{net} \mid \mu \,\rangle_{\chi}^{\rho'}$$

$$\text{if } h_2.a_2 \in \chi, \text{ and } \rho' = \rho \cup (\text{FV}(v) \cap \text{Dom}(\alpha))$$

$$\langle\, \alpha \mid \beta,\, [s]_{h_1},\, [s_n]_{net} \mid \mu \,\rangle_{\chi}^{\rho} \overset{t}{\mapsto} \langle\, \alpha \mid \beta,\, [T_{st}(t, s)]_{h_1},$$

$$[T_{st}(t, s_n)]_{net} \mid \mu, <h_1.a_1 \Leftarrow [v, r']>_{h_2.a_2}^{h_1} \,\rangle_{\chi \cup (\text{FV}(v) - \text{Dom}(\alpha))}^{\rho}$$

$$\text{if } h_1.a_1 \in \rho \text{ and } \text{FV}(v) \cap \text{Dom}(\alpha) \subseteq \rho$$

Finally we need a transition rule to represent the cost of an inactive agent residing at a host. As explained earlier, this cost is complicated by the fact that we do not want to charge an agent if the wait is caused by factors associated purely with the host itself. Essentially, we want to charge the agent if there is no message in the system for it, for the time that its co-agents are executing. This would make sense if the host's scheduler would schedule an application scheduler for each application, rather than scheduling individual agents directly. In this way, the rent for the memory being used can be charged only for the time for which the application is scheduled.

$$\left\langle \alpha, [R[\![\text{ready}(e)]\!], r]^{h_1}_{a_1} \mid \beta, [s]_{h_1} \mid \mu \right\rangle^{\rho}_{\chi} \overset{t}{\mapsto}$$

$$\left\langle \alpha, [R[\![\text{ready}(e)]\!], r - \epsilon]^{h_1}_{a_1} \mid \beta, [T_{st}(t, s)]_{h_1} \mid \mu \right\rangle^{\rho}_{\chi}$$

if $<h.a \Leftarrow [v, r']>^{h_2}_{h_2 . a_2} \notin \mu$ for any $v, r', a_2$ and $h_2$

and $t$ is a transition in some co-agent of $a_1$

---

## 12.5　Agent Ensembles

Individual agents are not much more powerful than conventional sequential programs. However, by exploiting parallelism, distribution and mobility, ensembles of agents promise orders of magnitude greater computational power than conventional programs. Before the promise can be realized, the dynamicity and uncertainty in such systems poses a number of problems. To allow agent ensembles to operate effectively, we need to provide the ability to organize groups of agents in interesting ways. Specifically, there are two kinds of concerns we have to address. First, the contexts in which they execute and interact need to be dynamically customizable. Second, the interactions of different, potentially overlapping groups of agents, need to be mediated to ensure shared protocols. We describe the programming model that has been developed to provide the requisite flexibility.

### 12.5.1　Customizing Execution Contexts

An agent traveling from node to node seeking affordable resources may find itself in environments that by default do not meet some of its requirements for execution. For example, an agent may need some helper agents that could be asked to perform specialized tasks, as is the case with a library of plug-ins. In order to ensure the appropriate execution context, the agent could ensure that an acceptable context already exists at the host before migrating there. Alternately, it could customize the context at arrival.

In some cases, the execution of an agent needs to be mediated, contained, scheduled, etc., to meet requirements such as security, real-time, or Quality of Service (QoS). Because the implementation of such requirements is dependent on the physical and logical resources available, the underlying architecture supporting agents must be customizable. It is essential for the ability to customize the execution context that the code for requirements such as QoS be implemented separately from the code for the application functionality. For example, if the agents encoding an

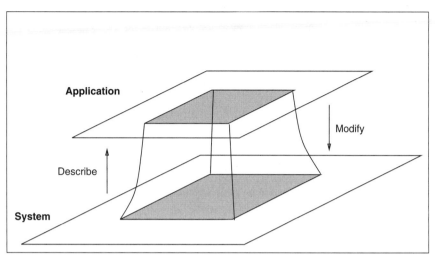

**Figure 12.2**   Computational Reflection

application are assigning their own priorities and schedules, it is not very feasible to schedule them in order to satisfy real-time requirements.

Customization of the execution context is accomplished using a technique called *reflection* [22]. Reflection allows an application to monitor the execution of the underlying system and to modify it dynamically (Figure 12.2).

### Reflection

In general, models of reflection enable interaction of higher level operations, such as real-time constraints, and lower level information about the execution environment, such as load distribution over a group of processors, available network bandwidth, etc.

Because the Actor model allows the state of the computation to be modeled directly, the computation environment called the *meta-level architecture* can be represented at an appropriate level of abstraction using the same base language [32]. Specifically, this allows use of reflection enabling an agent to have a continuous interaction with the environment to determine available resources and relate it to its own state to provide evolving resource consumption strategies.

In Rosette [31], a commercially developed object-oriented implementation of an Actor architecture, the architecture has an *interface layer* and a *system environment*. The interface layer provides *mechanisms* for monitoring and control of applications, where the system environment contains actor communities which implement resource management *policies*, providing monitoring, debugging, resource management, system simulation, and compilation/transformation facilities.

To support reflection of the interface layer, Rosette uses three classes of resource actors to abstractly implement an actor: *container, processor*, and *mailbox*. Containers model the storage local to actors, in a way similar to frames in knowledge-based systems. Each container is a set of associations (*slots*) of keys with values, which are both other actors. Additions and deletions of slots model allocations and deallocations of storage. Processor actors determine how to determine the method for responding to a message. Mailbox actors buffer incoming messages until they can be processed.

Suppose we want to ensure the availability of some agent where its absence may be catastrophic. We may replicate the service to ensure availability when the original server fails. In the following example adapted from [2], we will see how such a replication service may be provided.

### Example 12.6 Replicated Service

We can use meta-actors called *dispatchers* to trap out-going messages, and *mail-queue* meta-actors to trap in-coming messages, for every actor. When a service request arrives for the server, its dispatcher can forward a copy of the request to the alternate servers too. When the servers respond with results, their responses are tagged with an identifier for the request. At the client end, the mail-queue meta-actor can use the tag to discard extra copies of any response. A manager in charge of replicating a service takes the following actions to achieve the state shown in Figure 12.3:

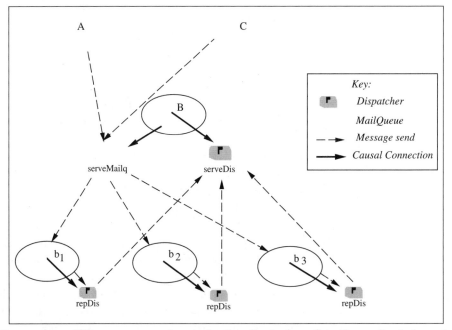

**Figure 12.3**   When a message is sent by the clients A or C to the replicated service B, the message is received by B's mail queue serveMailq (1). The message is then sent to each of the replicas (2).

1.  The specified server is replicated by a manager by creating actors with the same behavior and acquaintance list.

2.  A mail queue is installed for the original server to make it act as the *distributor* described above. Messages destined for the original server are broadcast to the replicas. A broadcast using `ssends` (synchronous sends) is done so that all replicas receive messages in the same order and thus solve the same task.

3.  The dispatcher of the original server is modified to act as the *collector* described above. The first message out of each set of replica responses is selected to be passed to the destination.

4.  The dispatchers of the replicas are changed to forward all messages being sent to the original server's dispatcher. In addition, the messages are tagged so that the original server's dispatcher can eliminate multiple copies of the same message.

The new mail queue for the original server is described using the following behaviors:

```
(defActor SERVEMAILQ (data members)
  (method get (who)
     ... )
  (method put (msg)
      ;; A bcaster actor broadcasts msg to members
      (bsend (newActor bcaster msg) members)))

(defActor BCASTER (msg)
  (method (l)
     (if (not (null? l))
         (ssend (car l) msg)
         (send self (cdr l)))))
```

Note that message order is being preserved in the broadcast. We use `ssend` function to guarantee consistent state at each replica. `bsend` is a remote procedure call (blocking send). Figure 12.3 shows the resulting actions occurring when a message is sent to the replicated service. The original server is actor $B$. When a message is received by the distributor, serveMailq ($B$'s new mail queue), the message is broadcast to the replicas $b_1$, $b_2$, $b_3$. Each of the replicated actors has the same base-level behavior as $B$. Therefore, upon receipt of the message, each $b_i$ responds in the same way $B$ would have. However, if the replicas respond to the message, the message destinations would be rerouted by the dispatchers *repDis* to the original server's dispatcher, *serveDis* (serving as the collector). For each response, *serveDis* gets three messages, one from each replica. It processes the three messages and sends out a single response to the original destination. Note that the base-level actor $B$ does not receive any messages now since all the incoming messages are redirected to the replicas by its mail queue *serveMailq* and the outgoing messages are sent by the dispatchers of the replicas directly to its dispatcher *serveDis*.                                                                          □

### 12.5.2    Interaction Protocols

Ability of the system to cope with new kinds of failures of a few nodes or parts of the network is essential in a distributed system. A variation of the problem appears when we are dealing with systems where "failure" is the norm, such as distributed systems using wireless communications where the network connectivity is essentially dynamic [15].

When introducing mechanisms for fault-tolerance, it is important to separate the fault-tolerance aspects of the code from the application for reasons of modularity and reusability. In this section we will discuss an abstraction over the primitive Actor model called *interaction policies*. Interaction policies determine what protocols to use in dealing with a failure situation.

An interaction policy may be expressed in terms of the interfaces of actors and implemented by using appropriate protocols to coordinate actors. A protocol imposes a certain role on each participating actor. In essence it mediates the interactions between actors to ensure that each relevant actor implements its end of the interaction policy.

Notice that the implementation of such protocols can be quite involved: it involves exchanging a number of messages between participating actors. Current techniques for developing distributed software require developers to implement interaction policies and application behavior together, significantly complicating code. The lack of modularity not only makes it hard to reason about code; it limits its reusability and portability. Moreover, the resulting code is brittle: modifying an interaction policy to satisfy changing requirements requires modifying the code of each relevant component and then reasoning about the entire system, essentially from scratch.

In the first place, in standard programming models, we cannot even express an interaction protocol as a program module; to do so we require the ability to write meta-programs with distributed scope. An interaction protocol imposes a role for each actor, specifically, trapping and tagging incoming and outgoing messages to implement the protocol. Such customization of an individual actor's mail system may be further limited only for the duration of an interaction.

Sturman and Agha have developed a language for describing and implementing interaction policies [29, 30]; using this language, a protocol abstraction may be instantiated by specifying a particular group of actors and other initialization parameters. The runtime system must then support specific forms of reflection, which are sufficiently powerful to enable dynamic modification of the mail system and to store and retrieve actor states, or other parts of the meta-architecture.

Now notice that the semantics of actor systems in the presence of protocols is quite different from the semantics of ordinary (the so-called base-level) actor systems. Our pragmatic experience suggests that reasoning about distributed applications is simplified by our meta-programming system; after all, code size is reduced by at least an order of magnitude, and the application is decomposed into more intuitive units corresponding to the requirements specification. However, the semantics of meta-level operations remains poorly understood. Recent research based on ac-

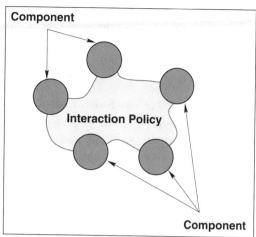

**Figure 12.4**  A distributed system consists of a set of components carrying out local computations and interacting in accordance with a set of *policies*.

tors has made progress on the problem of reasoning in the presence of meta-actors, specifically, by defining a reasoning system and using it to prove the correctness of a meta-level algorithm for taking a global snapshot of a running distributed system of actors [32].

### 12.5.3  Coordination

Dynamic, virtual organization of agents can be accomplished by using coordination mechanisms to express a wide variety of interactions. Coordination is a key design concern for a multiagent system. Since each problem-solving agent possesses only incomplete information which represents a local view of the overall system, and limited computational power, it must coordinate with other agents to achieve globally coherent and efficient solutions. Coordination can be viewed from three different perspectives: the information content, the exercise of control, and the coordination mechanisms [26]. The information used for coordination can be data, new facts discovered, partial solution/plan, preferences, or constraints. What one would like to develop are reusable abstractions for coordination which allow agents to play a richer variety of roles.

As a gross simplification, temporal coordination can be seen as an abstraction of synchronization, the problem of determining *when* actions take place rather than *what* individual actors do. Hence, coordination constraints are an abstraction of synchronization constraints, constraints on the order of actions.

It turns out that two types of synchronizations are often useful. The first type imposes precedence constraints on otherwise asynchronous events at different actors, and the other requires such events to be atomic (loosely speaking, to co-occur). By providing a language abstraction, called *synchronizer* to express these two types of constraints, we are able to show that the task of distributed programming may be further simplified [10]. Because synchronizers may be superimposed, and may be dynamically added or removed, implementing such a system efficiently proves to be a fairly challenging but is nevertheless feasible. The following example is due to Frolund [11].

### Example 12.7  Coordinating Robots

Consider two coordinating robots. Each robot has an arm and a hand, and it can grab a widget with its hand, and lift and move it using its arm.

A single robot can be modeled as a part-whole hierarchy where the robot object serves as an interface between a user and the robot components. When told to move a widget from point $p_1$ to point $p_2$, the interface tells the arm the hand to $p_1$, tells the hand to grab the object, tells the arm to move the hand to $p_2$, and finally tells the hand to release the object. At the completion of any request, the component (hand or arm) informs the robot object about the completion. For instance, the hand would send the message `releaseDone`

Here, we'll consider the case where two robots are to cooperate in moving widgets. The top level object is a logical robot `composed` that serves as an interface for the composed physical robots. These composed robots are allowed to share a widget that is at a position reachable to both. A request may involve movement of a single robot or it may need cross-robot movement. To service a latter type of request to move a widget from $p_1$ to $p_2$, the interface robot would tell robot closer to $p_1$ (the `passer`) to move it from $p_1$ to $p_s h$, the shared position, and next tell the other robot (the `receiver`) to move it from $p_s h$ to $p_2$. The `passer` would in turn communicate with `passerHand` and `passerArm` and so on. Depending on the physical details of the environment, cross-robot movement may have integrity requirements, such as:

- *Totality:* The top level message must send a move message to both or neither of the robots. If only one robot can be dispatched, the widget may get "stuck" at the shared position, preventing cross-robot movement involving other widgets.

- *Collision avoidance:* At most one widget may occupy the shared position at any time.

- *Sequencing:* During a cross-robot movement, the first robot must release the widget before the second robot grabs it.

A synchronizer to coordinate cross-robot movement would have to represent each of these requirements. The totality and collision-avoidance requirement are satisfied by putting an atomicity constraint, that requires `move` requests to both robots to be dispatched at the same time. The sequencing requirement is satisfied by disabling `receiver`'s hand from grabbing the widget while `passer` is active, and by installing triggers that would alternate the value of `passerActive` between `T` and `nil`, as it is dispatched `move` and `releaseDone` messages (by `composed` and `passerHand`, respectively).

```
(defSynch robots (passer receiver receiverHand start end shared)
  (let ((passerActive nil))
    (atomic (request-when (passer.move from to)
                 (and (= from start) (= to shared)))
            (request-when (receiver.move from to)
                 (and (= from shared) (= to end))))
    (disable (request-when receiverHand.grab passerActive))
    (trigger (-> (request-when (passer.move from to)
                         (and (= from start) (= to shared)))
                 (setf passerActive T)))
             (-> (request-when passer.releaseDone T)
                 (setf passerActive nil)))))
```

The `robots` synchronizer template is instantiated by the top-level object composed for each cross-robot movement.                                              □

Synchronizers can be very effective in enforcing system level coordination requirement such as the need to avoid redundant work. Note that in a multiagent system, multiple agents serving the same interest often end up performing the same execution sequences without knowing about each other. At the system level, such redundant activity could be avoided by using appropriate synchronization constraints to disable requests for an activity following the first one.

### Example 12.8  Real-Time Constraints

RTsynchronizers [24] offer one way of implementing real-time constraints using an abstraction similar to that for the declarative coordination constraints discussed earlier. RTsynchronizers are objects that enforce real-time constraints by constraining whether or not messages of a certain type can be delivered to an actor at a certain point in time.

Consider a variation of the Producer/Consumer problem where the produced object must lie in the buffer for a certain amount of time before being removed

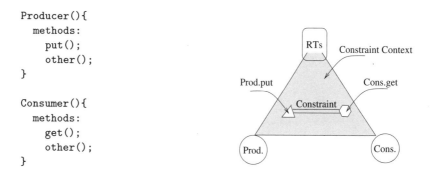

```
Producer(){
  methods:
    put();
    other();
}

Consumer(){
  methods:
    get();
    other();
}
```

**Figure 12.5**  Producer/Consumer with Time-Bounded Buffer.

by the consumer. A *Time Constrained Producer/Consumer* problem can be implemented by writing writing the code for the usual Producer/Consumer problem without explicitly considering the time constraint (Figure 12.5). Then, separately an RTsynchronizer can be declared with the time constraint that would prevent the Consumer's `get` request to be delivered until the required amount of time has elapsed. The declaration are translated into the correct scheduling of actors, if such a translation is feasible.                                                                      □

### 12.5.4   Naming and Groups

In multiagent systems, it is important to be able to access new services that become available and to know when existing servers no longer exist. This necessitates a pattern based naming scheme that identifies agents as being members of groups and allows communication with agents that are not individually known. These group identifiers can also be used in defining protocols.

Groups of agents are an important unit of representation; for example, in defining protocols we can assign roles to a group of agents rather than an individual agent. Moreover, it is often necessary to communicate with agents whose address is not previously known. In other words, we need support for a Yellow Pages service to find addresses of agents of a given type. Traders in object request broker architecture perform a similar function.

The ActorSpace model allows an abstract specification of a group of actors [7]. An actorspace associates an actor with specific attributes; the sender of a message specifies a destination pattern which is pattern-matched against the attributes of actors in the actorspace. The model may also be seen as providing a distributed version of the *blackboard*[8] system for broadcast communication. A simple analogy

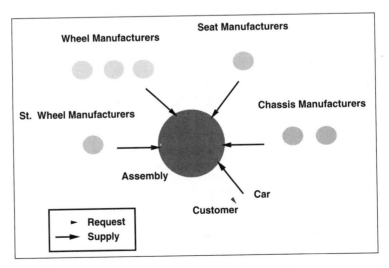

**Figure 12.6**   A car assembly factory. The assembly sends requests to actorspaces whose membership may dynamically change.

with set theory illustrates the difference between naming in actors and actorspaces. A set may be defined by enumerating its elements, or by specifying a characteristic function which defines a subset in a domain. The first method is analogous to actor communication (where an explicit collection of mail addresses of actors must be specified), whereas the second method corresponds to actorspace communication. Of course, in conventional mathematics the two ways of characterizing sets are equivalent since the properties of mathematical objects are static; by contrast, actors may dynamically change their attributes. Actorspace provides a transparent way of managing groups of actors. It generalizes the notion of ports in process calculi, where object identity is also not uniquely defined, but pattern are degenerate.

Figure 12.6 shows a simple example of an actorspace. A car assembly requires certain types of parts which may be available through different vendors, sets that may themselves be changing over time. Which vendor fills a request may not be germane to the assembly process. Such requests may be mediated through an actorspace. Finally, meta-level operations may be associated with an actorspace. For example, an actorspace manager may transparently schedule requests to ensure load balancing.

## 12.6 Related Work

There are two aspects to programming multiagent systems—the mechanisms defining an individual agent's behavior (its computational engine), and mechanisms to support coordination between agents. Computational engines of individual autonomous agents in DAI have traditionally piggybacked on advances in conventional AI. In addition, DAI research has addressed issues related to communication and coordination among agents. At the linguistic and system level, a focus of the DAI research has been to provide the abstractions and tools necessary to develop agents. We will call a system providing such linguistic and system level support an agent architecture.

One of the earliest testbeds for building agent architectures was provided by the MACE system [12], which executed in a distributed memory multiprocessing environment. Based on the experience of this research, Les Gasser [13] outlined the avenues of cooperation between the areas of DAI and concurrent programming, and how the two fields can be brought closer to each other. The current proposal draws part of its inspiration from the insights obtained by that research. More recently, an actor-based DAI system called InfoSleuth [35] has been developed at MCC.

Genesereth [14] defines an agent as an entity that is able to communicate correctly in an agent communication language, thereby emphasizing the expressiveness of such a language. Programs may be converted into software agents by rewriting them so that they have the needed communication ability, or by employing transducers or wrappers to achieve such functionality. Facilitators keeping track of capabilities of agents implement a federated system of communication providing a pattern-based message sending facility.

The Knowledge Query and Manipulation Language (KQML) [9, 21], described in detail in Chapter 2, is a message-handling protocol that aims to provide an effective platform for agent communication by addressing fundamental components of (i) a common language, (ii) a common understanding of exchange knowledge, and (iii) an ability to exchange the two. KQML messages communicate an attribute called *attitude* along with the message content. The language primitives, called *performatives*, define actions permissible to agents in communication. There are special agents called *facilitators* that provide support in identifying agents and services, brokering agreements, etc.

The term Agent Oriented Programming has been coined by Shoham [27] to refer to a specialization of Object Oriented Programming (as in actor programming), where the state of an actor (now called an agent) contains beliefs, capabilities, choices and similar *mental* notions, and the computation consists of agents' social interactions with each other, such as informing, offering, accepting, rejecting, competing, assisting, and so on. The latter idea is derived from speech act literature (e.g.[25]) which categorizes speech in similar ways. Each agent runs a loop in which it first reads the current message, updating its mental state, and then executes the commitments for the current time. Munindar Singh [28] has developed a theoretical framework for reasoning about intentions, know-how and communications.

A multi-level architecture for multiagent systems is described by Werner [33] where a meta-architecture is defined to formalize users', programmers' or designers' interactions with an open system. Michael Kolb's CooL (Cooperation Language) [19] provides a higher level of abstraction with respect to agent design than the actor paradigm, but it gives a knowledge and execution perspective on agents rather than employing mental states. It is possible to give a high level specification of cooperation by negotiating a cooperation object (e.g. goal, plan, schedule) or by synchronizing mutual execution of a plan.

Another context in which the term agent has recently been used is the world wide web (WWW), and there has been an explosion of interest in building agents, in this community too. The use of the term *agent* in DAI and in WWW has different but related meanings. In both contexts, agents are mobile, persistent pieces of code that execute autonomously. In DAI systems, agents may be more complex pieces of code exhibiting intelligence, either individually or collectively; while in the context of the WWW, this is not necessary. We give two examples to illustrate such agents.

A popular language that provides support for concurrent programming is Java. This language, however, is not based on any formal model of concurrency. It allows multiple threads to run concurrently, but unlike actors, Java objects and threads are separate entities, and its passive object model fails to abstract over units of concurrency. The `synchronize` primitive provided for enabling safe usage of concurrent threads is a very low-level facility and its overuse by paranoid programmers often results in deadlocks. This separation of object and thread also creates a problem for migration. By providing Actor primitives in the form of a library, the Actor Foundry [20] developed at OSL attempts to put a discipline for system development in Java.

The Mobile Agent Facility Specification by the Object Management Group [17] makes a case for standardizing areas of mobile agent technology to promote interoperability. These include agent management, transfer, naming (agent as well as agent system), agent system types and location syntax.

Telescript [34] addresses using a public network as a platform on which third-party developers can build their applications. This platform is based on a *remote programming* paradigm that uses Mobile Agents (MA) that can migrate from a client to a remote server and execute remotely on behalf of the client.

Cybenko's group at Dartmouth [16] addresses the issues in implementing mobile agents in an environment consisting of computers, which are often disconnected from the network. Cybenko's mobile agent system, AgentTcl reduces migration to a single instruction, provides transparent communication among agents (hiding all transmission details), and provides a simple scripting language as the main agent communication language while allowing straightforward addition of new languages and transport mechanisms.

## 12.7 Conclusions

The ability to coordinate the behavior of agents in agent ensembles is a key challenge for Distributed AI. We are just beginning to understand the concept of agent and the requirements for supporting their execution. A platform for supporting multiagent ensembles needs to provide scalable mechanisms for safe and efficient execution over open networks of computers. No such architectural platform currently exists today.

We have presented some basic notions that are necessary to support programming agents for DAI, but it is by no means the complete picture. In particular, the underlying platform must control ways in which resources are accessed and managed. The chapter has described how resource allocation policies may be represented at the agent level. Research on techniques for resource allocation continues and will be able to borrow from previous work in subject areas as diverse as operating systems and economics.

Our current understanding of agent semantics is still primitive. For example, there is no well developed equational theory of agents. Because such a theory would allow rigorous reasoning about the behavior of agents, it is very important to the problem of security. Specifically, nodes must be protected against malicious or buggy agents. One idea is that a host could verify the relevant properties of an agent before admitting the host in a less protected mode. Because finding a proof of a program is computationally very expensive (it can be intractable), agents could carry proofs of their programs that the hosts check. Checking an existing proof is computationally much less expensive.

Another approach to security is to *sandbox* the agents. This technique, partially employed by the programming language Java, physically separates the space occupied by an important piece of code (such as that for an agent), to prevent it from affecting the node's operation in any undesirable way. However, because Java's sandboxing model does not limit the physical or logical resources consumed by imported code, it is insufficient for preventing deleterious agents. A third possibility is authentication of agents. Hosts would allow access to agents based on prior knowledge or by checking certification provided by trusted registries.

From a different perspective, because agents can spawn other agents, multiagent systems must also be able to control the activity of ensembles of agents. The behavior of an individual member of an agent ensemble may be quite reasonable, but the behavior of a group of agents can be chaotic. We have a number of examples where the outcome of collections of autonomous processes result in this kind of phenomena. Consider two of them. A ferry sunk as all the passengers rushed to one side in response to a perceived emergency. A power outage in a small area caused a cascading outage. Economic models of control, such as those in markets, may be one approach here. However, for reasons that are apparently not entirely understood, the short term behavior of markets with human players can itself be quite chaotic.

The development of programming language constructs to allow high-level description of behavior for scalable agent ensembles must await a better understanding of what we need to represent. What is now better understood is how to separate the description of agents functional actions from that of other aspects such as naming, scheduling, and synchronization. These modularity and abstraction mechanisms that have been developed in concurrent programming in general go a long way towards providing the basis for designing and experimenting with powerful agent systems.

## 12.8   Exercises

1.   *[Level 1]* Security is an important concern in multiagent systems. Systems may be threatened by harmful activities of individual agents or by ensemble of agents affecting system performance by their collective activity. One such concern, resource consumptive behavior, has been discussed at some length in this chapter. Describe other specific ways in which security is threatened in such systems by collective behavior of agent ensembles.

2.   *[Level 1]* Download an Actor system and use it to implement a parallel search of a distributed n-ary tree. You can find a Java-based Actor system at <http://osl.cs.uiuc.edu>.

3.   *[Level 1]* Describe at least three different schemes for implementing actors in Java. Discuss the advantages and disadvantages of the design decisions in each scheme.

4.   *[Level 2]* Implement an interpreter for an actor language and develop a single processor simulation of actors for executing programs written in this language.

5.   *[Level 2]* Extend the semantics developed in this chapter to incorporate a yellow pages service. Specifically, provide a way of representing and maintaining

ActorSpaces, and write new transition rules needed to express communication in a system employing ActorSpaces.

6. *[Level 3]* In an actual implementation of an agent architecture, it may be unreasonable to assume that the resources needed to complete a task can be predicted reliably, requiring a more complex mechanism by which agents may request more resources from, or return unused resources, to a *sponsor*. These sponsors may be created by client agents as managers of resources available to a task. Extend the semantics described in this chapter to incorporate a reasonable scheme employing such sponsors. Note that potential frequency of sponsor-agent communication may preclude having remote sponsors; similarly, a naive scheme may result in the sponsors becoming a bottle-neck.

7. *[Level 3]* Agents in a multiagent system may be organized in different ways. An example would be a group of agents learning to solve an optimization problem using the genetic algorithm. Implement such a system and study its ensemble level behavior.

8. *[Level 3]* Consider several representative types of organizations of agents and study potentially chaotic behaviors that may result at the level of ensembles. Specifically, analyze systems organized as *markets* and *firms*. What types of desirable emergent behaviors can you expect to result from such organizations.

9. *[Level 4]* Design and implement an agent architecture. Document the assumptions you make about how agents and agent ensembles would use the architecture.

## 12.9  References

1. G. Agha. *Actors: A Model of Concurrent Computation in Distributed Systems.* MIT Press, Cambridge, Mass., 1986.

2. G. Agha, S. Frølund, R. Panwar, and D. Sturman. A linguistic framework for dynamic composition of dependability protocols. In *Proceedings of the 3rd IFIP Working Conference on Dependable Computing for Critical Applications*, September 1992.

3. G. Agha, C. Houck, and R. Panwar. Distributed execution of actor systems. In D. Gelernter, T. Gross, A. Nicolau, and D. Padua, editors, *Languages and Compilers for Parallel Computing*, number 589 in LNCS, pages 1–17. Springer-Verlag, 1992.

4. G. Agha, I. A. Mason, S. F. Smith, and C. L. Talcott. A foundation for actor computation. *Journal of Functional Programming*, 1996. to appear.

5. Gul Agha. Concurrent Object-Oriented Programming. *Communications of the ACM*, 33(9):125–141, September 1990.

6. Gregory R. Andrews. *Concurrent Programming: Principles and Practice.* Benjamin/Cummings, 1991.

7. C. J. Callsen and G. A. Agha. Open Heterogeneous Computing in ActorSpace. *Journal of Parallel and Distributed Computing*, pages 289–300, 1994.

8.   L. D. Erman, F. Hayes-Roth, V. R. Lesser, and R. D. Reddy. The hearsay-ii speech understanding system: Integrating knowledge to resolve uncertainty. *ACM Computing Surveys*, 12(2), 1980.

9.   Tim Finin, Yannis Labrou, and James Mayfield. Kqml as an agent communication language. In Jeffrey M. Bradshaw, editor, *Software Agents*, pages 291–316. MIT Press, 1997.

10.  S. Frølund and G. Agha. A language framework for multi-object coordination. In *Proceedings of ECOOP 1993*, volume 707 of *LNCS*. Springer Verlag, 1993.

11.  Svend Frølund. *Coordinating Distributed Objects: An Actor-Based Approach to Synchronization*. MIT Press, 1996.

12.  L. Gasser, C. Braganza, and N. Herman. Mace: A flexible testbed for distributed ai research. In M. N. Huhns, editor, *Distributed Artificial Intelligence*, pages 119–152. Pitman - Morgan Kaufmann, 1987.

13.  Les Gasser and Jean-Pierre Briot. Object-based concurrent programming and distributed artificial intelligence. In Nicholas M. Avouris and Les Gasser, editors, *Distributed Artificial Intelligence: Theory and Praxis*, pages 81–107. Kluwer Academic, 1992.

14.  Michael R. Genesereth. An agent-based framework for interoperability. In Jeffrey M. Bradshaw, editor, *Software Agents*, pages 317–346. MIT Press, 1997.

15.  Robert Gray, David Kotz, Saurab Nog, Daniela Rus, and George Cybenko. Mobile agents for mobile computing. Technical Report PCS-TR96-285, Department of Computer Science, Dartmouth College, Hanover, NH 03755, May 1996.

16.  Robert S. Gray. A flexible and secure mobile-agent system. In Mark Diekhans and Mark Roseman, editors, *Proceedings of the Fourth Annual Tcl/Tk Workshop (TCL '96)*, Monterey, California, July 1996.

17.  Crystaliz Inc., General Magic Inc., GMD FOKUS, and IBM Corporation. Mobile Agent Facility Specification. Technical report, Object Management Group, June 1997.

18.  W. Kim. *Thal: An Actor System for Efficient and Scalable Concurrent Computing*. PhD thesis, University of Illinois at Urbana-Champaign, 1997.

19.  Michael Kolb. A cooperation language. In *Proceedings: First International Conference on Multi-Agent Systems*, pages 233–238, San Francisco, CA, June 1995. AAAI, AAAI Press, MIT Press.

20.  Open Systems Laboratory. The actor foundry: A java-based actor programming environment. *Available for download at http://www-osl.cs.uiuc.edu/~astley/foundry.html*.

21.  Yannis Labrou and Tim Finin. A proposal for a new kqml specification. Technical Report CS-97-03, University of Maryland Baltimore County, February 1997.

22.  P. Maes. Computational reflection. Technical Report 87-2, Vrije University. Artificial Intelligence Laboratory, 1987.

23.  G. Plotkin. Call-by-name, call-by-value and the lambda calculus. *Theoretical Computer Science*, 1:125–159, 1975.

24.  S. Ren and G. Agha. RTSynchronizers: Language support for real-time specifications in distributed systems. In *Proceedings of ACM SIGPLAN 1995 Workshop on Languages, Compilers, and Tools for Real-time Systems*, pages 55–64, 1995.

25.  J. Searle. *Speech Acts*. Cambridge University Press, Cambridge, UK, 1969.

26.  M.J. Shaw and M.S. Fox. Distributed artificial intelligence for group decision support. *Decision Support Systems*, 9:349–367, 1993.

27.  Yoav Shoham. An overview of agent-oriented programming. In Jeffrey M. Bradshaw, editor, *Software Agents*, pages 271–290. MIT Press, 1997.

28.  Munindar P. Singh. *Multiagent Systems*. Number 799 in Lecture Notes in Artificial Intelligence. Springer-Verlag, 1994.

29.  D. Sturman and G Agha. A protocol description language for customizing failure semantics. In *The 13th Symposium on Reliable Distributed Systems, Dana Point, California*. IEEE, October 1994.

30.  Daniel C. Sturman. *Modular Specification of Interaction Policies in Distributed Computing*. PhD thesis, University of Illinois at Urbana-Champaign, May 1996.

31.  C. Tomlinson, W. Kim, M. Schevel, V. Singh, B. Will, and G. Agha. Rosette: An object oriented concurrent system architecture. *Sigplan Notices*, 24(4):91–93, 1989.

32.  N. Venkatasubramanian and C. L. Talcott. Reasoning about Meta Level Activities in Open Distributed Systems. In *Principles of Distributed Computing*, 1995.

33.  Eric Werner. The design of multi-agent systems. In Eric Werner and Yves Demazeau, editors, *Decentralized A.I. 3. Proceedings of the Third European Workshop on Modelling Autonomous Agents in a Multi- Agent World, Kaiserslautern, Germany*, pages 3–28. North-Holland, August 1992.

34.  James E. White. Mobile agents. In Jeffrey M. Bradshaw, editor, *Software Agents*, pages 437–472. MIT Press, 1997.

35.  D. Woelk, M. Huhns, and C. Tomlinson. InfoSleuth agents: The next generation of active objects. *Object Magazine*, July/August 1995.

# 13     Distributed Control Algorithms for AI

Gerard Tel

## 13.1   Introduction

Centralized intelligence currently makes place for networked, or distributed intelligence. The `Webster` program on my computer illustrates it all: it has no built-in dictionary, but responds my queries by Internet access to an American server, yet outperforms any lookup in a paper version. Collecting resources in any computer is uneconomical, specialized resource servers are easier to maintain, and access cost is low due to cheap communication technology.

**Network Computations.** Computations in networks of processing nodes, each holding a part of the inputs and/or resources initially, can roughly be classified into *centralized*, *duplicated*, or *distributed* computations. A centralized solution relies on one node being designated as the computer node and possessing the resources to process the entire application locally. All input data and relevant resources are sent to this node, and after local processing the computer sends the relevant output data to each of the other nodes. A duplicated solution sends all input data to each node, after which each node processes the entire application and throws away all output data except those it needs itself. The flagrant waste of computing resources can be economically justified only if the output data (which is not transported here) far exceeds the input data in size. Duplicated computation is used to compute routing tables in the Internet [24, Sec. 5.5].

This chapter concerns distributed solutions, where the processing steps of the application are divided among the participating nodes. Even when not explicitly based on a sequential algorithm, each distributed solution can be seen as containing a sequential one consisting of the combined computation steps of the participants. In addition the distributed solution contains communication actions for the exchange of intermediate results and coordination; our goal is to minimise communication and computation cost.

Afek and Ricklin [1] observe cost benefits of an intermediate strategy where computation is concentrated in several computing centres. Awerbuch and Peleg [4] reach similar conclusions, but a discussion of such solutions, though we would still consider them as distributed, is not possible in this chapter.

### 13.1.1   Model of Computation

The distributed model is characterised by a collection of autonomous processing elements, called *nodes*. In addition to some computing and storage resources, each node has the possibility to exchange information with some of the other nodes; these are referred to as its *neighbors* and the communication takes place through a *link* (also called *edge*).

We denote by $n$ the number of nodes (or *size*) of the network and by $m$ the number of links and thus the network can be represented as an undirected graph on $n$ vertices and with $m$ edges. We use $D$ for the *diameter* of this graph. We assume the graph to be connected, which implies $m \geq n - 1$. It is not assumed that the nodes know this graph; representing it in every node would be costly, and contradicts the aim of processing each bit of input where it belongs. Storing some derived topological information, such as $n$, $m$, or the diameter of the graph, would be feasible, but it is usually superfluous.

The neighbour relation can be defined by the hardware, for example in processor networks where the neighbors are those processors to which the node is physically connected. Alternatively, the application can define this relation, for example, in Belief Networks [31], where each node stores information about a stochastic variable and communicates with nodes storing some related variables.

**Symmetry.** In this chapter it is not necessary to make a distinction between nodes on the basis of their resources (computing or storage nodes) or role (such as clients or servers), but we do assume two distinctions. First, nodes are identified by unique, uninterpreted tags (names) and initially each node knows its own tag and those of its neighbors (*neighbourhood knowledge* is assumed). Second, a single node is distinguished to act as an initiator of computations; this only means that this node executes a special program (usually just an additional start procedure), not that is has extra capabilities or resources.

These assumptions are natural because they can be met at low cost when implementing a distributed system; distributed algorithms research has investigated their influence on the power of the model.

In terms of network computing power, one of these assumptions suffices and they are equivalent [28]. If only identities are given, we may use an *election* program to choose one node as an initiator; such a program should of course not rely on the existence of an initiator, and would output, for example, the largest identity [13, 29]. If no initial identifiers are known while an initiator is distinguished, it may start a network traversal to assign unique names. A different situation arises in *anonymous* networks, where neither identities nor initiator are given; Rosenstiehl *et al.* [21] established 25 years ago that these networks can compute fewer functions. No function that requires to break symmetry can be computed deterministically; with randomised algorithms, naming and election can be performed, but only if the nodes initially know the size of the network [27, Chap. 9].

**Communication.** In this chapter, the communication between nodes is by *message passing* and has two operations, *send* and *receive*. Parameters for the send are: the *recipient*, which is a neighbors of the calling node, and the *message*, which is some piece of information; it will be transported to the mailbox of the recipient. The receive operation removes a message from the node's mailbox; it can complete only if a message is available, and returns the message and its sender. If there are no messages the operation is suspended; if there is more than one message, either of them can be returned.

We further assume that communication is *asynchronous*, which means that the completion of a send operation does not imply that the message has been received, or even, that it was delivered in the recipient's mailbox. All we assume is that it will eventually be available for reception because we assume *reliable* communication. The time between sending a message and its delivery at the receiver is unpredictable and may vary between channels and even between messages.

Only one temporal relation can be derived, namely, that the message is sent *before* it is received; we also assume that each message is received only once. This distinguishes message passing from communication by writing and reading a shared variable; it is cumbersome to ensure that each item written to such a variable is read (and processed) by the reading node exactly once.

### 13.1.2  Complexity Measures

The asynchrony in the communication causes the execution model to be non-deterministic; indeed, a distributed program may allow different executions on the same data depending on the scheduling of the events. When discussing complexity we shall always consider the *worst case* over all possible schedules.

**Communication, Time, and Storage.** The first goal in analysis of distributed algorithms is to compute the amount of communication by the algorithm; usually, as the number of messages exchanged in a computation. Only if messages in some solution are exceptionally large (contain more than, say, a few data items), we must be more precise and count the bits in each message, for example, in the "linear" depth-first search algorithm of Section 13.2.1.

The time complexity represents the duration of the computation, and is expressed in terms of the *slowest* message in the computation. This compares with the classical sequential time complexity, which does not really measure time but instead counts consecutive operations. The parallelism in the distributed model complicates matters slightly. Consider node $p$ sending messages $m_1$ and $m_2$ to neighbors $q$ and $r$, respectively; after receiving $m_1$, node $q$ sends message $m_3$ to $r$ and this message arrives at $r$ before message $m_2$. This small example, illustrated by the *space-time diagram* of Figure 13.1, contains a *message chain* of length 2, namely message $m_1$ followed by $m_3$ (sent after receipt of the former). However, the entire chain is formed during the transmission of the single message $m_2$, and hence we say the time complexity of the example is 1.

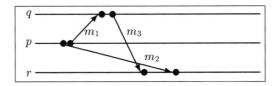

**Figure 13.1**    Two messages in one time unit.

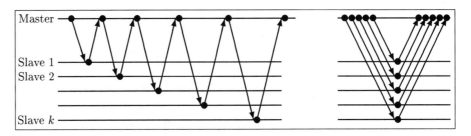

**Figure 13.2**    The local processing controversy.

We ignore local processing when computing time complexities; the time involved in processing is considered "small compared to the transmission delays." Two small examples may illustrate the controversy; see Figure 13.2. First, a server $p$ polls $k$ neighbors *one by one* by sending a message and receiving a reply; each request being sent upon receipt of the previous reply. The time complexity is $2k$ because polling each neighbors costs 2 time units, one for the request and one for the reply, and this repeats $k$ times. Ignoring the processing time between receiving a message and sending the next one appears acceptable, because no waiting is involved, and it does not change the asymptotical complexity.

Alternatively the server may poll its neighbors in parallel by sending a request to each and then collect the answers; *now the time complexity is 2* because all requests are sent without waiting, and the last reply must arrive at the server after at most 2 time units. The definition of time complexity assumes that the time for sending the $k$ requests, and the time for processing the $k$ replies, is negligible.

The *storage complexity* expresses the amount of memory used by the algorithm; sometimes computed in bits, but it is usually convenient to assume larger units, "words," each capable of storing an identifier or integer.

**Discussion.** We might be tempted to compare the complexity of a distributed algorithm to the complexity of sequential algorithms for the same problem. When comparing, sequential *time* should not be compared to distributed *time*, but to message complexity. Indeed, in the sequential model, "time" actually measures the total amount of "work" because time actually counts the instructions executed sequentially. In the distributed model, "work" corresponds to messages, because the work performed by nodes can usually be charged to sending and receiving messages; see Algorithm 13.15–13.18 for an example. Distributed time accounts for the speedup that is achieved by the parallelism inherent in the model, but also penalizes for nodes that must wait for data before continuing their execution.

It is usually observed that the communication complexity for processing the network topology is at least linear in $m$, which is the input size for topological problems. For graph exploration, for example, this can be shown formally [27, Chap. 6] because each link must carry at least one message. Task that require processing a constant amount of information for each node (such as a sum of distributed inputs, see Alg. 13.11) can be performed with $O(n)$ messages using spanning trees or cycles. A message complexity below $O(n)$ is not possible for tasks that require cooperation of each node.

The worst case w.r.t. time complexity occurs when all messages are exchanged one after the other, and the time complexity then equals the message complexity. A straight-forward distribution of a sequential algorithm (see Section 13.2.1) often results in both message and time complexity being equal to the sequential time complexity (i.e., $\Theta(m)$). If all processing for each node can be performed in constant time, the overall time complexity becomes *linear* in the size of the network ($n$) and this is often possible, as we will see.

A *fast* algorithm is one that uses sub-linear (i.e., $o(n)$) time. Fast computing is not easy; Garay *et al.* [11] present an algorithm for Minimal Spanning Tree that runs in $O(D + n^{0.614})$ time, but the solution appears a bit artificial. The message complexity of the fast solution is large (unknown though), while message optimal solutions (exchanging $O(n \log n + m)$ messages) exist with linear time complexity [3, 10]. We shall discuss a distributed depth-first search algorithm whose time is proportional to the depth of the DFS tree, while again message complexity rises sky-high.

The network diameter serves as a time lower bound for all tasks that require coordination between all nodes (including every task that requires consensus in the output), because no information can be communicated across the network in $o(D)$ time. Linial [15] gives examples of tasks (Maximal Independent Set, Colouring) that can be solved by *local computations*, i.e., in sub-diameter time, and Litovsky *et al.* [16] have further investigated the power of local computations.

### 13.1.3  Examples of Distributed Architectures in AI

Distribution may be driven by several factors, such as the wish to speed up computations by using more hardware, or the availability of resources.

**Multiprocessor computers.** Sometimes an application can be processed by a single computer (in a sequential model) but this is just too slow. The solution is a *multiprocessor computer*, such as an array of 16, 128, or more processors connected by a high-speed communication network. The steps of the computation must be allocated over the available machines, but as the architecture does not match the application, this is usually a difficult task. The ideal allocation shares the computation load as good as possible, while achieving a low communication overhead (due to the exchange of intermediate results). See Section 13.4.5.

**Resource distribution.** In some situations distribution is not a choice, but is enforced by the availability of necessary resources at different locations. Consider, for example, the problem of planning several university committee meetings. Committees that share a professor may not overlap their meetings, but to decide if some date is available, the member's agenda must be consulted. Finding out if the members can go from one meeting to the other in time requires inspection of bus and train time tables. To see if rooms are available, the cooperation of the room reservation systems at the various universities is necessary.

Each of the mentioned resources runs at a fixed location, so the planning application must include distributed problem solving; we shall consider distributed constraint satisfaction in Section 13.4.

**Belief Networks.** A Belief Network models hypotheses and statistical dependencies between them in a graph. The computations to update the information in this network are naturally distributed over the nodes, where each node may need information from its neighbors to do the update. Each node in the graph can be described as a process, communicating with its neighbors processes. The physical location of the processes then becomes irrelevant: for the application it does not matter if all nodes are on the same machine, or distributed over various machines. In Section 13.5 we show that processing the network structure (computation of a loop cutset) can be described in the same model.

---

## 13.2    Graph Exploration

This section describes algorithms to compute spanning trees in an undirected network, that is, partition the set of edges into *tree* edges (these will be directed from parent to child) and *non-tree* edges. At the end no node will see the entire tree, but only the status of its own links (tree or non-tree).

The problem of computing weight-minimal trees has received attention in the literature [10], but where unit-cost links are assumed all trees are weight-minimal and we shall not address this problem. We illustrate the algorithms by giving pseudocode with Pascal-like (mostly self-explanatory) syntax set in typewriter font. As a convention we shall use a subscript $u$ when reasoning about a variable of node $u$ (as in $la_u$), but because in a distributed algorithm a node can access only its own variables, the subscript is omitted from the pseudocode.

### 13.2.1   Depth-First Search

In the sequential setting, depth-first search has been in wide use since the late 1950's, especially in Artificial Intelligence, as a technique for exploring solution

```
                    var visited[u]: bool init false ;

                    procedure dfs(u):
                        if not visited[u]
                        then   begin visited[u] := true ;
                                    forall v in Neigh[u] do dfs(v)
                               end

                    Start the algorithm: dfs(u0)
```

**Algorithm 13.1**   Sequential depth-first search.

spaces for problems. Its importance for graph processing was recognised by Hopcroft and Tarjan and results from the simplicity of the algorithm ($O(m)$ sequential time) combined with an attractive structural property of the constructed tree, namely, that the two endpoints of any non-tree edge are connected by a *directed* path in the tree.

Sequential depth-first search is implemented by a short recursive procedure (Alg. 13.1); the first call of *dfs(u)* recurses on all neighbors, while subsequent calls return immediately. Calls to node $u$ may be nested, i.e., a second call to $u$ may occur while the first one is still active, but in this case the second call returns immediately because *visited*[u] is set when entering the procedure. The start node $u_0$ is the root of the constructed tree, and each other node becomes a child of the neighbor from which the first call of *dfs(u)* was made (this is not shown in Alg. 13.1). Alg. 13.1 makes two recursive calls through each edge.

**First distributed solution.** In the distributed model, control is passed from one node to the other by exchange of a message, so each recursive call uses two messages: one for the call and one for the return. Some saving can be achieved; node $u$ will *not* place a call to its father, and node $u$ will *not* call the procedure on neighbour $v$ if a call was earlier received *from* $v$ and returned. The reason is in both cases that the neighbour has already been visited and would return the call immediately.

To describe the operation of node $u$ in more detail, consider the receipt of a message from neighbour $v$. If $u$ has sent a message to $v$ earlier, the received message is a return message and $u$ selects a next neighbour for placing a call; when the neighbors are exhausted, $u$ sends a return message to its father or, if $u$ is the initiator, terminates. Otherwise, the message is a call from $v$; if this is the first call for $u$, designate $v$ as the *father* and send a message to another neighbour. If a call was received before, a return message is sent to $v$ immediately.

Alg. 13.2 uses variable $status_u[v]$ to indicate if the link from $u$ to $v$ is *unused*, *father*, or *cal* or *ret* if a call or return was sent through the link. It is not necessary to use different messages for a call and a return because the nature of the message can be derived from the context as argued above. Consequently, the algorithm uses only a single type of message, denoted [dfs].

```
        var   visited        bool   init false ;
              status[v]              init unused        (* for each neighbor *)


        Start the algorithm (initiator only!):
              visited := true ;
              for some w in Neigh do
                  begin send [dfs] to w ; status[w] := cal end


        Upon receipt of [dfs] from v:
              if not visited then
                  begin visited := true ; status[v] := father end ;
              if status[v] = unused then
                  begin send [dfs] to v ; status[v] := ret end
              else if there is a w with status[w] = unused then
                  begin send [dfs] to w ; status[w] := cal end
              else if there is a w with status[w] = father then
                  begin send [dfs] to w end
              else (* initiator *) stop
```

**Algorithm 13.2**   Distributed depth-first search (for $u$).

At the end, the link status is interpreted as follows. Each non-initiator has one *father* link, leading to its father in the constructed dfs tree. A *ret* link was used for returning a second or later call and hence indicates a non-tree link leading to a descendant in the dfs tree. A *cal* link was used for placing a call, and this link is either a tree link (if the call was the first one made on the neighbour) or a non-tree link leading to an ascendant. If nodes must be able to distinguish between downward tree links and upward non-tree links, this can be done by using two different return messages for returning the first and the subsequent calls.

Regarding the complexity of the algorithm, we observe that two messages are exchanged through each link, hence the communication complexity is $2.m$ messages. As they are exchanged one after the other, the time complexity is also $2.m$. The algorithm uses in each node a number of bits proportional to its degree.

**Awerbuch's linear-time solution.** Exactly $n - 1$ of the edges become tree edges, so in the case that $m$ significantly exceeds $n$, the time complexity of the algorithm is dominated by the calls and returns through *non-tree* edges. These calls do not construct edges of the dfs tree; so *if* node $u$ could be aware of its neighbour $v$ being visited already, the call to $v$ could be skipped without affecting the outcome, and the time complexity would be reduced significantly.

This is exploited in Awerbuch's algorithm [2]; each node informs its neighbors when it is visited for the first time, before forwarding any recursive calls. Of course we still communicate through each edge, but informing the neighbors can be parallelized and we save on time. When forwarding calls, the node now skips neighbors that are known to be visited already (status *done*); see Alg. 13.3.

```
        Start the algorithm (initiator only!):
            visited := true ;
            forall x in Neigh do send [visit] to x ;
            forall x in Neigh do receive [ack] from x ;
            for some w in Neigh do
                begin send [dfs] to w ; status[w] := cal end

    Upon receipt of [visit] from v :
            status[v] := done ; send [ack] to v

    Upon receipt of dfs from v:
            if not visited then (* first dfs is first call *)
                begin visited := true ; status[v] := father ;
                        forall x in Neigh – {v} do send [visit] to x ;
                        forall x in Neigh – {v} do receive [ack] from x
                end ;
            if there is a w in Neigh with status[w] = unused then
                    begin send [dfs] to w ; status[w] := cal end
            else if there is a w in Neigh with status[w] = father then
                    begin send [dfs] to w end
            else (* initiator *) stop
```

**Algorithm 13.3**   Awerbuch's distributed depth-first search.

It uses three types of messages, namely [dfs] as before for the calls and returns, [visit] messages to indicate that the sender was visited, and [ack] messages to acknowledge these. The status of a link can be *unused, father, cal,* or *done* to indicate that no [dfs] message was exchanged, but the neighbour has been visited. The *ret* status is not used because no node ever receives a second call message; the corresponding clause of Alg. 13.2 is removed from the response to a [dfs] message.

The algorithm still communicates only a constant number of bits per edge, but the message complexity is now $4.m$, which is seen as follows. On a tree edge $uv$, $u$ informs $v$ about being visited at the expense of two messages, and the call on $v$ by $u$ costs two messages; no [visit] message is sent by $v$ to its father. On a non-tree edge $uv$ the nodes $u$ and $v$ mutually inform each other of being visited, both at the cost of two messages.

The algorithm exchanges 2 [dfs] messages through $n - 1$ links, to a total of $2n - 2$ messages and these are exchanged in a chain. Each time a node is visited for the first time the flow of [dfs] messages is interrupted for exchanging [visit] and [ack] messages, which takes two time units. Hence the time complexity is bounded by $4n - 2$. A slightly better result was obtained by Cidon [6].

**Linear-message solution.** Calls and returns through non-tree edges can be avoided without sending additional messages; see Hélary *et al.* [12]. In these solutions a node is not informed about a neighbour being visited by receiving from that neighbour, but instead the call and return messages include a complete list

```
        Start the algorithm (initiator only!):
            S := { u } ;
            for some w in Neigh do
                begin send [dfs,S] to w ; status[w] := cal end

    Upon receipt of [dfs,S] from v :
            if not (u in S) then (* first message is first call *)
                begin S := S + {u} ; status[v] := father end ;
            if (exists w in Neigh with w notin S) then
                begin send [dfs,S] to w ; status[w] := cal end
            else if (exists w in Neigh with status[w] = father) then
                begin send [dfs,S] to w end
            else (* initiator *) stop
```

**Algorithm 13.4**    Linear-message depth-first search (node $u$).

of nodes already visited. Indeed, placing a call on any neighbour is avoided if that neighbour occurs in the list; see Algorithm 13.4, where we eliminated the *visited* variable because a node can inspect the message to find out if it was visited before.

The algorithm illustrates various observations regarding communication complexity and its relation to "amount of work." The total number of messages is reduced to $2(n-1)$, but at the expense of having very long messages; indeed the very last message received by the initiator contains the full list of all nodes. The total *length* of all transmitted lists is at least $n^2 - 1$ and at most $\frac{3}{2}n(n-1)$ node names; we observe a significant difference between *counting* messages (message complexity) and *weighing* them (bit complexity).

It is not reasonable to assume that Algorithm 13.4 requires only a constant amount of local processing per sent or received message, because the search for an unvisited neighbour requires to compare the received list of node names to the set of neighbors. Finally, the algorithm requires a lot of local storage to represent the $S$ set. Concluding, the high bit complexity and the considerable local processing and storage, make the algorithm unpractical in most realistic situations.

**Fast solution.** The fastest algorithm for distributively computing a depth-first search tree is not obtained by simulating the sequential dfs algorithm, but by exploiting a characterisation of the resulting type of tree.

### Definition 13.1
A rooted spanning tree of a graph satisfies the *dfs property* if for each edge $uv$, either $u$ is an ancestor of $v$ or $v$ is an ancestor of $u$.

(The usual definition of dfs trees is based on the construction procedure, from which this property can be derived.)

Now assume an ordering on node names is available, and represent a path from the initiator to a node as a string enumerating the nodes in the path.

```
            var la : string    init infty ;

        For the initiator only:
            la := u ;
            forall x in Neigh do send [path,la] to x


        Upon arrival of a [path,rho] message from v:
            receive [path,rho] from v ;
            if rho.u < la then
                begin la := rho.u ;
                        forall x in Neigh s.t. x not in la
                                do send [path,la] to x
            end
```

**Algorithm 13.5**   The Relaxation algorithm.

### Lemma 13.1

The set of edges formed by combining for all nodes $u$ the lexically minimal simple path (lmsp) from the initiator to $u$ is a dfs tree.

**Proof** (Sketch!) The selected edges connect the graph because for each node at least one path from the initiator is included. It is a tree because any prefix of the lmsp to $u$, say ending in vertex $v$, is the lmsp for $v$; this also implies that the tree path from the initiator to $u$ is the lmsp to $u$.

To show that the dfs property is satisfied, consider neighbors $u$ and $v$ and let their lmsp's be $lmsp(u)$ and $lmsp(v)$, respectively; assume without loss of generality that $lmsp(u) < lmsp(v)$. If node $v$ is in $lmsp(u)$, the prefix of $lmsp(u)$ up to $v$ is a path to $v$ that is lexically smaller than $lmsp(u)$, so assuming $lmsp(u) < lmsp(v)$, $v$ is not contained in $lmsp(u)$.

But then $lmsp(u)$ concatenated with $v$, denoted $lmsp(u) \cdot v$, is a simple path to $v$ and this implies $lmsp(v) \leq lmsp(u) \cdot v$. Consequently, $lmsp(u) < lmsp(v) \leq lmsp(u) \cdot v$, which implies that $lmsp(u)$ is a prefix of $lmsp(v)$, and $u$ is an ancestor of $v$. ∎

As a consequence, a dfs tree can be constructed with a variation of Chandy and Misra's algorithm [27, p. 120] for shortest path computation; see Alg. 13.5. Variable $la_u$ is node $u$'s *approximation* of its lmsp; the approximations are initialized to $\infty$, a string exceeding all other strings, and remain conservative in the sense that $la_u \geq lmsp(u)$.

The approximation is decreased when node $u$ obtains information about a simple path to $u$ that is lexically smaller than $la_u$; that is, upon receipt of a [path, $\rho$] message such that $\rho \cdot u < la_u$. The updated $la_u$ is propagated to the neighbors because the smaller path to $u$ may result in a smaller path to the neighbour also. This propagation and the subsequent processing of the message is called a *relaxation* over the edge to the neighbour.

Only finitely many messages are exchanged by the algorithm, because the messages sent by any node correspond to smaller and smaller paths, all of bounded length ($n - 1$ hops) because they are simple. It is not particularly hard to construct an example where exponentially many messages are exchanged.

We call node $u$ *ready* if $la_u = lmsp(u)$; no changes in $la_u$ occur after $u$ becomes ready, because no path smaller than $lmsp(u)$ is ever proposed to $u$. It can be shown that, for $v$ the second last node in $lmsp(u)$, if edge $vu$ is relaxed after $v$ becomes ready, then $u$ is ready also.

### Lemma 13.2

Within $t$ time units after the initialization by $u_0$, every node with an *lmsp* of length $t$ or smaller is ready.

**Proof**   This is done by induction on $t$; indeed, because no string starting with $u_0$ is ever lexically smaller than the string $u_0$, the initiator is ready immediately at the initialization.

Assume $u$ has an lmsp of $t + 1$ hops, with second last node $v$. Node $v$ has an lmsp of $t$ hops, hence at some point, within $t$ time units after initialization, there is a relaxation that makes $v$ ready. At this moment, $v$ sends its new estimate $la_v$, now $lmsp(v)$, to $u$ and this message is received within a time unit. After this relaxation, that is, within $t + 1$ time units from initialization, $u$ is ready.   ■

We conclude that the algorithm constructs a dfs tree exchanging a large, but finite, amount of messages in time proportional to the depth of the tree. The algorithm can be fast in some cases, but other graphs have a dfs tree of linear depth.

The relaxation algorithm introduces another problem in distributed computing, namely that no node can directly observe the termination of the construction. Indeed, all nodes will end in the receiving state, where their approximations equal the actual minimal paths, but the nodes are never sure that no smaller paths will ever be proposed. We study the *termination detection* problem in Section 13.3.

The algorithm can also be used without prior definition of an initiator; if all nodes execute the initiating code, the network will converge towards a spanning tree with the smallest node as the root. Indeed, the paths starting in this node are *all* lexically smaller than the paths starting in any other node, so every node eventually accepts a path from the smallest node as the lexically minimal one.

**Breadth-first search.** A spanning tree has the *breadth-first search* property if the tree path from the root to each node is a shortest path in the network. Sequential computation of such a tree is very efficient ($O(m)$ work) but makes use of a data structure, a queue, to temporarily store nodes that have been discovered, but were not yet visited. The data structure plays an important role to ensure that the nodes are visited in the correct order and the use of this queue makes breadth-first search surprisingly difficult to distribute.

The simplest algorithms explore the network by sending an explore message through each edge ($2m$ messages). To synchronise the exploration, coordination

```
            var rec    : integer ;
                father : neighbour ;

            Algorithm for the initiator:
                rec := 0 ;
                forall v in Neigh do send [echo] to v ;
                while rec < |Neigh| do
                        begin receive [echo] ; rec := rec + 1 end

            Algorithm for other nodes:
                receive [echo] from w ; father := w ; rec := 1 ;
                forall v in Neigh – {w} do send [echo] to v ;
                while rec < |Neigh| do
                        begin receive [echo] ; rec := rec + 1 end ;
                send [echo] to father
```

**Algorithm 13.6**   The Echo algorithm (for node $u$).

from the root takes place after each level (of which there can be $D$) at the expense of a linear number of messages. Consequently, the communication for the coordination is of order $D.n$. In the worst case, $D$ is linear in $n$, so the overhead is quadratic and dominates the message complexity.

By exploring $l$ levels between successive synchronisation rounds the number of coordination messages is reduced to $D.n/l$ but $l$ exploration messages may be sent through each edge. The resulting $D.n/l + ml$ message complexity is minimised to $\sqrt{D.n.m}$ with $l = \sqrt{D.n/m}$; choosing the best $l$ requires a priori knowledge of $D$ and $m$. Even more sophisticated algorithms are known, but their complexity still exceeds the complexity of the sequential algorithm significantly.

The bottom line is that in the design of distributed algorithms, breadth-first search should be avoided if possible; fortunately, there are alternatives.

### 13.2.2   Pseudo-Fast Exploration: the Echo Algorithm

In practice, a very fast exploration and spanning tree construction algorithm is obtained if each node forwards exploration messages to all its neighbors in parallel. The algorithm (Alg. 13.6) floods [echo] messages to all nodes, exchanges them over non-tree edges, and "echoes" them back through tree edges.

In more detail, the Echo algorithm (Alg. 13.6) operates as follows. The initiator start the *exploration phase* of the algorithm by sending messages to its neighbors. Upon receipt of the first message, a non-initiator forwards messages to all neighbors except the sender of that first message, thus messages are flooded to all nodes in the network. Each node stores the neighbour from which the first message was received, and the corresponding links form a spanning tree in the network.

The *echo phase* of the algorithm consists of the replies sent by each non-initiator to its father; a node replies to its father after receiving one message from each neighbour (condition $rec_u = |Neigh_u|$). It must be shown that node $u$ eventually receives a messages from each neighbour; for $u$'s father this is obvious (it is $u$'s first message) and for the non-tree links it is easy to see. Indeed, if $uv$ is a non-tree link, then $v$ sent a message to $u$ upon its first receipt, hence $u$ eventually receives this message.

We can now show that the echo phase starts from the leaves of the tree and propagates upwards to the initiator. Indeed, the leaves have no children and hence will send to their father by the argument in the previous paragraph. Then the nodes whose children are leaves can send to their fathers, and so on. This reasoning shows not only that *all* nodes will eventually receive from each neighbour, but also that the order in which this happens at the various nodes is determined by the tree shape, and the initiator is the last node to terminate.

The echo algorithm constructs an *arbitrary* spanning tree (it can be shown that *every* spanning tree of the network can be the result of the non-deterministic exploration), which limits its applicability. On the other hand, the algorithm is fast *in practice*; its time complexity in our model has frequently been misunderstood. Because the exploration phase forwards [echo] messages immediately, all nodes are reached by the exploration within $D$ time units after initialization. The echo phase returns messages over the same paths, and it is easy to be mislead in thinking that this phase will also terminate in $O(D)$ time. It is easy to show that the time consumption is $O(D)$ under very weak additional assumptions about the timing of messages, and this explains why the algorithm is empirically fast; see the exercises 4 and 5.

Unfortunately, our theoretical model allows for worse executions [27, p. 217]. The $O(D)$ construction time of the tree does not imply that its depth is $O(D)$ because exploration messages over a long path may bypass messages over shorter paths. That the echo phase sends messages over the same path does not imply that they take the same time, because our model does not induce relations between various transmission delays over the same link. Exploiting the first observation yields an execution where a tree of depth $\Theta(n)$ is constructed in $O(D)$ time, after which the echo phase takes linear time.

### 13.2.3   Searching for Connectivity Certificates

We have seen that the construction of a spanning tree requires at least $\Omega(m)$ communication; it was recently discovered that the same amount of communication can result in a much richer structure. This subsection defines (edge) *connectivity certificates* of networks, and we shall show how to construct certificates sequentially and distributively. We also give applications of certificates.

**Connectivity and Connectivity Certificates.** The *local connectivity* of nodes $u$ and $v$ in $G$, denoted $\lambda_G(u, v)$, is defined as the maximal number of edge disjoint paths connecting $u$ and $v$. (This function is related to transport capacity and reliability as explained at the end of this subsection.) A connectivity certificate is a subset of the edges preserving connectivity to a certain degree.

### Definition 13.2

A subset $E' \subseteq E$ is a *k-connectivity certificate* if, with $G' = (V, E')$, for all nodes $u, v \in V$ $\lambda_{G'}(u, v) \geq \min(k, \lambda_G(u, v))$.

For example, a maximal forest preserves 1-connectivity, because nodes that are connected (through a path) in $G$ are also connected in a maximal forest; nodes in different components of $G$ remain unconnected in the forest, of course. Nodes joined by multiple paths in $G$ are joined by only a single path in the forest, so higher connectivities are not certified by the forest. Now extend the forest to a set $E'$ of edges such that every edge contained in a cycle in $G$ is also contained in a cycle in $E'$. Then, if $u$ and $v$ are joined by *two* paths in $G$, the set $E'$ also contains two such paths, and hence $E'$ is a 2-certificate.

It is most attractive to have small size certificates, but the computation of minimal certificates is NP-Complete; a $k$-certificate is *sparse* if its size is $O(k.n)$.

**Computation of Sparse Certificates.** Nagamochi and Ibaraki have shown that sparse $k$-certificates can be computed efficiently, namely by computing and removing a maximal forest $k$ times.

### Theorem 13.1 [19]

Let $E_i$ be any maximal forest in $(V, E \setminus \cup_{j<i} E_j)$; then $\cup_{j \leq k} E_j$ is a sparse $k$-connectivity certificate.

Computing $k$ maximal forests can easily be done in $O(k.(n + m))$ time but Nagamochi and Ibaraki achieved an $O(n + m)$ algorithm by cleverly combining the construction of the various forests.

*Computing a maximal forest.* A maximal forest is obtained by starting with no edges ($E' = \emptyset$) and applying *test(e)* to every edge $e$ (in arbitrary order), where *test(e)* means:

```
if e introduces no cycle in E'
then E' := E' + {e} else reject e
```

Regardless of the test order the obtained structure is a maximal forest, but different test orders may yield different forests.

In general it could require some effort to see if $e$ introduces a cycle, but this effort is eliminated *by suitable test order strategy*. Call a node *active* if it has untested edges, and call a non-trivial tree of the forest active if it contains active nodes; the test strategy guarantees *at most one active tree* at any moment. The strategy is: if there is an active tree $T$, then select an active node $u$ from it and test *all its untested edges*; testing all untested edges of $u$ is called a *visit* to $u$. Then, if there is an active tree, adding some edges of $u$ to $E'$ only extends $T$ but does not introduce an extra active tree, and only if there is no active tree, adding an edge may introduce one.

The uniqueness of the active tree implies that in a visit to $u$, edge $uv$ introduces a cycle *if and only if $v$ is adjacent to an edge in $E'$*. Indeed, $v$ is adjacent to the untested edge $uv$, hence active, and so if it has an $E'$ edge it is in an active tree;

because there is only one active tree, $v$ is already connected to $u$ through $T$. The construction of the forest is: repeatedly select and visit an unvisited node, if possible one that already has an adjacent $E'$ edge. The visit to $u$ is: consider its untested edges $uv$ and include them if and only if $v$ has no $E'$ edges yet.

*Computing all forests simultaneously.* We start the construction with all forests empty ($E_i = \emptyset$) and apply a basic ranking step $rank(e)$ to every edge, where $rank(e)$ adds $e$ to the first forest where $e$ does not introduce a cycle.

```
i := smallest value s.t. e does not create a cycle in Ei ;
Ei := Ei + {e}
```

The ranking order will imply, as above, that every forest has at most one active tree, hence edge $uv$ creates a cycle in $E_j$ if and only if $v$ already has an edge ranked $j$. Thus, when edge $uv$ is ranked during a visit to $u$, its rank is the smallest rank at which $v$ has no adjacent edges yet. A crucial property follows: if any node has an edge ranked $i$, it also has edges ranked $j$ for all $j < i$; the highest rank of an edge of a node will be called the *level* of that node.

Each forest will have at most one active tree, and the mentioned property implies that a node active in forest $i$ is also active in forest $j$ for all $j < i$. Hence it suffices to select a node of maximal level and rank all its adjacent edges in order to construct the required sequence of maximal forests.

Nagamochi and Ibaraki have shown that the entire ranking can be completed in $O(n + m)$ time in the sequential model. Their solution uses a centralized data structure to store all unvisited nodes according to their level; the next visited node is selected from it in $O(1)$ time. Ranking an edge requires the data structure to be updated, because an unvisited node is increased in level; moving the node from one list to the list of next level is also done in $O(1)$ time.

**Distributed Certificate Algorithm.** At first sight the centralized data structure frustrates a distributed implementation, just as it is the case for breadth-first search. However, Evens *et al.* [9] showed that the central data structure can be replaced by a recursive search for unvisited nodes through the branches of the tree of the highest active level. To this end, if node $u$ receives a search message through an edge of rank $i$, it forwards the message through all unsearched edges of rank $i$ and higher, highest ranks first.

In Algorithm 13.7, node $u$ stores the rank of its adjacent edge $uv$ in $rank_u[v]$ (0 if the edge is unranked), and the flag $search_u[v]$ indicates if the search must still be forwarded to $v$. Verweij [32] shows that this search procedure indeed visits at each time the unvisited node of highest label. We summarise the properties of the algorithm.

### Theorem 13.2
Algorithm 13.7 exchanges $4m$ messages in $4m$ time and assigns a rank to each edge in such a way that for each $k$, the edges with ranks 1 to $k$ form a sparse $k$-connectivity certificate.

```
        var rank[v]    : int    init 0 ;
            visited    : bool   init false ;
            search[v]  : bool   init true ;

        procedure Visit:
            begin visited := true ;
                  forall v s.t. rank[v] = 0
                      do begin send [rnk] to v ;
                                receive [ranked,i] from v ;
                                rank[v] := i
                          end
            end

        procedure Search(v):
            begin if not visited then Visit ;
                  forall w s.t. search[w] and rank[w] >= rank[v],
                          in decreasing order of rank[w]
                      do begin search[w] := false ; send [srch] to w ;
                                receive [return] from w
                          end ;
                  if  v = u (* Initiator! *)
                      then construction is terminated
                      else send [return] to v
            end

        Upon receipt of [rnk] from v:
            rank[v] := smallest i>0 s.t. u has no edge ranked i ;
            send [ranked,rank[v]] to v

        Upon receipt of [srch] from v:
            Search(v)

        To initiate the search (Only the initiator!):
            Search(u0)
```

**Algorithm 13.7**   The distributed certificate algorithm (for node $u$).

Ranking the unvisited edges of $u$ (in procedure *Visit*) can be done in parallel to reduce the time complexity to $2m + 2n$. If only a certificate for one given value of $k$ is required, the edges ranked higher than $k$ need not be searched and the algorithm uses $2k.n + 2n$ time.

**Applications.** In communication networks, the local connectivity of $u$ and $v$ has two important operational meanings, related to *capacity* and to *reliability*. First, if each edge has a given data rate $\rho$, the existence of $k$ disjoint paths between $u$ and $v$ implies that an overall data flow of $k.\rho$ can be transported from $u$ to $v$. Second, the edge disjointness of the paths implies that, as long as $k - 1$ or fewer links fail, at least one path between $u$ and $v$ remains unaffected. Consequently, $\lambda_G(u, v)$ equals both the maximal data flow between $u$ and $v$, and the number of link failures that can partition $u$ from $v$.

*Determining local connectivity.* The local connectivity of $u$ and $v$ can be computed by repeatedly searching for an *augmenting path* in the graph, until no more paths are found. As this search may cost $O(m)$ messages, this way of computing the connectivity costs about $O(\lambda.m)$ messages ($\lambda = \lambda_G(u, v)$).

A better complexity is obtained with certificates; after ranking all the edges, the first $uv$ path is searched in the edges of rank 1. The second augmenting path is searched among the edges ranked 1 and 2, and the $i^{\text{th}}$ augmenting path is searched among edges of rank up to $i$. Indeed, if $i$ paths exist in $G$, the certificate property guarantees that they exist in the union of the first $i$ forests, so the restricted search does not terminate inappropriately. Because the $i^{\text{th}}$ path is searched in a restricted network with less than $i.n$ edges, the total cost is $O(\lambda^2.n)$, which is usually smaller than $\lambda.m$.

*Testing global connectivity.* Algorithms for computing 2- or 3-connected components may profit from execution on a 2- or 3-connectivity certificate [14]. The certificate can be computed in $O(m)$ time and messages, and guarantees that the subsequent connectivity algorithm has to consider only $O(n)$ edges.

---

## 13.3   Termination Detection

A distributed algorithm terminates when it reaches a global state (configuration) in which no event of the algorithm is applicable. However, such a terminal configuration does not imply that each node is in a terminal state, that is, a (local) state from which no events are applicable, as is illustrated by Algorithm 13.5. Each node awaits the arrival of messages in a receiving state, and reacts to their arrival by sending some (possibly zero) messages. While a node always returns to a receiving state (hence not explicitly terminated) the computation as a whole halts when all nodes are simultaneously in this state and no messages are in transit.

This section discusses techniques to make termination explicit by distributively detecting that the program has reached a terminal configuration. A description of the problem is given in Section 13.3.1, and we discuss two classes of solutions in Sections 13.3.2 and 13.3.3.

### 13.3.1   Problem Definition

The description of the termination detection problem abstracts away from the purpose and operations of the computation in question, but concentrates on the aspects relevant for termination. A node is assumed to be in either an *active* or a *passive* state, where in an active state the node may send messages and in a passive state it may not. (In Alg. 13.5 a node receiving a message immediately sends the

```
var   state : (act, pas) ;

Su: { state = act }
      send [mes]

Ru: { A message [mes] arrives at u }
      receive [mes] ; state := act

Iu: { state = act }
      state := pas
```

**Algorithm 13.8**   Steps of distributed computation (node *u*).

resulting message and becomes receiving (passive) again. Here we model a slightly more general situation where a node may already receive while still processing previous messages.) The transition from active to passive may occur spontaneously (namely, when the active node finishes its current activities), but a passive node can *only* be awakened by receiving a message. The operation is modelled by the transitions in Alg. 13.8; again, the actual computation as well as the content of the exchanged message are abstracted away from.

Receiving messages is impossible if no messages are in transit, and sending messages is impossible if all nodes are passive; becoming passive is clearly also impossible in this case, and hence termination of Alg. 13.8 occurs when *simultaneously* all nodes are passive and all channels are empty.

A *termination detection algorithm* is added to a distributed computation and requires to make termination explicit. Detection requires executing some extra statements with the operations of the computation, as well as exchanging some extra messages for the detection purpose only. (These additional *control* message do not render a passive node active, of course.) Correctness requires that (1) if the computation terminates, this is detected within finite time thereafter (liveness) and (2) termination is not detected prematurely (safety).

The detection algorithms roughly fall in two categories. *Tracing* algorithms follow the computation flow by tracing active nodes along the message chains that activated them, and call termination when all traced activity has ceased. *Probe* algorithms rely on global (coordinated) scans of the network state and call termination when no activity is found. The distinction can be compared to that between reference counting and mark-and-sweep type garbage collectors [30].

### 13.3.2   Tracing Algorithms

A tracing algorithm relies on knowledge of the set of initially active nodes, because all activity of the computation originates from these nodes by message chains. Dijkstra and Scholten's algorithm [8] assumes that initially exactly one node is active; we call this node the *root* node.

```
        var  state : (act, pas)  init if u=u0 then act else pas ;
             cc    : integer      init 0 ;
             fat   : node         init if u=u0 then u else undef ;

   Su: { state = act }
        send [mes] ; cc := cc + 1

   Ru: { A message [mes] from v arrives at u }
        receive [mes] ; state := act ;
        if fat = undef then fat := v
                       else send [sig] to v

   Iu: { state = act }
        state := pas

   Au: { A message [sig] arrives at u }
        receive [sig] ; cc := cc - 1

   Tu: { cc = 0 and state = pas and fat != undef }
        if fat = u (* Root node! *)
           then Detect
           else  send [sig] to fat ; fat := undef
```

**Algorithm 13.9** Dijkstra and Scholten's algorithm (node $u$).

**Global description: Computation tree.** The detection algorithm maintains, during the distributed computation, a *computation tree $T$*, whose vertices are nodes of the network and messages in transit; the root node is the root of $T$. Steps of the computation trigger updates in the tree structure aimed at preserving the crucial property of $T$:

> at any time, *all active nodes* as well as *all* [mes] *in transit* are vertices of $T$.

In addition, control messages and passive nodes may be in $T$, but their presence serves the maintenance of the tree rather than the correctness of the algorithm directly. In view of this property, termination can be concluded if the root node is passive and has no children. Indeed, the root node having no children implies $T$ contains only the root, so no [mes] are in transit and no node other than the root is active; if the root is also passive we have termination.

**Detailed description.** Variable $fat_u$ is *undef* if $u$ is not in the tree, points to $u$ itself if $u$ is the root node, and points to $u$'s father if $u$ is a non-root tree node; $cc_u$ counts the children of $u$ in $T$. When active node $u$ sends a [mes], this message becomes a child of $u$ hence $cc_u$ is incremented (action $\mathbf{S}_u$ in Alg. 13.9). When $u$ is activated (action $\mathbf{R}_u$) its membership of $T$ must be ensured and this can be done by assuming the sender of the [mes] as its father; the father $cc$ is unaltered as $u$ replaces the [mes] as a child. If $u$ is already in the tree, the [mes] is removed

```
var la  : string     init infty ;
    cc  : integer    init 0 ;
    fat : node       init undef ;

For the initiator only:
    la := u ; fat := u ;
    forall x in Neigh
        do begin send [path,la] to x ; cc := cc + 1 end

Upon arrival of a [path,rho] message from v:
    receive [path,rho] from v ;
    if fat = undef then fat := v
                   else send [sig] to v ;
    if rho.u < la then
        begin la := rho.u ;
                forall x in Neigh s.t. x not in la
                    do begin send [path,la] to x ; cc := cc + 1 end
        end

Au: { A message [sig] arrives at u }
    receive [sig] ; cc := cc - 1

Tu: { cc = 0 and fat != undef }
    if fat = u (* Root node! *)
        then Detect: construction completed
        else send [sig] to fat ; fat := undef
```

**Algorithm 13.10**   Relaxation with Termination Detection (node $u$).

from the tree and a `[sig]` message is sent to its father to decrease the $cc$. Observe that a passive node remains in the tree if it has children, and a childless node remains in the tree if it is active; only if a passive, childless node is in the tree the withdrawal action $\mathbf{T}_u$ takes place. A non-root node sends a `[sig]` to its father so as to decrement the latter's $cc$, while the root node calls termination in this case.

**Correctness, variations, discussion.** It is far from trivial to firmly establish that the algorithm is correct and operates as described above, even under the most exotic scenarios of the computation and its timing. The basic techniques (invariant properties and variant functions) and their application to this algorithm are discussed in [27, Sec. 8.1] but are outside the scope of this chapter. Actually, the termination detection problem and the publication of several incorrect solutions strongly motivated research in verification techniques for distributed algorithms.

The algorithm can be applied to computations like Alg. 13.5, where the active state is not explicit. The resulting fast DFS algorithm with termination detection is shown as Alg. 13.10. The requirement that only one node initiates the computation was relaxed by Shavit and Francez [22]; in their algorithm each initiator of the computation traces a subset of the activity, and one round of global communication

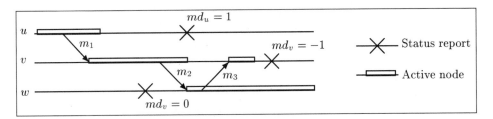

**Figure 13.3**   Compensated behind-the-back activation.

is used to determine that all traced activity has ceased.

The number of exchanged control messages equals the number of messages exchanged by the underlying computation, and this was shown to be optimal in the worst case. If a computation is started from a single node and the number of exchanged messages is relatively small (linear in $n$ or $m$, say), the Dijkstra–Scholten algorithm is the termination detector of choice.

### 13.3.3   Probe Algorithms

Probe algorithms repeatedly scan the entire network for active nodes and computation messages; they are based on the principle laid out by Dijkstra, Feijen, and Van Gasteren [7]. For simplicity of explanation we shall assume a special node (the *controller*) to coordinate detection; the controller exchanges status reports with all nodes.

In order to establish the absence of computation messages, each node maintains a *message deficit*, being the number of messages it has sent so far minus the number of messages it received so far. At any time, the number of messages in transit equals the sum of all deficits, hence empty channels mean zero deficit sum. In reply to a request ([req] message) from the coordinator, each node sends a status report ([stat, $m$, $c$] message), but defers sending it until it is passive.

It is tempting to believe that, because the nodes were passive when sending the report, the controller can detect termination if it receives status reports from all nodes and the deficits add to zero. However, unsafety results from the status reports being produced at different times, as is illustrated in the space-time diagram of Figure 13.3. Node $w$ was activated "behind-the-back" of the controller, but the activating message $m_2$ causes no negative deficit because the deficit was compensated for by receiving $m_3$ from $w$! Message $m_2$ *crosses* the probe because it was sent before the status report of its sender, but received after the status report of its receiver, and $m_3$ is said to cross the probe *backwards*.

Taking the status reports can be coordinated so as to prevent any message from crossing the probe backwards, which would render the algorithm safe; the status reports would then form a *consistent snapshot* cf. [5]. It is easier however, to detect the possibility of any compensated behind-the-back activation; to this end, each node also includes in its status report, whether any [mes] message was

```
var   state    : (act, pas) ;
      md       : int      init 0 ;
      rec      : bool     init false ;

Su:   { state = act }
      send [mes] ; md := md + 1

Ru:   { A message [mes] arrives at u }
      receive [mes] ; state := act ;
      rec := true ; md := md – 1

Iu:   { state = act }
      state := pas

Au:   { state = pas and a [req] message has arrived. }
      send [stat,md,rec] to controller ; rec := false

Code for the controller:
      repeat t := false ; s := 0 ;
             forall u do send [req] to u ;
             forall u do
                    begin receive [stat,m,r] ;
                          t := (t and r) ; s := s+m
                    end
      until ( t = false and s = 0 ) ;
      Detect termination
```

**Algorithm 13.11**   Probe based termination detection (node $u$).

received since sending the previous report. If this is the case, termination is not concluded; thus the receipt of a compensating backward message prevents detection; the resulting algorithm is shown as Alg. 13.11.

**Variations, complexity, discussion.** The various probe based algorithms differ considerably, mainly in their treatment of in-transit messages, and the collection of the status reports [25, 26]. Instead of *counting* messages as we have shown, acknowledgements or time-outs can be used.

Instead of direct communication with the controller as in Alg. 13.11, probe propagation through a Hamiltonian Cycle, or the Echo algorithm can be used for status communication. To implement the latter possibility, the controller acts as the initiator in the Echo algorithm. Status reports are sent upward in the constructed spanning tree in an accumulated fashion, i.e., each node reports the sum over all $md_u$ and the conjunction over all $rec_u$ of the nodes $u$ in its subtree.

Instead of having an additional controller, one of the nodes of the computation will perform the controller task in addition to the computation proper. In this way it is not necessary to add either nodes or channels to the network solely for the purpose of detection.

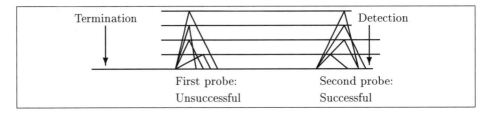

**Figure 13.4**   The detection delay.

Probe algorithms are the detectors of choice in computations that exchange a lot of messages, especially if many are exchanged in parallel. The reason is that probe algorithms exchange a fixed number of control messages *per probe*, independent of the number of basic messages. A good balance between detection overhead and detection delay can be achieved by starting probes under the control of a timer (as in [20].) Assume a fixed delay of $\Delta$ is introduced between the end of an unsuccessful probe and the start of the next one, and that the duration of the probe is small compared to $\Delta$. After termination occurs, some of the nodes may have *rec = true* so that the first probe started after termination fails to detect. The next probe finds all nodes with *rec = false* and thus termination is detected after at most $2\Delta$ delay.

## 13.4   Distributed Arc Consistency and CSP

To demonstrate the application of the distributed algorithm techniques to distributed AI problems, we shall now study the distributed Arc Consistency algorithm DisAC4; see also [20]. The Constraint Satisfaction Problem and consistency filters were also discussed in Chapter 4.

The Constraint Satisfaction Problem (CSP) and Arc Consistency (AC) are defined in Section 13.4.1, and the sequential AC4 algorithm is outlined in Section 13.4.2. We then consider a resource distributed model, where the resources for checking the consistency of a variable are located at a particular node. Section 13.4.3 gives the resulting algorithm, where each node is assumed responsible for one model variable, and Section 13.4.4 discusses termination detection for this version. An alternative computational model, a multiprocessor computer, where each node holds a subset of the variables, is considered in Section 13.4.5. Section 13.4.6 discusses how the distributed AC algorithm can be extended to be used in distributed backtracking CSP algorithms.

### 13.4.1   Constraint Satisfaction and Arc Consistency

A Constraint Satisfaction Problem is defined by a set of *variables* $Z = \{x_1, \ldots, x_n\}$, where $x_i$ must be assigned a value $v_i$ from a *domain* $D_i$ but subject to *constraints*. The constraints are a collection of binary predicates $C_{ij}$ where $C_{ij}(v, w)$ indicates if assigning $v$ to $x_i$ is legitimate w.r.t. $C_{ij}$ if value $w$ is assigned to $x_j$. A *solution* to the problem is an assignment that is simultaneously legitimate for all constraints, or, equivalently, in which no constraint is violated. It is usually assumed that constraints are symmetric (that is, $C_{ij}(v, w) = C_{ji}(w, v)$), but symmetry is not used in the algorithms of this section.

Finding a solution is computationally hard (the problem is NP complete) and generally involves testing all or many possible assignments. The size of each domain is assumed finite (in order to express complexities we assume a uniform upper bound $|D_i| \leq a$), but the number of possibilities is still exponential in $n$.

Arc Consistency is a polynomial technique that may help to reduce the search space considerably; it deletes a value from a domain if some constraint is seen to be unfulfillable with this value. More specifically, consider constraint $C_{ij}$ and assume that for some $v \in D_i$ there is *no* $w \in D_j$ for which $C_{ij}(v, w)$ is true. As $C_{ij}$ can not be fulfilled with $x_i = v$, the value $v$ in $D_i$ is redundant and can be eliminated for further consideration. This elimination may lead to other values becoming redundant in turn. A problem is called *arc consistent* if it has no redundant domain values. The *Arc Consistency* problem is to restrict all domains in a constraint satisfaction problem, so as to make the problem arc consistent but without eliminating possible solutions.

Formally, given domains $D_1$ through $D_n$, the Arc Consistency problem requires to find $D'_1$ through $D'_n$ such that:

1. The domains are restricted: $D'_i \subseteq D_i$.

2. The restricted problem is arc consistent: No $D'_i$ contains a redundant value.

3. The output is maximally arc consistent: if sets $D''_i$ with $D'_i \subseteq D''_i \subseteq D_i$ are arc consistent, then $D''_i = D'_i$ for each $i$.

The third requirement implies that no solutions are eliminated: if $(v_1, \ldots, v_n)$ is a satisfying assignment, then $v_i \in D'_i$ for each $i$.

Usually not every pair of variables has a non-trivial constraint (a constraint different from *true*). The problem is modelled as a directed graph where the variables are the nodes, and there is an edge from $x_i$ to $x_j$ if $C_{ji}$ is non-trivial. Let $Succ_i$ denote the successors and $Pred_i$ the predecessors of $i$ in this graph and $m$ the number of edges.

### 13.4.2  The AC4 Algorithm

Mohr and Henderson [18] proposed the following data structures and algorithm for detecting redundant values; see Alg. 13.12. For each $x_i$, and each $v \in D_i$, an array of counters is maintained, where the counter $cnt[i, v, j]$ exists for each $j$ for which a constraint $C_{ij}$ exists. The counter $cnt[i, v, j]$ expresses the number of values $w \in D_j$ for which $D_{ij}(v, w)$ is true. When some counter $cnt[i, v, j]$ equals zero, the value $v$ is redundant and is removed from $D_i$. As a result, $cnt[j, w, i]$ should be decremented for all $j, w$ such that $C_{ji}(w, v)$ and to this end the pair $(i, v)$ is queued for later processing. In this processing it is not necessary to evaluate the

```
            (* Initialize counters and support structures *)
            forall Cij
                 do forall v in Di
                        do forall w in Dj
                              do if Cij(v,w)
                                   then begin cnt[i,v,j] +:= 1 ;
                                              Insert( Supp[j,w], <i,v> )
                                   end ;

            (* Check for initially redundant values *)
            forall Cij
                 do forall v in Di
                      do if cnt[i,v,j] = 0
                         then begin Enque (Q,<i,v>) ; Delete(Di, v) end ;


            (* Main loop *)
            while not Empty(Q)
                 do begin Deque(Q, <j,w>) ;
                     forall <i,v> in Supp[j,w]
                          do if v in Di
                              then begin cnt[i,v,j] := cnt[i,v,j] − 1 ;
                                         if cnt[i,v,j]=0
                                         then begin Enque (Q,<i,v>) ;
                                                    Delete( Di, v)
                                              end
                              end
                     end
            end
```

**Algorithm 13.12**    Sequential AC4.

$C_{ji}$ predicate again, because all relevant information is stored in additional support data structures $Supp[j, w]$. The set $Supp[j, w]$ contains all pairs $\langle i, v \rangle$ for which $C_{ij}(v, w)$ is *true*, or, equivalently, for which $w$ is counted in $cnt[i, v, j]$. The main loop of Alg. 13.12 shows how the relevant counters are decremented and how this may make other values redundant in turn.

The size of the *cnt* arrays is at most $m.a$ integers because $(i, j)$ ranges over edges of the graph. The size of the support structure is larger because for each constraint $C_{ij}$, all values in $D_j$ may support all values in $D_i$, in which case the *Supp* lists together have $m.a^2$ pairs. As each pair $(i, v)$ is queued at most once, the queue never holds more than $n.a$ pairs. Thus, the storage complexity of AC4 is dominated by the support structures.

Initialization of the data structures costs $m.a^2$ time, the initial check for redundant values takes $m.a$ time, and the main loop may again take $m.a^2$ time. The resulting $O(m.a^2)$ time complexity is optimal for Arc Consistency [18].

### 13.4.3   The Distributed AC4 Algorithm

In this subsection we shall describe a distributed implementation of the AC4 algorithm, first assuming that there is one computing node for each variable. Thus, node $i$ maintains the domain $D_i$ and holds the resources for evaluating $C_{ij}$; this makes node $i$ the place of choice to maintain $cnt[i, v, j]$ as well. Neighbouring nodes will communicate the elimination of nodes in order to enforce decrementing the counters.

We shall now discuss the storage of the support structures. One possibility is to store $Supp[j, w]$ in node $j$ and have $j$ send a message to node $i$ for each $\langle i, v \rangle$ found in $Supp[j, w]$. However, if node $j$ sends just one message to node $i$ when $w$ is eliminated, node $i$ must still evaluate $C_{ij}$ to find out for which $v$ $cnt[i, v, j]$ must be decremented. If $j$ sends a list of values $v$ for which this is the case, the communication complexity becomes very high.

Another possibility is to split $Supp[j, w]$ over the various neighbors: the pairs $\langle i, v \rangle$ are stored in node $i$. When node $j$ eliminates $w$ it will inform node $i$ with a single message, and on receipt of this message node $i$ must consider all its pairs of $Supp[j, w]$. This possibility is chosen in [20].

However, we observe that the support structure can be eliminated completely without significantly increasing the computational complexity of the algorithm. Indeed, for each $j$, $w$ the set $Supp[j, w]$ is read just *at most* once, namely, when $j$ is eliminated from $D_j$. Our distributed implementation therefore uses a different decrement policy. When $w$ is eliminated from $D_j$, rather than enumerating a stored set $Supp[j, w]$, we will test for each $i$, $v$ if $C_{ij}(v, w)$ is true, and, if so, decrement $cnt[i, v, j]$,

The queue of the sequential algorithm is distributed over all nodes as the receive queues ($RQ$) and send queues ($SQ$). Whenever node $i$ detects $v$ to be redundant, $v$ is placed in the local send queue $SQ_i$. An independent subprocess $\mathbf{S}_i$ is responsible for taking all values out of this queue and informs the neighbors by sending a [remove, $v$] message. Incoming messages are buffered in the receive queue; an independent subprocess $\mathbf{R}_i$ inserts all received values in this queue, and the worker process $\mathbf{W}_i$ reads its input from this queue.

The elimination of support data structures reduces the storage requirements: Algorithm 13.13 stores an array of $a$ counters $cnt_i[*, j]$ (in node $i$) for each constraint $C_{ij}$, hence the overall storage requirement is $O(m.a)$.

The initialization requires $O(m.a^2)$ time (as does the sequential algorithm) and exchanges no messages. (If $\delta_i$ is the in-degree of node $i$, the computation for node $i$ is $O(\delta_i.a^2)$.) To this end we assume that node $i$ knows the initial domain $D_j$, denoted as $D_j^0$, and counts, for each $v$, the number of supporters in this initial domain.

To assess the communication and computation cost of the processing phase, first observe that each value $w \in D_j^0$ is deleted from $D_j$ and queued in $SQ_j$ *at most once* because of the test in procedure *Redundant*. Consequently, each arc in the constraint graph carries at most $a$ messages, to a total message complexity of $O(m.a)$. Each

```
        var    D        init Di   (* Domain *)
               cnt[v,j]            (* Count support *)
               SQ,RQ              (* Send and Receive queue *)

        procedure Redundant (v):
            if v in D then
                begin Delete(D, v) ; Enque(SQ, v) end

        Initialization (for each node):
            forall j in Pred
                do forall v in D
                    do begin cnt[v,j] := 0 ;
                            forall w in Dj^0
                                (* Node i knows the initial set Dj *)
                            do  if Cij(v,w)
                                    then cnt[v,j] := cnt[v,j] + 1 ;
                            if  cnt[v,j] = 0
                                then Redundant(v)
                    end

    Wi:  { Receive queue RQ is not empty }
         Deque (RQ, <j,w> ) ;
         forall v in D
             do if Cij(v,w)
                 then begin cnt[v,j] := cnt[v,j] – 1 ;
                            if cnt[v,j] = 0
                                then Redundant (v)
                 end

    Ri:  { receive [remove,w] from node j }
         Enque (RQ, <j,w> )

    Si:  { SQ is not empty }
         Deque ( SQ, v) ;
         forall j in Succ do send [remove,v] to j
```

**Algorithm 13.13**   Distributed AC4 Algorithm (node $i$).

value received is enqueued for later processing, and this processing (action $\mathbf{W}_i$) consists of a loop over (at most) $a$ values in $D_i$. The local computation cost is therefore bounded by $O(m.a^2)$ steps, hence the initialization phase still dominates the computation.

The distributed time complexity is $O(n.a)$; indeed, at most this many values are eliminated altogether, and the redundancy of some value is detected at most one time unit after its last supporter was eliminated.

### 13.4.4   Termination Detection

Termination of Alg. 13.13 is implicit, because after the elimination of all redundant values the nodes will be in a receiving state, ready to receive and process further [remove, *] messages. Fortunately, application of the results of Section 13.3 is straightforward. Define *pas*(*i*) to be the following predicate:

$SQ_i$ is empty $\land$ $RQ_i$ is empty $\land$ initialization is completed in node $i$

We observe the following.

1. *If pas*(*i*) *holds, it can be falsified only by the receipt of a* [remove, *w*] *message.* After initialization, the only steps for node $i$ are $\mathbf{W}_i$, $\mathbf{S}_i$, and $\mathbf{R}_i$, but processing and sending are not possible when the receive and send queue are empty. So only receipt is possible in this case, and will place a value in the receive queue, thereby falsifying *pas*(*i*).

2. *If pas*(*i*) *holds, node i cannot send a* [remove, *] *message.* The empty send queue disables the send action.

3. *If simultaneously for all i pas*(*i*) *holds and no channel contains a* [remove, *] *message, the algorithm has terminated.* In this case, no processing or sending is possible because all queues are empty, and no receiving is possible because no messages are in transit.

Thus the assumptions for the termination detection problem are satisfied, and we can apply the algorithms of Section 13.3 to make termination explicit. The tracing algorithm (Alg. 13.3.2) is not appropriate here. First, it requires that there is exactly one initiator, which is not the case in Alg. 13.13 (generalizations to more initiators exist, though). The main reason is the overhead of control messages; tracing algorithms double the communication, while probe algorithms can have a much lower communication overhead if the distributed computation exchanges a lot of messages in parallel.

Thus, the Distributed AC4 algorithm should be combined with a probe based termination detection algorithm, such as Alg. 13.11. We shall not give the combined algorithm here.

On termination of the distributed AC4 algorithm, the remaining domains $D_i$ are maximally arc consistent and two special situations deserve our attention.

1. **Contradiction:** *On termination, some* $D_i$ *is empty.*
   Clearly, the product space is also empty, and because no solution to the problem is eliminated by the Arc Consistency algorithm, this condition implies that there exists no assignment satisfying all constraints.

2. **Solution:** *On termination, each* $D_i$ *is reduced to a singleton* $\{v_i\}$.
   In this case the product space contains just a single assignment, namely $(x_1, \ldots, x_n) = (v_1, \ldots, v_n)$. Because the domains are arc consistent, this assignment is easily seen to satisfy all constraints. Indeed, consider constraint

$C_{ji}$ and observe that, because $v_i$ was not removed from $D_i$, there is at least one $w$ in $D_j$ for which $C_{ji}(w, v_i)$ is true. But $D_i$ is the singleton $\{v_j\}$, so $C_{ji}(v_j, v_i)$ is true.

Evaluating these conditions can easily be done by augmenting the termination detection algorithm; in addition to reporting the $rec_i$ and $md_i$ information, node $i$ states if $D_i$ is a singleton, and if $D_i$ is empty.

### 13.4.5   Partitioning for Multiprocessor Computers

We have so far assumed that there is a given, one-to-one correspondence between nodes and variables; a natural assumption if the resources for checking consistency are distributed and expensive to reallocate. Other applications may allow to freely allocate variables of the problem to processing nodes, for example, when a multi-processor machine is used to solve a CSP (with all resources at hand).

We first discuss the execution of Algorithm 13.13 in this case, especially if more than one variable is assigned to any machine node. Node $u$ maintains the administration for a collection $Z_u \subset Z$ and will execute all computations of Alg. 13.13 for the relevant variables, with only two twists that are not completely trivial. First, if node $i$ sends a message to node $j$ while $i$ and $j$ are in the same machine, no message is sent but the eliminated value is placed in the queue locally. Second, a machine can use a single receive queue, rather than a separate one for each of the variables it holds.

Thus the execution of the Arc Consistency itself is not very complicated, but the interesting question is to find a good allocation of variables over nodes. This distribution should have a favourable processor load, and need as little communication as possible. Fortunately, as a result of the analysis in the previous subsection, the load and communication of a distribution can be computed.

Let node $i$ of the Arc Consistency Problem be allocated to processor $p(i)$ of the machine. As node $i$ of the problem requires $O(\delta_i.a^2)$ work, the total load of processor $p$ is $\sum_{i:p(i)=p} \delta_i.a^2$. As $O(a)$ messages are exchanged through each edge of the problem, the total amount of communication will be $O(a).|\{ij \in E : p(i) \neq p(j)\}|$. Minimising load and communication (over all allocations) is NP-hard, so an approximation algorithm is needed; see for example the work by Lo [17].

### 13.4.6   Distributed Constraint Satisfaction Algorithm

We shall now briefly discuss how Distributed Arc Consistency can be used in distributed solutions for Constraint Satisfaction Problems. A CSP is usually solved by backtracking, where parts of the solution space are eliminated from search by hypothesis generation. A hypothesis for variable $x_i$ specifies a subset of the domain $D_i$ and restricts the search to tuples for which $x_i$ is in the subset. The current problem instance is narrowed down with the additional restriction that $x_i$ is in the subset, yielding a new problem instance. More generally, a hypothesis can itself be a binary predicate assuming a constraint on combinations of $x_i$ and $x_j$ values.

If **solution** occurs in the restricted search space, the problem is solved and the found tuple is the solution. (It satisfies all the original constraints plus the current collection of hypotheses.) If **contradiction** is found, a backtracking step is taken: the hypothesis is replaced by its negation because the hypothesis is found to be inconsistent with the problem (including earlier hypotheses) and search is continued. If neither of these situations occurs, a next hypothesis is generated to narrow down the search space further.

The evaluation of the problem instances uses Arc Consistency: after each generation of a hypothesis or its replacement by its negation, the domains are further restricted by the Arc Consistency algorithm. We have seen that the AC algorithm reduces the domains to the maximally arc consistent subsets, and allows to conclude if **solution** or **contradiction** occurs.

A distributed CSP solver alternates hypothesis generation, hypothesis evaluation (by means of arc consistency), and hypothesis elimination (backtracking) in a coordinated way. To decide what hypothesis to generate, we assume that each node can locally evaluate the attractiveness of hypotheses it can generate. For example, generating a hypothesis concerning a variable with 20 possible values may be less attractive than one concerning a variable with 2 possible values. After termination of each arc consistency phase, the controller coordinates a global search for the node with the most attractive hypothesis. This does not require that the controller has access to all information or even that it can communicate with each node directly. In the next section we show (in the context of a graph processing algorithm) how such an evaluation is possible in a network of arbitrary topology using broadcasts and convergecast over a spanning tree.

**More detailed description.** When detecting termination of the arc consistency phase, the controller also evaluates if **solution** or **contradiction** occurs and informs the nodes.

If the search space is still too large, all nodes stack the current value of their domain $D_i$ and the support structures $cnt_i[v, j]$. They evaluate the attractiveness of any hypothesis they can generate, and report the most attractive one. The convergecast allows the coordinator to find the most attractive hypothesis, and informs the node that submitted this hypothesis. This hypothesis is added to the constraints, after which Arc Consistency is started again.

In case of **solution**, the computed assignment is the output of the problem and the whole algorithm is terminated.

In case of **contradiction**, a backtrack step is taken. All nodes restore the previous values of $D_i$ and $cnt_i[v, j]$ and in addition, the node that generated the most recently added hypothesis replaces it by its negation. After this, arc consistency is started again.

```
C := empty ;
while V != empty
      do begin if there is v in V with deg(v) = 1
                   then remove v from G
                   else  begin K := { v in V | indeg(v) <= 1 } ;
                               v := node of highest degree in K ;
                               C := C + {v} ;
                               remove v from G
                         end
             end
      end
```

**Algorithm 13.14**   Suermondt and Cooper Loop Cutset.

## 13.5   Distributed Graph Processing

We shall demonstrate various techniques for distributed processing of the network topology by a distributed algorithm that has the topology as the input graph. The example worked out is the computation of a loop cutset in a Belief Network, which is a necessary preprocessing stage for the application of loop cutset conditioning in these networks. The aim of this section is to show how a sequential algorithm (by Suermondt and Cooper [23]) can be modified for distributed execution.

### 13.5.1   The Problem: Loop Cutset

A *Belief Network* is a directed acyclic graph in which the nodes represent various hypotheses and the arcs represent known statistical dependencies. Let $\vec{G} = (V, \vec{E})$ denote the directed graph, and $G = (V, E)$ the underlying undirected graph. The algorithms for updating the probability distribution of the hypotheses assume that $G$ is free of cycles, and hence to apply these algorithms, cycles must be eliminated. A vertex in an undirected cycle is called a *pit* if both of its adjacent cycle arcs are incoming, and we require each cycle to be broken by the removal of at least one non-pit vertex.

**Definition 13.3**
A *loop cutset* is a subset $C \subseteq V$ such that for each cycle in $G$, $C$ contains at least one node of the cycle that is not a pit of that cycle.

**Algorithm of Suermondt and Cooper.** For efficiency reasons, the cutset should be small, but computation of an optimal cutset is NP hard. The best-known heuristic for computing small cutsets (Suermondt and Cooper [23]) includes vertices in $C$ one by one, trying to choose vertices that cut as many loops as possible. This is done by choosing a vertex with maximal degree, but to avoid cutting a cycle by removal of a pit, the chosen node must have in-degree zero or one. Because nodes of degree one are never part of a cycle, these nodes are removed (repeatedly) before searching for a cut-node; see Alg 13.14.

### 13.5.2  Distributed Execution of the Algorithm

The distributed algorithm does not represent the cut set in any central place; instead, at the end each node will know whether it is itself a cutnode or not. Algorithm 13.14 is simulated by two alternating phases, each under control of a coordinating node, which is the root of a spanning tree in the network. The spanning tree is used for control purposes, and an edge of the network can be part of it regardless whether it was already eliminated by the Suermondt/Cooper algorithm.

A *leaf trim* phase removes as many degree-one nodes as possible, and repeatedly; that is, if the removal of a node causes the degree of another node to drop to one, the latter is removed in the same phase. A *cut node search* is initiated when there are no more leaves, and searches the network for the highest degree node (with in-degree zero or one). When identified, the cut node becomes the new controller; a *shift controller* phase moves the root of the spanning tree to this node and hands control to the next leave trim phase. This phase has no counterpart in Alg. 13.14, and neither has the initial phase that constructs the control spanning tree.

**Part one: Variables and leaf trim.** Algorithm 13.15 shows the variables and constants used by the node $u$. The constants $In_u$ and $Out_u$ represent the incoming and outgoing neighbors of $u$ in the graph; in the algorithms, $x$ and $y$ will range over neighbors of $u$, i.e., over $In_u \cup Out_u$.

To construct and maintain the control tree, each adjacent edge $ux$ has a *link control status* $lcs_u[x]$ with the following meaning. The initial status is *basic*; when $x$ is a child or the father of $u$ the status is *son* or *fat*; and when the edge was rejected for the spanning tree, its status is *frond*.

The removal of edges and nodes by the Suermondt/Cooper algorithm is represented by the *link activity status* and *node activity status* $las_u[x]$ and $nas_u$. Initially the link is active (status is *yes*) but upon removal of $x$ or $u$, $las_u[x]$ becomes *no*. The nodes are also initially active ($nas_u = yes$), but they can be removed either as a leaf or as a cut node, and $nas_u$ becomes either *noncut* or *cut*.

The variables $mydeg_u$, $bestdeg_u$, and $bestbranch_u$ are used to determine the next cut node; $mydeg_u$ is the degree of $u$, $bestdeg_u$ the highest degree in $u$'s subtree, and $bestbranch_u$ points to the location in the tree where the highest degree is found.

Algorithm 13.15 also presents the procedures for removal of leaves. The *TrimTest* procedure verifies if $u$ has degree one, and if so, $u$ becomes *noncut*; a [remove] message is sent to the only neighbour to inform it of the removal, and the procedure terminates after receipt of an acknowledgement [sig]. Receipt of the [remove] message causes the carrying edge to be non-active ($las = no$), and the node performs

```
    cons  In                           (* Incoming neighbors *) ;
          Out                          (* Outgoing neighbors *) ;

    var   lcs[x]      init basic       (* Link control status *) ;
          las[x]      init yes         (* Link activity status *) ;
          nas         init yes         (* Node activity status *) ;
          mydeg                        (* Compute degree of u *) ;
          bestdeg                      (* Highest degree in subtree *) ;
          bestbranch                   (* Point to best degree *) ;

    procedure TrimTest:
        if | { x : las[x] = yes } | = 1
        then begin x := neighbour s.t. las[x] = yes ;
                   nas := noncut ; las[x] := no ;
                   send [remove] to x ;
                   receive [sig] or [remove] from x
                           (* Optimisation, see text *)
              end

    Upon receipt of [remove] from y:
        las[y] := no ; TrimTest ; send [sig] to y
```

**Algorithm 13.15**　Variables and Leaf Trim.

*Trim Test* itself. If a [remove] message is sent as a result, the replying [sig] message is deferred until a reply was received, according to the Dijkstra/Scholten principle. A slight twist is the possibility to receive a [remove] message instead of a [sig]; this will happen where two nodes ($v$ and $w$) connected by a single edge remain at some point in the execution. Both nodes call *Trim Test* and decide to remove themselves and send a [remove] message over the edge. Rather than having both nodes reply to the other's message with a [sig], each one treats the received message as the reply, thus saving the two extra messages. *I do not know how many messages are saved* in this way, but with this modification it is possible to compute the overall number of messages easily; see Section 13.5.3.

**Part two: Control tree construction.** The initial control tree is constructed by executing the echo algorithm from the initiator; this is shown in Alg 13.16. Procedure *ConstructSubtree* sends [construct, 0] messages through all *basic* edges and awaits the receipt of a [construct, $i$] message. The construct messages of the exploration stage have $i = 0$, while the replies to the father have $i = 1$; thus upon receipt of the message, the edge is recognised as either *son* or *frond*. Upon completion of the subtree a message (with $i = 1$ of course) is returned to the father.

Nodes run *Trim Test* in parallel with the construction of the subtree and await its return before replying to the father. Consequently, when the construction terminates at the initiator, the first round of leaf elimination was completed, and the search for the node of highest degree is initiated by calling the procedure

```
procedure ConstructSubtree:
    forall x s.t. lcs[x] = basic
        do send [construct,0] to x ;
    while exists x : lcs[x] = basic
        do begin receive [construct,i] from y ;
                if i=0  then lcs[y] := frond
                        else lcs[y] := son
        end


The initiator starts the algorithm:
    pardo ConstructSubtree & TrimTest odrap ;
    InitSearchCutnode


The others, upon arrival of the first [construct,i] message:
                (* i=0 in the first message, because the
                first message is certainly NOT a reply. *)
    receive [construct,0] from x ; lcs[x] := fat ;
    pardo ConstructSubtree & TrimTest odrap ;
    send [construct,1] to x
```

**Algorithm 13.16**   Construction of control spanning tree.


*InitSearchCutnode.*

**Part three: Search for cut node.** The procedure *NodeSearch*, called in node $u$, computes the highest node degree in the subtree of $u$ (with the restriction, of course, that only nodes with in-degree zero or one are taken into account). This procedure computes the degree of $u$ itself and initiates a recursive computation in the subtrees by sending [search] messages to the sons of $u$. The procedure terminates only after receipt of a [bestis, $d$] message from each child; the order in which these messages arrive is not relevant. While processing the replies, $u$ maintains the highest degree seen in the variable $bestdeg_u$ and $bestbranch_u$ points to either $u$ itself or to the subtree reporting the highest degree.

This computation and the exchange of [search] and [bestis, $d$] messages over a spanning tree are a typical example of the *broadcast/convergecast* mechanism. By changing the local computation, the same mechanism can be used to compute other functions, such as summation or conjunction and disjunction, as the application requires.

The coordinator of the round initiates the search by calling *InitSearchCutnode*, and all other nodes become involved upon receipt of a [search] message (from their father necessarily). In the latter case, after completion of *NodeSearch* the result value is sent to the father in a [bestis, $d$] message, where $d$ is the computed degree ($bestdeg_u$). When the *NodeSearch* procedure terminates in the coordinator, the stored value is the overall highest degree. A value 0 at this point indicates that there are no nodes left with in-degree bounded by 1; actually a termination condition for the algorithm, as any non-empty directed acyclic graph has such

```
procedure NodeSearch:
    if   | { x in In : las[x] =yes } | <= 1
         then mydeg := | { x : las[x] =yes } |
         else mydeg := 0 ;
    bestdeg := mydeg ; bestbranch := u ;
    forall x s.t. lcs[x] = son
         do send [search] to x ;
    forall x s.t. lcs[x] = son
         do (* in order of message arrival !! *)
             begin receive [bestis,d] from x ;
                 if d > bestdeg
                     then begin bestdeg := d ;
                                bestbranch := x
                          end
             end

procedure InitSearchCutnode:
    NodeSearch ;
    if bestdeg = 0 then Terminate
                   else ChangeRoot


Upon receipt of [search] from x:
                    (* x is the father *)
    NodeSearch ;
    send [bestis,bestdeg] to x
```

**Algorithm 13.17**  Search for cut node.

nodes. If *NodeSearch* leads to a positive value, this is the maximal node degree, and a node of this degree can be chosen as the next cut node. To pass control to such a node, the current coordinator calls the procedure *ChangeRoot*.

**Part four: Controller shift.** Because the newly selected cutnode is at the center of the leaf-trim activity of the next round, we prefer to make it the new controller.

After the execution of *NodeSearch*, each node $u$ has the pointer $bestbranch_u$ pointing to the highest degree node in the subtree of $u$. The procedure *ChangeRoot* is called only in nodes for which the subtree contains the globally highest degree. Indeed, the first call to *ChangeRoot* occurs in the controller (after completion of *NodeSearch*) and the subtree of the controller contains the entire network.

We now consider the procedure *ChangeRoot*; if $bestbranch_u = u$, then the maximum over $u$'s subtree occurs at $u$, and because this maximum equals the global maximum, node $u$ itself is chosen as the next cut node. Otherwise a [changeroot] message is sent to the son that reported the highest degree (pointed by $bestbranch_u$) because this subtree must contain the globally maximal degree. The direction of all control tree edges through which the [changeroot] message is forwarded is reversed so that the new controller becomes the root of this tree.

Finally we discuss the removal of the cut node from the network. The node

```
                procedure ChangeRoot:
                    if bestbranch = u
                    then begin nas := cut ;
                                (* Coordinate next round *)
                                TrimFromNeighbors ;
                                InitSearchCutnode
                        end
                    else begin lcs[bestbranch] := fat ;
                                send [changeroot] to bestbranch
                        end

                Upon receipt of [changeroot] from x:
                    lcs[x] := son ; ChangeRoot

                procedure TrimFromNeighbors:
                    forall x s.t. las[x] = yes
                        do send [remove] to x ;
                    forall x s.t. las[x] = yes
                        do (* In order of arrival of the messages *)
                            begin receive [sig] or [remove] from x ;
                                    las[x] := no
                            end
```

**Algorithm 13.18**  Controller shift.

becomes a cut node ($nas_u := cut$) and informs its neighbors about its removal by calling *TrimFromNeighbors*. If removing one of the edges decreases the degree of a neighbour to 1, trimming of this new leaf is performed immediately, and termination of the whole procedure is detected as before.

Observe that *before* removal of the cut node there were no leaves (as a result of the previous trimming round), and only the neighbors of the cut node decrement their degree. Consequently, if there are any leaves at this point, they are contained in the neighbors of the cut node, and hence *TrimTest* need only be initiated in these neighbors.

After termination of this trimming round the controller initiates the search for the next cut node by calling *InitSearchCutnode*.

### 13.5.3  Complexity and Conclusions

To evaluate the complexity of the distributed algorithm, we introduce some parameters; $n$ and $m$ are the number of nodes and edges of $G$ as usual, let $s$ be the size of the computed cutset, and $d$ the diameter of the control tree (worst case: $n - 1$). We then observe that in all procedures of the algorithm, at most a constant amount of work is associated with receiving or sending a message. Thus, the computation complexity of the algorithm is asymptotically equal to the number of messages exchanged by the algorithm. As remarked before, this is usually the case in distributed graph algorithms.

For the communication complexity we consider how many messages of each type are exchanged. For the construction of the control tree, two [construct, $i$] messages are sent through each edge of the graph to a total of $2m$ messages. Each edge is deactivated exactly once at the expense of two messages, so the total amount of [remove]/[sig] messages is also $2m$. The evaluation of the highest degree node requires the exchange of one [search] and one [bestis, ...] message through each edge of the control tree, which is $2(n-1)$ messages. This evaluation is performed $s+1$ times (the last evaluation yields 0 but is used to detect the end of the algorithm), so the overall number of [search] and [bestis, $d$] messages is $2(s+1)(n-1)$. Finally, the execution shifts the controller $s$ times, which requires [changeroot] messages to be sent through a path in the control tree; the total number of [changeroot] messages is bounded by $s.d$. We thus see that $2m + 2m + 2(s + 1)(n - 1) + s.d$ messages are exchanged, which is about $4m + 2s.n$.

When evaluating the amount of time used by the algorithm we must realize that we have no guarantee of any actual parallelism occurring in the trimming of leaves. If we *ignore* leaf trimming, the construction of the control tree takes at most $2d$ time, a search for a cut node takes at most $2d$ time, and changing the root to the new cut node takes at most $d$ time. These procedures together take $(3s + 4).d$ time, but their progress can be delayed when nodes wait for leaf trimming to terminate. However, in the worst case all trimming is done sequentially and the exchange of [remove]/[sig] messages takes 2 time units per node, so the other procedures are delayed at most $(n - s).2$ time units, and the overall time complexity is bounded by $(3s + 4).d + 2(n - s)$.

Our example of a distributed graph processing algorithm was taken from the Artificial Intelligence domain, namely loop cutset computation. Other graph algorithms can be treated in a similar way to yield distributed versions; known examples include Shortest Path [27, Sec. 4.2], Minimum Spanning Tree [10], Maximum Flow [32], Connectivity problems [14].

## 13.6   Conclusions

This chapter gives an overview of the most important techniques of distributed algorithm design for Distributed Artificial Intelligence applications. Important issues in this domain are the distributed control of computations, and the distributed processing of the network graph.

We have seen two important control paradigms. Termination detection is necessary to observe when some subcomputation has ended, and a new phase of the application can start. Examples included termination of arc consistency in distributed Constraint Satisfaction, and the leaf trimming sub-phase of Suermondt and Cooper's loop cutset algorithm. Distributed coordination can be issued by a controller using broadcast and convergecast over a spanning tree. Such a tree can be constructed using the echo algorithm, and can be used to broadcast computation states, to convergecast maximal values or sums, and the root of the tree can move. All these techniques were used in Suermondt and Cooper's algorithm, and are applicable to the distributed CSP algorithm outlined in Section 13.4.6. The interested reader is referred to [27] to read about more paradigms, such as leader election, control for anonymous networks, snapshots, synchronous algorithms; I consider them of lesser importance for the AI community.

Distributed graph processing is based on sequential techniques for the same problem, and distributed graph exploration is an important step. We have seen several depth-first search algorithms, and studied an algorithm for connectivity certificates. Breadth-first search is notoriously difficult to implement in distributed algorithms.

We have not addressed any issues related to failure and recovery of nodes; fault tolerance is an important area in distributed algorithms research, but the results are not easily transferred to the Artificial Intelligence application domain.

## 13.7   Exercises

1. *[Level 2]* Prove that the time complexity of a distributed algorithm is bounded by its message complexity.

2. *[Level 1]* Prove that the total length of the $2n - 2$ lists exchanged by Algorithm 13.5 is between $n^2 - 1$ and $\frac{3}{2}n(n - 1)$.

3. *[Level 1]* How does the Relaxation Algorithm (Alg. 13.5) prevent the formation of paths that are not simple?

4. *[Level 1]* Prove that the time complexity of the Echo algorithm (Alg. 13.6) is $O(D/\alpha)$ if message delay is not only upper bounded by one time unit, but also lower bounded by $\alpha$ time units ($0 < \alpha \leq 1$).

5. *[Level 2]* Prove that the time complexity of the Echo algorithm (Alg. 13.6) is $O(D.\beta)$ if the ratio between the delays, suffered by two messages sent through the same link (even in different directions) is bounded by a constant $\beta$.

6. *[Level 2]* The *detection delay* of a termination detection algorithm is the maximum time that can elapse between termination and its detection. Prove that the detection delay of the Dijkstra–Scholten algorithm is $\Theta(n)$. Prove that $\Omega(D)$ is a lower bound on the detection delay.

7. *[Level 2]* Algorithm 13.11 is not exactly fault-tolerant: it will already fail in case of a *single* error where one node erroneously increments its *md* counter without sending a message. Describe what happens in this case, and argue why this behaviour is inevitable for termination detection algorithms.

8. *[Level 4]* Develop termination detection algorithms that can work even if nodes may crash. You will find out that detecting termination in spite of $t$ possible crashes requires that a passive node can only be activated by receiving at least $t + 1$ activation messages.

9. *[Level 3]* Work out all the details and give a complete algorithm for the distributed Constraint Satisfaction Problem.

10. *[Level 2]* Write a distributed algorithm to test if the network graph is bipartite (2-colorable) and uses $O(m)$ messages and $O(n)$ time.

11. *[Level 3]* Write a distributed algorithm to construct a Maximal Independent Set (MIS) in the network graph.

12. *[Level 3]* Develop a distributed algorithm that works on a directed acyclic graph and computes a topological sort. At the end, each node knows its sequence number in the topological sort.

13. *[Level 4]* The Distributed Cutset Algorithm (Alg. 13.15–13.18) can be improved. A change of a node's degree during a leaf-trim round occurs only if it is a neighbor of a node trimmed in that round. Consequently, the global search for the highest-degree node (Alg. 13.17) can be replaced by a contest between neighbors of trimmed leaves and the previously highest-degree nodes. Develop an improved algorithm along these lines and analyse its complexity (messages and time).

## 13.8   References

1. Yehuda Afek and Moty Ricklin. Sparser: A paradigm for running distributed algorithms. In Adrian Segall and Shmuel Zaks, editors, *6th Int. Workshop on Distributed Algorithms*, volume 647 of *Lecture Notes in Computer Science*, pages 1–10, Haifa, November 1992. Springer Verlag.

2. Baruch Awerbuch. A new distributed depth-first search algorithm. *Information Processing Letters*, 20:147–150, 1985.

3. Baruch Awerbuch. Optimal distributed algorithms for minimum weight spanning tree, counting, leader election and related problems. In *Symp. on Theory of Computing*, pages 230–240, May 1987.

4. Baruch Awerbuch and David Peleg. Routing with polynomial communication-space trade-off. *SIAM J. Discr. Math.*, 5(2):151–162, May 1992.

5. K. Mani Chandy and Leslie Lamport. Distributed snapshots: Determining global states of distributed systems. *ACM Transactions on Computer Systems*, 3(1):63–75, February 1985.

6. Israel Cidon. Yet another distributed depth-first search algorithm. *Information Processing Letters*, 26:301–305, January 1988.

7. Edsger W. Dijkstra, Wim H. J. Feijen, and A. J. M. van Gasteren. Derivation of a termination detection algorithm for distributed computations. *Information Processing Letters*, 16(5):217–219, June 1983.

8. Edsger W. Dijkstra and Carel S. Scholten. Termination detection for diffusing computations. *Information Processing Letters*, 11(1):1–4, August 1980.

9. Shimon Even, Gene Itkis, and Sergio Rajsbaum. On mixed connectivity certificates. In Paul Spirakis, editor, *European Symposium on Algorithms*, volume

979 of *Lecture Notes in Computer Science*, pages 1–16. Springer Verlag, 1995.

10. Robert G. Gallager, Pierre A. Humblet, and P. M. Spira. A distributed algorithm for minimum weight spanning trees. *ACM Transactions on Programming Languages and Systems*, 5:67–77, 1983.

11. Juan A. Garay, Shay Kutten, and David Peleg. A sub-linear time distributed algorithm for minimum-weight spanning trees. In *Symp. on Theory of Computing*, pages 659–668, 1993.

12. Jean-Michel Hélary, Aomar Maddi, and Michel Raynal. Calcul distribué d'un extremum et du routage associé dans un réseau quelconque. Technical Report 516, INRIA, Rennes, April 1986.

13. Lisa Higham and Teresa Przytycka. A simple, efficient algorithm for maximum finding on rings. In André Schiper, editor, *7th Int. Workshop on Distributed Algorithms*, volume 725 of *Lecture Notes in Computer Science*, pages 249–263. Springer Verlag, September 1993.

14. Esther Jennings. *Distributed Graph Connectivity Algorithms*. PhD thesis, Dept of Elec. Eng., Luleå Un. (Sw.), Sept. 22, 1997.

15. Nathan Linial. Distributive graph algorithms: Global solutions from local data. In *Foundations of Computer Science*, pages 331–335. IEEE, 1987.

16. Igor Litovsky, Yves Métivier, and Wiesław Zielonka. On the recognition of families of graphs with local computations. *Information and Computation*, 118(1):110–119, April 1995.

17. Virginia Mary Lo. Heuristic algorithms for task assignment in distributed systems. *IEEE Trans. on Computers*, 37(11):1384–1397, November 1988.

18. R. Mohr and T. C. Henderson. Arc and path consistency revisited. *Artif. Intell.*, 28:225–233, 1986.

19. Hiroshi Nagamochi and Toshihide Ibaraki. A linear-time algorithm for finding a sparse $k$-connected spanning subgraph of a $k$-connected graph. *Algorithmica*, 7:583–596, 1992.

20. Thang Nguyen and Yves Deville. A distributed arc-consistency algorithm. Technical report, Dépt Informatique, Univ. Cath. de Louvain, 1348 Louvain-la-Neuve, Belgium, September 1995.

21. Pierre Rosenstiehl, J. R. Fiksel, and A. Holliger. Intelligent graphs: Networks of finite automata capable of solving graph problems. In R. C. Read, editor, *Graph Theory and Computing*, pages 219–265. Academic Press, 1972.

22. Nir Shavit and Nissim Francez. A new approach to the detection of locally indicative stability. In Laurent Kott, editor, *Int. Colloq. on Automata, Languages, and Programming*, volume 226 of *Lecture Notes in Computer Science*, pages 344–358. Springer Verlag, 1986.

23. H. J. Suermondt and G. F. Cooper. Probabilistic inference in multiply connected belief networks using loop cutsets. *Int. J. of Approximate Reasoning*, 4:283–306, 1990.

24. Andrew S. Tanenbaum. *Computer Networks*. Prentice Hall, 3rd edition, 1996.

25. Gerard Tel. Distributed infimum approximation. Technical Report RUU–CS–86–12, Dept of Computer Science, Utrecht Univ., 1986. URL http://www.cs.ruu.nl/~gerard/liter/dia.dvi.

26. Gerard Tel. Total algorithms. *Algorithms Review*, 1(1):13–42, January 1990.

27. Gerard Tel. *Introduction to Distributed Algorithms*. Cambridge University Press,

Cambridge, U.K., 1994.

28. Gerard Tel. Network orientation. *Int. Journal on Foundations of Computer Science*, 5(1):23–57, March 1994.

29. Gerard Tel. Linear election in hypercubes. *Parallel Processing Letters*, 5(3):357–366, 1995.

30. Gerard Tel and Friedemann Mattern. The derivation of termination detection algorithms from garbage collection schemes. *ACM Transactions on Programming Languages and Systems*, 15(1):1–35, January 1993.

31. Linda C. van der Gaag. Bayesian belief networks: Odds and ends. *The Computer Journal*, 39(2):97–113, 1996.

32. Bram Verweij. Distributed edge depletion for maximum flows. Master's thesis, Dept of Computer Science, Utrecht Univ., July 1996.

# Glossary

# Subject Index

# Glossary

The Glossary is a joint effort of the chapter authors. The initials in the square brackets indicate the names of the contributing authors as listed at the end of this glossary. If multiple authors contributed to the same entry, then the different contributions were combined by the editor. The glossary overviews relevant terms in the field of multiagent systems and DAI. References to related literature can be found for most entries via the subject index. A list of DAI systems and tools is presented in the *Readings in Distributed Artificial Intelligence*, ed. by Alan H. Bond and Les Gasser, Morgan Kaufmann Publ., pp. 41–42, 1988. A list of agent-specific key terms and systems is provided in *Intelligent Agents*, ed. by Wooldridge and Jennings, Springer-Verlag, Lecture Notes in Artificial Intelligence, Vol. 890, pp. 22–28, 1995.

**AAIS** – An expert system which predicts organizational performance from a set of rules about the interaction among various organizational design features. [KMC,LG]

**Accessible Environment** – An environment in which an agent can obtain complete, accurate, up to date information about the environment's state. [MW]

**ACL** – Agent Communication Language. *See also* KQML, KIF.

**ACT** – A plan content language structured to be shared between independent plan generation and plan execution subsystems. [EHD]

**ACTION** – The successor to (*see*) HITOP-A: a highly detailed, industry-used analysis and design system for exploring interactions between managerial strategy and TOP-integrated organizational configuration, developed with a $10M 5-year investment from major industrial sponsors. *See also* TOP-MODELER. [KMC,LG]

**Actors** – Autonomous, interacting computing elements, which encapsulate a behavior (data and procedures) and a process, and communicate by message-passing. Sometimes "actor" and (*see*) "agent" are used synonymously. [GAA,NJ]

**ActorSpace** – A naming model for abstract specification of groups of (*see*) actors. ActorSpace allows communication between actors who do not know previously know each other. [GAA,NJ]

**Adaptation** – Broadly speaking, the change in the behavior of a system so that it becomes suitable to a new situation. *See* learning. [SS,GW]

**Agent** – An *autonomous, reactive, pro-active* computer system, typically with a central locus of control, that is at least able to communicate with other agents via some kind of communication language. Another common view of an agent is that of an active object or a bounded process with the ability to perceive, reason, and act. Various attributes are discussed in the context of agent-based systems: *see*, e.g., autonomy, benevolence, introspection, mobility, pro-active, rational, reactive, situatedness, social ability, veracity. *See also* actor, agent architecture, body, head, information agent, interface agent, software agent. [MNH,LNS,MW]

**Agent0** – A prototype agent-oriented programming language, developed by Yoav Shoham. [MW]

**Agent Architecture** – A particular methodology for building agents. More generally, the term is used to denote a particular arrangement of data structures, algorithms, and control flows, which an agent uses in order to decide what to do. Agent architectures can be characterized by the nature of their decision making. Example types of agent architecture include logical-based architectures (in which decision making is achieved via logical deduction), reactive architectures (in which decision making is achieved via simple mapping from perception to action), belief-desire-intention architectures (in which decision making is viewed as practical reasoning of the type that we perform every day in furtherance of our goals), and layered architectures (in which decision making is realized via the interaction of a number of task accomplishing layers). *See also* BDI architecture, deliberative architecture, INTERRAP, IRMA, layered architecture, reactive architecture, subsumption architecture. [MW]

**Agent Oriented Programming** – An approach to building agents, which proposes programming them in terms of mentalistic notions such as belief, desire, and intention. *See also* Agent0, behavior language, mental attitude. [MW]

**All-Pay Auction** – Auction protocol where all bidders have to pay some amount even if they do not win the item. [TS]

**Architecture** – *See* agent architecture, organizational structure.

**Arrow's Impossibility Theorem** – A result regarding truthful voting that states that no social choice rule has a particular set of intuitively desirable features. [TS]

**Asynchronous Search Algorithm** – An algorithm for solving a search problem represented by a graph. An asynchronous search algorithm solves a problem by accumulating local computations for each node in the graph. The execution order of these local computations can be arbitrary or highly flexible, and can be executed asynchronously and concurrently. [TI,MY]

**Auction** – *See* all-pay auction, common values auction, correlated values auction, descending (Dutch) auction, first-price open-cry (English) auction, first-price sealed-bid auction, private values auction, revenue equivalence, second-price sealed-bid (Vickrey) auction.

**Autonomy** – Generally, autonomy means "under self-control." More specifically, the assumption that, although we generally intend agents to act on our behalf, they nevertheless act without direct human or other intervention, and have control over their internal state and actions. [MW]

**Axiomatic Bargaining** – An approach to solving bargaining problems by postulating desiderata, and proving that a particular solution (uniquely) satisfies them. [TS]

**Bargaining** — *See* axiomatic bargaining, Nash bargaining solution, Rubinstein bargaining model, strategic bargaining.

**BDI Agent** — An agent with a (*see*) BDI architecture.

**BDI Architecture** — A type of (*see*) agent architecture containing explicit representations of beliefs, desires, and intentions. Beliefs are the information an agent has about its environment, which may be false; desires are those things that the agent would like to see achieved, and intentions are those things the agent is either committed to doing (intending *to*) or committed to bringing about (intending *that*). The architecture addresses how the beliefs, desires, and intentions of the agents are represented, updated, and processed to determine the agent's actions. In BDI architectures, decision-making mirrors the practical reasoning that we each carry out every day in furtherance of our goals. *See also* belief, desires, intentions. [MW]

**BDI Concepts** — The concepts of (*see*) belief, (*see*) desire, and (*see*) intention, as applied in the modeling of agents in DAI. *See also* BDI architecture, hybrid approaches, modal approaches, sentential approaches. [MPS,ASR,MPG]

**Behavior Language** — Generally, a language for specifying an agent in terms of its (desired) behavior. An example is the BEHAVIOR LANGUAGE developed at MIT in the context of the (*see*) subsumption architecture. [GW]

**Belief** — A concept describing the states of the world that the agent cannot discriminate among. *See also* BDI architecture, mutual belief. [MPS,ASR,MPG]

**Benevolence** — The assumption that an agent always does, or tries to do, what is asked of it by other agents or humans. [GW]

**Binary Protocol** — Voting protocol where the candidates are voted on pairwise, and the loser is always eliminated. [TS]

**Blackboard** — An information processing structure composed of several cooperating knowledge sources (each containing any kind of algorithm, rules, data, and so forth), a separate control element (determining the order in which the knowledge sources are executed), and the blackboard itself (the locus of communication and global memory). [GW]

**Blackboard Architecture** — Specifically, an agent architecture built according to the blackboard paradigm; *see* blackboard. Generally, an agent architecture whose centerpiece is a shared repository called a blackboard, which permits undirected information exchanges between independent knowledge sources. [EHD]

**Block Pushing** — An application involving multiple agents (typically two robots) which must push a box from a starting to a goal location. The box is assumed to be large enough so that none of the individual agents can solve this task.

**Body** — The portion of an agent not responsible for communication. *See also* head. [HVDP]

**Borda Protocol** — Voting protocol where each voter can give $|O|$ votes to one candidate, $|O| - 1$ votes to another, and so on. The candidate with the highest sum of votes gets chosen. [TS]

**Broadcast/Convergecast** – Technique to exercise control in a network where a spanning tree is available. The root of the tree initiates sending request messages down all branches of the tree (broadcast). Each reply message summarizes the information of the entire subtree of the sender. Before replying, each node awaits the replies from all of its children. [GT]

**Case Theory** – A linguistic model of sentence structure that focuses on the roles supported by each verb and the nouns that can fill those roles. [HVDP]

**CFG** – (*See*) Characteristic Function Game.

**Characteristic Function Game (CFG)** – An abstract, common setting for studying (*see*) coalition formation. Each potential coalition has a value associated with it. That value is assumed independent of the actions of nonmembers. [TS]

**Cluster (C) Contract** – Contract where more than one item is moved atomically from an agent to another. *See also* OCSM-contract. [TS]

**Coalition** – A set of agents that work together to solve a joint problem. Often used as a synonym for (*see*) ensemble, (*see*) group, and (*see*) team. *See also* coalition formation. [GW]

**Coalition Formation** – The process where agents form (*see*) coalitions that work together to solve a joint problem via coordinating their actions within each coalition. Each agent belongs to exactly one coalition. Coalition formation includes three activities: (*see*) coalition structure generation, optimization within each coalition, and payoff division among agents. Forming a coalition has much to do with finding an appropriate (*see*) organizational structure. *See also* characteristic function game, coalition structure generation, COALITION-STRUCTURE-SEARCH-1, core, merging algorithm, Shapley value, splitting algorithm. [TS]

**Coalition Structure Generation** – The process of partitioning agents into exhaustive, disjoint (*see*) coalitions. [TS]

**COALITION-STRUCTURE-SEARCH-1** – A particular anytime algorithm for (*see*) coalition structure generation. Motivated by the goal of minimizing the worst case ratio bound from optimum. [TS]

**Cognitive Concepts** – Concepts applied in DAI that are inspired from folk psychology. These include the three (*see*) BDI concepts, but also others such as know-how and (*see*) commitments. [MPS,ASR,MPG]

**Cognitive Primitives** – Any of the concepts borrowed from psychology. [MPS,ASR, MPG]

**Coherence** – The property or state of acting as a unit. A measure of how well a system behaves as a unit. Evaluation criteria for coherence are, e.g., efficiency, solution quality, and graceful degradation in the presence of failure. *See also* competence. [MNH,LNS,GW]

**Collaboration** – Generally, "working together." Collaboration often refers to forms of high-level (*see*) cooperation that require (the development of) a mutual understanding and a shared view of the task being solved by several interacting entities.

Sometimes the terms collaboration and cooperation are used in the same sense. *See also* competition, coordination, interaction. [GW]

**Collaborative Technology** – *See* groupware.

**Commitments** – Pledges by an agent to undertake a specified course of action. Commitments may be (*see*) psychological or (*see*) social. *See also* conventions. [MNH]

**Common Knowledge** – Same as (*see*) mutual belief, but where it is (*see*) knowledge that is nested all the way. [MPS,ASR,MPG]

**Common Object Request Broker Architecture (CORBA)** – Interoperable architecture promoted and standardized by the OMG (Object Management Group) consortium. This architecture defines client/server middleware that allows objects to interoperate. [GW]

**Common Values Auction** – Auction setting where each agent's valuation is completely determined by (same as) the others' valuations. [TS]

**Communication** – How information is exchanged among agents but discount incidental interactions through the environment. The intentional exchange of information on the basis of a shared system of signs. *See also* head, ontology. [MPS,ASR,MPG,GW]

**Communication Complexity** – Amount of communication necessary to execute an application, or to solve a problem; usually expressed as the number of messages exchanged (message complexity). To give long messages a higher weight than short messages, the communication can be expressed in terms of the overall number of bits or words in the messages (bit complexity). [GT]

**Communityware** – The methodologies and tools for creating, maintaining, and evolving social interaction in communities. Communityware supports diverse and amorphous groups of people. Compared with (*see*) groupware, communityware focuses on an earlier stage of collaboration: group formation from a wide variety of people. *See also* computer supported collaborative work. [TI]

**Competence** – The ability to do a task well. Contrasted with (*see*) coherence which is the ability to work together well, regardless of whether the work is useful. [EHD]

**Competition** – A variety of (*see*) coordination in which the success of one participant implies the failure of others. *See also* cooperation, interaction. [HVDP]

**Computer Supported Cooperative Work (CSCW)** – Research area that studies the use of computing and communications technologies to support group activities. This area concerns both software development and social factors in group work. *See also* communityware, groupware. [CSE,JW]

**Computational Economics (Agent-Based)** – The computational study of economies. Often it is assumed that the economies are modelled as evolving distributed systems of interacting (*see*) agents. [GW]

**Computational Organization Theory (COT)** – Computational theorizing about organizations or organizing. *See also* organizational structure. [KMC,LG]

**Concordia** – A commercial Java-based mobile agent platform from Mitsubishi. *See also* Odyssey, Voyager. [TS]

**Concurrent METATEM** – A logic-based agent programming language, in which agents are programmed by giving them a temporal logic specification of the behaviour that it is intended they should exhibit; agents directly execute their specification in order to generate their behaviour. [MW]

**Connection Problem** – The problem of finding an appropriate assignment between available agents and tasks to be executed. [GW]

**Constraint Propagation** – May be viewed as a mechanism for coordination that involves the passing of symbolic information among entities. [HVDP]

**Constraint Satisfaction Problem (CSP)** – The problem of finding an assignment of values (taken from finite, discrete domains) to variables such that constraints among the variables are satisfied. Backtracking algorithms and consistency algorithms can be used for solving constraint satisfaction problems. *See also* distributed constraint satisfaction problem, search. [TI,MY]

**Content Language** – The language in which the contents of message structures are encoded. [EHD]

**Contingency Contract** – Contract where the obligations are made conditional on future events. Enables contracts and improves their Pareto efficiency. Requires an event verification mechanism and knowledge of possible future events. [TS]

**Contingency Planning** – The development of conditional plans in which responses to possible contingencies have been accounted for and included. *See* planning. [EHD]

**Contract** – An agreement between several agents on carrying out or refraining from specific activities. Usually contracts are task-oriented, and imply (*see*) commitments. *See* contract net protocol, leveled commitment contract. [GW]

**Contract Net Protocol** – An influential protocol for supporting the search for connecting tasks to be done with agents (contractors) that are willing and able to do them. "Contract net" usually refers to a negotiation-based task allocation algorithm. *See also* contingency contract, leveled commitment contract, mutual selection, OCSM-contract. [EHD,TS]

**Conventions** – Mechanisms for managing (*see*) commitments in changing circumstances. [MNH]

**Conversation** – A series of (*see*) communications among different agents; typically following a (*see*) protocol and with some purpose. [MPS,ASR,MPG]

**Cooperation** – (*See*) coordination among nonantagonistic agents. A variety of coordination in which the participants succeed or fail together. *See also* competition, interaction. [MNH]

**Cooperative Planning** – The formation of a plan through the cooperative efforts of multiple planning specialists, each of whom contributes to the overall plan. *See* planning. [EHD]

**Cooperative Protocol** – A (*see*) protocol that specifies how agents have to cooperate in order to achieve a common goal. *See* cooperation. [GW]

**Cooperative State-Changing Rules** – Rules of "good citizenship" that guide agents into taking actions that contribute to the collective rather than to self-interest. [EHD]

**Coordination** – Refers to the state of a community of agents in which actions of some agents fit in well with each other, as well as to the process of achieving this state. The degree of coordination is the extent to which they avoid extraneous activity by reducing resource contention, avoiding livelock and deadlock, and maintaining applicable safety conditions. Much work in DAI is concerned with coordination as a specific form of (*see*) interaction. Two manifestations of coordination that play particularly important roles in DAI are (*see*) competition and (*see*) cooperation. *See also* collaboration, constraint propagation, dissipative field, heterarchy, hierarchy, negotiation, synchronization. [MNH,LNS,GW]

**CORBA** – (*See*) Common Object Request Broker Architecture.

**Core** – A criterion of dividing payoff among agents in (*see*) coalition formation (CFGs) in a way that the resulting payoff configuration is stable. Guarantees that no subgroup of agents is motivated to move out of the coalition structure. In some games the core is empty, i.e. no stable payoff division exists. [TS]

**CORP** – A simple intellective model of organizational performance in which each agent can learn through experience or follow standard operating procedures, are organized into either a team or hierarchical structure, and and in which the set of agents are working in a distributed fashion on a classification task. [KMC,LG]

**Correlated Values Auction** – Auction setting that has both private value and common value features. [TS]

**COT** – (*See*) Computational Organization Theory.

**Credit-Assignment Problem** – Also known as the fundamental learning problem. The problem of determining the degree to which each activity in a set of activities (carried out by a single or several agents in sequence or in parallel) deserves credit or blame for the final outcome. In the context of DAI systems, this problem can be decomposed into the (*see*) inter-agent credit-assignment problem and the (*see*) intra-agent credit-assignment problem. *See* learning. [GW]

**CSCW** – (*See*) Computer Supported Cooperative Work.

**CSP** – (*See*) Constraint Satisfaction Problem.

**Cultural Transmission** – An intellective model of organizational performance which explores the relation between knowledge, culture, and organizational design. [KMC,LG]

**DAI** – (*See*) Distributed Artificial Intelligence.

**DARES** – A distributed theorem proving system.

**DCHS** – (*See*) Distributed Constrained Heuristic Search.

**DCSP** – (*See*) Distributed Constraint Satisfaction Problem.

**DD** – (*See*) Distributed Delivery.

**Decision Making (Distributed, Rational)** – Distributed decision making is the process of making decisions by, and usually for, multiple agents. This is difficult because agents often have different preferences and incomplete information. Distributed decision making is useful because many situations are not zero-sum games, and the social welfare can be increased by joint decision making that leads to more desirably coordinated actions. Key techniques include voting, auctions, bargaining, market mechanisms, contracting, and coalition formation. [TS]

**Decision Support System (DSS)** – A decision support system provides an information environment that assists the decison-making of personnel in control of complex natural or artificial systems such as installations or organizations, with the aim of maximizing efficiency and minimizing the negative impact of faults. Knowledge-based decision support systems use symbolic representations of expert knowledge to (i) analyze a given situation by identifying its advantageous and problematic aspects; (ii) predict the short-term behavior of the system in different scenarios; and (iii) recommend and justify plans of control actions. [JC,SO]

**Deliberative** – Based on or requiring the manipulation of symbols. Usually contrasted with (*see*) reactive. [GW]

**Deliberative Architecture** – An (*see*) agent architecture that requires an agent to manipulate symbols. Usually contrasted with (*see*) reactive architectures. [GW]

**Descending (Dutch) Auction** – Auction protocol where the price starts high, and is lowered by the auctioneer. The auction stops when some bidder takes the item at the current price. [TS]

**Design-To-Time Algorithm** – An algorithm that is tailored to the execution time that is at its disposal. [TS]

**Desires** – The states of affairs toward which the agent has a positive disposition. *See also* BDI architecture [MPS,ASR,MPG]

**Deterministic Environment** – An environment in which there is no uncertainty about the effect an action will have. Few real-world environments are deterministic. [MW]

**Dialogue** – Same as (*see*) conversation.

**Discrete Environment** – An environment in which percepts and actions are discrete, as opposed to continuous. [MW]

**Dissipative Field** – A mechanism for coordination in which agents sense the gradient or flow of a scalar value and orient themselves accordingly. [HVDP]

**Distraction** – The phenomenon of changing the course of an agents search due to received messages. Usually considered undesirable (negative distraction), although positive distraction also can occur. [EHD]

**Distributed Artificial Intelligence (DAI)** – Most broadly construed, the study and construction of systems composed of interacting, intelligent entities. DAI is much concerned with (*see*) agents and (*see*) coordination. [HVDP,GW]

**Distributed Constrained Heuristic Search (DCHS)** – A combination of distributed constraint satisfaction and heuristic search, where heuristics guide the variable and value ordering decisions. Applied to distributed scheduling. *See* distributed constraint satisfaction problem. [EHD]

**Distributed Constraint Satisfaction Problem (DCSP)** – A (*see*) constraint satisfaction problem where variables and constraints are distributed among agents. Solving such a problem can be considered as achieving (*see*) coherence among the agents. [TI,MY]

**Distributed Delivery (DD)** – An application involving multiple delivery robots which must make timely deliveries without excess travel and without colliding.

**Distributed Hierachical Planning** – An extension of hierarchical planning (i.e., planning at different levels of abstraction) into a distributed environment. *See* planning. [EHD]

**Distributed Meeting Scheduling** – An application involving multiple calendar managers that must cooperatively search for a meeting time.

**Distributed Sensor Network Establishment (DSNE)** – An application in which a selection of geographically-distributed sensors is chosen in order to monitor an overall region.

**Distributed Vehicle Monitoring (DVM)** – An application in which geographically-distributed sensors cooperatively map the movements of vehicles across their sensed regions.

**Dominant Strategy** – An agent's (*see*) strategy that is best for the agent no matter what others do. [TS]

**DSNE** – (*See*) Distributed Sensor Network Establishment.

**DSS** – (*See*) Decision Support System.

**DVM** – (*See*) Distributed Vehicle Monitoring.

**Dynamic Logic** – Propositional logic enhanced with a regular expression language of actions or programs, which can be used to model the necessary and possible results of performing different programs. [MPS,ASR,MPG]

**Echo Algorithm** – Technique to construct an arbitrary spanning tree in a network by flooding messages through all edges. Each node acknowledges the first message it received, but only after receipt of a message through each other channel. Information can be dispersed and collected as in the (*see*) broadcast/convergecast technique. [GT]

**EDI** – Electronic Data Interchange. A set of (*see*) protocols for exhanging business data electronically among trading partners. [HVDP]

**Ensemble** – A multiagent system, especially one whose agents pursuing a collective goal. Often used as a synonym for (*see*) coalition, (*see*) group, and (*see*) team. [GAA,NJ]

**Environment** – *See* accessible environment, deterministic environment, discréte environment, episodic environment, static environment. *See also* reactive, situatedness.

**Episodic Environment** – An environment in which an agent's tasks are divided into a number of discrete episodes, with the performance of the agent in one episode having no effect on other episodes. Episodic environments simplify an agent's decision making process, as they relieve the agent of the need to reason about the interaction between current and future behaviour. [MW]

**ESPRIT** – The joint R&D program of the European Community.

**Favor Relations** – Opportunities in which one agent can accomplish a goal that another agent desires. [EHD]

**Feedback (Learning Feedback)** – A measure indicating the level of performance achieved so far by a learning system. *See* learning. [SS,GW]

**FIPA** – Foundation for Intelligent Physical Agents; a consortium that is developing standards for agents.

**First-Price Open-Cry (English) Auction** – Auction protocol where each bidder is allowed to keep raising his bid based on others' bids. The auction ends when no one wants to raise, and the highest bidder gets the item at the price of his bid. [TS]

**First-Price Sealed-Bid Auction** – Auction protocol where each bidder is allowed to send in a bid without seeing the others' bids. The highest bidder gets the item at the price of his bid. [TS]

**Focal Points** – Landmarks in a solution space that stand out as candidate solutions that are more likely to be mutually chosen. [EHD]

**Functionally Accurate Cooperation** – In contrast to completely accurate, independent problem solving, functionally-accurate cooperation assumes agents might make mistakes when solving their tasks and need to engage in a cooperative exchange of results to overcome their individual errors and converge on an acceptable solution. [EHD]

**Garbage Can** – An intellective model of organizational behavior in which problems, choices, and solutions flow through the system. [KMC,LG]

**General Equilibrium** – A solution for a market where supply meets demand on each commodity, consumers maximize their preferences within their budget, and producers maximize profits within their production possibilities. Not a game theoretic solution concept. *See* Newtonian price tâtonnement algorithm, price-taking assumption, price tâtonnement algorithm, quantity-based algorithms. [TS]

**Gibbard-Satterthwaite Impossibility Theorem** – A result regarding insincere (strategic) voting. It basically states that with unrestricted preferences, each deterministic protocol that has truth-telling as the dominant strategy, is dictatorial. [TS]

**Goals** – A mutually consistent set of (*see*) desires. [MPS,ASR,MPG]

**Grafcet** – A graphical language for describing the control of a distributed system, based on Petri nets. [HVDP]

**Group** – A multiagent system, especially one that is viewed (or acts or is intended to act) as a single agent. Often used as a synonym for (*see*) coalition, (*see*) ensemble, and (*see*) team. [MPS,ASR,MPG]

**Group Intention** – An intention that is shared by a group of agents. [MPS,ASR,MPG]

**Groupware** – Computing and communications technology based systems that assist groups of participants, and help to support a shared environment. The term *collaborative technology* is of used in this sense. *See also* communityware, computer supported cooperative work. [CSE,JW]

**Head** – That portion of an agent that enbles it to communicate with other agents. *See also* body. [HVDP]

**Heterarchy** – A structure of (*see*) coordination in which an agent may constrain the same other agents by which it is itself constrained. *See also* hierarchy. [HVDP]

**Hierarchical Behavior-Space Search** – A coordination strategy where agents represent themselves to each other in terms of how they will behave at an abstract level, and then iteratively exchange more details only in relevant parts of their behavior descriptions. Coordination can occur at any level of behavioral abstraction. [EHD]

**Hierarchy** – A structure of (*see*) coordination in which an agent does not constrain those agents by which it is itself constrained *See also* heterachy. [HVDP]

**HITOP-A** – A detailed industry-funded organizational design and analysis tool focusing on tight integration of technology, organizational and people (TOP) perspectives. *See* ACTION. [KMC,LG]

**Host** – A physically or economically distinct boundary (e.g., a processor) on which an entity (e.g., a (*see*) software agent) may reside and execute. [GAA,NJ]

**Hybrid Approaches to the BDI Concepts.** – Semantical approaches that are based on a combination of modal logics and explicit representation of sentences of a formal language. *See* BDI concepts. [MPS,ASR,MPG]

**IBIS** – (*See*) Issue Based Information System.

**Illocution** – The aspect of a (*see*) speech act that deals with its core meaning; in between its locution and perlocution. [MPS,ASR,MPG]

**Information Agent** – Information agents are (*see*) that have access to multiple, potentially heterogeneous and geographically distributed information sources. Information agents have to cope with the increasing complexity of modern information environments, ranging from relatively simple in-house information systems, through large-scale multidatabase systems, to the visionary Infosphere in the Internet. One of the main tasks of the agents is an active search for relevant information in non-local domains on behalf of their users or other agents. This includes retrieving, analyzing, manipulating, and integrating information available from different information sources. [GW]

**Insincere Voting** – Voting where agents lie about their preferences if that increases their expected utility. [TS]

**Intentions** – (*See*) goals that the agent is currently working on, i.e., those leading to the agent's actions. *See also* BDI architecture, group intention. [MPS,ASR,MPG]

**Interaction** – Generally, everything that occurs "between" agents (agent-agent interaction) and "between" agents and their environment (agent-environment interaction). Agents can interact directly via—verbal—(*see*) communication (by exchanging information) and indirectly via their (*see*) environment (by passively observing one another or by actively carrying out actions that modify the environmental state). Interaction may result in changes in the (*see*) internal state and the future course of activity of an agent. Interaction can be characterized according to its frequency, persistence, pattern, purpose, and so forth. A common distinction is that between deliberative and reactive interaction (*see* deliberative, reactive). Much work in DAI is concerned with interaction between agents. Forms of interaction that play an important role in DAI are (*see*) cooperation and (*see*) competition. A type of interaction that plays an important role in human contexts, but not in technical systems, is para- and non-verbal communication (e.g., by intonation and gesture). [GW]

**Interaction Analysis** – During plan merging, the process of identifying conflicting interactions among the plan steps of different agents. *See* planning. [EHD]

**Interaction Protocol** – *See* protocol.

**Inter-Agent Credit-Assignment Problem** – The problem of assigning credit or blame for overall system performance to the external actions carried out by the system components. *See* credit-assignment problem. [GW]

**Interface Agent** – An agent, typically a (*see*) software agent, that supports its user(s) in fulfilling certain tasks. For instance, an interface agent may hide the complexity of a difficult task, train and teach a human user, and perform sub-tasks on a user's behalf. The terms *software assistant* and *personal assistant* are often used in this sense. Interface agents also play an important role in (*see*) computer supported cooperative work. [GW]

**Internal State** – *See* mental attitude.

**Internet** – The collection of computers, networks, and routers that use the TCP/IP suite and function as a single large internetwork. In the groupware context, the Internet can be described in terms of the hardware that supports it, the software that facilitates it, and the demographics of the people that populate it. [CSE,JW]

**INTERRAP** – A vertically layered two-pass (*see*) agent architecture. [MW]

**Intra-Agent Credit-Assignment Problem** – The problem of assigning credit or blame for a particular action carried out by a system component to the component's internal inferences and decisions leading to this action. *See* credit-assignment problem. [GW]

**Introspection** – The ability of an agent to examine and reflect its own thoughts, ideas, plans, goals, and so forth. [GW]

**IRMA** – An influential (*see*) BDI agent architecture. [MW]

**Issue Based Information System (IBIS)** − A model and methodology for system design and decision making in which strict argumentation categories are utilized. The decision making methodology consists of three phases, divergence, convergence, and decision. The model supports argumentation via a clear separation between issues, positions, and arguments. [CSE,JW]

**JAAPI** − Java Aglet API. An object framework developed by IBM that is built on top of Java and that supports the construction of mobile (*see*) software agents. [GW]

**Job Shop** − A manufacturing facility in which the routing of a part from one machine to another is not physically fixed. [HVDP]

**KIF** − Knowledge Interchange Format. A computer-oriented language for the interchange of knowledge among disparate programs. It has declarative semantics and is logically comprehensive. Moreover, it provides for (i) the representation of knowledge about the representation of knowledge, (ii) the representation of non-monotonic reasoning rules, and (iii) the definition of objects, relations, and functions. KIF is part of the (*see*) Knowledge Sharing Effort. [GW]

**Know-How** − The ability of an agent to knowingly achieve some (typically intended) state of affairs. [MPS,ASR,MPG]

**Knowledge** − From the point of view of logics, knowledge is often defined as true (*see*) belief or, more specifically, true justified belief. *See also* common knowledge. [MPS,ASR,MPG]

**Knowledge Level** − A level of describing the knowledge and reasoning of an individual agent that abstracts away from the form and mechanisms used to represent this knowledge; the level below the (*see*) social level. [HVDP]

**Knowledge Sharing Effort (KSE)** − Sponsored by the Advanced Research Projects Agency (ARPA). A consortium and initiative to develop methodology and software for the sharing and reuse of knowledge. Examples of major outcomes of the Knowledge Sharing Effort are (*see*) KIF, (*see*) KQML, and (*see*) Ontolingua. [GW]

**KQML** − Knowledge Query and Manipulation Language. A language and protocol for exchanging information and knowledge. KQML can be thought of as consisting of three layers. The content layer bears the actual content of the message. The communication layer encodes message features which describe low-level communication parameters (e.g., identity of sender). The message layer determines the kind of interactions one can have with a KQML-speaking agent, and its primary function is to identify the (*see*) protocol to be used for message delivery and to supply the (*see*) speech act attached to the content. KQML is part of the (*see*) Knowledge Sharing Effort. [GW]

**Layered Architecture** − An (*see*) agent architecture that is structured into a number of layers, each of which typically represents an increased level of abstraction from the layer beneath it. Two types of layered architectures can be distinguished: horizontally layered (i.e., each layer is directly connected to the sensory input and action output), and vertically layered (i.e., sensory input and action output are dealt with by at most one layer each). Examples include (*see*) TOURINGMACHINES and (*see*) INTERRAP. [MW]

**Learning (Distributed)** – Broadly speaking, learning refers to self-improvement of future behavior based on past experience. "Distributed" means that several entities (agents) are involved in the same learning process, where each entity contributes to the solution of the overall learning task according to its individual abilities or preferences. The distribution may concern the identification of sub-tasks of the overall learning task, their execution, or both. *See also* adaptation, credit-assignment problem, feedback, multiagent learning, organizational adaptation. [GW]

**Legacy System** – A existing system that is not included within the scope of a new system development effort, but that must interoperate with the new system. [HVDP]

**Leveled Commitment Contract** – Contract where each party can decommit by paying a prenegotiated penalty. Enables contracts and improves their Pareto efficiency. Does not require an event verification mechanism or knowledge of possible future events. *See* contract. [TS]

**Life Cycle** – A series of stages through which an industrial project passes, from the time it is first considered until it has been retired from service. [HVDP]

**Linkages (in an Organization)** – The set of relations among nodes in a (*see*) network. For example, if the nodes are people the linkages might be friendship, advice, or works with. Such linkages are often called ties by organizational theorists and arcs by mathematicians. [KMC,LG]

**Locution** – The surface form of a (*see*) speech act; that which is actually transmitted. [MPS,ASR,MPG]

**Logic** – *See* dynamic logic, modal logic, predicate logic, propositional logic, temporal logic. [MPS,ASR,MPG]

**MACE** – A domain-independent modeling and simulation testbed for multiagent systems. MACE embodies a high-level social theory and uses concurrent agents for all phases of system construction and simulation. [KMC,LG]

**Mental Attitude** – A property ascribed to an agent describing its internal state. It is usually distinguished between information or cognitive states (e.g., belief and knowledge), deliberative or conative states (e.g., intention and commitment), and motivational or affective states (e.g., desire, choice, preference, and goal). [GW]

**Merging Algorithm** – A particular anytime algorithm for (*see*) coalition structure generation. Starts from agents operating individually, and constructively builds coalitions. *See also* splitting algorithm. [TS]

**Message** – Generally, a piece of data, the elementary unit of communication. More specifically, a piece of data which possibly includes the representation of an (*see*) actor behavior, that is sent from one actor to another. *See also* communication complexity, space-time diagram. [GAA,NJ]

**Message-Passing** – A communication paradigm where entities interact by sending explicit messages to each other. *See also* communication, interaction. [GAA,NJ]

**Meta-Level Organization** – An organizational structure specifying agents' (*see*) roles in the coordination process. *See also* coordination. [EHD]

**Migration** – Transfering a possibly active computation from one processing unit (e.g., a computer or agent) to another. [GAA,NJ]

**Mobility** – An agent's ability to change its physical position. [GW]

**Modal Approaches to the BDI concepts** – Semantical approaches that are based on (*see*) modal logics. *See* BDI concepts. [MPS,ASR,MPG]

**Modal Logic** – The logic of necessity and possibility. This forms the basis of a number of the logics of (*see*) BDI concepts. [MPS,ASR,MPG]

**MRP** – Manufacturing Resource Planning; a widely-used process for planning the availability of parts and machines in manufacturing. [HVDP]

**Multiagent (M) Contract** – Contract where tasks are atomically reallocated among more than two agents. *See also* OCSM-contract. [TS]

**Multiagent Foraging** – An application involving multiple agents which have to collect food in a confined area and take it to a predefined region.

**Multiagent Learning** – In its stronger meaning, this term refers to situations in which several agents collectively pursue a common learning goal. In its weaker meaning, this term broadly refers to situations in which an agent pursues its own learning goal, but is affected in its learning by other agents (e.g., their knowledge, beliefs, intentions, and so forth). *See* learning. [GW]

**Multiagent Soar** – Any of the models of organizational behavior in which each of the agents is modeled as a Soar agent. *See also* Soar. [KMC,LG]

**Multiagent System** – A system composed of multiple, interacting (*see*) agents. *See also* interaction. [GW]

**Multistage Negotiation** – Negotiation-based cooperative resolution of conflicts, where several cycles or "rounds" take place in which the participants e.g. send requests, locally examine solutions, and generate alternative views. An advanced form of distributed problem solving and planning. *See* negotiation. [GW]

**Murmuring** – To counter possible message losses, murmuring means that agents periodically repeat themselves until they receive evidence that the message has been received. [EHD]

**Mutual Belief** – A (*see*) belief about a proposition that is shared by a set of agents in such a way that the agents (i) belief the same proposition, (ii) believe that each of the others believes it, and (iii) have similar nested beliefs about each other's beliefs to an arbitrary level of nesting. [MPS,ASR,MPG]

**Mutual Selection** – When an agent that passes a task to another, and the other that is accepting the task, each chooses to engage in this transaction. Usually used to describe the (*see*) contract net protocol. [EHD]

**Nash Bargaining Solution** – A particular solution in the family of axiomatic bargaining solutions. The product maximizing solution. [TS]

**Nash Equilibrium** – A profile of (*see*) strategies (one for each agent) such that no agent is motivated to change its strategy given that others do not change. *See also* strong Nash equilibrium. [TS]

**Negotiated Search** − An approach in which multiple agents can propose partial or complete solutions, from which agents engage in iterative elaboration and critiquing. In overconstrained situations, agents can compromise by relaxing their solution requirements. *See* negotiation. [EHD]

**Negotiation** − (*See*) interaction among agents based on (*see*) communication for the purpose of coming to an agreement. Negotiation has much to do with distributed conflict resolution and decision making, and requires that the agents use a common language (*see* agent communication language). In the course of negotiation an agent makes a proposal which then is commented (e.g., refined, criticized, or refuted) by other agents. Negotiation may be interpreted as (*see*) coordination among competitive or simply self-interested agents. Another common interpretation of negotiation is that of a distributed, communication-based (*see*) search through a space of possible solutions. *See also* multistage negotiation, negotiated search. [MNH,LNS,GW]

**Network (Organizational)** − A collection of nodes and the relations among them. Within the organization there are many networks, including the social network (who likes or communicates with whom) and the task network (which subtasks must be done before or simultaneously with which other subtasks). *See* linkages. [KMC,LG]

**Newtonian Price Tâtonnement Algorithm** − A variable step size (*see*) price tâtonnement algorithm. [TS]

**NII** − National Information Infrastructure (US).

**NIIIP** − National Industrial Information Infrastructure Project (US).

**Observation-Based Plan Coordination** − The use of observations about others actions, rather than explicit (*see*) communication, to sychronize and otherwise coordinate plans. [EHD]

**OCSM-Contract** − Powerful complex contract type that allows moving from any task allocation to any other. *See* cluster (C) contract, multiagent (M) contract, original (O) contract, swap (S) contract. *See also* contract net protocol. [TS]

**Odyssey** − A commercial Java-based mobile agent platform from General Magic. *See also* Concordia, Voyager. [TS]

**OEM** − Original Equipment Manufacturer; the company at the top of a supply chain, which manufactures the finished product. [HVDP]

**Ontolingua** − A set of tools, written in Common Lisp, for analyzing and translating ontologies (*see* ontology). It uses (*see*) KIF as the interlingua and is portable over several representation systems. It includes a KIF parser and syntax checker, a cross reference utility, a set of translators from KIF into implemented representation systems, and a HTML report generator. Ontolingua is part of the (*see*) Knowledge Sharing Effort. [GW]

**Ontology** − Generally, A specification of the objects, concepts, classes, functions and relationships in an area of interest. For a given area, the ontology may be explicitly represented or implicitly encoded in an agent. More specifically, to support the sharing and reuse of formally represented knowledge among AI systems, it is useful to define the common vocabulary in which shared knowledge is represented; a specification of such a common vocabulary for a shared domain of discourse is called an ontology. *See also* ontolingua, ontology sharing problem. [GW]

**Ontology Sharing Problem** – The problem that agents need a shared (*see*) ontology to be able to communicate meaningful. [GW]

**Open System** – A system composed of a variable number of parts that interact although typically they are developed independently, that act concurrently and asynchronously, that have a decentralized control, that possess limited knowledge, and that have limited and potentially inconsistent views of the overall system. [GW]

**ORGAHEAD** – An intellective model in which the agents learn from experience as they work in distributed fashion on an classification or assessment task, and the chief executive officer (modeled as an annealer) also learns how to alter the organization's structure as the set of tasks potentially changes. [KMC,LG]

**Organization** – A system composed of interacting agents, together with the relationships that exist between them. *See also* organizational structure. [GW]

**Organizational Adaptation** – A change in the organization or its personnel that results in the maintenance of or improvements in performance regardless of whether or not there are changes in the environment. *See* learning. [KMC,LG]

**Organizational Consultant** – A detailed expert system for exploring the potential impact of different organizational designs and tasks on various aspects of performance from a management choice perspective. [KMC,LG]

**Organizational Design** – The organization's design is the set of processes and (*see*) networks that comprise the organization. [KMC,LG]

**Organizational Structure** – Generally, the "architecture" of a multiagent system, the pattern of information and control relationships between agents. Specifically, a specification and assignment of (*see*) roles and responsibilities to participants in a cooperative planning and/or problem- solving endeavor. The set of (*see*) networks that comprise the organization. *See also* coalition formation. [KMC,EHD,LG,GW]

**Original (O) Contract** – Contract where one item is moved from an agent to another. See also OCSM-contract. [TS]

**OSI** – Open Systems Interconnection; a standard layered architecture for computer communications. [HVDP]

**PACT** – Palo Alto Collaboration Testbed. PACT is a laboratory for joint experiments in computer-aided concurrent engineering being pursued by research groups at Stanford University, Lockheed, Hewlett-Packard, and Enterprise Integration Technologies.

**Pareto Efficiency** – A criterion for evaluating outcomes. A solution is Pareto efficient (Pareto optimal) if there exists no other solution where no agent is worse off and some agent is better off. [TS]

**Parallel Search for Insincere Agents** – A method for motivating self-interested agents to follow a particular global search strategy. [TS]

**Partial Global Planning (PGP)** – A coordination approach in which agents iteratively form, coordinate, and execute their plans, which allows changing goals and plans, tolerates inconsistent views of collective effort, and supports task passing. *See* planning. [EHD]

**Partial Order Planner** – A planner that constructs a partial order plan, in which the temporal ordering of plan steps is only committed to to the minimal extent needed to ensure proper performance. *See* planning. [EHD]

**Path-Finding Problem** – The problem of finding a path from a start node to a goal node in a graph. A graph consists of a set of nodes, each of which represents a state, and a set of directed links between nodes, each of which represents an operator available to a problem solving agent. *See* search. [TI,MY]

**Perlocution** – The aspect of a (*see*) speech act dealing with its effect upon a recipient. [MPS,ASR,MPG]

**Personal Assistant** – A (*see*) software agent that acts for and on behalf of one or several users. To be able to do so, personal assistants often are intended to model their users' interests, intentions, goals, and so forth. *See* interface agent. [GW]

**Petri Net** – A modeling technique for distributed systems. [HVDP]

**PGP** – (*See*) partial global planning.

**Plan Combination Search** – A distributed planning approach in which agents individually formulate feasible sets of plans for their goals, and then engage in distributed search to prune these sets to converge on an acceptable combination of their individual plans. *See* planning. [EHD]

**Plan Merging** – A distributed planning approach in which each agent formulates is desired plan, and then these plans are merged into a collective plan. *See also* planning. [EHD]

**Plan Synchronization** – The insertion of synchronization actions into plans to avoid conflicting actions. *See also* planning. [EHD]

**Planning (Distributed)** – Generally, the formulation of a scheme (plan) for the attainment of a goal. Planning can be thought of as a specialization of (*see*) problem solving, where the problem to be solved is to find an appropriate plan. "Distributed" planning means that several entities are involved in plan formulation, plan execution, or both. *See also* ACT, contingency planning, cooperative planning, distributed hierachical planning, interaction analysis, multistage negotiation, observation-based plan coordination, partial global planning, partial order planner, plan combination search, plan merging, plan synchronization, team plan. [EHD,GW]

**Plural-Soar** – An intellective model of organizational performance in which each agent is a Soar agent and the agents are working collectively to fill orders from the goods in a warehouse. *See also* Soar. [KMC,LG]

**Plurality Protocol** – Voting protocol where the candidates are voted on all at once, and the one with the most votes wins. [TS]

**Pragmatics** – How the symbols of communication are interpreted. [MNH,LNS,LNS]

**Predicate Logic** – (*See*) propositional logic enhanced with variables and quantifiers to make statements about all or some objects in a given domain of discourse. [MPS,ASR,MPG]

**Price-Taking Assumption** – Assumption made in general equilibrium theory. Agents are assumed to act as if their supply and demand decisions did not affect the market prices. Becomes approximately valid as the agent's size in the market becomes negligible. [TS]

**Private Values Auction** – Auction setting where each agent's valuation is independent of others' valuations. [TS]

**Price Tâtonnement Algorithm** – An iterative search algorithm for finding a general equilibrium. At every iteration, the auctioneer increases the price of goods that were over-demanded, and decreases the price of goods that were under-demanded. [TS]

**Pro-Active** – Capable of taking the initiative; not driven solely by events, but capable of generating goals and acting rationally to achieve them. [MW]

**Problem Solving (Distributed)** – Generally, the identification and execution of a sequence of activities that transform a start state into a desirable state. "Distributed" means that the identification, the execution, or both, are distributed over several entities. *See* result sharing, result synthesis, task accomplishment, task allocation, task decomposition, task sharing. *See also* multistage negotiation, planning, search. [EHD,GW]

**Propositional Logic** – The simplest form of logic dealing with elementary facts and boolean combinations of them. [MPS,ASR,MPG]

**Protocol** – A structured exchange of messages leading to some defined outcome. The rules of the interaction that describe what actions each agent can take at each time. A protocol prescribes how (*see*) communication and (*see*) synchronization between a group of agents takes place. *See also* Borda protocol, binary protocol, cooperation protocol, interaction, plurality protocol, strategy. [GAA,EHD,TS,NJ]

**Psychological Commitments** – The extent to which an agent will not reconsider its beliefs or intentions. These appear suboptimal in the narrow sense, but give stability to the agent's actions, and are essential for agents of limited reasoning power. *See* commitments. [MPS,ASR,MPG]

**Quantity-Based Algorithms** – Search algorithms for finding a general equilibrium. They can be constructed to operate as anytime algorithms where feasibility is maintained at every iteration. *See also* search. [TS]

**QuestMap** – A commercial (*see*) groupware product implementing a version of (*see*) IBIS as a graphical shared hypertext map. Each graphical map, constructed and edited in an ongoing fashion by end users, contains nodes representing issues, positions, and arguments which are variously connected by colored graph links. [CSE,JW]

**Rational** – To behave in a way that is suitable or even optimal for goal attainment. [GW]

**Reactive** – (Of agent behaviour) Capable of maintaining an ongoing interaction with the environment, and responding *in a timely fashion* to changes that occur in it. (Of agent architectures.) An architecture that includes no symbolic representations and does no symbolic reasoning. [MW]

**Reactive Architecture** – A (*see*) agent architecture that does not rely on symbol manipulation. Usually contrasted with (*see*) deliberative architectures. [GW]

**Remote Creation** – Creating a new actor or agent at a remote (*see*) host. [GAA,NJ]

**Resources** – Physical resources (processor, memory, etc.) and logical resources (channels, threads) that are used in the course of a computation. [GAA,NJ]

**Result Sharing** – Cooperative problem solving through iterative exchange of partial results in the search for an overall result to a problem. [EHD]

**Result Synthesis** – The stage in distributed problem solving where agents are combining partial results of others (and themselves) into more comprehensive results. [EHD]

**Revelation Principle** – A central principle in mechanism design. It says that any outcome that can be supported in equilibrium with a complex protocol, can be supported in (truth-telling) equilibrium via a single-shot protocol. [TS]

**Revenue Equivalence** – Theorem regarding auctions. It says that with risk neutral bidders in private value auctions, a large number of auction protocols surprisingly have the same expected revenue to the auctioneer, despite the fact that the bidding strategies are different. [TS]

**Role** – The functional or social part which an agent, embedded in a multiagent environment, plays in a (joint) process like problem solving, planning, or learning. Typically roles include permissions and responsibilities, and are associated with specific behavioral patterns. Roles are often thought of as being defined through (*see*) social laws or (*see*) strategies. *See also* meta-level organization, organizational structure, team. [GW]

**Rubinstein Bargaining Model** – An alternating offers bargaining protocol used in conjunction with subgame perfect equilibrium analysis. [TS]

**SDML** – Strictly Declarative Modeling Language, can be used with multiple agent models and has facilities for examining team interaction. [KMC,LG]

**Search** – An umbrella term for various problem solving techniques in AI, where the sequence of actions required for solving a problem is not known in advance but must be determined by a trial-and-error exploration of alternatives. Search problems may be divided into three classes: (*see*) path-finding problems, (*see*) constraint satisfaction problems, and (*see*) two-player games. *See also* asynchronous search algorithm, problem solving, quantity-based algorithms. [TI,MY]

**Second-Price Sealed-Bid (Vickrey) Auction** – Auction protocol where each bidder is allowed to send in a bid without seeing the others' bids. The highest bidder gets the item at the price of the second highest bid. [TS]

**Semantics** – What the symbols of communication denote. [MNH]

**Sentential Approaches to the BDI Concepts** – Semantical approaches that are based on the explicit representation by the agent of sentences of a formal language. *See* BDI concepts. [MPS,ASR,MPG]

**Shapley Value** – A way of dividing payoff among agents in coalition formation (CFGs). The Shapley value exists for every characteristic function game, but does not guarantee as strong stability as the core. [TS]

**Sincere Voting** – Voting where agents reveal their true preferences. [TS]

**Situatedness** – An agent's ability to continuously interact with, or to be embedded in, its environment. [GW]

**Soar** – A general, rule-based problem solving architecture. [GW]

**Social Ability** – The ability to interact with other agents, typically by exchanging information via some language. [GW]

**Social Commitments** – The broad class of (*see*) commitments referring to the obligation of an agent to another agent. They may involve witnesses or context groups. [MPS,ASR,MPG]

**Social Concepts** – Concepts applied in DAI that are inspired from sociology. for instance, (*see*) group, (*see*) role. [GW]

**Social Laws** – Generally, behavior-prescribing specifications. Rules that specify how an agent embedded in a society of agents should behave. More specifically, a set of constraints on individual actions in particular contexts such that, if all agents follow the laws, the agent system will avoid undesirable states. *See also* role, strategy. [EHD,GW]

**Social Level** – A level of describing the interactions of multiple agents that abstracts away from their individual cognitive processes; one level higher than the (*see*) knowledge level. [HVDP]

**Social Primitives** – Any of the concepts borrowed from sociology. [MPS,ASR,MPG]

**Software Agent** – An agent that is implemented in software. *See also* interface agent. [GW]

**Software Assistant** – *See* interface agent.

**Softbot** – SOFTware roBOT.

**Space-Time Diagram** – Graphical representation of the interaction between several nodes by the exchange of messages. The diagram shows the execution of each involved node as a straight line and the exchanged messages as arrows. [GT]

**Spawn** – A distributed operating system where computation is allocated based on a repeated Vickrey auction (*see* second-price sealed-bid auction). [TS]

**Speech Act** – A communication viewed as a combination of its (*see*) locution, (*see*) illocution, and (*see*) perlocution. [MPS,ASR,MPG]

**Speech Act Theory** – The view of natural language as actions. The basic claim is that utterances are actions that result in (or are intended by the speaker to result in) changes in the internal state (*see* mental attitudes) of a hearer. "Verbal actions" of this kind are called (*see*) speech acts. [MNH,LNS,GW]

**Splitting Algorithm** – A particular anytime algorithm for (*see*) coalition structure generation. Starts from all agents operating together, and splits off coalitions. *See also* merging algorithm. [TS]

**Static Environment** – An environment that is guaranteed to change only via the action of the agent in it. [MW]

**Strategic Bargaining** – An approach to solving bargaining problems by defining the protocol and carrying out game theoretic equilibrium analysis. [TS]

**Strategy** – Agent's mapping from state history to action; a way to use the (*see*) protocol. *See also* dominant strategy, Nash equilibrium, role, social law. [TS]

**STRIPS Operator** – A specification of an action in terms of the preconditions that must hold for the action to apply, and the effects the action has on the state of the world once it is executed. [EHD]

**Strong Nash Equilibrium** – A solution concept for games that requires that no subgroup is motivated to change their strategies in a coordinated manner. *See* Nash equilibrium. [TS]

**Subsumption Architecture** – Developed by Rodney Brooks, a reactive (*see*) agent architecture in which agent decision making is achieved through the interaction of a number of task accomplishing "behaviors," each of which is an independent activity-producing system in its own right. Layers typically interract by "inhibition" and "suppression," and are extremely economical in computational terms, making no use of symbolic representation or reasoning mechanisms. [MW]

**Sugarscape** – An artificial life model in which very simple agents consume resources, migrate, and reproduce. [KMC,LG]

**Swap (S) Contract** – Contract where agents swap a pair of tasks atomically. *See also* OCSM-contract. [TS]

**SWARM** – A multiagent simulation language for modeling collections of concurrently interacting agents in a dynamic environment. [KMC,LG]

**Synchronization** – A specification of the constraints on the order of events occuring in a system. Synchronization may be viewed as an elementary (*see*) coordination mechanism. [GAA,NJ,GW]

**Syntax** – How the symbols of comunication are structured. [MNH,LNS]

**TAC Air Soar** – A model of distributed teamwork in which each of the agents are modeled in (*see*) Soar and the organizational structure is embedded as a set of predefined procedures in the knowledge base. [KMC,LG]

**TAEMS** – A system for modeling, analyzing, and simulating multiagent systems based on the structure of the multiagent tasks and the relationships between the distributed subtasks. [EHD]

**Task Accomplishment** – The stage in distributed (*see*) problem solving where agents are accomplishing their own local tasks. [EHD]

**Task Allocation** – The stage in distributed (*see*) problem solving where agents are deciding where tasks will be done. [EHD]

**Task Decomposition** – The stage in distributed (*see*) problem solving where agents are breaking large tasks into smaller tasks to be distributed to others. [EHD]

**Task Sharing** – Cooperative (*see*) problem solving through the decomposition of large tasks and the enlistment of other agents to accomplish the subtasks. [EHD]

**Team** – A multiagent system, especially one whose members play different (*see*) roles and work together to achieve some common goals. Often used as a synonym for (*see*) coaliltion, (*see*) ensemble, and (*see*) group. [MPS,ASR,MPG]

**Team Plan** – An explicit representation of how multiple agents should work together in accomplishing a goal. [EHD]

**Telescript** – A commercial development environment for agent-based applications from General Magic. [GW]

**Temporal Logic** – (*See*) propositional logic augmented with operators to make claims about the truth of different conditions at different times. [MPS,ASR,MPG]

**Termination Detection** – The determination that a distributed computation has come to a halt. The issue is not always trivial because termination could be a property of the global state, while each node only observes its own local state. Detection then requires a mechanism to ensure that communication channels are empty, and exchange of information about the local states. [GT]

**ToH** – (*See*) Tower of Hanoi.

**TOP-MODELER** – The commercial, PC-based tool developed from (*see*) ACTION. [KMC,LG]

**TOURINGMACHINES** – A horizontally layered (*see*) agent architecture. *See* layered architecture. [MW]

**Tower of Hanoi (ToH)** – A classic AI problem involving moving a stack of disks from one peg to another under constraints on actions. The space of possible plans is exponential. [EHD]

**TRACONET** – TRAnsportation COoperation NEt. The system that introduced a sound marginal cost-based decision making criterion into the contract net protocol. A distributed implementation that was tested on a real world multienterprise vehicle routing problem with 771 tasks and 77 vehicles. [TS]

**Two-Player Game** – For instance, chess and checkers. A two-player game can be represented by a tree called a game tree, which represents the sequence of possible moves. The minimax procedure is a method for finding a good move by creating only a reasonable portion of a game tree, and the alpha-beta pruning method can be used to speed up the minimax procedure without any loss of information. *See* search, asynchronous search algorithm. [TI,MY]

**Vacuum Cleaning World Application** – An application involving multiple agents which have to clean up a predefined region (e.g., a house).

**VDT** – An emulation model of performance for teams dealing with routine design tasks. [KMC,LG]

**Veracity** – The assumption that an agent is truthful and does not provide information of which it thinks that it is false. [GW]

**Voting** – *See* Arrow's impossibility theorem, Gibbard-Satterthwaite impossibility theorem, sincere voting, Insincere (strategic) voting, protocol.

**Voyager** – A commercial Java-based mobile agent platform from ObjectSpace. *See also* Concordia, Odyssey. [TS]

**Walras** – (1.) L. Walras, economist. Forefather of general equilibrium theory. (2.) A simulated computational market economy based on general equilibrium theory, and a variant of the price tâtonnement algorithm. [TS]

**Watchdog** – An agent whose sensory scope is wider than that of most other agents in the community, but whose only action is raising signals to which other agents respond. [HVDP]

**Whiteboard** – Shared writing and drawing surface that allows multiple participants to view and work upon an information artifact simultaneously, without inhibiting each other. *See also* blackboard. [CSE,JW]

**Workflow Management System** – Networked control system that assists in analyzing, coordinating, and executing business processes. It typically consists of two sub-systems:(1) A modelling subsystem which allows organizational administrators and analysts to construct procedural models of the flow of work among people and tasks; and (2) An enactment subsystem which uses the model to coordinate task executions by various participants at various workstations connected to a network. [CSE,JW]

**Wrapper** – Software (and possibly dedicated hardware) that enables a system constructed according to one architecture to interoperate with a system of a different architecture. [HVDP]

**WWW** – The World Wide Web.

**W3C** – The World Wide Web consortium hosted at MIT.

## Contributors to the Glossary:

| | |
|---|---|
| ASR | Anand S. Rao |
| CSE | Clarence (Skip) Ellis |
| EHD | Edmund H. Durfee |
| GAA | Gul A. Agha |
| GT | Gerard Tel |
| GW | Gerhard Weiss |
| HVDP | H. Van Dyke Parunak |
| JC | Jose Cuena |
| JW | Jacques Wainer |
| KMC | Kathleen M. Carley |
| LG | Les Gasser |
| LNS | Larry N. Stephens |
| MNH | Michael N. Huhns |
| MPG | Michael P. Georgeff |
| MPS | Munindar P. Singh |
| MW | Mike Wooldridge |
| MY | Makoto Yokoo |
| NJ | Nadeem Jamali |
| SO | Sascha Ossowski |
| SS | Sandip Sen |
| TI | Toru Ishida |
| TS | Tuomas Sandholm |

# Subject Index

—— **D**

—— **E**

—— **F**

# ——— W

# ——— X, Y, Z